The Named God
and the Question of Being

THE NAMED GOD
AND THE QUESTION OF BEING

A Trinitarian Theo-Ontology

Stanley J. Grenz

WESTMINSTER
JOHN KNOX PRESS
LOUISVILLE • KENTUCKY

Scripture quotations from the New Revised Standard Version of the Bible are copyright © 1989 by the Division of Christian Education of the National Council of the Churches of Christ in the U.S.A. and are used by permission.

Book design by Sharon Adams
Cover design by Night & Day Design

First edition
Published by Westminster John Knox Press
Louisville, Kentucky

This book is printed on acid-free paper that meets the American National Standards Institute Z39.48 standard. ∞

PRINTED IN THE UNITED STATES OF AMERICA

05 06 07 08 09 10 11 12 13 14 — 10 9 8 7 6 5 4 3 2 1

Library of Congress Cataloging-in-Publication Data

Grenz, Stanley J. (Stanley James)
    The named God and the question of being : a trinitarian theo-ontology / Stanley J. Grenz.—1st ed.
        p. cm. — (The matrix of Christian theology)
    Includes bibliographical references and index.
    ISBN 0-664-22204-8
    1. Philosophical theology.   2. Ontology.   3. Trinity.   4. God—Name.
I. Title.

BT55.G74   2005
231'.044—dc22   2005047927

Contents

Introduction: The Saga of a Name   1

PART ONE

THE SAGA OF BEING

1 From *To On* to the *Ipsum Esse*:
  The Christianization of Being   15
2 From the First Cause to the Infinite:
  The Secularization of Being   51
3 From Onto-Theology to Theo-Ontology:
  The Demise of Being   90

PART TWO

THE SAGA OF THE I AM

4 From Exodus to Exile:
  The Covenanted I AM   133
5 From Jacob's Well to Calvary's Cross:
  The Incarnate I AM   174
6 From the Future to the Eternal:
  The Exalted I AM   207

PART THREE

THE SAGA OF THE TRIUNE NAME

7 From the I AM to the Trinity:
  The Meaning of the Divine Name   249
8 From the Trinity to Being:
  The Ontology of the Divine Name   291
9 From God's Triune Be-ing to Human Being:
  Our Inclusion into the Divine Name   342

Index   374

Introduction

The Saga of a Name

Christian theology and the discipline of Western philosophy known as metaphysics have enjoyed a continuous, close, and mutually enriching relationship since the patristic era. In his Lowell Lectures of 1926, Alfred North Whitehead noted one direction in which the mutual enrichment that has historically been involved in the connection between the two intellectual endeavors has flowed. "Christianity," he wrote, "has always been a religion seeking a metaphysic."[1] In 1942, George Santayana, in turn, hinted at the basically religious character of philosophy, at least as he pursued it. He declared, "My philosophy is like that of the ancients a discipline of the mind and heart, a lay religion."[2] In keeping with this acknowledgment, Santayana's own philosophical construction—especially

---

1. Alfred North Whitehead, *Religion in the Making* (New York: World Publishing, 1960), 50.
2. George Santayana, *Realms of Being* (New York: Charles Scribner's Sons, 1942), 827.

his delineation of the triad of power, essence, and spirit—evidences striking parallels to basic aspects of the Christian doctrine of the Trinity.[3]

Even while Whitehead and Santayana were voicing these perspectives, however, their colleagues were engaging in what became a protracted debate regarding one participant in this historically lively relationship between theology and philosophy. The philosophical guild was wracked by disputes regarding not only the nature of but also the very propriety of metaphysics as an intellectual pursuit. So unsettling had the questioning become by the middle decades of the twentieth century that in 1963 the neoscholastic thinker Joseph Owens could conclude, "Today metaphysics is not to be approached as though it had a generally accepted field and method."[4]

The questioning of metaphysics that rocked the guild throughout most of the early twentieth century was spearheaded by logical positivists, who claimed that its assertions are cognitively meaningless in that they are not empirically verifiable. Their attack was later joined by scientifically oriented philosophers, who concluded that science provides the sole pathway to genuine knowledge.[5] In recent decades, the chorus of negative voices has been augmented by thinkers who reject metaphysics under the guise of deconstruction or by appeal to postmodern sensibilities. Yet despite the widespread questioning of the discipline, metaphysical exploration has not died. On the contrary, it continues to be pursued by a variety of professional philosophers to the extent that some observers speak (albeit cautiously) about a modest revival in metaphysics.[6]

Traditionally, philosophy has been divided into a variety of topics. Nevertheless, most of its traditionally minded practitioners see at the heart of this intellectual pursuit three crucial inquiries: the exploration of the nature of existence (metaphysics), the nature of knowledge (epistemology), and the nature of values (axiology).[7] The phrase from which the first of these disciplines initially derived its name means simply "what comes after the physical"[8] (ta meta ta physika). Some historians suggest that the term was coined by Aristotle's immediate successors.[9] A more popular account of its origin postulates that the term did not emerge until

---

3. See especially Santayana, *Realms of Being*, 846–53.

4. Joseph Owens, *An Elementary Christian Metaphysics* (Milwaukee: Bruce Publishing Co., 1963), 12.

5. For a synopsis of and short engagement with these perspectives, see Panayot Butchvarov, "Metaphysics," in *The Cambridge Dictionary of Philosophy*, 2nd ed., ed. Robert Audi (Cambridge: Cambridge University Press, 1999), 563.

6. For this judgment, see E. J. Lowe, "Metaphysics, Opposition to," in *The Oxford Companion to Philosophy*, ed. Ted Honderich (New York: Oxford University Press, 1995), 559.

7. For this description, see Archie J. Bahm, *Metaphysics: An Introduction* (Albuquerque: World Books, 1983), 3.

8. For this observation, see Owens, *Elementary Christian Metaphysics*, 1.

9. An example is Owens, *Elementary Christian Metaphysics*, 1.

the first century BC, when Andronicus of Rhodes collected and edited Aristotle's writings. Andronicus grouped together under the label *ta physika* (the treatises on material natures) Aristotle's eight books that explore the natures of things in the visible world. He placed after these works the writings of the great Greek thinker that engage with the nature and properties of reality in its most general, nonmaterial aspects. For want of an accurately descriptive name, the theory concludes, Andronicus labeled these works *ta meta ta physika* (studies placed after the treatises on material natures).[10] Paul Glenn offers this appraisal of the appropriateness of the designation "metaphysics" (*meta-physika*), which supposedly arose in this manner: "Now, by almost miraculous good fortune, this name, which originated in the accident of an editor's arrangement of books, suits perfectly the science to which it is applied. For metaphysics treats of that which comes after, or lies beyond, the separate objects grasped by the sense and the sciences which treat of such objects."[11]

Despite the ambiguity surrounding the origin of the name, metaphysics has come to be seen as involving a relatively stable set of questions. The discipline is typically described as "the philosophical investigation of the nature, constitution, and structure of reality"[12] or as the "philosophical study whose object it is to determine the real nature of things—to determine the meaning, structure, and principles of whatever is insofar as it is."[13] This latter definition suggests that the primary topic of metaphysics is existence[14] and that the primary question that metaphysicians explore is, "What *kind* of concept is expressed by 'existence' and its cognates?"[15]

Louis de Raeymaeker proposes a slightly different, and widely followed, understanding. He defines metaphysics as "the philosophical discipline which seeks to discover the fundamental explanation of the whole complexity of beings."[16] Like its Greek counterpart, *on*, the English word "being" is a participle of the verb "to be." And similar to *on*, it can function grammatically both as a participle and as a noun. The meaning of "being" as a philosophical term, therefore, is closely connected to the use of "to be" to mean

---

10. For an example of a philosopher who rejects this historical reconstruction, see Owens, *Elementary Christian Metaphysics*, 3.

11. Paul J. Glenn, *Ontology: A Class Manual in Fundamental Metaphysics* (St. Louis: B. Herder Book Co., 1947), 2.

12. Butchvarov, "Metaphysics," 563. A somewhat similar definition reads: "a philosophical inquiry into the most basic and general features of reality and our place in it." Jaegwon Kim and Ernest Sosa, "Preface," in *Metaphysics: An Anthology*, ed. Jaegwon Kim and Ernest Sosa (Oxford: Blackwell, 1999), ix.

13. "Metaphysics," in *The New Encyclopedia Britannica* (Chicago: Encyclopedia Britannica, 1994), 12:10.

14. This focus is even more pronounced in Bahm's definition that reads: the "inquiry into existence and its categories." Bahm, *Metaphysics*, 6.

15. Jaegwon Kim and Ernest Sosa, "Introduction to Part 1," in Kim and Sosa, *Metaphysics*, 3.

16. Louis de Raeymaeker, *The Philosophy of Being: A Synthesis of Metaphysics*, trans. Edmund H. Ziegelmeyer (St. Louis: B. Herder Book Co., 1954), 28.

"to exist" or "to have existence." As a participle, "being" carries the idea of "existing" or "having existence," understood in an active rather than a merely passive sense. In its metaphysical sense, "being" is usually used substantively to designate "that whose act is 'to be,'" "that which has existence" or more simply "that which is."[17] As such, "being" differs from the related word "essence," which is often defined as "that by which a thing is what it is."[18]

Many metaphysicians, however, understand the word "being" in a somewhat wider sense. Celestine Bittle offers a classic description:

> The term "being"... includes anything that has a *positive reference to existence*, whether this existence be actual or merely possible. The common element in actual and possible beings is their *capacity for existence*. Hence, "being" in general means something capable of existing, *existible*; something capable of being actualized, *actualizable*; something capable of being realized, *realizable*.[19]

Similarly, Glenn declares:

> By *being* we mean reality. And by *reality* we mean whatever exists or can exist. Anything that now exists, or that has existed in the past, or that will exist in the future, or can be thought of as existing even though it never actually existed and never will—any such thing is a *reality*, a *thing*, a *being*. Any such thing *has* being, that is, it has existibility.[20]

Being, understood in this manner, is deemed by many traditional philosophers to comprise the central concern of metaphysics. In keeping with the centrality of being to this intellectual endeavor, Etienne Gilson concludes, "Since *being* is the first principle of human knowledge, it is *a fortiori* the first principle of metaphysics."[21] Yet "being" is more readily connected to an intellectual pursuit that is traditionally seen as comprising one subdiscipline of metaphysics: ontology.

The designation "ontology" is derived from the Greek terms *on* and *logos*. Its etymology leads naturally to the common description of the philosophical discipline as "the science of being." With this general definition in view, philosophers routinely describe ontology as the study of being as such,[22] being in itself, being in its most general aspects,[23] or being simply

17. See Celestine N. Bittle, *The Domain of Being: Ontology* (Milwaukee: Bruce Publishing Co., 1939), 12; Henry J. Koren, *An Introduction to the Science of Metaphysics* (St. Louis: B. Herder Book Co., 1955), 22.
18. Koren, *Introduction to the Science of Metaphysics*, 131.
19. Bittle, *Domain of Being*, 13.
20. Glenn, *Ontology*, 3–4.
21. Etienne Gilson, *Being and Some Philosophers*, 2nd ed. (Toronto: Pontifical Institute of Mediaeval Studies, 1952), 2.
22. Glenn, *Ontology*, 3.
23. Bittle, *Domain of Being*, 6.

as being.[24] Many philosophers further divide ontology into three major parts. The first inquires into being and its primary determinations, including the concept of being, the kinds of being, and matters relating to change, essence, and existence. The second looks at the transcendental attributes of being (e.g., oneness, identity and distinction, truth, goodness and beauty). The study is then rounded out in the third division by considering the categories of being, among which are quality, relation, and causality.[25]

The German philosopher Christian Wolff (1679–1754) is often credited with popularizing the designation "ontology" as the study of being. Wolff divided metaphysics into two basic subdisciplines: general metaphysics or ontology, and special metaphysics (which included theodicy, cosmology, and psychology).[26] Wolff's work, however, was predated by that of an early German devotee of Cartesian philosophy, Johann Clauberg (1622–1665). In the prolegomenon to his book on ontology (which he termed "ontosophiae"), Clauberg declared, "Since the science which is about God calls itself *Theosophy* or *Theology*, it would seem fitting to call *Ontosophy* or *Ontology* that science which does not deal with this and that being, as distinct from the others owing to its special name of properties, but with being in general."[27] Regarding this statement, Gilson declares, "This text may be held, in the present state of historical knowledge, for the birth certificate of ontology as a science conceived after the pattern of theology, yet radically distinct from it, since being *qua* being is held there as indifferent to all its conceivable determinations."[28]

In a sense, *The Named God and the Question of Being* is a study in the central subdiscipline of metaphysics called ontology. This is evident even in the title itself, which promises that the overarching topic to be explored in the ensuing nine chapters is the question that lies at the heart of ontology. Yet what follows is not a delineation of, nor an engagement with, the plethora of issues that philosophers who explore the ontological concept of being routinely raise. Instead, the focus of this volume is the one fundamental issue with which ontology itself rises or falls. The book raises from one particular perspective the question regarding the propriety of speaking of Being itself. More specifically, it looks at the longstanding trajectory of thought that has not only equated this concept with the God of the Bible but in so doing has claimed that the ontological category of Being provides the conceptuality in the context of which the biblical God

24. Glenn, *Ontology*, 6. Henri Renard likewise offers this as the definition of metaphysics. Renard, *The Philosophy of Being*, 2nd ed. (Milwaukee: Bruce Publishing Co., 1946), 13.

25. For this division, see Bittle, *Domain of Being*, 10.

26. Koren, *Introduction to the Science of Metaphysics*, 2. For a slightly different delineation of Wolff's divisions, see Owens, *Elementary Christian Metaphysics*, 7.

27. Johann Clauberg, *Elementa philosophiae sive Ontosophiae* (1647), as cited in Gilson, *Being and Some Philosophers*, 112.

28. Gilson, *Being and Some Philosophers*, 112.

is to be understood. Thus, one intent of the following chapters is to engage the possibility that the wedding of philosophy and theology in what has become the traditional and accepted manner is no longer appropriate (if it ever was). In so doing, the volume builds from those recent thinkers who in various ways have heralded the demise of onto-theology. But moving against the conclusions drawn by many of these voices, the book seeks to show that this demise does not spell the end of fruitful engagement between Christian theology and the Western philosophical tradition.

Furthermore, in the spirit of Johann Clauberg, *The Named God and the Question of Being* pursues the inquiry into the ontological question from a self-consciously theological perspective. We might say that the argument set forth in the following chapters begins by demonstrating the historical validity of Whitehead's claim that Christianity has been a religion in search of a metaphysics. But the book as a whole rejects any suggestion that this search, and hence the purported dependence of Christian theology on Western ontology, is inevitable or necessitated by something inherent in theology itself. At the same time, the book could be seen as a case study in the possibility of a mutually enriching conversation between the two intellectual endeavors.

In the recent past, any conversation of this type between theology and ontology would have drawn the ire of a high percentage of theoreticians in both disciplines. Yet the situation appears to be changing. Rebecca Chopp reflects the presence of such a change among theologians when she advises, "The refusal to continue foundationalism does not let us beg off the metaphysical question, it seems to me. Precisely as we attempt to move away from foundationalism to theology, we need to employ some kind of revised metaphysical inquiry."[29] One goal of the following chapters is to indicate the contours of an ontological inquiry that might arise when due consideration is given to one particular insight from Christian theology. Again the title identifies this insight. As is evident in the first three words, *The Named God*, the book seeks to engage with ontology from the vantage point that arises out of the realization that the biblical God is named.

This characterization correctly infers that the inquiry that comprises this book is not generically theological in orientation. Rather, the argument presented here seeks to advance a conversation with ontology on the basis of one particular orientation point. The theological context in which the ensuing discussion transpires is that of a commitment to a thoroughgoing Trinitarian theology.

The rebirth of Trinitarian theology is one of the most far-reaching theological developments of the last hundred years.[30] One crucial issue that

29. Rebecca S. Chopp, "Feminist Queries and Metaphysical Musings," in *Rethinking Metaphysics*, ed. L. Gregory Jones and Stephen E. Fowl (Oxford: Blackwell, 1995), 47–48.

30. I delineated the history of this development in Stanley J. Grenz, *Rediscovering the Triune God: The Trinity in Contemporary Theology* (Minneapolis: Fortress, 2004).

has emerged from this rebirth is the question of the kind of engagement with ontology that is opened through the displacement of the older focus on the divine unity by a concern for the triunity of God. The assumption that God's unity precedes the divine threeness has fit well with the various substantialist ontologies that have reigned during much of the history of Western philosophy. If this book gives evidence of pursuing the kind of search for a metaphysics that Whitehead saw as inherent in Christianity, then the quest would be for an ontology that is appropriate to the theological conviction that God is triune.

Nevertheless, the central concern of *The Named God and the Question of Being* is not the development of a Trinitarian ontology as such. Rather, the intent of this volume is to pursue the deeper question of ontology from a thoroughgoing Trinitarian perspective. This means that rather than asking about the implications of ontology for theology, the book seeks to ascertain the implications of the Christian conception of God as triune for the question of ontology. And it does so cognizant that the context in which any such conversation now occurs is one in which metaphysics itself has become suspect, at least in many circles. Moreover, the central insight that the book brings to the table as it engages in this task is the realization that the Trinitarian God of the Bible is named. For this reason, the named character of God emerges as the central motif that is unpacked throughout the book.

At the heart of *The Named God and the Question of Being*, therefore, is the explication of a central theme of Scripture by means of a Trinitarian rubric. Drawing from the observation that the God of the biblical story is named, the book sets forth the idea that the plot of the Bible can be told as the unfolding of the self-naming of the triune God that occurs through the interplay of the three Trinitarian members. The book is motivated by the belief that the theme of the self-naming God, viewed in this manner, provides a promising basis for an enriching conversation with the central question of ontology, the question of Being.

To accomplish this goal, the nine chapters of the book are organized into a triad of triads. Each triad, in turn, comprises a particular "saga." And each of these is a saga of one particular name. The word "saga" was deliberately chosen as the heading for each of the three parts of the book because of the narrative overtones that it conveys. Denoting each of the three parts as a "saga" is intended to indicate that each triad of chapters tells a specific story or depicts a particular drama. The three sagas, in turn, form an overarching story: the saga of the intended interplay of the named character of God and the question of Being, and hence the intended interplay of theology and ontology.

The triad of chapters that constitute part 1 is entitled "The Saga of Being." These chapters depict the drama of the concept of Being through three major acts. Act 1 (chapter 1) traces the story of Being from its advent among the pre-Socratic philosophers to its thorough Christianization, which occurred by means of its perceived link to the biblical God who bears the name I AM. The Christianization of Being reached its apex in the high Middle Ages. The second chapter follows the pathway of Being through the twists and turns that were inaugurated in the wake of the demise of the Thomistic synthesis through the Romantic movement. The exploits of Being during the scenes that make up act 2 of the saga facilitate the eventual secularization of the concept. Chapter 3, in turn, explores the story of how the fortunes of Being eventually resulted in its apparent demise at the hands of those who called for the end of onto-theology.

At the heart of the saga of Being that is narrated in these three chapters is a delineation of two distinct ways of relating the biblical God to Being and hence of connecting Christian theology to Greek ontology. The first of these, the Neoplatonic and Augustine proposal, links God to the inward quest of the human soul. Under this rubric, God comes to be seen as the ultimate goal of our search for personal identity and, by extension, as the fulfillment of our spiritual nature. This perspective opens the way to the philosophical conception of God as the infinite. The second trajectory, one that is generally associated with Aristotle and Aquinas, sees God as the ground of the cosmos. Consequently, God is perceived as the ultimate goal of the human quest for knowledge of the world and, as such, as the fulfillment of our intellectual nature. Connected to this understanding is the idea that God is the First Cause of the world.

Implicit in the three chapters that constitute the saga of Being is a particular understanding of the great achievement and the dire tragedy of the synthesis of God and Being. This far-reaching innovation in theological and philosophical history gave impetus to the triumph of rationality and aided the birth of science. Yet it also abetted the rise of irrationality and opened the door to the secularization process. The saga delineated in these chapters concludes by describing what might be called the last gasp of Being, which occurred with the shift from static to dynamic Being. This is followed by the last gasp of ontology itself, which comes in the form of the ontology of existence (or being-in-the-world). Taken as a whole, therefore, "The Saga of Being" raises the crucial ontological question: Was the invention of "Being" a mistake? And if so, what are the implications of its apparent demise? This question forms, at least initially, the central problem that *The Named God and the Question of Being* sets itself to address.

In part 2, the genre of the book shifts from historical narrative to exegesis. Yet the exegesis that comprises the second triad of chapters does not take the traditional form of looking closely at a series of isolated texts. Instead, the exegesis of texts occurs within an overarching narrative. In fact, the exegesis of the chosen texts serves to develop the plot of the drama that these three chapters seek to unfold. In this manner, the exegesis of the I AM texts that constitute the second triad form a second unified story.

The various texts that are selected as elements in the story are woven together so as to narrate "The Saga of the I AM." The central moments of this story are revelation, incarnation, exaltation.

The I AM is chosen as the hero of this second saga precisely because the patristic and medieval Christian theologians perceived in this name the means to link the biblical God to the Greek concept of Being. For this reason, the immediate purpose of the saga of the I AM is to determine whether or not the forging of this link was biblically warranted. More importantly, however, "The Saga of the I AM" comprises the central section of the book—standing between "The Saga of Being" and the theological engagement of part 3—so that it might present the biblical story line of the divine name as an alternative to the story of the philosophical, onto-theological use of that name. In so doing, the saga also lays the foundation for the attempt to launch the new engagement between theology and ontology, via the divine name, that becomes the explicit goal of the final three chapters of the book. To fulfill its role in the overall structure of the volume, chapters 4, 5, and 6 repeatedly draw from two prominent features of the biblical narrative: intertextuality and the schema of promise and fulfillment.

The first chapter of the triad that makes up "The Saga of the I AM" (chapter 4) focuses on the Old Testament segment of the story. Act 1 of this particular drama presents the Old Testament segment by means of three scenes, which pursue the themes of covenantal revelation (exodus), revocation (exile) and renewal (new exodus). As the drama of the chapter opens, we catch a glimpse of the largely nonphilosophical character of the divine name. Moreover, we see that the name is initially indeterminate, for it anticipates a future, deeper disclosure of meaning. And yet its very meaning entails the promise of God's "be-ing present" with Israel. Scene 2 discloses that the divine name can be revoked, although even its revocation carries with it the promise of renewal. This indicates that in the absence of the divine name, the character of the name as "be-ing present" is still evident. In the final Old Testament scene, the revocation of the divine name emerges as itself revokable, a movement that involves a kind of double negative. This revocation of the revocation is possible, in that God's very being is to be present everywhere in the narrative, even where God is absent, and in this sense God's be-ing involves being "first and last."

Chapter 5 turns our attention to Jesus' I AM sayings, which are exegeted in an order that reveals an inherent flow of the drama from ambiguity to clarity. This second act of the second saga traces through Jesus' sayings the perspective that Jesus' claims to be the I AM form a double entendre. In so doing, the main character of this act of the drama leaves the matter of his identity open and invites the eyes of faith to see who he truly is. Although it presents Jesus as the I AM throughout his life, the Fourth Gospel elevates as the event in which Jesus' disclosure of the I AM is especially vivid in his death on the cross. Yet here as elsewhere, at the heart of his I AM claim is Jesus' declaration that he participates in God's life, in life from above or eternal life, and therefore he has the prerogative to mediate life to others. In his life and death, Jesus both possesses and reveals the divine name, which is the Father's own name.

The exegetical narrative of chapter 6 shifts the focus to the Synoptics and the Apocalypse, and thereby facilitates the story line in moving from the eschatological to the eternal dimensions of the story of the incarnate I AM. Advancing a theme with which the Old Testament section of the drama ended, the narrative set forth here indicates how even the pronouncement of the I AM is an eschatological event. The claim to be the I AM entails a declaration of sovereignty over history, for the eschatological presence of the I AM demonstrates that inherent in the name itself is the act of be-ing present to all of history. The drama reaches its climax with the portrayal of the divine name as shared among the three Trinitarian members and the promise that it will be shared with us as well.

If part 2 sets the framework, in the form of an alternative story, for a renewed conversation between theology and ontology, part 3 of the book seeks to bring the two preceding sagas into just such a meaningful conversation. To this end, the three chapters that constitute this final triad make use of the two distinct genres that characterize the first two triads: historical survey and exegesis. To these, however, is added a third: theological reflection. Hence, this triad of chapters seeks to unify what was juxtaposed in parts 1 and 2 by means of the theological purposes, for which it appropriates the historical and exegetical materials.

What results from this engagement is likewise a kind of narrative. To indicate this basic characteristic, part 3 also carries the label "saga." More specifically, it comprises "The Saga of the Triune Name." Nevertheless, the approach in these chapters is neither the seemingly straightforward narration of part 1, nor the stylized exegetical narrative found in part 2. Rather, the chapters bring together both of these genres in the task of advancing an integrative theological conversation.

The goal of part 3 is to provide the basis for, and the contours of, a theo-ontology. This goal is pursued in a manner that is in keeping with the focus of the book, which arises out of the observation that the God of the Bible is named. To this end, the triad begins with a chapter that focuses on the theory of naming (chapter 7). In this chapter, an initial historical sketch reveals the scant interest in the divine name shown by theologians, which observation raises the question regarding the name of God in the New Testament. The search for this name, in turn, leads to the realization that the I AM is a shared name. A sketch of the debate about the significance of proper names then launches a theological discussion, based on secular theories of naming, about the meaning of the divine name. The narrative of Jesus' baptism, read in the context of this discussion, forms the basis for concluding that the divine naming is a triune event. In this manner, chapter 7 lays the conceptual groundwork for the delineation of a theo-ontology based on the concept of God as the self-naming triunity that follows in chapter 8.

To set forth this theo-ontology, the middle chapter of the triad begins with a lengthy historical sketch of the rise of the doctrine of the Trinity as it emerged from the theological engagement with Platonism that characterized the patristic era. As depicted here, this trajectory in theological history reached its apex with the significant alteration of Platonism that developed in the work of Marius Victorinus and Augustine. The chapter then engages with the question of the significance of apophatic theology, which has been especially important in the Eastern Orthodox tradition, for the development of a theo-ontology. Although at first glance the negative approach would seem to put an end to any idea of looking to the divine name as the starting point for a theo-ontology, the opposite turns out to be the case. Apophatic theology actually provides the very basis for such a theo-ontology. It fulfills this role, because it opens the door to revelation and because it elevates the category of Other as the central feature of reality and, more importantly, even of God.

This contribution of the apophatic tradition opens the way for the ensuing theological discussion of the concept of Otherness as it relates primarily to God but by extension to the world as well. The chapter then brings the various threads of the discussion together to set forth the resultant theo-ontology. To this end, it appropriates the Victorinian-Augustinian insights that the initial historical sketch unveiled. More specifically, the horizontal triad that they developed out of Platonism opens the door to speaking about the eternal self-naming of God as a dynamic of knowing and being known. The Augustinian model of Trinitarian love, in turn, occasions the conclusion that inclusion in the dynamic of "gift" is the ultimate character of "being" and that this gifting is ultimately a Trinitarian-pneumatological reality.

In this manner, chapter 8 forms the apex of the book, for it marks the end of the journey toward a theo-ontology. Yet with the completion of this journey, the narrative of the book is still not at its end. Rather, the theo-ontology set forth in the eighth chapter invites a ninth as an epilogue that speaks about the incorporation of human being into the divine story. To accomplish this task, chapter 9 looks to Paul's Areopagitica as the basis for an inclusion-oriented theo-ontology, which speaks of the reception of being as a divinely bestowed gift. On this basis, the chapter then draws together three far-reaching themes that come together to form the anthropological dimension of the theo-ontology that is connected to the process of naming: the *imago Dei*, viewed as the human vocation as given through the universal significance of Jesus Christ as the true Adam; *theosis*, understood in terms of our divinely given human destiny to be participants in—and hence to find our existence in—the life of the triune God; and the Spirit as eschatological gift, as the gift who is the *telos* of the triune life and the life of the world. In this manner, the chapter links the theo-ontology of the book to the central insights of the first volume of this series and anticipates what will be explored in subsequent volumes.

Eduard Schweizer recalls Whitehead declaring at one point, "The doctrine of the Trinity is one of the greatest achievements of the human intellect."[31] Perhaps by delineating the manner in which the saga of the name of the triune God can be seen to interface with what has remained the perennial concern of Western ontology, an engagement that in our day has become even more crucial, *The Named God and the Question of Being* might be able to bring us to catch a small glimpse of the greatness of this achievement. And perhaps in the process we will be led to see ourselves more clearly as those upon whom the gift of being is bestowed so that we might be drawn into the story of the self-naming, triune God.

---

31. Eduard Schweizer, *The Good News according to Matthew*, trans. David E. Green (Atlanta: John Knox, 1975), 534.

PART ONE
THE SAGA OF BEING

Chapter One

From *To On* to the *Ipsum Esse*

The Christianization of Being

Prior to the sixth century BC, Being—as the overarching topic of inquiry in ontology—did not exist.

In part, Being was linguistically birthed. One of its progenitors was a peculiar characteristic of the ancient language known as Indo-European. This language sports a root word, *es-* (in English, the verb "to be") that functions in a variety of ways, including as a verb of predication (e.g., "I am male"), location (e.g., "I am here") and existence ("I am").[1] That the root word *es-*, and with it the Greek verb *einai*, is already weighted in the direction of Being is evident in the fact that the verb functions as a stative copula. This means that *einai* ("to be") can be conjugated in the durative tenses—the present and the imperfect—but not in the punctiliar or non-durative aorist tense. Thereby, it forms a linguistic contrast to the mutative

---

1. Charles H. Kahn, "Retrospect on the Verb 'To Be' and the Concept of Being," in *The Logic of Being*, ed. Simo Knuuttila and Jaakko Hintikka (Dordrecht: D. Reidel Publishing Co., 1985), 3.

copula ("to become") with its predisposition toward the alternative ontological idea of Becoming.[2]

Yet the aspect of the verb "to be" that ultimately facilitated the emergence
of Being was its veridical use ("It is [true] that I am male"), which in a sense
simply makes explicit the truth claim implicit in the verb's functioning as a
declarative copula. As Charles Kahn concludes from his study of *einai*:

> Thus the Greek concept of Being takes its rise from that naive, pre-
> philosophic notion of "reality" as whatever it is in the world that makes
> some statements true and others false, some opinions correct and oth-
> ers mistaken. . . . What is peculiar to Greek (and Indo-European) is
> that a locution for "reality" in this sense should be provided by a verb
> whose primary function is to express predication and sentencehood
> for statements of the form X is Y.[3]

The nuances of the verb "to be" may have provided the basis for the
emergence of Being. But the impetus for its appearance on the intellectual stage of the ancient Mediterranean world lay in the questions of cosmology—inquiries into the nature of the "stuff" of things, the dynamics
of change and the basis for the unity of the cosmos—that were pursued
by a diverse group of thinkers in the ancient Greek world. Above all, these
thinkers wanted to determine what this ultimate Reality is that remains
constant despite the changes that can be readily observed in the world.[4]

Once birthed, Being quickly grew to occupy center stage within the
scholarly discourse that flourished in the ancient Mediterranean societies.
Since its advent, Being has enjoyed a long reign as the queen of the discipline of metaphysics and, above all, monarch of that particular aspect of
metaphysical inquiry known as ontology.

The Coming into Being of Being

Prior to the birth of Being, the perennial questions regarding the nature
and source of the phenomena that people noticed in the cosmos around
them were routinely answered by appeal to the actions of deities and to
stories that narrated the exploits of the gods. Being was the product of the
reflections of those thinkers who sought to shift the task of making sense
of life away from the commonly followed method of attributing fate to
the decisions and antics of a multitude of whimsical deities. Instead of
invoking the gods to explain the mysteries of life, these thinkers, who
beginning with Pythagoras came be known as philosophers (i.e., "lovers

2. For this observation, see Kahn, "Retrospect on the Verb 'To Be,'" 7.

3. Kahn, "Retrospect on the Verb 'To Be,'" 22.

4. For a similar summarization of the basic pre-Socratic philosophical query, see Martin J. Walsh,
A History of Philosophy (London: Geoffrey Chapman, 1985), 14.

of wisdom"),[5] looked to some underlying principle, logic, or *logos*, that could be postulated as providing order to the universe.[6]

Being's Beginnings

Samuel Enoch Stumpf reflects what has become the standard historiography regarding Western philosophical history when he cites the seaport town of Miletus, located on the western shores of Ionia in Asia Minor as the "birthplace of philosophy." Moreover, following a tradition that likely dates to Aristotle,[7] he elevates Thales of Miletus (c. 625–547) as the "first philosopher,"[8] an accolade that parallels the repeatedly articulated designation of Thales as the "father of philosophy."[9]

The Gestation of Being

Regardless of when and by whom the philosophical quest was inaugurated,[10] at its inception, philosophy sought to account for several conclusions that appear to arise immediately from observation: the cosmos seems to be composed of many different kinds of things; some of these things change from time to time into something else; certain things share a resemblance to each other.

Thales concluded from his inquiry into these matters that a single ingredient lay at the basis of the various things in the cosmos and that by means of this fundamental element the manifold and diverse things were related to each other. In his estimation, this basic element not only comprises the underlying "stuff" present in all things, but it also forms the dynamic that gives rise to all that is. Hence, it constitutes the basic dimension of reality that undergoes change and thereby produces all the various objects that we find in the world.

If Aristotle is a trustworthy guide to the teachings of his predecessors, then Thales postulated that this first principle of all things is water.[11] In

5. For this conclusion, see Robert C. Solomon and Kathleen M. Higgins, *A Short History of Philosophy* (New York: Oxford University Press, 1996), 28.

6. For a similar perspective, see Solomon and Higgins, *Short History of Philosophy*, 8.

7. For this judgment, see William L. Reese, "Thales," in *Dictionary of Philosophy and Religion* (Atlantic Highlands, NJ: Humanities Press, 1980), 573.

8. Samuel Enoch Stumpf, *Socrates to Sartre: A History of Philosophy*, 4th ed. (New York: McGraw-Hill, 1988), 3, 5.

9. See, for example, W. T. Jones, *A History of Western Philosophy* (New York: Harcourt, Brace & Co., 1952), 34. See also Frederick Mayer, *A History of Ancient and Medieval Philosophy* (New York: American Book Co., 1950), 16.

10. For an interesting perspective regarding the fluidity of the beginnings of philosophy in general and Western philosophy in particular, see Solomon and Higgins, *Short History of Philosophy*, 25–29. Solomon and Higgins suggest that Pythagoras may rank as the first philosopher.

11. See Aristotle, *Metaphysics* I.3.983b20, trans. Richard Hope (New York: Columbia University Press, 1952), 10. For a discussion of the possible sources of Thales' cosmology, see G. S. Kirk and J. E. Raven, *The Presocratic Philosophers: A Critical History with a Selection of Texts* (Cambridge: Cambridge University Press, 1957), 87–98.

so doing, he stood at the head of the list of a group of thinkers who are often designated as the Milesian materialists. These early philosophers earned the designation "materialists" because they offered naturalistic accounts of the cosmos that posited one or more physical elements as forming the fundamental reality that accounts for the manifold things present in the cosmos.

More important than the exact answer that Thales proposed were the assumptions that motivated his considerations. These suppositions determined the kind of answer that he was anticipating when he posed the question as to the unity lying behind the diversity present in the world.[12] In formulating his answer, Thales avoided reciting stories about the actions of the gods, proposing instead that the diversity of reality was the result of a single unifying principle and that this principle lay within the cosmos and its processes. In so doing, he not only reflected what came to be the central concern of Greek metaphysics in general, but he also stood at the beginning of the monist tradition in philosophy, which declares that one elementary principle is the cause of everything in the universe. Moreover, Thales assumed that the elemental building block of the cosmos is inherently active, in that it contains within itself the principle of change or transformation that gives rise to the manifold things that we observe around us. Like many of the other pre-Socratic thinkers, he believed that the cosmos is in a certain sense "alive," that it possesses what might be called a "soul."[13] In any case, by seeking the "one" by means of which the "many" are both caused and ultimately related, Thales embarked on a quest not only for what could be termed a naturalistic cosmology, but also for what later came to be called Being. In this manner, we could say that Thales stood on the verge of launching the discipline of ontology.

Anaximander (611–546), Thales' immediate successor in Miletus and the thinker with whom D. W. Hamlyn believes philosophy was born,[14] offered what is often viewed as a more sophisticated proposal than that of his predecessor. Anaximander asserted that the first principle of all reality is an eternal, imperishable, undifferentiated mass of matter out of which all things are made and to which they return. Even though he conceived of this unbounded mass as a concrete substance, what he postulated as the first principle of the cosmos was something that is not observable by the senses. Rather than being one of the elements in the cosmos,[15] as is

---

12. For a somewhat similar exposition of Thales' assumptions, see Jones, *History of Western Philosophy*, 34.

13. For this commonly held judgment regarding the pre-Socratic thinkers, see D. W. Hamlyn, *A History of Western Philosophy* (New York: Viking, 1987), 16.

14. Hamlyn, *History of Western Philosophy*, 17.

15. For this judgment, see Frank Thilly, *A History of Philosophy*, 3rd ed., rev. Ledger Wood (New York: Henry Holt, 1957), 26.

the case of the subject of Thales' proposal, Anaximander's Boundless, Infinite, or Indefinite is more akin to what came to be known as Being.[16]

One particular query that Thales had raised carried special significance for the philosophical endeavor: the conceptual difficulty posed by the seemingly opposite tendencies capsulated in the concepts of permanence and change, together with the question as to how the "one" can change into the "many." One paradigmatic answer to this question was offered by an Ephesian aristocrat named Heraclitus (544–484), whom in his classic study of Greek philosophy Eduard Zeller lauds as "the profoundest and most powerful of the pre-Socratic philosophers."[17] Central to Heraclitus's perspective was the observation that change is always occurring, that everything is in flux. He encapsulated his resultant philosophical perspective in his famous saying, "Upon those who step into the same rivers, different and [again] different waters flow,"[18] which is often paraphrased as the dictum, "One cannot step into the same river twice."

Actually, Heraclitus was less interested in asserting that Becoming is the fundamental characteristic of all reality (which in one sense he did, of course, claim) than in accounting for the basic unity that lies behind and persists through the never-ending change that is observable in the world.[19] Change, he postulated, entails a unity in diversity; change involves something that is transformed into something else. Heraclitus's goal was not only that of pinpointing what this "something"—this basic element of all reality—is, but also of discovering the principle of change itself. His deliberations led him to conclude that the oneness of the cosmos lies in the orderliness and regularity of change; it consists in "change according to the measures," to cite Heraclitus's description.[20] Although he may not have drawn this conclusion himself, Heraclitus's perspective suggests that the unity of the cosmos is to be found in a unity of order within the change evident in the cosmos rather than in a oneness produced by some material that supposedly lies behind the cosmos.

In any case, Heraclitus depicted the cosmos as an ever living fire. In his estimation, fire formed an especially appropriate candidate for the depiction of change in that fire is a process by means of which what is consumed is transformed into something else in such a manner that a balance

---

16. For a short discussion of the meaning of the term *to apeiron* in Anaximander's thought, see Kirk and Raven, *Presocratic Philosophers*, 108–10.

17. Eduard Zeller, *Outlines of the History of Greek Philosophy*, 13th ed., Wilhelm Nestle, trans. L. R. Palmer (New York: Meridian Books, 1957), 64.

18. Heraclitus, fragment 12. For this translation, see Kirk and Raven, *Presocratic Philosophers*, 196.

19. In this respect, the typical heuristic contrasting of Heraclitus and Parmenides must be seen as historically questionable. For an example of the use of the two figures as a heuristic device, see Colin E. Gunton, *The One, the Three and the Many: God, Creation, and the Culture of Modernity* (Cambridge: Cambridge University Press, 1993), 16–21.

20. For this saying of Heraclitus, see Jones, *History of Western Philosophy*, 38.

is maintained between the in-come and the out-go of the process. As Samuel Stumpf explains, the result "is a stability in the universe because of the orderly and balanced process of change or flux, the same 'measure' coming out as going in, as if reality were a huge fire that inhaled and exhaled equal amounts, preserving all the while an even inventory in the world."[21]

Perhaps Heraclitus did not intend to suggest that everything was made of fire in a literal sense. He was likely not a materialist after the pattern of the Milesian thinkers. Rather, he possibly purposed that fire function metaphorically. His use of the term "fire" provided a way of conceptualizing how the cosmos could be characterized by the one apparent constant: change. Regardless of the exact manner in which he viewed the image of "fire," Heraclitus introduced the idea of the presence of an overarching unity—a *logos*—beneath the flux, and he postulated that this *logos* provides an undergirding order to the observable chaos.

The Birth of Being

Heraclitus's elevation of the importance of change in understanding reality has enjoyed far-reaching influence throughout the history of philosophy. Nevertheless, the honor of being the actual progenitor of Being, and hence of ontology as the study of Being, belongs to another fifth-century Greek philosopher, a younger contemporary of Heraclitus, who spent most of his life in Elea, a town south of Naples, Italy. Parmenides (540–470) is routinely hailed as the first philosopher to view all reality under the common aspect of Being.[22] He delineated his conception of Being in a poem, which according to historian Anthony Kenny is "the founding charter of ontology."[23]

Parmenides' poem is divided into two sections, preceded by an introduction. Of the two major parts, the first, entitled the "Way of Truth," is the more significant for the development of the concept of Being. In this section, Parmenides argues that the correct understanding of "what is," the perspective afforded by reason, differs greatly from what is commonly held to be the case, which, as he suggests in the second major part of the poem, arises from the senses. In drawing this distinction, Parmenides follows the lead of Heraclitus in differentiating between appearance and reality, and in suggesting that what is perceived by the senses is not always what is actually the case.

Parmenides' approach in the "Way of Truth" marks what many historians see as a far-reaching innovation in argumentation that lies at the

21. Stumpf, *Socrates to Sartre*, 13–14.

22. For an example of a philosopher who grants this status to Parmenides, see Henry J. Koren, *Introduction to the Science of Metaphysics* (St. Louis: Herder, 1955), 13.

23. Anthony Kenny, *A Brief History of Western Philosophy* (Oxford: Blackwell, 1998), 8.

heart of philosophical discourse: the basing of an argument on the method of deductive reasoning. The poet begins his deliberations by stating premises that he claims are necessarily true; he then deduces from these premises conclusions that he believes must be accepted as true as well. Furthermore, Parmenides shifted the focus of argumentation to the analysis of the most basic bits of language, especially the verb "to be." According to Solomon and Higgins, Parmenides (together with his student Zeno) thereby "removed philosophy from the hands of mere sages, visionaries, and speculators and turned it into a discipline, a difficult set of skills to be mastered only with considerable intelligence and patience."[24]

Parmenides' overarching goal was that of drawing out the implications of the widely held belief among the pre-Socratic philosophers that reality is constituted by a single element (monism). Yet his reflections on this belief led him to a conclusion that differed markedly from the perspective that Heraclitus had offered. His analysis of the concept of change suggested that the idea of a single, cosmic unity that undergoes change is self-contradictory. Parmenides argued that in contrast to what observations of the cosmos might suggest, change is not the fundamental characteristic of reality. Instead, change is illusionary.

The basic topic that Parmenides treats in his poem is *to on*, that is, the class of things that are be-ing or whatever is engaged in be-ing. Kahn highlights the importance of this aspect of Parmenides' work: "It was Parmenides who first introduced 'what is' (*to on*) as a central topic for philosophical discussion, and the paradoxical argument by which he developed his thesis turned out to be one of the most creative innovations in the history of Western thought."[25]

Parmenides begins his discussion of the "Way of Truth" by contrasting two types of inquiry, which can be expressed as "It is" (i.e., Being) and "It is not" (i.e., Unbeing or Not-being), or as two seemingly self-evident statements: "What is, is" and "What is not, is not." Parmenides writes:

> Come now, and I will tell thee . . . the only ways of enquiry that can be thought of: the one way, that it *is* and cannot not-be, is the path of Persuasion, for it attends upon Truth; the other, that it *is-not* and needs must not-be, that I tell thee is a path altogether unthinkable. For thou couldst not know that which is-not (that is impossible) nor utter it; for the same thing can be thought as can be.[26]

His conception of be-ing includes the idea of existing, of course. Yet it carries a much more all-encompassing meaning that brings into its purview an engagement with the fact that a thing has any characteristics

---

24. Solomon and Higgins, *Short History of Philosophy*, 34.
25. Kahn, "Retrospect on the Verb 'To Be,'" 4.
26. Parmenides, fragment 2. For this translation, see Kirk and Raven, *Presocratic Philosophers*, 269.

whatsoever. Stated in another manner, his interest is not limited to the use of the verb "to be" or "is" in the existential sense of "to exist." Rather, his concern extends to the word "is" in all its uses, including the copulative in which "is" joins a subject with a predicate ("X is Y"). Hence, in his use of the term, Being encompasses all those things to which something can be ascribed as true. Unbeing, in contrast, is that to which nothing can be ascribed as true.

According to Parmenides, it is impossible to think or to say, "It is not," because to do so is to contradict oneself. Not only does Unbeing not exist, insofar as no predicate can be ascribed to it, Unbeing cannot be the object of thought. In this manner, Parmenides linked being-thought and actual being.

The contrast between Being and Unbeing is closely connected to what many historians have cited as the main postulate of Parmenides' perspective: the static character of Being. We might say that Parmenides extended the stative-durative aspect of the verb "to be" to "*what is*" (*to on*), concluding that, like the meaning of the verb itself, "*what is*" must also be stative and durative.[27] As a consequence, he argued that Being has no beginning or end; nor is it subject to change. To suggest that Being has a beginning entails the supposition that it emerges from Unbeing, and to suggest that Being comes to an end requires that it turn into Unbeing. According to Parmenides, both of these proposals are impossible, simply because there is no such thing as Unbeing. Similarly, any change of Being would involve a change from Being to Unbeing, which is likewise nonsense.

The logic of his argument led Parmenides to reject as well any temporal or spatial distinctions in "what is." He thereby replaced the concept of time with the "eternal now." He also explicated the impossibility of special differentiation by likening "what is" to a sphere.[28]

Parmenides admitted, of course, that change does in some sense occur. What he denied is that such changes constitute changes *of* Being. Instead, he asserted that they are changes *within* Being. In so doing, he drew a conclusion from the common observation—that some things appear to be unchanging whereas other things seem to be in a constant state of flux—that differed greatly from his predecessors and contemporaries. Heraclitus attempted to solve the problem of the relationship between the seemingly opposite aspects of enduring and changing by postulating that in fact all things were in flux and that the fundamental characteristic of all reality is change. Parmenides, in contrast, asserted that at a fundamental level all things are static and therefore that unchangeability is the basic principle of reality.

27. For this suggestion, see Kahn, "Retrospect on the Verb 'To Be,'" 4.
28. For a helpful explication of Parmenides' arguments regarding these two points, see Hamlyn, *History of Western Philosophy*, 24.

When Parmenides drew this conclusion, Being was born. Yet the being that was birthed thereby was largely unknowable, for the final conclusion of Parmenides' argument was that the only declaration that could be made about "what is" is this: "It is."[29]

Being's Promotion to the Center of Philosophical Inquiry

The story of pre-Socratic philosophy does not end with Parmenides, of course. But the story of Being among the pre-Socratic thinkers does. The assumption that had driven the proto-ontology of Thales as well as the fledgling ontology of Parmenides was the belief that the cosmos was unified by means of the participation of all things in one fundamental principle that in turn is responsible for the diversity and change evident to the senses. Yet not everyone in the era prior to Socrates accepted this basic outlook. Some thinkers, such as Empedocles, Anaxagoras, and Leucippus, as well as the younger contemporary of Socrates, Democritus, rejected the idea of a unified cosmos in favor of a plurality of underlying elements.

Viewed from the perspective of philosophical materialism, the pre-Socratic era reached its high point with the latter of these, Democritus (c. 460–370). He postulated that the cosmos consisted of a host of elements, none of which could be further divided or cut into even more basic elements. Each of these "atoms" (from *a* = not and *tom* = cut), he added, was eternal. Moreover, these independent atoms produce all that is by randomly moving and combining in the void or empty space of the universe.

The pathway that Being trod, however, followed a trajectory that moved in a direction quite different from what Democritus's theorizing suggested. The philosopher who rescued the fledgling life of Being from a Democritizing fate was the fourth-century Athenian, Plato (428–348).

Being and the Realm of the Forms

Writing in 1952, W. T. Jones articulated the seemingly audacious claim that "whether we like it or not, we are, all of us, more or less Platonists." He then explained, "Even if we reject Plato's conclusion, our views are shaped by the way in which he stated his problems."[30] Jones included within this claim a host of people ranging from poets to politicians. Although this may be the case, the chief area of Plato's influence lies in philosophy in general and ontology in particular. Plato provides a crucial link in the history of Being.

Although Plato was by no means the first Greek philosopher, he has been credited with being the first to write extensively on the various problems of philosophy.[31] Solomon and Higgins go so far as to call him the

---

29. For this point, see Hamlyn, *History of Western Philosophy*, 24.
30. Jones, *History of Western Philosophy*, 92.
31. Vernon J. Bourke, *History of Ethics* (Garden City, NY: Doubleday, 1970), 1:24.

"greatest writer in philosophy" and to declare, "Compared to virtually any philosopher before or since, Plato was more brilliant, more moving, funnier, and more profound."[32] Similarly, Rex Warner lauds Plato as "a genuine innovator on a scale to which succeeding centuries offer no parallel."[33] Despite his great skill as an innovative thinker, Plato was deeply indebted to the pre-Socratic philosophers. Frank Thilly offers a helpful summary of the connection:

> Plato's system incorporates and transforms the doctrines of his predecessors. Plato shares the skepticism of the Sophists regarding knowledge of sense appearances, and agrees with Socrates that genuine knowledge is always by concepts. He accepts Heraclitus' doctrine that the world is in constant change, but restricts its application to the world of sensuous appearances. With the Eleatics, he agrees that the real world is unchangeable, but substitutes for Parmenides' unchanging being his world of eternal ideas. With the atomists, he agrees that reality is manifold, but replaces a plurality of atoms by a plurality of forms or ideas . . . and finally he agrees with nearly all Greek philosophers that reality is basically rational.[34]

Plato's place in the history of being rests largely with his well-known theory of forms, which is routinely hailed as Plato's "most significant philosophic contribution"[35] and "most original philosophical achievement."[36] This theory provides the basis not only for his ontology but for other aspects of his philosophical thinking as well, including his perspective on such matters as epistemology, politics, aesthetics, and ethics.[37]

Scholars routinely divide Plato's dialogues into three groups, reflecting three periods in his literary career. The first group consists of the Socratic dialogues, so named because in them Socrates appears in his historical role of deflating illegitimate claims to knowledge. These dialogues set the stage for the development of Plato's theory of forms. In the second group, Socrates is presented as a teacher expounding philosophical insights, chief among which is the theory of forms. Although Socrates is sometimes the central character in the dialogues that constitute the final group, more often his role is either diminished or nonexistent. Most significantly, these late dialogues often take a critical stance toward the theory of forms, an observation that leads some interpreters to conclude that Plato had come to abandon all or part of the theory. Whether or not Plato actually repudi-

32. Solomon and Higgins, Short History of Philosophy, 49.
33. Rex Warner, The Greek Philosophers (New York: Mentor Books, 1958), 72.
34. Thilly, History of Philosophy, 73.
35. Stumpf, Socrates to Sartre, 58.
36. Thilly, History of Philosophy, 81.
37. See, for example, the conclusion of Hamlyn, History of Western Philosophy, 58. For the author's synopsis of Plato's ethic, see Stanley J. Grenz, The Moral Quest: Foundations of Christian Ethics (Downers Grove, IL: InterVarsity Press, 1997), 65–67.

ated late in life the perspective that he so painstakingly developed during the middle period of his literary career, it is indeed the case, as Anthony Kenny points out, that "it is difficult to find any other philosopher in the history of the subject who has presented with similar clarity and eloquence such powerful arguments against his own most darling theories."[38]

Some commentators suggest that Plato's theory of forms may have been an outgrowth of his interest in ethics. He may have concluded that Socrates' questions about the nature of the virtues can only be answered by appeal to some perceived absolute standard—virtue as virtue, virtue as such, or virtue in itself—that defined the essence of each of the virtues and determined that they are indeed virtues.[39] An equally likely source was in the problem of epistemology that he inherited from his predecessors, whom he perceived as having rightly differentiated between appearance and reality, as well as from the distinction that Socrates drew between opinion and truth.

The world as perceived by the senses is changing constantly. Things come into existence, take on new characteristics, and pass away. In Plato's estimation, this situation cannot give rise to genuine knowledge, which by its very nature as the conformity of thought with reality is static, universal, and eternal. Following his mentor Socrates, Plato pointed out that the changeable character of things in the material world means that sense experience can only lead to opinion. Only the kind of intellectual perception that is able to lay hold of unchangeable objects can lead to knowledge.

To provide a way forward in this situation, Plato theorized that reality consists of two aspects. On the "surface," as it were, is the realm of perception or sense experience. This is the realm of the many, which includes individual things or objects. This is also the realm of change, impermanence or "becoming." In this "world of becoming," Plato acknowledged, everything is indeed in flux, as Heraclitus had pointed out. According to Plato, however, there is another world, the intelligible realm, the realm of the forms or the ideas (from the Greek terms *ideai* or *eidoi*, which refer to kinds or species rather than to mental ideas or concepts). Insofar as the forms are eternal, unchangeable and static, the realm of the forms is the "world of being" that coheres with Parmenides' vision.

Yet one additional aspect was necessary to bring the two pre-Socratic proposals together. Plato declared that the two worlds were connected. The many individual objects that we encounter through our senses *participate* in their corresponding forms. Objects exemplify—even if partially and inadequately—the forms.[40] Not only are the forms the essential

---

38. Kenny, *Brief History of Western Philosophy*, 55.
39. See, for example, Hamlyn, *History of Western Philosophy*, 49.
40. Hence, Stumpf describes Plato's forms as "those changeless, eternal, and nonmaterial essences or patterns of which the actual visible objects we see are only poor copies." Stumpf, *Socrates to Sartre*, 58.

archetypes that make things what they are, they also constitute the basis by means of which things can be judged to be what they are. To cite two examples, the forms of Beauty and Goodness are not only the archetypes that all things that are either beautiful or good exemplify, they are the unchanging standards by means of which things can be deemed beautiful or good.

Following the lead of his materialist predecessors would have led Plato to conclude that their immaterial character results in the forms being less real than objects in the world of becoming. Instead, he asserted that the eternal forms are more real than the changeable objects we encounter. They are more real, he argued, if for no other reason than because we must presuppose them in all our explanations of the world. Furthermore, they continue to exist eternally, persisting even as their particular exemplars perish. In addition, the forms are more real because they, and not the changeable things in the sensual world, are the objects of thought and hence of knowledge.

In this manner, Plato ascribed logical priority to the forms and elevated the realm of being above the world of becoming. At the same time, he did not relegate the world of becoming to mere illusion, but viewed it as a level of reality that is lower than the realm of being. The world of becoming holds this inferior status in that the things in the sensual realm are products not only of the forms but also of a second principle, "matter."[41] According to Plato, matter is the indefinable, formless, and imperceptible substratum that is responsible for the perishable, imperfect, and changeable aspects of things in the world of becoming. Whereas the presence in things of the forms mediates to them their participation in being, matter is the cause of the diversity and imperfection of the manifold exemplars that embody the same form.

The postulate that objects participate in their corresponding forms which logically precede them opened the way not only for Plato's conception of knowledge but also for his belief that knowledge is possible. He theorized that knowledge is ultimately concerned with the forms that changeable things reflect and that the quest for knowledge is a quest to know these unchangeable realities. To cite one example, Plato argued that the concept of circularity antedates our ability to identify circular objects.[42] Our idea of circularity does not correspond to anything in the physical world, because all such objects are subject to change over time. Instead, actual knowledge must be of the particular unchanging, nontemporal reality exemplified in all circular objects, namely, the form of Circularity. Because knowledge is knowledge of the forms, such knowledge is absolute, universal, and objective.

---

41. For a helpful synopsis of this aspect of Plato's thought, see Thilly, *History of Philosophy*, 82–83.

42. This example is drawn from Ethel M. Albert, Theodore C. Denise, and Sheldon P. Peterfreund, *Great Traditions in Ethics: An Introduction* (New York: American Book Co., 1953), 12–13.

Plato's thesis that everything in the world of becoming exemplifies its corresponding form also leads naturally to his understanding of the good. "Good" means simply "exemplifying the corresponding form." Hence, a particular tree is "good" if it exemplifies the form of Tree or Treeness. A good chair is one that exemplifies Chairness. Similarly, the good for humans consists of exemplifying the human form or Humanness.

According to Plato, what sets humans apart from the animals is the possession of reason, and hence he believed that humans are inherently intellectual beings. By means of the power of reason, humans can attain true knowledge, knowledge of the eternal realm beyond the changeable, physical objects present to the senses and hence beyond the realm of becoming. By using the power of reason, humans can contemplate the forms and thereby gain access to the eternal realm of Being. As they do, people exemplify the human form. In this context, Plato elevates the philosopher as the person who has developed the intellectual skills necessary to accomplish this task.

Plato took the theory of forms a step further. He noted that the forms participate in each other, thereby forming an organic unity. Furthermore, this participation leads to a hierarchical ordering among the forms that resembles a pyramid. The various human intellectual disciplines, in turn, have as their goal that of progressing upward in the pyramid of knowledge. Hence, a botanist, for example, moves from the study of a particular daisy to the study of the form Daisy, but then progresses to the higher form Flower.

Ultimately, the manifold plurality of the forms all participate in something that they have in common, namely, the form of forms, that stands at the apex of the hierarchical arrangement. Plato termed this highest form "the form of the Good." In this manner, he linked together the truly real and the truly good. Insofar as the ultimate human intellectual enterprise consists in knowing the Form of the Good, metaphysics and all other aspects of the human quest converge. Knowing the forms, and above all the form of the Good, satisfies not only our quest for truth but also our desire for beauty and virtue. In Plato's ontology, therefore, Being comes into its own as the all-encompassing eternal reality that gives meaning to everything else.

Being as Self-Absorbed Thinking

Centuries after his death, Plato's greatest pupil,[43] Aristotle (384–322), was hailed by Dante as "the master of those who know."[44] This epitaph was

43. Clifford L. Barrett, *Ethics: An Introduction to the Philosophy of Moral Values* (New York: Harper & Brothers, 1933), 140.

44. Louise Ropes Loomis, introduction to *Aristotle: On Man and the Universe*, ed. Louise Ropes Loomis (Roslyn, NY: Walter J. Black, 1943), xxxvi.

well deserved, for the breadth of topics about which Aristotle wrote—
ranging across the natural sciences, all aspects of philosophical inquiry,
the history of sport and the theater, as well as the history of ideas[45]—indicates that he was the paradigmatic "Renaissance man," if we might use
this term anachronistically. In the annals of the history of Being, however,
Aristotle is chiefly important as a master ontologist. Parmenides may be
heralded as the first metaphysician, insofar as he was the first thinker to
consider all things under the aspect of Being. Nevertheless, the status of
being the first person "to systematize a comprehensive theory of being"
belongs to Aristotle.[46]

Beginning in the Renaissance, commentators tended to regard Plato
and Aristotle as representing two opposite philosophical outlooks. This is
evident, for example, in Raphael's fresco that since 1620 has been known
as *The School of Athens*. The artist depicts Plato wearing the ethereal colors of fire and air (e.g., red and maroon or purple), carrying a copy of the
Timaeus (in which he sets forth his cosmology, including the theory of
forms), gesturing toward heaven, with his feet nearly suspended above the
steps. Aristotle, in contrast, is clothed in the tones of earth and water
(brown and blue), with the palm of his outstretched hand turned toward
the earth. He is carrying a copy of his *Ethics*, and his feet are firmly planted
on the floor. The twentieth-century historian of theology Samuel Stumpf
follows the traditional perspective on the two Greek philosophers when
he writes, "It could be said . . . that Aristotle oriented his thought to the
dynamic realm of *becoming*, whereas Plato's thought was fixed more upon
the static realm of timeless *Being*."[47] In recent years scholars have tended
to note the overlap between the two thinkers and to view Aristotle's perspective as more a modification than a refutation or abandonment of the
perspective proposed by his teacher.[48] Yet the similarities between the two
ought not to overshadow the important differences that separate them. In
the history of Being, Aristotle offered a far-reaching alternative to the perspective advanced by his mentor.

Aristotle is routinely hailed as the "the father of logic"[49] or the person
who "invented" formal logic in the sense that he was the first to develop
the study of deductive inference (syllogism).[50] His interest in logic (which
he designated as the science of analytics) was closely linked to his desire to
advance the sciences, which Aristotle understood in a broad manner that

45. For a list of the topics about which Aristotle wrote, see Kenny, *Brief History of Western Philosophy*, 58.
46. Koren, *Introduction to the Science of Metaphysics*, 13.
47. Stumpf, *Socrates to Sartre*, 81.
48. See, for example, the judgment of Kenny, *Brief History of Western Philosophy*, 57.
49. Walsh, *History of Philosophy*, 47.
50. For an example of the first accolade, see Stumpf, *Socrates to Sartre*, 83. The more circumspect
appraisal is found in David Charles, "Aristotle," in *The Oxford Companion to Philosophy*, ed. Ted
Honderich (New York: Oxford University Press, 1995), 53.

allowed him to include under this umbrella not only such obvious disciplines as physics but also politics, ethics, and aesthetics. He viewed logic as a tool by means of which the language of scientific analysis—understood as devising true statements regarding both *what* things are and *why* they are what they are or behave as they do—could be properly formulated.

For Aristotle, logic entails the attempt to set forth the basis for the development of the kind of language that could represent reality adequately. This quest, however, led seamlessly to metaphysics.

Aristotle noted that logical discourse proceeds by stipulating the kind of thing that is under discussion, that is, its "substance." In Aristotle's writings, "substance" can carry several meanings, but basically it refers to the enduring reality of a thing, including what it actually is, to which certain characteristics are predicated. These predicates can be either intrinsic or extrinsic to the substance to which they are predicated. The former are "essential" characteristics, whereas the latter are "accidental." A substance, then, may be described as the permanent substratum that underlies the characteristics, such as color, texture, and size, that are predicated of a particular thing. These characteristics, Aristotle added, can be grouped under several types or "categories," including quantity, quality, relation, action, affection, place, time, position, and endowments. In Aristotle's understanding, substances and categories are not simply mental constructs; they actually exist outside the mind (albeit only within actual things). Because these terms, which are among the topics that Aristotle's logic explores, are ontological as well as logical categories, the logic that he devised required an ontological underpinning.

Aristotle's designation for the discipline that later came to be known as metaphysics is "first philosophy." Metaphysics holds this rank—it is premier among the sciences—for several reasons. In his estimation, metaphysics is foundational to the scientific enterprise in that it is concerned with the "first principles and causes" from which the principles of the various sciences are derived and hence from which all other things come to be known. Moreover, metaphysics inquires into knowledge at the highest level—knowledge of what is universal rather than particular. In so doing, it goes beyond the questions of the other sciences, which inquire about what specific species of things are and why they are what they are. The task of metaphysics is to explore the universal or foundational question regarding what it means to be anything at all, that is, what it means for anything to be. For this reason, Aristotle concluded that first philosophy is the science of Being as Being. He provided the following succinct description:

> There is a science which studies Being *qua* Being, and the properties inherent in it in virtue of its own nature. This science is not the same as any of the so-called particular sciences, for none of the others contemplates Being generally *qua* Being; they divide off some portion of it and study the attribute of this portion. . . . But since it is for the

first principles and the most ultimate causes that we are searching, clearly they must belong to something in virtue of its own nature. Hence if these principles were investigated by those also who investigated the elements of existing things, the elements must be elements of Being not incidentally, but *qua* Being. Therefore it is of Being *qua* Being that we too must grasp the first causes.[51]

At the heart of his exploration into Being is Aristotle's repeated use of the postulate that objects are a unity of form and matter. In drawing from the language of form and matter, Aristotle was following the lead of Plato, who likewise attributed the existence of individual things to these two principles. Nevertheless, Aristotle's proposal marked a seemingly slight yet far-reaching alteration of his mentor's understanding of reality. The younger thinker agreed that the unchangeable, eternal forms are more perfect than changeable objects. But Aristotle rejected his mentor's suggestion that the forms exist outside of specific objects. Rather than existing in some separate realm of being, Aristotle averred, the forms "exist" only in the individual things in the cosmos in which they adhere. In short, in his estimation, form is never without matter, and matter is never without form.

His rejection of Plato's postulating of a realm of the forms meant that Aristotle invested greater importance in determining the philosophical dynamics involved in the process of change. In fact, his task was largely that of dealing with the problem of change as it had been bequeathed to him by his forebears. Rather than viewing existing things as static entities, he regarded them as ongoing activities.[52] Every substance, Aristotle explained, moves, changes, and acts; consequently, every substance is a subsisting energy—an act[53]—and hence an actuality. In this manner, he linked the being of a thing with its substance, understood both as what it is and as that whereby it is an act. Substance, therefore, understood in terms of act and not existence served as the key to Aristotle's ontology. Consequently, for him, Being took the form of a verb rather than a noun, as had been the case in Plato's ontological perspective.

This perspective on the significance of change led Aristotle to list "causes" with the "first principles" that the philosopher is seeking. Everything that is, Aristotle said, is what it is because of four causes (understood as principles that carry explanatory power).[54] He labeled these four the material, the formal, the efficient, and the final causes. Aristotle articulates his understanding of causation already in his *Physics*, a work that con-

51. Aristotle, *Metaphysics* VI.1.731–732. This idea is evident in the focus on the concept of the "first mover" that plays such a crucial role in Aristotle's thought. See, for example, Aristotle, *Metaphysics* IV.11–12.1018b9–1020a8 (pp. 102–7).

52. For a somewhat similar characterization, see Walsh, *History of Philosophy*, 52.

53. For a similar description, see Etienne Gilson, *Being and Some Philosophers*, 2nd ed. (Toronto: Pontifical Institute of Mediaeval Studies, 1952), 44.

54. For a succinct summary of the four causes, see Loomis, introduction to *Aristotle*, xvi.

stitutes what might be called a philosophy of nature or natural philoso-phy.[55] Stated simply, the material cause is the specific material elements of which the object is composed; the formal cause is the archetype or essence that comprises what the object actually is (such as what makes a ceramic bowl a bowl rather than merely a lump of clay); the efficient cause is the agent (e.g., the potter), whose activity caused the change that pro-duced the object as it now is; and the final cause is the goal that deter-mines the purpose or *telos* of the object, its raison d'etre.[56] Although these four are distinct, Aristotle observes that the latter three often coincide,[57] thereby setting up what becomes the fundamental polarity in his ontol-ogy: the distinction between form and matter.

In the *Metaphysics*, Aristotle repeats the findings of his *Physics*. Revers-ing the order of the first two causes, he describes them in the following succinct manner: "Now there are four recognized kinds of cause. Of these we hold that one is the essence or essential nature of the thing . . . ; another is the matter or substrate; the third is the source of motion; and the fourth is . . . the purpose or 'good'; for this is the end of every generative or motive process."[58] Consequently, Aristotle's four causes function as explanations for four aspects of any thing: what it is, from what it is made, by what (or whom) it is made, and the intention or goal for which it is made.[59]

Aristotle's conception of a dynamic involving form and matter and his perspective on the four causes as constituting the explanation for change coalesced in his understanding of the distinction between potentiality (*dynamis*) and actuality (*energeia*) or fulfillment (*entelecheia*). According to Aristotle, all objects are potentially whatever they have the capacity to become even before they attain or fulfill their potential. An acorn, for example, already is a potential oak tree before it takes root and grows. For Aristotle, actuality takes logical precedence over potentiality. Moreover, he equated "matter" with the potentiality that can become an actuality when it takes on form. In this sense, the actual (the form) logically pre-cedes the potential (the matter). Furthermore, he postulated that move-ment from potentiality to actuality requires that there already be something actual. Hence, the chicken precedes the egg—not temporally,

55. Aristotle, *Physics* II.3.194b 23–33, in *Introduction to Aristotle*, ed. Richard McKeon (New York: Random House, 1947), 122–23.

56. Walsh offers a quite different characterization of Aristotle's perspective: "The *material* cause or raw material (*hyle*) of any particular being is the power (*dynamis*) within the physical entity empow-ering its primary activity of being. The *formal* cause is the activity of being (*energia*) which is ener-getically going on within the particular reality or entity. The *efficient* cause is the agent that initiates a transition from an inner activity of one kind to a new and changed activity of another kind; thus, certain juices added to wine will change the wine into vinegar. The *final* cause is the goal-directed cause of a natural being's development." Walsh, *History of Philosophy*, 52–53.

57. Aristotle, *Physics* II.7.198a 26–29 (McKeon, *Introduction to Aristotle*, 132).

58. Aristotle, *Metaphysics* I.3.983a–983b 21–33 (McKeon, *Introduction to Aristotle*, 9).

59. For a statement of this approach, see Stumpf, *Socrates to Sartre*, 92–93.

but logically—because the chicken is the goal that is latent in the egg; it is the actuality of which the egg is a potentially. And for there to be an egg, there must have been a chicken that (logically speaking) preceded it.

The manner in which Aristotle describes the various causes leads inevitably to a close link between the final and formal causes. Insofar as the final cause stipulates what a thing is for, it determines what the thing is. At the same time, the *telos* toward which a thing strives is in a sense present within its formal cause. This connection lends an emphasis on what might be termed "internal finality" in Aristotle's ontology. Things strive to fulfill a goal that is latent in what they are, and yet what they are is conditioned by the *telos* that they are striving to actualize.

Because all things are caught up in the movement from potentiality to actuality and insofar as potentiality presupposes something that is actual, Aristotle concluded that some pure actuality must be presumed. There must be something that is purely actual, something whose "very nature is to be in act,"[60] an *actus purus* that is thereby the fullness of being. There must be something that is the ultimate cause of the movement from potentiality to actuality but does not participate in this movement itself. Aristotle termed this pure actuality, this eternal principle of motion, the Unmoved Mover. He likened the Unmoved Mover to the form of the world, which, in turn, he viewed as a substance. Furthermore, the Unmoved Mover is the final cause of the cosmos. By being the ultimate object of the desire of all that is, the Unmoved Mover moves, or draws, the cosmos toward its natural end, toward the fullness of its being, and hence toward the Unmoved Mover itself.

On the basis of the dictum that the "purely actual" cannot be involved in change, Aristotle's metaphysical reflections led him to postulate what must characterize the Unmoved Mover. He surmised that this actuality must entail the activity of thinking. Furthermore, the Unmoved Mover could only contemplate what is "most divine and precious." Consequently, the "divine thought" could only think about itself. "Its thinking," therefore, "is a thinking on thinking," as Aristotle himself declared.[61] This suggests that the Unmoved Mover, which is pure thinking and hence pure being, is "thought-thinking-thought," to cite Thilly's helpful quip regarding Aristotle's proposal.[62] Or, as Walsh states even more poignantly, the Unmoved Mover is "conscious Being being conscious."[63]

Insofar as the Unmoved Mover is the act of self-reflection, it is passive in the world-creating process. Etienne Gilson offers a telling characterization of Aristotle's perspective:

60. Aristotle, *Metaphysics* XII.6.1071b 20 (McKeon, *Introduction to Aristotle*, 132).
61. Aristotle, *Metaphysics* XII.9.1074b 26–27, 32–33 (McKeon, *Introduction to Aristotle*, 291, 292).
62. Thilly, *History of Philosophy*, 109.
63. Walsh, *History of Philosophy*, 65.

> As a World-Maker, the God of Aristotle can insure the permanence of substances, but nothing else, because He Himself is an eternally subsisting substance, that is, a substantial act, but nothing else. His actuality is a self-contained one. He is an act to himself alone, and this is why what happens outside Himself is not due to the fact that He loves, for He loves himself only, but to the fact that He is love.[64]

Aristotle's willingness to describe the Unmoved Mover as "thinking on thinking" leads to the conclusion that in the ontology—in the "comprehensive theory of being"—set forth so painstakingly by his reflections on Being qua Being, Being has not turned out to be nothing whatsoever, as some commentators seem to suggest.[65] Rather, Being has become reflective thought.[66] In bringing Being into the very center of metaphysics, "the philosopher's philosopher"[67] transformed the *to on* of the pre-Socratic thinkers into the Self-absorbed Intellect.

Being Becomes Christian

In Eduard Zeller's estimation, "Aristotle's philosophy denotes a beginning and an end."[68] This was clearly the case with respect to the history of Being. Together with his mentor Plato, Aristotle stands at the apex of the trajectory of ontological thought that began with Thales. At the same time, his alteration of Plato's metaphysical proposal set the stage for the next chapter of the ongoing saga of philosophical speculation regarding Being. As Solomon and Higgins rightly note, Aristotle's "ingenious metaphysics . . . in competition with Plato's theory of Forms, set the agenda for at least sixty generations,"[69] so much so that "the entire Western philosophical tradition is . . . an elaborate extension of the debate between Plato and Aristotle."[70] The prominent characters in that chapter were no longer pagan Greek philosophers, however, but a new breed of thinkers who sought to determine the relationship between the Greek concept of Being and the God of the Bible.

Initially, the attitude of Christian leaders to the Greek philosophical heritage was mixed. The second-century apologists, such as Justin Martyr, expressed sympathy for philosophy, while elevating Christianity as the true philosophy, the true pathway to wisdom.[71] Early in the third century,

---

64. Gilson, *Being and Some Philosophers*, 71.
65. See, for example, Kenny, *Brief History of Western Philosophy*, 80.
66. For this description, see Thilly, *History of Philosophy*, 101.
67. For this epitaph, see Solomon and Higgins, *Short History of Philosophy*, 56.
68. Zeller, *Outline of the History of Greek Philosophy*, 219.
69. Solomon and Higgins, *Short History of Philosophy*, 59.
70. Ibid., 67–68.
71. For a helpful summary, see Roger E. Olson, *The Story of Christian Theology: Twenty Centuries of Tradition and Reform* (Downers Grove, IL: InterVarsity Press, 1999), 54–67.

Clement of Alexandria, whom Kenny credits with providing "the first substantial attempt . . . to harmonize Christianity with Greek philosophy,"[72] went so far as to suggest that Greek philosophy served as a "schoolmaster" bringing the Greeks to Christ, a perspective that was echoed seventeen centuries later by Frederick Copleston.[73] Clement even advised that philosophical study was imperative for every educated Christian:

> Accordingly, before the advent of the Lord, philosophy was necessary to the Greeks for righteousness. And now it becomes conducive to piety; being a kind of preparatory training to those who attain to faith through demonstration. "For thy foot," it is said, "will not stumble, if thou refer what is good, whether belonging to the Greeks or to us, to Providence." For God is the cause of all good things; but of some primarily, as of the Old and the New Testament; and of others by consequence, as philosophy. Perchance, too, philosophy was given to the Greeks directly and primarily, till the Lord should call the Greeks. For this was a schoolmaster to bring "the Hellenic mind," as the law, the Hebrews, "to Christ." Philosophy, therefore, was a preparation, paving the way for him who is perfected in Christ.[74]

Not all patristic thinkers agreed with this appraisal, as is evident in Tertullian's famous rhetorical question "What does Athens have to do with Jerusalem?"[75] Nevertheless, the followers of Justin and Clement eventually gained the upper hand. Insofar as Christian theologians carried forward the trajectory of ontological reflection bequeathed to them by their Greek philosophical forebears, the fortunes of Being came to be tied up with their speculations.

Being and the Soul's Desire

The first Christians to fly the banner of Greek philosophy were more indebted to Plato than to Aristotle. This is evident already in the work of Clement. It is perhaps even more pronounced in his younger Alexandrian contemporary, Origen (185–254), who drew from philosophical arguments in his vigorous defense of Christianity aimed at his pagan fellow Platonist, Celsus. Yet the kind of Platonism that proved to be the most influential on the subsequent Christian philosophical tradi-

---

72. Kenny, *Brief History of Western Philosophy*, 95.

73. Frederick Copleston, *A History of Philosophy*, vol. 1, *Greece and Rome* (1946; repr., New York: Image Books, 1985), 503.

74. Clement of Alexandria, *The Stromata*, in *Ante-Nicene Fathers*, vol. 2, *Fathers of the Second Century: Hermas, Tatian, Athenagoras, Theophilus, and Clement of Alexandria*, ed. Alexander Roberts and James Donaldson (1887; repr., Peabody, MA: Hendrickson, 1995), 305.

75. Tertullian, *The Prescription against Heretics* 7. It might be an overstatement to say that Tertullian espoused a radical rejection of classical philosophy and culture per se. What he objected to were the heresies that often resulted from the syncretism of pagan philosophy and Christian theology. See Justo L. González, *The Story of Christianity* (San Francisco: Harper & Row, 1984), 1:53–54.

tion tended to be imported from a Greek philosophical source known as Neoplatonism.

The One beyond Being

The term "Neoplatonism" was coined by German scholars in the mid-nineteenth century as a means to differentiate the views of Plato from those of his ancient followers. Yet the designation is often used in a more specific sense to refer to the particular variety of Platonism inaugurated by Plotinus (204–270), whom Kenny elevates as "the last great pagan philosopher,"[76] and carried further by his disciple Porphyry (234–c. 305). This outlook is sometimes contrasted with the eclectic versions of Platonic philosophy that flourished from the first century BC to the second century AD, which are commonly grouped together under the designation "Middle Platonism."

Plotinus sought to overcome Aristotle's objections to Plato's philosophy by reshaping Plato's basic teachings into a new metaphysical system that resembles Aristotle's.[77] What resulted was a far-reaching alteration of Plato's ontology, especially his account of the form of the Good and the attendant understanding of the possibility of knowledge of ultimate reality.

On at least one occasion, Plato suggested that the form of the Good lies beyond the realm of the forms and consequently beyond Being itself (understood in the intellectual manner indicative of the ancient Greek philosophers). He declared, "The objects of knowledge not only receive from the presence of the good their being known, but their very existence and essence is derived to them from it, but of their being and essence, though the good itself is not essence but transcends essence in dignity and surpassing power."[78] Plotinus took this declaration seriously. In fact, this aspect of Plato's legacy formed the heart of Plotinus's Neoplatonism.

Paralleling the form of the Good in Plotinus's outlook is his concept of the One. According to Plotinus, the One is not an essence (*ousia*), but is beyond essences. It is not a being, but is prior to all beings. In fact, it is beyond Being as well.[79] Moreover, the One transcends all predicates, even the predicate "is," which means that it is completely ineffable and indescribable. Plotinus chose the term "the One" cognizant that no name actually suits this reality and only because the attempt to speak about it requires that some name be used.[80]

76. Kenny, *Brief History of Western Philosophy*, 96.

77. For this judgment, see R. Bain Harris, "Neoplatonism," in the *Oxford Companion to Philosophy*, ed. Ted Honderich (New York: Oxford University Press, 1995), 613.

78. Plato, *Republic* VI.509b, in the *Collected Dialogues of Plato*, ed. Edith Hamilton and Huntington Cairns (Princeton, NJ: Princeton University Press, 1961), 744.

79. Plotinus, *Enneads* VI.9.2–3, in *The Essential Plotinus*, trans. Elmer O'Brien (New York: Mentor Books, 1964), 74–78.

80. Plotinus, *Enneads*, VI.9.5 (*Essential Plotinus*, 80).

According to Plato, anything is knowable to the extent that it is real. Consequently, as the mind advances from particular things in the senses to abstract essences, thought becomes more definite and clear. Hence, when we look at a particular tree our conception of "treeness" is not fully crystallized, because that tree is not a perfect representation of treeness. But as our mind moves from particular trees to the Form of Treeness our conception becomes clearer, because we are now contemplating Treeness in its pure form apart from the deficiencies that characterize every particular tree, each of which is less real than the corresponding form. Moreover, Plato believed that the human mind could come to know the highest form, the form of the Good, and thereby actualize the highest mode of human existence. Plotinus disagreed. He observed that all thought involves duality, namely, the duality of the thinker and the object thought. For this reason, all thought is conditioned, in contrast to ultimate reality, which is unconditioned, and therefore thought is inadequate to the task of knowing. On this basis, Plotinus concluded that what is ultimate—the One—cannot be apprehended through the power of thought alone.

Plato also declares that the form of the Good is the source of the being of all things. Plotinus picked up on this Platonic theme as well. He taught that the One serves as the eternal source of all that is, as well as the measure of all things. Yet he added that the One does not create the cosmos, for creation implies activity, which in turn entails change. According to his cosmology, all that is flows or "emanates" from the One in a manner similar to the way that light emanates from the sun. Consequently, everything manifests the One, even though nothing is equal to or can be equated with it. Moreover, the emanations that form the cosmos arise in a (logically) sequential series that form a hierarchy. The first of these emanations, and hence the one that is most like the One, is Intelligence (*nous*), which comprises the underlying rationality of the cosmos and is somewhat comparable to the realm of Plato's forms (or perhaps the contemplation of the forms). Plotinus linked Intelligence (and not the One) to the concept of Being.[81] Emanating from Intelligence is Soul (*psyche*), which we might view on one level as the life principle animating the entire physical universe in which we participate through our personal soul. At the end of the chain of emanations is Matter, which is devoid of form and, because it is furthest away from the One, lies close to darkness.

Plato postulated that insofar as sensible objects belong to the realm of becoming, they simply cannot reflect the forms perfectly. He suggested that such objects are evil only in a negative way, namely, in that they lack goodness. Plato's followers, however, came to view matter as in some sense being itself evil. Plotinus explained that in keeping with the chain of emanations, material things are disposed to move downward by means of

---

81. Plotinus, *Enneads*, V.9.8 (*Essential Plotinus*, 53).

engaging in motion that is not directed rationally. In this respect, he viewed matter as the principle of evil, even speaking of formless matter as the "first evil." Humans find themselves in the middle of this hierarchy of being.[82] As composite beings consisting of soul and matter, they belong partially to the realm of spirit and partially to the realm of matter. Yet their true being does not lie in the material dimension, but in the intellectual or spiritual. Although Plotinus acknowledged that humans are intellectual creatures, he declared that true fulfillment does not come through satisfying the human intellectual curiosity. More than seekers of knowledge, humans are essentially "desire,"[83] and the true object of the human soul's desire is the One. The soul desires the One as the perfection that it lacks. In this way, the One is the "source" of the soul. Nevertheless, because humans are caught within material bodies, the soul does not necessarily look upward to the higher realm. Instead, humans tend to orient themselves by looking downward to the lower regions of matter. In this manner, the body emerges as the "second evil," for the influence of the material body, with its tendency toward the absence of order, is the cause of the evil that emerges in the soul's existence. As a consequence, for Plotinus the struggle against evil "is therefore not against some outside force but against the tendency to be undone within, to become disordered, to lose control of the passions," to cite Stumpf's helpful characterization.[84]

According to Plotinus, all creation is a cyclic movement *from* the One and *to* the One. More importantly, because the soul is a microcosm of the universe, the cyclic rhythm perceivable throughout the universe is imbedded in the ontological structure of the human person. The soul is designed to return to the One, by means of a turning inward, an "introspection" or a journey into the "center of the soul," to cite Plotinus's words.[85] This journey involves three stages. The first is a negative movement that consists of the separation of the self from the realm of multiplicity or sense experience so as to enter into the intelligible realm.[86] This step entails forsaking the world of matter for the interior world of thought. But because the soul does not return to the One through the pursuit of knowledge alone, a second stage must follow, which involves a separation from an even loftier multiplicity, namely, from reasoning itself. In this stage, the soul moves deeper within, entering a realm in which even thought disappears. Insofar as these two steps lead to an interiority in which the soul has attained the point of utmost simplicity within itself, they prepare the way for the third stage: union with the One.

82. Plotinus, *Enneads*, IV.8.4, trans. Stephen Mackenna (New York: Penguin Books, 1991), 338–39.

83. Elmer O'Brien, introduction to *Essential Plotinus*, 31.

84. Stumpf, *Socrates to Sartre*, 129.

85. Plotinus, *Enneads* VI.9.8 (Mackenna, 544).

86. Plotinus, *Enneads* I.6.9; IV.7.34 (Mackenna, 54–55, 502–3).

Plotinus likened the union of the soul with the One to inebriation. Or, to use another analogy, it is similar to being so absorbed in the task of reading that the reader is no longer aware that he or she is reading.[87] Such a union involves the intellect going beyond itself into the nonintelligible. But the most appropriate word to describe the experience is "ecstasy," understood in the original sense of "standing outside oneself."[88] In the return to the One, the last veil of multiplicity is lifted. The soul takes flight to its true home, the One, from which it came. Because it involves the overcoming of the subject-object dualism, the experience is closer to sensing a "presence transcending knowledge"[89] than engaging in an act of knowledge. When this occurs, Plotinus declared, "the contemplative is suddenly swept by the wave of The Intelligence beneath and carried on high and sees, never knowing how; vision floods the eyes with light but it is not light that shows some other thing; the light is itself the vision."[90] In its ecstatic union with the One, the soul becomes in a sense divine itself.[91]

Being as the Desire of the Christian Soul

Neoplatonism flourished for several centuries after the deaths of Plotinus and Porphyry. It even found a home in Athens at a philosophical school that at one point was headed by Proclus (412–485), who systematized Neoplatonism and synthesized it with other proposals. Many Christians in the patristic era viewed Greek philosophy in general and Neoplatonism in particular with suspicion, however, an attitude that climaxed in the emperor Justinian issuing an order in 529 forbidding the teaching of philosophy at the Athenian school. Despite this act, that according to some historians signaled the end of an age,[92] aspects of Neoplatonism seeped into Christian thought. Proclus influenced the Christian writer Dionysius the Areopagite, now known as Pseudo-Dionysius, who introduced into Byzantine theology an apophatic approach to knowledge that was fashioned out of the Neoplatonic heritage. Even more important, however, in infusing Christian thought—especially its Latin variety—with impulses from the Greek philosophical tradition and thereby setting the stage for the intellectual pursuits of the Middle Ages was the work of the great bishop of Hippo, Augustine (354–430). As Anne Fremantle observes, "At the very beginning of medieval philosophy stands St. Augustine, and, in a way, he stands also at its end."[93]

87. Plotinus, *Enneads* I.4.10 (Mackenna, 40–41).

88. Plotinus, *Enneads* VI.9.11; VI.7.17 (Mackenna, 547–49, 486–88).

89. Plotinus, *Enneads* VI.9.4 (Mackenna, 539).

90. Plotinus, *Enneads* VI.7.36 (Mackenna, 505).

91. Plotinus, *Enneads* V.1.3 (Mackenna, 350).

92. Mayer, *History of Ancient and Medieval Philosophy*, 335.

93. Anne Fremantle, *The Age of Belief: The Medieval Philosophers* (New York: Mentor Books, 1954), 23.

Like his Greek philosophical forebears, Augustine explored the metaphysical question about the nature of reality. Furthermore, the Neoplatonism that he encountered through the Latin translations of the writings of Plotinus and Porphyry while a professor of rhetoric in Milan influenced his understanding of Christianity.[94] Nevertheless, the overriding consideration that determined his perspective on reality was the Christian faith. Consequently, rather than being purely philosophical, his interest in the nature of the real was overwhelmingly religious. As Jones observes, "It was not, for instance, a desire to solve the problem of knowledge that led him to investigate the nature of reality. . . . With him the motive was a desire for the soul's salvation and a search for a satisfactory object of religious faith."[95] In keeping with this perspective, Augustine declared, "God and the soul, that is what I desire to know. Nothing more? Nothing more."[96]

With Augustine, therefore, the self in its relationship to God emerges as the central philosophical problem.[97] In elevating the soul in this manner, he offered a new, theological twist to the Socratic dictum, "Know thyself."[98] Augustine viewed the journey inward both as an odyssey of the soul and as a pilgrimage into the soul that marked the quest for God. The goal of this inward journey toward God, which involves both the cognitive and the affective dimensions of the soul, is to bring the soul to love what the mind contemplates, so that the soul might be affected by what it in love possesses.[99] As this occurs, the soul experiences the eternal life that comes through knowing (John 17:3) and loving God (Matt. 22:37),[100] namely, union with God. In short, Augustine turned to the soul, because he was convinced that the inward journey marks the pathway to the eternal God, who alone can bestow true happiness.[101]

In keeping with the task of "faith seeking understanding," Augustine's delineation of the soul's journey to God required a rational apologetic for the existence of the God in whom Christians believe. He was convinced, however, that before postulating the certainty of God's existence, the philosopher must establish the trustworthiness of reason, or the possibility of certitude in general, by proving that it is possible to know something

94. Alasdair MacIntyre offers a somewhat unique description of this indebtedness: "The Platonic dichotomy between the world of sense perception and the realm of Forms is Christianized by St. Augustine into a dichotomy between the world of the natural desires and the realm of divine order." MacIntyre, *A Short History of Ethics* (New York: Macmillan, 1966), 117.

95. Jones, *History of Western Philosophy*, 353.

96. As quoted in *Philosophy in the Middle Ages: The Christian, Islamic, and Jewish Traditions*, ed. Arthur Hyman and James J. Walsh (Indianapolis: Hackett Publishing Co., 1973), 16.

97. Mayer, *History of Ancient and Medieval Philosophy*, 367.

98. For this judgment, see Etienne Gilson, *The Christian Philosophy of Saint Augustine*, trans. L. E. M. Lynch (New York: Random House, 1960), 3.

99. Augustine, *Eighty-Three Different Questions* 35.2, trans. David L. Mosher, in *The Fathers of the Church*, ed. Ludwig Schopp (New York: CIMA Publishing, 1948), 70:65–66.

100. Augustine, *Eighty-Three Different Questions* 35.2 (Schopp, *Fathers of the Church*, 70:66–67).

101. Augustine, *The Happy Life* 2.11 (Schopp, *Fathers of the Church*, 5:58–59).

at all. For this reason, the actual starting point for Augustine's reflections lay in his response to the Greek philosophical skepticism that he had at one point embraced but then abandoned upon his discovery of Neoplatonism and against which he wrote soon after his conversion to Christianity. Augustine countered the skeptics' assertion that the human mind is incapable of comprehending any truth by arguing that the act of doubting (or the state of being deceived) itself yields certainty, if only the certainty that one is doubting (or is deceived).[102] This realization entails as well the certainty of one's own existence.[103] In *The City of God*, he offered this variation of the *cogito* that is sprinkled throughout his writings:

> If I am deceived I am. For he who is not cannot be deceived; and if
> I am deceived, by this same token I am. And since I am if I am
> deceived, how am I deceived in believing that I am? for it is certain
> that I am if I am deceived. Since, therefore, I, the person deceived,
> should be, even if I were deceived, certainly I am not deceived in this
> knowledge that I am.[104]

In his rebuttal of skepticism, Augustine claimed a degree of certainty for what is known within the soul. Thereby, the Augustinian turn inward elevated the cognitive aspect of the soul—that is, the mind—and opened the door to what Charles Taylor calls "the stance of radical reflexivity or adopting the first-person standpoint,"[105] that is, the turn toward one's own act of being aware. Moreover, as Etienne Gilson points out, by means of this process of freeing itself "of doubt by the certainty of its own existence" the mind is led to see itself "as a vital activity of a higher order." In short, the "mind sees itself as soul."[106]

What emerges as Augustine's ensuing concern, however, is not whether a person can gain certainty, but rather the manner in which certainty is attained: how the finite, changeable human mind can attain indubitable knowledge of eternal truths, which govern the mind itself and therefore

102. Augustine, *On the True Religion* 39.73; *The Free Choice of the Will* 2.3.7, trans. Robert P. Russell, in *The Fathers of the Church: A New Translation* (Washington, DC: Catholic University of America Press, 1968), 59:113–15.

103. See Augustine, *The Happy Life* 2.7 (Schopp, *Fathers of the Church*, 5:51 n. 1), regarding which the editor remarks, "It is here for the first time that Augustine seeks to establish the absolute certitude of one's own consciousness as the essential basis of knowledge"; Augustine, *Soliloquies* 2.1, in *Nicene and Post-Nicene Fathers*, 1st series, 7:547–48; Augustine, *Free Choice of the Will* 2.3.7 in *Augustine: Early Writings*, ed. John Burleigh, vol. 6, The Library of Christian Classics (Philadelphia: Westminster Press, 1953), 109. See also Augustine, *Confessions* 5.10.19, in *Nicene and Post-Nicene Fathers*, 1st series, ed. Philip Schaff (1887; Peabody, MA: Hendrickson, 1995), 1:86; Augustine, *On the Trinity* 15.12.21, in *Nicene and Post-Nicene Fathers*, 1st series, ed. Philip Schaff (1886; Peabody, MA: Hendrickson, 1995), 3:210–12. (Hereafter this work will be abbreviated *NPNF*.)

104. Augustine, *The City of God* 11.26, in *NPNF*, 1st series, 1:220.

105. Charles Taylor, *Sources of the Self: The Making of the Modern Identity* (Cambridge, MA: Harvard University Press, 1989), 130.

106. Gilson, *The Christian Philosophy of Saint Augustine*, 44.

transcend it.[107] Yet he did not begin immediately with the knowledge present in the mind, but with what in his estimation constitutes the lowest level of knowledge: knowledge that arises from the senses. Such knowledge carries the least degree of certainty, Augustine theorized, in that both the objects that we sense and the organs by means of which we sense them are constantly changing.

More important for Augustine's program than whatever actual knowledge sense experience might be able to produce, however, is the role of sensation in pointing the mind beyond the objects of sense to the immaterial objects or ideas (such as beauty or the truths of mathematics) that the mind uses in making judgments about sensed objects.[108] As sensation directs the mind "upward" in this manner, the pathway of knowledge moves from the less certain level (knowledge of, or truths about, sensed objects) to the more certain level (general or eternal truths, which do not reside in the objects themselves but in the comprehending mind or reason). In this manner, Augustinian thought follows a path leading "from things outward to inward, from lower to higher,"[109] as Augustine himself said, or "from the exterior to the interior and from the interior to the superior," to cite Gilson's interpretation of Augustine's statement.[110]

Augustine's question as to how the mind, which is finite, can grasp with certainty truths that are eternal had also exercised Plato and Aristotle. In his response, Plato theorized that the soul comes to recollect what it knew before entering the body. Aristotle, in turn, suggested that the intellect comes to know the forms by seeing their presence in particular things. In contrast to both (albeit nevertheless drawing from an analogy articulated by Plato), Augustine appealed to the concept of illumination. Just as the eye is able to perceive objects that are illumined by light from the sun, so also the mind is able to see eternal truths "in a certain incorporeal light which is *sui generis.*"[111] According to Augustine, the "incorporeal light" that facilitates the finite human mind in its epistemological task is God. Furthermore, in contrast to Plato but pursuing a direction somewhat similar to Plotinus, Augustine concluded that the immutable ideas exist in the mind of God and consequently that the goal of the search for truth is the God who not only facilitates the mind in understanding truth but is also Truth itself. In this manner, Augustine demonstrated that the attaining of truths, including the certitude of one's own existence, leads the

107. For a similar characterization of Augustine's concern, see Frederick Copleston, *A History of Philosophy*, vol. 2, *Mediaeval Philosophy* (1950; repr., New York: Image Books, 1985), 52.

108. Augustine, *On the Trinity* 9.6.9–11; 12.14.22–23; 12.15.24, in *NPNF*, 1st series, 1:129–30, 163–64; Augustine, *The Free Choice of the Will* 2.13.35; 2.8.20–24.

109. Augustine, *On Psalms* 146 (145). 2, in *NPNF*, 1st series, 8:662. See also Augustine, *On the Trinity* 14.3.5, in *NPNF*, 1st series, 3:185.

110. Gilson, *Christian Philosophy of Saint Augustine*, 20.

111. Augustine, *On the Trinity* 12.15.24, in *NPNF*, 1st series, 3:164. See also Augustine, *Soliloquies* 1.8.15; 1.1.3, in *NPNF*, 1st series, 7:539, 7:538.

mind to seek a unity higher than itself, that is, to search for the Truth that illumines everyone who comes into the world (John 1:9).[112] In short, the presence of truth in the mind is the surest sign of the presence of God—who is immutable Truth—in the soul.

In addition to the cognitive, Augustine's inward turn involved a strong affective or volitional dimension. According to Augustine, every operation of one's cognitive powers is under the control of the will, and consequently each movement of the soul depends on the will.[113] Building on the Aristotelian idea that every physical entity is drawn to its own appropriate location by a type of natural weight, Augustine asserted that the soul is drawn to its natural place of rest. He termed the soul's "weight"—the desire that produces every movement of the will—"love" or "charity," understood as the natural tendency toward some good.[114] In a manner that parallels his epistemological move from truths in the mind to the reality of God as Truth, Augustine argued that God, understood as the highest Good, lies behind and beyond the movement of the will toward specific goods. Drawing from the Johannine declaration "God is love" (1 John 4:8), he declared that God is the object of charity, as well as being Charity itself.[115] God is both the ultimate Good that the human person desires and, as the true object of the soul's desire, the one who constitutes the true essence of the will. In this manner, Augustine viewed the will as the dominant faculty of the human soul and the key to the soul's journey toward God. In his estimation, if the will turns away from its divine end it cuts the whole person off from that goal, whereas if the will adheres to its true goal it binds the entire person to it as well.[116]

The appropriation of the Neoplatonic focus on ultimate knowledge as a mystical intuition of the divine that lay at the heart of Augustine's philosophical program[117] was tied to a basically Neoplatonic ontology that conceived of reality as a hierarchy of being resembling a pyramid and that equated being with the good and nonbeing with evil. Yet in adapting the ontology that he inherited from the Neoplatonists, Augustine replaced the One at the apex of Plotinus's hierarchy of reality with the Christian God, who, according to Augustine, is likewise the highest good.[118] On this basis, Augustine asserted that the human *summum bonum* is God, or perhaps better stated, the enjoyment of God. Augustine postulated that humans seek after God by nature. And we find blessedness only as we are

112. Augustine, *De Vera Religione* 39.73.
113. Gilson, *Christian Philosophy of Saint Augustine*, 132–33.
114. Augustine, *Confessions* 13.9.10; *Letters* 55.10.18; *City of God* 11.28.
115. Augustine, *Homilies on the First Epistle of John* IX.1 in *NPNF*, 1st series, 7:513–14.
116. Gilson, *Christian Philosophy of Saint Augustine*, 237.
117. Albert et al., *Great Traditions in Ethics*, 107.
118. Augustine, *Concerning the Nature of Good*, in *Basic Writings of Saint Augustine*, trans. A. H. Newman, ed. Whitney J. Oates (New York: Random House, 1948), 1:431.

"inwardly illuminated and occupied by his truth and holiness."[119] Only then do our strivings cease, for in both the contemplation of God and affection for God we find the goal of our existence. Augustine voiced this sublime idea in the eloquent prayer found in his *Confessions*, "You have formed us for Yourself, and our hearts are restless till they find rest in You."[120]

Augustine's adaptation of Neoplatonism also provided the foundation for his response to the problem of evil. Insofar as God created everything that is, all beings (including the devil) are good.[121] Evil, therefore, is not something that actually exists; it is not an objective reality. Instead, evil is purely negative; it is a privation of being or of goodness that "exists" only in beings which are themselves good. As Augustine declared, "There is no efficient cause of evil, but merely a deficient one, for evil is not effected, but a defection."[122] The negativity that is evil can take the form of the disruption of order in nature or the disordering of nature. Hence, evil occurs when any being is deprived of its order or when its original nature as God created it becomes corrupted. Moral evil, in turn, emerges as good creatures fall away from their true moral nature and therefore lack the moral goodness that ought to characterize them. The source of evil deeds lies in human passion[123] and ultimately in a privation within the human will. Evil arises from a will that is not what it ought to be, for instead of desiring God it is directed toward something that is not God. The solution for this concupiscence, in turn, is a redirection of the will toward God that arises with the setting of the affections on God alone.

At one crucial point, however, Augustine's ontology differs significantly from that of Plotinus, namely, in the latter's contention that the One is beyond Being. Augustine was moved to disagree with Plotinus by his reading of Scripture. More particularly, he was influenced by the divine act of self-naming given to Moses. The God of Israel is "I am what I am," which Augustine took to mean, "the one who exists," that is, Being. In addition, Augustine observed that nearly everyone conceives of God as "something than which nothing more excellent or more sublime exists" or "that which excels in dignity all other objects."[124] In keeping with considerations such as these, Augustine concluded that God is the highest being, the perfect being, or even Being itself. The one who is both Being itself and the source of being and truth is both eternal and all-knowing.

---

119. Augustine, *On the Morals of the Catholic Church* 11.18, trans. Richard Stothert and Albert H. Newman, in *St. Augustine: The Writings against the Manichaeans and against the Donatists*, in *NPNF*, 4:46.

120. Augustine, *Confessions* 1.1.1, in *NPNF*, 1st series, 1:45.

121. Augustine, *Enchiridion* XII, in *NPNF*, 1st series, 3:240.

122. Augustine, *City of God* 12.7, in *NPNF*, 1st series, 2:230.

123. Augustine, *The Problem of Free Choice (On Free Will)* 1.3.8, trans. Dom Mark Pontifex, vol. 22 of *Ancient Christian Writers*, ed. Johannes Quasten and Joseph C. Plumpe (New York: Newman Press, 1955), 41.

124. Augustine, *On Christian Doctrine* 1.7.7, in *NPNF*, 1st series, 2:524.

As the all-knowing source of all that is, Augustine added, God contemplates eternally his own essence. In this manner, God sees in himself all possible finite reflections of his infinite perfection, which thereby are eternally present in the divine mind as the divine ideas or exemplars. According to Augustine, then, all things are finite reflections of God's eternal thought[125] and have ontological truth insofar as they embody the exemplars in the divine mind.

In Augustine's proposal, therefore, following as it did on the heels of Plotinus's work, the Being of Greek philosophy became the God who is the soul's desire. As such, the biblical God—the one disclosed as the great I AM—is Being itself.

Being as the *Ipsum Esse*

The thousand years between the fall of Rome to the barbarians in the fifth century to the fall of Constantinople to the Turks in the fifteenth century are often lumped together as forming an epoch known as the Middle Ages.[126] Samuel Stumpf paints an especially bleak picture of the first half of this era:

> The fall of the Roman Empire in 476 ushered in a period of intellectual darkness. The barbarians who destroyed the political might of Rome also shattered the institutions of culture in Western Europe. Learning came almost to a halt. Virtually the whole body of ancient literature was lost. For the next five or six centuries, philosophy was kept alive by Christian scholars who became the channels through which the works of the ancient Greeks were transmitted to the West.[127]

The wars, invasions, and migrations that plagued Europe beginning in the final years of Augustine's life did indeed exact an immense toll on the intellectual life of the Western world. Yet the bleakness of these centuries was punctuated by the work of such luminaries as Boethius (c. 480–524)—whom the fifteenth century humanist Lorenzo Valla characterized as the last of the Romans and the first of the scholastics[128]—and John Scotus Erigena (c. 810–c. 877). Moreover, regardless of how "dark" they may have been, the centuries that have often been characterized as the Dark Ages eventually gave way to the great burst of intellectual creativity that resulted in the rebirth of philosophy during the late eleventh through the early fourteenth centuries. Regarding this era, Anne Fre-

125. See Stumpf, *From Socrates to Sartre*, 141–42.

126. For this judgment, see Fremantle, *Age of Belief*, 72.

127. Stumpf, *From Socrates to Sartre*, 151. For a similar perspective, see Mayer, *History of Ancient and Medieval Philosophy*, 370.

128. Henry Chadwick, *Boethius: The Consolations of Music, Logic, Theology, and Philosophy* (Oxford: Clarendon, 1981), xi.

mantle declares, "Then it was that Christian culture produced such a feast of learning and literature, of law and art, as made it one of the glorious golden ages of man."[129]

Intellectual activity flourished in these centuries, largely because this era was characterized by what Edward Grant calls "a new self-conscious emphasis on reason," the role of which was deemed to be that of elucidating the natural and the supernatural worlds. Grant explains the importance of this development: "In all the history of human civilization, reason had never been accorded such a central role, one that involved so many people over such a wide area for such an extended period."[130]

The approach to philosophical and theological questions pursued by Christian thinkers in the Middle Ages, especially by those who were associated with the cathedral schools, came to be known as scholasticism. At the heart of scholasticism was the belief that Christian faith and human reason were not inimical. Rather, as Augustine had suggested, the God of the Bible had endowed humans with the faculty of reason. One consequence of this divine gift was that reason could assist believers in coming to understand more clearly the truths that they had already accepted by faith. A long list of significant thinkers—beginning in the eleventh century with theologians such as Anselm, who is sometimes credited with being the father of scholasticism[131]—concluded that it was not only appropriate but even necessary to apply reason to the mysteries of the Christian faith. Yet the central figure who drew from this approach in the task of advancing the history of Being was the theologian who in the estimation of most historians stands at the apex of medieval philosophy: Thomas Aquinas (1225–1274).[132]

Aquinas's perspective on the nature of Being emerged out of his monumental synthesis of Christian theology and the heritage of Greek philosophy. This synthesis was made possible because the medieval master postulated that a partial overlap in subject matter exists between theology and philosophy, especially insofar as the latter climaxes in natural theology. Viewed from this perspective, both theology and philosophy speak about God's creation of the cosmos and of the human *telos*, an outlook that eventually led to Aquinas's linking of the First Cause of the world with the God of the Bible.

Aquinas acknowledged that the two disciplines are formally distinct, for they view the objects that they study from two quite different perspectives: Philosophy studies created things as they are in themselves, whereas theology considers them as in some way representing

---

129. Fremantle, *Age of Belief*, 73.
130. Edward Grant, *God and Reason in the Middle Ages* (Cambridge: Cambridge University Press, 2001), 2–3.
131. Grant, *God and Reason in the Middle Ages*, 56.
132. For this judgment, see Stumpf, *From Socrates to Sartre*, 173.

God.[133] Philosophy explores what is knowable by the light of reason, whereas theology speaks about what is known by divine revelation.[134] Nevertheless, Aquinas countenanced no ultimate disparity between theology and philosophy.

Aquinas's rationale for this assumption arose in part out of the general scholastic perspective that postulated a harmony between faith and reason. Rather than being inimical to nature, he argued, the gifts of grace, including religious faith, are added to nature in such a manner that they perfect it. Furthermore, in that both faith and reason are given by God, the light of faith does not destroy the light of natural reason.[135] Moreover, because God is the author of both, nothing that is instilled in us by nature can ultimately contradict what has been revealed by God and is known to us through faith. For Aquinas, this meant that matters pertaining to philosophy, which is grounded in the natural light of reason, cannot contradict or oppose matters pertaining to the sacred teaching explored by theology. On the contrary, theology completes philosophy.

Although he was a theologian by profession, Aquinas was well versed in both Platonism and Aristotelianism, and both influenced his thought.[136] Indeed, Henry Sidgwick characterizes his perspective as "Aristotelianism with a Neo-Platonic tinge, interpreted and supplemented by a view of Christian doctrine derived chiefly from Augustine."[137] Of the two impulses, however, that of Aristotle served to be the stronger. Aquinas participated in the renaissance of interest in Aristotle that was developing during the thirteenth century. He was, of course, no slavish devotee to his Greek forebear.[138] Nevertheless, in his attempts to move against what had hitherto been the central strand of the medieval tradition, which had been dominated by the legacy of Augustine and, by extension, the philosophical method that originated with Plato, Aquinas drew heavily from Aristotle, whom he repeatedly designated simply as "the Philosopher."

Although he was indebted to Platonism at certain points, Aquinas rejected what he saw as the "Platonic errors" that he was convinced were

133. Thomas Aquinas, *Summa Contra Gentiles* II.4, in Thomas Aquinas, *On the Truth of the Catholic Faith*, vol. 2, *Creation*, trans. James F. Anderson (Garden City, NY: Image Books, 1956), 34–36.

134. Thomas Aquinas, *Summa Theologica* Ia.1.1, trans. Fathers of the Dominican Province (1911; repr., Westminster, MD: Christian Classics, 1981), 1.

135. *Leon.* 50.98.114–18, as cited in John F. Wipple, *The Metaphysical Thought of Thomas Aquinas: From Finite Being to Uncreated Being* (Washington, DC: Catholic University of America Press, 2000), xxii.

136. For this judgment, see Jan A. Aertsen, "Aquinas's Philosophy in Its Historical Setting," in *The Cambridge Companion to Aquinas*, ed. Norman Kretzmann and Eleonore Stump (Cambridge: Cambridge University Press, 1993), 13–14.

137. Henry Sidgwick, *Outlines of the History of Ethics* (Boston: Beacon, 1960), 141.

138. For a helpful engagement with the question of the dependency of Aquinas on Aristotle, see Joseph Owens, "Aristotle and Aquinas," in Kretzmann and Stump, *Cambridge Companion to Aquinas*, 38–59.

responsible for the philosophical aberrations of his day. At the heart of these errors was the "flight from existence."[139] In Aquinas's estimation, by postulating the two worlds—the realm of the forms and the realm of sensible objects—Plato had erroneously separated "being" from "becoming" and had in effect declared that reality is fundamentally essence rather than existence. As a consequence, Aquinas added, Plato had falsely concluded that the senses, which only yield knowledge of changeable particular objects, were epistemologically separated from the attainment of knowledge of the changeless eternal forms.

In forming a response, Aquinas drew from Aristotle's claim that objects in reality (or substances) consist of "form" plus "matter." At the same time, he offered an innovative expansion of Aristotle. He widened the basic Aristotelian ontology to include the idea that things are also a composition of "essence" (or substance) plus "existence." For Aquinas, substance is what is or has being, whereas "existence is that in virtue of which a substance is called a being."[140] As that in virtue of which a substance is a real being (*ens*), existence (*esse*) stands in relation to essence as actuality to potentiality. Joseph Owens summarizes the radical ontological shift that this Thomistic postulate entailed: "For Aristotle the things were actual through their form. For Aquinas the composite of form and matter was made actual by existence. Existence was in this way the ultimate actuality of every finite thing, and always distinct from the thing's nature."[141]

Aquinas's central ontological principle, that a thing has being insofar as it is a composition of essence and existence, placed contingency at the heart of all finite being. Because things are essence plus existence, their being is not necessary; they do not need to exist. This discovery of a contingency lying at the core of all reality, in turn, allowed Aquinas to postulate the existence of a Being that is the author of all things, yet cannot itself be a composition of existence and essence but must have existence as its very essence and thereby exists by necessity. Aquinas found that this philosophical conclusion cohered with the meaning of the divine name as "I am who I am" that God disclosed to Moses (which Augustine had likewise noted), for the biblical text indicates that God's very nature is that of existing. This means that being belongs to God's own nature. Insofar as God's very essence is to be, in God existence and essence coincide. God, in short, is *ipsum esse*.

In contrast to Aristotle's perspective, Aquinas postulated that the coincidence of essence and existence is the case only with respect to God. In

139. For a helpful discussion of this point, see Anton C. Pegis, introduction to *Introduction to Saint Thomas Aquinas,* by Thomas Aquinas, ed. Anton C. Pegis (New York: Modern Library, 1945), xi–xii; and Ralph McInerny, *St. Thomas Aquinas* (Notre Dame, IN: University of Notre Dame Press, 1977), xv–xxvii.

140. Aquinas, *Summa Contra Gentiles* 2.54.

141. Owens, "Aristotle and Aquinas," 48.

all created things, in contrast, essence and existence are separable.[142] Not only is God the primary instance of Being, God also becomes the one who, in turn, bestows being on all that is. In reaching this conclusion, Aquinas—like Christian theologians before him—replaced the Greek idea that the cosmos was eternal with the biblical notion of the divine creation of the world "in the beginning." In so doing he transformed Aristotle's Unmoved Mover, who can only be the final cause of the world, into the Creator God of the Bible, understood not only as the world's final cause but also its efficient cause. As the first efficient cause of all things, this God is the cause of their being. God is therefore the *ipsum esse* from whom all things derive their *esse*. Aquinas's postulate that God is the First Cause of the world had the additional advantage of allowing him to conclude that rather than merely contemplating the divine reality itself (as is the case with Aristotle's Unmoved Mover), the God who creates all things also knows every detail about created things and exercises providential care over them.

The distinction that he posited between essence and existence facilitated Aquinas in taking an epistemological step beyond Aristotle as well. The medieval theologian concluded that the mental activity in grasping a thing's nature (*what* it is), namely, the activity of conceptualization, differs from that involved in judging that the thing exists (*that* it is).[143] Moreover, this ontological perspective gave rise to a this-world based, naturalistic or concretely focused epistemology. Aquinas considered the senses to be the gateway to knowledge.[144] Furthermore, on the basis of the presence of natural light within the intellect, he dispensed with the Augustinian idea that divine illumination is necessary for knowledge of truths.[145]

Aquinas's basically Aristotelian metaphysical assumption that all things are a composite of form and matter occasioned his understanding of the nature of the human person. In contrast to the Platonic anthropology with its focus on the soul coming to know apart from the body, Aquinas declared that the human person is soul plus body,[146] a composite in which the soul is the form of the body.[147] Aquinas added that the soul is the spiritual substance through which the composite human individual exists.

Aquinas agreed with his Greek forebears that the fundamental human purpose is knowing. He agreed wholeheartedly with the famous opening

142. For an extended treatment of this distinction in Aquinas's writings, see John F. Wipple, *The Metaphysical Thought of Thomas Aquinas: From Finite Being to Uncreated Being* (Washington, DC: Catholic University of America Press, 2000), 132–76.

143. For a helpful delineation of this Thomistic innovation, see Owens, "Aristotle and Aquinas," 48–49.

144. Aquinas, *Summa Theologica* 1.1.9; see also 1.85.3.

145. See, for example, Aquinas, *Summa Theologica* Ia.79.4 and IaIIae.109.1.

146. Aquinas, *Summa Theologica*, 1.75.4.

147. Ibid., 1.76.1.

line of Aristotle's *Metaphysics*: "All human beings by nature desire to know."[148] This agreement put him at odds with an outlook propagated by certain medieval Augustinians, such as Bernard of Clairvaux (1090–1153), who condemned the idea that knowledge should be pursued for its own sake.[149] Despite his basic agreement with the Greek philosophical tradition, Aquinas asserted against its Platonist branch that the soul is unequal to its task apart from the body. Because the soul knows truth only as it comes to know objects in the senses, knowing is mediated through sense experience. Insofar as the knower is not "pure mind" but a composite of soul and body, the activity of the human person consists in "knowing the world of sensible things" rather than "thinking abstract thoughts in separation from existence," to cite Anton Pegis's characterization of Aquinas's position.[150]

In defending the idea that knowing lies at the heart of human nature, Aquinas drew from the basic Aristotelian insight that agents always act with a specific end in view: "Every agent, by its action, intends an end. For in those things which clearly act for an end, we declare the end to be that towards which the movement of the agent tends."[151] Each existing thing has a purpose, each is designed to act for some specific goal, and each naturally "tends" toward this purpose; it strives to fulfill its *telos* or to actualize its potential, which in turn comprises its "good." Because the soul is an intellectual substance, Aquinas added, the goal of human existence is not merely physical maturity but intellectual knowledge. Or perhaps more appropriately stated, the activity that most actualizes the human purpose is knowing.

Aquinas's focus on existence and essence facilitated him in elevating the vision of God as the *telos* of human existence as a knowing creature. In a manner reminiscent of certain impulses derived not only from Aristotle but also from Neoplatonism, he declared that the highest "object" we can know—and thus the goal or object of our epistemological quest—is God.[152] He derived this conclusion from the idea that the perfection of an effect consists in returning to its principle or to that from which it comes. According to Aquinas, the Creator of all things, and hence the one who is their final end, is God. More particularly, "the end of the intellectual creature" (i.e., the human person) is to come to know the First Cause.[153] Ultimately, knowing the First Cause entails understanding *what* God is by means of the contemplation of God's essence. It involves

---

148. Aristotle, *Metaphysics* I.1.980a21 (Hope, 3).
149. For a short discussion of this, see Aertsen, "Aquinas's Philosophy," 28.
150. Pegis, introduction to *Introduction to Saint Thomas Aquinas*, xxiv.
151. Aquinas, *Summa Contra Gentiles* 3.2.
152. For a discussion of the reason that the contemplation of God is the end of the human person, see McInerny, *St. Thomas Aquinas*, 59.
153. Aquinas, *Summa Contra Gentiles* 3.25; see also 3.37.

nothing less than the vision of God (*visio Dei*). Although Aquinas admitted that this "possession of God" is primarily an intellectual activity, in his estimation it also involves the satisfaction of the will, which in the process is moved by reason toward the only true good. This situation, Aquinas concluded, constitutes true happiness.[154]

Aquinas quickly added that the attainment of such blessedness is not possible in this life.[155] In the here and now, we simply cannot see God face to face.[156] Nor does the beatific vision that comes with the reception of eternal life arise apart from divine grace, for the natural light of reason is limited in what it can come to know about God.[157] According to Aquinas, human reason can move from sense experience of the world to a demonstration of God's existence (i.e., *that* God is). Reason can also determine to a limited extent *what* God is, insofar as reason concludes what must be deemed to be true about God as the First Cause of the world.[158] Yet this movement proceeds from created things, which can represent only in part what God is. Consequently, Aquinas concluded, the affirmations that we make about God on the basis of the perfections that we see manifested imperfectly in creatures are not univocal but only analogical. And, of course, reason is inadequate to discover the truths about God that are given by revelation and to which we have access only through faith. For complete theological knowledge, therefore, and hence for attaining the beatific vision of God, we are dependent upon divine revelation.[159]

In this manner, in Aquinas's theologically informed system of the intellectual disciplines that facilitated his synthesis of Christian theology and Greek philosophy, faith becomes the divine gift that perfects our intellectual nature. Moreover, theology—which includes the study of the truths regarding the Creator God of the Bible—thereby becomes the crucial discipline that completes philosophy, understood as the exploration of Being qua Being. As Frederick Copleston concludes regarding Aquinas's perspective, "Metaphysics has its own object . . . and a certain autonomy of its own, but it points upwards and needs to be crowned by theology."[160] In the process, however, Aquinas pressed the God of the Bible into the service of ontology. As the *ipsum esse*, God has become the self-existent First Cause of the world, as well as Being qua Being.[161]

154. Ibid., 3.26.
155. Ibid., 3.48.
156. Aquinas, *Summa Theologica*, 3.51.
157. Ibid., 1–II.109.5.
158. Aquinas, *Summa Contra Gentiles* 1.3.2–3.
159. Aquinas, *Summa Theologica*, 1.1.1.
160. Copleston, *History of Philosophy*, 2:311.
161. For a similar conclusion voiced by a twentieth-century Thomist, see Etienne Gilson, *Being and Some Philosophers*, 2nd ed. (Toronto: Pontifical Institute of Mediaeval Studies, 1952), 157.

Chapter Two

From the First Cause
to the Infinite

The Secularization of Being

The classical era of Greek culture witnessed the rise and flowering of philosophy in general and metaphysics in particular. The reflections of three centuries of Greek intellectuals, climaxing in the work of Aristotle, resulted in a well-developed ontology that placed the concept of Being at the center of the philosophical understanding of reality. After some initial hesitation, Christian theologians took upon themselves the role of guardians of this treasure. In the West, a tradition of philosophical theology, or theological philosophy, emerged that rivaled—even surpassed—the trajectory charted by the ancient Greek masters. From Augustine to Aquinas, Christian thinkers busied themselves with the task of determining how the God whom they served fit together with the Greek conception of Being.

The link between the Greek and Christian perspectives—between the idea of the First Principle of all that is and the "I AM who I AM" of the Exodus narrative—was forged in a variety of basilicas, monasteries, and university lecture halls of Christendom. Yet perhaps the greatest of the Christian theological blacksmiths was Thomas Aquinas. His elevation of natural theology as the point of overlap between the philosophical and theological disciplines facilitated his efforts to claim that the First Cause of the world that Aristotle had discovered through his philosophical ruminations was none other than the biblical God who had created the world *ex nihilo*. With Aquinas, therefore, it appeared that the vexing questions of ontology had been resolved and, consequently, that the story of metaphysics had reached its proverbial "happy ending." Yet the narrative turned out to be no fairy tale, and its happy ending was short-lived. The turning of the page of the book of ontology did not reveal the anticipated closing words "the end" but a stark "to be continued . . ."

At issue in part two of the saga would be the very manner in which God and Being are to be conceived. Some thinkers would pursue a pathway similar to the one that Aquinas, following Aristotle, had trod and offer variations and permutations of the idea of God as the First Cause of the world. Others, in contrast, would opt in a direction that was more in keeping with Plato and Augustine and appeal instead to the concept of the Infinite. In the end, however, ontology would move far afield of the marriage of the Greek and the Christian visions that was consummated in the Middle Ages. Indeed, the discussion would lead to what might be characterized as the demise of the "Christian" Being or the secularization of Being.

The Demise of the Scientific God

The Thomistic synthesis did not simply constitute the climax of nineteen centuries of Western philosophical reflection. Rather than marking the end of ontology, the work of Aquinas served to launch a renewed discussion about the nature of Being and, with it, of the connection between the Christian God and the Greek idea of a First Principle of the cosmos. The genius of Aquinas was his ability to set forth a conception of theology and philosophy that presented God as a necessary aspect of both disciplines. Because the God of Christian theology was in fact the First Cause of the world, he maintained, this God was not only the topic of Christian theology but was also the first principle—that is, the *telos*—of philosophical inquiry. In this manner, Aquinas presented the I AM of Scripture as a scientific God. As theologians and philosophers began the descent from the heights of medieval thought, however, this assertion came to be hotly contested. When the dust settled, the scientific God had been dethroned, a development that constituted a significant chapter in the larger story of the demise of the "Christian" Being and Being's secularization.

The Undoing of the Thomistic Synthesis

Already during Aquinas's life, intellectual (and political) strife had pitted Augustinians against Aristotelians. This discord intensified after Aquinas's death in 1274. At stake in the dispute was nothing less than the grand synthesis of theology and philosophy that he had so carefully crafted. Regarding this development, Etienne Gilson declared tersely, "After a short honeymoon, theology and philosophy thought they had discovered that their marriage had been a mistake."[1]

The Undermining of the Intelligible God

One theologian who stood between the Aristotelians and their Augustinian critics was a thinker whose sophisticated intellectualizing earned him the nickname "the subtle doctor," namely, John Duns Scotus (c. 1266–1308). D. J. B. Hawkins lauds Scotus as "a systematic thinker in the grand manner, second only to St. Thomas in the middle ages, and presenting another synthesis of Augustine and Aristotle."[2] Allan B. Wolter, in turn, declares that Scotus "brought many of Augustine's insights, treasured by his Franciscan predecessors, into the mainstream of the Aristotelianism of his day."[3]

As these accolades suggest, Scotus was above all a Christian theologian whose main interest was to make room for Christian doctrine within the context of the Aristotelian philosophical framework. To this end, his goal was not that of simply criticizing Aquinas—in fact, his criticisms more often are directed toward other targets—but rather that of correcting and completing the synthesizing work that Aquinas had advanced.[4] Although he believed that in the process he was preserving the basics of Aristotelian philosophy, his tinkering with the proposal of his Greek mentor was sufficiently radical to produce what in the end was a thoroughgoing revision not only of Aristotle but, by extension, of Aquinas as well.[5]

Scotus's tinkering with Aristotle and Aquinas arose out of his concern to safeguard the objectivity of knowledge and validate the claim that the human intellect possesses genuine knowledge.[6] He accepted the general Aristotelian epistemology that views knowledge as moving from particulars to the universals embedded in them. He agreed as well that the primary natural object of the intellect is Being qua Being. But in contrast to Aristotle and Aquinas, Scotus denied that the human mind was limited

---

1. As quoted in Anthony Kenny, *A Brief History of Western Philosophy* (Oxford: Blackwell, 1998), 152. For a similar sentiment, see Etienne Gilson, *The Spirit of Medieval Philosophy,* trans. A. H. C. Downes (Notre Dame, IN: University of Notre Dame Press, 1936), 18.

2. D. J. B. Hawkins, *A Sketch of Medieval Philosophy* (New York: Sheed & Ward, 1947), 101.

3. Allan B. Wolter, "Duns Scotus, John," in *The Cambridge Dictionary of Philosophy*, 2nd ed., ed. Robert Audi (Cambridge: Cambridge University Press, 1999), 247.

4. For a similar judgment, see Martin J. Walsh, *A History of Philosophy* (London: Geoffrey Chapman, 1985), 151.

5. See Martin M. Tweedale, "Duns Scotus, John," in *A Companion to Metaphysics*, ed. Jaegwon Kim and Ernest Sosa (Oxford: Blackwell, 1995), 126.

6. For a similar judgment, see W. T. Jones, *A History of Western Philosophy* (New York: Harcourt, Brace & Co., 1952), 511.

by nature to knowledge derived from sense experience. In his estimation, this would undermine metaphysics as the science of Being qua Being. Or to state the point from the perspective of Christian metaphysics, it would make any natural knowledge of God impossible, thereby casting us on revelation alone in the task of knowing God.

Nor did Scotus find admissible Aquinas's appeal to analogical language as the means whereby the philosopher could move from knowledge of creatures to truth about God. He asserted that the "transcendental" concepts that we gain from sensible things and then apply to God—including perfections such as wisdom, knowledge, truth, beatitude, freedom, and benevolence—must be postulated of both in a univocal manner, for otherwise we could not draw inferences from what we know to be true of creatures to what must be true about God. Scotus extended this principle to the concept of being, as well as to the attributes of being (one, true, good), all of which, he concluded, must likewise be univocal.[7] In short, Scotus's tinkering suggested that despite Aquinas's good intentions, his epistemology had undermined the possibility of any natural knowledge of God and in so doing had actually opened the door to skepticism and agnosticism.

Rather than following Aristotle and Aquinas, Scotus asserted that the mind naturally possesses the ability to grasp knowledge of Being as such, and not merely material being. Yet in keeping with the extension to epistemology of Christian teaching regarding human sinfulness that he acquired through Augustine, he quickly added that this capability is severely limited in the mind's present fallen state. Furthermore, Scotus set much stiffer criteria for what constitutes a valid demonstration of a logical argument than Aquinas had done. More specifically, he did not agree with his predecessor that inferences that move from effects to their cause can be conclusive. As a result of his more careful approach coupled with his voluntarism, Scotus concluded that Aquinas had been overly optimistic about what can be known about God through philosophy (in the form of natural theology).

An additional difficulty that Scotus detected in the Thomistic epistemology was concerned with our knowledge of individuals. Following Aristotle, Aquinas postulated that matter is the individuating principle in all physical creatures. But if matter is unknowable and knowledge is only of forms, as Aquinas also taught, then how can the mind gain knowledge of individual things?

Scotus attempted to resolve this difficulty that he found inherent in Thomism by replacing matter as the principle of individuality with an additional element, which he designated *entitas individualis* or *haecceitas*

---

7. For a helpful summary of Scotus's enumeration of the transcendental attributes, see Walsh, *History of Philosophy*, 153.

("thisness").[8] According to Scotus, a thing's "haeccity" or "thisness" is inseparable from, yet nevertheless distinct from, the form or nature that determines the thing's "whatness" (*quidditas*) and is shared by other things of the same kind. In the knowing process, in turn, the mind abstracts from the haeccity of a thing the form or common nature that it shares with others. Hence, the *haecceitas* and the *quidditas* form what Scotus, following an approach that was common among the Franciscan thinkers of his day, called an objective formal distinction (*distinctio formalis a parte rei*), that is, a distinction that the mind makes when it distinguishes in an object two or more formal elements that are objectively distinct but are in fact ultimately inseparable from one another.[9] For example, whereas soul and body are ultimately separable from each other, the essence "human" and the instantiation of humanness in a particular human being are not.

The effect of this proposal was far-reaching. Aquinas had declared that insofar as things are composites of essence and existence, in all finite beings essence and existence are distinct. Scotus denied this. His argument was based in part on the act of cognition itself: "Nor should a distinction be made between the knowledge of *whether a thing is and what it is.* . . . For I never know of anything *whether it is* unless I have some concept of that which I know to be, and this inquiry is about that concept."[10] Scotus took the matter a step further. His perspective effectually eliminated the necessity for a finite essence to be imbedded in matter to be individuated and in that sense to exist. Rather, an essence qua essence is already in fact individualized. Insofar as neither essence nor existence accounted for the individuality of real things, Scotus could simply do away with any significance that might arise from distinguishing them, or possibly even eliminate the distinction between them completely.[11] Hence, he declared forthrightly, "it is simply false, that existence (*esse*) is something different from essence."[12]

As this conclusion suggests, Scotus's tinkering extended to ontology as well. He accepted Aristotle's basic description of metaphysics as the science of Being qua Being. But rather than taking up Aristotle's interest in

8. Duns Scotus, *Opus Oxoniense* [*The Oxford Commentary on the Four Books of the Sentences*], 2.3.5, no.1, and 2.3.6, as cited in Frederick Copleston, *A History of Philosophy*, vol. 2, *Mediaeval Philosophy* (1950; repr., New York: Image Books, 1985), 516; Duns Scotus, *Quaestiones in libros Metaphysicorum* 7.13, nos. 9, 26, as cited in Copleston, *History of Philosophy*, 2:517.

9. For a similar description, see Copleston, *History of Philosophy*, 2:508.

10. Duns Scotus, *Opus Oxoniense* [*The Oxford Commentary on the Four Books of the Sentences*], book I, distinction III, questions 1–2, in *Philosophy in the Middle Ages: The Christian, Islamic, and Jewish Traditions*, ed. Arthur Hyman and James J. Walsh (Indianapolis: Hackett Publishing Co., 1978), 561.

11. Fremantle, for example, makes this stronger claim: "Duns Scotus denied the distinction between essence and existence, because neither accounted for the individuality of real things." Anne Fremantle, *The Age of Belief: The Medieval Philosophers* (New York: Mentor Books, 1954), 183.

12. Duns Scotus, *Opus Oxoniense* 4.13.1, no. 38, as cited in Copleston, *History of Philosophy*, 2:510.

the four causes, Scotus, perhaps following the Islamic philosopher Avicenna, devoted his attention to the questions that surround the idea and nature of being.[13] Moreover, as a Christian, he viewed the ultimate goal of this science to be the pursuit of what can be said about the God who revealed himself to Moses as "I AM WHO I AM." To this end, Scotus revamped the proofs for God's existence that had been set forth by his theological predecessors, especially Anselm and Aquinas. In his estimation, the proofs lead to the supposition that God is the uncaused, nondependent transcendent cause of all finite beings; above all, God is the one who is infinite. Insofar as "infinite," in contrast to "being," cannot be predicated of creatures but of God alone, Scotus concluded, "infinite" signifies God's intrinsic, distinct mode of being. In short, God is the infinitely perfect being.

This perspective, in turn, leads to what is perhaps the most widely known aspect of Scotus's proposal and one that clearly placed him at odds with Aquinas: his defense of what is often termed "voluntarism." Aquinas had argued that in both God and the human person, the intellect is the primary power and that this power moves the will. The theological implication of this position is that God acts in accordance with the eternal exemplars that exist within the divine intellect, rather than by some mysterious or unknowable determination of the divine will. Scotus was less enamored than Aquinas with the Greek perspective that described the will largely in terms of appetite. Instead, he linked the will, as the power of volition, to freedom, a shift in emphasis that allowed him to declare categorically, "Nothing other than the will is the total cause of volition in the will."[14] Furthermore, insofar as the one who is Infinite Being must be characterized by complete liberty, God's actions are not contingent on anything beyond the divine will. On this basis (and more in keeping with Augustine), Scotus gave far more credence to the role of the will in moving the intellect. As a result, he was far less convinced than Aquinas that the universe is thoroughly rational or intelligible.

Anne Fremantle insightfully declares, "For St. Thomas . . . God is the infinite *being*, for Duns Scotus, He is the *infinite* being."[15] This shift in emphasis, although grammatically slight, when coupled with the introduction of "thisness" as a central ontological concept, was philosophically far-reaching. It marked, in effect, not only the shift in focus from existence to essence but the subsuming of existence under essence that lay at the heart of Scotus's tinkering with the Thomistic synthesis. This is evident, for example, in *The Oxford Commentary on the Four Books of the Sentences* (*Opus Oxoniense*), in which Scotus declares that to know God is to

---

13. See, for example, Copleston, *History of Philosophy*, 2:483.
14. Duns Scotus, *Opus Oxoniense*, book II, distinction XXV, the Single Question, in Hyman and Walsh, *Philosophy in the Middle Ages*, 599.
15. Fremantle, *Age of Belief*, 185.

know God as this particular essence which necessarily exists.[16] His use of the proofs for God's existence leads to the conception of God as the one who is both first in the order of being and infinite being. Because being first and being infinite can be postulated of God alone, they constitute God's uniqueness and hence God's "thisness." Insofar as the "thisness" of God is in this manner determined, so also is God's existence, which thereby becomes an intrinsic mode of the divine essence.[17]

In short, Scotus's exploration of Being qua Being nets the conclusion that existence is ultimately a mode of individuality or individualized essence, and the one who is the most fully individual of all and hence who exists most necessarily is the one whose essence is that of being infinite. This Infinite Being, whose existence is an intrinsic mode of his essence, is the one whom theology in turn equates with the "I AM WHO I AM" of the Bible. In offering this proposal, Scotus took a first step away from the idea of a rational First Cause of the world that had played such a crucial role in the Thomistic synthesis and a step toward the conception of God as the volitional Infinite that would emerge as a central motif in later ontological presentations.

The Undermining of Natural Theology

Frank Thilly, reflecting the historiography that by the turn of the twentieth century had become the standard narrative,[18] declares that scholasticism moved through three stages, each of which was characterized by a unique understanding of the meaning of universals. During the formative period, the ninth to the twelfth centuries, scholasticism reflected the Platonic idea that universals comprise the essences of things and therefore exist (logically speaking) *prior to* things. In the thirteenth century, which formed the culmination or completion[19] of scholasticism, the Aristotelian outlook predominated, so that universals were considered to be real, yet as existing *in* things rather than prior to them. Then during the period of the eclipse[20] or decline of scholasticism that ensued in the fourteenth century, many philosophers came to conclude that universals are not real in either of the ways articulated by their realist forebears but "exist" only in the knowing mind and hence solely *after* things.[21]

16. Duns Scotus, *Opus Oxoniense*, lib. 1, dis. 2, q. 1–2, no. 4, as cited in Gilson, *Spirit of Medieval Philosophy*, 93.

17. For a detailed development of this argument, see Etienne Gilson, *Being and Some Philosophers*, 2nd ed. (Toronto: Pontifical Institute of Mediaeval Studies, 1952), 93–94.

18. This historiography is articulated, for example, by Patrick J. Foote in his "Outline History of Scholastic Philosophy," which was added to the 1923 edition of Shallo's standard textbook of scholastic philosophy initially published in 1905. See Michael W. Shallo, *Lessons in Scholastic Philosophy* (Philadelphia: Peter Reilly, 1923), 3–21.

19. This is Foote's preferred term. Foote, "Outline History of Scholastic Philosophy," 11.

20. This is Foote's preferred term. Foote, "Outline History of Scholastic Philosophy," 17.

21. Frank Thilly, *A History of Philosophy*, 3rd ed., rev. Ledger Wood (New York: Henry Holt, 1957), 191–92.

The transition from the thirteenth to the fourteenth centuries, and hence from the culmination to the decline of scholasticism, was already heralded by Duns Scotus. Indeed, Aquinas's writings were hardly dry when Scotus inaugurated what would become a long line of philosophers who modified the great medieval thinker's vision of the reasonableness of the universe and of the God who had created it by shifting the focus away from the divine reason to the divine will.[22] Despite his voluntarism, however, Scotus remained a thoroughgoing realist. Consequently, the person who more than any other embodied the far-reaching philosophical transformation that was underfoot was not Scotus but William of Ockham (c. 1285–1349).

According to D. W. Hamlyn, Ockham represented "the last peak of medieval philosophy."[23] Similarly, Anne Fremantle describes him as standing, "if any single man can claim such a position, at the end of the Middle Ages as the great iconoclast, clearing the encumbered ground and preparing a beach-head for the philosophers of the Renaissance."[24] Above all, Ockham contributed to the destruction of the scientific God (and with it the demise of "Christian" Being) by launching a process that led to the decoupling of the Christian God from the Greek philosophical idea of the First Cause. The basis for doing so lay in his unwavering allegiance to the primacy of revelation in theology, which had the effect of undermining the synthesis of philosophy and theology that had formed the legacy of Aquinas and the other scholastic thinkers of the high Middle Ages.

As Fremantle's appraisal suggests, Ockham is routinely considered a philosopher. Yet he saw himself above all as a theologian. Moreover, as a theologian, he was preoccupied with a desire, in the words of Frederick Copleston, "to purge Christian theology and philosophy of all traces of Greek necessitarianism, particularly of the theory of essences, which in his opinion endangered the Christian doctrines of the divine liberty and omnipotence."[25] Ockham understood God's omnipotence to mean that God can do anything that God chooses to do. This emphasis formed a stark contrast to the implications inherent in the older metaphysic of essences, which suggested that God was governed by (and therefore, in Ockham's estimation, limited by) the eternal ideas or essences.[26]

His concern to defend the omnipotence and freedom of God launched Ockham along the road to voluntarism that Scotus had charted. Ock-

22. Henry Sidgwick offers the controversial conclusion that according to Duns Scotus, God's will lies beyond reason and consequently that God's ordering of the world is absolutely arbitrary. Sidgwick, *Outlines of the History of Ethics* (Boston: Beacon, 1960), 147.

23. D. W. Hamlyn, *A History of Western Philosophy* (New York: Viking, 1987), 122.

24. Fremantle, *Age of Belief,* 201.

25. Frederick Copleston, *A History of Philosophy,* vol. 3, *Late Mediaeval and Renaissance Philosophy* (1953; repr., New York: Image Books, 1985), 3:47–48.

26. Copleston, *History of Philosophy,* 3:50.

ham's voluntarism is evident, for example, in his declaration that God could have chosen to become incarnate as an animal, such as an ox or a donkey, rather than as a human being.[27] This seemingly crass statement articulates Ockham's conviction that the incarnation, like God's ways in general, is the product of an arbitrary act of the divine will, rather than the outworking of a rational plan. Like other aspects of the faith, therefore, the doctrine of the incarnation is ultimately a mystery that cannot be exhaustively understood through rational reflection. As this example suggests, Ockham rejected the claim implicit in Thomism that divine and human reason are so close that if we were able to gain access to God's mind we could understand its operative logic. In Ockham's estimation, this assumption was tantamount to transforming the living God of the Bible into a "civilized Aristotelian." Rather than being the epitome of rationality and logic, Ockham concluded, God is inscrutable will.

Ockham's theological agenda was paralleled by his rethinking of the basis of scientific knowledge. His goal was nothing short of simplifying the semantic framework of the theoretical sciences by eliminating what he considered to be the unnecessary accretions foisted upon it by the scholastics. In this project, he considered himself to be a consistent follower of Aristotle;[28] his intent was simply that of returning the scientific endeavor to its Aristotelian roots.[29] Yet in many respects Ockham was not merely a slavish follower of the Greek master. Rather, he "bent" Aristotle's natural philosophy to his own purposes, one of which was that of working out his theological voluntarism.[30]

One philosophical question that was immediately affected by Ockham's theological voluntarism was that of the mechanisms of cognition. He affirmed the standard medieval concept of intuitive knowledge as the immediate intellectual apprehension of a thing, caused by the thing itself, by means of which the mind judges that the thing exists or concludes something about it (such as its color).[31] But he went against the grain of common belief when he asserted that in theory God could produce in a person intuitive knowledge about a nonexistent object.[32] For example, although I might naturally assume from my perception of my desk that it exists and is the cause of the perception, in fact the desk need not exist.

---

27. For a concise yet helpful summary of Ockham's voluntarism, see Copleston, *History of Philosophy*, 3:67–68.

28. For this judgment, see Copleston, *History of Philosophy*, 3:42.

29. Ernest A. Moody, *The Logic of William of Ockham* (New York: Sheed & Ward, 1935), 26–30.

30. For this judgment, see Andre Goddu, "Ockham's Philosophy of Nature," in *The Cambridge Companion to Ockham*, ed. Paul Vincent Spade (Cambridge: Cambridge University Press, 1999), 144–55.

31. Ockham, Prologue to the *Ordinatio Ockham* I.2, as cited in Copleston, *History of Philosophy*, 3:62.

32. William of Ockham, *Quodlibetal Questions* 6.6, trans. Alfred J. Fredos and Francis E. Kelley, Yale Library of Medieval Philosophy (New Haven, CT: Yale University Press, 1991), 506.

The omnipotent God, by a sheer act of the divine will, might have destroyed the desk and yet caused me to have the same perception of the desk's presence that I would have if the desk actually existed. According to Ockham, therefore, although God generally works through other causes, God is capable of bypassing them by a sheer act of the divine will. It should be added that Ockham believed as well that God's act in causing in a person an intuitive cognition of a nonexistent thing would also cause that person to judge that the thing did not exist.[33]

Ockham's elevation of the divine will above the divine intellect precipitated his most important contribution to ontology. Ockham advocated what is commonly termed a "nominalist" understanding of universals, although he never used this designation to describe himself.[34]

As a philosophical perspective, nominalism predates Ockham's work. In fact, it formed one of the general positions that emerged in the ongoing controversy in medieval philosophy that was ignited by a sentence found in Boethius's Latin version of Porphyry's *Isagoge* (an introduction to Aristotle's *Categories*): "Next as to *genera* and *species*, do they actually subsist, or are they merely thoughts existing in the understanding alone; if they subsist are they corporeal or incorporeal; are they separate from sensible things or only in and of them? I refuse to answer; these are very lofty questions unsuited to an elementary work."[35] The eleventh-century French monk Roscelin is sometimes credited for being the first person to defend what came to be known as the nominalist perspective.[36] Roscelin even drew from this understanding an innovative interpretation of the doctrine of the Trinity, albeit one that was subsequently deemed heretical by the Council of Soissons (1092). He argued that insofar as only particular substances exist and general concepts are merely designations for particular objects, there can be no single reality corresponding to the general name "God." Rather than there being a single divine substance, he theorized, the three persons of the Trinity comprise three particular substances who nevertheless are one in will and power.[37] Despite the presence of proponents of varieties of nominalism throughout the Middle Ages, until the fourteenth century this proposal remained a minority viewpoint.

The majority of Ockham's predecessors, including Aquinas and Scotus, had retained the older concept of universals as well as the attendant realism. They were motivated in part by the assumption that the existence

33. See Eleonore Stump, "The Mechanisms of Cognition: Ockham on Mediating Species," in Spade, *Cambridge Companion to Ockham*, 184–88; and Elizabeth Karger, "Ockham's Misunderstood Theory of Intuitive and Abstract Cognition," in Spade, *Cambridge Companion to Ockham*, 211–13.
34. Paul Vincent Spade, "Ockham's Nominalist Metaphysics: Some Main Themes," in Spade, *Cambridge Companion to Ockham*, 113 n. 1. Some historians, such as Foote, deny that Ockham was a nominalist. See Shallo, *Lessons in Scholastic Philosophy*, 21.
35. As cited in Thilly, *History of Philosophy*, 199–200.
36. For this judgment, see Foote, "Outline History of Scholastic Philosophy," 6–7.
37. As cited in Thilly, *History of Philosophy*, 206.

of universals is necessary for the scientific endeavor. According to the medieval understanding, science focuses on general assertions, which are *ipso facto* statements about universals. In Ockham's estimation, however, his predecessors had not exorcised sufficiently the Platonism that elevated a supposed realm of universals above the realm of the senses (even if the higher realm was nothing more than the divine mind) and that claimed that knowledge is dependent on some kind of supernatural illumination. To remedy this situation, Ockham proposed an understanding of science that did not require the existence of universals.

Ockham denied the contention shared by theologians from Augustine to Aquinas that universals are existent realities present in the mind of God in the form of the divine Ideas. This denial emerged as the outcome of a fundamental ontological perspective that lay at the heart of his philosophical proposal. All that exists, he averred, are individual things or singular beings, that is, substances and their sensible qualities. To exist means to be an individual.[38] Rather than being actual entities that exist outside the human mind and inhere in things,[39] what philosophers denote as "universals" are linguistic signs that represent individual things.[40] Or as Samuel Stumpf points out, for Ockham universals are tools that the mind uses in the task of "thinking in an orderly way about particular things."[41] These universals arise, Ockham added, as we abstract from individual things the qualities we find common to them. For this reason, to ascribe actual existence to universals is (among other errors) to make mental abstractions into existent entities and thereby to violate what came to be known as "Ockham's razor."[42] This axiom—also known as the principle of parsimony (the *lex parsimoniae*)—which has been expressed in various formulations, including "Entities are not to be multiplied without necessity"[43] or "Plurality need not be posited unless it is necessary to posit it,"[44] repeatedly found its way into Ockham's writings.[45]

---

38. See, for example, Ockham's discussion of this point in William of Ockham, *Commentary on the Sentences*, bk. 1, distinction 2, question 6, in Hyman and Walsh, *Philosophy in the Middle Ages*, 624–26.

39. Ockham declared unequivocally, "No universal is anything existing in any way outside the soul." I Sent., 2.8.Q, as cited in Copleston, *History of Philosophy*, 3:56.

40. Ockham, *Summa Logicae* I.14–15.

41. Samuel Enoch Stumpf, *Socrates to Sartre: A History of Philosophy*, 4th ed. (New York: McGraw-Hill, 1988), 197.

42. Although this principle has come to be associated with Ockham, it predates the fourteenth-century philosopher, for it was likely derived by Robert Grosseteste from a statement in book 5 of Aristotle's *Physics* that nature operates in the shortest way possible. For this account, see Fremantle, *Age of Belief*, 202.

43. For this statement of the principle, see Fremantle, *Age of Belief*, 202. For a slightly different rendering, see Thilly, *History of Philosophy*, 248.

44. For this statement of the principle, see Paul Vignaux, *Philosophy in the Middle Ages: An Introduction*, trans. E. C. Hall (New York: Meridian Books, 1959), 174.

45. See, for example, Marilyn McCord Adams, *William Ockham*, 2 vols. (Notre Dame, IN: University of Notre Dame Press, 1987), 156–61.

Ockham's nominalistic perspective regarding universals extended to his understanding of the ontological category of Being. Like other universals, "Being" is not an entity outside the mind and hence a reality in which things participate, he argued. Rather, "Being" is simply a mental tool, a term, similar to the concept of "something."

Because it is the science of Being, Ockham concluded, metaphysics is not concerned with any actual thing, but merely with a mental or logical concept.[46] At the same time, he acknowledged that the task of metaphysics extends to an exploration of one particular being, the highest being—God. Moreover, he agreed with Scotus that the word "being" is used univocally of God and creatures. This univocal use is necessary, Ockham asserted, if we are to be able to conceive of the existence of a being called "God."[47] He quickly added, however, that God and creatures are not to be thought of as alike in either substance or accidents.[48]

As a good late medieval philosopher, Ockham accepted the theory of fourfold causation that stood at the heart of Aristotle's ontology.[49] Yet he gave the whole understanding a radical empiricist flavor, arguing that causality cannot be discovered through a priori reasoning but only through experience of the world. As a result, rather than speaking of the material and formal causes as metaphysical principles of being, he understood them in purely physical terms, the former comprising the actual spatial body of an object and the latter being the form, shape, or structure of its material parts. Similarly, Ockham altered the understanding of final causality, suggesting that it is simply a metaphorical way of speaking about things that are acting uniformly by natural necessity. But perhaps the most significant alteration occurred in the manner in which he viewed efficient causality. According to Ockham, this dimension is to be understood chiefly (albeit not solely) as denoting a regular succession or a particular sequence within the pattern of the behavior of objects, whose regularity is dependent on God's freely chosen ordering of creation and is known experientially or through observation.

The world that Ockham's nominalist revision of Aristotle's theory of causality led him to envision consisted of distinct entities or "absolutes," each of which exists by the divine will but none of which is connected to any other in any necessary manner. Relations, in turn, like all concepts, are not realities that exist outside the mind. They are not metaphysical entities that are distinct in some realist sense from existing things, but are mental abstractions that speak about empirically observable interactions between or among existing things. Giorgio de Santillana offers the following telling

46. Ockham, 3 Sent., 9.T, as cited in Copleston, *History of Philosophy*, 3:78.
47. Ibid.
48. Ockham, 3 Sent., 9.Q, as cited in Copleston, *History of Philosophy*, 3:80.
49. For a succinct summary of Ockham's proposal, see Walsh, *History of Philosophy*, 173.

characterization of the picture of reality that emerges from Ockham's proposal: "We have there a world of carefully defined and utterly separate ('absolute') entities, connected only by an abstract order, a discontinuous universe where even cause and effect become shadowy with respect to clear distinction and sharp separation of the objects of thought."[50]

Even more significant for the history of Being, however, was the innovation—precipitated by Ockham's alteration of the Aristotelian understanding of efficient causality—in the proof for the existence of God as the first efficient cause of the world that the medieval theologians had developed out of Aristotle's metaphysics.[51] Ockham perceived insightfully that the idea should be divided into two aspects. "First efficient cause" can refer to the original agent responsible for the coming into being of all things as well as the temporal genesis of motion in the world. Ockham denied that the existence of God as the first cause in this sense can be proved. Just as a human being is generated from noneternal human parents, he averred, so also the first creature or the first movement in the temporal sequence of the world could have been generated from a noneternal source that has in the meantime lapsed into nothingness.[52] Ockham noted, however, that in addition to suggesting a divine *producer* of the world, "first efficient cause" can also be used in the sense of a divine *conserver*, who is ultimately responsible for upholding all things and for maintaining motion in each present moment. Lying behind this aspect of the idea of a first cause is the premodern belief that a body can remain in motion only if it is maintained in motion by a moving power that continues to exist so long as the movement persists.

Although Ockham believed that the existence of a first cause in the sense of conserver could be philosophically demonstrated, he denied that knowledge about the nature of that first cause could be determined by reason alone. Nor could reason demonstrate the divine unicity, the quality of being one or a unity.[53] These matters, Ockham concluded, belong to the realm of revelation and faith.

Whether or not Ockham actually intended to undermine the synthesis between theology and philosophy that his forebears had so skillfully constructed is debatable.[54] Nevertheless, his nominalism drove a wedge between science and theology (or between reason and revelation) and bestowed upon each of them a degree of autonomy over against the other.

50. Giorgio de Santillana, *The Age of Adventure: The Renaissance Philosophers* (New York: Mentor Books, 1956), 11.

51. For a helpful delineation of the significance of Ockham in the history of this concept, see Wolfhart Pannenberg, *The Idea of God and Human Freedom*, trans. R. A. Wilson (Philadelphia: Westminster, 1973), 82–83.

52. Ockham, *Quodlibetal Questions* 2.1 (Fredos and Kelley, 93–96).

53. Ockham, *Quodlibetal Questions* 1.1 (Fredos and Kelley, 5–12).

54. Copleston, for example, claims that this was not Ockham's intent. Copleston, *History of Philosophy*, 3:84.

Regarding the realm of reason, Ockham declared that the general assertions toward which science strives are not general insofar as they reflect knowledge of universals as such but in that they assert what is true of many individuals. In so doing, he eliminated the need for supernatural illumination to bring the mind from sense perception to knowledge of some supposedly supersensible forms, and as a consequence he eliminated the need for revelation to enlighten the pathway of science. In short, he devised what W. T. Jones terms a "secular" science, that is, one in which science reaches "its own kind of truth in its own kind of way."[55] At the same time, by concluding that experience is the sole source of scientific knowledge, Ockham relegated all knowledge that transcends experience to the realm of revelation and faith. As a consequence, philosophy could no longer lead the inquirer to truths of natural theology, for theological truth ultimately comes only through revelation.

In fairness, it must be pointed out that Ockham was not motivated by a desire to procure for science an autonomy from theology. Rather, his intent was to preserve the primacy of faith within the theological enterprise. In contrast to Aquinas, who viewed faith as supplementing and perfecting reason, Ockham was convinced that faith and reason are distinct even to the point that on occasion they can actually contradict each other. In his estimation, certain mysteries of the faith might not simply lie beyond natural reason; they might even run contrary to reason.[56] Ockham wanted to ensure that if such contradiction occurs, Christians will follow the pathway that faith charts, even if it appears irrational.

Thilly reached an insightful conclusion regarding the extent to which Ockham's proposal served to divide the two aspects of the human knowing project that the medieval Christian philosophers had sought to synthesize: "We find in these views the abandonment of the fundamental principles of the entire scholastic enterprise, the original goal of which had been the rationalization of the Christian faith, the union of philosophy and theology. The whole undertaking is now declared to be not only presumptuous, but futile; scholastic theology is a pseudo-science, the entire contents of faith are inaccessible to reason."[57] Henry Koren takes the matter further. He contends that the proposals of thinkers such as Ockham ultimately undermine ontology itself: "The nominalists and conceptualists consider the concept of being as a pure figment of our intellect and therefore without any objective values. This position makes true metaphysics impossible."[58]

55. Jones, *History of Western Philosophy*, 521.
56. For this conclusion, see Alfred J. Freddoso, "Ockham on Faith and Reason," in Spade, *Cambridge Companion to Ockham*, 345.
57. Thilly, *History of Philosophy*, 249.
58. Henry J. Koren, *An Introduction to the Science of Metaphysics* (St. Louis: B. Herder Book Co., 1955), 23.

The Undoing of the First Cause

Koren's prediction that nominalism would inevitably undermine the entire metaphysical project did not come to pass immediately. Nevertheless, Ockham's work contributed to a climate that encouraged philosophers to consider other approaches to the question of Being than the one that had reigned (if only briefly) in the high Middle Ages.

God as the Coincidence of Opposites

One such alternative to the medieval synthesis that traversed a trajectory quite different from the pathway Ockham had trod was offered by the lawyer turned theologian and Catholic cardinal, Nicholas of Cusa (1401–1464). Thilly lauds Nicholas's work as comprising "the only system of thought to come out of the fifteenth century . . . which does not follow the beaten track of scholasticism."[59] Similarly, Giorgio de Santillana notes, "There is no doubt that with Nicholas . . . German philosophy has entered the scene full-fledged, with some of its powerful characteristics well in evidence."[60] Above all, however, Nicholas provided a proposal that elevated to center stage a focus on the Infinite that went beyond what even Scotus had envisioned.

Nicholas voiced fundamental agreement with the nominalists' contention that reason cannot lead to knowledge of God. But he disagreed with them regarding the cure that this situation demands. Instead of looking to logic and seeking to refashion the conceptual edifice underlying theoretical science as Ockham had proposed, Nicholas returned to the Neoplatonic heritage, including the writings of Dionysus the Areopagite, that had been submerged during the ascendancy of Aristotelianism in the high Middle Ages. Reminiscent of his Neoplatonic forebears, Nicholas extolled the possibility of an immediate intuition of God in the form of an ecstatic "vision without comprehension."[61] This occurs, he asserted, by means of what he called "learned ignorance" (*doctra ignorantia*), that is, through a realization that ignorance is in fact the greatest learning. According to Nicholas, knowledge of one's ignorance can lead to a coincidence of opposites—the coincidence of knowing and not-knowing—that facilitates a grasping of God as "that simplicity where contradictories coincide."[62]

Like the nominalists, Nicholas pointed out that the Aristotelian scholastics had failed to see that the Being they had elevated to center stage in their metaphysical deliberations was merely a grammatical category.

59. Thilly, *History of Philosophy*, 264.

60. De Santillana, *Age of Adventure*, 48.

61. Nicholas of Cusa, *On the Vision of God* 16.69, in *Selected Spiritual Writings*, trans. H. Lawrence Bond, The Classics of Western Spirituality (Mahwah, NJ: Paulist Press, 1997), 266.

62. Nicholas of Cusa, *On Learned Ignorance* 3.264 (*Selected Spiritual Writings*, 206).

But he took the matter a step further. Nicholas added that the Thomists had also not understood that the "way of reason," which they esteemed as the pathway to knowledge of Being and hence of God, could not serve this purpose. To this end, he noted that knowledge progresses from the lowest stage, sense experience, which is merely affirmative (in that the senses only affirm), to discursive reason, which entails both affirmation and denial and which thereby is bounded and governed by the law of non-contradiction (that is, the mutual exclusion of opposites). Because the human intellect cannot grasp any truth with perfect accuracy, Nicholas added, knowledge must proceed through this process of affirming contradictories and opposites. But the pathway must move beyond discursive reason to a superior intellectual activity, an intellectual vision, that denies the oppositions of reason so as to apprehend the Infinite that transcends all contradictions and encompasses all opposites as the "coincidence of opposites."[63]

In setting forth his proposal, Nicholas drew from a far-reaching rethinking of the nature of mathematics. According to the medieval philosophers, mathematics is chiefly concerned with magnitude—it is a science that deals with "more" and "less"—and for this reason is of little assistance in a quest for knowledge that busies itself with essences that are deemed to be either wholly present in or wholly absent from existing things. Nicholas, in contrast, presented mathematics as the science of the infinite. Furthermore, he was convinced that if infinity lies at the core of all being and even characterizes the divine essence, as Scotus and other medieval theorists had claimed, then mathematics (as the science of the infinite) becomes a potential pathway to the discovery of truth. Consequently, following the ancient Greek philosopher Pythagoras, he looked to the order, to the harmony in multiplicity, and, above all, to the coincidence of opposites (*coincidentia oppositorum*) symbolized by numbers for the key to ultimate truth.[64]

Nicholas found in mathematics a series of metaphors that aided theological reflection. Many of these found their basis in the fact that the concept of the "infinite" presents to the mind a series of illuminating paradoxes, for when extended to infinity conceptions that have been rejected as impossible suddenly become possible and plausible. Hence, when "maximum" and "minimum" are freed from the quantifying notions of large and small—that is, when they are viewed from the perspective of infinity—the two coincide.[65] Nicholas likewise observed that if one side of a triangle is extended to infinity, the other two sides coincide with it.

63. Hamlyn goes so far as to claim that this constitutes Nicholas's "key idea." Hamlyn, *History of Western Philosophy*, 124.

64. On this point, see Walsh, *History of Philosophy*, 187; and de Santillana, *Age of Adventure*, 49.

65. Nicholas of Cusa, *On Learned Ignorance* 1.4.11 (*Selected Spiritual Writings*, 91).

Similar observations led him to conclude that "the infinite line is the maximum triangle, circle, and sphere," which geometric figures he saw as lying
at the basis of all reality.[66] He then drew from the manner in which the max-
imally straight line is in fact inherent in any finite line to indicate how infinity is present (or "contracted") in each finite thing and forms the measure
of its very essence.[67] In this manner, then, mathematics led Nicholas to elevate infinity as the standpoint from which to view and solve problems and
to look to the coincidence of opposites as the method for discovering truth.
As H. Lawrence Bond explains, "At infinity thoroughgoing coincidence
occurs. . . . The coincidence of opposites provides a method that resolves
contradictions without violating the integrity of the contrary elements and
without diminishing the reality or the force of their contradiction."[68]

Nicholas maintained that, like the divine Infinite, the universe is infinite, albeit in a "contracted" manner.[69] As such, it reflects the "absolute
maximum" that is God, who is the *complicatio* or enfolding as well as the
explicatio or unfolding of all things.[70] Moreover, like an infinite sphere,
the universe has no center and no circumference, which suggested to
Nicholas that God is both its center and its circumference. Consequently,
the universe is also a unity in plurality, a coincidence of opposites that
derives from the coincidence of opposites that characterizes the infinite
God. In this manner, the metaphorical theology of Nicholas served to
explode the closed sphere of the Aristotelian world.[71]

Nicholas's elevation of mathematics as the science of the infinite cast
him as a harbinger of things to come. He prefigured the shift to mathematics that characterized not only René Descartes' attempt to launch philosophy upon a new foundation but also the empiricist approach to the
scientific study of nature that dominated the intellectual culture that began
to emerge in the Renaissance. Yet of perhaps even greater significance for
the history of Being, Nicholas's articulation of the rich theme of the unfolding of the infinite in the finite and the enfolding of the finite in the infinite served as a foretaste of the kind of philosophy of nature that would
flower four hundred years later in the Romantic movement.[72] In both
cases, Nicholas's thought offered an ontological perspective from which to
understand God as the cause of the world in a manner that provided a
promising alternative to the Aristotelian perspective of God as first efficient
cause that had played such an important role in the medieval synthesis.

66. Nicholas of Cusa, *On Learned Ignorance* 1.13.36 (*Selected Spiritual Writings*, 103).
67. Nicholas of Cusa, *On Learned Ignorance* 1.15.40–41 (*Selected Spiritual Writings*, 105–6).
68. H. Lawrence Bond, introduction to Nicholas of Cusa, *Selected Spiritual Writings*, 22.
69. Nicholas of Cusa, *On Learned Ignorance* 2.11.150 (*Selected Spiritual Writings*, 154–55).
70. This is explicated in Nicholas of Cusa, *On Learned Ignorance* 2.1.91–2.4.116 (*Selected Spiritual Writings*, 128–40).
71. For this characterization, see de Santillana, *Age of Adventure*, 53.
72. Bond, Introduction to *Selected Spiritual Writings*, 19.

God and the Mechanistic Universe

The Renaissance intensified the move from final to efficient causality, together with the elevation of mathematics, that had begun already in the late Middle Ages. Yet it did so in a manner that signaled a sharp turn away from the direction that had been so carefully charted by Nicholas of Cusa. Beginning in the Renaissance, philosophers became increasingly interested in nature as a unified, dynamic system of bodies that moved in accordance with an underlying intelligible structure.[73] They believed that the structure immanent within nature can be expressed mathematically and that nature can be studied without immediate reference to God. As a consequence, the philosophies of nature that the Renaissance scientists and their successors developed no longer sought to present the material world as a revelation of its divine ground, a goal that had not only provided such a strong impulse to the thinking of the medieval thinkers but had formed the basis for Nicholas's reformulation of Christian Neoplatonism as well. The fledgling scientific approach to the world, in contrast, had as its goal the discovery of an inherent structure of nature that could be brought to light by means of measurement, observation, and experimentation. As the scientific enterprise grew, therefore, physics increasingly replaced metaphysics as the central topic of natural philosophy.

The rise of the scientific mentality was dependent on a monumental shift in the basic conceptual language used to talk about the world, namely, the shift from qualitative to quantitative terminology. In keeping with Aristotle's understanding, medieval science had looked to "natural principles"—the idea that every object follows a "natural" tendency to fulfill its own inner purpose—to explain movement and change in the world. The architects of the new scientific perspective rejected such language as mere metaphysical speculation. In their estimation, the proper approach to the study of natural processes was to focus on what could be quantified and measured and thereby to seek to discover the uniform laws of nature that lie at the basis of the motion observed in the world.

The rising scientific approach with its attendant emphasis on the quantitative dimensions of reality is rightly associated with names such as Johann Kepler (1571–1630) and Galileo Galilei (1564–1642). Nevertheless, the person who perhaps more than any other stands at the apex of this development was born in the year following Galileo's death: Isaac Newton (1643–1727).[74]

---

73. For a helpful summary of this development, see Frederick Copleston, *A History of Philosophy*, vol. 4, *Descartes to Leibniz* (1960; repr., New York: Image Books, 1985), 8–10.

74. Hence, Hamlyn declares, "The new movement in physics had its culmination in Isaac Newton's *Principia* (1687)." Hamlyn, *History of Western Philosophy*, 144. This judgment finds echo in Walsh, who declares, "The revolutionary thinking of Renaissance physical theory reached its apex in the achievements of Sir Isaac Newton." Walsh, *History of Philosophy*, 264.

Newton is generally credited with setting the direction that would govern the pattern of science for the next several centuries. Isaiah Berlin encapsulates the transformation that Newton inaugurated: "If the model that dominated the seventeenth century was mathematical, it is the mechanical model, more particularly that of the Newtonian system that is everywhere imitated in the century that followed."[75] Building from the assumption that the basic processes of nature can be quantified and described mathematically, Newton postulated that nature consists of bodies in motion and furthermore that everything from the largest objects in the heavens to the smallest particles on earth exhibit the same laws of motion. In Newton's wake every aspect of the universe, including human thought, came to be explained in accordance with a mechanical or mechanistic understanding. Insofar as the mechanistic model was applied to all disciplines of knowledge—encompassing politics, ethics, metaphysics, and even theology—all fields of the human endeavor became, in effect, branches of natural science.

In the eyes of many, Newton stands nearly in a class by himself. Solomon and Higgins suggest that he was not only "the greatest physicist of the time" but perhaps "the greatest scientist ever."[76] Kenny goes so far as to assert that Newton's *Philosophiae naturalis principia mathematica* (1687) "caused a revolution in science of much more enduring importance than the Glorious Revolution of the following year."[77] Walsh notes that Newton was even "idolized in his own age,"[78] an idolizing that is evident in the words of Newton's older contemporary John Locke (1632–1704), who spoke of him as "the incomparable Mr. Newton."[79] Newton's widely acknowledged stature led Alexander Pope to pen a tongue-in-cheek quip:

> Nature and Nature's laws lay hid in Night
> God said, "Let Newton be!" and all was Light.[80]

Despite Newton's far-reaching importance to all aspects of the human knowing project, historians of philosophy generally do not list Newton among the discipline's luminaries, but rather tend to relegate him to the annals of the history of science.[81] Frederick Copleston reflects the outlook of many of his fellow historians when he declares regarding Newton, "He

75. Isaiah Berlin, *The Age of Enlightenment: The Eighteenth-Century Philosophers* (New York: Mentor Books, 1956), 14.

76. Robert C. Solomon and Kathleen M. Higgins, *A Short History of Philosophy* (New York: Oxford University Press, 1996), 191.

77. Kenny, *Brief History of Western Philosophy*, 215.

78. Walsh, *History of Philosophy*, 264.

79. John Locke, *An Essay concerning Human Understanding*, ed. Roger Woodhouse (New York: Penguin, 1996), 11.

80. As cited in John Herman Randall Jr., introduction to *Newton's Philosophy of Nature: Selections from His Writings*, ed. H. S. Thayer (New York: Hafner, 1953), xiv.

81. For an example of this tendency, see Kenny, *Brief History of Western Philosophy*, 216.

was not, of course, primarily a philosopher, as we understand the word today. . . . His great importance consists in the fact that he completed to all intents and purposes the classical scientific conception of the world which Galileo in particular had done so much to promote."[82] Yet it should be pointed out that until the eighteenth century, philosophy and the natural sciences were not clearly separated. On the contrary, physics and metaphysics were often viewed as belonging together under the common rubric of "natural philosophy," and one of the tasks of metaphysics was deemed to be that of delineating the proper conceptual and explanatory system for scientific investigations of nature.[83] In keeping with this more unified view of science and philosophy, Newton viewed himself as a philosopher of nature, even though he described his discipline in what we would likely see as more scientific terms: "Natural philosophy consists in discovering the frame and operations of nature, and reducing them, as far as may be, to general rules or laws—establishing these rules by observations and experiments, and thence deducing the causes and effects of things."[84]

Often cited as Newton's greatest scientific achievement was the discovery of the principle of gravitation.[85] By postulating that the motion of both celestial and terrestrial bodies are governed by the same law, this discovery dealt the final deathblow to Aristotelian physics.[86] Furthermore, Newton's mechanistic perspective regarding the movement of both celestial and terrestrial bodies presupposed that such movement occurred on an immense stage or within a kind of infinitely big box that consisted of an infinite empty void (space) and an infinite temporal stretch (time).[87] Hence, Newton proposed the controversial idea that space and time are to be conceived in an absolute manner, that is, as infinitely extended continua that possess properties of their own.[88] Yet of even greater importance for the history of

82. Copleston, *History of Philosophy*, 4:32.
83. Stuart Hampshire, *The Age of Reason: The Seventeenth-Century Philosophers* (New York: Mentor Books, 1956), 14.
84. This statement is from Newton's "Scheme for Establishing the Royal Society." See Isaac Newton, *Philosophical Writings*, ed. Andrew Janiak, Cambridge Texts in the History of Philosophy (Cambridge: Cambridge University Press, 2004), ix.
85. Newton defined this principle in the following manner: "If spheres be however dissimilar (as to density of matter and attractive force) in the same ratio onward from the center to the circumference, but everywhere similar at every given distance from the center, on all sides round about; and the attractive force of every point decreases as the square of the distance of the body attracted: I say that the whole force with which one of these spheres attracts the other will be inversely proportional to the square of the distance of the centers." Isaac Newton, *The Principia* 5, On Gravity Proposition 76, as cited in Randall, introduction to *Newton's Philosophy of Nature*, 105.
86. Kenny, *Brief History of Western Philosophy*, 216.
87. See, for example, Isaac Newton, *The Principia: Mathematical Principles of Natural Philosophy*, Scholium to the Definitions, 1–3, trans. I. Bernard Cohen and Anne Whitman (Berkeley: University of California Press, 1999), 408–9.
88. It should be pointed out that although Newton's idea of absolute space and time became a commonplace understanding of the universe, it was by no means unchallenged even in the seven-

Being was Newton's articulation of another law, inertia, which he listed as the first axiom of motion[89] and which he postulated is due to a force innate within matter itself: "Inherent force of matter is the power of resisting by which every body, so far as it is able, preserves in its state either of resting or of moving uniformly straight forward."[90]

In Newton's estimation, rather than undermining Christian belief, the laws of motion that he had postulated actually pointed to the existence of God. For example, Newton believed that the law of gravity necessitated God's existence, for God was the one who had determined that some matter would coalesce into shining bodies (stars) and other matter into opaque bodies (e.g., planets). God was likewise the one responsible for setting the planets in their orbits and for initially causing their motions.[91] In this manner, Newton resurrected the notion of God as the first efficient cause of the world in the temporal sense, which understanding Ockham had shown to be suspect 350 years earlier. This aspect of Newton's natural philosophy would eventually lead to deism, on the one hand, and to David Hume's skeptical agnosticism, on the other.

Although the law of gravity led Newton to affirm the aspect of God as first efficient cause that Ockham had denied (God as the first temporal cause), the law of inertia undermined the other aspect, the conserver God, that Ockham's reflections had left intact.[92] If a principle inherent in matter itself empowers every thing in the universe to persist in the state in which it presently is, whether that state be one of motion or rest, unless and until it is acted upon by other forces, then once a state of existence or of motion has come into being, its continuance is not dependent on the simultaneity of any particular cause external to the thing itself, let alone a prime cause that stands at the beginning of a great chain of causation. By eliminating the need for God as the conserver or prime mover in each moment of time, the law of inertia obviated the necessity of the postulate of God as an explanatory principle in the realm of physics.

In short, Newton had—perhaps unwittingly—in effect completed the undermining of the concept of God as the first efficient cause that Ockham had begun three and a half centuries earlier. Although this did not occur as the immediate aftermath of Newton's work, the ultimate outworking of this development would be the demise of the scientific God.

---

teenth and eighteenth centuries. Leibniz, for example, argued that rather than being absolute and static, and existing independent of human perception, space and time were relative terms denoting a relational structure, a way of speaking about the relationships between bodies (space) and events (time). According to Leibniz, "space" refers to the order of coexistence of bodies and "time" to the order of succession of events.

89. Newton, *Principia* 1, "Axioms, or The Laws of Motion," 416.

90. Newton, *Principia* 1, Definition 3, 404.

91. See, for example, Isaac Newton, "Four Letters to Richard Bentley," in *Opera Omnia* 4:429–42, as cited in Thayer, *Newton's Philosophy of Nature*, 46–58.

92. I am indebted for this observation to Pannenberg, *Idea of God and Human Freedom*, 82–83.

The Reconception of Being

The discoveries of Newton, coming as they did on the heels of the work of Kepler and Galileo, proved fatal to the Aristotelian-inspired medieval conception of reality. The emerging scientific mentality with its empirical and experimental approach had little use for metaphysical categories such as "substance," "form," and "accident" that for centuries had provided the linguistic tools for describing the world. Furthermore, astronomy and the new physics rendered the notion of God superfluous to an orderly account of reality. Newton had reintroduced the idea of a first temporal cause of the world into his cosmology. But the victory for the Christian faith that this move appeared to have won was short-lived. In effect, Newton had reduced God to a mere inference from the natural order of mechanical causes. The die was thereby cast for a wholesale elimination of God from the reigning scientific cosmology. Indeed, as the eighteenth century unfolded and then gave way to the nineteenth, many thinkers came to see that if the universe could sustain itself without divine help, then it might just as easily originate itself as well.

For all its explanatory power, the mechanistic picture of the universe endemic to Newtonian physics with its focus on self-contained particles that act upon each other in an external manner did not offer a completely satisfying cosmology. Newton was well aware that experimental science suggested the presence in the material world of relational forces (such as attraction and repulsion) that seemed to act at a distance. He likewise knew that the presence of these forces means that matter does not act solely in a mechanistic manner but is also essentially active and relational. Despite his valiant efforts, Newton was not able to reconcile the relational and the mechanistic dimensions of the universe. Consequently, he bequeathed to his successors not only the burden of finding a place for God in the new cosmology but also the seemingly more mundane task of bringing together these apparently disparate aspects of reality.

Being-in-General and the Triune God

Perhaps the most illustrious person in the generation immediately after Newton to busy himself with both of these challenges, at least in the American colonies, was Jonathan Edwards (1703–1758). Although Edwards was a pastor by vocation, he has routinely been hailed as a great philosophical thinker.[93] This designation is not unwarranted, for he was knowledgeable in philosophy, science, mathematics, and literature, as well as theology. Moreover, in his theological writings he drew insight from the

---

93. Arthur Cushman McGiffert, *Protestant Thought before Kant* (London: Duckworth, 1911), 177.

leading philosophical voices of the day, including John Locke, Francis Hutcheson, and the Cambridge Platonists.[94]

Nevertheless, Edwards was above all a theologian who sought to resolve the theological issues that plagued the church in eighteenth-century New England. As a consequence, the philosophical and scientific pursuits that sparked his interest early in his educational experience were soon pressed into the service of his theological purposes. Edwards turned his intellectual endeavors to the goal of recasting the Calvinist theology that he had inherited from his Puritan forebears in the light of the philosophical and scientific concerns of the Enlightenment natural philosophers, especially Newton and Locke, for the sake of the renewal of the church.[95] For this reason, Edwards had little impact on the shape of American philosophy.[96] But his influence on American theology has been so great that in the wake of the mid-twentieth-century renaissance of interest in Edwards's work,[97] Robert Jenson could state without fear of contradiction that Edwards is "America's greatest theologian."[98]

Despite the fact that his own overriding interest was theological and not philosophical, Edwards made a crucial contribution to the history of Being. In his thought, philosophy and theology were intricately interwoven. Edwards himself realized that any attempt to recast Calvinism in the wake of the Enlightenment required that it be placed on a more overtly ontological foundation, one that conceived of God as unconditional Being rather than simply as absolute Will. The result of his efforts was nothing short of a thoroughgoing reconceptualization of the nature of reality itself. He replaced the traditional Western metaphysics of substance and form with a conception of reality as a dynamic network of dispositional forces and habits,[99] at the heart of which is the Christian God, whom Edwards, following the medieval scholastic synthesizers, pressed into service as his central metaphysical conceptuality.

94. Conrad Cherry, *The Theology of Jonathan Edwards: A Reappraisal* (Bloomington, IN: Indiana University Press, 1966), 4.

95. For a helpful treatment of the manner in which Edwards's work parallels that of the leading figures in Enlightenment philosophy, see Leon Chai, *Jonathan Edwards and the Limits of Enlightenment Philosophy* (New York: Oxford University Press, 1998).

96. William J. Wainwright, "Edwards, Jonathan," in *The Cambridge Dictionary of Philosophy*, 2nd ed., ed. Robert Audi (Cambridge: Cambridge University Press, 1999), 253.

97. The renewal of interest in Edwards is generally attributed to the work of Perry Miller. For example, Jenson declares, "It was Perry Miller's virtuosic *Jonathan Edwards* which in 1949 inspired the contemporary rediscovery of Edwards." Robert W. Jenson, *America's Theologian: A Recommendation of Jonathan Edwards* (New York: Oxford University Press, 1988), vii. Similarly, Lee cites Perry Miller as the one "who is largely responsible for the recent revival of interest in Jonathan Edwards." Sang Hyun Lee, *The Philosophical Theology of Jonathan Edwards*, expanded ed. (Princeton, NJ: Princeton University Press, 2000), 3.

98. Jenson, *America's Theologian*, 3.

99. Lee, *Philosophical Theology of Jonathan Edwards*, 3–4.

The ontological category that Edwards used to denote God was "Being-in-general." He may have borrowed this designation from the French philosopher Nicholas Malebranche (1638–1715), whose influential treatise *Search after Truth* was translated and published in England in 1694. Nevertheless, Edwards developed his own description of how the mind arrives at this conception. By beginning with any particular object to which the verb "to be" may be applied, and then divesting the object of all the primary and secondary characteristics that make it particular rather than universal, the mind finds itself left with the mysterious "something" to which philosophers attach the present participle "being."[100] This philosophical exercise led Edwards to affirm the "the absolute, universally unconditional, necessity of God's being,"[101] which Douglas J. Elwood suggests formed the most fundamental philosophical assumption of his thinking.[102]

Edwards's affirmation of the absolute necessity of Being-in-general formed the philosophical analogue to his theological focus on a particular understanding of the divine sovereignty. Roger Olson offers a helpful characterization of this understanding, while pinpointing the central role that it played in Edwards's perspective:

> No theologian in the history of Christianity held a higher or stronger view of God's majesty, sovereignty, glory and power than Jonathan Edwards. Edwards focused his entire thought on those themes and demanded stringently that every idea be brought back to them and tested by them. For him, God is the all-determining reality in the most unconditional sense possible and always acts for his own glory and honor.[103]

As Olson points out, Edwards claimed that the ultimate goal of God's activity is the divine glory. As Edwards himself declared, "It appears that all that is ever spoken of in the Scripture as an ultimate end of God's works is included in that one phrase, 'the glory of God'; which is the name by which the last end of God's works is most commonly called in Scripture."[104] This goal is accomplished, he added—drawing on the motif of harmony that had been central to the Newtonian understanding of the

---

100. Jonathan Edwards, "Of Being," in *The Works of Jonathan Edwards*, vol. 6, *Scientific and Philosophical Writings*, ed. Wallace Anderson (New Haven, CT: Yale University Press, 1980), 202–7. For a similar description, see Douglas J. Elwood, *The Philosophical Theology of Jonathan Edwards* (New York: Columbia University Press, 1960), 12–13.

101. Edwards, "Of Being," 203.

102. Elwood, *Philosophical Theology of Jonathan Edwards*, 24.

103. Roger E. Olson, *The Story of Christian Theology: Twenty Centuries of Tradition and Reform* (Downers Grove, IL: InterVarsity Press, 1999), 506.

104. Jonathan Edwards, "Concerning the End for Which God Created the World," in *The Works of Jonathan Edwards*, vol. 8, *Ethical Writings*, ed. Paul Ramsey (New Haven, CT: Yale University Press, 1989), 526.

universe—as every part of creation fulfills its destiny so that the whole reflects the harmony that characterizes God's own being. Because love is what unites all things into a harmonious whole,[105] Edwards concluded, humans fulfill their destiny above all as they love God wholly.

This focus on God as the all-determining reality entailed a cosmology that offered a radical alternative to the proposals of Edwards's Newtonian contemporaries. Newton had discovered a universe that is ordered by natural laws of motion. His followers, in turn, tended to conceive of these natural laws as fixed principles or permanent characteristics of nature. This perspective facilitated an understanding of the teaching of *creatio ex nihilo* (which the patristic thinkers had devised to counter the Platonic idea of the demiurge) in a manner that removed God from direct involvement with the universe in any continuous way. The result was the nascent deism that emerged in Edwards's day. Jenson offers a caustic yet not wholly inappropriate characterization of the deistic cosmology: "The God of the eighteenth century's reception of Newton was an omniscient and omnipotent Engineer, who had fashioned a universal machine for his own pleasure and to be the maintenance-free mill of his blessings for others."[106]

Edwards, however, was not content to view God as the distant originator of the universe, as the one who had merely established "nature's laws." He averred that God is creatively present and directly communicative everywhere and at all times. This God does not simply speak creation into existence in the primordial past. Rather, creation emerges out of the divine infinity, and it does so continuously, as God expresses himself in an outgoing movement. Edwards offered the following summary of this aspect of his understanding of the divine creative activity:

> Thus it appears reasonable to suppose, that it was what God had respect to as an ultimate end of his creating the world, to communicate of His own infinite fullness of good; or rather it was His last end, that there might be a glorious and abundant emanation of his infinite fullness of good *ad extra*, or without Himself; and the disposition to communicate Himself, or diffuse his own *Fullness*, which we must conceive of as being originally in God as a perfection of his nature was what moved Him to create the world.[107]

Lying behind this statement is a particular understanding of the Christian teaching that God created the world out of nothing. In contrast to the use to which the deists were putting the classical doctrine of *creatio ex nihilo*,[108] Edwards's commitment to the absolute necessity of God as

105. Herbert Wallace Schneider, *The Puritan Mind* (London: Constable, 1931), 144.
106. Jenson, *American's Theologian*, 25.
107. Edwards, "Concerning the End for Which God Created the World," 433–34.
108. For a helpful discussion of this connection, see Elwood, *Philosophical Theology of Jonathan Edwards*, 35–37.

Being-in-general led him to read into this Christian teaching the idea of *creatio continua*.[109] In his estimation, "the very being, and the manner of being, and the whole, of bodies depends *immediately* on the Divine Being," to the extent that without God's upholding influence "the whole universe would in a moment vanish into nothing." In short, "not only the well-being of the world" but also its "very *being*"[110] depends on "a present immediate operation of God on the creation."[111] In fact, he took the idea of *creatio continua* to the point of asserting that the very "existence of created substances, in each successive moment, must be the effect of the immediate agency, will, and power of God," who creates the entire universe in each moment out of his own inexhaustible Being.[112]

Edwards was well aware that his understanding of *creatio continua* meant that the world as a whole, together with everything in it, both ceases to exist and is renewed in existence at every moment. Hence, in his treatise on *Original Sin*, he declared:

> If the existence of created substance, in each successive moment, be wholly the effect of God's immediate power, in that moment, without any dependence on prior existence, as much as the first creation out of nothing, then what exists at this moment, by this power, is *a new effect*; and simply and absolutely considered, not the same with any past existence, though it be like it, and follows it according to a certain established method.[113]

Earlier in the same treatise, Edwards offered a more detailed explication:

> For it does not at all necessarily follow, that because there was sound, or light or color, or resistance, or gravity, or thought, or consciousness, or any other dependent thing the last moment, that therefore there shall be the like at the next. *All dependent existence whatsoever is in a constant flux, ever passing and returning; renewed every moment*, as the colors of the bodies are every moment renewed by the light that shines upon them; and *all is constantly proceeding from God*, as light from the sun. "In him we live and move, and have our being!"[114]

As this appeal to Paul's use of an anonymous Greek source indicates, Edwards sought to provide an alternative to the post-Newtonian dualism of nonmaterial force versus material substance, and to do so by introduc-

---

109. Jonathan Edwards, *The Works of Jonathan Edwards*, vol. 3, *Original Sin*, ed. Clyde Holbrook (New Haven, CT: Yale University Press, 1970), 401.

110. Jonathan Edwards, "Notes on Science," in *Works*, 6:238.

111. Jonathan Edwards, *The Works of Jonathan Edwards*, vol. 23, *The Miscellanies 1153–1360*, ed. Douglas Sweeney (New Haven, CT: Yale University Press, 2004), 201.

112. Edwards, *Works*, 3:401.

113. Edwards, *Works*, 3:402. Edwards offers a similar statement in his short treatment of God's existence in "Miscellanies," 125 [a]. See Jonathan Edwards, *The Works of Jonathan Edwards*, vol. 13, *The Miscellanies a–500*, ed. Thomas A. Schafer (New Haven, CT: Yale University Press, 1994), 288.

114. Edwards, *Works*, 3:304.

ing the idea of a divine, all-inclusive Being, who forms the Reality in whom all finite beings are grounded.[115] At one point in his *Notes on the Mind*, he suggested that the Newtonian concept of space is the best analogy to this mystical presence of God. En route to concluding simply that "space is God," Edwards offered the following explanation: "Space is this necessary, eternal, infinite and omnipresent being. We find that we can with ease conceive how all other beings should not be. We can remove them out of our minds, and place some other in the room of them; but space is the very thing that we can never remove and conceive of its not being."[116]

Perhaps of greater importance for the history of Being than the specific analogy that Edwards proposed to understand the connection between God and the world was his appeal to the being of God itself for the basis for the divine creative activity. To this end, he offered a far-reaching alteration of the standard conception of God as *actus purus*. According to Edwards, the divine being is not merely pure actuality, but is simultaneously both actual and dispositional. Edwards depicted the divine Being as "a disposition to communicate Himself,"[117] that is, as a disposition to repeat and even enlarge the divine essence. Although this disposition is already fully actualized in the divine life *ad intra*, Edwards added, it leads naturally to the actualization of that essence *ad extra*. So central is this idea in marking the innovative character of Edwards's proposal that Sang Hyun Lee rightly concludes, "It is Edwards's dispositional ontology of the divine self-enlargement (and not, as is sometimes suggested, Neoplatonic philosophy) that explains the logic of the ongoing purposive and creative activity of an already truly actual and sovereign God."[118]

This observation leads to a final, and perhaps surprising, aspect of Edwards's proposal: its inherent Trinitarianism. As is well known, the doctrine of the Trinity as such was not prominent in Edwards's preaching or in the writings that were published in his lifetime.[119] Yet the understanding of God as triune provided the necessary undergirding not only for his thought in general,[120] but more importantly for his ontology. The centrality of this doctrine as an underlying motif of his theological and philosophical reflections set Edwards apart not only from the deists of his day but also from the seventeenth- and eighteenth-century Puritans, who, as Jenson notes, "did not dispute the doctrine" but simply "did not much use it."[121]

---

115. Elwood, *Philosophical Theology of Jonathan Edwards*, 41.

116. Edwards, "Of Being," 203. See also Edwards, "Notes on the Mind," in *Works*, 6:339–40.

117. Edwards, "Miscellanies," no. 107, in *Works*, 13:277–78.

118. Lee, *Philosophical Theology of Jonathan Edwards*, 8.

119. Amy Plantinga Pauw, *The Supreme Harmony of All: The Trinitarian Theology of Jonathan Edwards* (Grand Rapids: Eerdmans, 2002), 2.

120. Bruce M. Stephens, *God's Last Metaphor: The Doctrine of the Trinity in New England Theology* (Chico, CA: Scholars Press, 1981), 8.

121. Jenson, *America's Theologian*, 18.

Edwards looked to the doctrine of the Trinity for the key for understanding how in God the divine disposition and the divine actuality not
only coincide but also are completely present within the life of the triune
God *ad intra*. Insofar as the Son and the Spirit comprise the perfect repetition of the primordial actuality of the Father, both the divine actuality
and the divine disposition to repeat that actuality are complete within the
divine life.[122] Yet in keeping with the divine essence as the disposition to
self-enlargement through repetition, God exercises the divine essence
externally in time and space by creating the world. In this manner, creation emerges from God as the repetition in space and time—that is, *ad
extra*—of the everlasting process of God's self-enlargement of what God
already is.[123]

In this manner, then, Edwards reconnected the link between the God
of the Bible and the Greek ontological conception of Being that formed
the center of the medieval synthesis but that had been undermined by the
developments in both theology and natural philosophy that were giving
birth to modernity. Unlike his medieval forebears, however, Edwards realized that ultimately such a synthesis could not be forged except on the
basis of an acknowledgment of the specifically Christian teaching regarding God. In short, Edwards showed that the one who is Being-in-general
can be none other than the God who is triune. In so doing, however, he
also anticipated the discussion of the relationship between the spatial-
temporal world in which we live and a supposed eternal realm lying
beyond our perceptions that exercised the minds of the great German idealists of the next century.

The Triumph of the Infinite

Edwards was not the only thinker to draw inspiration from the scientific
world that emerged from the work of such luminaries as Isaac Newton.
Others, beginning with the Continental rationalists and the British empiricists, likewise took up the challenge that Newton had bequeathed to his
intellectual heirs. Like Edwards, some of these thinkers maintained the link
between Being and the God of the Bible. Yet for an increasing number of
intellectuals, the latter served no necessary philosophical purpose.

John Locke (1632–1704) exemplifies this tendency. In his *Essay concerning Human Understanding* (1689), he set forth what came to be the
central tenets of the empirical method that many philosophers of the day
deemed to be demanded by the scientific approach that had become such

---

122. For a helpful summary of Edwards's understanding of the immanent Trinity, see Sang Hyun
Lee, "Edwards on God and Nature: Resources for Contemporary Theology," in *Edwards in Our Time:
Jonathan Edwards and the Shaping of American Religion*, ed. Sang Hyun Lee and Allen C. Guelzo
(Grand Rapids: Eerdmans, 1999), 18–19.
123. Lee, *Philosophical Theology of Jonathan Edwards*, 6.

an important aspect of the Enlightenment. Contra Descartes and the Continental rationalists, Locke asserted that all knowledge begins with experience. Moreover, in contrast to the rationalists who suggested that the mind is characterized by a complex structure that includes a set of innate ideas, Locke added that the mind begins as a *tabula rasa*, a blank tablet, that is completely passive in the knowing process. The mind simply receives "impressions" or sensations from the external world via the senses, from which it then formulates ideas.

Despite his adherence to empiricism, Locke accepted the older metaphysical concept of substance. We infer the existence of substances in which properties inhere, Locke conceded, because we cannot conceive of the existence of properties except as properties of something. Furthermore, despite Locke's own personal religious stance and his attempts to provide rational credibility for the belief in God and Christianity, his empiricism actually moved in quite another direction. Not only was God superfluous to his epistemology, but Locke's focus on sense experience as providing the sole basis for knowledge actually vitiated against any claim to philosophical knowledge of God.[124]

As the 1700s drew to a close, thinkers such as George Berkeley (1685–1753) and David Hume (1711–1776) saw through the concession that Locke had made to traditional metaphysics. Hume was especially forceful in drawing out the implications of empiricism, for he showed that this epistemological program led to a thoroughgoing skepticism. He concluded that following a purely empirical method cannot lead to knowledge of certain features of reality that we take for granted. If all we know are our perceptions, he declared, we lack a sufficient foundation for many of our most commonplace concepts, such as causality and substance. Hume acknowledged that we continually gain perceptions of the coincidence of the sequence of events from which we induce the relationship of causality. He pointed out, however, that we do not actually experience causality itself. In a similar manner, Hume argued that our imagination attributes to objects the experiences that we have of series of impressions (size, color, etc.), so that our supposed knowledge of "substances" is due merely to the habits of the mind rather than being connected to actual metaphysical entities.

Hume's epistemological skepticism not only eliminated a variety of metaphysical entities, it also called into question the deistic version of religion in general and Christianity in particular that had emerged from the work of the early scientifically inclined theologians and philosophers of nature. His assertion that we have no actual experience of causation undercut the basis of the cosmological argument, which states that the reality of the world demands the existence of a Creator as its first cause. Similarly,

124. For a similar perspective, see Solomon and Higgins, *Short History of Philosophy*, 196.

his conclusion that the concept of substance is merely a mental habit undermined the basis for the deistic belief in the immortality of the soul.[125]

Ultimately, Hume's work tended toward a philosophical agnosticism that had little place for metaphysical notions such as God, and it found even the concept of Being no longer necessary to the philosophical enterprise. In the wake of Hume's skepticism, the survival of ontology itself could only occur by means of a drastic reordering of the very character of metaphysical reflection.

God and Transcendental Idealism

Hume's writings piqued the creative genius of the great German thinker Immanuel Kant (1724–1804), whom W. T. Jones claims was the first professional philosopher, that is, "the first thinker for whom philosophy was a trade instead of a sophisticated hobby."[126] Kant found Hume's radical skepticism challenging to the extent that it awakened him from his own "dogmatic slumber." Kant's probing of the problem of knowledge that Hume had pinpointed led him to agree with his predecessor's cautious assessment of the human epistemological process. With Hume, he concluded that pure empiricism alone could not lead to a comprehensive theory of knowledge. Nor could it provide a sound basis for the scientific enterprise that had been advanced by such luminaries as Newton.[127] Unlike Hume, however, Kant believed that this limitation did not inevitably lead to skepticism. Nor did it demand the rejection of all metaphysical concepts, such as God and the soul. To show that this is the case, Kant set before himself the goal of placing metaphysics on firmer footing.

Kant's efforts resulted in what he considered to be a "Copernican Revolution" in philosophy, delineated in his first great "critique," the *Critique of Pure Reason* (1781, 1787). Just as the great Polish astronomer Nicolas Copernicus (1473–1543) had argued against the wisdom of his day and asserted that the planets revolve around the sun, so also Kant rejected the widely held empiricist assumption that the mind is passive in the epistemological process and instead elevated the mind to the center of the act of knowing. He argued that in the act of knowing the mind is not conformed to the object that is known, as the empiricists had asserted; instead, the object is conformed to the operations of the mind.[128]

According to Kant, knowledge of the external world is not the product of sense experience alone, for the senses merely furnish the "raw data" that the mind systematizes. The process of organizing sensations (i.e., the attain-

---

125. These arguments are put forth in Hume's essays *Providence and a Future State* (1748), *Dialogues concerning Natural Religion* (1779), and *Natural History of Religion* (1757).

126. Jones, *History of Western Philosophy*, 812.

127. For this perspective, see Walsh, *History of Philosophy*, 307–8, 316.

128. Walsh, *History of Philosophy*, 312.

ing of "knowledge") is made possible by certain formal concepts present in the mind, which act as a type of grid or filter that makes knowing possible.[129] Kant determined that two of the various formal concepts were foundational: space and time.[130] He argued that space and time are not properties that inhere in things but that they belong to the ordering that the mind imposes on the world it encounters. Therefore, objects may not actually exist "in space and time," yet we simply cannot know the external world of sense experience in any other way than by means of these two concepts. Solomon and Higgins offer the following summary of Kant's basic thesis: "We 'constitute' the objects of our experience out of our intuitions, locating these objects in space and time and in causal relationships with other objects."[131]

The hypothesis that the mind is active in the epistemological process had the effect of limiting this kind of knowledge to the realm of personal experience, that is, to objects as they are present in experience. Consequently, Kant distinguished between objects present in the experience of the human knower (which he termed "phenomena") and objects lying beyond experience (which he labeled "noumena").[132] Generally Kant uses the term noumenon to refer to an object as it exists apart from any relation to a knowing subject, although at times he speaks of a noumenon as an object for which we simply lack the needed apparatus to detect. In either case, we have no sense experience, and hence no direct knowledge, of noumena. Because our knowledge is limited to phenomena (that is, to objects as they are present in our experience), we can gain no knowledge of things in themselves, at least not through sense experience and the scientific method. To cite Kant's summary statement: "We can . . . have no knowledge of any object as thing in itself, but only in so far as it is an object of sensible intuition, that is, an appearance."[133]

Like Hume's epistemology, Kant's theory of knowing placed strict limits on the ability of theologians and philosophers to argue from sense experience to transcendent realities (such as God, the soul, and the cosmos).[134] Insofar as such realities lie beyond the categories lodged within the human mind, especially space and time, they cannot be known through the scientific enterprise.

Kant's goal, however, was not to deny these metaphysical realities but to establish them on a more secure foundation. To this end, he noted that

129. Hume agreed that such concepts were necessary for human knowing but declared that they were deduced from experience. Kant, in contrast, claimed that these concepts "sprang from the pure understanding." Immanuel Kant, *Prolegomena to Any Future Metaphysics*, trans. and ed. Paul Carus (Illinois: Open Court, 1967), 7.

130. See Immanuel Kant, *Critique of Pure Reason*, trans. Norman Kemp Smith (New York: St. Martin's, 1929), 67–82.

131. Solomon and Higgins, *Short History of Philosophy*, 208.

132. Kant, *Critique of Pure Reason*, 264–69.

133. Ibid., 27.

134. See, for example, Kant, *Critique of Pure Reason*, 29.

humans naturally tend to seek to unify their experiences and cognitions. They do so, Kant observed, by appeal to what he cited as the three transcendental regulative ideas of pure reason: the idea of self (or ego) as the totality-in-unity of the thinking subject, the idea of the cosmos (or world) as the totality-in-unity of the cosmic series of all phenomena, and the idea of God as the being of all beings that forms the absolute ground and condition of all objects of thought.[135] Although these concepts do not correspond to any object that we encounter in sense experience, they emerge as we follow our natural mental disposition to devise a coherent synthesis of our experience. They stand at the apex of the transcendental conditions that must be true for knowledge of phenomena to be possible.

In his second major treatise, the *Critique of Practical Reason* (1788), Kant continued this enterprise of devising a firmer grounding for the metaphysical realm. He observed that the human person is not only a creature capable of sense experience but is also a moral being. Moreover, he noted that the world is not merely an object for human scientific exploration but is also a stage on which humans act—that is, it is a realm of moral value. Like the realm explored by pure or theoretical reason, this moral dimension of human existence is fundamentally rational. Hence, Kant spoke of it as the subject matter of "pure practical reason" or the topic of the "practical" (i.e., moral) use of pure reason.[136] Consequently, in Kant's estimation, the goal of reason extends beyond inquiring into "theoretical knowledge" (i.e., "knowledge of what *is*") to include "practical knowledge" (that is, "the representation of what *ought to be*").[137] Similar to the unifying impulse found within pure reason, the practical use of reason requires that the philosopher postulate the reality of three metaphysical realities—God, immortality, and freedom—even though these three lie beyond the pale of sense experience. The postulates of practical reason, in turn, correspond to the three transcendental regulative ideas of pure reason.

By reintroducing the metaphysical realm that the empirical method had dispelled, Kant opened the way for a return of God into the purview of critical philosophy. He even described his work, in keeping with his stance as a confessional Lutheran, as that of denying "*knowledge*, in order to make room for *faith*."[138] Yet despite Kant's personal adherence to Christianity, the God whom he reintroduced into metaphysics differed considerably from the God that Edwards had posited at the heart of his philosophical system. Ultimately, the God of Kant's metaphysics is both a regulative principle of theoretical or "pure" reason and the one whom practical reason demands as the guarantor that happiness will eventually be distributed in accordance

135. See Kant, *Critique of Pure Reason*, 492.
136. Kant, *Critique of Pure Reason*, 26.
137. Ibid., 526.
138. Ibid., 29.

with virtue. In both cases, the God demanded by philosophy is a far cry from the God depicted in Christian theology and served by Christian piety. In his philosophical reflections, Kant came close to replacing the personal God of the Christian tradition with a God who is little more than a metaphysical value. Jones provides the following telling observation:

> God, it would seem, is the same sort of value we attribute to ourselves as persons, the supreme example of that reason we respect in ourselves. What distinguishes God from man, on this view, is the difference between right and duty. When, that is, we recognize this value in ourselves, we experience it under the form of a compulsion. . . . When we think of this value in its own right, as a good to be realized, not as an obligation imposed on us, we call it "God."[139]

The "Infinite" of Romanticism

Martin Walsh concludes that Kant's philosophical system "was a rich amalgam of incongruous elements" which unsurprisingly "disintegrated quickly after its original formulation."[140] This disintegration began already among the younger thinkers who followed in Kant's wake and contended with each other as to who was his legitimate successor.

The point of tension that separated some second-generation Kantian idealists from their master was his postulate of the thing-in-itself, which they viewed as an unwarranted concession to an outmoded metaphysic. One claimant to the post-Kantian throne, Johann Gottlieb Fichte (1762–1814), remedied this situation by simply kicking out the Kantian thing-in-itself, to cite Arthur Schopenhauer's characterization of Fichte's work.[141] Actually, Fichte's intent was to correct what he saw as the glaring deficiency in Kant's critical idealism by unifying what he deemed to be its two antithetical aspects, namely, the epistemology of the first *Critique* and the moral philosophy of the second. To this end, he elevated the moral dimension (which he labeled "idealism") above the scientific (and in his estimation "dogmatic") aspect.

In his own major philosophical treatise, *The Science of Knowledge* (1794), Fichte set aside the problem of the subject's apprehension of the external world that Kant had tackled in the *Critique of Pure Reason*, in favor of an inquiry into the "I" (ego or self), understood not as static but, drawing an impulse from Kant and expressed in the typical Romantic manner, as a process whereby the self apprehends itself and thereby both posits itself and creates its world.[142] To this end, he offered a detailed

139. Jones, *History of Western Philosophy*, 866–67.
140. Walsh, *History of Philosophy*, 335.
141. Arthur Schopenhauer, *The World as Will and Representation*, trans. E. F. J. Payne (New York: Dover, 1969), 1:436.
142. George H. Mead, *Movements of Thought in the Nineteenth Century*, ed. Merritt H. Moore (Chicago: University of Chicago Press, 1936), 87.

philosophical argument showing that this process involves the "I" (or the self) positing something other than itself (the not-self), which it views both as determining the self and as being determined by the self.[143]

In setting forth this thesis that the knowing self creates and determines its own external world, Fichte appealed to what his predecessor denoted as "practical reason." Following Kant, Fichte identified the self with its moral task, in that the self realizes itself in freely doing its duty. Yet he differed with his mentor regarding the manner in which this occurs. For Fichte, the knowing self determines its external world for the purpose of providing a field for one's moral endeavors, by means of which one knows oneself and constitutes onself as a self. He summarized the point in *The Vocation of Man* (1800): "My world is the object and sphere of my duties, and absolutely nothing more; there is no other world for me, and no other qualities of my world than what are implied in this."[144] Or to cite George Herbert Mead's characterization of Fichte's proposal, "The self throws up the world as a field within which action must take place; and, in setting up the world as a field of action, it realizes itself."[145] For Fichte, therefore, creation is ultimately of value because it facilitates the self in doing its duty.[146] In this manner, he transposed the realm that Kant claimed to know through "pure" reason (the world of sense perception) into the product of "practical" reason. By depriving thereby the noumenal realm of its philosophical importance, he in effect kicked out the "thing-in-itself."

Fichte's jettisoning of "thing-in-itself" cut the one remaining link to an absolutely external reality that Kant had retained. Moreover, it opened the way for the creation of what some philosophers refer to as "alternative conceptual frameworks." Whereas Kant applied the concept of human freedom to the realm of ethical action alone, Fichte elevated what he considered to be an even more important focus of freedom, namely, the realm of thought or the play of the imagination. This freedom means that rather than being limited by necessity to a single way of understanding the world,[147] each of us may possibly describe objects by means of different sets of concepts or different "conceptual frameworks," by means of which we, in effect, create different worlds for ourselves.

Although this implication has proven to be a lasting contribution of German idealism, of more immediate importance in the history of Being is the connection to the concept of the Infinite that Fichte's "corrective"

143. Johann Gottlieb Fichte, *The Science of Knowledge*, trans. Peter Heath and John Lachs (New York: Meredith, 1970), 120–27. For a concise summary of this aspect of Fichte's thought, see M. J. Inwood, "Fichte, Johann Gottlieb," in *Oxford Companion to Philosophy*, 278.

144. Johann Gottlieb Fichte, *The Vocation of Man*, trans. William Smith (LaSalle, IL: Open Court, 1965), 108.

145. Mead, *Movements of Thought*, 90.

146. Peter Heath and John Lachs, preface to Fichte, *Science of Knowledge*, xviii.

147. Robert C. Solomon, *Continental Philosophy since 1750: The Rise and Fall of the Self* (Oxford: Oxford University Press, 1988), 50.

of Kant instantiated. The self-positing action of the self served in Fichte's thought as a bridge to the concept of the Infinite, which formed the heart of Romantic philosophy. According to Fichte, the self cannot posit itself as a finite self without simultaneously positing the "Absolute Self" or "World-Spirit,"[148] that is, the Infinite of which the self is the finite expression.[149] The act of self-positing entails the centering of the self on the infinite or Absolute Self.[150] This idea lies behind Fichte's terse declaration, "I create God every day."[151] According to Fichte, the Absolute Self is the ultimate source of the not-self, the seemingly objective world. The Self posits this world as its task—as the Self's moral obligation and as the place in which the Self acts. In good Romantic fashion, Fichte linked the Absolute Self, as well as its creation of the world, to the finite self through which the Absolute Self expresses itself:

> That Eternal Will is thus assuredly the Creator of the World, in the only way in which He can be so, and in the only way in which it needs creation:—in the finite reason. . . . Only in our minds has He created a world; at least that *from which* we unfold it, and that *by which* we unfold it;—the voice of duty, and harmonious feelings, intuitions, and laws of thought.[152]

As this statement indicates, Fichte viewed the self as characterized ultimately by will and considered the exercise of the moral will to be the connection between the finite self and the Infinite Will. In keeping with the Romantic pattern of linking the "voice within" with the revelation of the infinite, he considered the human conscience to be the point of access to the Infinite Will and thereby the source that discloses the place of the particular self in the grand scheme of the cosmos:

> Thus do I approach—the mortal must speak in his own language— thus do I approach that Infinite Will; and the voice of conscience in my soul, which teaches me in every situation of life what I have there to do, is the channel through which again His influence descends upon me. That voice, sensualized by my environment, and translated into my language, is the oracle of the Eternal World which announces to me how I am to perform my part in the order of the spiritual universe, or in the Infinite Will who is Himself that order.[153]

Fichte's introduction of the concept of will set the stage for what emerged as a crucial aspect of nineteenth-century German Romanticism.

148. Fichte, *Vocation of Man*, 133.
149. For an interesting discussion of this, see Mead, *Movements of Thought*, 101.
150. For this point, see Mead, *Movements of Thought*, 95.
151. As cited in Mead, *Movements of Thought*, 95.
152. Fichte, *Vocation of Man*, 157–58.
153. Ibid., 152–53.

The poets and philosophers who contributed to this intellectual development, which Solomon and Higgins characterize as a "misshapen but enthusiastic movement,"[154] welcomed Kant's underscoring of the limits of rational knowledge as well as his insistence on the existence of a realm behind or beyond the phenomenal world. Yet they refused to accede to his conclusion that we have no access to this noumenal realm, which according to Kant remains unknowable to us. In their attempts to resolve the seemingly thorny intellectual conundrum that Kant had bequeathed to his offspring, the Romantics drew inspiration from his third *Critique*, the *Critique of Judgment* (1790), in which he spoke of the purposefulness of the cosmos as well as of the aesthetic dimension of life. Many of them, in turn, gravitated to the idea of the will that Fichte had brought to the fore. What the Romantics required in this process was a philosopher of Kant's genius who could articulate a view of the world that fit the cosmic yet often tragic Romantic sensibilities. Eventually such a philosopher was discovered: Arthur Schopenhauer (1788–1860),[155] who, in the estimation of DeWitt H. Parker, "carried the philosophy of romanticism further than it had been carried before."[156]

Like Fichte, Schopenhauer's goal was to correct what he saw as the insufficiencies in Kant's philosophy.[157] Schopenhauer agreed with Kant's distinction between the phenomenal and the noumenal realms, but he disagreed with his predecessor's claim that the latter is unknowable. Like Fichte, Schopenhauer was interested in the "transcendental subject" that posits or determines the world as its object. Nevertheless, he disagreed that this subject was best characterized as an "I," a self, or an ego. Rather, Schopenhauer replaced Fichte's transcendental self with a transcendental will, thereby proposing what Walsh terms "transcendental voluntaristic idealism."[158]

Schopenhauer set forth his perspective in his book *The World as Will and Idea* (1818). Drawing from a viewpoint reminiscent of the medieval nominalists, he pointed out that the conceptual or scientific way of thinking, such as the classification of colors into the categories of green and blue, is cognitively inadequate, for it leads us to lump together things that are in fact different (e.g., shades of blue) and to separate things that are in fact similar (e.g., shades of blue-green). Furthermore, this manner of thinking can lead us astray in the practice of living. Instead, Schopenhauer

154. Solomon and Higgins, *Short History of Philosophy*, 221.
155. For a similar judgment, see Solomon and Higgins, *Short History of Philosophy*, 223.
156. DeWitt H. Parker, "Arthur Schopenhauer," in *Schopenhauer Selections* (New York: Charles Scribner's Sons, 1928), xviii.
157. Schopenhauer offers a lengthy appraisal of Kant in *World as Will and Representation*, 1:413–534. For the conclusion that Schopenhauer saw his own work as the continuation and completion of Kant's, see E. F. J. Payne, "Translator's Introduction," in Schopenhauer, *World as Will and Representation*, 1:vi.
158. Walsh, *History of Philosophy*, 356.

advised us to look to feeling, immediacy, and intuition. He believed that we gain an intuition of the inner nature of reality—of the thing-in-itself—from an examination of self-consciousness. The self perceives of itself as both an external (i.e., spatial and temporal) object and an inward immediacy that involves being a willing, active agent. In short, the self intuits itself as "will."[159] In Schopenhauer's estimation, our observable behavior, our body, and even our mind are all expressions of our fundamental volition.

Schopenhauer's conception of will ought not to be confused with the idea of "purposing." He offered a comprehensive yet fluid[160] conception that viewed will as involving "all striving, wishing, shunning, hoping, fearing, loving, hating."[161] Indeed, he declared that "all that directly constitutes our own weal and woe, desire and aversion, is clearly only affection of the will, is an excitation, a modification, of willing and non-willing, is just that which, if it takes outward effect, exhibits itself as an act of will proper."[162] Above all, however, will is a forceful dynamic, at the heart of which is the idea of striving.

In a typical Romantic manner, Schopenhauer extended the concept of will to the universe as a whole. On the basis of his assumption that the forces in nature are essentially akin to the human will,[163] he concluded that all phenomena, whether deliberate human conduct or the seeming blindly acting forces of nature, are manifestations of a cosmic will that forms an underlying unity and comprises the thing-in-itself.[164] The world, in turn, is the "representation" or "mirror" of the will. As such, it reveals that what it wills is "nothing but this world, life, precisely as it exists," so that the will is best termed "the will-to-live."[165] Thus, as T. L. S. Sprigge notes, for Schopenhauer, "the universe is a single, 'vast,' cosmic Will to Exist which experiences itself through an apparent diversity of conscious beings in a spatio-temporal and deterministic world."[166]

As has already been noted, Schopenhauer did not invent the will; nor was the elevation of the will unique to his proposal. Kant and especially Fichte had developed the concept. Yet they linked it to reason and therefore viewed the will as reasonable. Fichte, for example, asserted, "The will is the living principle of reason." Moreover, he spoke of "Infinite Reason" and defined will as "self-active reason."[167] It was precisely here that Schopenhauer parted company from his predecessors. He claimed that

159. Schopenhauer, *World as Will and Representation*, 1:100.
160. Patrick Gardener, *Schopenhauer* (Baltimore: Penguin Books, 1963), 152.
161. Schopenhauer, *World as Will and Representation*, 2:204.
162. Ibid., 2:202.
163. Guenter Zoeller, "Schopenhauer on the Self," in *The Cambridge Companion to Schopenhauer*, 2nd ed., ed. Robert Audi (Cambridge: Cambridge University Press, 1999), 31–32.
164. Schopenhauer, *World as Will and Representation*, 1:109–10, 143, 162.
165. Ibid., 1:275.
166. T. L. S. Sprigge, "Schopenhauer, Arthur," in *Oxford Companion to Philosophy*, 803.
167. Fichte, *Vocation of Man*, 140–41, 151.

the will is nonrational, arational, or even irrational. The will "is not deter-mined as consequent by a reason or ground, and so it knows no necessity; in other words, it is *free*." The cosmic will is not characterized by any particular goal or purpose. Instead, it is simply *blind* striving.[168] Rather than the will being under the rule of reason, reason is secondary to the will, he argued, for reason cannot formulate or prescribe its ends.[169] Nor does the will merely supplement the intellect in the constitution of the human self; it is the source of the self's own being.[170] Contra both Kant and Fichte, therefore, Schopenhauer denied the fundamental rationality of the thing-in-itself or the transcendental subject, arguing instead that it is irrational will.

Nevertheless, Schopenhauer did not view the goal of existence as willful self-aggrandizement. Instead, he claimed that this goal is the abolition of the will. Rather than simply surrendering to the will to live, he declared, the self must recognize that as an expression of the cosmic will, it is ultimately identical with every other self, every other creature, and even the whole of nature. This recognition, in turn, requires that the self overcome its fixation on its own individuality; it must surmount the *principium individuationis*.

Like other Romantics, Schopenhauer suggested that aesthetic experi-ence contributes to this process. Not only does the aesthetic allow us to recognize the presence of the universal within the particular, it also serves to quiet the will within us. Yet of even greater significance, as the self-as-will comes to "the knowledge of its own inner nature,"[171] that is, the knowledge "that our true self exists not only in our own person . . . but in everything that lives,"[172] the person embarks along the road toward sainthood. This pathway includes the pursuit of justice and equality; a loving, sympathetic compassion that views the suffering of others[173] as one's own; an asceticism that facilitates the elimination of egoism; and finally the resignation of the will itself.[174]

His embracing of the pathway toward saintliness led Schopenhauer beyond the pale of Christianity; indeed, it drew him beyond adherence to any particular religion. In a manner that anticipated twentieth-century plu-ralism, he concluded that he had discovered an intuition that lies beneath the dogmatic articulations of the various religions, all of which are merely attempts to express in the kind of abstract terms that reason can accept the fundamental truth regarding the world that is directly apprehended by intuition. In keeping with this perspective, Schopenhauer wrote:

168. Zoeller, "Schopenhauer on the Self," 18.
169. Parker, "Arthur Schopenhauer," xviii.
170. Zoeller, "Schopenhauer on the Self," 19.
171. Schopenhauer, *World as Will and Representation*, 1:404.
172. Ibid., 1:373.
173. Ibid., 1:375–78.
174. Ibid., 1:408.

What I have described here with feeble tongue, and only in general terms, is not some philosophical fable, invented by myself, and only of today. No, it was the enviable life of so many saints and great souls among the Christians, and even more among the Hindus and Buddhists, and also among the believers of other religions. Different as were the dogmas that were impressed on their faculty of reason, the inner, direct, and intuitive knowledge from which alone all virtue and holiness can come is nevertheless expressed in precisely the same way in the conduct of life.[175]

The intuition of the unity of all reality as an expression of the transcendental will kept some type of conception of God at the center of the philosophical picture that Schopenhauer painted. Yet the infinite Will that he perceived to be present within the finite, willful agent bore little resemblance to the conceptions of the divine that had been articulated in the tradition at the end of which Schopenhauer himself stood. Any resemblance between the Infinite of the philosophers and the I AM of the Exodus narrative had evaporated. The connection between Being and the God of Christian theology—a connection that had been so carefully forged in the Middle Ages and the residue of which had continued to structure the philosophical discussion long after the medieval synthesis had been undermined—had now been completely severed. In Schopenhauer's proposal, the triumph of the Infinite was complete, and with this triumph Being was completely secularized.

175. Schopenhauer, *World as Will and Representation*, 4:68, trans. E. F. J. Payne, 2 vols. (Indian Hills, CO: Falcon's Wing Press, 1958), 1:383.

Chapter Three

From Onto-Theology
to Theo-Ontology
The Demise of Being

One prominent trajectory in the Age of Reason reshaped philosophy into the image of natural science and thereby hoped to find truth—and God—in the realm of nature, which was viewed as static and complete. Contrary to the intentions of its chief architects, this approach eventually undermined the link between the Christian God and the Greek concept of the First Cause of the world. And this, in turn, opened the way for the triumph of the idea of the Infinite. Ultimately, the process netted a "secularized" version of Being that in many respects resembled the classical tradition of ancient Greek philosophy.

Chroniclers of the history of philosophy routinely elevate René Descartes as the thinker who above all others carried the classical tradition into the modern era.[1] Descartes retained the classical principles of

---

1. For a similar characterization of the history of modern philosophy, see Douglas Browning, "Preface to the First Edition," in *Philosophers of Process*, ed. Douglas Browning and William T. Myers (New York: Fordham University Press, 1998), xii–xiii.

substance and causality, including the postulate that all appearances are attributes inhering in a substance, as well as the axiom that nothing can be present in an effect that did not already inhere in its cause. In addition, he went beyond his forebears in postulating the existence of three basic types of substance: mind, matter, and God.[2] The dualism between the natural substances of mind and matter endemic to the Cartesian proposal taxed the thinking of philosophers for the next three hundred years. Descartes' heirs puzzled over the metaphysical question of how the mind and the body are able to affect each other and the epistemological problem regarding the possibility of knowledge of the external world. In response, some of Descartes' successors attempted to explain how the distinct substances interact. But others working in his wake, especially those who stood in what is often called the "rationalist" tradition, concluded that the solution required a jettisoning of two of the three substances. Yet they differed as to which of the three ought to be retained: matter (e.g., Hobbes and the French *philosophes*), mind (e.g., Berkeley and Leibniz) or God (e.g., Spinoza).

Already in the Enlightenment era, the entire Cartesian tradition came under strict scrutiny. The most intense attack came from David Hume, who critiqued the epistemological claims of all the various rationalist proposals, as well as those of his empiricist forebears. In the wake of Hume's challenge, Kant attempted to reinstate the concepts of substance and causality by relegating them to the constructive mind. Despite his valiant efforts, as the nineteenth century unfolded and then gave way to the twentieth, the entire tradition of invoking the language of substance and causality came under fire. The ultimate outworking of these developments was the inauguration of a trajectory that led to the demise of Being.

The Dynamic Being

Being's demise did not happen immediately. Before the philosophical Armageddon occurred, Western intellectual history witnessed a renaissance of metaphysical speculation. Of greatest importance were the several attempts to renew metaphysics by changing the rules of the ontological game. The most significant rule change occurred as philosophers exchanged the language of substance and causality for that of process and creativity, a move that comprised the final chapter in the larger story of the shift from a static to a dynamic ontology. The two most far-reaching and

2. A concise, helpful sketch of the Cartesian innovation in postulating the substantial status of matter is found in Ivor Leclerc, "Whitehead and the Dichotomy of Rationalism and Empiricism," in *Whitehead's Metaphysics of Creativity*, ed. Friedrich Rapp and Reiner Wiehl (Albany: State University of New York Press, 1990), 2–4.

influential proposals that reflect the new dynamic approach to metaphysics were offered by Georg W. F. Hegel and Alfred North Whitehead.

The Ontology of the Unfolding Absolute

The first major modern philosopher to propose what we might describe as a dynamic ontology was the German idealist Georg W. F. Hegel (1770–1831). Hegel's lasting philosophical legacy is evidenced by the fact that nearly 125 years after his death, Robert S. Franks lauded his proposal as "the most completely rounded philosophical system of modern times,"[3] and twenty-five years later, Avrum Stroll and Richard H. Popkin could still refer to Hegel as the "most famous modern metaphysician."[4]

Similar to many other philosophical systems offered in the Romantic era, Hegel's "completely rounded" program was motivated to a great degree by the central difficulty that Kant's successors saw in the work of their predecessor: his postulate of an unknowable thing-in-itself. Like others who worked in the wake of Kant, Hegel was convinced that human reason can—and must—transcend the limits that his predecessor had set. He stood apart from his contemporaries, however, in the exact manner in which he proposed to solve this perceived problem. The innovative solution that Hegel devised catapulted him above his peers and gained for him the status of being "the dominant figure of post-Kantian thought," to cite D. W. Hamlyn's accolade.[5]

At the heart of Hegel's philosophical proposal was his declaration that reality forms one, all-encompassing, active, developing process, and that this ongoing dynamic is the unfolding of the principle of rationality that is being concretized in the world process itself. The innovative character of Hegel's proposal is evident when it is viewed in the context of the various idealistic philosophies that had been proposed by his predecessors. These metaphysical offerings invariably considered the higher realm of ideas, by virtue of its eternal character, to be static and populated by an eternally existing, unchangeable set of ideas. Into this basic understanding Fichte introduced a dynamic element, insofar as he suggested that the transcendent Self (or Ego) was responsible for both the subjective and objective aspects of our experience. Hegel, however, took this proposal to the limit.

Furthermore, Fichte's colleagues in the Romantic movement tended to portray whatever transcendent reality they posited as irrational or even completely meaningless. Hegel, in contrast, presented a vision of an all-encompassing dynamic that is orderly and purposive. The world process

3. Robert S. Franks, *The Doctrine of the Trinity* (London: Duckworth, 1953), 160.
4. Avrum Stroll and Richard H. Popkin, *Introduction to Philosophy*, 3rd ed. (New York: Holt, Rinehart & Winston, 1979), 159.
5. D. W. Hamlyn, *A History of Western Philosophy* (New York: Viking, 1987), 245.

is rational, he declared, and consequently it can be thought. In fact, Hegel believed that the pattern of thought and the pattern of reality coincide. Viewed from this perspective, we might say that for him the dynamic of the world process (i.e., the Absolute) is Thinking in the ultimate sense, Thinking knowing itself, or Thinking coming to think of itself through the object that is being thought.[6] In this manner, Hegel can rightly be characterized as having "developed Fichte's subjective idealism into the all-encompassing theory of objective or absolute idealism,"[7] to cite Stroll and Popkin's description.

Yet Hegel took the matter an additional step. He linked the principle that forms the dynamic of both thought and reality with the God of Christianity. In so doing, he revived in modern form the grand vision of a synthesis between philosophy and theology—and hence between Being and God—that had been forged by the medieval scholastics.

Reality and Thought as Dynamic Movement

In launching his corrective of Kant, Hegel chose a similar starting point to that proposed by Fichte, namely, the phenomenon of consciousness and the discovery of what is evident to our consciousness. Consciousness plays this role in Hegel's programmatic and, in the opinion of many historians, greatest book, *Phenomenology of Spirit* (1807).[8] This book forms a kind of prologue to the philosophical system set forth in his subsequent volumes, which Solomon and Higgins describe as "a magnificent conceptual odyssey that carries us from the most elementary to the most all-encompassing and complex conceptions of human consciousness."[9] Despite the shared starting point in consciousness, Hegel's work moves in a direction quite different from the one that Fichte had trod. Fichte's philosophical deliberations commence with the presence within consciousness of self-consciousness (or the self) as a given. For Hegel, in contrast, self-consciousness—or self-knowledge—looms as the goal of the world process; it forms the *telos* toward which the dynamic Absolute moves.[10]

This difference provided the basis for the particularly Hegelian manner of refuting Kant's positing of an unknowable thing-in-itself. In the introduction of *Phenomenology of Spirit*, Hegel contrasts the status of objects of consciousness (which he termed "being for consciousness" and deemed to be a form of "being for another") to that of what supposedly

6. For a somewhat similar characterization, see W. T. Jones, *A History of Western Philosophy* (New York: Harcourt, Brace & Co., 1952), 879.

7. Stroll and Popkin, *Introduction to Philosophy*, 159.

8. See, for example, Robert C. Solomon and Kathleen M. Higgins, *A Short History of Philosophy* (New York: Oxford University Press, 1996), 216.

9. Solomon and Higgins, *Short History of Philosophy*, 216.

10. For a similar characterization, see Frank Thilly, *A History of Philosophy*, 3rd ed., rev. Ledger Wood (New York: Henry Holt, 1957), 478.

exists independently of consciousness (i.e., "being in itself"). He argues that insofar as the only basis for claiming that anything exists lies in consciousness itself and the very idea of something existing in itself derives from consciousness, the distinction between "being for another" and "being in itself" likewise exists only in consciousness. Therefore, Hegel concluded, the idea of a thing-in-itself—that is, of something that exists apart from consciousness—is self-contradictory.[11]

The goal of *Phenomenology of Spirit*, however, is not simply to refute and correct Kant, but to set the stage for Hegel's own philosophical proposal. To this end, the book narrates what might be called the journey of consciousness, a journey that climaxes in the "absolute knowing" that occurs as self-consciousness becomes aware of itself as self-consciousness and becomes cognizant of all its objects as part of itself. This, in Hegel's estimation, is the beginning point of philosophy.[12]

Hegel's larger proposal, in turn, involves an attempt to delineate the movement that is inherent in pure thought and is at the same time the goal-directed process immanent in nature, understood as the world as a whole. He is confident that such a philosophical project is possible, because philosophy is ultimately humankind thinking Thinking's thought of itself, and in and through the human spirit the Absolute comes to know itself or becomes conscious of itself. On this basis, Hegel divided philosophy into three major parts: logic (i.e., the study of *logos* or thought itself), philosophy of nature, and philosophy of mind. As Martin J. Walsh notes regarding Hegel's system, "These three studies give us a complete reconstruction, in conceptual form, of the self-actualization or life of the Absolute."[13]

Crucial to Hegel's understanding of the dynamic of thought, and, by extension, of the world process as well, is his contention that the movement of philosophical reasoning creates the various stages of its own history as it passes through them. Moreover, in each, the preceding stage is carried into the next as its basis while being negated in the process, so that the previous stage is both preserved and suspended in the latter. Hegel presented this innovative understanding of the character of thought as the solution to the problem of the coincidence of thesis and antithesis that Kant explored in his *Critique of Pure Reason*, as well as the resolution to the condition of the "coincidence of opposites" at work in nature and human history that had been noted by the Romantic philosophers. Whereas Kant concluded from this phenomenon that "pure" reason is epistemologically

11. G. W. F. Hegel, *The Phenomenology of Mind*, trans. J. B. Baillie (New York: Harper & Row, 1967), 33–34, 206.

12. For example, near the end of the book, Hegel writes, "As to the actual existence of this notion, science does not appear in time and in reality till spirit has arrived at this stage of being conscious regarding itself." Hegel, *Phenomenology of Mind*, 798; see also p. 805.

13. Martin J. Walsh, *A History of Philosophy* (London: Geoffrey Chapman, 1985), 346.

limited, Hegel declared that both thesis and antithesis can be affirmed when understood in the light of a more inclusive proposition—their synthesis—in which both are canceled out and yet preserved.

Hegel is often interpreted as asserting that the dynamic of thought is an ongoing movement through the three stages of thesis, antithesis, and synthesis. This characterization, which is commonly known as the "Hegelian dialectic" (although he likely inherited it from Fichte[14] or Schelling[15]), has some merit. Yet Hegel's actual proposal was somewhat more complex,[16] especially in that he gave a much more prominent place to the act of negation than the typical descriptions tend to imply.[17] "The simple point of negative self-relation," he declared, is "the innermost source of all activity, of living and spiritual self-movement, the dialectic soul, which all truth has in it and through which it alone is truth."[18] In keeping with this perspective, Hegel conceived of thought as moving through a kind of double act of negation: the negating that posits the opposite (antithesis) and the negating of the opposition (synthesis). Horst Althaus explains the significance of this Hegelian innovation in logic:

> That A (preserved in B) = non-A, and that the infinite should become the infinite through the power of the negative, is something that before Hegel perhaps only Heraclitus could have claimed with equal boldness. What was new about the self-confessedly abstruse treatment characteristic of Hegel's book was that such a formula and all its implications would henceforth belong amongst the indubitable first principles of logic itself.[19]

What Hegel uncovered as the central characteristic of the movement of abstract thought he deemed to be operative in the world process as well. To cite his terse assertion, "What is rational is actual and what is actual is rational."[20] In fact, this intimate connection between thought and life is what gave importance to the dynamic of double negation—of differentiation and reconciliation—that he found at the center of the movement of

14. For this opinion, see Claude Welch, *Protestant Thought in the Nineteenth Century*, vol. 1, *1799–1870* (New Haven, CT: Yale University Press, 1972), 90.

15. For this judgment, see Franks, *Doctrine of the Trinity*, 160.

16. For a similar judgment as well as an identification of the historical root of the popular simplification of Hegel's own view, see Robert B. Pippin, "Hegel, Georg Wilhelm Friedrich," in *The Cambridge Dictionary of Philosophy*, 2nd ed., ed. Robert Audi (Cambridge: Cambridge University Press, 1999), 368.

17. See, for example, the helpful characterization in William Young, *Hegel's Dialectical Method: Its Origins and Religious Significance* (Nutley, NJ: Craig Press, 1972), 9.

18. G. W. F. Hegel, *The Science of Logic*, trans. W. H. Johnston and L. G. Struthrers (London: George Allen & Unwin, 1929), 2:477.

19. Horst Althaus, *Hegel: An Intellectual Biography*, trans. Michael Tarsh (Cambridge: Polity Press, 2000), 132.

20. G. W. F. Hegel, *Philosophy of Right*, trans. T. M. Knox (London: Oxford University Press, 1967), 10.

thought. For Hegel, therefore, reason is not something that is externally brought to life. Rather, it emerges out of experience, especially experience as a whole.[21] This understanding carried far-reaching implications for philosophy. It meant that philosophical reflection leads not only to the discovery but also to the coming into being of ultimate truth, and that this coming into being is historical.[22] Moreover, rather than being the rational conclusions reached from the use of the proper reasoning pattern (as had been the concern of philosophy at least since Descartes), truth is connected, at least structurally, to the process itself, viewed as a whole. Truth is found in the ebb and flow, the twists and turns of the process of reasoning that eventually leads to resolution. Hegel noticed likewise that the reasoning process does not consider its object to be ultimately external to itself, but sees it as contained within itself. He called this activity of reason grasping its object "conception," and he termed the ultimate conception, the gathering of all conceptions into a connected whole, "the Idea" or the conception of the Absolute.

The Modern Synthesis of Philosophy and Theology

Hegel's primary designation for the dynamic present in both thought and reality that brings reality into a unified whole (the Absolute) was the German word *Geist*. This term served his purposes well, in that it combines the concept of rationality reflected in the English word "mind" with the dimension of the supramaterial bound up with the idea of "spirit." Above all, *Geist* is an active subject, an activity, a process that is reflected by and realized in the all-encompassing world process. *Geist* takes on objective form and comes to full awareness of itself through the historical process, the stages of which *Geist*—like the dynamic of thought—creates as it passes through them. Above all, the different epochs in human history form the stages through which *Geist* passes en route to self-discovery.[23] Consequently, the history of human culture not only involves the human spirit encountering its own conscious life,[24] but *Geist* realizing itself and coming to know itself through humankind, especially the religious dimension of the human phenomenon.

Hegel's use of the term *Geist* to name the Absolute that realizes itself in the world process in accordance with a movement of dialectical logic opened the way for him to posit an intrinsic connection between this

21. Emil L. Fackenheim, *The Religious Dimension in Hegel's Thought* (Chicago: University of Chicago Press, 1967), 98.
22. Aiken asserts that Hegel's program constituted the first "thoroughgoing attempt to view all philosophical problems and concepts, including the concept of reason itself, in essentially historical terms." Henry D. Aiken, *The Age of Ideology* (New York: Mentor Books, 1956), 72.
23. Hegel, *Phenomenology of Mind*, 807–8. See also his poetic statement on p. 91.
24. George Lichtheim, introduction to Hegel, *Phenomenology of Mind*, xxvi.

ongoing dynamic and the divine.[25] This marked an important break from the Enlightenment philosophical theologians, who had looked to nature to find the footprints of its aloof, transcendent Designer. In contrast to this approach, Hegel sought the divine in the totality of the processes of nature and history, which he believed formed a unified whole and thereby manifested an underlying, self-actualizing principle that is both rational and spiritual.

When viewed from the religious perspective, *Geist* is the God who reveals himself and who actualizes himself in the ongoing process that is present within both rational thought and history. Indeed, Hegel's God can only be conceived as existing in the sense of this rational and historical unfolding. Hegel's goal, therefore, was not simply to speak about dialectical movement as an abstract principle of logic, but to articulate the dynamic of the self-disclosure of the living God. Hans Küng explains the connection: "God himself contains antithesis within himself, and he himself reconciles this antithesis. He is the dialectic. This is the God, proceeding through polarity toward reconciliation, whom Hegel intends to describe—not in abstract propositions, but in a living process, focussing not on an abstract, dead divine essence, but on the concrete, living act that God himself is."[26]

Hegel concluded that the human religious phenomenon reaches its fullness in Christianity in general and in its modern Protestant version in particular,[27] which he believed sets forth in representational form the basic philosophical theme of *Geist* coming to self-consciousness through the activity of the human spirit. He found the connection between the Christian God and *Geist* in the doctrine of the Trinity, which he understood as denoting God as dynamically active. For Hegel, this doctrine is not merely a religious teaching, but "the concrete determination and nature of God as spirit."[28] In fact, he went so far as to declare that *Geist* remains an empty word, if it is not understood in accordance with the Christian doctrine of the Trinity.[29]

In his *Lectures on the Philosophy of Religion*, Hegel offered what became a widely influential articulation of the doctrine of the Trinity: "God is thus grasped as what he is for himself within himself; God [the Father] makes himself an object for himself (the Son); then, in this object, God remains

25. See, for example, Carl J. Friedrich, introduction to *The Philosophy of Hegel*, by G. W. F. Hegel, ed. Carl J. Friedrich (New York: Random House, 1954), xliii; J. B. Baillie, "Translators Introduction," in Hegel, *Phenomenology of Mind*, 37–39; and Hegel, *Phenomenology of Mind*, 88.

26. Hans Küng, *The Incarnation of God: An Introduction to Hegel's Thought as Prolegomena to a Future Christology*, trans. J. R. Stephenson (New York: Crossroad, 1987), 362.

27. For a similar judgment, see Fackenheim, *Religious Dimension in Hegel's Thought*, 22.

28. G. W. F. Hegel, *Lectures on the Philosophy of Religion*, ed. Peter C. Hodgson, trans. R. F. Brown, P. C. Hodgson, and J. M. Stewart (Berkeley: University of California Press, 1984–1985), 1:127.

29. Ibid.

the undivided essence within this differentiation of himself within himself, and in the differentiation of himself loves himself, i.e., remains identical with himself—this is God as Spirit."[30] Although this expression of the doctrine (the Absolute itself [Father], its being-other [Son], and its unity with itself [Spirit]),[31] can be understood as speaking about a dynamic solely within the eternal God apart from the world, Hegel cautioned against conceiving of God as a divine being who exists as three persons apart from the world. Rather, he considered this articulation of the doctrine to be a representational way of speaking about the dynamic of thought in an abstract manner. It represents the dialectical movement of differentiation and reconciliation that the philosopher explores under the rubric of the science of logic.[32] John Burbidge offers this characterization of Hegel's perspective: "God before creation is the self-determining universal that, like the self-contained process of conceiving, eternally differentiates (or particularizes) the Son from the Father while yet negating that negation to give God concrete individuality or singularity as spirit."[33]

According to Hegel, *Geist* cannot be left merely on the level of pure abstraction. Instead, timeless truth unfolds necessarily in history. Charles Taylor explains the thoroughgoing nature of Hegel's commitment to this idea: "Historical events are not an irrelevant by-play, at best illustrating or dramatizing universal truth, but the inescapable medium in which these truths realize and manifest themselves."[34] For this reason, the abstract God comprises only the first logical moment in the divine dynamic. Because *Geist* is integrally related to the world process, the abstract Trinity must move to the Trinity in history, that is, to the self-revelation and self-actualization of God.

In this historical process, Hegel saw three moments of the divine reality: Essential Being, explicit Self-existence, and Self-knowledge. The first involves abstract or pure Being and hence God in God's essential reality. The second marks the entrance of abstract *Geist* into existence through the creation of the world, as God enters into relation with what is other. According to Hegel, this "objectively existent spirit" (the world) is characterized on the one hand by being "the Son" (that which "knows itself to be essential Being") and on the other hand by alienation and abandonment (evil). The third moment is *Geist* passing into self-consciousness, which occurs above all in human history and in the endeavors of the

30. Ibid., 1:126–27.

31. For the suggestion of this language, see Küng, *Incarnation of God*, 277.

32. For a similar characterization, see Samuel Powell, *The Trinity in German Thought* (Cambridge: Cambridge University Press, 2001), 121–22.

33. John W. Burbidge, *Hegel on Logic and Religion: The Reasonableness of Christianity* (Albany: State University of New York Press, 1992), 133. (See also Hegel, *Encyclopedia of the Philosophical Sciences*, § 567 in *Philosophy of Mind*, 299.) For an excerpt of the latter, see Peter G. Hodgson, *G. W. F. Hegel: Theologian of the Spirit* (Minneapolis: Fortress, 1997).

34. Charles Taylor, *Hegel* (Cambridge: Cambridge University Press, 1975), 493.

human spirit, especially human knowledge of God (i.e., religion). As Hegel declared, "God is only God so far as he knows himself; his self-knowledge is, further, a self-consciousness in man, and man's knowledge *of* God which proceeds to man's self-knowledge *in* God."[35] This third moment marks the completion of the dynamic of differentiation and reconciliation, and hence the fullness of *Geist* or Absolute Spirit.

The triadic process, together with the connection between God and humanity so central to Hegel's thinking, forms the interface between the Christian story and the philosophical truth which it represents. Viewed from this perspective, the three moments of the divine reality are somewhat analogous to the three persons in the Christian concept of the Trinity as disclosed in the biblical narrative.[36] The first moment is God in his essential being. The second moment appears as God moves outside himself and enters into relation with what is other than himself, as is evident in his bringing the universe into being. In the encounter with humankind, God returns to himself, for the religious life in which humankind comes to know God corresponds to God knowing God's own self.[37] This third moment, therefore, marks the completion of reconciliation within reality.

Because Hegel was concerned with the self-actualization of God in the historical process and especially the self-disclosure of God in the endeavors of the human spirit, the philosophical truth at the center of his thinking was the union of God and humanity. Stated in theological terms, his system could be interpreted as a grand declaration of the metaphor of the incarnation.[38] Jesus is crucial to this process, because in him the idea of the unity of God and humankind has been made explicit in history. In the incarnation of Jesus, the universal philosophical truth of the divine-human unity has been actualized in a particular historical individual. Because history is the actual unfolding of reality, this event has significance not only for creation but for God as well. In Christ, God has actually passed from abstract idea into historical particularity, and as a result "the pure or non-actual Spirit of bare thought has become actual."[39]

---

35. G. W. F. Hegel, *Philosophy of Mind: Being Part Three of the Encyclopedia of the Philosophical Sciences*, trans. William Wallace, Together with the Zusätze in Boumann's Text (1845), trans. A. V. Miller (Oxford: Clarendon, 1971), no. 564, p. 298. Elsewhere he declares, "That Man knows God implies, in accordance with the essential idea of communion or fellowship, that there is a community of knowledge; that is to say, Man knows God only insofar as God Himself knows Himself in Man." G. W. F. Hegel, *Lectures on the Philosophy of Religion: Together with a Work on the Proofs of the Existence of God*, trans. Rev. E. B. Speirs and J. Burdon Sanderson (1895; repr., London: Routledge & Kegan Paul, 1962), 3:303.

36. For Hegel's understanding of the Trinity, see Hegel, *Philosophy of Mind*, no. 381, p. 12; no. 567, p. 299.

37. According to Hegel, humankind knows God, because in humanity God knows God's own self. See, for example, Hegel, *Lectures on the Philosophy of Religion* (Speirs and Sanderson), 3:303.

38. Friedrich, introduction to *The Philosophy of Hegel*, xxxvi.

39. Hegel, *Phenomenology of Mind*, 781.

Hegel found this truth most clearly expressed in the crucifixion. In his estimation, this event speaks about God taking on radical finitude, the highest form of which is death, and thus about the death of the abstract God: "The death of the mediator is death not merely of his *natural* aspect, of his particular self-existence: what dies is not merely the outer encasement, which, being stripped of essential Being is *eo ipso* dead, but also the abstraction of the Divine Being."[40] At the same time, the crucifixion constitutes the reconciliation of creation with God and thereby reconciliation within God.[41] Furthermore, in the Christian story Christ's death sets the stage for the resurrection. In Hegel's understanding, this event effects the advent of the universal or Absolute Spirit and of the kingdom of the Spirit, which is not only the goal of history but also constitutes God's full historical self-realization.

As this summary suggests, the link that Hegel forged between the philosophical idea of *Geist* and the theological doctrine of God as triune facilitated him in reaching not only an *entente cordiale* but a full reconciliation between theology and philosophy.[42] Hegel found such a reconciliation possible because he was convinced that philosophy and religion express the same content, God, in different ways. Insofar as religion and philosophy share the same "object," namely, "the eternal truth, God and nothing but God and the explication of God," the two ultimately "coincide in one."[43] Whereas religion speaks about God by means of images (*Vorstellungen*), Hegel explained, philosophy uses concepts (*Begriffe*), and consequently its chief aim is to conceptualize what is given in religion as images.[44] Hegel's proposed synthesis or reconciliation, therefore, "consisted in a transition from representational thinking to conceptual thinking, a transition that involves transcending the non-essential representational form, retrieving the truth contained in the representations, and restating that truth in conceptual terms," as Samuel Powell explains.[45]

In the end, his bold attempt at intellectual reconciliation marks the great and lasting appeal of Hegel's system. The nineteenth was a century of iconoclasts who overturned and undermined reigning authorities. But it was also a century of innovators and grand system builders who sought new ways to conceive of reality as a whole. As had been the case during the high Middle Ages, in the early nineteenth century the time was ripe for the articulation

40. Ibid.

41. Hegel, *Lectures on the Philosophy of Religion* (Hodgson), 3:220.

42. Hegel noted at the conclusion of his lectures on the philosophy of religion in 1824 that his goal was "to reconcile reason with religion in its manifold forms, and to recognize them as at least necessary." Hegel, *Lectures on the Philosophy of Religion* (Hodgson), 3:247. Cf. Hegel, *Lectures on the Philosophy of Religion* (Speirs and Sanderson), 3:151.

43. Hegel, *Lectures on the Philosophy of Religion* (Hodgson), 1:152–53. Cf. Hegel, *Lectures on the Philosophy of Religion* (Speirs and Sanderson), 1:19–20.

44. For a discussion of this point, see Paul Tillich, *A History of Christian Thought*, ed. Carl Braaten (New York: Simon & Schuster, 1968), 424.

45. Powell, *Trinity in German Thought*, 108.

of an all-encompassing, rational account of the world. By stepping into the gap and seizing the moment, Hegel became the man of the hour. Working under the shadow of Romanticism, he was able to create a new, thoroughly modern synthesis that drew from the legacy of Enlightenment rationalism, mediated through Kant, and the lingering intellectual and spiritual residue of Christianity, formed in him by his Lutheran heritage. In forging this synthesis, Hegel did more than attain his own goal of refurbishing the rationalistic ideal. In overcoming Kant's dilemma of an unknowable thing-in-itself by positing a transcendental Rationality that is ultimately suprarational and spiritual, he bequeathed to his heirs a Romantic rationalism[46] in the form of a dynamic ontology that provided a new way of bringing together the Greek interest in Being and the Christian concern for God. But in so doing, he both forestalled and facilitated Being's eventual demise.

Being in the Process of Becoming

Hegel was arguably the first modern philosopher to propose a dynamic metaphysic. Yet his proposal is not generally cited as an example of process philosophy. Rather, this term is reserved for a movement that developed subsequent to Hegel, when the nineteenth century was giving way to the twentieth.

The pathway for the rise of process philosophy was paved by thinkers such as Henri Bergson, Charles Sanders Peirce, and William James. David Hume had questioned only the epistemological claims of the classical philosophical tradition. These thinkers, in contrast, launched an even more radical attack on Cartesian rationalism. They called into question the explanatory value, and hence the metaphysical propriety, of the language of substance and causality that Descartes had mediated to modern philosophy. In the early twentieth century, this attack gave rise to a constructive, comprehensive philosophical proposal that carries the designation "process philosophy."

Although the twentieth century witnessed the development of several process philosophies, the most prominent expression was that of the mathematician-turned-philosopher Alfred North Whitehead (1861–1947).[47] So significant has Whitehead's work been that his name has become almost synonymous with process thought.[48] Moreover, his articulation of

46. For a somewhat similar judgment, see W. T. Jones, *A History of Western Philosophy* (New York: Harcourt, Brace & Co., 1952), 903.

47. A succinct summary of Whitehead's philosophy is offered by Rosemary T. Curran, "Whitehead's Notion of the Person and the Saving of the Past," *Scottish Journal of Theology* 36, no. 3 (1983): 363–85. Also important has been the work of Charles Hartshorne. A short but helpful summary of Hartshorne's contribution is found in Alan Gragg, "Charles Hartshorne," in *The Makers of the Modern Theological Mind*, ed. Bob E. Patterson (Waco, TX: Word, 1973).

48. For a parallel sketch of Whitehead's philosophy in the context of its ramifications for process theology, see Stanley J. Grenz and Roger E. Olson, *Twentieth-Century Theology: God and the World in a Transitional Age* (Downers Grove, IL: InterVarsity Press, 1992), 134–37.

process philosophy has won him the accolades of historians of philosophy. William Reese, for example, asserted that Whitehead "produced the most impressive metaphysical system of the 20th century."[49] Robert Neville hailed Whitehead's magnum opus, *Process and Reality*, as "the single most important book of speculative metaphysics in the twentieth century."[50] Rasvihary Das, in turn, offered a more detailed explanation of Whitehead's importance: "When metaphysics is looked upon with distrust by many and its very possibility is disputed by some, Whitehead has rendered a signal service to the cause of pure thought by demonstrating not only the possibility but also the necessity and great value of metaphysical speculation."[51]

The Contours of Process Philosophy

As Das's accolade suggests, Whitehead's overarching goal was to reestablish the importance of metaphysics in the context of a scientifically oriented, antimetaphysical environment. Science is necessary, he maintained, but it must be based on a proper cosmology, for every science tacitly presupposes a metaphysical system.[52] Consequently, he saw himself as engaging in what for him was the traditional task of speculative philosophy, namely, "the endeavour to frame a coherent, logical, necessary system of general ideas in terms of which every element of our experience can be interpreted."[53] At the same time, he acknowledged the limitations of every metaphysical proposal, for he also described philosophy as an "attempt to express the infinity of the universe in terms of the limitations of language"[54] or "the endeavour to find a conventional phraseology for the vivid suggestiveness of a poet."[55]

To establish an ontology that was in tune with the times, Whitehead found it necessary to set himself against the cosmology that had dominated modern thought since the time of Galileo, Descartes, and Newton.[56] This perspective, which Whitehead called "scientific materialism," is erroneous because it "presupposes the ultimate fact of an irreducible brute matter, or material, spread through space."[57] By postulating that every material

---

49. William L. Reese, "Whitehead," in *Dictionary of Philosophy and Religion* (Atlantic Highlands, NJ: Humanities Press, 1980), 622.

50. Robert C. Neville, foreword to *The Metaphysics of Experience: A Companion to Whitehead's Process and Reality*, 2nd ed., by Elizabeth M. Kraus (New York: Fordham University Press, 1998), xv.

51. Rasvihary Das, *The Philosophy of Whitehead* (1928; repr., New York: Russell & Russell, 1964), 195.

52. See Alfred North Whitehead, *Adventures of Ideas* (New York: Mentor Books, 1955), 147–50, 158; Whitehead, *Religion in the Making* (New York: World Publishing, 1960), 76, 83.

53. Whitehead, *Adventures of Ideas*, 223. See also the discussion in Alfred North Whitehead, *Process and Reality*, corrected ed., ed. David R. Griffin and Donald W. Sherburne (New York: Free Press, 1978), 3–17.

54. Alfred North Whitehead, *Essays in Science and Philosophy* (New York: Philosophical Library, 1947), 14.

55. Alfred North Whitehead, *Modes of Thought* (1938; repr., New York: Capricorn, 1958), 68–69.

56. For a confirmation of this opinion, see Thilly, *History of Philosophy*, 612.

57. Alfred North Whitehead, *Science and the Modern World* (New York: Free Press, 1967), 17.

object occupies a determinate, bounded space and persists through a well-defined time interval, scientific materialism claims that an object's essential property is its "simple location" in space and time. To do so, Whitehead averred, is to mistake an abstraction for a concrete reality, that is, to be guilty of what he denoted "the fallacy of misplaced concreteness."

Whitehead's goal was not to eschew naturalism as such, but to devise a metaphysical proposal that reflected the scientific advances that had occurred in the late nineteenth and early twentieth centuries. The new physics replaced the idea of simple location with the concept of energy—work done—and it described reality in terms of power, so that in time all things are connected through the history of efficient causation. Whitehead sought to work out the underlying metaphysics of this newer view.[58] Yet he rejected the modern reduction of causality to efficient causation. He claimed that the physicists' notion of physical energy was merely an abstraction of a more complex energy found in every event.[59] His goal, therefore, was that of constructing a theory of internal relations that could conceive of the "now" as internally connected to both the past and the future, because it finds its basis in both.

In his *History of Western Philosophy*, D. W. Hamlyn voiced the sentiments of many when he quipped, "Certainly one needs a considerable readjustment of one's ordinary categories to understand Whitehead."[60] Grasping Whitehead's philosophy is difficult for linguistic reasons.[61] But equally challenging is the fact that his ontology marks a turn to becoming, relationality, and an organic model of reality. As Douglas Browning notes, the basic doctrine of process philosophy "is that the universe is essentially to be understood as creative, organic, and temporal."[62]

Whitehead saw himself as standing within the philosophical tradition that runs from Descartes to Hume.[63] He affirmed this trajectory, because it had discovered in subjective experience the clue to the fundamental nature of the human essence.[64] But he moved beyond this tradition, in that he was convinced that our experiences yield dynamic rather than static processes. And they reveal interrelated entities rather than separate, independent ones. He believed that the trajectory from Aristotle through the medieval scholastics to Descartes, in contrast, had introduced into Western philosophy the erroneous idea of the self-sufficient substance,

---

58. In accordance with the new physics, Whitehead abandoned "the notion that simple location is the primary way in which things are involved in space-time. In a certain sense, everything is everywhere at all times." Whitehead, *Science and the Modern World*, 91.

59. Whitehead, *Adventures of Ideas*, 188.

60. Hamlyn, *History of Western Philosophy*, 302.

61. For a comment on this aspect, see Kraus, *Metaphysics of Experience*, 3–7.

62. Browning, "Preface to the First Edition," xii.

63. Whitehead, *Process and Reality*, ix.

64. Whitehead, *Adventures of Ideas*, 177–78. This view is elaborated throughout *Process and Reality*; see, for example, 162.

that is, that a substance requires nothing other than itself to exist.[65] As Elizabeth Kraus points out, Whitehead found this error problematic, in part because "it exalts the categories of quality and quantity over the category of relation, failing to realize that the former themselves are relational in that they express the ways in which substances *are for* other substances, and are not attributes of isolated substances."[66]

Moreover, Whitehead asserted that the subjective or emotional experience ("feeling") indicative of human existence is not only present in humans but is inherent in all reality.[67] Hence, Whitehead saw "feeling," dynamic movement, and "being present in another entity" in every existing thing.[68] He contended that reality could be better understood by discovering in organisms—in "dynamic, creative, interdependent entities in the process of development"[69]—rather than in mechanisms the fundamental way of characterizing the universe. Consequently, Whitehead described his metaphysical proposal as "organic mechanism" or "philosophy of organism."[70]

For Whitehead, reality is not static essence, but process. Alluding to the maxim of Heraclitus, he wrote, "The ancient doctrine that 'no one crosses the same river twice' is extended. No thinker thinks twice; and, to put the matter more generally, no subject experiences twice."[71] Or as Robert B. Mellert observed, "Whitehead's basic insight is that reality is a series of interrelated becomings."[72] But Whitehead took the matter a step further. In his estimation, existence and dynamic process are intertwined. Consequently, his central concern was not what things are, or what they are made of; instead, what he considered is how they become. And his metaphysic is not based on the idea of "substance" but on a consideration of the events of which he believed the universe consists.[73] To cite Whitehead's words, "*How* an actual entity *becomes* constitutes *what* that actual entity *is*: so that the two descriptions of an actual entity are not independent. Its 'being' is constituted by its 'becoming.' This is the 'principle of process.'"[74]

It should be pointed out that Whitehead did not jettison the concept of being in favor of becoming, or elevate change over permanence. Rather, he sought to highlight how being and becoming, permanence and change,

65. See, for example, Whitehead, *Process and Reality*, 50.

66. Kraus, *Metaphysics of Experience*, 2.

67. Whitehead, *Process and Reality*, 53, 166–67, 176–77. He wrote, "Apart from the experiences of subjects, there is nothing, nothing, nothing, bare nothingness." *Process and Reality*, 167.

68. Ibid., 50.

69. Stroll and Popkin, *Introduction to Philosophy*, 169.

70. In *Science and the Modern World* he offered his system of "organic mechanism" as a replacement for scientific materialism. See Whitehead, *Science and the Modern World*, 76.

71. Whitehead, *Process and Reality*, 29.

72. Robert B. Mellert, *What Is Process Theology?* (New York: Paulist Press, 1975), 20.

73. Peter Hamilton, *The Living God and the Modern World* (London: Hodder & Stoughton, 1967), 73.

74. Whitehead, *Process and Reality*, 23.

are to be given equal status in metaphysics, because both are equally present in experience.[75] In *Process and Reality*, he asserted clearly the interrelationship of being and becoming: "In the inescapable flux, there is something that abides; in the overwhelming permanence, there is an element that escapes into flux. Permanence can be snatched only out of flux; and the passing moment can find its adequate intensity only by its submission to permanence." Whitehead then indicated the experiential basis for his conclusion: "Those who would disjoin the two elements can find no interpretation of patent facts."[76]

Whitehead's preference for an organic model of reality and his focus on becoming give a relational character to his proposal. Drawing these themes together, Donald W. Sherburne offers a helpful characterization of the process ontology: "Whitehead's metaphysics is something like what would result if one took the metaphysics of Aristotle and instead of making the category of substance primary, made the category of relation primary. Unlike a Cartesian being, which requires nothing but itself in order to exist, a Whiteheadian being . . . in an important sense *is* its relations to other beings."[77]

Whitehead postulated that reality is built from four ultimate concepts: actual occasions (or actual entities), eternal objects, God, and creativity.[78] Actual occasions, which comprise the fundamental building blocks of reality, are not permanently enduring things, but transient "occasions of experience" or "drops of experience."[79] Moreover, all actual entities are alike. As Whitehead asserted somewhat poetically, "God is an actual entity, and so is the most trivial puff of existence in far-off empty space."[80] And because the macroscopic and microscopic processes mirror each other, the nature of all reality can be depicted by any one entity. In fact, Jorge Luis Nobo goes so far as to claim that this principle constitutes Whitehead's fundamental vision of the ultimate nature of reality. He characterizes Whitehead's vision of universal solidarity as declaring that "the entire universe is somehow to be found within each of its ultimate concrete components or, equivalently, that the final real actualities of which the universe is composed are each in all and all in each."[81]

Actual occasions are not neutral, objective, purely material substances. Instead, they are value oriented, for each is a striving toward the realization

75. For this judgment, see Kraus, *Metaphysics of Experience*, 1.
76. Whitehead, *Process and Reality*, 338.
77. Donald W. Sherburne, "Whitehead, Alfred North," in *A Companion to Metaphysics*, ed. Jaegwon Kim and Ernest Sosa (Oxford: Blackwell, 1995), 511.
78. Huston Smith, "Has Process Theology Dismantled Classical Theism?" *Theology Digest* 35, no. 4 (1988): 310.
79. Whitehead, *Process and Reality*, 18.
80. Ibid., 28–29.
81. Jorge Luis Nobo, *Whitehead's Metaphysics of Extension and Solidarity* (Albany: State University of New York Press, 1986), xiv.

of some value.[82] Each occasion is an activity of becoming, a bringing together into a unity of "feeling" (which Whitehead called "satisfaction") responses to the relevant past and the reachable future. Hence, each is dipolar, consisting of a "physical" pole (the past) and a "mental" pole (the achievable possibility). Moreover, although each actual occasion creates itself in the process of experiencing,[83] each is also embedded in a stream of occasions on which it is dependent.[84] Each is in part the product of past occasions of experience, for it accepts and rejects dimensions from its antecedent.[85] Whitehead used the term "prehension" to speak of the movement from past to present, that is, of the relatedness of each occasion to the antecedent universe.

An actual occasion is a fleeting reality. Once it has attained a unity of experience, it passes from the "privacy" of becoming to its "public" function as an object to be used by others in their becoming. It "perishes." Yet it is prehended by its successor. We might say, citing Kraus's helpful description, that an actual entity is

> a drop of process, a pulse, a throb or existence, an event, a happening
> of value which sacrifices its immediacy in the instant it is gained, in the
> same manner as any "now" loses its nowness to a subsequent "now"....
> By the same token, just as the content of any "now" becomes an his-
> torical "then" to be taken into account by all future "nows," so the
> structure of the subjectivity achieved by an actual entity in its process
> is transformed into objectively functioning, stubborn, past fact.[86]

Whitehead termed the process whereby an actual occasion becomes an object for subsequent entities "superject." To emphasize this movement from subject to object, he referred to the actual entity as a "subject-superject."

Prehension ensures a continuation of past into present. Yet each occasion is also unique and new, for it arises from what is already given without being limited to that given. It is free to accept or reject prehensions from the past. Not only does each occasion prehend antecedent occasions, it also selects and rejects eternal objects in the process of creating itself. Eternal objects are patterns and qualities—geometric relationships, colors, emotions, pleasures, pains—somewhat similar to Plato's Forms.[87] Yet unlike Plato, Whitehead did not view eternal objects as existing realities.[88]

82. Alan Gragg, "Charles Hartshorne," 31.
83. Whitehead, *Process and Reality*, 25. See also Victor Lowe, *Understanding Whitehead* (Baltimore: Johns Hopkins Press, 1962), 38–41.
84. Whitehead, *Process and Reality*, 203.
85. Ibid., 23–24.
86. Kraus, *Metaphysics of Experience*, 3.
87. For this connection, see Walter E. Stokes, "God for Today and Tomorrow," in *Process Philosophy and Christian Thought*, ed. Delwin Brown, Ralph E. James Jr., and Gene Reeves (Indianapolis: Bobbs-Merrill Co., 1971), 257.
88. Whitehead postulates no reality for any principles except insofar as they are exemplified by actual occasions. This is what he meant by his widely known "ontological principle," which states that "actual entities are the only reasons; so that a search for a reason is a search for one or more actual entities." Whitehead, *Process and Reality*, 37.

Rather, they are the "pure potentials" that an actual occasion could reflect.[89] In this way, they function as the formal categories that give shape to the world, which consists of the actual occasions.[90]

Actual occasions that share a common element tying them together into a self-sustaining whole form a "society of occasions."[91] Societies come in various types, including "living societies."[92] Yet the most unique is that of the human person. Each human is a society that can remember its past, anticipate its future, and weave the two together. Ultimately, a human remains a finite society, for its experience incorporates a limited past and a limited future. This leads to the concept of an unbounded society, that is, to the idea of God.[93]

The God of Process Philosophy

In Whitehead's proposal, God is the unbounded society of occasions, who remembers all experiences and envisions all possibilities and who weaves past and future together in a never-ending process. Central to Whitehead's elaborate understanding of the Deity is the presupposition that God is an entity among the other entities in the world.[94] Like all actual entities, God is dipolar, consisting of a primordial and a consequent dimension.[95] Furthermore, this God is an integral and necessary aspect of reality, Whitehead asserts, for in his dipolar nature God fulfills two foundational roles in the dynamic of the universe.

The first role that God plays is connected to the becoming of each actual occasion. In the entire process of its becoming, each occasion is confronted by an "initial aim," consisting of the best possible combination for the now-forming occasion, which it is free to accept or reject.[96] By means of the initial aim, the occasion is lured to create an enjoyable experience and to be creative of the future by making a contribution to the enjoyment of others. This initial aim, according to Whitehead, is provided by God. More specifically, it is connected to God's primordial nature (or the nontemporal, "mental" pole), which is bound up with

89. Whitehead, *Process and Reality*, 34.

90. Whitehead, *Religion in the Making*, 87; see pp. 87–88.

91. Whitehead, *Process and Reality*, 20; Whitehead, *Adventures of Ideas*, 204.

92. See Whitehead, *Process and Reality*, 103ff.

93. Whether Whitehead thought of God as an unbounded society or an actual entity has been debated by subsequent process thinkers. See Gene Reeves and Delwin Brown, "The Development of Process Theology," in Brown et al., *Process Philosophy and Christian Thought*, 39–40.

94. Whitehead writes, "God is not to be treated as an exception to all metaphysical principles, invoked to save their collapse. He is their chief exemplification." Whitehead, *Process and Reality*, 343.

95. The dipolar nature of God in relation to the world is delineated in Whitehead, *Process and Reality*, 342–51. Whitehead also referred to God as displaying a threefold character: primordial, consequent, and superject. *Process and Reality*, 87.

96. Whitehead, *Process and Reality*, 85, 244–45.

God's role as the principle of the process of the world.[97] God envisages the infinite variety of eternal objects, functions as the primordial valuation of all possibilities,[98] and supplies the lure to the actual entities in the process of becoming.[99] Hence, God contains the entire range of possibilities and is thereby the foundation of novelty.[100]

Yet in his primordial nature, God is not complete. God's feelings lack the fullness of actuality. As a result, another dimension of God is also necessary, a dimension that is connected to the second function that God performs in the world. Once an occasion arises, it immediately perishes. Yet it is not lost.[101] It not only forms the predecessor for the next occasion, but it also adds to God's experience. There it remains embedded forever, attaining what Whitehead calls "objective immortality." This dynamic leads to the second aspect of the dipolar God: God's consequent nature (or the temporal, "physical" pole). As "God consequent," God prehends the temporal world; God functions as the location of all perishing actual entities and in so doing forms the world into a unity. In this way, God retains the novelties achieved as the future becomes the present and vanishes into the past.[102] This activity completes God's nature in "a fullness of physical feeling."[103] As a result, God becomes "the great companion— the fellow-sufferer who understands."[104]

These two dimensions of the divine reality produce an integral relation between God and the world. Both need the other, and both are bound up with the other. As Whitehead concluded, "Each temporal occasion embodies God, and is embodied in God."[105]

Many of Whitehead's followers extol this close connection between God and the world as one of the great strengths of his metaphysical system. Theologian Norman Pittenger, for example, notes that God is thereby characterized by "relationship." He then adds:

> God's perfection is not that of abstract being but is to be found in his capacity for, and actualization of, his relationships with that which is not himself. Hence the model for God is not some self-contained being who requires nothing for his self-existence save his own iden-

97. In Whitehead's words, God is "the unlimited conceptual realization of the absolute wealth of potentiality . . . not *before* all creation, but *with* all creation." Whitehead, *Process and Reality*, 343–44.
98. Whitehead, *Religion in the Making*, 148.
99. Whitehead, *Process and Reality*, 189.
100. Norman Pittenger, "Whitehead on God," *Encounter* 45, no. 4 (1984): 329.
101. The immortality of every actual entity is required by Whitehead's "ontological principle," for "everything in the actual world is referable to some actual entity." God functions as the ontological principle that fulfils this necessity. Whitehead, *Process and Reality*, 244.
102. See Reese, "Whitehead," 624.
103. Whitehead, *Process and Reality*, 345.
104. Ibid., 351.
105. Ibid., 348. Whitehead adds, "The World's nature is a primordial datum for God; and God's nature is a primordial datum for the World."

tity. The model is a richly related being whose innermost nature or quality is in his ceaseless participation and sharing. Hence, since love is relationship, sharing, being affected by, and caring, God essentially is Love.[106]

Das, in turn, lauds the rejection of the classical idea of God as the divine despot inherent in Whitehead's proposal[107] as a great advance over traditional theistic metaphysical perspectives:

> Sometimes we have systems of philosophy which introduce the notion of God merely to tide over their inherent metaphysical difficulties. What happens mostly in such cases is that God, like a despotic ruler, administers metaphysical laws to other entities, but himself remains outside the operation of those laws. He is made to support a system without Himself becoming a part of the system. The system works with His help, but His functions do not flow, as obligatory duties, from the system. The very reverse of this is the case with God in Whitehead's system. It is truer to say that God is supported on the system than that the system is supported on God. He does not determine how the system is to work, His functions are rather defined by the system. All this implies that God is not the ultimate principle in Whitehead's philosophy. The ultimate principle is creativity, and it is exemplified in God as well as in other actual entities.[108]

Das's statement indicates that yet another ultimate concept, creativity, stands at the foundation of Whitehead's entire system.[109] Creativity is not another existing "thing," but is rather the principle of unity behind the multiplicity of the actual entities.[110] It is, in the words of Jan Van der Veken, "the principle that explains the existence of a unified, dynamic universe."[111] Creativity is likewise the principle of novelty displayed by each of the actual entities and the source of the individuality of each as a participant in the "creative advance" that characterizes the process as a whole.[112] In this way, creativity displaces even God as the ultimate

106. Norman Pittenger, *Alfred North Whitehead* (Richmond, VA: John Knox, 1969), 34.

107. Whitehead claimed that by accepting the idea of God as the divine despot, "the Church gave unto God the attributes which belonged exclusively to Caesar." Whitehead, *Process and Reality*, 343.

108. Das, *Philosophy of Whitehead*, 156–57.

109. For a discussion of the relationship between God and creativity, see John B. Cobb, *A Christian Natural Theology* (Philadelphia: Westminster, 1965), 203–14.

110. Whitehead, *Process and Reality*, 21.

111. Jan Van der Veken, "Creativity as Universal Activity," in *Whitehead's Metaphysics of Creativity*, ed. Friedrich Rapp and Reiner Wiehl (Albany: State University of New York Press, 1990), 182.

112. Whitehead, *Process and Reality*, 21. Whitehead concluded *Process and Reality* by delineating four phases of creativity in the process of the actualizing of the universe. The first is the phase of conceptual origination, which lies in the primordial God. Next comes the temporal phase of physical origination, the rise of individual occasions lacking in solidarity. This is followed by the phase of perfected actuality, as the many are unified in the immediate consciousness of God. The final is the phase of the completion of the creative activity, as the "perfected actuality" is passed back to the temporal world so that each temporal actuality may include it "as an immediate fact of relevant experience." This, Whitehead added, is the love of God for the world. *Process and Reality*, 351.

metaphysical principle of Whitehead's philosophy. As Friedrich Rapp observes, "God as a transcendent creator is replaced by Whitehead with the supreme principle of creativity, which determines all being and is conceived as purely immanent."[113]

Whitehead elevated creativity as the ultimate principle of dynamism in the cosmos. But this elevation of creativity came at the expense not only of God but also of Being itself. In this manner and perhaps contrary to his own intentions, Whitehead's dynamic ontology, to an even greater extent than Hegel's, not only forestalled but also contributed to the demise of Being.

The De(con)struction of Onto-Theology

By introducing becoming into the concept of Being, the dynamic, relational, organic ontologies of the nineteenth and early twentieth centuries changed the rules of the metaphysical game. As the twentieth century unfolded, some philosophers ventured even further down the road of ontological change. Convinced that ontology could only be rescued by ridding it of what they called "onto-theology," these revisionists set out on a quest to dismantle the entire Western metaphysical tradition. Although their goal (unlike that of the analytical philosophers) was to salvage Being, in the end Being became a casualty of their philosophical crusade. The names most closely associated with this development are Martin Heidegger and Jacques Derrida.[114]

Clearing the Ground for a New Beginning

Perhaps no twentieth-century philosopher has found his political views more controversial and his intellectual proposals more variously understood than Martin Heidegger (1884–1976). Heidegger's interpreters customarily divide his literary activities into two segments and in the process contrast the "earlier" existentialist Heidegger with the "later" poetic Heidegger. In this aspect of his work, Walter Kaufmann finds a parallel between Heidegger and Schelling, and then explains its significance:

> There are two Heideggers as once there were two Schellings: the early and the late one. In both cases the late philosophy has esoteric, if not mystic, touches and is supported by the most tremendous sense of a historic mission. Unlike Kant, Fichte, and Hegel who felt that it was

---

113. Friedrich Rapp, "Whitehead's Concept of Creativity and Modern Science," in *Whitehead's Metaphysics of Creativity*, 71.

114. For parallel sketches of Heidegger and Derrida in the context of their importance for postmodernism, see Stanley J. Grenz, *A Primer on Postmdernism* (Grand Rapids: Eerdmans, 1996), 103–8, 138–50.

given to them to bring to an end a long and remarkable development, Heidegger claims, as Schelling did, that he is making a new start and that with him a new age is beginning.[115]

Some commentators see in the lectures that he gave around 1930 (but published only later) an indication that Heidegger abandoned many of his earlier views.[116] Solomon and Higgins claim that he came to realize that, contrary to his desire to start from scratch (i.e., "without presuppositions"), his early work was "still mired in the suppositions of traditional metaphysics."[117] Other interpreters, in keeping with Heidegger's own denials that his later thought differed greatly from what he set forth in his early works,[118] highlight the continuity, rather than disjuncture, that they find running through his literary career.[119]

In any case, for much of the twentieth century, Heidegger's importance was deemed to lie in his supposed status as the "father of German existentialism," a designation that he himself eschewed.[120] The "early" or "existentialist" Heidegger was widely acclaimed for his penetrating insight into the existential implications of the fact that humans are conscious of their own impending death.[121] Even theologians such as Rudolf Bultmann, John Macquarrie, and to some extent Paul Tillich got in the act, for they looked to the "early" Heidegger for the philosophical foundation for an existentialist theology. With the postmodern turn came a shift in focus away from the "early" to the "later" Heidegger. In contrast to his existentialist followers, postmodern philosophers tend to prefer the poetic Heidegger, whom they consider to be one of the first "to take Nietzsche seriously as a thinker."[122]

---

115. Walter Kaufmann, "Existentialism from Dostoevsky to Sartre," in *Existentialism from Dostoevsky to Sartre*, ed. Walter Kaufmann (Cleveland: Meridian Books, 1956), 36.

116. M. J. Inwood, "Heidegger, Martin," in *The Oxford Companion to Philosophy*, ed. Ted Honderich (New York: Oxford University Press, 1995), 348.

117. Solomon and Higgins, *Short History of Philosophy*, 270.

118. See, for example, Inwood, "Heidegger, Martin," 348–49.

119. Adamczewski, for example, sees the continuity in Heidegger's "continual striving to ask about the enshrouded matter of being." Zygmunt Adamczewski, "Questions in Heidegger's Thought about Being," in *The Question of Being: East-West Perspectives*, ed. Mervyn Sprung (University Park: Pennsylvania State University Press, 1978), 55; cf. p. 62. Adamczewski does find, however, certain ambiguities between Heidegger's earlier and later thought; see pp. 63–65.

120. For his reasons why he is not an existentialist, see Martin Heidegger, "Letter on Humanism," trans. Frank A. Capuzzi and J. Glenn Gray, in *Basic Writings*, rev. and expanded ed., ed. D. F. Krell (San Francisco: HarperCollins, 1993), 213–65. See also Allen Megill, *Prophets of Extremity: Neitzsche, Heidegger, Foucault, Derrida* (Berkeley: University of California Press, 1985), 150–51.

121. Heidegger speaks of authentic living as being "free for death," which occurs as we anticipate our death. See Martin Heidegger, *Being and Time*, trans. John Macquarrie and Edward Robinson (New York: Harper & Row, 1962), 435, 436.

122. See Martin Heidegger, *The Question concerning Technology and Other Essays*, trans. William Lovitt (New York: Harper & Row, 1977), 54–55.

The Question of Being

Early in his career, Heidegger declared that the fundamental question of metaphysics, and therefore the basic question of his own thought, is the question of Being: "Why is there anything at all rather than nothing?"[123] Posing the question in this manner allowed him to pinpoint what he deemed to be the fundamental flaw in the entire Western philosophical tradition, which in turn paved the way for his own alternative.

Although philosophers from the pre-Socratic Greeks to Hegel and Nietzsche were informed by the question of Being and even formulated questions about Being, Heidegger declares that they failed to raise the question about Being itself. He explains that philosophers and scientists alike seek definitive judgments about things-in-being (or things "out there"). They devise substance ontologies that describe objects by defining them, that is, by listing the attributes or characteristics of each particular substance. They try to discover essential categories by analyzing the opposites of Being (e.g., becoming and appearance), hoping to transcend these opposites and arrive at Being. Moreover, they attempt to understand human existence by appeal to the same set of ontological categories (e.g., substance) that they apply to animals and inanimate objects, thereby treating humans in the same way as other beings.

In so doing, Heidegger asserts, these thinkers miss the deep ontological structures of human existence. They fail to note the fundamental difference that separates humans and other beings. Humans cannot be described by formulating a list of human attributes, he avers. In contrast to the being of other beings, the being of a human person includes the awareness of one's being. Therefore, Heidegger concludes, only humans can raise the question about their being and about Being itself. As a consequence of this grave mistake within Western intellectual history, humans misunderstand the nature of their existence. In fact, they even flee from their own basic identity, which is linked to "being there" or being-in-the-world.[124]

Taken as a whole, Heidegger's writings display a single, overarching goal, namely, to clear the philosophical ground that has been polluted by this basic mistake, so that he might begin anew by means of the development of an "ontology in general" or a "fundamental ontology." To this end, he engages in what he calls a "destruction" (*Destruktion*) of the history of ontology. His purpose is to peel off the layers of calcified tradition so that he might retrieve the basic, but long forgotten, sources of understanding that lie at the core of Western philosophical thought.[125] Actu-

---

123. See Martin Heidegger, *An Introduction to Metaphysics*, trans. Ralph Manheim (New York: Doubleday Anchor Books, 1961), 1.

124. On this point, see Herman Philipse, *Heidegger's Philosophy of Being* (Princeton, NJ: Princeton University Press, 1998), 19, cf. 375.

125. For this description, see Charles Guignon, "Heidegger, Martin," in Kim and Sosa, *Companion to Metaphysics*, 203.

ally, Heidegger borrowed the concept of "destruction" from Luther. The great Reformer had used the word to designate his attempt to dismantle the tradition of the medieval scholastics, who in his estimation had perverted the pristine Christian faith by conceptualizing it in accordance with the concerns of the Greek philosophical tradition.[126] In a manner reminiscent of Luther's attack on medieval theology, Heidegger set out to dismantle the Western philosophical tradition so that he could make a new start that would discover, "unconceal," or "recall" Being (or what he later calls "a new ground of meaning"[127]) through a study of authentic human existence.

Heidegger launched his fundamental-ontological project in what turned out to be his lengthiest book, *Being and Time* (1927).[128] Stroll and Popkin claim that this volume "is one of the most complicated ever written in philosophy."[129] Herman Philipse, in turn, characterizes it as "a systematic treatise in the grand manner of German philosophy, with pretensions so high as Germany had not seen since Hegel's *Phänomenologie des Geistes*."[130] As lofty as its author's aspirations may have been, the work is not as long as Heidegger initially planned. As he notes in the eighth section of the book, he intended to produce a volume consisting of an introduction and two parts of three divisions each. Part 1 was to be largely systematic and constructive, whereas part 2 was to contain his "destruction" of the history of ontology on the basis of the problem of temporality. In its published form, however, *Being and Time* contains only the introduction and the first two divisions of part 1.[131]

Despite its brevity, at least in comparison to Heidegger's initial plan, the book explicates a far-reaching and influential metaphysical proposal. Philipse notes that the ontology of human existence contained in the two published sections "profoundly transformed the European philosophical scene in the second and third quarters of the twentieth century."[132] Stumpf takes this appraisal a step further, suggesting that Heidegger's proposal has exercised an influence beyond the boundaries of philosophy: "In a remarkable way, Heidegger transformed the concept of Being from a highly abstract and remote concept into a subject of intense concern to every human being."[133]

---

126. Philipse, *Heidegger's Philosophy of Being*, 21.

127. For a discussion of this change, see John M. Anderson, introduction to *Discourse on Thinking*, by Martin Heidegger, trans. John M. Anderson and E. Hans Freund (New York: Harper & Row, 1966), 19–21.

128. For a helpful, concise overview of *Being and Time*, see Michael Inwood, *Heidegger: A Very Short Introduction* (New York: Oxford University Press, 1997).

129. Stroll and Popkin, *Introduction to Philosophy*, 432.

130. Philipse, *Heidegger's Philosophy of Being*, 377, cf. xv.

131. For a helpful summary of where Heidegger later addressed the other topics, see Inwood, *Heidegger*, 11.

132. Philipse, *Heidegger's Philosophy of Being*, 16.

133. Stumpf, *Socrates to Sartre*, 497.

In *Being and Time*, Heidegger followed a phenomenological method, derived (albeit in altered form) from his teacher Edmund Husserl. This method uses as its starting point the one who raises the question of Being or those for whom truth is manifest, that is, human beings.[134] This method gave rise to a term that formed the cornerstone of Heidegger's early work, the difficult, nearly undefinable concept of *Dasein* (literally, "being there").[135] Although at first glance the term might appear to be a general designation for Being, Heidegger links *Dasein* closely with human existence. *Dasein* is that reality which is concerned with the nature of its own being. *Dasein* wonders, What am I? How did I come to be? And what does my existence mean? Above all, *Dasein* is the being who asks the philosophical question of Being.

According to Heidegger, *Dasein* arises from the "facticity" or "factuality" of human existence, the realization that we are thrown into a world which is ours even though it is not of our own making. Because *Dasein* is always raising the basic philosophical questions, no final answers ever emerge. Instead, we have to "work out," rather than simply "find out," who (or what) we are. And we do this through living in the world. Rather than a static "thing," therefore, *Dasein* is an activity, the outworking of living in the world. *Dasein*, therefore, means basically "being-in," or "being-in-the-world," understood in this dynamic sense.[136]

Dasein encapsulates Heidegger's bold rejection of the Cartesian-Kantian idea of the self as the knowing subject that encounters the world as object.[137] According to Heidegger, the starting point for philosophy is not the self-conscious, thinking being (not the Cartesian *cogito*), but simply a "being there." And the human being is not primarily a thinking self, a subject who engages in cognitive acts. Instead, we are above all beings in the world who are enmeshed in social networks. In the world, we carry out our various tasks. As we do so, we encounter things, at least initially, as "tools" that we use, rather than as objects.

Heidegger is convinced that replacing the thinking self confronting its object with "being-in" the world overcomes what in his estimation is the wrongheaded question of the relationship between the subject and the object that has plagued modern philosophy. He proposes that the subject-object dualism and the resultant two-part experience of "self" and "world"

134. For a detailed description of this approach, see Catriona Hanley, *Being and God in Aristotle and Heidegger: The Role of Method in Thinking the Infinite* (Lanham, MD: Rowman & Littlefield, 2000), 105–20.

135. Concerning *Dasein* Solomon declares, "It is an intentially vague, non-descriptive, almost vacuous designation, virtually a pointing gesture rather than a proper subject for a philosophy." Robert C. Solomon, *Continental Philosophy since 1750: The Rise and Fall of the Self* (Oxford: Oxford University Press, 1988), 154.

136. Heidegger, *Being and Time*, 78.

137. Martin Heidegger, *Basic Problems of Phenomenology*, trans. Albert Hofstadter (Bloomington: Indiana University Press, 1982), 122–40.

give way to a unitary phenomenon, the "being-present-at-hand-together" of subject and object.[138] This vision of being-in-the-world as a seamless whole enables Heidegger to wage a relentless attack on the dualisms that he sees as besetting philosophy (and literary theory) since Descartes:[139] mind and body, self and world, subject and object, self and other.[140] Heidegger's attack likewise seeks to subvert the view of the subject as an independent substance, existing above time and human society or inhabiting some eternal, transcendent realm detached from life.[141]

In Heidegger's estimation, the structure of our existence can only be understood in connection to finite time or temporality. Moreover, *Dasein* must be viewed in connection with all three dimensions of temporality—past, present, and future—in contrast to the focus on the present that characterizes the substance ontology that has predominated in the Western philosophical tradition. Heidegger claims that philosophers since Plato have seen existence from the perspective of a single temporal mode, "the present." They declare that things exist insofar as they present themselves to us in the here and now.[142] They assume that reality is static, enduring presence. What is ultimately real, they theorize, is what persists through change or remains present in the midst of change. In so doing, they confuse Being with "presence." We might say that such philosophers devise a "metaphysics of presence" (although Heidegger himself likely never used this particular term[143]). Heidegger objects to this focus on the present, because it reinforces the fatal Cartesian dichotomy between subject and object. It maintains the distinction between ourselves as conscious, thinking selves and the physical world, which we see as the object of our knowing. According to Heidegger, an existing thing is not merely what presents itself in the present. It is also what is not now present, because it is either past or future. Consequently, Being includes absence as well as presence.

Heidegger's ontology of temporality leads as well to what many commentators elevate as the central insight of his philosophical proposal. Acknowledging our temporal finiteness implies that we must confront our own death; we must realize that we are "being-unto-death." This confrontation, Heidegger adds, involves a particular mood (or state of mind signifying the human condition): *Angst* ("dread"). *Angst* is not only the realization that our life as a whole is pointing toward death, but is also the

138. Heidegger, *Being and Time*, 221.
139. Frank Lentricchia, *After the New Criticism* (Chicago: University of Chicago Press, 1980), 81.
140. Solomon, *Continental Philosophy since 1750*, 156.
141. Lentricchia, *After the New Criticism*, 81, 85.
142. See, for example, Heidegger, *Being and Time*, 47, 101; Martin Heidegger, *On Time and Being*, trans. Joan Stambaugh (New York: Harper & Row, 1972), 3, 12–15.
143. For this judgment, see Jean-Luc Marion, "In the Name: How to Avoid Speaking of 'Negative Theology,'" trans. Jeffrey L. Kosky, in *God, the Gift, and Postmodernism*, ed. John D. Caputo and Michael J. Scanlon (Bloomington: Indiana University Press, 1999), 20.

resultant feeling of nothingness with regard to being in the world.[144] Heidegger theorizes that the terrifying nature of the confrontation with our own death leads us to try to hide our finiteness from ourselves by engaging frantically in matters pertaining to everyday life. Although we implicitly understand our own being, we attempt to escape from this self-understanding and from accepting our condition as it is. Moreover, we relinquish the task of defining ourselves to the social context in which we find ourselves or to the roles that others cast us in. In short, we acquiesce to "others," to a fuzzy, indeterminate "they." Thereby, we become, to use Heidegger's term, *Das Man*.

According to Heidegger, the flight from our finiteness as revealed in *Angst* into worldly occupations entails *Dasein*'s "falling" (*Verfallen*). This situation sets up the fundamental existential choice with which *Dasein* is confronted, the choice between authentic and inauthentic existence, between being oneself and fleeing from oneself. Authentic existence, Heidegger adds, involves a resolute anticipation of our own death. Such authenticity enables us to integrate the various phases of our life into a meaningful whole. We are able to appropriate our unique past and anticipate our unique future, and then integrate them into a present that we affirm as the opportunity for decisive action. In this manner, resoluteness enables us to be our self as a whole. Without resoluteness, in contrast, one's life is dispersed into disparate parts.[145]

Rescuing Being from Onto-Theology

Writing in 1956, Walter Kaufmann characterized Heidegger as belonging "to the contemporary revolt against representation." Moreover, he concluded that Heidegger's goal was to replace representational thinking with "a thinking that recalls."[146] This appraisal is especially appropriate to Heidegger's later writings, in which he explores the implications of the temporality of existence for the nature of truth and language.[147]

Heidegger bemoans the transformation of truth into the certainty of representational thinking he finds characteristic of the Western tradition.[148] Furthermore, he refuses to reduce truth to the seemingly self-evident correspondence understanding that dominates our thinking. Truth is not merely the correspondence of our statements to a fully formed reality that exists outside of us, he avers. In fact, reducing our focus

144. For this description, see Stroll and Popkin, *Introduction to Philosophy*, 433–34.

145. See, for example, Heidegger, *Being and Time*, 312–82.

146. Kaufmann, "Existentialism from Dostoevsky to Sartre," 39.

147. For a book-length treatment of the later Heidegger, see Joseph J. Kockelmans, *On the Truth of Being: Reflections on Heidegger's Later Philosophy* (Bloomington: Indiana University Press, 1984).

148. Martin Heidegger, *The End of Philosophy*, trans. Joan Stambaugh (New York: Harper & Row, 1973), 19–26.

to the demand for certainty that is connected with the correspondence theory posits a nonsensical external world. It fails to see that the only world we have is the world of experience in which we are embedded as participants and therefore that we can speak about truth only insofar as we are "in" it, rather than searching for it outside of experience.

These considerations lead Heidegger to conclude that truth is not absolute and self-standing, but is relational.[149] Even more significant is his assertion that rather than the quest for certainty of propositions, truth has to do with "revelation," with the "disclosure" of Being. To gain such truth, he adds, requires an "openness to the mystery" that occurs only as we move away from our modern fixation with calculative thinking and engage in what he calls "meditative thinking."[150] This transition is necessary, he believes, because our vaunted conceptual categories are insufficient to help us come to grips with the truth of Being.[151] It must be replaced by a new, more rigorous type of thinking that is neither merely theoretical nor practical but precedes that distinction.[152] Such a thinking "recalls the truth of Being." Through such thinking, Being shines; Being, which otherwise remains concealed, becomes unconcealed.

In attempting to describe the thinking that "recalls," Heidegger returns to the aesthetic approach pioneered by Friedrich Nietzsche. Like his predecessor, Heidegger looks beyond conceptual discourse to artistic expression.[153] Not only is art a vehicle for the revelation of truth and hence of Being, it even becomes the means for the creation of truth.[154] He writes, "Art then is the becoming and happening of truth. Does truth, then, arise out of nothing? It does indeed if by nothing is meant the mere not of that which is, and if we here think of that which is as an object present in the ordinary way, and thereafter comes to light and is challenged by the existence of the work as only presumptively a true being."[155] Heidegger goes so far as to suggest that a work of art creates its own world.

Yet for Heidegger, art is not the ultimate world-creating power. Like Nietzsche, he moves to language,[156] and especially poetry, as the quintessential creative expression.[157] Language takes precedence over art, because of its closer connection with thought. In fact, according to Heidegger, language

---

149. Heidegger criticizes the demand for certainty because it seeks a basis for truth "which no longer depends upon a relation to something else but rather is absolved from the very beginning from this relation, and rests within itself." Heidegger, *End of Philosophy*, 26.

150. Heidegger, *Discourse on Thinking*, 55, 46.

151. See Martin Heidegger, "Letter on Humanism," in *Basic Writings*, 236.

152. Heidegger, "Letter on Humanism," 236.

153. For a summary of Heidegger's turn to art and then to poetry, see Inwood, *Heidegger*, 121–28.

154. For a discussion of his dimension of Heidegger's thought, see Megill, *Prophets of Extremity*, 157–62.

155. Martin Heidegger, *Poetry, Language, Thought*, trans. Albert Hofstadter (New York: Harper & Row, 1971), 71.

156. For a discussion of this point, see Megill, *Prophets of Extremity*, 162–70.

157. See Heidegger, *Poetry, Language, Thought*, 73–74.

and thought are nearly reciprocal, in that the experience of language is thought's experience of itself.[158] Like Nietzsche, Heidegger believes that through its connection with thought, language plays a crucial role in bringing the human world into existence.[159] To announce this, he coins the word "thinging": "In the naming, the things named are called into their thinging. Thinging, they unfold world, in which things abide and so are abiding ones."[160]

Here, however, Heidegger appears to step farther than even Nietzsche dared to tread. For Heidegger, we do not so much create language as move within it. Our "being-in" language allows us to discover that language gives itself to us, and hence is reality or Being.[161] As we enter into this kind of genuine experience with language, we are transformed.[162]

In taking this additional step, Heidegger has, in effect, cut language free from the artist. Some commentators conclude that in so doing he leaves us with "a view from nowhere."[163] Regardless of whether or not such an appraisal is valid, Heidegger's intent appears to be that of leading his readers to a mystical encounter which is neither objective nor subjective.[164] Only such an encounter, he avers, can facilitate the philosopher in moving behind metaphysics, with its concern for beings, to what lies at its basis, namely, the recalling of the truth of Being itself, which in Heidegger's estimation "has remained concealed from metaphysics during its long history from Anaximander to Nietzsche."[165]

Michael J. Inwood points out that Heidegger "is alternately worshipped, reviled, or sympathetically assimilated to other, more accessible philosophers."[166] Yet "worshipers" and "revilers" alike are unsure whether what we might call Heidegger's "mysticism of Being" is in fact able to provide the answer to the quest for a "new beginning," or whether his contribution is much more modest in scope.[167] In either case, Heidegger's central importance for the story of Being lies in the manner in which his

158. Megill, *Prophets of Extremity*, 164.

159. Heidegger writes, "The word alone gives Being to the thing." Martin Heidegger, *On the Way to Language*, trans. Peter D. Hertz (New York: Harper & Row, 1971), 62.

160. Heidegger, *Poetry, Language, Thought*, 199–200.

161. Martin Heidegger, *What Is Called Thinking?* trans. Fred D. Wieck and J. Glenn Gray (New York: Harper & Row, 1968), 192.

162. Martin Heidegger, *On the Way to Language*, trans. Peter D. Hertz (New York: Harper & Row, 1971), 57.

163. This catchy phrase has even become the title of a book: Thomas Nagel, *The View from Nowhere* (New York: Oxford University Press, 1986).

164. Solomon, *Continental Philosophy since 1750*, 167.

165. Martin Heidegger, "The Way Back into the Ground of Metaphysics," in Kaufmann, *Existentialism from Dostoevsky to Sartre*, 210.

166. Inwood, "Heidegger, Martin," 348.

167. For a succinct statement of the discussion of Heidegger's contribution as well as his own contention that both his friends and his foes have misunderstood his work, see Kaufmann, "Existentialism from Dostoevsky to Sartre," 35–36.

critique of traditional metaphysics opens the way to the mystical idea of Being as mystery.

Heidegger's "destruction" of the Western metaphysical tradition depicts the history of metaphysics as a story of forgetfulness or conceal- ment. He places the blame for such concealment at the feet of the sub- stance ontology of Western philosophy, which tradition he came to refer to by the cryptic designation "onto-theology." This descriptor goes back at least to Kant, who uses it to describe the attempt to prove the existence of God "through mere concepts, without the help of any experience what- soever."[168] Heidegger, however, decries the God of onto-theology. This God, he claims, enters the scene "only insofar as philosophy, of its own accord and by its own nature, requires and determines how the deity enters into it."[169] Furthermore, we "can neither pray nor sacrifice to this god [of philosophy]. Before the *causa sui*, man can neither fall to his knees in awe nor can he play music and dance before this god."[170] In short, the God of onto-theology—that is, the God of reason or philosophy—is not the God of religious devotion, to whom devotees pray and with whom they enter into a relationship of trust.

It would be a mistake, however, to conclude that Heidegger's rejection of onto-theology is a critique of all God-talk. Rather than eliminating the- ological discourse as such, his critique focuses on "those that have sold their soul to philosophy's project of rendering the whole of reality intelli- gible to human understanding," to cite Merold Westphal's characteriza- tion. Westphal explains: "Their fault does not consist in affirming that there is a highest Being who is the clue to the meaning of the whole of being. It consists in the chutzpa of permitting this God to enter the scene only in the service of their project, human mastery of the real."[171]

Heidegger accuses the Christian metaphysical tradition of this kind of chutzpa. In his estimation, Christian onto-theology shares in the mistake that characterizes the metaphysical tradition as a whole, namely, that of con- ceiving of Being as an entity, as a being—God. In so doing, it conceals rather than reveals the truth of the source of significance and transcendence.

In Heidegger's estimation, by not paying attention to the ontological difference between Being and beings, the metaphysical tradition of onto- theology marked the oblivion of Being. Yet this characterization of the fail- ure of onto-theology provides the occasion for his ultimate goal. Heidegger views his project as that of inaugurating a new beginning. At the heart of

168. Immanuel Kant, *Critique of Pure Reason*, A632 = B660, trans. Norman Kemp Smith (New York: St. Martin's, 1965), 525.

169. Martin Heidegger, *Identity and Difference*, trans. Joan Stambaugh (New York: Harper & Row, 1969), 56.

170. Ibid., 72.

171. Merold Westphal, *Overcoming Onto-Theology: Toward a Postmodern Christian Faith* (New York: Fordham University Press, 2001), 4.

this new beginning is the desire to bring us to the point in which we can recall the truth of Being. The reawakened awareness or recollection of Being to which Heidegger seeks to call us (and which George Connell aptly characterizes as "maddeningly elusive"[172]) is not so much conceptual as experiential. It is not an understanding but an experiencing, an experience of astonishment or wonder. This experience, Heidegger adds, lies at the core not only of philosophy but of humanness itself, and it marks the uniqueness of human beings: "Man alone of all beings, when addressed by the voice of Being experiences the marvel of all marvels: that what-is is."[173]

The new beginning that Heidegger envisions, therefore, is connected to a mystical encounter with Being, which he sees as ultimately mystery. In this sense, Heidegger's program carries a significance that is profoundly religious. Philipse pinpoints this well: "Interpreting the history of metaphysics *as* the history of oblivion of Being is not primarily a contribution to historical scholarship in philosophy. Rather, it is an act of repentance, which is needed to prepare a new 'event' or advent of Being." Philipse then offers this poignant conclusion: "Heidegger's entire later philosophy is an attempt to rescue religion in an age of atheism."[174]

Deconstructing Logocentrism

Heidegger's *Destruktion* of the Western metaphysical tradition and, by extension, of onto-theology opened the way for a quest for an encounter with Being that, because of its mystical character, may be said to be ultimately religious. Observers are less sure that the same claim can be made for Jacques Derrida's program of deconstruction, which Merold Westphal says is— together with postmodern philosophy in general—"rightly perceived as the most sustained critique of metaphysics since logical positivism."[175]

Christina Howells, who hails Derrida as "one of the most significant and brilliant French philosophers of the twentieth century," admits that the "sheer difficulty" of his texts is "legendary."[176] Since the publication in 1974 of his book *Glas*, it has become increasingly customary among commentators (including Richard Rorty[177]) to speak of an "earlier" and

172. George Connell, "Against Idolatry: Heidegger and Natural Theology," in *Postmodern Theology and Christian Thought*, ed. Merold Westphal (Bloomington: Indiana University Press, 1999), 146.
173. Martin Heidegger, "What Is Metaphysics?" in *Existentialism from Dostoevsky to Sartre*, rev. ed., ed. Walter Kaufmann (New York: New American Library, 1975), 261.
174. Philipse, *Heidegger's Philosophy of Being*, 382.
175. Westphal, *Overcoming Onto-Theology*, 219.
176. Christina Howells, *Derrida: Deconstruction from Phenomenology to Ethics* (Cambridge: Polity Press, 1999), 1.
177. See, for example, Richard Rorty, *Contingency, Irony, and Solidarity* (New York: Cambridge University Press, 1989), 123–87; Richard Rorty, *Philosophical Papers*, vol. 2, *Essays on Heidegger and Others* (New York: Cambridge University Press, 1991), 93–128. For an engagement with Rorty's perspective on Derrida, see Rodolphe Gasché, *Inventions of Difference: On Jacques Derrida* (Cambridge, MA: Harvard University Press, 1994), 3–13.

a "later" Derrida.[178] Richard Kearney, for example, suggests that Derrida's initial interest in an epistemological version of deconstruction gave way to a focus on ethical responsibility, that is, for a "determination to reread the deconstructive turn in the light of an ethical re-turn." Kearney maintains, however, that these two aspects are in fact integrally related, that they are moments in Derrida's overarching concern for the "other" or for what he himself calls "the indispensable notion of responsibility."[179]

Within this larger framework, Derrida has waged a campaign against the traditional metaphysical dualism that separates philosophy and literature. His legendarily difficult publications reveal his desire to call philosophy to task for its tendency to stand in judgment over other literary expressions while resisting the suggestion that it is itself a kind of writing. He challenges what he sees as the incredulous claim of philosophers that they are objective observers to whom is given the prerogative to raise foundational questions about other disciplines such as "What is literature?" or "What is poetry?" In responding to this claim, Derrida draws other forms (such as poetry) into the domain of the philosopher, thereby indirectly and discreetly interrogating philosophy's attempt to divide one type of writing from another.[180] Hence, Howells points out that a "feature of the Derridean strategy is to undo the conventional distinction between literature and philosophy and the hierarchy which subordinates the former to the latter."[181] What makes this attack on the philosophical tradition crucial for the story of Being is the fact that it entails a concerted attempt to undermine "logocentrism" and with it, the traditional conception of Being itself.

Questioning Logocentrism

At the heart of Derrida's program is his interest in the question of how language derives its meaning. And he is not happy with the answer that he finds in Western philosophy. Philosophers, especially in the modern era, erroneously locate meaning in the ability of our thoughts and statements to represent an objective, given reality. Moreover, they view writing as a representation of speech.[182] To undermine this tendency in modern philosophy, Derrida wages a ruthless war against the so-called realist understanding of language, which assumes that our statements are representations of the world as it actually is apart from human activity.

178. For an engagement with the "later Derrida," see Herman Rapaport, *Later Derrida: Reading the Recent Work* (New York: Routledge, 2003).

179. Richard Kearney, "Derrida's Ethical Re-Turn," in *Working through Derrida*, ed. Gary B. Madison (Evanston, IL: Northwestern University Press, 1993), 28, 31. See also Christopher Norris, *Derrida* (Cambridge, MA: Harvard University Press, 1987), 196–97.

180. See Peggy Kamuf's remarks in Derrida, *A Derrida Reader: Between the Blinds*, ed. Peggy Kamuf (New York: Columbia University Press, 1991), 143–44.

181. Howells, *Derrida*, 71.

182. Norris, *Derrida*, 121.

He denies that language has a fixed meaning connected to a fixed reality or that it unveils definitive truth.

In Derrida's estimation, linguistic realism is closely connected to a mistaken understanding of literature that has characterized Western thought. To expose this, he contrasts "speech" and "writing." Actually, these two dimensions of language function in his critique as metaphors for a deeper contrast that Derrida seeks to illumine: "Speech" stands for the possibility of direct contact with truth, whereas "writing" is the realization that we have no such immediate connection. By its very nature, speaking is more closely connected with its source than writing is. When we speak, what we say is broadcast immediately into the world, but then it quickly disappears. Speech, therefore, carries a sense of immediacy. When we write, in contrast, our writing quickly becomes disengaged from us. It is no longer dependent on us for its existence. In fact, what we have written can remain long after we are gone. Because writing is not dependent on the presence of its origin, it is removed from the immediacy that speech connotes.[183]

Derrida criticizes Western philosophy for eschewing "writing" in the pursuit of "speech."[184] He notes that philosophy takes the form of writing. Although writing is the mode of language that indicates absence, not presence, modern thinkers assume that their literary efforts can bring to light an immediately present truth or meaning. Derrida labels this tendency in Western philosophy to look to the word or language (especially written language)—that is, to the *logos*—as the carrier of meaning, "logocentrism."

Logocentrism, in turn, is connected to what Derrida calls the "metaphysics of presence." His use of this phrase is, of course, reminiscent of Heidegger, and in that sense he might be said to be continuing the program that Heidegger began. Yet Derrida charges that his predecessor did not go far enough in his attempt to "destruct" onto-theology, for he failed to realize that onto-theology is an expression of a metaphysics of presence. Consequently, in Derrida's estimation, even Heidegger operated within a metaphysics of presence.[185]

Derrida is convinced that the metaphysics of presence leads to "metaphysical determinations of truth." By these phrases, he has in view the perspective of philosophers who assume the existence of a domain of objects or acts to which we have direct epistemological access.[186] These philosophers believe that such a "presence" of being, or a presence of an essence

183. Jacques Derrida, *Of Grammatology*, trans. Gayatri Chakravorty Spivak (Baltimore: Johns Hopkins University Press, 1976), 37.

184. Ibid., 35.

185. For this judgment, see Henry Ruf, "The Origin of the Debate over Ontotheology and Deconstruction in the Texts of Wittgenstein and Derrida," in *Religion, Ontotheology, and Deconstruction*, ed. Henry Ruf (New York: Paragon, 1989), 21, 35–37.

186. For this description of "presence" theory, see Samuel C. Wheeler III, *Deconstruction as Analytic Philosophy* (Stanford, CA: Stanford University Press, 2000), 17.

that we can come to know, lies at the foundation of language.[187] Hence, they are convinced that language (the system of linguistic "signs") is able to "signify" or represent this given reality in its essential nature. The order of language that this perspective assumes begins with an "origin" or "sense" (the "transcendental signified") that comes to voice through expressive communication, that is, through the *logos* (the "transcendental signifier"), to which writing might be added as a third element that is distanced from the first two.

Derrida writes, "All the metaphysical determinations of truth . . . are more or less immediately inseparable from the instance of logos, or of a reason thought within the lineage of the logos, in whatever sense it is understood."[188] Robert Magliola offers the following helpful commentary on this statement: "By 'metaphysical determinations of truth,' Jacques Derrida means all judgments and measurements of 'truth' which are *logocentric*, that is, centered on a concept of truth as logos. And by 'logos' he means truth defined as the *expression* (or 'signifier') of an originating *factor* (or 'signified'), no matter what that factor may be." Magliola then adds, "and it is clear that Derrida holds that the whole Western tradition, in one way or another, is logocentric."[189]

Philosophers who adhere to the metaphysics of presence search for some ultimate "word," presence, essence, truth, or reality that can form the foundation for our thought, language, and experience.[190] When expanded to the grand scale of the world as a whole, such philosophical speculation leads theorists to offer a variety of labels for that ultimate foundation: God, the Idea, the World Spirit, the Self. In keeping with this perspective, some philosophers assert that we have access to the divine mind or to the infinite understanding that God possesses, whereas others assume the existence of an infinitely creative subjectivity or a human self present to, and fully known to, itself.[191] Imbued with the "myth of presence," Derrida adds, these thinkers make claims that they cannot possibly defend and exude a confidence that their writings cannot possibly sustain. This "onto-theological tradition" refuses to consider the possibility that there is no ultimate grounding for our systems of thought and language.

The initial object of Derrida's attack on logocentrism was the phenomenology of Edmund Husserl.[192] Howells goes so far as to declare that

187. Derrida, *Of Grammatology*, 11–12. See also Gayatri Chakravorty Spivak, "Translator's Preface," in *Of Grammatology*, lxviii.

188. Derrida, *Of Grammatology*, 10–11.

189. Robert Magliola, *Derrida on the Mend* (West Lafayette, IN: Purdue University Press, 1984), 3.

190. Derrida, *Of Grammatology*, 49.

191. Ibid., 73.

192. Derrida's relationship to Husserl is variously understood by commentators. For a collection of essays that focus on this problem, see William R. McKenna and J. Claude Evans, eds., *Derrida and Phenomenology* (Dordrecht: Kluwer, 1995).

"Derrida's whole philosophical programme seems to spring from his tussle with phenomenology." She then adds, "It is the phenomenological attempt to ground knowledge in experience, evidence and self-presence, and its apparent failure that leads him to the conclusion that the attempt itself is fundamentally misconceived."[193]

Husserl renewed the perennial modern attempt to provide an indisputable foundation for reason and language. Reminiscent of Descartes, he set out to discover the primordial structures of thought and perception. He was convinced that this is facilitated by elevating knowledge that arises from authentic "self-presence" above knowledge based on memory, anticipation, or traces of an absent experience. This differentiation, in turn, requires a demarcation between the "now," where the subject is located, and the receding horizons of past and future. Central to Husserl's project is a distinction between two modes of language. "Expressive" signs indicate personal intention, whereas "indicative" signs signify, but are not the carriers of, animating intention. Hence, dark clouds may portend a storm, but they do not indicate that someone intends to rain on a planned parade. For Husserl, expressive signs—and not indicative signs—offer the key to understanding the meaning of language.[194] Consequently, he argued that the study of language must focus on the self-reflective, solitary consciousness—the individual mental life—and not the realm of interpersonal discourse.

Making a *Différance*

At the heart of Derrida's challenge to Husserl's "logic of presence" is his discovery of the indeterminacy of language.[195] To develop this, Derrida picks up on the concept of "difference" pioneered by Ferdinand de Saussure and others, including Heidegger.[196] But he adds an interesting, playful twist. He changes *différence* to *différance*, a move that Joseph Margolis deems to be "Derrida's joking way of exposing, by imitation, the transcendentalist's own strategy."[197] The noun *différance* is, of course, Derrida's own coinage. Its etymological root lies in the French verb *différer*, which means both "to differ" and "to defer." By introducing the *ance*-ending, which in French produces verbal nouns, he constructs a new form that means both "differing" and "deferring."

193. Howells, *Derrida*, 7.
194. Christopher Norris, *What's Wrong with Postmodernism: Critical Theory and the Ends of Philosophy* (Baltimore: Johns Hopkins University Press, 1990), 201–2.
195. For a helpful engagement with this aspect of Derrida's thought, see Wheeler, *Deconstruction as Analytic Philosophy*, 15–35.
196. Derrida, *Of Grammatology*, 52. For this discussion, see, for example, Heidegger, *Poetry, Language, Thought*, 202–10.
197. Joseph Margolis, "Differing to Derrida's Difference," in *European Philosophy and the American Academy*, ed. Barry Smith (LaSalle, IL: Hegeler Institute, 1994), 209. For an example of Derrida's description of the term *différance*, see Jacques Derrida, *Margins of Philosophy*, trans. Alan Bass (Chicago: University of Chicago Press, 1982), 1–27.

Derrida appeals to Saussure's observation that a linguistic signifier (e.g., a word) does not possess a fixed meaning within itself. A linguistic sign does not have any intrinsic characteristics that determine its meaning. Instead, a signifier derives its meaning from its relations within the language system.[198] Consequently, a linguistic signifier cannot by itself "force" a particular interpretation; nor can it be self-interpreting. Meaning, in contrast, is produced by the difference between signifiers in the language chain. Language, in turn, is not a composite of independently meaningful units. Rather, the signs we use to express intention are caught up in a network of linguistic relations. And a language system is a system of differences, for every concept in the system is defined by its differences from other concepts.

On the basis of this understanding of language as involving difference, Derrida concludes that meaning cannot lie buried within Husserl's isolated, self-reflective consciousness. Nor are Husserl's "presence" (or the meaning of the present) and the self autonomous givens. Both are contextual, for they arise from their positive and negative relations to other elements.

Différance does not only entail "differing," however, but also "deferring." Following Saussure's lead, Derrida differentiates between a phonic "signifier" (i.e., the word itself) and its corresponding mental "signified" (the concept, idea, perception, emotion to which the word is connected).[199] Our use of phonic signifiers to express mental signifieds creates a crucial difference between language and the mental process to which we seek to give expression. The meanings of the words we use arise out of their relations within the immediate context in which they appear (their "textual location") and not necessarily from any connection to mental signifieds. Derrida concludes that in the end language is merely "self-referential." A sign, he argues, will always lead to another sign. Thus, a language is a chain of signifiers referring to other signifiers, in which each signifier in turn becomes what is signified by another signifier. And because the textual location in which a signifier is embedded constantly changes, its meaning can never be fully determined. For Derrida, therefore, meaning is never static. It is never given once for all. Instead, meaning changes over time and with changing contexts. For this reason, we must continually "defer" or postpone our tendency to attribute meaning.[200]

Crucial to Derrida's view is his observation that both meaning and consciousness are dependent on language. There is no "signified" (i.e., no mental concept) that exists apart from the "signifier" (i.e., the word that

198. Ferdinand de Saussure, *Course in General Linguistics*, trans. W. Baskin (New York: Philosophical Library, 1959), 120.

199. E.g., Derrida, *Of Grammatology*, 63; Charlene Spretnak, *States of Grace: The Recovery of Meaning in the Postmodern Age* (San Francisco: HarperCollins, 1991), 234.

200. Jacques Derrida, *Positions*, rev. ed., trans. Alan Bass (New York: Continuum, 2002), 28–29.

we attach to that thought).[201] Because of this link between mental activity and language, *différance*—the interplay of passive differing and active deferring—provides a radical critique of the concept of the self as an entity existing apart from its context. There is no self that stands beneath or precedes linguistic activity. Derrida acknowledges that each of us does indeed experience himself or herself as existing as a self in the "now," but he avers that the experience of a singular, objective "present" is in fact an illusion. What we experience in the present is actually the result of a complex web of meanings that is constantly changing. Through language and concepts, we impose the sense of objective meaning on the flux of experience.

To see how this is so, let us suppose that I claim to see a mug on a desk in a room.[202] Our tendency is to assume that this is an objective, given occurrence. Yet there is no single correct statement that objectively describes the experience. On the contrary, I could offer many possible descriptions of it, and each description would actually alter and color the experience itself. Depending on the circumstances, I may anticipate enjoying a refreshing drink in my work area, see another example of my son's untidiness, or view the situation as an opportunity to hurl a missile at an attacker. Derrida's goal is to bring to light this dimension of language, especially of written language. He wants to chasten the modern pretension of assigning fixed meanings to the flux of experience.

The change from *différence* to *différance* serves other functions as well. The replacement of the "e" with an "a" is not readily noticeable in speaking, but is evident only when the word is written. Consequently, Derrida's use of the *différance* serves as a parody of the classical Western idea that writing is simply the representation of human speech, which is more foundational and immediate. In this playful manner, he seeks to subvert the classical theory of meaning, which moves from thought to speech to written language.[203] Furthermore, through Derrida's series of "misspellings" of *différence*, *différance* reminds the reader that the perfectly spelled word is absent from the text while its meaning remains present.[204] This phenomenon illustrates his thesis, drawn from Heidegger, that the meaning of writing arises from an interplay between presence and absence. Meaning occurs because of the presence of a "trace" of a now absent reality or a trace of its former connections to other elements.[205]

---

201. Lentricchia, *After the New Criticism*, 168.

202. For the basis of this example, see Hilary Lawson, "Stories about Stories," in *Dismantling Truth: Reality in the Post-Modern World*, ed. Hilary Lawson and Lisa Appignanesi (New York: St. Martin's Press, 1989), xxv.

203. Jonathan Culler, *On Deconstruction: Theory and Criticism after Structuralism* (Ithaca, NY: Cornell University Press, 1982), 97.

204. Spivak, "Translator's Preface," xliii.

205. Derrida's new style of writing seeks to expose this situation. See, for example, Derrida, *Positions*, 26.

Undercutting the Quest for Being

Derrida's mentor in his attack on the logocentrism that he finds in much of Western philosophy is Heidegger, or perhaps better stated, Nietzsche as read by Heidegger.[206] But in contrast to his predecessors, the French philosopher is not a new mythmaker.[207] He does not attempt to construct something new on the foundation of the old. Rather, his goal appears to be largely negative or destructive. He wants to disavow the tradition of its logocentrism with its attendant assumptions that philosophy is pure, disinterested inquiry and that our language matches an "outside" world. J. Claude Evans claims that Derrida even undercuts Heidegger himself, insofar as Derrida claims that "there are no 'original experiences' which we could uncover by 'destructuring,' or that there are no 'master words' that can express the very event of the manifestation of Being."[208]

The weapon that Derrida unsheathes to accomplish this goal is a process that he terms "deconstruction." "Deconstruction" is a notoriously difficult word to define.[209] In fact, it defies definition, if for no other reason than that Derrida has shrewdly placed obstacles along the path. He claims that deconstruction is not a method, a technique, a style of literary critique, or even a procedure for textual interpretation.[210] In his spirited critique of the use of deconstruction in American universities, Dallas Willard underscores this perspective. He declares bluntly, "'Deconstruction' is not a *method* of thought. It is at best a set of *claims about* thought and discourse and their meanings."[211] For his part, Derrida warns against replacing the actual activity of deconstructive reading with a description or conceptualized understanding of that activity.[212]

Despite the difficulty of describing what Derrida means by the term "deconstruction," commentators have not been unwilling to say something about it. For example, in a lengthy explanatory essay, Rodolphe Gasché offers the following crisp description: "Deconstruction is an operation which accounts for and simultaneously undoes self-reflection."[213]

---

206. For an example of his evaluation of Heidegger, see Jacques Derrida, *Of Spirit: Heidegger and the Question*, trans. Geoffrey Bennington and Rachel Bowlby (Chicago: University of Chicago Press, 1989). For an example of Derrida's use of Nietzsche, see Jacques Derrida, *Margins of Philosophy*, trans. Alan Bass (Chicago: University of Chicago Press, 1982), 109–36. Regarding the point that Derrida is drawing from Nietzsche as read by Heidegger, see Spivak, "Translator's Preface," xxxiii.

207. For this conclusion, see Megill, *Prophets of Extremity*, 333.

208. J. Claude Evans, "The Rigors of Deconstruction," in Smith, *European Philosophy and the American Academy*, 82.

209. For a somewhat lengthy characterization of the term, see Jacques Derrida, *Margins of Philosophy*, 329–30.

210. Jacques Derrida, "Letter to a Japanese Friend," in *A Derrida Reader*, 273.

211. Dallas Willard, "The Unhinging of the American Mind: Derrida as Pretext," in Smith, *European Philosophy and the American Academy*, 17. For a critical engagement with Derrida, see Dallas Willard, "Predication as Originary Violence: A Phenomenological Critique of Derrida's View of Intentionality," in Madison, *Working through Derrida*, 120–36.

212. See Norris, *Derrida*, 20.

213. Gasché, *Inventions of Difference*, 40.

Derrida declares that deconstruction cannot be reduced to any one way or method, but must be spoken of in the plural.[214] Viewed from one perspective, we might say that deconstruction is an assault upon logocentrism, understood as the assumption that something lies beyond our system of linguistic signs to which a written work can refer so that it might be able to substantiate its claim to be an authentic statement.[215] Derrida seeks to divest us of logocentrism by showing the impossibility of drawing a firm line between reality and our linguistic representations. His chief focus, of course, is written language—texts. To wean us from too quickly assuming that we can discover the meaning inherent in a text, he demonstrates the difficulties of any theory that defines meaning in a univocal way, whether by appeal to what the author intends, to what literary conventions determine, or even to what a reader experiences.[216] After all our theorizing, he observes, there still remains "the free play of meaning," which is the result of what Derrida calls "the play of the world." The text always provides further connections, correlations, and contexts; hence, it is always open to further meanings.

The immediate target of this kind of deconstruction is, of course, philosophy. Derrida believes that the Western philosophical tradition is hopelessly logocentric in that it engages in a search for an ultimate grounding for our language. Deconstruction shows the fallacy of this search. Derrida's goal, therefore, is to alter the entire program of philosophy. No written work is held static by a metaphysical anchor. Writing has no extralinguistic referent. Consequently, any attempt to construct such a referent inevitably leads only to the construction of a fiction created out of words. Rather than the search for the one unifying truth, Derrida concludes that philosophy's "first principle" is a system of symbols that is not propped up by anything outside language. And the purpose of philosophy is not to defend or account for these systems, but to deconstruct them.[217]

The implications of deconstruction, however, run deeper. Saussure's insight that linguistic meaning arises from structures of relations and not in some ideal correspondence between sound and sense cannot be limited to written language. Rather, language—including spoken language—is always a system of differential signs. As a consequence, we might say that all speech is really writing, for every use of language is subject to interpretation in the way that writing is. Not only does the classical definition

214. Jacques Derrida, *Psyche: Inventions de l'autre* (Paris: Galilee, 1987), 390–91, as cited in Gasché, *Inventions of Difference*, 61.

215. See Walter Truett Anderson, *Reality Isn't What It Used to Be: Theatrical Politics, Ready-to-Wear Religion, Global Myths, Primitive Chic, and Other Wonders of the Postmodern World* (San Francisco: Harper & Row, 1990), 90.

216. Culler, *On Deconstruction*, 131–34.

217. Anderson, *Reality Isn't What It Used to Be*, 91; Solomon, *Continental Philosophy since 1750*, 201.

of writing apply to every form of language, but it applies even to thinking itself.[218]

This leads us back to Derrida's basic goal, namely, to disavow us of the "metaphysics of presence." There is no "presence" to which we have direct access, which presence can give a static, determinable meaning to our linguistic utterances. For this reason, he advises us to abandon the logocentric quest for a meaning that exists outside and beyond the differential play of language (i.e, the quest for the "transcendental signified"). Deconstruction is a perpetual reminder that the origin of language lies with writing (the "sign of a sign") and not with some assumed immediate experience of the correspondence of thought with object. Indeed, not even thought can escape the endless supplementarity of the linguistic system.

But where does this leave concepts such as God and Being?

Derrida has said of himself, "I quite rightly pass for an atheist."[219] Despite comments such as this, his actual relationship to religion in general, to his Jewish heritage, and to God-language is more complicated. In 1994, two years before the appearance of "Faith and Knowledge: The Two Sources of 'Religion' and the Limits of Reason Alone," which Gil Anidjar considers to be "Derrida's most explicit treatment of 'religion,'"[220] Rodolphe Gasché declared, "Although Derrida's texts directly broach neither the question of God nor man's relations to God, these questions make themselves felt in a contextual, oblique manner through Derrida's more explicit investigations into the relations and the commerce between different, seemingly exclusive types of discourses."[221]

Since Gasché offered his comment, John Caputo and others have mused about a theological and even mystical dimension in Derrida's later works.[222] In an essay in which he brings deconstruction into conversation with radical orthodoxy, Caputo takes the matter a step further. In a telling statement in which he contrasts Derrida and Augustine, he observes:

> The difference is that Augustine has seized and settled upon a determinate historical name for the object of his faith and hope and love, that he has "entrusted" or "delivered" himself over to the proper names that have been transmitted to him by his tradition, while for Derrida faith and hope and love make their way in the night as best they can. For night is their element, and the particular figures in which our faith and hope and love take shape can always be determined otherwise.[223]

218. Derrida, *Of Grammatology*, 50.

219. As quoted in John D. Caputo, "What Do I Love When I Love My God? Deconstruction and Radical Orthodoxy," in *Questioning God*, ed. John D. Caputo, Mark Dooley, and Michael J. Scanlon (Bloomington: Indiana University Press, 2001), 308.

220. Gil Anidjar, "Introduction: 'Once More, Once More': Derrida, the Arab, the Jew," in Jacques Derrida, *Acts of Religion*, ed. Gil Anidjar (New York: Routledge, 2002), 40.

221. Gasché, *Inventions of Difference*, 150.

222. See John D. Caputo, *The Prayers and Tears of Jacques Derrida: Religion without Religion* (Bloomington: Indiana University Press, 1997).

223. Caputo, "What Do I Love When I Love My God?" 311.

Caputo's characterization fits well with a declaration that Derrida himself wrote in response to his mother's question as to whether he believes in God: "The endurance of God in my life goes under other names—so much so that I'm taken quite understandly for an atheist—the omnipresence in me of what I call God in my absolved language . . . being . . . the secret from which I am excluded."[224]

Regardless of the final outcome of the debate over the extent to which Derrida is "religious," his persistent deconstructing of logocentrism stands at the end of a lengthy trajectory in Western philosophical history. The loss of the metaphysics of presence that characterizes Derrida's perspective and the indeterminacy to which his philosophical and theological insights—in contrast to those of Augustine—consign us appear to undercut any ontology that conceives of Being coming to expression in human language; indeed, it would undercut any quest for Being whatsoever. In short, Derrida's deconstruction of the Western philosophical tradition marks the demise of Being, at least as Being has been understood throughout much of history.

Derridian indeterminacy seems to carry another implication as well. It appears to spell the end of theology. In Derrida's estimation, it undermines specifically the Hegelian onto-theology "which determines absolute knowledge as the truth of religion,"[225] although he is open to the possibility that theologians might replace the onto-theological fetish of God with a "God beyond God."[226] By extension, Derridian indeterminacy would seem to undermine as well the classic Christian theological conception that draws its vision of God from the image of the originating Father who speaks his Logos in creation and incarnation.

Yet we might discover that in the end the death of onto-theology does not necessitate the demise of constructive theology itself. On the contrary, the victory of indeterminacy might in fact occasion a rebirth of that aspect of the Augustinian option that looks to a self-naming God, rather than a supposedly universally accessible structure of being, for the source of, and the recipient of, human faith, hope, and love. In this way, the death of onto-theology, at least in the form in which it has predominated throughout much of Western history, might actually open the way to a truly appropriate theo-ontology. In any case, the quest for such a theo-ontology is the task that the demise of Being bequeaths to theology.

224. Jacques Derrida, "Circonfession," in *Jacques Derrida*, by Geoffrey Bennington and Jacques Derrida, trans. Geoffrey Bennington (Chicago: University of Chicago Press, 1993), 146–47.

225. Derrida, *Acts of Religion*, 53.

226. Derrida, "Comment ne pas parler," in *Psyche*, 560–61; Derrida, *De l'esprit: Heidegger et la question* (Paris: Galilee, 1987), 179–84, as cited in Kearney, "Derrida's Ethical Re-Turn," 44.

PART TWO
THE SAGA OF THE I AM

Chapter Four

From Exodus to Exile

The Covenanted I AM

From Augustine to Aquinas, Christian theologians have connected the God of the Bible with the Greek conception of Being. Moreover, in their estimation, the link between Christian theology and Greek philosophy was forged by the biblical assertion that the God of the Bible is the great I AM. Under the influence of Greek philosophical thinking, theologians understood this designation as indicating that the biblical God is characterized first and foremost by philosophical traits such as self-existence, eternality, unchangeability, and, consequently, absolute being. Jerome spoke for many when he declared, alluding to God's annunciation of the divine name to Moses:

> There is one nature of God and one only; and this, and this alone, truly is. For absolute being is derived from no other source but is all its own. All things besides, that is, all things created, although they appear to be, soon are not. For there was a time when they were not, and that which once was not may again cease to be. God alone who is eternal, that is to say, who has no beginning, really deserves to be

called an essence. Therefore also he says of him, "I am has sent me."
As the angels, the sky, the earth, the seas all existed at the time, it
must have been as the absolute being that God claimed for himself
that name of essence, which apparently was common to all.[1]

Similarly, Jerome's younger contemporary, Hilary of Poitiers, in speaking
about his encounter with Exodus 3:14, declared:

> I confess that I was amazed to find in them an indication concern-
> ing God so exact that it expressed in the terms best adapted to human
> understanding an unattainable insight into the mystery of the Divine
> nature. For no property of God which the mind can grasp is more
> characteristic of Him than existence, since existence, in the absolute
> sense, cannot be predicated of that which shall come to an end, or of
> that which has had a beginning. . . . Wherefore, since God's eternity
> is inseparable from Himself, it was worthy of Him to reveal this one
> thing, that He is, as the assurance of His absolute eternity.[2]

The long-standing tendency to see in the designation I AM the link
between the biblical God and the philosophical idea of Being raises the
possibility that the journey of the I AM through the biblical narrative
might provide the basis for a renewed engagement of theology with ontology. Determining the extent to which the concept of the I AM holds
promise for such an engagement requires that we retrace this trajectory.

The Revelation of the Divine Name

The first two books of the Pentateuch suggest that the early patriarchs
used a plethora of names to speak of the one whom they worshiped. Some
scholars find in the repeated use of the designation 'el or 'elohim an indication that the ancestors of the Hebrews paid homage to the Mesopo-
tamian high god, El, whom they believed had entered into covenant with
them. Although the final redactor of Genesis readily identifies El with
Yahweh, the God of Israel, the biblical narrator continues to use the name
"El" in the dialogue sections in Genesis.[3] In the early chapters of Exodus,
however, the situation changes radically.

The Genesis narrator asserts that the name "Yahweh" came into use
early in human religious history (Gen. 4:26). Exodus, in contrast, links
the revelation of the divine name (or at least the revelation of its significance) with Yahweh's call of Moses. As Yahweh explains to Moses when

---

1. Jerome, *Letter* 15.4, in *Nicene and Post-Nicene Fathers*, 2nd series, ed. Philip Schaff and Henry
Wace (1893; repr., Peabody, MA: Hendrickson, 1994), 6:19.
2. Hilary of Poitiers, *On the Trinity* 1.5, in *Nicene and Post-Nicene Fathers*, 2nd series, 9:41.
3. Christopher Wright, "Christian and Other Religions: The Biblical Evidence," *Themelios* 9, no.
2 (1984): 6.

this call is subsequently reconfirmed, "I appeared to Abraham, to Isaac and to Jacob as God Almighty [El-Shaddai], but by my name the LORD [Yahweh] I did not make myself known to them" (Exod. 6:3). Therefore, the story of the I AM, at least insofar as this designation forms in some sense an explanation of the name "Yahweh," begins with the call of Moses.

The Revealing of the Name: I AM

The central text in which the significance of "Yahweh" comes to the fore is Exodus 3:14. In fact, John Durham claims that this text comprises "the only explanation of this unique divine name to be found in the OT."[4] Consequently, in his estimation, this verse is "supremely a theological text, one of the most theological texts in the entire Bible."[5] Despite its theological importance, the verse is an exegetical conundrum. Terrence Fretheim understates the situation when he remarks, "Exodus 3:14 is one of the most puzzled over verses in the entire Hebrew Bible."[6] Brevard Childs presents a more straightforward assessment: "Few verses in the entire Old Testament have evoked such heated controversy and such widely divergent interpretations."[7]

The Narrative Context: The Concern for the Divine Identity

The explication of the central Old Testament name for the God of Israel occurs within the narrative of Yahweh's call of Moses from the burning bush. More specifically, the dialogue between Yahweh and Moses that forms the heart of the narrative provides the context for the revelation of the meaning of the divine name. In the dialogue, Yahweh not only reveals his identity as the I AM, but in the process alludes to the divine self-declaratory phrase "I am Yahweh" that is found so often in the Old Testament.

Already at the beginning of the incident, the identity of the God who calls Moses is central. The scene opens with the angel (or messenger) of Yahweh appearing to Moses as a flame in a bush. Immediately, however, this enigmatic figure gives way to "Yahweh" and "God" as the designations of the one who converses with Moses. Here, as in similar texts, exegetes do not generally find the interplay of Yahweh and Yahweh's messenger problematic, but simply posit a close link between the two.[8] The older exegetical tradition accomplished this by concluding that the angel

---

4. John I. Durham, *Exodus*, Word Biblical Commentary (Waco, TX: Word, 1987), 33.

5. Ibid., 37.

6. Terence E. Fretheim, *Exodus, Interpretation: A Bible Commentary for Teaching and Preaching* (Louisville: KY: John Knox, 1991), 63.

7. Brevard S. Childs, *The Book of Exodus: A Critical, Theological Commentary* (Philadelphia: Westminster, 1974), 61.

8. See, for example, Cornelis Houtman, *Exodus*, trans. Johan Rebel and Sierd Woudstra, 4 vols., Historical Commentary on the Old Testament (Kampen, Netherlands: Kok, 1993–), 1:336.

of Yahweh is a christophany, a preincarnate appearance of Christ.[9] Contemporary exegetes tend to be more circumspect in their treatment of this Old Testament figure. Some see the angel of Yahweh as simply God "in manifestation," to cite A. B. Davidson's characterization.[10] Others connect this figure to the divine Word, rather than directly to Christ as the Word. George Knight, for example, declares, "The messenger is in effect the living Word of God reaching through to us in a thought-pattern that the human mind can grasp."[11] This conclusion is in keeping with Werner Schmidt's findings: "The self-revelation of God in his word is a basic characteristic of the Old Testament understanding of God."[12]

As Moses approaches the burning bush, Yahweh offers the first self-identifying statement of the narrative: "I am the God of your father, the God of Abraham, the God of Isaac and the God of Jacob" (v. 6). The singularity of the first designation, "the God of your father," might be understood as Yahweh's way of connecting his identity with the religious heritage that Moses inherited from his own family[13] or from his father-in-law (if the Kenite-Midianite theory, discussed later in this section, is correct). In any case, by means of this statement Yahweh claims to be the God who stands behind a lineage of religious devotion that runs back to the patriarchs. Yahweh's first self-designation, therefore, underscores continuity with a past relationship that links him both to Moses and to Israel.

In response to Yahweh's declaration that he intends to send Moses to Pharaoh to bring the Israelites out of Egypt (v. 10), Moses raises a series of four objections as to why he is not an appropriate agent of deliverance. The first (3:11) and the fourth (4:10) center on his unsuitability for the task, whereas the second (3:13) and third (4:1) mention the likelihood that Israel will not accept his leadership.[14] Yahweh listens to and answers each of these objections in turn (3:12, 14–22; 4:2–9, 11–12).

Yahweh's second indication of his identity comes in his response to Moses' first objection, "Who am I that I should go to Pharaoh, and bring

9. See, for example, Albert Knudson, *The Religious Teaching of the Old Testament* (New York: Abingdon-Cokesbury, 1918), 200; E. W. Hengstenberg, *Christology of the Old Testament* (1847; repr., Grand Rapids: Kregel, 1970), 282–87.

10. A. B. Davidson, *The Theology of the Old Testament*, ed. S. D. F. Salmond (New York: Charles Scribner's Sons, 1917), 69.

11. George A. F. Knight, *Theology as Narration: A Commentary on the Book of Exodus* (Grand Rapids: Eerdmans, 1976), 17.

12. Werner H. Schmidt, *The Faith of the Old Testament: A History*, trans. John Sturdy (Philadelphia: Westminster, 1983), 53.

13. Durham, *Exodus*, 31. Keil, in contrast, declares, "In the expression 'thy father,' the three patriarchs are classed together as one." C. F. Keil and F. Delitzsch, *Biblical Commentary on the Old Testament*, trans. James Martin et al., 10 vols. (Grand Rapids: Eerdmans, 1951), 1:440.

14. For this enumeration, see Houtman, *Exodus*, 1:324–25. Hyatt, in contrast, offers a slightly different list, which sees this verse as the first objection, which is followed by three others (4:1, 10, 13). J. Philip Hyatt, "Commentary on Exodus," in *The New Century Bible* (London: Marshall, Morgan & Scott, 1971), 74.

the Israelites out of Egypt?" (v. 11). The divine conversation partner assures Moses of his personal presence: "I will be [or I am] with you" (v. 12). Thereby, Yahweh indicates that the question is not about who Moses is, but who is with Moses. By repeating the "I am" (*'ehyeh*) of verse 6 and anticipating its use in verses 14–15, the narrative moves a step closer to the explication of the divine name. As Ronald Clements rightly observes, "There is already a play here upon the meaning of the divine name which is yet to be disclosed."[15] Moreover, this text hints that the theme of God being present with Israel and, through Israel, with all humankind will characterize the biblical narrative from this point forward. In fact, the promise of this text will eventually form part of the background for the profound shift of the declaration from the first to the third person in the promise of the coming of Immanuel (Isa. 7:14), which the New Testament writers see as a prophecy of the advent of Jesus Christ.[16]

The narrative now moves to the pivotal point in the conversation. Moses indicates that his task in leading Israel out of Egypt will require that Israel acknowledge his leadership. To this end, he will need to be able to tell the people the name of the God who has sent him. In response to Moses' query, "What shall I say to them?" (v. 13), Yahweh offers three self-identifying designations: "I AM WHO I AM" (*'ehyeh 'aser 'ehyeh* [v. 14a]), I AM (*'ehyeh* [v. 14b]) and, reminiscent of his initial self-designation but now adding the divine name, "Yahweh, the God of your ancestors, the God of Abraham, the God of Isaac, and the God of Jacob" (v. 15).

Moses' query raises the preliminary exegetical question of why knowing the divine name was deemed to be so important. One proposal theorizes that he is anticipating being interrogated by the Israelites about whether God truly is able to intervene on their behalf. Durham explicates this perspective:

> What Moses asks, then, has to do with whether God can accomplish what he is promising. What is there in his reputation that lends credibility to the claim in his call? How, suddenly, can he be expected to deal with a host of powerful Egyptian deities against whom, across so many years, he has apparently won no victory for his people? The Israelites in Egypt, oppressed savagely across many years and crying out with no letup to their God, have every reason to want to know, "What can *He* do?"—or perhaps better, "What *can* He do?"[17]

In this case, the divine name could reveal the character and power of the God who promises to liberate his people.

---

15. Ronald E. Clements, *Exodus*, Cambridge Bible Commentary (Cambridge: Cambridge University Press, 1972), 21.

16. For a similar connection, see Knight, *Theology as Narration*, 22.

17. Durham, *Exodus*, 38.

A second possibility is that Moses is anticipating that the Israelites will question his status as the messenger of the God of the fathers. In such a situation, knowing the divine name would provide him with the credentials he needs. His knowledge of God's character as revealed in the divine name would substantiate that Moses enjoys a special relationship or close bond with the God of the patriarchs.[18] Or by means of his disclosure of the divine name, Moses would be able to demonstrate that he has been sent by the God of the fathers, for he is thereby able to show the people that he has received a new revelation from the ancestral God regarding his saving activity, which revelation is confirmed and summed up in the disclosure of a new title for this God.[19] As Fretheim explains, "The assumption seems to be that, if Moses has been commissioned to bring the people out of Egypt, Moses should have a divine name commensurate with this new development in God's relationship with Israel."[20]

Underlying both of these suggestions is a particular understanding of the significance of names. The ancient Semite peoples believed that names were closely, even essentially, related to their bearers. In fact, a name was deemed to indicate the nature and character of, or at least the power connected to, its bearer. This connection was viewed as especially important in situations in which a person believed that he or she had come into contact with a deity. Ancient people accepted without question the idea that they were surrounded by divine powers which determined their lives. Furthermore, they were convinced that gaining the name of a particular deity was beneficial, in that by so doing they would be in a position to call upon the power of the deity.[21] In wanting to know the name of the God who had spoken out of the burning bush, therefore, Moses, and by extension the Israelites, would be seeking a means by which they might call upon the deity who had appeared to his servant and had promised to bring them out of bondage in Egypt.

Regardless of which of these dynamics might be at work in the narrative, what is crucial for our purposes is Yahweh's response to Moses' request.

The Meaning of the I AM Self-Designation

Moses' query elicits a declaration of the divine name, "Yahweh." But Yahweh prefaces this enunciation by voicing a statement that appears to encapsulate a description to which the name is to be linked, "I AM WHO I AM" (*'ehyeh 'aser 'ehyeh*). This declaration comprises the only attempt in

---

18. Houtman, *Exodus*, 1:366.

19. R. Alan Cole, *Exodus: An Introduction and Commentary*, Tyndale Old Testament Commentaries, ed. D. J. Wiseman (Downers Grove, IL: InterVarsity Press, 1973), 69.

20. Fretheim, *Exodus*, 63.

21. For a discussion of this belief and its application to Exod. 3:14, see Hyatt, "Commentary on Exodus," 75; Gerhard von Rad, *Theology of the Old Testament*, trans. D. M. G. Stalker, 2 vols. (New York: Harper & Row, 1962, 1965), 1:181–82; Schmidt, *Faith of the Old Testament*, 53.

the Old Testament to provide insight into the significance of the divine name. Moreover, with the possible exception of Hosea 1:9, the sentence in Exodus 3:14 is never invoked in the Old Testament.[22]

The most immediately evident feature of the sentence itself is its repetition of the verb *'ehyeh*. Some commentators (but by no means all[23]) deem this to be an example of a Hebrew syntactical construction known as *idem per idem*. In this construction, which is found several times in Exodus (e.g., 4:13; 16:23; 33:19) as well as in other Old Testament texts (e.g., 1 Sam. 23:13; 2 Sam. 15:20; 2 Kgs. 8:1; Ezek. 12:25), the verb of a main clause is repeated in a relative clause. The *idem per idem* construction indicates that the writer (or speaker) is being intentionally indefinite or imprecise, because he or she is either unwilling or unable to be definite or precise,[24] or is seeking to express something that cannot be defined more closely.[25]

The enigmatic character of the divine declaration, evidenced by the *idem per idem* construction, has led a few exegetes to conclude that Yahweh's response indicates an unwillingness to comply with Moses' request by being intentionally evasive. Some proponents of this view speculate that Yahweh's refusal to answer the question directly may be due to the fact that the divine nature, being incomprehensible or incomparable, cannot be fully expressed in a name.[26] In keeping with this idea, Richard Coggins suggests that the best reading of Yahweh's response "is to see here an element of the reaction found in the other theophanies, a refusal to let mere humans know the name and thereby too much of the character of God."[27] Houtman, in turn, draws from the Hebrew syntactical construction to conclude that the sentence could be rendered, "I am whosoever I am" or "What does it matter who I am?"[28] He then expands the interpretation, suggesting that God is in effect saying to Moses, "I am so great and so incomparable that what I am cannot be articulated in a single term; it cannot be expressed by a name; do not ask concerning his name; one cannot speak about me at the level of 'What is his name?'"[29] Other exegetes theorize that Yahweh's hesitation arises out of his desire to prevent humans from acquiring the power or control over him that knowing his name

22. Hyatt, "Commentary on Exodus," 78.

23. See, for example, the alternative proposed in E. Schild, "On Exodus 3:14—'I am that I am,'" in *Vetus Testamentum* 4 (1954): 296–304. For a rebuttal of this position, see Peter R. Ackroyd and Barnabas Lindars, eds., *Words and Meanings: Essays Presented to David Winton Thomas on His Retirement from the Regius Professorship of Hebrew in the University of Cambridge, 1968* (London: Cambridge University Press, 1968), 15–28.

24. Hyatt, "Commentary on Exodus," 75–76.

25. Martin Noth, *Exodus: A Commentary*, trans. J. S. Bowden (Philadelphia: Westminster, 1962), 45.

26. See, for example, Roy L. Honeycutt, Jr., "Exodus," in *The Broadman Bible Commentary*, ed. Clifton J. Allen, 12 vols. (Nashville: Broadman, 1969–1972), 1:315.

27. Richard Coggins, *The Book of Exodus* (Peterborough, UK: Epworth, 2000), 18.

28. Houtman, *Exodus*, 1:95–96.

29. Ibid., 1:95.

would facilitate. God's declaration to Moses, therefore, could be rendered, "I am who I am, and it is not your business to know my name."[30]

This perspective is surely correct, insofar as it reflects the idea that in his response to Moses, Yahweh intentionally retains his sovereign freedom and prerogatives as the divine one. In keeping with this insight, Gerhard von Rad points out that Yahweh's statement contains an implicit censure of Moses' question. Von Rad then adds, "In giving the information which he does, Jahweh reserves his freedom to himself, a freedom which will be displayed precisely in his being there, in his efficacious presence."[31] Yet as von Rad also indicates, contextual considerations suggest that Yahweh is doing more than censuring Moses. His intention appears to be that of offering Moses insight into the identity of the God who has called him and who promises to deliver Israel. Fretheim points out that the fact that the name "Yahweh" is immediately used in apposition to "the God of your fathers" in verses 15–16 militates against the idea that God is being purposely evasive.[32] But if Yahweh is indeed offering Moses insight into the meaning of the divine name, the problem remains as to the significance of this seemingly strange self-designation.

The perplexity that exegetes sense in their attempt to determine the meaning of the divine self-designation is evident in the fact that a variety of suggestions have emerged for how the statement ought to be rendered. Each of these reflects a particular interpretation of the content of what God thereby discloses to Moses. The standard, traditional, familiar translation of the Hebrew sentence *'ehyeh 'aser 'ehyeh* is simply, "I AM WHO I AM" (e.g., NRSV). The New English Bible, in turn, proposes a variation on this rendering, one that is influenced by the shortening of the sentence to *'ehyeh* that follows in the verse: "I AM; that is who I am." In addition to these, a host of more complex proposals have surfaced. Some give a future sense to the verb, such as "I will be what (who) I will be," "I will be what I intend to be," or perhaps even "I will be who I am/I am who I will be."[33] Others treat the verb as carrying a causative sense: "I will cause to be what I will cause to be" or "I create whatever I create."[34]

As the variety of the proposed translations indicates, the Hebrew text involves grammatically unresolvable uncertainties. One of these has to do with the intended meaning of the word *'aser* that connects the two verbs. This term is a particle of relation with a wide variety of possible meanings, including "who/what," "he who/that which." It also can serve as a conjunction, meaning "that," "so that," "forasmuch as," or "because."[35]

30. Fretheim, *Exodus*, 64.
31. Von Rad, *Theology of the Old Testament*, 1:181–82.
32. Fretheim, *Exodus*, 64.
33. Ibid., 63.
34. D. N. Freeman, "yhwh," in *Theological Dictionary of the Old Testament*, ed. G. Johannes Botterweck and Helmer Ringgren, trans. David E. Green (Grand Rapids: Eerdmans, 1977–), 516.
35. *A Hebrew and English Lexicon of the Old Testament*, ed. Francis Brown, S. R. Driver, and Charles A. Briggs (Oxford: Clarendon, 1962), 81–84.

More difficult, however, are the questions surrounding the verb *'ehyeh*. For example, is it to be treated as a simple qal or as a causative hiphil? The final two suggested translations noted above view the Hebrew verb as a hiphil. This rendering of *'ehyeh* suggests that Exodus 3:14 explicitly links Yahweh with the idea of the Creator God. Despite the sympathetic hearing that this perspective has enjoyed since it was articulated by William R. Arnold and W. F. Albright early in the twentieth century,[36] it has not been able to supplant the older conclusion that the verb is best seen as a qal.[37] In fact, the idea that the verb is a hiphil has been rejected outright by some exegetes,[38] such as Houtman, who dismisses it as a "rather improbable theory."[39]

Even if we conclude that *'ehyeh* is best seen as a qal, we have not yet solved the exegetical problem that the verb poses. Because *'ehyeh* is in the imperfect tense, it refers simply to incomplete action. Hence, it can carry either a present or a future sense. Understanding *'ehyeh* as a future[40] suggests that the statement carries the idea that God is the master of his own destiny and consequently that God's self-disclosure will come in the future, as he is active in the life and history of Moses and Israel.[41] In keeping with this idea, Childs declares, "The formula is paradoxically both an answer and a refusal of an answer. . . . God announces that his intentions will be revealed in his future acts, which he now refuses to explain. . . . God's intention for Moses is an expression of his being God and will be manifest according to his own plan."[42] Similarly, Cole raises the possibility that the sentence means, "I will only be understood by My own subsequent acts and words of revelation." Cole then adds, "This would seem to fit the biblical pattern, for in all subsequent Israelite history God would be known as the One who brought Israel from Egypt (Ex. 20:2)."[43] Martin Noth draws from the indefiniteness of the supposed *idem per idem* construction the conclusion that the sentence entails a certain kind of indefiniteness:

36. See William R. Arnold, "The Divine Name in Exodus 3:14," *Journal of Biblical Literature* 24 (1905): 107–65; W. F. Albright, "The Name Yahweh," *Journal of Biblical Literature* 43 (1924): 370–78. Cf. David N. Freedman, "The Name of the God of Moses," *Journal of Biblical Literature* 79 (1960): 152; S. Mowinckel, "The Name of the God of Moses," *Hebrew Union College Annual* 32 (1961): 121–33.

37. Even David N. Freeman, who favors the hiphil rendering admits, "Whether the verb was originally a qal or a hiphil formation is not entirely clear." Freeman, "yhwh," 5:500, cf. 513.

38. See, for example, von Rad, *Theology of the Old Testament*, 1:11. See also Walther Eichrodt, *Theology of the Old Testament*, trans. J. A. Baker, 2 vols. (Philadelphia: Westminster, 1961, 1967), 1:189.

39. Houtman, *Exodus*, 1:95.

40. The popularity of this option is evident by the fact that a variant of this translation, "I shall be what I shall be," is simply assumed by Avivah Gottlieb Zornberg, *The Particulars of Rapture: Reflections on Exodus* (New York: Doubleday, 2001), 74.

41. For a statement of his position, see Hyatt, "Commentary on Exodus," 76.

42. Childs, *Book of Exodus*, 76.

43. Cole, *Exodus*, 70.

> Here perhaps the meaning is less one of pure indefiniteness ("I am someone or other"), than of that kind of indefiniteness in which something definite is envisaged but is not meant to be expressed ("I am something, but it will only turn out later what I am"). Most likely, however, that kind of indefiniteness is expressed which leaves open a large number of possibilities ("I am whatever I mean to be").[44]

The kind of open-ended indefiniteness that Noth and others find in the future sense of the verb indicates that the sentence expresses more than a deep theological truth about the God who promises to deliver Israel. It carries as well an implicit call to Moses and the people to respond to the divine promise with trust.[45] Yet, despite the importance of the insight that it implies, to focus solely on the future sense of the verb would be to reduce the meaning of the divine self-disclosure that came to Moses. For this reason, we must invoke the interpretation that has predominated throughout the centuries, namely, the understanding that renders 'ehyeh in the present tense.

Many exegetes are convinced that if the verb is understood in this manner, "I am who I am" becomes "I am the one who is," in keeping with the Septuagint (*ego eimi to on*), and thereby carries the idea that this God is the only one who has real existence. (Alternatively, the sentence might read "I am because I am," that is, the one who is self-caused or for whom there is no cause outside of himself.) Writing in the *Pulpit Commentary*, George Rowlinson reflects this interpretation. In his estimation, the sentence explains the true meaning of the divine name as "'The Alone Existent'—the source of all existence." Rowlinson then explains, "The idea expressed by the name is . . . that of real, perfect, unconditioned, independent existence."[46] Similarly, John J. Davis concludes, "If the simple Qal sense is maintained, it carries the fundamental idea of the self-existence of God, and simply means 'I am the One who is.'"[47]

Despite the impressive pedigree of what has become the traditional view, most contemporary commentators doubt that the sentence can carry such a philosophically oriented understanding. Noth, for example, asserts unequivocally, "The verb *hyh* in Hebrew does not express pure 'being,' pure 'existing' but an 'active being.'"[48] Von Rad is equally adamant:

> Nothing is farther from what is envisaged in this etymology of the name of Jahweh than a definition of his nature in the sense of a philosophical statement about his being . . . a suggestion, for example, of

44. Noth, *Exodus*, 45.

45. For a similar conclusion, see Cole, *Exodus*, 70.

46. George Rawlinson, *Exodus*, 2 vols., in *The Pulpit Commentary*, ed. H. D. M. Spence and Joseph Exell (New York: Funk & Wagnalls, n.d.), 1:57.

47. John J. Davis, *Moses and the Gods of Egypt: Studies in the Book of Exodus* (Grand Rapids: Baker, 1977), 65.

48. Noth, *Exodus*, 45.

his absoluteness, aseity, etc. Such a thing would be altogether out of keeping with the Old Testament. The whole narrative context leads right away to the expectation that Jahweh intends to impart something—but this is not what he is, but what he will show himself to be to Israel.[49]

Hyatt takes the matter a step further, finding the emergence of a near-consensus regarding the text: "Most critics who comment upon this sentence agree that in Hebrew thought the emphasis is not upon pure or abstract being, but rather upon active being and positive manifestation of the Deity in activity. Specifically, the stress is upon God's presence with Moses and Israel; his 'being' is a 'being with,' a divine presence."[50]

As these quotations indicate, contemporary scholars generally conclude that 'ehyeh ought to be understood in an "active," rather than a "static," present sense. Moreover, the imperfect tense of the verb indicates that Yahweh's act is continuous and, in that sense, not yet finished. The continuous present depicted by the verb is one that enfolds past and future into an ongoing present act of be-ing, or "is-ing," to borrow Durham's term.[51] This suggests that the divine existence or "being" conveyed in Yahweh's self-depiction as I AM is dynamic rather than static, conceptual or abstract. We might describe the divine being as a purposeful "being there," a "being present" that is efficacious. By extension, it is an active presence that entails a "being with."

Moreover, Yahweh's continuous act of be-ing entails his active presence in the human realm, above all in the history of Israel.[52] In his promise to Moses, "I will be (I am) with you," Yahweh revealed to his servant that the active be-ing bound up with the name I AM entails his active presence in Moses' unfolding mission. Moses, in turn, is to announce to the Israelites that the God who is active be-ing is also efficaciously present in the midst of their plight (cf. Exod. 2:24–25; 3:7). To the oppressed Israelites in Egypt, Yahweh may have seemed absent, yet he is the God who continuously and actively is, and this active be-ing means that he is indeed present.[53]

Twice in the chapter, Yahweh claims that he is the God of the patriarchs. The inclusion of this epithet is intended to declare that the God who is present with Moses and the Israelites is the one who was also present with the patriarchs. As Werner Schmidt notes, when read in the context of Yahweh's I AM declaration, this claim confirms the all-encompassing nature of the present sense of 'ehyeh. Therefore, as Schmidt rightly observes, the future that is inherent in the Hebrew verb "is not inaugurated later, after

49. Von Rad, *Theology of the Old Testament*, 1:180.
50. Hyatt, "Commentary on Exodus," 75–76.
51. Durham, *Exodus*, 39.
52. Noth, *Exodus*, 45.
53. For a similar idea, see Durham, *Exodus*, 39.

some specific passing of time, but it begins already with—or works its way into—the declaration in the present. Just as in the self-presentation 'I am the God of your fathers' (v. 6) past and present are linked, so also in the promise in v. 14 an unbounded future and the present are seen as a unity."[54]

But there remains an additional significance of Yahweh's claim. "I am," in the sense of "being present," is precisely the explication of the meaning of the name that Yahweh offers Moses in response to his request that the divine name be revealed to him. The mark that identifies the God who commissioned Moses as the God of the patriarchs is in fact given in the meaning of his name as I AM, that is, as "being present." Because Moses can only offer the Israelites the explication of Yahweh as I AM, he is not bringing any new revelation about the character of their God. Nor is he acting on behalf of any other deity than the God of the fathers. Moses is simply confirming to them what the patriarchs had already come to know experientially about their God.[55]

The connection to the past bound up with Yahweh's declaration that as the I am he is the God of the patriarchs provides a final clue to the meaning of the longer divine self-description, 'ehyeh 'aser 'ehyeh. In Yahweh's continuous act of be-ing, an act that confirms him as the God both of the patriarchs and of Israel in Egypt, Yahweh remains always faithful to himself. Not only does Yahweh's act of be-ing involve a pledge to Moses and Israel that "I am [I will be] there (for you),"[56] it entails the promise that "I am [I will be] who I am (for you)." Hence, the addition of the relative clause in the statement indicates that Yahweh is not simply the one who is present, but the one who is *faithfully* present. In his continuous act of being present, Yahweh remains always faithful to his own character. Fretheim captures the essence of this idea: "God will be God with and for the people at all times and places. The formulation suggests a divine faithfulness to self: wherever God is being God, God will be the kind of God God is. . . . God can be counted on to be who God is."[57] Viewed in this light, we might elevate Walther Eichrodt's rendering as the most insightful paraphrase of Yahweh's explication of the divine name: "I am really and truly present, ready to help and to act, as I have always been."[58]

Yet even in stating this point, we dare not lose sight of the kind of indefiniteness in the statement to which Noth has alerted us. What Yahweh has given in the explication of the divine name as I AM, as the one whose active be-ing means his presence with Israel, is merely the promise that his pres-

---

54. Werner H. Schmidt, *Exodus*, vol. 2 of *Biblischer Kommentar Altes Testament*, ed. Siegfried Herrmann, Werner H. Schmidt, and Hans Walter Wolff (Neukirchen-Vluyn: Neukirchener Verlag, 1988), 1:178 (translation mine).

55. Houtman, *Exodus*, 1:95–96.

56. Von Rad, *Theology of the Old Testament*, 1:180.

57. Fretheim, *Exodus*, 63.

58. Eichrodt, *Theology of the Old Testament*, 1:190.

ence in each moment of Israel's history is always faithful to his presence in every other moment, including the moments that make up the proto-history formed by his presence with the patriarchs. As the story unfolds, the Exodus narrative forms an immediate exposition of the I AM of Exodus 3:14,[59] which subsequently overflows into the entire story of Israel, giving texture to the divine name even as the name explicated in this verse shapes that story.[60] But beyond that, the name "Yahweh," understood in the sense of active be-ing or being present, remains the name by which God will be known in the biblical narrative forever, in fulfillment of Yahweh's own intention (Exod. 3:15).

The Revealed Name: "I Am Yahweh"

Yahweh's response to Moses' request moves from the double designation that explicates the name (I AM WHO I AM) and its shorter form (I AM) to the giving of the name itself. Moses is instructed to tell the Israelites that he had been sent by 'EHYEH (I AM), that is, by "Yahweh," the God of the patriarchs. From that point on, the divine declaration, "I am Yahweh," moves to center stage in the narrative of Israel.[61] To an ancient Hebrew audience, the phonic connection between "Yahweh" and I AM would be obvious, for it merely involves a transition from the first-person verbal form to the third.[62]

The close connection between the sound of the two words signals the link between the two designations for the Deity, together with the claim that he is the God of the "fathers." The I AM and, with it, the "I AM WHO I AM" declarations are to form the basis for understanding the meaning of the name. In fact, this meaning is to be taken as inherent in the name itself. Eichrodt observed insightfully, "If the saying *nomina sunt realia* is valid in any context, it is surely that of the divine name in the ancient world."[63] What remains is for us to explore this connection between name and meaning more explicitly.

Meaning and the Origin of the Divine Name

It would appear that the place to begin is with the historical and etymological origins of the divine name. The attempt to determine the meaning of the name through an exploration of the origins of "Yahweh" is hampered, however, by the fact that its origins are shrouded in mystery.

---

59. Walter Brueggemann, *Theology of the Old Testament: Testimony, Dispute, Advocacy* (Minneapolis: Fortress, 1997), 124 n. 17.

60. For a similar idea, see Fretheim, *Exodus*, 63–64.

61. Von Rad notes that the name Yahweh is found "some 6700 times" in the Old Testament. Von Rad, *Theology of the Old Testament*, 1:186.

62. Noth, *Exodus*, 43.

63. Eichrodt, *Theology of the Old Testament*, 1:178.

The presence of the word or of its shorter form (e.g., *yh*, *yhh*, or *yhw*) in extrabiblical writings, names, and inscriptions suggests that the designation is not limited to Israel. In fact, the name "Yahweh," or at least the shorter form of the name,[64] was probably not originally devised by the Hebrews but was in use long before the establishment of Israel as a people (cf. Gen. 4:26). This conclusion has launched some scholars on a quest to discover among other ancient Near Eastern peoples whatever historical source mediated the name to Moses and thereby facilitated him in (re)introducing "Yahweh" to the Hebrews in Egypt. The Exodus narrative itself seems to support this hypothesis. In the second commissioning of Moses, Yahweh declares that the patriarchs had not known him by this name but only as "El Shaddai" (Exod. 6:3).

One widely held proposal is that Yahweh was originally a deity worshiped by the Kenites, who were a clan within the Midianites. Moses, in turn, became acquainted with the worship of Yahweh through his relationship with this clan. This relationship may have come through his father-in-law, who was a Midianite priest, or through his mother, whose name (Jochebed) is a compound in which "Yahweh" forms a component.[65] Another theory finds a clue in Yahweh's declaration to Moses, "I am the God of your father" (Exod. 3:6; cf. 15:2; 18:4), read in the light of the ancient practice of worshiping patron deities. In ancient times, particular deities would become patrons of specific patriarchs by revealing themselves to them. When a son, in turn, followed in this worship, the patron deity became known as "the god of my father."[66] Yahweh, the theory postulates, was originally the patron god of one of Moses' ancestors.[67] At that time, he was likely known as "Yahweh-A" (with "A" symbolizing the name of this unknown ancestor), a name that means, "He causes A to live" or "the Sustainer of A." Yahweh later became the deity of the clan of Moses and, through Moses, of Israel. During this process, the ancestor's name was dropped, and Israel's god came to be known simply as "Yahweh."

Other exegetes attempt to gain insight into the meaning of the name "Yahweh" by seeking its etymological rather than historical roots. One such proposal looks to the root *hwh* ("fall"), which is found frequently in the Aramaic and Arabic dialects.[68] This connection can possibly suggest that the name carries the meaning "the one who blows away or causes to fall" (i.e., "the hurler of lightning"). In this way, Yahweh comes to be char-

64. For the question as to which form is older, see Eichrodt, *Theology of the Old Testament*, 1:187–89; and von Rad, *Theology of the Old Testament*, 1:10.
65. For a short discussion of this theory, see Houtman, *Exodus*, 1:96–97. See also Davidson, *Theology of the Old Testament*, 50–53.
66. For an explication of this practice, see Albrecht Alt, *Essays on Old Testament History and Religion*, trans. R. A. Wilson (Oxford: Blackwell, 1966), 1–66.
67. For a longer exposition of this theory, see Hyatt, "Commentary on Exodus," 79–80.
68. Noth, *Exodus*, 44.

acterized as a weather god or a storm god.[69] More likely is the view that links the stem *hwh* to the Hebrew root *hwy*, later *hyh*, which is often rendered "be at hand," "exist" (phenomenally), or "come to pass."[70] The strength of this possible connection has led many commentators to conclude that "Yahweh" is a verbal form of this root, so that its basic meaning is, "He is." Noth proposes a variant on this theme. Although the verbal meaning is likely reflected in Exodus 3:14, he theorizes, the name was perhaps originally a noun formed by the addition of the prefix *ya* being added to the root *hwh*, which suggests the meaning "the being one."[71]

Many commentators question whether either of these approaches can in fact shed light on the significance of the divine name. Some are convinced that because the actual derivation and meaning of "Yahweh" are unknown, the connection that the Exodus narrator makes between the name and the verb *hyh* is not intended to be an actual account of the name's origin, but a wordplay that serves to connect a meaning to the name.[72] Indeed, Schmidt points out that "if the name Yahweh was already in existence and taken over by the Old Testament, its basic meaning may have been unintelligible for a long time back."[73] Clements, in turn, explains, "Most probably the author of the account did not know its real origin, and simply used its similarity in sound and appearance to the Hebrew verb 'to be' as a point to be explained. This he does by allowing God to introduce himself as the great 'I AM.'"[74] Childs takes the matter a step further:

> An alternative solution is to take seriously Israel's own tradition when it interprets the divine name in a manner which is in striking discontinuity with the Ancient Near Eastern parallels. Such a view would certainly recognize the Ancient Near Eastern cognates of the divine name and even reckon with a long prehistory of the name before its entrance into Israel, but it remains open to the possibility that a totally new meaning was attached to the name by Israel.[75]

Finally, Eichrodt points in the direction in which that new meaning was to emerge: "In Israel there was less interest in the etymological significance of the divine name than in the concrete content which it conveyed, and which was to be deduced from quite a different source, namely the demonstrations in history of the power of its owner."[76]

---

69. For this possibility, see Schmidt, *Faith of the Old Testament*, 59. Schmidt does not consider this to be the best interpretation. He adds, "In the end, the simplest solution seems to be most likely: 'he is, shows himself, is at work.'"

70. Freeman, "yhwh," 5:500, cf. 513.

71. Noth, *Exodus*, 44 n.

72. For this view, see Davidson, *Theology of the Old Testament*, 45–46, 53–55.

73. Schmidt, *Faith of the Old Testament*, 58–59.

74. Clements, *Exodus*, 23.

75. Childs, *Exodus*, 64.

76. Eichrodt, *Theology of the Old Testament*, 1:187.

The Meaning of the Giving of the Divine Name

A "new meaning" of the name "Yahweh" does indeed unfold, as the God of Israel demonstrates his power in the narrative of this people. Yet we would be mistaken if we were to see in the biblical story the development of "a totally new meaning." At least we could not draw this conclusion from the Exodus narrative. The goal of the narrator is clearly not that of arguing for complete discontinuity between the Mosaic worship of Yahweh and the faith of the fathers. This is the case even in Exodus 6:3, which in a sense provides a fuller delineation of what is inherent in the divine name disclosed to Moses at the burning bush. The narrator's overarching concern in this text remains the same as that evidenced in Exodus 3, namely, claiming that Yahweh is none other than the God of the patriarchs.

The mention of the name "El Shaddai" in Exodus 6:3 recalls the incident in which Yahweh appeared to Abraham as El Shaddai (Gen. 17:1) and entered into a covenant with him and his offspring. This covenant included the promise that El Shaddai would "be God" to Abraham and to his offspring, that he would give the land of Canaan to them, and that he would "be their God" (vv. 7–8). According to the Exodus narrator, the covenant made with the patriarchs is not only still in effect, but, more importantly, it is now about to be fulfilled. The covenanting God is about to act in history in delivering Israel from bondage in Egypt and then in bringing the people into the promised land.[77] In fact, the narrator points out that the unfolding of covenant has already begun in that the covenanting God has already heard the sighing of the Israelites and has remembered the covenant (Exod. 3:5). Moreover, in the subsequent instruction to Moses as to what he should say about the God who has reiterated his call to his servant, Yahweh repeats the central feature of the covenant that had been made with Abraham, "I will take you as my people and I will be your God," and then adds, "You shall know that I am Yahweh your God" (v. 7).

The change in names declared in Exodus 6:3 and 7, therefore, marks a new stage in the divine program with Abraham and his offspring. El Shaddai, the promising God, is now to be known as Yahweh, the God who remembers the covenant and acts to bring the covenantal promise to completion.[78] Houtman, therefore, is surely correct when he concludes regarding this text that

> it is unlikely that in 6:3 the author/editor of Exodus aimed to notify readers concerning how the name YHWH became known. The conception rooted in the pre-critical phase of biblical exegesis, which holds that God did not make his name known to Moses, but told him instead that from now on He would manifest himself with other qualities than was the case during the period of the patriarchs, does

77. For a similar perspective on this verse, see Durham, *Exodus*, 74; Childs, *Exodus*, 113–14.
78. For a similar understanding, see Childs, *Exodus*, 114–15.

the most justice to the text of Exodus in its present form. God manifested himself to the fathers as El Shaddai, as the one who made promises (Gen. 17:1ff.; 35:11ff.; cf. 28:3f.; 48:3f.). As YHWH, He acts to accomplish those promises.[79]

At the same time, viewed from another perspective, we might say that Yahweh's ongoing relationship with Israel does reveal something new. In this saga, Yahweh discloses further the significance of the divine name, yet always in keeping with the revelation given to Moses at the burning bush. A question that often forms the basis for new (or further) disclosures of what is inherent in the divine name concerns whether or not Yahweh chooses to remain true to his own nature as the "be-ing one," that is, as the one who is present with Israel.

This characteristic of the biblical story is exemplified by a telling incident in the Exodus narrative (Exod. 33:12–23) that occurs soon after Israel's great apostasy in creating a golden calf for cultic worship. At issue in this text is whether or not Yahweh will go with Israel as they leave Sinai. The theme of the divine presence is introduced by Yahweh's declaration that he will not accompany the Israelites as they depart for the promised land (v. 3). This theme is reiterated as in response to Moses' entreaty that he remember that Israel is his people (v. 13) Yahweh revokes the threat: "My presence will go with you, and I will give you rest" (v. 14). Then, desirous of a sign assuring him that Yahweh will truly be present in Israel's ongoing story, Moses requests that he might see the divine glory (v. 18), a term which in the Old Testament "is a recognized way of expressing the divine presence," as Coggins points out.[80] This evokes Yahweh's response: "I will make all my goodness pass before you, and will proclaim before you the name, 'Yahweh,'" which is followed by the cryptic assertion, "and I will be gracious to whom I will be gracious, and will show mercy on whom I will show mercy" (v. 19).

The shift in terminology from "glory" to "goodness" is significant. More important for Moses than a manifestation of Yahweh's appearance is that he learn what kind of a God Yahweh is. To this end, Yahweh declares that he will reveal to Moses the depth of the character of the one who has promised his presence, a declaration that suggests that God's glory is bound up with his character as the one who is fully good. Yahweh adds that his self-disclosure will include speaking the divine name, which in this case is linked to compassion. Regarding this verse, Childs notes, "The name of God, which like his glory and his face are vehicles of his essential nature, is defined in terms of his compassionate acts of mercy."[81] The pronouncing of the name "Yahweh" becomes the means by which God

79. Houtman, *Exodus*, 1:101–2.
80. Coggins, *Book of Exodus*, 123.
81. Childs, *Exodus*, 596.

confirms that he will be gracious to Israel despite the apostasy of his people. Consequently, Moses must use his ears, as well as his eyes, to gain the assurance that he desires.

The connection between the divine name and compassion is repeated in the incident that follows next in the narrative. Moses returns to Mount Sinai to receive the commandments that Yahweh will write on stone tablets. Upon Moses' arrival at the top of the mountain, Yahweh descends from a cloud, stands with his servant, and again declares the divine name: "Yahweh, Yahweh, a God merciful [compassionate] and gracious, slow to anger, and abounding in steadfast love and faithfulness" (Exod. 34:6). The declaration that Yahweh abounds in love and is filled with compassion is found so often (e.g., Neh. 9:17; Ps. 86:15; 103:8; 111:4; 116:5; 145:8; Joel 2:13; Jonah 4:2; Isa. 54:10) that it forms a central theological theme of the Old Testament. Williston Walker concludes regarding this formula, "Nothing therefore is more prominent in the OT than the ascription of compassion, pity, mercy, etc., to God; the people may be said to have gloried in it."[82] The ever new disclosure of the compassionate character of the presence of Yahweh, therefore, forms as a crucial dimension of the narrative of the ongoing revelation of the meaning of the divine name.

If these observations are correct, the genius of Exodus 3:14 may well lie less in any supposed connection to the actual etymological roots of the name that it supposedly brings to the surface than in the link drawn here between the divine name and the Hebrew verb that denotes active be-ing and dynamic presence. The ongoing drama of the story of Israel, beginning with the deliverance from Egypt and the entrance into Canaan, becomes the theater in which the name—and hence the character—of Yahweh unfolds. But what comes to the fore in this ongoing drama is the continual presence of the one who was already present with the patriarchs and hence whose very name denotes such a never-ending and hence covenant-remembering presence.

Herein, then, lies the unity of name and reality. As the divine name, "Yahweh" already contains who Yahweh "is." Whether it is etymologically or merely phonetically connected to *hyh*, the wordplay in Exodus 3:14 is meant to announce that Yahweh is the one who "is." The repeated self-designation "I am Yahweh" entails the claim, "I am the one who is." And this "is" involves active be-ing, active presence in every moment of the ongoing saga of God's history with Israel.

The act of giving the divine name carries yet an additional significance. This act invokes and evokes relationship. Just as withholding one's name reflects an unwillingness to enter into relationship and, in fact, precludes true relationship, so also giving one's name invites and fosters relation-

82. W. L. Walker, "Compassion," in *International Standard Bible Encyclopedia*, rev. ed., ed. Geoffrey W. Bromiley, 4 vols. (Grand Rapids: Eerdmans, 1979), 1:755.

ship. In giving the divine name to Moses and by extension to Israel, Yahweh links himself to his people and to their story.[83] The reciting of the divine name, in turn, becomes both an expression of gratitude for past experiences of the divine presence and a petition for this presence in the here and now.

The Reiteration of the Divine Name

Despite its glorious beginning, the story of Israel, and with it the saga of the I AM, did not unfold smoothly. On the contrary, the history of the relationship between Yahweh and Israel might be described as a drama in three scenes, which in turn forms act 1 of the larger drama of the I AM. Scene 1 of this first act focuses on the joyous revelation of the divine name to a people in whose history Yahweh desires to reveal his very identity as the one whose be-ing entails being present with them. The glorious first scene, however, soon draws to a close. And the tragedy to which it gives way in scene 2 is in one sense wholly unexpected. Yet perhaps even more unexpected, at least when viewed from the human perspective, is the final scene of act 1, with which the Old Testament half of the drama of the I AM draws to a close. In these two scenes the divine name comes to be reiterated. This reiteration occurs as the I AM revokes his name but then revokes this revocation.

The Revoking of the Divine Name: "Not Your I AM"

Exodus 6:3 portrays Yahweh as recalling that as El Shaddai, he had entered into a covenant with Abraham and his offspring in which he promised that he would "be God" to them, that he would give the land of Canaan to them, and that he would "be their God" (Gen. 17:1, 7–8). The covenanting God then reaffirms this promise to the Israelites in Egypt immediately prior to his intervention on their behalf: "I will take you as my people and I will be your God" (Exod. 6:7). In this manner, the text becomes an extension or elaboration of the declaration of the meaning of the divine name revealed in Exodus 3:14. Read in the light of its expansion in Exodus 33:19 (and elsewhere), Yahweh's self-disclosure at the time of the call of Moses presents the divine name as indicating that Yahweh is the I AM, the one who is present—compassionately—with his people at each point along their journey.

Lodged within three chapters that Francis Andersen and David Freedman describe as "an elaborate *recapitulatio* of the Exodus,"[84] Hosea 1:2–9

83. For a somewhat similar suggestion, see Fretheim, *Exodus*, 65.

84. Francis I. Andersen and David Noel Freedman, *Hosea: A New Translation with Introduction and Commentary*, Anchor Bible (Garden City, NY: Doubleday, 1980), 131.

is possibly the only place in the entire Old Testament in which the sentence in Exodus 3:14 is explicitly invoked.[85] Yet its invocation here is not for the purpose of reaffirming the validity of the divine name in Israel's experience. On the contrary, it is invoked so that it might be revoked. In this text, Yahweh declares that because of Israel's sin, the relationship between the people and their God has changed. In response to Israel's sin, Yahweh—"the one who is"—no longer is I AM.

The Context: The Relationship between Israel and Yahweh

That the Israelites were unfaithful covenant partners of Yahweh was not a new development in the eighth century BC. National apostasy did not suddenly emerge during the course of Hosea's lifetime. On the contrary, throughout the history of the nation, Israel had proven to be a wayward and stiff-necked people. As a result, prophets had repeatedly decried Israel's sin and idolatry, and had warned them that Yahweh would not tolerate forever their breech of the covenant. The new development that does emerge in the story of Israel in the eighth century is God's decision to deal with his covenant people through divine judgment by ejecting them from the land of promise. Hosea, the only "writing prophet" of the northern kingdom,[86] is one of those voices who find themselves called to be the heralds of impending doom.[87] Indeed, as Douglas Stuart declares with a hint of understatement, "Because of the characteristics of (northern) Israel in the mid-eighth century B.C., God's prophetic word could hardly have been predominately positive."[88]

The mention of Hezekiah in the opening verse of the book implies that Hosea's prophetic ministry continued at least until the final years before the fall of Samaria.[89] His initial message, however, was not merely negative but may have focused on a call for national repentance with the hope of avoiding the threatened disaster (2:2–3). In any case, he came to see that such a severe judgment was not only inevitable but could even become the occasion for a recapitulation of the ancient exodus story, in which Yahweh revives his people and enters again into covenant with them.

The feature of worship in Israel that drew Hosea's fire was epitomized in the practice of referring to Yahweh as "my Baal" (2:16). Insofar as *ba'al*

---

85. The suggestion that Hosea 1:9 is an allusion to Exod. 3:14 dates at least to W. Robertson Smith, *The Prophets of Israel and Their Place in History to the Close of the Eighth Century B.C.: Eight Lectures* (New York: D. Appleton, 1882), 388.

86. For this designation, see von Rad, *Theology of the Old Testament*, 2:139.

87. For a succinct description of the eighth-century prophets, see Andersen and Freedman, *Hosea*, 40–44.

88. Douglas Stuart, *Hosea-Jonah*, Word Biblical Commentary (Waco, TX: Word, 1987), 7.

89. G. I. Davies, *Hosea*, New Century Bible Commentary (Grand Rapids: Eerdmans, 1992), 24–25. For a more detailed discussion of the dates of Hosea's ministry, see Andersen and Freedman, *Hosea*, 147–49.

was a common Hebrew term for "lord" or "husband," it might have gained credence as an attractive vehicle for expressing reverence for and devotion to Yahweh. Moreover, at one stage in Canaanite history, the term was a generic word that could designate any deity. In Hosea's estimation, however, the designation was tainted beyond repair, because it was encumbered with pagan Canaanite religious overtones.[90] Not only had *ba'al* come to be used in a narrower sense to refer to the various gods of the Canaanites, but it functioned as the actual name of the most prominent of the Canaanite gods.[91]

The Canaanite religion that proved to be such a strong rival to the worship of Yahweh centered on a mythical understanding of the source of fertility and life.[92] The Canaanites believed that fertility in Palestine was dependent on the high god (or *ba'al*), Hadad, the god of storm and rain. This Baal Hadad was believed to be manifested as local baals at cult places throughout the country. Through them, Hadad supposedly impregnated the land, or perhaps a mother earth goddess, by means of rain that caused the earth to produce crops, and he caused humans to produce offspring as well. Worshipers at the religious cites could coax Baal to bestow fertility by reenacting the copulation between the fertility god and the land. Aspects of Baal worship such as these no doubt were instrumental in leading Hosea to see that the use of the language of *ba'al* among Israelites and the intrusion of elements of Canaanite cult practices into the worship life of Israel, whose God was Yahweh, was a sign of a syncretistic acceptance of an alien religion.[93] In fact, this kind of syncretism led to what Hans Walter Wolff aptly calls "a 'Baalization' of Yahweh himself."[94]

Despite the theological errors that Hosea saw in the Canaanite cult, the incorporation of *ba'al* into the worshiping life of Israel provided the motif—paternal or conjugal love—into which the prophet translated the meaning of the covenant between Yahweh and Israel that had played such a crucial role in determining the self-identity of the nation throughout its history. The cult of Baal had an idea of God as love, but understood it in sexual terms. Hosea was able to salvage from this mistaken perspective the realization that Yahweh resembled an aggrieved yet faithful husband who yearns for his covenant partner[95] (as well as a heartbroken but steadfast

90. For a discussion of the struggle between Yahwism and Baalism, see von Rad, *Theology of the Old Testament*, 1:25–30.

91. For this array of meanings, see Henry McKeating, *The Books of Amos, Hosea, and Micah*, Cambridge Bible Commentary (Cambridge: Cambridge University Press, 1971), 86–87.

92. For a helpful summary of Canaanite myth, see Elizabeth Achtemeier, *Minor Prophets I*, New International Biblical Commentary (Peabody, MA: Hendrickson, 1996), 15. See also Roy L. Honeycutt, Jr., "Hosea," in *Broadman Bible Commentary*, 7:3–4.

93. For this conclusion, see Andersen and Freedman, *Hosea*, 169.

94. Hans Walter Wolff, *Hosea: A Commentary on the Book of the Prophet Hosea*, trans. Gary Stansell, ed. Paul D. Hanson (Philadelphia: Fortress, 1974), 16.

95. For a similar depiction, see McKeating, *Books of Amos, Hosea, and Micah*, 71–73.

father), which the prophet placed within a larger context of an ongoing love story between Yahweh and the covenant people whom he loves.[96] As David Allan Hubbard explains, "Hosea's answer to the harlotry with the Baals was not a prudish rejection of the love relationship but an absolute claim to it. It was not the *love* that was wrong, nor the symbolic marriage to deity; it was the ritual prostitution in which the relationship was expressed."[97]

This marked, however, a decisive step—indeed, a radical innovation—in ancient Hebrew theology. Until the eighth century the promoters of Yahwism had avoided sexual motifs in speaking about God.[98] Hosea, in contrast, appropriated the myth of the divine marriage as a way of telling the story of Yahweh's relationship to Israel. In so doing, he became the first of the prophets to elevate marriage as a fitting symbol for the relationship between Yahweh and Israel.[99] At the same time, he was also the first to articulate the related idea that Israel's acceptance of the Canaanite mythical nature religion was "harlotry."[100] Hubbard underscores the significance that the first of these twin aspects of Hosea's message carried:

> No-one before had spoken so repeatedly of God's love (*'hb*) for his people, and no-one had cast divine grace in the vocabulary of marital intimacy. Neither the realm of international treaties nor of mercantile contracts gave adequate depth, breadth, length and height to the love of God. Only the realm of the family, which Hosea knew at its worst in his marriage and sensed at its best in his understanding of God's constancy, could do that.[101]

Yet in the process of appropriating the Canaanite motif, Hosea drastically altered its central features. Thereby he sought to direct Israel away from the mythical perspective regarding fertility that was indicative of the Baal cult. The giver of life, he averred, is not a mythical nature deity, but the God who had entered into covenant with Israel and had journeyed with them throughout their history since delivering them from bondage in Egypt. Furthermore, Yahweh's marriage partner is not some mythical female goddess, Hosea declared, but the historical nation of Israel. Moreover, he added, the marriage relationship that Yahweh enjoys with the land/nation is not physical but moral in character.[102] In this manner, Hosea shifted the context in which the relationship between Yahweh and Israel was to be understood

---

96. For a delineation of this story, see Achtemeier, *Minor Prophets I*, 3–4.

97. David Allan Hubbard, *Hosea: An Introduction and Commentary*, Tyndale Old Testament Commentaries (Leichester, UK: InterVarsity Press, 1989), 29.

98. See, for example, von Rad, *Theology of the Old Testament*, 1:27.

99. For this observation, see Honeycutt, "Hosea," 9.

100. Von Rad, *Theology of the Old Testament*, 2:142.

101. Hubbard, *Hosea*, 29.

102. For this conclusion, see James M. Ward, *Hosea: A Theological Commentary* (New York: Harper & Row, 1966), 11–12.

away from the magical realm connected to the cycles of nature. In its stead, he elevated the historical events involving Yahweh and the nation,[103] as well as the moral structure of the historical covenant.[104] As James Luther Mays aptly concludes, "Nature is pre-empted by history as the sphere of God's action."[105]

The Divine Revocation

Hosea's own relationship with Gomer and his experience in raising children provided him with an intimate, firsthand perspective that provided the basis for his message to the nation. Regarding this connection, Roy Honeycutt observes, "Seldom is the revelation of God mediated through such depth of personal anguish and suffering."[106] The opening chapter of the book encapsulates the sad tale of this aspect of the prophet's life. The theme is picked up again in the third chapter.

Exegetical uncertainties abound in these two texts, as well as in the three chapters of Hosea of which they are a significant part. James Ward notes that these chapters "have probably provoked more discussion than any other segments of the prophetic literature, except perhaps the oracles concerning Immanuel and the Suffering Servant." He then explains, "One of the reasons for this massive interest is the theological importance of the material."[107]

One crucial exegetical question concerns the relationship between the two stories.[108] Do they narrate different events involving different women? Do they refer to two stages in Hosea's relationship to Gomer, and if so, in what order did they occur?[109] Or do the two narratives simply recount the same events? Equally difficult is the question regarding the nature of Hosea's relationship to Gomer. G. I. Davies, for example, suggests that Hosea became a client of a prostitute named Gomer and procreated children with her outside of marriage. This historical reconstruction, in turn, leads to the conclusion that the prophet represents Baal, not Yahweh, in the religious drama to which the narrative points.[110] More widely held is the view that Hosea married Gomer. But this conclusion leads to the subsequent question of whether her immorality had already occurred prior to the marriage,[111] and if so whether Hosea was aware of

103. For this perspective, see Achtemeier, *Minor Prophets I*, 15.

104. For a similar observation, see James Luther Mays, *Hosea: A Commentary* (Philadelphia: Westminster, 1969), 9.

105. Mays, *Hosea*, 11.

106. Honeycutt, "Hosea," 1.

107. Ward, *Hosea*, 8–9.

108. For a helpful summary of the options, see McKeating, *Books of Amos, Hosea, and Micah*, 75–77.

109. For this view, see Achtemeier, *Minor Prophets I*, 6.

110. Davies, *Hosea*, 50–51, 108.

111. For this view, see Achtemeier, *Minor Prophets I*, 5.

it.[112] It is also possible that Gomer commenced her wayward ways only after their union was consummated.[113] Also left undisclosed in the text is the exact nature of her immorality. Was it connected to the rituals surrounding the worship of the Canaanite fertility god,[114] perhaps involving a marriage-initiatory fertility rite introduced into Israelite worship from Canaanite practices?[115] Or did it entail overt promiscuity or adultery,[116] albeit possibly within the context of officially approved Baal worship?[117] Fortunately, finding answers to such questions, while not irrelevant to the exegetical task, is not a prerequisite to gaining a sense of the central message of the text.[118]

Although the focus of Hosea 1:2–9 is on the human actors, the active agent in the drama narrated in the chapter is neither the prophet nor Gomer, but Yahweh. Four times in the text Yahweh speaks, instructing his prophet to engage in a prophetic action. The initial instruction sets the stage for what follows. Hosea is to take "a wife of whoredom" and to raise children, an act that symbolizes the "great whoredom" being committed by "the land" in forsaking Yahweh (v. 2). The subsequent imperatives relate to the symbolic naming of the three children whose births follow in succession.

Yahweh commands Hosea to name his first child, a son, Jezreel (vv. 4–5). The name itself is composed of the imperfect of the verb *zare'* ("to sow") plus *'el*, the word for "God." Hence, the word means "God will sow" or "God will scatter seed."[119] Jezreel was also the name of both a town and a particularly fertile valley located in the northern kingdom, whose beauty had been marred by several bloody battles and other acts of violence. The name Jezreel, therefore, had come to carry deep emotive overtones in eighth-century Israel. Hosea's prophecy anticipates that Jezreel will soon witness another military conflict. But this time it will involve an event of judgment that will spell the end of the northern kingdom itself. Moreover, because of its phonetic similarity to the word "Israel" (*yizre'el* versus *yisra'el*), Jezreel forms a wordplay that suggests that the giving of this name to Hosea's son does not merely entail a prophecy regarding the specific place that shares the name. It also symbolizes the nation as a whole that is ripe for judgment.

The names of the second and third children, beginning as they do with the negative particle *lo'*, form a stark contrast to the general practice in

---

112. McKeating, *Books of Amos, Hosea, and Micah*, 77.
113. For this view, see Andersen and Freedman, *Hosea*, 116.
114. For an exposition of this alternative, see Achtemeier, *Minor Prophets I*, 15.
115. Wolff, *Hosea*, 13–15.
116. For a defense of this conclusion, see Andersen and Freedman, *Hosea*, 157–67.
117. Andersen and Freedman, *Hosea*, 116.
118. For this judgment, see Stuart, *Hosea-Jonah*, 11.
119. Hubbard, *Hosea*, 62.

Israel to give children positive names.[120] The second child is to receive the ominous name *lo' ruhamah*—"Not pitied" or "No compassion." The word is a perfect tense, pual verb that implies a completed act of rejection occurring at some past point in time. This suggests that beyond the basic meaning, "She is not pitied," the name carries the idea, "She has been expelled from a relationship of compassion" or even "of love."[121]

A few exegetes speculate that the giving of this name, when seen in the light of the absence of any reference to Hosea as the girl's father, suggests that the prophet did not recognize this child as his own offspring.[122] In any case, the name displays an unmistakable illusion to Israel's cherished belief that their God acts toward them with the compassionate care drawn from a deep love that a father extends toward his children (cf. Ps. 103:13). By commanding Hosea to name Gomer's daughter "Not pitied," Yahweh is voicing a sharp critique of the presumption that had come to characterize the nation. More significantly, he is announcing a change in his attitude toward his people. Compassion or pity, Yahweh declares, is now giving way to judgment. In this sense, Yahweh is revoking the compassionate presence with Israel that ever since his appearance to Moses (Exod. 33:19) he had shown to be inherent in his name.

The most poignant of the names that Hosea gives to Gomer's children, however, is the third. Yahweh commands the prophet to name the third child "Not my people" (*lo' 'ammi* [v. 9]). The gravity of this name ought not to be overlooked. Andersen and Freedman point out that "'My people' was perhaps the most beloved title conferred on Israel by Yahweh," who "was acclaimed with pride as 'our God.'"[123] The name of Gomer's second son signals that the relationship between Yahweh and Israel has completely unraveled. Israel has been acting as if they are not God's people, and in response Yahweh now declares that he is no longer their God. The relationship that dates to the exodus has been completely breached. Elizabeth Achtemeier summarizes the grave reality that is involved in this divine pronouncement: "Yahweh, the God of the covenant, upon whom Israel's very life depends, is declaring his covenant bond null and void, divorcing his wife Israel, deserting his beloved people. There can be no other outcome of that word of God than the death of Israel."[124] James Limburg, in turn, indicates the gravity of Israel's situation by noting the "terrifying progression" in the sequence of the three names: "The first announced a future when Israel would have to live without a king, the second a future without God's compassion, and the third a future without God."[125]

120. Stuart, *Hosea-Jonah*, 31.

121. Andersen and Freedman, *Hosea*, 188.

122. For this possibility, see McKeating, *Books of Amos, Hosea, and Micah*, 79.

123. Andersen and Freedman, *Hosea*, 197.

124. Achtemeier, *Minor Prophets I*, 18.

125. James Limburg, *Hosea-Micah* (Atlanta: John Knox, 1988), 9. For a longer treatment of this theme, see J. J. Given, *Hosea*, in Spence and Excell, *Pulpit Commentary*, 7–8.

The poignancy of the symbolism bound up with this name is enhanced by the explanation that ensues. Up to this point in the chapter, Yahweh has spoken to Hosea *about* Israel. Now, after commanding the prophet to name Gomer's son "Not my people," Yahweh directs his words *to* Israel, whom he addresses in the second-person plural: "for you are not my people, and I am not your God." This sentence, which Wolff deems to be a divorce formula,[126] consists of a direct negation of the covenant formula that is reiterated in one form or another throughout the Old Testament: "I will be your God and you will be my people" (e.g., Exod. 6:7; Lev. 26:12; Deut. 26:17–19; 2 Sam. 7:24; Jer. 7:23; 11:4). Consequently, the declaration, like the name of Gomer's son, marks the revocation of the covenantal promise that Yahweh had made to Abraham and had reiterated to Israel just prior to the exodus (e.g., Exod. 6:7). Of even greater importance, however, it explicitly revokes the meaning inherent in the divine name itself that was already implicitly negated in the name of the second child.

Crucial to this revocation is the last clause in the divine statement. Following the Hebrew word order strictly yields the following rendering: "I (am) not I am to you" (*'enki lo'-'ehyeh lakem*). However, this translation does not reflect fully the sense that the declaration carries. The Masoretic Text sheds additional light.[127] The Masoretes added a *maqqeph* between *lo'* ("not") and *'ehyeh* (I AM), indicating that the two words are to be linked together into one vocalized unit, and they vocalized *'hyh* in the same manner as in Exodus 3:14. This suggests that the Masoretes (like the translators of the LXX) did not consider the word *'hyh* in Hosea 1:9 to be a simple verb but saw it as a repetition of the divine name (I AM) disclosed in Exodus 3:14. Furthermore, the *lakem* that comes at the end of the clause can function simply as a grammatical alternative to the suffixed possessive pronoun. If these observations are correct—if "I am" is read as a noun rather than a verb and if *lakem* is seen as a possessive rather than a prepositional phrase—then the word order of the second clause of the divine divorce pronouncement parallels that of the first clause, for both display the following form: connecting word ("for"/"and"), nominative pronoun ("you"/"I"), negative particle ("not"/"not"), noun ("people"/ "I am"), possessive ("my"/"your"). Thereby, the declaration becomes, "I am not your I AM."[128] In this manner, "Not-your-I-AM" becomes a fourth name, along with "Jezreel," "Not pitied," and "Not my people," that speaks of the breaking of the covenant and the impending judgment on Israel.

126. Wolff, *Hosea*, 21.

127. For the perspective that I take in this paragraph, see also Stuart, *Hosea-Jonah*, 33; Wolff, *Hosea*, 21–22.

128. For an elaboration of the basis of this rendering, see Wolff, *Hosea*, 21–22; Stuart, *Hosea-Jonah*, 33.

That Hosea can incorporate the language of Exodus 3:14 into this pro-nouncement indicates that the connection between the name "Yahweh" and the verb *'hyh*, whether it was etymological or simply phonetic, was still present to the minds of the Israelites of his day. The vivid recollection of Yahweh's self-disclosure in his call to Moses adds poignancy to the nega-tion of the divine name in Hosea 1:9. The declaration of judgment, cli-maxing in the revocation not only of the covenant but also of Yahweh's willingness to remain Israel's I AM leaves the nation completely without hope. Its demise is now inevitable, and, with it, the status of Israel's God is called into question as well.

The Message of Hope

The declaration of impending judgment on a nation that has become "Not my people," announced by a God who is now "Not your I AM," does not exhaust the message of the first section of the book of Hosea. On the con-trary, the prophet moves from his powerful warning of impending judg-ment to an announcement of his hope for a restoration of the covenant.

The hopeful character of the prophecy is evident in the literary struc-ture of the section itself. Following Hubbard's helpful schema, we can divide Hosea 1–3 into a two-part narrative (1:2–9; 3:1–5) within which is placed a three-part oracle (1:10–2:1; 2:2–13; 2:14–23). The result is a five-part literary unit that follows an A B' B B' A' structure. The unit begins with a story whose point is judgment (A [1:2–9]). Next comes an oracle proclaiming hope (B' [1:10–2:1]), followed by an oracle announc-ing judgment (B [2:2–13]) and then a second hopeful oracle (B' [2:14–23]). Finally, a narrative whose point is hope (A' [3:1–5]) rounds out the literary unit.[129]

The first oracle (1:10–2:1) looks forward to a day when the names of Hosea's children, as vivid symbols of the nation, are reversed and hence when Israel's covenant relationship to Yahweh is restored. This covenant renewal will mark a reversal of every aspect of the divine judgment that Hosea announces throughout the book.[130] It will entail the restoration of Yahweh's promises to his people, specifically the promise that Israel will become an innumerable host of people (cf. Gen. 22:17). Moreover, Israel will now be called "children of the living God," a designation that is unique to Hosea and therefore is likely his imaginative insight.[131] In addi-tion, the two kingdoms will be reunited, and together they will be sown (planted) by God.

The most significant feature of the two oracles of hope is the play on the names of Gomer's children that occurs in both. According to the second

---

129. Hubbard, *Hosea*, 51–52.
130. For a delineation of this, see Achtemeier, *Minor Prophets I*, 19.
131. Stuart, *Hosea-Jonah*, 38; Wolff, *Hosea*, 27.

oracle (2:14–23), on the glorious future day of restoration, Jezreel will take on the positive meaning connected to its etymology. God will "sow" Israel in the land (2:22–23). Because it has this inherently positive connotation, in the oracles of hope the name "Jezreel" remains unchanged from its use in the narrative of judgment. The names of the other two children, in contrast, do not. At the end of the first oracle, the "not" (*lo'-*) prefix in both names is dropped, as Jezreel-Israel is encouraged to name the other two *'ammi* and *ruhamah* (2:1). We might say that the negation of the covenant between Yahweh and Israel is thereby itself negated. By means of this renaming—that is, by means of the negation of the initial negative naming—the sense of the names of the children is shifted from negative to positive. In the second oracle of hope, the basis for this name change is delineated. Yahweh promises to have pity on "Not pitied" and to say to "Not my people," "You are my people," who will say in response, "You are my God" (2:23). Thereby this negation of the negative naming entails the reversal of the divorce pronouncements that had been made by Israel and Yahweh.

Viewed from the perspective of the depth of the judgment that Yahweh metes on wayward Israel, the renewal of the covenant is nothing short of life from the dead. In this sense, it comprises "resurrection." This meaning is suggested by the Hebrew clause *we'alu min ha'eres*, which is unhelpfully rendered in the NRSV as "and they shall take possession of the land" (1:11). Stuart declares that this clause "provides the most dramatic wording of the verse, one that may well have dual connotations: both return from exile and resurrection from 'death.'"[132] The coming "great day of Jezreel" will be a time when "God will sow" Israel in the land. The replanting of the nation that had been dispersed from the land and in that sense died is nothing short of life from the dead, that is, resurrection. Moreover, the act of resurrection or restoration will be carried out by the one who is truly I AM and therefore is able to remain faithfully and compassionately present in the story of his people, even in the face of their unfaithfulness. The second oracle of hope expands the idea. When the promised renewal occurs, Yahweh will restore fruitful presence in the land and compassion and peoplehood to the nation from whom they had been removed (2:21–23).

The three names, therefore—Jezreel, "Not pitied," and "Not my people"—are well chosen. Inherent in each is the implicit hope that Israel can once again enjoy a covenant relationship with Yahweh, even if the anticipated restoration requires the negation of the negation entailed in judgment. And when this happens, Yahweh's name, the fourth and climactic name in the text, will be restored as well. The one who in Hosea's prophecy is "Not your I AM" will again be I AM in and through Israel. Yahweh will

---

132. Stuart, *Hosea-Jonah*, 39.

again be the one whose very name signifies active be-ing—active, compassionate presence among his people.

The Renewing of the Name: "He, the First and the Last"

The middle section of the canonical book of Isaiah (chaps. 36–39) comprises a historical interlude, excerpted from 2 Kings 18–20, that divides the chapters that precede it from those that follow. The excerpt describes the events in and around Jerusalem at the close of Isaiah's ministry and climaxes with a warning regarding what the descendants of Hezekiah can anticipate from the Babylonians. The chapters that immediately follow (40–55), which are commonly grouped together and denoted "Deutero-Isaiah" or "Second Isaiah," address this particular situation.

In 1965, George A. F. Knight declared, "No section of the Old Testament has attracted more attention than has Isa. 40–55."[133] Despite this attention, he adds, little *theological* interest has been paid to these chapters, largely because scholars have been wrapped up with the critical issues surrounding them. Thirty-six years later, Brevard Childs echoed this complaint. He noted that despite the large number of recently written commentaries devoted to these chapters, "tremendous confusion still reigns regarding virtually every serious problem of interpretation."[134]

One issue that has vexed interpreters is the relationship of Isaiah 40–55 to the first part of the book. The traditional answer assumed that all sixty-six chapters formed a unity because they were the product of the eighth-century prophet for whom the book is named.[135] Most modern exegetes reject this view. Some argue that chapters 40–55 are the work of an anonymous prophet who directed his words to Jewish exiles in Babylon a century later. More recently, a growing number of scholars have sought new interpretive methods that allow the entire book to be read as a canonical whole.[136] To this end, some suggest that Isaiah in its current form dates to the late fifth century.[137]

---

133. George A. F. Knight, *Deutero-Isaiah: A Theological Commentary on Isaiah 40–55* (New York: Abingdon, 1965), 9.

134. Brevard S. Childs, *Isaiah*, Old Testament Library (Louisville, KY: Westminster John Knox, 2001), xi.

135. For a succinct, recent argument for the unity of Isaiah, see J. Alec Motyer, *The Prophecy of Isaiah: An Introduction and Commentary* (Downers Grove, IL: InterVarsity Press, 1993), 25–33. See also Edward J. Young, *The Book of Isaiah: The English Text, with Introduction, Exposition, and Notes*, 3 vols., New International Commentary on the Old Testament (Grand Rapids: Eerdmans, 1963–1972), 538–49. See also Charles Cutler Torrey, *The Second Isaiah: A New Interpretation* (New York: Charles Scribner's Sons, 1928); Oswald T. Allis, *The Unity of Isaiah* (Philadelphia: Reformed Publishing Co., 1950); Edward J. Young, *Studies in Isaiah* (London: Tyndale, 1955); Edward J. Young, *Who Wrote Isaiah?* (Grand Rapids: Eerdmans, 1958).

136. See, for example, Walter Brueggemann, *Isaiah 40–66*, Westminster Bible Companion (Louisville, KY: Westminster John Knox, 1998), 4–5.

137. John D. W. Watts, *Isaiah 34–66*, Word Biblical Commentary (Waco, TX: Word, 1987), 71.

Regardless of who was ultimately responsible for the writing of Isaiah 40–55, the setting and focus of these chapters clearly differ from those of the first half of the canonical book. This far-reaching difference forms the basis for the crucial place of the writings of Second Isaiah, whom Knight lauds as "the greatest mind of all the prophets of the OT"[138] in the ongoing saga of the I AM.

The Revocation of the Revocation of the Covenant

Assyria was the foreign threat that loomed on the horizon during the initial ministry of Isaiah. The dominant power that concerns the chapters that constitute Second Isaiah, in contrast, is Babylon, or more specifically, the Babylon that is soon to collapse (47:1–15) before the might of the Persian king Cyrus (44:28–45:7). This political change provides the historical context that cradles the dramatic difference in message that sets Second Isaiah off from the eighth-century "prophets of doom."

Like Hosea, Amos, and Micah, Isaiah (initially) denounces the people for their sins and announces to them Yahweh's decreed destruction of the nation. Far from disagreeing with the eighth-century prophets of doom, Second Isaiah presupposes the correctness of their predictions. In so doing, he follows their astounding theology of history. In contrast to the "standard" wisdom of the ancient world that connected success in battle to a corresponding victory among the gods, these prophets declare that the unseen hand of Yahweh, and not the deities that the great world conquerors worshiped, lay behind their military successes. Israel and then Judah did not meet with defeat at the hands of pagan conquerors because the gods of the conquering nations had vanquished Yahweh. Rather, Yahweh himself had sent his people into exile, and he had done so in response to their sins.

Second Isaiah addresses a people who have lost faith in their God. Insofar as they were no longer able to believe that Yahweh was either willing or able to help them in the midst of their sorry plight, they resemble the slaves in Egypt. The parallel between Israel in bondage and Israel in exile opens the way for the emergence of what comes to be a predominant anticipation in Second Isaiah, a new exodus in the form of an end to the Babylonian exile. Although the eighth-century prophets such as Hosea had incorporated this motif, nothing in their writings rivals the intensity and fullness of the exodus symbolism in these chapters.[139] Second Isaiah does not merely draw from the exodus story, however; he places it within the context of Yahweh's promises to the patriarchs and even within Israelite traditions about Yahweh's act of creation itself.

---

138. Knight, *Deutero-Isaiah*, 11.
139. Watts, *Isaiah 34–66*, 81.

To despairing Jews in Babylon, Second Isaiah offers a message of hope predicated on the insertion of a new situation between chapters 39 and 40. The sovereign Lord of human history and of all creation declares that Israel's punishment is complete, and he promises the new beginning that eighth-century voices such as Hosea have anticipated. Moreover, just as Yahweh had used foreign nations to punish Israel, so now they would be his instrument in rescuing his people. Specifically, Yahweh had appointed Cyrus to destroy the oppressors of the exiled Jews and thereby to bring to an end their sufferings, which had now been sufficient.[140] Second Isaiah is convinced that the exiles in Babylon will soon witness glorious events happening around them that are nothing less than the work of Yahweh (43:10–15), who intends to bring about the restoration of his people to the promised land (43:5–7; 48:20) as well as the rebuilding of Jerusalem (52:1–2; 54:11–13)—all of this for the sake of his own glory (48:11).

These themes are disclosed in embryonic form in the first eleven verses of Isaiah 40, which serve as a type of prologue to the entire section of the canonical book.[141] Some commentators see in these verses an outline of the prophet's call and commission, although they admit that the form that the text takes differs from other call narratives.[142] Other exegetes, such as John D. W. Watts, view the text as a series of "urgent calls for messengers to represent Yahweh and the heavenly court in spreading the word of Yahweh's decisions and coming actions."[143] In any case, Second Isaiah begins with an exhortation based on Yahweh's promise that he will soon act to bring about a new exodus that will be even greater than the exodus from Egypt. Furthermore, Yahweh, whom Ezekiel had pictured as abandoning Jerusalem (Ezek. 9–11), will again be taking up residence in the holy city.[144] At this point in the history of Israel, therefore, the prophetic mission can only be one of announcing comfort to Israel in view of the imminent revelation of the glory of Yahweh (Isa. 40:1–5), which, in turn, is associated with the fulfillment of the divine promise of salvation.

In the exhortation, which is attributed to God himself, Israel and Yahweh are both depicted in language reminiscent of the ancient covenant. The nation is "my people," and Yahweh is "your God." In this manner, the opening verses of Isaiah 40 announce the crucial theological theme that is expanded and elaborated in the ensuing chapters. The one who had formerly declared to Israel, "You are not my people," will now speak of the exiles as "my sons" and "my daughters" and as those who "are called by my name" (43:6–7); he will now declare to them, "You are mine"

---

140. For a similar description, see R. N. Whybray, *Isaiah 40–66*, New Century Bible Commentary (London: Marshall, Morgan & Scott, 1981), 35.

141. For a discussion of the canonical function of the prologue, see Childs, *Isaiah*, 303–4.

142. Whybray, *Isaiah 40–66*, 48.

143. Watts, *Isaiah 34–66*, 79.

144. For this interpretation of Isa. 40:3, see Watts, *Isaiah 34–66*, 80.

(43:1). In this manner, the one who had announced "I am not your I AM" is once again about to act as I AM for his people. In short, Second Isaiah focuses on the divine revoking of the revocation of the covenant that Yahweh had declared through preexilic prophets, including Hosea. As this occurs, what Moses implored Yahweh that he might see, namely, the divine glory, will now be made plainly evident not only in Israel but before all humankind (40:5).

Second Isaiah offers two designations for the God who is now revoking the revocation of the covenant that are important for the saga of the I AM. On several occasions in these chapters Yahweh declares, "I am he" ('ani hu') and "I am the first and I am the last" ('ani ri'shon wa'ani 'aharon'). The first of these self-designations did not originate with Second Isaiah. On the contrary, already in Deuteronomy, Yahweh announced, "See now that I, even I, am he; there is no god besides me" (Deut. 32:39). Franz Delitzsch goes so far as to assert that since the time of Deuteronomy, the statement "Yahweh is he" was "the fundamental clause of the Old Testament *credo*."[145] In contrast to the "I am he" designation, the self-predication, "I am the first and I am the last," might rightly be attributed to Second Isaiah's theological acumen. In any case, taken together, the addition of these two descriptions to Israel's ongoing reflection on the divine name constitutes Second Isaiah's chief contribution to the saga of the I AM.

By means of these two designations, Second Isaiah "came as near to the concept of eternity as was possible within the limits of his theological world of thought," to cite R. N. Whybray's conclusion.[146] Although this may be the case, the question remains as to the manner in which the work of revoking the revocation of the covenant is inherent in the divine name. We must therefore ask, In what sense is Yahweh eternal?

The I AM Who Is "He"

Many scholars point out that Second Isaiah draws from several rhetorical strategies to advance his message. One such strategy is the use of "oracles of salvation" or "oracles of assurance of salvation" (41:17–20; 42:14–17; 43:16–21; 46:1–13; 48:1–11, 12–17). Of greater importance for the I AM saga is his use of "trial-speeches"[147] or "speeches of disputation"[148] (41:1–5, 21–29; 43:8–15; 44:6–8; 45:20–25).[149]

145. Franz Delitzsch, *Biblical Commentary on the Prophecies of Isaiah*, trans. James Martin, 2 vols. (Edinburgh: T. & T. Clark, 1867), 2:251.
146. Whybray, *Isaiah 40–66*, 37.
147. For this term, see Whybray, *Isaiah 40–66*, 35.
148. Brueggemann, *Isaiah 40–66*, 29.
149. For these enumerations, see John Scullion, *Isaiah 40–66*, Old Testament Message (Wilmington, DE: Michael Glazier, 1982), 33. For a more detailed discussion of the genres of Second Isaiah, see Antoon Schoors, *I Am God Your Savior: A Form-Critical Study of the Main Genres in Is. XL–LV* (Leiden: Brill, 1973).

The disputations of Second Isaiah set Yahweh's claims in conflict with the ideological claims of Babylon. One technique that is used in these is to invite Israel and/or the nations to appraise the rival claims of Yahweh and the Babylonian gods to control historical events in keeping with some purpose. To adjudicate this controversy, Yahweh (through the prophet) sets up the criterion of prophecy and fulfillment, that is, the ability of either party to announce in advance his intention to bring about a specific event, an event that subsequently occurs.

Second Isaiah also sets out this case in the context of rival understandings of creation. The prophet maintains that Israelite traditions regarding Yahweh's creation of the world are more credible than the Babylonian creation myths. To this end, Second Isaiah speaks of creation as an unaided act of the one God (40:13–14) and of the heavenly bodies as creatures rather than gods (40:26). Moreover, the prophet elevates the fact that in contrast to the Babylonian creator god Marduk, whose parents are named and play a role in the act of creation, Yahweh has no parentage but was sole God from the beginning. By drawing from this idea, Second Isaiah finds the basis for his prophecy regarding the future in the role of Yahweh in the act of creation itself. This wider "battle of God and the gods" forms the context for Yahweh's repeated declaration, "I am he."

Isaiah 43:8–13, which Watts denotes as "a trial speech against gods who do not exist and hence cannot be present,"[150] resumes a tribunal scene that was announced already in chapter 41. Here Yahweh summons the people of Israel to be his witnesses among the nations. Israel is Yahweh's chosen servant so that the truth about Yahweh might be known. In the ensuing verses, Yahweh articulates his own cause, which is directed toward Israel itself. In stating his case, he announces, "I am he," three times.

The first occurrence comes in the context of Yahweh's declaration of his longevity in comparison with the fleeting gods of the nations: "so that you may know and believe me and understand that I am he. Before me no god was formed, nor shall there be any after me" (43:10).[151] The gods of the nations, especially the Babylonian deities who stood in genealogical succession, Yahweh asserts, do not rival him. Rather than being one member within a genealogy of gods, he predates all such gods and does not beget any god that will continue after him. Delitzsch draws out the immediate meaning of the divine statement: "His being has no beginning and no end; so that any being apart from his, which could have gone before or could follow after, so as to be regarded as divine (in other words, the deity of the artificial and temporal images that are called gods by the

---

150. Watts, *Isaiah 34–66*, 128.
151. Koole, however, renders the statement, "It is I." Jan L. Koole, *Isaiah III*, 3 vols., Historical Commentary on the Old Testament (Kampen: Kok Pharos, 1997–2001), 1:308.

heathen), is a contradiction in itself."[152] Viewed in this context, therefore, "I am he" is connected to the singularity of God. As in Deuteronomy 32:39, the assertion "I am he" entails the claim that the only God is Yahweh, the God of Israel.

In the wake of this declaration, Yahweh identifies himself as the one, true, saving God (Isa. 43:11). Verse 11 begins with the long form of the first person pronoun ('anoki), which is then repeated for emphasis and is followed by the divine name: "I, I, Yahweh." The assertion that Yahweh is the only savior leads to the second instance of the use of the declaration "I am he." This time the assertion occurs in the context of Yahweh's claim that no one can thwart his work: "I am God, and also henceforth I am He; there is no one who can deliver from my hand; I work and who can hinder it?" (v. 13).

This announcement of the self-designation "I am he" raises an exegetical difficulty: What is the meaning of the *gam miyom* that precedes the cryptic self-reference *'ani hu'*? The older exegesis sees these words as referring to the first day (that is, when time began) and hence as carrying the idea that "as long as time has existed He is God and has so manifested Himself," to cite Edward Young's rendering of the phrase.[153] A variation translates the words, "even before the day was," and thereby finds in them a reference to God's eternality.[154] Recent translations, in contrast, reflect the exegetical conclusion that the words indicate that from this moment onward Yahweh will show that he is the true God.[155] The point of the text, therefore, is that past experiences of God's reliability (v. 12) should lead Israel to entrust the future to Yahweh as well.

Viewed in this light the self-designation "I am he" in this verse (and in v. 10 as well) denotes Yahweh's ability to fulfill his promise. In this sense, the divine self-designation functions as an elaboration of the divine name. It speaks of Yahweh's "being-present" in the future as in the past and therefore at all moments in Israel's history. As we have already seen, in the context of chapter 43 in particular and Second Isaiah in general, "I am he" takes on an additional, albeit related, sense. The God who is sovereignly and savingly present in Israel's story is the sole God. As Jan Koole points out, "On account of the preceding *'emi-'el*, the expression also becomes a claim to complete exclusiveness: Yahweh is not a god but the God, not just the same one but the Only One."[156] These themes coalesce in the idea that

152. Delitzsch, *Biblical Commentary on the Prophecies of Isaiah*, 2:193.

153. Young, *Book of Isaiah*, 3:151.

154. See, for example, John Calvin, *Commentary on the Book of the Prophet Isaiah*, trans. William Pringle (Grand Rapids: Eerdmans, 1948), 3:335.

155. Christopher R. North, *The Second Isaiah: Introduction, Translation, and Commentary to Chapters XL–LV* (Oxford: Clarendon, 1964), 121. This rendering is even supported by Delitzsch. See Delitzsch, *Biblical Commentary on the Prophecies of Isaiah*, 2:194.

156. Koole, *Isaiah III*, 1:314–15.

as the savior of Israel, as the one who acts in the story of his people and because he acts in this manner, Yahweh is the true God and the only God.

The salvific theme connected to the "I am he" declaration is even more pronounced in the third statement in the chapter: "I, I am He who blots out your transgressions for my own sake" (v. 25). This assertion occurs in the context of yet another trial speech, albeit one (and the only one) in which Yahweh opposes Israel.[157] The self-designation once again begins with the emphatic double use of the long first-person pronoun. This time, however, the construction is not followed by the divine name but by the third-person pronoun *hu'* ("he"). Young rightly concludes that the "emphasis is upon God alone as the One who blots out transgressions."[158]

The theme is picked up again in Isaiah 46:4. As a preparation for the dismissal of the political power of Babylon that comes in chapter 47, Isaiah 46 moves to dismiss the gods that guarantee and authorize that power.[159] To this end, Second Isaiah paints a vivid contrast between the lifeless, passive gods Bel and Nebo, and Yahweh. The idols must be carried by their devotees in the solemn religious processions connected to the worshiping life of the Babylonians[160] (or carried by fugitives who are fleeing the advancing army of Cyrus).[161] Rather than being *carried by* his devotees as is the case with the Babylonian gods, Yahweh *carries* his people. And he does so like a loving mother carries her children (cf. Exod. 19:4; Deut. 1:31; 32:11; Isa. 63:9). In Isaiah 46:3–4, Yahweh points out that he has carried Israel from the "womb," a word that is linked to the verb meaning "to show compassion,"[162] and he promises that he will continue to do so "even when you turn gray." In this context, Yahweh declares, "even to your old age I am he" (v. 4).

Some commentators see this instance of the statement "I am he" as merely an alternative way of saying, "I am the same."[163] Yet the word order in the Hebrew suggests that the declaration ought to be seen as another occurrence of the cryptic designation of the divine name. Yahweh is pledging that even to the farthest future, he will remain "I am he" to Israel.[164]

157. Claus Westermann, *Das Buch Jesaja: Übersetzt und erklärt*, 3rd ed. (Göttingen: Vandenhoeck & Ruprecht, 1976), 107; Childs, *Isaiah*, 341.

158. Young, *Book of Isaiah*, 3:162.

159. For this interpretation, see Brueggemann, *Isaiah 40–66*, 86–87.

160. For this interpretation, see Paul D. Hanson, *Isaiah 40–66*, Interpretation: A Bible Commentary for Teaching and Preaching (Louisville, KY: John Knox, 1995), 113; and John L. MacKenzie, *Second Isaiah, Introduction, Translation, and Notes*, Anchor Bible (Garden City, NY: Doubleday, 1967), 87.

161. This position is presented in Childs, *Isaiah*, 359; and North, *Second Isaiah*, 163–64.

162. Brown, Driver, and Briggs, *Hebrew and English Lexicon of the Old Testament*, 933.

163. See, for example, Conrad von Orelli, *The Prophecies of Isaiah*, trans. J. S. Banks (Edinburgh: T. & T. Clark, 1889), 260. Whybray is slightly more cautious. He declares, "Here this characteristic phrase comes close to meaning 'I am the same.'" Whybray, *Isaiah 40–66*, 115.

164. For a similar interpretation, see Knight, *Deutero-Isaiah*, 149.

That is, Yahweh pledges to be the one who is present in Israel's story as the only true and saving God even in the distant future.

The theme of compassion is even stronger in the final occurrence of the self-designation "I am he" in Second Isaiah (Isa. 51:12). Now, however, Yahweh's statement is placed in the context of his work of comforting Israel, a theme which was announced in the very first verse of the prologue. The God of Israel declares, "I, I am he who comforts you." Whybray explains that in this verse, "Yahweh indignantly refutes the charge of inactivity." And as in 40:1, so also here "'comfort' is not just a matter of speaking soothing words, but of bringing the nation's suffering to an end."[165] The grammatical construction underscores the focus on Yahweh as the one making this claim,[166] and it facilitates the emphatic nature of Yahweh's declaration. As Young helpfully notes, "By repeating the personal pronoun the Lord draws attention to Himself as the only sure source of comfort. This fact is also strengthened by the third person pronoun."[167]

The texts in Second Isaiah that echo Deuteronomy 32:39 by presenting Yahweh as declaring, "I am he," allude as well to the theme announced in Deuteronomy, namely, that Yahweh is the one whose very be-ing is to be ever present in Israel's story. At this stage of the story in which Israel is in exile in Babylon, Yahweh's presence entails a revocation of the revocation of the covenant. For this reason, the divine presence may be said to be an active, saving presence, and, at least for the exiles, it is consequently a comforting presence. Moreover, as the one who is savingly present throughout Israel's journey, Yahweh alone is God. Therein lies the divine eternality entailed in the divine name that is explicated as "I am he." This theme is articulated in an even stronger manner in the divine self-designation that finds its genesis in Second Isaiah: Yahweh as the first and the last.

The I AM Who Is First and Last

The initial occurrence of the divine self-designation as first and last is found in the trial speech with which the main body of Second Isaiah commences and therefore which marks the first point where the prophecy takes the form of a court of law (Isa. 41).[168] In this text, Yahweh summons the gods to the tribunal to defend their claims to divine power.[169] In the tribunal, the deities are represented by their subjects, the nations.

As the scene commences, Yahweh challenges the nations to consider the question of who is behind the rise of a victor from the east (41:2).

---

165. Whybray, *Isaiah 40–66*, 160.
166. Delitzsch, *Biblical Commentary on the Prophecies of Isaiah*, 2:289.
167. Young, *Book of Isaiah*, 3:315.
168. A. S. Herbert, *The Book of the Prophet Isaiah, Chapters 40–66*, Cambridge Bible Commentary (Cambridge: Cambridge University Press, 1975), 28.
169. Hanson, *Isaiah 40–66*, 35.

Although some commentators interpret the verse as referring to Abraham,[170] the overwhelming majority conclude that it points to Cyrus.[171] Yahweh invites the nations to consider who is actually at work in Cyrus's military victories. After repeating his query, "Who has performed and done this?" (v. 4), Yahweh either broadens it to include the idea of controlling the forces of history from the beginning of time[172] ("calling the generations from the beginning"), or responds to the query by declaring that the active agent is the one "who calls the generations"[173] or who has "called (into being) the generations (of man) from the beginning (of the world),"[174] namely, Yahweh himself. In either case, the claim of the text as a whole is that the hidden force behind these world-shaping events is none other than the questioner himself.

In staking his claim, God identifies himself in an emphatic manner: "I, Yahweh, am first, and will be with the last" (v. 4). The immediate implication is obvious. Yahweh stands behind Cyrus's meteoric rise to power. Not so straightforward is the implication of the self-designation for Yahweh's own nature.

The older exegetical tradition tended to find in the self-designation a reaffirmation of the meaning of the divine name that had been disclosed to Moses at the burning bush. A few exegetes take the matter even further and conclude that as such the verse entails a declaration of the eternality of God, which they see inherent in the divine name. Delitzsch, for example, declares, "It is the full meaning of the name Jehovah which is unfolded here; for God is called Jehovah as the absolute I, the absolutely free Being, pervading all history, and yet above all history, as He who is Lord of His own absolute being, in revealing which He is purely self-determined; in a word, as the unconditionally free and unchangeably eternal personality."[175]

Despite the attractiveness of explanations such as Delitzsch's, it is unlikely that Second Isaiah had such a highly philosophically oriented understanding in view, at least not in this verse. Calvin seems to be on the right track when he asserts regarding the divine self-designation, "This relates not only to the eternity of essence, but to the government which he

---

170. Calvin, for example, held to this view. Calvin, *Commentary on the Book of the Prophet Isaiah*, 3:246–50.

171. Even Young is to be included among the list of supporters of this view. Young, *Book of Isaiah*, 3:75.

172. Watts, *Isaiah 34–66*, 103.

173. For this translation, see Whybray, *Isaiah 40–66*, 61.

174. George Rawlinson, *Isaiah*, 2 vols., in Spence and Exell, *Pulpit Commentary*, 2:96. See also Delitzsch, *Biblical Commentary on the Prophecies of Isaiah*, 2:160. Ridderbos offers a slightly different suggestion, namely, that the phrase refers to the one who "called the nations into existence and assigned a special place in history to each." J. Ridderbos, *Isaiah*, trans. John Vriend, Bible Student's Commentary (Grand Rapids: Zondervan, 1984), 353.

175. Delitzsch, *Biblical Commentary on the Prophecies of Isaiah*, 2:160–61.

exercises on earth; as if he had said, that God does not grow old by any length of time, and never will surrender his authority; for he does not sit unemployed in heaven, but from his throne, on the contrary, he regulates the affairs of this world."[176] Claus Westermann, in turn, concludes that the text is "not a statement about Being in the sense of our Western way of thinking. Declared here is not the continuation of a static, existing divine being, but God's being over against everything that occurs. . . . What is declared here is a divine eternality that is connected to history and not theoretically placed over against it."[177] Similarly, Karl Elliger says regarding the latter part of the statement, which he sees as illuminating the former, that this "is therefore no assertion about God's Being as such, God's eternality, but about his always-being-present, even with the last humans."[178]

In keeping with this historical or narratival focus, some commentators view the statement as referring to Yahweh's presence in the human story from beginning to end. In keeping with this understanding, Christopher North declares, "The meaning is not exactly that Yahweh is 'eternal' but that he is contemporary with all history, from its beginning to its *eschaton*."[179] Watts narrows the field of vision slightly when he renders the statement, "I, Yahweh, was with the first," thereby suggesting the idea that God "is 'with' Cyrus, as he has been with successful rulers from the beginning of time."[180] Similarly, Koole places the statement within the context of the theology of history prominent at that time. He explains: "For the nations, the question of what powers bring about the rise and fall of empires is easy to answer. Gods supplant each other; the god Ashur was followed by the Babylonian Marduk, and now the Persian Ahuramazda threatens to gain supremacy. Against these the god of Israel sets his claim that he alone directs world history, in all periods."[181]

Yet an even narrower focus might be in view here. The divine self-designation appears to be tied closely to the narrative of Yahweh's covenant with Israel. Second Isaiah is probably thinking of Yahweh as the active, purposeful agent in Israel's story. This agent has been active ever since the first, which might in this context refer to the exodus itself.[182] And Yahweh will likewise be active with the events or persons that will bring the story to its glorious conclusion.

Regardless of the exact exegetical details, the purpose of the statement is evident. The prophet's goal is to assure the exiled Israelites that Cyrus's

---

176. Calvin, *Commentary on the Book of the Prophet Isaiah*, 3:250.
177. Westermann, *Das Buch Jessja* (translation mine).
178. Karl Elliger, *Deuterojesaja*, vol. 1, *Jesaia 40,1–45,7* (Neukirchen-Vluyn: Neukirchener Verlag, 1978), 125.
179. North, *Second Isaiah*, 94. See also Childs, *Isaiah*, 318.
180. Watts, *Isaiah 34–66*, 103.
181. Koole, *Isaiah III*, 1:142–43.
182. For this view, see Knight, *Deutero-Isaiah*, 49.

rise to power is not a cause for Israel to fear. Using language that reaffirms the meaning of the divine name in connection with his people and directly revoking the revocation of his name that he spoke earlier through prophets such as Hosea, Yahweh declares the reason that such fear is unwarranted: "I am with you. . . . I am your God" (41:10). The divine name, which since the burning bush had been closely bound with Yahweh's be-ing with Israel, now carries with it connotations of an all-encompassing presence. Because Israel's God is present at the beginning and the end of their story, the divine presence encloses the entire story, including not only the banishment of his people into exile but also the political forces that will mark their return—and that of his glory—to Jerusalem.[183]

The next occurrence of the divine claim to be first and last comes in Isaiah 44:6–8, which comprises yet another speech of disputation, albeit one that is followed by a vivid taunting of those who worship manufactured idols (44:9–20). In this speech, Yahweh again encourages Israel not to fear, basing the admonition on his status as the one who alone is God. The disputation begins with the divine Judge speaking on his own behalf and offering a clear assertion of his uniqueness or singularity: "Thus says Yahweh, the King of Israel, and his Redeemer, Yahweh of hosts: I am the first and I am the last; besides me there is no god" (v. 6).[184] This statement is enhanced by Yahweh's reminder of his ability to foretell the future. Indeed, he alone has "announced from of old the things to come" (v. 7).

It is not uncommon for commentators to find in this instance of the divine self-designation an unambiguous declaration of Yahweh's eternality. Young, for example, declares unabashedly, "He is the first in that He is before all creation as well as in the beginning of human history, but He is also the last in that He is above human history. The two expressions are designed to show His eternity and His complete independence of the creation. Before human history began He is, and when it shall finish, He is, the unending, eternal, and true God."[185] Other commentators, however, are less confident. Even Calvin is reticent to read too much into the verse: "By these words he does not assert God's eternity, but shows that He is always like himself, that they may hope that He will be to them in the future what they have found him to be in the past."[186] John L. MacKenzie, in turn, is so subdued in his appraisal that he can only say, "The reference is probably not to creation and eschatology, but simply designates an enumeration of which there is only one member."[187]

---

183. For a somewhat similar characterization, see Knight, *Deutero-Isaiah*, 50–51.
184. Whybray sees in the last phrase of the declaration "an even clearer assertion of Yahweh's uniqueness than 43:10–11." Whybray, *Isaiah 40–66*, 96.
185. Young, *Book of Isaiah*, 3:170.
186. Calvin, *Commentary on the Book of the Prophet Isaiah*, 3:364–65. I have slightly revised the translation to bring it in line with contemporary word usage.
187. MacKenzie, *Second Isaiah*, 63.

Perhaps Paul Hanson is on the right track when he affixes a theological importance to the statement: "Here the monotheistic principle is stated with unambiguous clarity, thereby marking the culminating stage in Israel's emergence from ancient Near Eastern polytheism to belief in one God as Creator and Ruler of the entire universe."[188] Yet the "monotheistic formula," as Elliger prefers to call it, cannot be separated from Yahweh's presence in and to Israel's story.[189] In fact, this principle not only proclaims the singularity of God, but it entails a specific characteristic of what it means to be God, namely, the ability to exercise power in and over history.[190] In this sense, the declaration "I am the first and I am the last" reiterates what was given as the meaning of the divine name in Exodus 3:14, namely, the presence of the Be-ing One in the history of Israel, especially as that story commences with the exodus.

Chapter 48 forms a climax to this section of Isaiah. It recapitulates many of the themes that were explicated in the chapters that precede and voices Yahweh's explicit call to Israel to flee from Babylon and return home (v. 20).[191] The chapter opens with a summons to hear (vv. 1–2), followed by declarations regarding "former things" (vv. 3–5) and "new things" (vv. 6–8), and an affirmation of Yahweh's self-regard (vv. 9–11). Yahweh announces that he is about to engage in a "new act" that he will accomplish for the sake of his own glory. Verses 12–16, which form another summons to hear, set this act of deliverance in the context of Yahweh's work in creation as well as in the obedience that creation offers to its Creator. In this manner, the prophecy points out that the one who is sovereign over creation is the sole ruler of history.

In the context of this latter summons, Yahweh offers a self-designation that brings together the two previously announced declarations, "I am he" and "I am the first, and I am the last" (v. 12). Yet in this verse, the grammar differs slightly from what is evident in the other occurrences of these divine self-designations. The Masoretes added a *maqqeph* between the two words of the first declaration, *'ani* ("I [am]") and *hu'* ("he"), thereby drawing them together into a single vocalized unit and indicating the close connection in meaning that the words carry. In the second assertion, the conjunction *'aph* has been substituted for the usual *wa* ("and") between the two clauses *'ani ri'shon* ("I am the first") and *'ani 'aharon* ("I am the last"). This conjunction generally denotes the addition of something greater, surprising, or unexpected. Thus, it can carry the idea of "how much more" or "the more so."[192] The use of *'aph* in this assertion suggests a gradation that continues into the next verse. The text could thus be ren-

---

188. Hanson, *Isaiah 40–66*, 87.
189. Elliger, *Deuterojesaja*, 1:125.
190. For this idea, see Elliger, *Deuterojesaja*, 1:125, 401.
191. Herbert, *Book of the Prophet Isaiah*, 82.
192. See Brown, Driver, and Briggs, *Hebrew and English Lexicon of the Old Testament*, 64–65.

dered, "I am the first. Even more so, I am the last. And even more so, my hand laid the foundation of the earth."

It is no surprise that some commentators draw out of Isaiah 48:12 the basis for finding in the divine self-designation a philosophical conception of eternality. Young provides a clear example: "The words, *I am He* . . . mean 'I am the One who is, the actual, living, true God.' The words *first* and *last* suggest that God is the beginning and ending of all things, and explain the statement *I am He*. . . . Unlike man and the creation, which are temporal and change, God is eternal and changes not."[193] Calvin, in contrast, sees instead a reference to "God's constant and unvarying will toward us." He continues: "But here it ought also to be observed, that Isaiah does not speak of God's eternal essence, but applies this doctrine to our use, that we may know that he will be to us the same that he has always been."[194]

Many of the exegetical questions surrounding this text (as well as the related verses in Second Isaiah) remain unresolved. What seems clear, however, is that in these verses the link between Yahweh's be-ing present in Israel's story is explicitly expanded and placed in the context of his be-ing present in all creation from the very inception of creation "in the beginning." Second Isaiah does not draw out all the theological implications of this expanding sense of the divine eternality. Nevertheless, the theological reflections contained in these chapters regarding the significance of the name of the one who is not only "I am he" but perhaps even more importantly "I am the first, and I am the last" will be expanded on the other side of the incarnation of the I AM.

---

193. Young, *Book of Isaiah*, 3:255.
194. Calvin, *Commentary on the Book of the Prophet Isaiah*, 3:477–78.

Chapter Five

From Jacob's Well to Calvary's Cross

The Incarnate I AM

Until the rise of the modern historical-critical approach to the Bible, it was quite common for commentators to suggest that the one who appeared to Moses at the burning bush was Christ. Moreover, Christ's presence was not simply relegated to the figure of the angel of Yahweh. Instead, many church theologians concluded that the entire incident was a christophany, an appearance of the preincarnate Christ. In naming Christ as the divine actor in this scene, Ambrose, for example, wrote, "This is the God of Abraham, the God of Isaac, the God of Jacob, who appeared to Moses in the bush, concerning whom Moses says, 'He who is has sent me.'" Ambrose then declared in no uncertain terms, "It was not the Father who spake to Moses in the bush, or in the desert, but the Son."[1]

---

1. Ambrose, *On the Christian Faith* 1.13.83, in *Nicene and Post-Nicene Fathers*, 2nd series, ed. Philip Schaff and Henry Wace (1893; Peabody, MA: Hendrickson, 1994), 10:215. See also *On the Christian Faith* 5.1.26, in *Nicene and Post-Nicene Fathers*, 2nd series, 10:287.

Such direct associations of Christ to the I AM in the Old Testament are, of course, exegetically problematic. Nevertheless, the New Testament seems to connect Jesus Christ as the incarnate Word with the I AM name that was given to Moses, revoked immediately prior to the dispersion, but then reiterated in the new exodus that came in the form of the return to the land of promise.

The standard Greek rendering of the Hebrew *'ehyeh* in the Septuagint is *ego eimi*, which is grammatically an emphatic construction emphasizing the subject (hence, "I myself am"). In keeping with this pattern, the divine declaration in Exodus 3:14 was translated into Greek as *ego eimi to on*, although the subsequent *'ehyeh* was rendered *to on* rather than *ego eimi*. In addition, *ego eimi* served as the standard Greek translation for the "I am he" (*'ani hu'*) statements in Second Isaiah. As a consequence of its linguistic associations with the Old Testament designations of the divine name, *ego eimi* became particularly useful for the New Testament writers. It allowed them to bring together into a single declaration the meanings that had come to be represented by both Hebrew expressions of the divine self-designation.

In the Gospels, the incarnate Jesus Christ is presented as voicing the *ego eimi* in a variety of texts. The Synoptics use the expression only meagerly. In the Fourth Gospel, however, the situation changes dramatically. The *ego eimi*, replete with its Old Testament overtones, is found repeatedly in John. In fact, the inclusion of the *ego eimi* is a characteristic feature of the style of the revelatory speeches that constitute the major portion of Jesus' preaching in the Fourth Gospel.[2] In this manner, John elevated a phrase, which in everyday language is quite commonplace, into a leitmotiv of his Gospel. In the Fourth Gospel, the *ego eimi* becomes the manner in which Jesus not only identifies himself, but in which he does so by associating himself with the God of the story of Israel.[3]

The Life-Giving I AM

The various utterances of the *ego eimi* that John places on Jesus' lips are often grouped together as the "I AM sayings of Jesus." In many of these sayings the "I am" serves as what Barnabas Lindars calls a "revelation-formula" (or a "recognition formula," to cite Rudolf

2. Ethelbert Stauffer, "ego," in *Theological Dictionary of the New Testament*, ed. Gerhard Kittel and Gerhard Friedrich, trans. Geoffrey W. Bromiley, 10 vols. (Grand Rapids: Eerdmans, 1964–1976), 2:349.

3. For a somewhat similar conclusion, see Raymond E. Brown, *The Gospel according to John: Introduction, Translation, and Notes*, 2 vols., Anchor Bible (Garden City, NY: Doubleday, 1966, 1970), 1:254.

Bultmann's designation[4]), because it is typically found in reports of theophanies.[5] The Old Testament basis for this understanding is solid. As J. H. Bernard notes, from Genesis to Isaiah, *ego eimi* "is often the style of Deity, and its impressiveness is unmistakable."[6] In the Fourth Gospel, the I AM sayings carry great rhetorical significance. They invite the reader to move beyond the physical humanness of Jesus to his origin in God and then to understand Jesus' person and mission in the light of that origin.[7] Bultmann puts it well when he declares, "Whoever hears these words spoken by the Revealer is faced with the ultimate decision: the *ego eimi* lays absolute claim to faith."[8] But in which instances is the *ego eimi* to be understood as a revelation formula?

The Double Meaning I AM Sayings

Grammatically, the I AM sayings of Jesus in the Fourth Gospel come in two basic varieties, based on whether the *ego eimi* is followed by a predicate noun that completes the meaning of the assertion or stands alone without any such expressed predicate. The second variety can be further divided into two subgroups. Sometimes the context suggests an implied predicate. On other occasions, no obvious candidate emerges from the context, leaving the *ego eimi* standing alone and carrying what is often termed "the absolute sense."

The most theologically significant instances of the *ego eimi*-plus-predicate construction are found in those situations in which Jesus is presented as making a unique claim about himself by stating an assertion regarding his person, generally by means of metaphor, in an emphatic manner. Seven such sayings occur in the Fourth Gospel. Jesus claims to be the bread of life (6:35, 41, 48, 51), the light of the world (8:12), the gate for the sheep (10:7, 9), the good shepherd (10:11, 14), the resurrection and the life (11:25), the true vine (15:1, 2), and the way, the truth, and the life (14:6). The copulative use of *eimi* in these statements indicates that in such situations Jesus is likely not alluding to the divine name directly. Moreover, these statements are not primarily ontological, but soteriological in tone.[9] As soteriological assertions they are all connected

---

4. Rudolf Bultmann, *The Gospel of John: A Commentary*, trans. G. R. Beasely-Murray, R. W. N. Hoare, and J. K. Riches (Philadelphia: Westminster, 1971), 225 n. 3. For a rejection of Bultmann's schema, see Luise Schottroff, "ego," in *Exegetical Dictionary of the New Testament*, ed. Horst Balz and Gerhard Schneider, 3 vols. (Grand Rapids: Eerdmans, 1990–1993), 1:379.

5. Barnabas Lindars, *The Gospel of John*, New Century Bible (London: Marshall, Morgan & Scott, 1972), 191.

6. J. H. Bernard, *A Critical and Exegetical Commentary on the Gospel according to St. John*, International Critical Commentary, 2 vols. (Edinburgh: T. & T. Clark, 1928), 1:cxvii.

7. For a similar characterization, see Lindars, *Gospel of John*, 191.

8. Bultmann, *Gospel of John*, 192.

9. Charles H. Talbert, *Reading John: A Literary and Theological Commentary on the Fourth Gospel and the Johannine Epistles* (New York: Crossroad, 1994), 152.

to the quality of "life"—eternal life—that Jesus claims to be able to mediate to anyone who believes in him.[10]

As assertions that embody Jesus' claim to be the one who both possesses and dispenses true life,[11] the the *ego eimi*-plus-predicate sayings elaborate the significance of his understanding of himself as the I AM. Taken together, they present Jesus as the agent of the Father in bringing salvation—that is, life—to his people.

More significant for the saga of the I AM are the verses in which the *ego eimi* has no explicitly stated predicate. Whenever the context suggests an implied predicate, the *eimi* can be read as merely a copulative. The "I am," in turn, can be interpreted as carrying simply the "everyday" meaning of the phrase ("It is I" or "I am the one"), as is the case in the one instance in which the *ego eimi* appears without an expressed predicate on the lips of a person other than Jesus (9:9). If the meaning of the *ego eimi* is to be limited to its everyday use in these texts, then Jesus' declarations need not be seen as references to the divine name.

Yet the situation is not quite so straightforward. It is not always obvious that a predicate is indeed to be supplied from the context; nor is it evident what that implied predicate is. Equally important is the theological difficulty that these texts can entail. At work in instances of the *ego eimi*-plus-implied-predicate structure can be what Lindars calls "richer, awe-inspiring overtones."[12] Hence, John might be intending that the *ego eimi* carry a double entendre (to cite Craig Keener's designation), a double meaning perceivable to the eyes of faith.

The I AM in Samaria

The first significant occurrence of the *ego eimi*-plus-implied-predicate construction is found in Jesus' conversation with the Samaritan woman at Jacob's well. If this text is to be viewed as alluding to the Old Testament divine name, we might say that this is the first time in which the incarnate I AM hints at this aspect of his identity.

In response to her declaration that the Messiah is coming, he declares, *ego eimi*, "I myself am [he]" (John 4:26). At first glance, his statement appears to be nothing more than an emphatic announcement that he is the Messiah whom the woman is anticipating,[13] and not a direct claim to

---

10. For a discussion of this, see Rudolf Schnackenburg, *The Gospel according to John*, trans. Cecily Hastings et al., 3 vols. (New York: Seabury, 1980–82), 2:80.

11. For a similar characterization, see Stanley B. Marrow, *The Gospel of John: A Reading* (New York: Paulist Press, 1995), 125.

12. Lindars, *Gospel of John*, 541.

13. See, for example, C. H. Dodd, *The Interpretation of the Fourth Gospel* (Cambridge: Cambridge University Press, 1953), 314–15. This interpretation was popular in the Middle Ages and the Reformation. Hence, see Thomas Aquinas, *Commentary on the Gospel of St. John*, vol. 4 of *Aquinas Scripture Series*, trans. James A. Weisheipl and Fabian R. Larcher, 4 vols. (Albany, NY: Magi Books, 1980),

be the I AM of the Old Testament.[14] Hence, D. A. Carson declares confidently, "This instance of *ego eimi* is not theologically loaded.[15] And Raymond Brown asserts, "It is not possible that this use is intended in the style of divinity."[16] Lindars, in turn, adds a word of explanation. Regarding this self-disclosure on the part of Jesus, he concludes, "That is in itself revelation enough for the time being."[17]

Most commentators, however, sense the presence of overtones of a deeper meaning in the text.[18] Keener, for example, suggests that the *ego eimi* might involve "double entendre pointing to a deeper identity."[19] William E. Hull takes the matter a step further. He surmises, "This use of 'I am' anticipates its explicit use later as a revelatory formula announcing the presence of the eternal God in the midst of history."[20] Thomas Brodie finds an even stronger connection between this text and the Old Testament. He sees in Jesus' words "an evocation of the central revelation of God to Moses" in Exodus 3:14, which leads him to conclude, "Jesus' self-identification as the expected Messiah is so formulated that it indicates the presence of God. And that God is calling for a reply."[21] Yet it is Francis Moloney who lifts the matter to the heights. Seeing here the presence of the "formula of revelation" that discloses an identity that "reaches beyond a Messiah-Christ," he renders the verse, "'I Am' [is] the one speaking to you."[22]

That John might have a deeper meaning of the *ego eimi* in view here is indicated by a particular grammatical feature of Jesus' response. The Greek construction, *ego eimi ho lalon soi*, can either be read, "I am the one speaking to you," which in this context would seem quite senseless, or "I am, the one speaking to you." In the latter case, "the one speaking to you" does not function as a predicate, but stands in apposition to the subject "I" of the *ego eimi*. This observation invites the supplying of the implied predicate, "the Christ," from the context.

1:252; John Calvin, *The Gospel according to St. John*, trans. T. H. L. Parker, ed. David W. Torrance and Thomas F. Torrance, 2 vols. (Edinburgh: Oliver & Boyd, 1959), 1:102.

14. See, for example, Colin G. Kruse, *The Gospel according to John: An Introduction and Commentary*, Tyndale New Testament Commentaries (Grand Rapids: Eerdmans, 2003), 135.

15. D. A. Carson, *The Gospel according to John*, Pillar New Testament Commentary (Grand Rapids: Eerdmans, 1991), 227.

16. Brown, *Gospel according to John*, 1:172.

17. Lindars, *Gospel of John*, 191.

18. See, for example, C. K. Barrett, *The Gospel according to St. John: An Introduction with Commentary and Notes on the Greek Text* (London: SPCK, 1965), 200; Edwyn Clement Hoskyns, *The Fourth Gospel*, ed. Francis Noel Davey (London: Faber & Faber, 1947), 244.

19. Craig S. Keener, *The Gospel of John: A Commentary*, 2 vols. (Peabody, MA: Hendrickson, 2003), 1:620.

20. William E. Hull, "John," in *The Broadman Bible Commentary*, ed. Clifton J. Allen, 12 vols. (Nashville: Broadman, 1969–1972), 9:254.

21. Thomas L. Brodie, *The Gospel according to John: A Literary and Theological Commentary* (New York: Oxford University Press, 1993), 224.

22. Francis J. Moloney, *The Gospel of John*, vol. 4 of *Sacra Pagina*, ed. Daniel J. Harrington (Collegeville, MN: Liturgical Press, 1998), 130.

Yet the *ego eimi* can also carry the absolute sense. If so, then John might be intending that the reader understand Jesus' assertion in connection with the Old Testament theophanic formula, *'ani hu'*.[23] The case for the latter is strengthened by the possible parallel to a verse in which Yahweh utters the nearly identical statement, *'ani hu' hamedabber*, which is rendered in the Septuagint as *ego eimi autos ho lalon* (Isa. 52:6).[24] In the Isaiah text, Yahweh promises a coming day when his people will know his name and, consequently, know that he is the one who is speaking. The similarity in construction might not only link Jesus' appearance as the fulfillment of this promise but also indicate a connection between the *ego eimi* in John 4:26 and the *'ani hu'* so prominent in Second Isaiah. In fact, it was the rendering of this construction in the Septuagint that resulted in *ego eimi* coming to be understood not only as a declaration of the divine singularity, which lay at the heart of several of the Isaiah texts, but also as a divine name.[25]

The I AM on the Sea of Galilee

The *ego eimi* with an implied predicate occurs again in Jesus' statement of reassurance spoken to his terrified disciples who see him walking on the Sea of Galilee (John 6:20). This incident is not unique to the Fourth Gospel, but is one of the few occasions in which Jesus utters the *ego eimi* in the Synoptics (see Mark 6:50; Matt. 14:27).

Although the incident has been dismissed by some commentators as "a pious legend," to cite B. Harvie Branscomb's appraisal of the Marcan story,[26] the presence of the pericope in Mark attests to its antiquity. Stauffer explains:

> This story must derive from a very old, much discussed, and widely disseminated tradition. For in Mark 6,49, we find the Evangelist plainly combating a polemic account which evidently tried to dismiss the whole affair as a ghost story. And in Mark 6,50, the reader is informed that all the persons in the boat saw the miracle and can testify to it. All this is reminiscent of the Easter controversy with its problem of ghostly appearances and its lists of witnesses.[27]

Philip Harner, in turn, suggests that this incident might have been the source in the Synoptic tradition from which John derived the absolute use of the *ego eimi*.[28]

---

23. For a helpful discussion of this connection, see Ethelbert Stauffer, *Jesus and His Story*, trans. Richard and Clara Winston (New York: Alfred A. Knopf, 1959), 174–95.

24. Bernard, *Critical ad Exegetical Commentary on the Gospel according to St. John*, 1:151. For a defense of the absolute sense of the *ego eimi* in John 4:26, see Stauffer, *Jesus and His Story*, 186–87.

25. Brown, *Gospel according to John*, 1:536.

26. B. Harvie Branscomb, *The Gospel of Mark*, Moffatt New Testament Commentary (New York: Harper & Brothers, n.d.), 117.

27. Stauffer, *Jesus and His Story*, 183.

28. Philip B. Harner, *The "I Am" of the Fourth Gospel: A Study in Johannine Usage and Thought* (Philadelphia: Fortress, 1970), 47.

At first glance, John 6:20 seems to be a straightforward example of the *ego eimi*-plus-implied-predicate construction that can be readily rendered into English as a simple self-identification. Jesus appears to be merely identifying himself to his disciples, who according to the accounts in the Synoptics fear that he is a ghost. In an attempt to reassure them and calm their fears, he declares, "It is I." F. F. Bruce speaks for those who take this cautious approach to the text: "There are places in this Gospel where the words *ego eimi* have the nature of a divine designation . . . but here they simply mean 'It is I.'"[29]

Many contemporary commentators, however, do not consider the matter to be quite so simple. Brown concludes that this is a "borderline case where one cannot be certain if a divine formula is meant."[30] Others, such as Carson, find in the text "an anticipation of a clearer self-disclosure by Jesus."[31]

Yet there might be an even stronger, double meaning intended here. Lindars is an example of those exegetes who move in this direction. After agreeing that the *ego eimi* "cannot be taken as the divine name of Exod. 3.14; it is simply self-identification," he then adds, "But, as the climax of the story, it brings Jesus to the centre of thought as the Saviour, and so we cannot exclude the possibility that John regarded it as an anticipation of the 'I am' saying of the discourse (verse 35)."[32] C. H. Dodd is even less cautious. He concludes that "Christ appears to them 'upon the waters,' and He pronounces the sacred formula, *Ego eimi*." Dodd then explains, "In view of the importance which the formula bears in other Johannine passages it seems more than probable that it is to be understood here as elsewhere as the equivalent of the divine name *'ami hu'*, I AM."[33] Similarly, in Rudolf Schnackenburg's estimation, "the evangelist . . . who has already led up to this (17b), makes the saying Jesus' full proclamation of himself, a revelation of himself as divine. For him it is not just the climax of the story, but the main reason for his inclusion of it in his narrative."[34]

In the Fourth Gospel the incident on the Sea of Galilee opens the way for the "bread of life discourse" that follows immediately in the narrative. In this discourse, which focuses on one of the soteriological *ego eimi*-plus-predicate sayings, Jesus draws from the material image of eating to announce his claim

29. F. F. Bruce, *The Gospel of John: Introduction, Exposition, and Notes* (Grand Rapids: Eerdmans, 1983), 148. See also Bernard, *Critical and Exegetical Commentary on the Gospel according to St. John*, 1:187; Kruse, *Gospel according to John*, 165; Leon Morris, *The Gospel according to John*, rev. ed., New International Commentary on the New Testament (Grand Rapids: Eerdmans, 1995), 310 n. 44.

30. Brown, *Gospel according to John*, 1:252.

31. Carson, *Gospel according to John*, 276. This comes in the wake of his basic rejection of an exalted meaning in this text, set forth on p. 275.

32. Lindars, *Gospel of John*, 247.

33. Dodd, *Interpretation of the Fourth Gospel*, 345. See also Brodie, *Gospel according to John*, 264; Moloney, *Gospel of John*, 203.

34. Schnackenburg, *Gospel according to John*, 2:27.

to be the one who brings spiritual sustenance—eternal life—to his follow-ers. Consequently, the declaration of assurance that Jesus voices to his disci-ples forms the narratival bridge between the feeding of the five thousand and Jesus' theological explication of the meaning of that miracle presented in the ensuing discourse.

As important as its role as a vital link connecting these lengthier seg-ments of John's narrative might be, the main basis for seeing in the *ego eimi* overtones of the divine name lies in the possibility that this incident entails a divine epiphany or a theophany.[35] The theophanic character of the pericope is indicated by the larger statement in which the *ego eimi* for-mula is articulated. Old Testament theophanies often include Yahweh announcing his name and admonishing his hearers not to fear. In chap-ter 4, we saw examples of this phenomenon in several of the texts in Sec-ond Isaiah (cf. Isa. 41:10, 14; 43:1, 5; 44:2; 51:12). This parallel would open the way to seeing in Jesus' "I am" statement overtones of the divine self-designation in Second Isaiah.

The theophanic character of the incident is even stronger in the Marcan version of the story, which in Robert Guelich's estimation "combines the characteristics of a true epiphany and rescue story."[36] In Mark, Jesus speaks the identifying *ego eimi* to his disciples as he attempts to pass by them (Mark 6:48). Some commentators have looked to the exodus for the Old Testa-ment background to Mark's account, viewing this account as a symbolic repetition of the crossing of the Red Sea.[37] Yet Jesus' passing by the boat more readily links the pericope to the theophany in which Yahweh passes by Moses and in the process the divine name is revealed (Exod. 33:22; cf. Elijah's similar experience in 1 Kgs. 19:11).[38] In the Synoptic version of the story, the theophanic pronouncement formula is likewise stronger than its parallel in the Fourth Gospel. In Mark (and Matthew) Jesus speaks the *ego eimi* between two admonitions: "Take heart, it is I; do not be afraid."

There might be yet another connection between this incident and the divine self-designation in Second Isaiah. In all three Gospels the event is closely connected to two situations in which Jesus shows his power over creation. It comes on the heels of the miraculous feeding of the five

---

35. See, for example, Herman N. Ridderbos, *The Gospel according to John: A Theological Com-mentary*, trans. John Vriend (Grand Rapids: Eerdmans, 1997), 217. Bultmann claims that Jesus' state-ment "is the traditional formula of greeting used by the deity in his epiphany." Bultmann, *Gospel of John*, 216.

36. Robert A. Guelich, *Mark 1–8:26*, Word Biblical Commentary (Dallas: Word, 1989), 346.

37. For this interpretation, see Morna D. Hooker, *The Gospel according to Saint Mark*, Black's New Testament Commentary (London: A. & C. Black, 1991), 170.

38. See, for example, A. M. Denis, "Jesus' Walking on the Waters: A Contribution to the His-tory of the Pericope in the Gospel Tradition," *Louvain Studies* 1 (1967): 284–97; J. Schneider, "par-erchomai," in *Theological Dictionary of the New Testament*, 2:681–82. See also Guelich, *Mark 1–8:26*, 350; William L. Lane, *The Gospel of Mark: The English Text with Introduction, Exposition, and Notes*, New International Commentary on the New Testament (Grand Rapids: Eerdmans, 1974), 237.

thousand, which, incidently, Mark, but especially John, suggest took place near the time of Passover. And of course, the declaration forms the climax to the incident in which Jesus walks on the Sea of Galilee. In several texts in Second Isaiah, Yahweh's declaration "I am he" is connected to his role as sovereign. The main theme of the prophetic writing is his sovereignty over history, of course, but mentioned as well is his status as the Creator whom all creation obeys. The Old Testament Creator motif is on occasion related to the idea of Yahweh's victory over the chaos, which, in turn, is at times represented by the sea (cf. Job 9:8; Ps. 74:12–14). In Isa. 51:9–11, this imagery is brought together with the Passover or exodus motif in anticipation of the new exodus of Israel from exile by means of the parting of the sea. The incident on the Sea of Galilee might carry overtones of this composite Old Testament theme. The act of walking on the water could be a way of connecting Jesus to the one who shows himself to be sovereign over the chaos in the act of creation and who promises a new deliverance of his people from bondage to sin.[39]

The I AM in the Garden

A similar verdict can be rendered for an incident that occurs much later in John's Gospel. At the time of his arrest, Jesus voices the *ego eimi* twice (18:5, 8). This pericope marks the final use of the *ego eimi* in connection with a Jesus saying in the Fourth Gospel.

The simplest reading of these verses sees the use of the *ego eimi* merely as Jesus' indication to his captors that he is the Jesus of Nazareth whom they are seeking. This appears to be clearly the case in the second of the two utterances, where the context suggests that the *ego eimi* might be nothing more than the means by which Jesus acknowledges his identity as the one being sought.[40] Even Dodd, who finds overtones of the divine name in many of the I AM sayings, takes a cautious view in this case. He concludes that the idea that the *ego eimi* in verse 5 is intended to carry deeper overtones "is in no way essential to the narrative; nor need the recoil of the assailants . . . of necessity imply an *Allmachtswunder*."[41] Yet in these verses a double meaning might also be intended to lead the reader to view Jesus in connection with the divine name.[42]

The case for this interpretation of the first utterance of the *ego eimi* is especially strong. Lindars notes that John's repetition of Jesus' statement in the narration in verse 6 "makes the *ego eimi* stand out so effectively."[43]

---

39. For this perspective, see Harner, *"I Am" of the Fourth Gospel*, 34–35.
40. This is admitted even by Lindars. Lindars, *Gospel of John*, 541–42.
41. Dodd, *Interpretation of the Fourth Gospel*, 426 n. 1. See also Bernard, *Critical and Exegetical Commentary on the Gospel according to St. John*, 2:587.
42. See, for example, Kruse, *Gospel according to John*, 350–51.
43. Lindars, *Gospel of John*, 541.

Even more noteworthy, however, is John's comment that at the sound of these words, Jesus' would-be captors "stepped back and fell to the ground." John's inclusion of this detail suggests that this is a revelatory event, even an "epiphany of Deity,"[44] that can only leave the arresting party prostrate before God.[45] George Beasley-Murray highlights the double meaning inherent in the evangelist's remark: "The reply of Jesus, 'I am (he),' may be seen as a normal self-identification, but we are almost certainly intended to recognize its overtones."[46] Harner, in turn, brings to the surface the Gospel writer's intent: "In this way John wishes to express his belief that such an attitude of awe and reverence is the only fitting response to Jesus' words, *ego eimi*."[47]

Upon closer inspection, the second utterance can likewise be seen as intended to carry a double meaning. The deeper aspect is again suggested by an explanatory comment that John adds. After Jesus' declaration, "So if you are looking for me, let these men go," the narrator links the implied outcome with an Old Testament prophecy: "This was to fulfill the word that he had spoken, 'I did not lose a single one of those whom you gave me'" (v. 9). Moreover, Jesus' high-priestly prayer anticipated this outcome in a theologically charged declaration: "While I was with them, I protected them in your name that you have given me. I guarded them, and not one of them was lost except the one destined to be lost, so that the scripture might be fulfilled" (17:12).

Regarding John's explanatory statement, Harner declares, "In this way John connects the words *ego eimi* with the belief that in Jesus men find deliverance and receive life itself."[48] Although this understanding is possible, in the context of the farewell discourse and the passion narrative it seems theologically weak. John's intent is likely more closely connected to a theme that is central to this segment of the arrest narrative (and comes repeatedly to the fore throughout the entire Fourth Gospel). As the *ego eimi*, as the one who is sovereign over history, Jesus is at all times in control of his own destiny. For John, this sovereignty is nowhere more evident than in the important matter of the timing of his death, which is crucial insofar as in the Fourth Gospel (as in the New Testament in general) Jesus' sufferings are completely voluntary. As the one who is sovereign over his own life and death, he is also able to protect those whom the Father has put into his care, even as he declared in his prayer in the upper room. In this sense, the "I am" declaration in John 18:8 carries similar theological significance as

---

44. Bultmann, *Gospel of John*, 639.

45. Gary M. Burge, "'I Am' Sayings," in *Dictionary of Jesus and the Gospels*, ed. Joel B. Green and Scot McKnight (Downers Grove, IL: InterVarsity Press, 1992), 355; Harner, *"I Am" of the Fourth Gospel*, 45.

46. George R. Beasley-Murray, *John*, Word Biblical Commentary (Waco, TX: Word, 1987), 322.

47. Harner, *"I Am" of the Fourth Gospel*, 45.

48. Ibid.

the "I am the good shepherd" saying. In fact, insofar as Jesus ensures the safety of his disciples by turning himself over to his assailants, the act becomes at this point in the narrative an "acted parable" in which "the good shepherd lays down his life for the sheep" (10:11) and thereby a fore-shadowing of his impending passion.[49]

The "I Am (He)" Sayings

The occurrences of the *ego eimi* in these texts carry overtones of the Old Testament divine self-designation by virtue of their ability to function as instances of double entendre. In several other texts, Jesus' I AM sayings incorporate the *ego eimi* without an implied predicate. In these texts, the *ego eimi* is to be understood in the absolute sense. Regarding the meaning of such texts, scholars have reached a near consensus. As Brown asserts, "Since this usage goes far beyond ordinary parlance, all recognize that the absolute *ego eimi* has a special revelatory function in John."[50] Exegetes do not speak with one voice, however, as to which specific occurrences fall under this category. Yet most find at least one case in the lengthy discussion between Jesus and his hearers narrated in John 8, which is often designated the sixth discourse of the Fourth Gospel. In these verses, the *ego eimi* occurs without an explicit predicate three times.

The Contextual and Narratival Background

John 8 forms the center section within a larger thought unit that consists of John 7–9. An introduction (7:1–13) leads to two discourse sections (7:14–52 and 8:12–59) followed by a narrative of a sign (9:1–41).[51] The materials are occasioned by the Feast of Tabernacles, which provides the basis for the two major motifs that Jesus announces in the two discourses, namely, the living water and the light of the world. The second main section, which E. C. Hoskyns characterizes as "the second great discourse concerning the unbelief of the Jews,"[52] can be divided into five smaller thought units (vv. 12–20, 21–30, 31–40, 41–50, 51–59), each of which follows the basic pattern: a provocative statement by Jesus, the response of his Jewish hearers, and then Jesus' retort in the form of either a monologue or a dialogue.[53]

According to John's account, as a result of Jesus' presence in Jerusalem, the last day of the Feast of Tabernacles concludes on a note of discord or division (7:43). Upon hearing his teaching and seeing the signs that he

---

49. For this interpretation, see Barrett, *Gospel according to St. John*, 435. See also Bernard, *Critical and Exegetical Commentary on the Gospel according to St. John*, 2:587.
50. Brown, *Gospel according to John*, 1:533.
51. For this grouping of these chapters of the Fourth Gospel, see Talbert, *Reading John*, 143.
52. Hoskyns, *Fourth Gospel*, 327.
53. For this observation, see Talbert, *Reading John*, 152.

had given, many people come to believe that he is the Messiah (vv. 31, 40–41). The Pharisees and the chief priests, in contrast, have grown ever more certain that the people are being deceived (v. 47). In the midst of this discordant situation, John situates an extended interaction that initially pits Jesus against the Pharisees but quickly develops into a dispute between him and those whom John labels "the Jews."

The imagery of the Feast of Tabernacles incorporates both water and light. On the final day of the feast, Jesus draws from the first of these (vv. 37–38). At that point, his pedigree as one who hails from Galilee rather than Bethlehem, and not his words as such, is what evokes division among his hearers. The controversy that emerges in the sixth discourse, in turn, is ignited by his use of the second image, drawn perhaps in part from the brightly illuminated temple precincts.[54] Jesus voices a saying that in Stanley B. Marrow's estimation "sums up all that he is and all that he does in the world and for it."[55] The statement in John's Gospel reflects one typical structure of the I AM sayings. Here the *ego eimi* occurs with an explicit predicate. Jesus declares, "I am the light of the world" (8:12).[56] In this claim, which launches the first subunit of the chapter (vv. 12–20), Jesus connects light and life, both of which are reiterated in some form or another in the subsequent discourse, although with the focus increasingly moving toward the latter. Both motifs, but especially the idea of eternal life, provide the context in which the *ego eimi* declarations of the chapter gain their meaning.

Once again, Jesus' actual words do not initially become the point of the dispute. Rather than engaging with him regarding the content of his audacious theological claim, the Pharisees focus on a legal technicality. They charge Jesus with what might be called inappropriate witness. Jesus' testimony has no legal standing, they declare, because he is bearing witness to himself, which violates the rabbinic teaching that testimony to oneself is not acceptable in a court of law (v. 13). In response, Jesus declares that the Pharisees are not in a position to comment about his witness because they are ignorant of his origin and destiny (v. 14), and therefore they can only judge in accordance with human standards (v. 15). With these words, Jesus hints at his self-awareness as a person on a mission, namely, to be the one sent from the Father, a sense of mission that is central to the I AM sayings. Insofar as this comment implies that his connection to his (heavenly) source is so close that his testimony carries the authority of God himself and therefore does not need human validation,[57]

---

54. See, for example, Bruce, *Gospel of John*, 188. For a short description of this aspect of the feast, see Hull, "John," 289; Talbert, *Reading John*, 152–53; Schnackenburg, *Gospel according to John*, 2:189–90.

55. Marrow, *Gospel of John*, 125.

56. For an alternate understanding, see Morris, *Gospel according to John*, 388.

57. For similar interpretations, see Kruse, *Gospel according to John*, 203; Lindars, *Gospel of John*, 316.

it sets the stage for the discussion of Jesus' relationship to his Father that follows later in the discourse and informs the meaning of the *ego eimi* declarations in the chapter.

What he claims about himself is true, Jesus adds, in that, in accordance with Old Testament law, it is confirmed by two witnesses: himself and his Father, who has sent him (vv. 17–18). Schnackenburg points out the paradox that is involved here: "As God's representative he himself gives totally adequate evidence because in him the Father speaks (v. 14). On the other hand, as God's representative he can be distinguished from the one who sent him, and so there are two witnesses."[58] This paradox, in turn, suggests the manner in which Jesus can appropriate to his person the divine name, while still differentiating himself from the Father, a theme to which we must return at the end of the chapter.

In voicing the claim that two witnesses are at work, Jesus speaks the *ego eimi*. In this instance, the phrase is immediately followed by a predicate. The sentence can be rendered, "I myself am the one witnessing concerning myself, and witnessing concerning me [is] the one who sent me, the Father." Bernard finds this to be an example of the use of *ego eimi* in solemn affirmation and concludes that this "is the style of Deity."[59] Yet the statement might best be taken as carrying overtones of Jesus' close connection with his Father and not of the divine name as such. In any case, his hearers do not latch on to this aspect of his assertion, but rather zero in on his claim regarding his Father.

The Pharisees' biting query, "Where is your Father?" (v. 19), perhaps triggered by their assumption that he was invoking his human father,[60] brings to the surface what emerges as the central theme of the dispute, the relationship between Jesus and the one whom he claimed to be his Father. The conversation resumes with Jesus's second provocative statement, which inaugurates the chapter's second subunit (vv. 21–30). He is going away; they, in turn, will search for him but will die in their sins; they cannot come to where he is going (v. 21). In this statement, Jesus introduces an issue—dying in sin versus receiving eternal life—that will take on increasing importance as the discourse moves steadily forward to Jesus' final "I am" claim.

The hearers, whom John now designates simply as "the Jews," are understandably perplexed (v. 22). Jesus continues by drawing a crucial contrast between himself and them. He and they differ radically in origin. Building from his declaration that they do not know either his origin or his destiny, he now adds that they are "from below," that is, "of this world." He, in contrast, is "from above." For Jesus, of course, these phrases

58. Schnackenburg, *Gospel according to John*, 2:194.
59. Bernard, *Critical and Exegetical Commentary on the Gospel according to St. John*, 2:296.
60. Kruse, *Gospel according to John*, 204.

have less to do with the material than the spiritual. In keeping with a theme that recurs throughout the Johannine literature, the idea most likely being expressed here is that Jesus' hearers belong to a realm in which darkness, death, and Satan hold sway (cf. 1 John 1:5–7; 5:19), whereas he belongs to the realm of light and life inhabited by his Father. This declaration forms the context for the first "I am" statement: "If you do not believe that I am, you will indeed die in your sins" (John 8:24 NIV).

The I AM Lifted Up

The meaning of the *ego eimi* in this verse is not readily evident. The grammatical construction might suggest an implied predicate, such as "the one I claim to be," as the NIV renders the text. In this case, Jesus is saying that his hearers will die in their sins if they do not believe that he is the one whom he has just described himself to be, that is, the one whose origin is from above. Even this meaning of the "I am" would carry deep christological overtones regarding his close connection to his Father. Yet the construction might also be an instance of the absolute use of *ego eimi*. If this is the case, then Bruce is correct in concluding that more than simple self-identification is at work here. Jesus is then "saying something important about his person."[61] But what?

The response of the Jews, "Who are you?" does not shed much light on the matter. The question does not necessarily reflect hostility on the part of his hearers, who might simply be voicing an honest question.[62] Perhaps bewildered by his indefinite, open-ended, cryptic self-designation, "I am," his hearers are merely wanting Jesus to elaborate, to tell them who he is, in fact, claiming to be.[63] Harner explains the reflective dynamic involved: "They mentally supply a predicate. But since they are uncertain exactly what this predicate should be, they ask, 'Who are you?'"[64] Yet the *su* ("you") at the beginning of the question is emphatic. This construction suggests that by their question, Jesus' hearers are intending to voice a strong challenge against, even rejection of, his claim.[65] The "You, who are you?" of the text, therefore, might mean something like "Who do you think you are!"

Even more exegetically problematic is Jesus' immediate response, *ten archen ho ti lalo hymin*, which Bruce characterizes as "perhaps the most difficult clause to translate in this whole Gospel."[66] The difficulties surround the meaning of *ten archen*, which could be read as either a noun in the

---

61. Bruce, *Gospel of John*, 193.
62. For this interpretation, see Moloney, *Gospel of John*, 271.
63. See Barrett, *Gospel according to St. John*, 282.
64. Harner, *"I Am" of the Fourth Gospel*, 43.
65. Schnackenburg, *Gospel according to John*, 2:200.
66. Bruce, *Gospel of John*, 193. Barrett, in contrast, finds that the difficulty of the sentence has been "exaggerated." Barrett, *Gospel according to St. John*, 283. For a summary of the exegetical options, see Morris, *Gospel according to John*, 398–400.

accusative ("the beginning") or as an adverbial phrase ("at all"), and of *ho ti* or *hoti*, which could be rendered either "what" or "why." Consequently, the sentence can be read in a variety of ways.[67] One interpretation takes Jesus' words to be an expression of exasperation: "Why do I speak to you at all?" (NRSV).[68] The statement might also be intended to serve as a reminder to them that he has been consistently declaring his identity since the beginning (perhaps of his public ministry): "Just what I have been claiming all along" (NIV).[69] In any case, the text suggests that at this point in the discourse Jesus' hearers do not appear to see in his words an explicit appropriation of the divine name. Whatever allusion to the divine I AM might be intended in this verse, therefore, is subtle.

Yet we are not left completely in the dark regarding the significance of Jesus' use of the *ego eimi* here. When read in the light of the discourse as a whole, Jesus' statement indicates that belief is a matter of life and death. He declares that unbelief results in spiritual death, thereby implying the parallel idea that belief leads to eternal life. The clue to the meaning of this utterance of the *ego eimi*, therefore, seems to lie in the link that Jesus makes between his claim regarding himself and his role in mediating to his followers the quality of life that God alone provides. In keeping with this idea, Marianne Meye Thompson paraphrases Jesus' lofty claim in this way: "Jesus participates in the life of God and therefore in God's purposes of giving life to the world."[70]

In verse 24, Jesus emphasizes the contrast between life and death. As the discourse unfolds, he focuses on the related idea that he is the one sent by the Father with the mission of bringing eternal life. A step in the direction of this mission focus occurs in the words that follow. Jesus declares that he speaks what he has heard from the one who has sent him (v. 26). John interjects into the narrative that his hearers do not understand that he is talking about the Father (v. 27). For this reason, Jesus adds an explanatory comment that embodies the second use of the *ego eimi*: "When you have lifted up the Son of Man, then you will realize that I am [he]" (v. 28).

On two other occasions in John, Jesus uses the verb "lift up" (*hupsoo*) to denote his impending crucifixion (3:14; 12:32). *Hupsoo*, however, is not a common expression for the act of crucifixion. In fact, its use in this connotation is unique to the Fourth Gospel. This Greek verb means "lift up," "raise high," and, figuratively, "exalt."[71] Consequently, Jesus' declaration is

---

67. For a succinct summary of the major alternatives, see Beasley-Murray, *John*, 125–26. For a more detailed engagement, see Hoskyns, *Fourth Gospel*, 335–36.

68. For a cogent defense of this rendering, see Schnackenburg, *Gospel according to John*, 2:200–201.

69. For a helpful delineation of this conclusion, see Brodie, *Gospel according to John*, 327. For the basis for a similar interpretation to the NIV, see Bruce, *Gospel of John*, 194.

70. Marianne Meye Thompson, *The God of the Gospel of John* (Grand Rapids: Eerdmans, 2001), 91.

71. William F. Arndt and F. Wilbur Gingrich, *A Greek-English Lexicon of the New Testament and Other Early Christian Literature*, 4th ed. (Chicago: University of Chicago Press, 1957), 858.

likely a double entendre. For John, Jesus' crucifixion, his being "lifted up" on the cross, is simultaneously his exaltation (cf. 12:23; 13:31–32; 17:1),[72] because the cross marks the depth of Jesus' obedience to the Father's will.[73] Consequently, "lifted up" is John's technical expression for the idea that Jesus' passion is the point at which his divine glory is disclosed.[74] Jesus likely has this understanding of the significance of his crucifixion in view in the statement uttered here. Yet the meaning of the *ego eimi* in this I AM saying is not unambiguous.

One exegetical question that contributes to the ambiguity has to do with the connection between the two independent clauses of the verse. Is the second clause ("and [that] I do nothing on my own, but I speak these things as the Father instructed me") a continuation of what Jesus anticipates his hearers will know after his crucifixion? Or does it begin a new, independent statement? It should be noted that the inclusion of "that" after the conjunction "and" found in many English translations is an interpretive interpolation, which is at best implied by the Greek text. Following the Greek itself (without the interpolation) yields an alternative rendering that places the "and" at the beginning of a new sentence in which Jesus voices a declaration, in keeping with what he says in verse 26, about what he continually does.[75] Both interpretations advance the same christological point: Jesus' close connection to the Father. Both likewise leave open the question of whether Jesus is explicitly invoking the divine name in this verse.

The likelihood that "I am" is meant to be taken as a direct citation of the divine name is diminished by the fact that viewing it in this manner requires that *ego eimi* be understood as the object of belief. Were this the case, we would expect the verse to read, "unless you believe that I am the 'I am.'"[76] Considerations such as this led Calvin to conclude against the ancient interpretation of the text that the *ego eimi* does not refer to Christ's essence but to his office or work on behalf of humankind.[77] Herman Ridderbos, following Calvin, concludes that the words "do not refer to the ontological relationship of the Son with the Father but to his action as the one sent by the Father."[78] According to Calvin and Ridderbos, then, the *ego eimi* here serves as a way of referring to Jesus' work in our salvation.

While agreeing that the point of the text is to affirm Jesus' role in giving eternal life to his followers, other commentators nevertheless do find

---

72. Lüdemann erroneously declares that the cross simultaneously means Jesus' exaltation into heaven. In the Fourth Gospel, the cross is the point of Jesus' glorification, but this does not entail an ascension. See Gerd Lüdemann, "hupsoo," in *Exegetical Dictionary of the New Testament*, 3:410.

73. For a statement of this aspect, see Keener, *Gospel of John*, 1:745.

74. For a similar description, see Lindars, *Gospel of John*, 322.

75. For this view, see Morris, *Gospel according to John*, 401.

76. For a declaration of this argument, see Ridderbos, *Gospel according to John*, 301.

77. Calvin, *Gospel according to St. John*, 1:216.

78. Ridderbos, *Gospel according to John*, 301.

allusions to the divine name in this verse (as well as in v. 24). More specifically, they see in these occurrences an echo of Second Isaiah (rather than of Exod. 3:14).[79] This connection to the "I am he" of Isaiah 40–55, in turn, is crucial in understanding the meaning of these two occurrences of the *ego eimi*. As I noted in chapter 4, the ancient prophet saw in the rise of the Persian conqueror Cyrus the work of Yahweh, who was inaugurating a new exodus. As the savior of Israel—as the one who is present with his people in a saving manner—Yahweh, who is also the creator of the world, repeatedly declared to the remnant in Babylon, "I am he," which the Septuagint renders *ego eimi*. In these two occurrences of the *ego eimi*, in turn, Jesus voices the I AM in a situation that parallels the pronouncement of the "I am he" in Second Isaiah. Read in the context of the Fourth Gospel as a whole, therefore, this statement suggests that Jesus, who is the incarnation of the Word through whom the world was created, is about to inaugurate a new exodus, one that involves not only salvation for the Jews but also the liberation of humankind from bondage to sin.[80]

The connection between John 8:28 and Second Isaiah sheds light on this I AM saying in another manner as well. I indicated in chapter 4 that in Second Isaiah, Yahweh presents himself as the true God and claims that this status is confirmed by the fact that he alone has foreknowledge of future saving events (e.g., Isa. 43:9–13). For this reason, he can declare himself to be the only God, the "I am he." A similar theology seems to be operative in John 8:28. This time, however, the saving act of God that inaugurates a new exodus is not the military success of any earthly conqueror but the "lifting up" of Jesus in his imminent crucifixion.

The link between John 8 and Second Isaiah is enhanced as well by the prescribed response of the respective hearers in each text. In Isaiah 43:10, Yahweh summons Israel to serve as his witnesses in the tribunal that he has called together. He states as the goal of their witnessing act, "so that you might know and believe me and understand that I am he" (*'ani hu'*; LXX *ego eimi*). The language "know and believe me . . . that I am he" reappears in these two verses of the Fourth Gospel. Jesus' hearers will die unless they "believe that I am he" (v. 24), and when they have lifted him up, they will "know that I am" (v. 28).

The connection between Jesus' "I am" assertions and the *'ani hu'* of Second Isaiah evident in these two verses is repeated in the occurrence of the *ego eimi* in John's account of the Last Supper. Prior to his betrayal at the hand of Judas, Jesus shows his concern for his disciples by forewarning them that such an event was soon to transpire.[81] He then explains, "I tell

---

79. For this judgment, see, for example, Bruce, *Gospel of John*, 193; Carson, *Gospel according to John*, 343.

80. For a similar interpretation, see Lindars, *Gospel of John*, 320–21.

81. For this interpretation, see Kruse, *Gospel according to John*, 286.

you this now, so that when it does occur, you may believe that I am he" (John 13:19). If the theology of Second Isaiah does form the background for this "I am" saying,[82] then we ought to interpret this verse, like John 8:28, as Jesus' invitation to his hearers to see in the impending fulfillment of his prophecy concerning his saving death a confirmation of his claim to be the I AM (the *'ani hu'*) of Israel, the one who is the only God. Moreover, the declaration, reminiscent of Isaiah 43:10 (and John 8:24, 28), reflects Jesus intention that his hearers *believe* "that I am" (cf. 14:29).

The introduction of the prophetic aspect places within these two instances a future orientation that is not as evident in most other I AM sayings. The eschatological aspect is enhanced in John 8:28 by Jesus' linking of himself to the figure of the Son of Man. We will return to this theme in chapter 6. For now, it is sufficient to draw from these occurrences the observation that the close connection that John posits between Jesus' *ego eimi* claim and the faith present in his hearers underscores the cryptic sense that it carries, whenever it is found on his lips in the Fourth Gospel. Harner is surely on the right track when he concludes regarding these sayings, "In this way John underlies its solemn nature as an authoritative statement that only Jesus can make and only those who believe in him can understand."[83] In relegating to himself the divine I AM designation, Jesus is declaring that he has been sent by the Father—by the God of the story of Israel—to mediate life to his hearers, and this life comes as they receive it from him by faith. Not only this, but he is also linking himself with the saving God of Israel in the closest possible way. In short, that he is the I AM will be most fully disclosed in his death on the cross, by means of which he makes salvation available to all who believe in him.

The Eternal I AM

The second subunit of the sixth discourse ends on a positive note: "As he was saying these things, many believed in him" (8:30). The final outcome of the chapter, in contrast, is quite different. In fact, beginning with the third subunit (vv. 31–40) the discussion between Jesus and "the Jews" becomes even more confrontational. The bitterness of the accusations that come to be voiced in the ensuing dispute leads Moloney to conclude that the remainder of the eighth chapter of John is "the most difficult section of the Gospel."[84] The issue that launches this round of the altercation and carries through to the end of the chapter focuses on the question of who can claim to be the legitimate heir of Abraham. At the end of the discourse, Jesus voices the final, climactic utterance of the *ego eimi* found in the chapter.

82. Lindars, *Gospel of John*, 455.
83. Harner, *"I Am" of the Fourth Gospel*, 37.
84. Moloney, *Gospel of John*, 274.

The Absolute I AM Saying

The I AM saying that occurs in John 8:58 is unique from all the others in
that it has no possible implied predicate. Hence, it is the one unambiguous occurrence of the *ego eimi* in the absolute sense.[85] For this reason, it
stands out as the single most defining instance for the meaning of Jesus'
appropriation of the divine name. It is consequently central to the saga of
the I AM.

The Narratival Context

Jesus' hearers, who at this point are identified by John as "the Jews who
had believed in him," are the ones who inject Abraham into the conversation. The third subunit, which then flows into the fourth, begins with
Jesus' provocative statement in which he declares that by following him
they will know the truth and thereby be set free (vv. 31–32). His hearers,
however, retort that insofar as they are Abraham's children (which had
become a standard way for Jews to understand their uniqueness as a people[86]), they have no need to be set free (v. 33). Moreover, they not only
have Abraham but also God as their father (v. 41). Yet their desire to kill
him and their inability to accept his word (or teaching) leads Jesus to
accuse his hearers of being children of the devil (v. 44). In so doing, he
brings into the open his underlying point that physical paternity is not
the crucial consideration for one's spiritual standing.

Couched within this growing parting of ways is Jesus' ongoing attempt
to cast the salvation he offers in terms reminiscent of the exodus and to
speak about the status of a "son" in a father's household. Overtones of the
exodus motif are suggested by Jesus' declaration that those who commit
sin are indeed slaves; they are in slavery to sin (v. 32). He links this theme
to the household motif by declaring that because the son has a permanent
place in the household, the son can bring genuine freedom to slaves (v. 36).
This declaration serves as a clear reference to himself and his role in bringing salvation. He then adds that the source of his teaching is what he has
seen "in the Father's presence" (v. 38) and "heard from God" (v. 40). These
assertions entail a claim that he stands in the closest possible connection
to God, a claim that he then repeats in the simple declaration, "I came
from God" (v. 42).[87]

85. Some commentators conclude that John 13:19 is likewise a case of the *ego eimi* in the absolute
sense. See, for example, Bernard, *Critical and Exegetical Commentary on the Gospel according to St.
John*, 2:468; Harner, *"I Am" of the Fourth Gospel*, 37. This is a possible understanding. Yet even here,
some connection to the assertions regarding himself in the surrounding materials remains possible.
Moreover, the *ego eimi* in this verse can be readily rendered with the implied predicate "he"; hence,
"I am he." This is not the case in John 8:58, where "I am he" is simply not a possible translation.

86. For an elaboration of this point, see Hoskyns, *Fourth Gospel*, 339–40.

87. For the two possible interpretations of this phrase, see Bruce, *Gospel of John*, 200.

The discourse also follows another aspect of the statement that Jesus made regarding the son and slaves, namely, the assertion that the son has a place in the father's household forever (v. 35). Here John's description of Jesus' opponents shifts to "the Jews," who hurl further insults at him. They suggest that he is a Samaritan and has a demon (vv. 48, 52), perhaps thereby indicating that they placed him in the category of the Samaritan prophets who made audacious claims but were dismissed by the Jews as being demon possessed (cf. Acts 8:9).[88]

Jesus' response, which inaugurates the fifth subunit of the discourse, voices the implication of what the status of "sons" entails for his followers: Those who keep his word will "never see death" (v. 51).[89] This statement follows the typically Johannine pattern of expressing a positive claim by means of a negative statement. In this case, Jesus is claiming to be the source and mediator of eternal life.[90] Some commentators see in this declaration yet another attempt to call his hearers to change their minds about him and pay attention to his words.[91] In any case, the statement is a reiteration of his claim that he has been sent with the mission of mediating a particular kind of life—avoidance of death or eternal life in the face of death, and hence continuation in the Father's household—to those who respond positively to his message.

The Jews, who assumed that Jesus was referring to physical death, retort by pointing out that Abraham and the prophets all died and then querying him, "Are you greater than our father Abraham who died? Who do you claim to be?" (v. 53). Literally, the latter question reads, "Who are you making yourself?" Hence, it raises the matter of who Jesus is exalting himself to be,[92] a pointed query that comes as no surprise in that Jesus' opponents repeatedly voiced the suspicion that he was "making himself equal to God" (cf. 5:18; 10:33).

The actual goal of Jesus' critics in raising this matter is unclear. Some exegetes postulate that his hearers are assuming that such pointed questions will lead Jesus to realize the erroneous implications of what he is saying. Schnackenburg, in contrast, theorizes that they "are accusing Jesus of blasphemy, and they are pushing him further in this direction until they have indisputable proof from his own lips that he claims divine status."[93] Jesus' declaration that he has the prerogative of granting eternal life does, of course, suggest that he is claiming to be superior to Abraham, perhaps even setting himself alongside God, who alone is eternally alive and the giver of life. Nevertheless, Jesus responds by denying that he is glorifying

---

88. Kruse, *Gospel according to John*, 215.
89. For a helpful delineation of this connection, see Lindars, *Gospel of John*, 331.
90. For a similar characterization, see Brodie, *Gospel according to John*, 334.
91. Kruse, *Gospel according to John*, 215.
92. For this understanding, see Beasley-Murray, *John*, 137.
93. Schnackenburg, *Gospel according to St. John*, 2:220.

himself. He is not making himself to be anyone.[94] Rather, his Father is the one who glorifies him (v. 54).

Jesus then indicates that even Abraham would confirm his claims. He declares that the great patriarch rejoiced to see his day, that "he saw it and was glad" (v. 56).[95] To his hearers, however, this remark appeared to make Jesus a contemporary of Abraham. It suggested that Jesus was claiming to have somehow been alive when Abraham walked the earth. In response to this incredulous suggestion, they voice one final, exasperated query, "You are not yet fifty years old, and have you seen Abraham?" (v. 57), which Schnackenburg renders as "How can you, at your young age, presume to claim dealings with the venerable Abraham?"[96] The stage is now set for Jesus' climactic declaration. In response, he evokes the *ego eimi* in an unmistakably emphatic manner: "Very truly, I tell you, before Abraham was, I am" (v. 58).

The Meaning of the Ego Eimi

Is the *ego eimi* here an allusion to Exodus 3:14? Was Jesus finally explicitly claiming for himself the divine name revealed to Moses at the burning bush? Some commentators are not convinced that this is the case. For example, Ridderbos declares unabashedly, "It is questionable . . . whether the reference in the 'I am' here is to the ontological category of divine being." In his estimation, the context of the verse indicates that the I AM refers to "the eschatological Redeemer promised and sent by God."[97] Lindars, citing Bultmann, explains that interpreting the *ego eimi* as a declaration of the divine name "would deprive the phrase of its verbal force, making it simply a name, so that the phrase would have to be an elliptical way of saying 'I am the I AM.'"[98] Other exegetes, in contrast, see in this verse clear overtones of the divine name revealed to Moses.[99] In fact, Brown asserts, "No clearer implication of divinity is found in the Gospel tradition."[100]

The case for this interpretation is based in part on the differences between the Greek verbs that are used to delineate the contrast between Abraham and Jesus. The verb used in conjunction with the former is *ginomai*, the basic meaning of which is "become." In speaking about himself, in contrast, Jesus uses the more static verb *eimi*. Alvah Hovey notes that

---

94. For this interpretation, see see Beasley-Murray, *John*, 137.

95. For a helpful summary of the possible meanings of this claim, as well as the Rabbinical background to the idea, see Beasley-Murray, *John*, 138–39. See also Schnackenburg, *Gospel according to John*, 2:221–23.

96. Schnackenburg, *Gospel according to St. John*, 2:223.

97. Ridderbos, *Gospel according to John*, 323.

98. Lindars, *Gospel of John*, 336. It should be noted, however, that Lindars nevertheless sees in the *ego eimi* "timeless preexistence" and "the timeless condition of eternal existence."

99. See, for example, Schnackenburg, *Gospel according to St. John*, 2:84, 224.

100. Brown, *Gospel according to John*, 1:367.

these two verbs carry quite different connotations. The former "signifies an existence which has an origin, and might be rendered in this case, *came to be*," whereas the latter "denotes existence simply and absolutely, without any reference to origin."[101]

Noteworthy as well is the difference in the tenses of the two verbs. The latter is in the present tense, in contrast to the aorist of the former. A long line of commentators since Chrysostom have found weighty significance in the use of the present tense "I am" rather than the past tense "I was."[102] Leon Morris, for example, concludes from this grammatical feature that "a mode of being that has a definite beginning is contrasted with one that is eternal," so that "'I am' must here have the fullest significance it can bear."[103] Similarly, Hovey suggests that the *eimi* is in "the timeless present," indicating that Jesus is claiming for himself "the same eternal, unsuccessive, absolute being, which was claimed by Jehovah, when he said to Moses: 'I am that I am.'"[104] Schnackenburg, in turn, writes, "Jesus speaks in the present, which places him in God's existence beyond time, in his eternal present."[105] Keener pushes the matter further. He offers a fuller explanation of the implication of the difference in tense between the two verbs: "The most natural way to express simple preexistence (e.g., for divine Wisdom) would have been to have claimed existence in the past tense before Abraham; the use of the present, by contrast, constitutes a deliberate citation of the divine name. As in the prologue, *eimi* is opposed to *ginomai* in such a way as to imply Jesus' deity."[106]

Keener's concluding statement embodies another important observation. The contrast between Jesus and Abraham voiced in John 8:58 echoes the opening two verses of the Johannine prologue. In John 1:1–2, the being-with-God of the Word is denoted by *eimi*, whereas the coming into existence of all created things is spoken of by means of *ginomai*.[107] This contrast also appears to echo the language of the psalmist's declaration of the divine eternality in comparison to creation: "Before the mountains *came into being* . . . from age to age you *are*" (Ps. 90:2).[108]

Equally important is the observation that John 8:58 appears to be an example of the absolute use of the *ego eimi*. In Keener's estimation, this grammatical characteristic of the text is conclusive. "When 'I am' lacks even an implied predicate," he declares, "it becomes unintelligible except as an allusion to God's name in the Hebrew Bible or LXX."[109]

101. Alvah Hovey, *Commentary on the Gospel of John*, An American Commentary on the New Testament (Philadelphia: American Baptist Publication Society, 1885), 200.

102. See, for example, Calvin, *Gospel according to St. John*, 1:236.

103. Morris, *The Gospel according to John*, 419.

104. Hovey, *Commentary on the Gospel of John*, 200.

105. Schnackenburg, *Gospel according to St. John*, 2:223.

106. Keener, *Gospel of John*, 1:770. See also Moloney, *Gospel of John*, 284–85.

107. For a similar observation, see Brodie, *Gospel according to John*, 336.

108. For this insight, see, for example, Brown, *Gospel according to John*, 1:360.

109. Keener, *Gospel of John*, 1:769–70.

That Jesus was drawing the divine name into his statement is also suggested by the response that his words evoked from his Jewish hearers. They appear to have sensed that he had crossed over the line into blasphemy, for at this point in the narrative, they disengage from the verbal sparring and take action. They pick up stones to kill him, apparently seeking thereby to execute him as a blasphemer. Kruse offers this appraisal of the gravity of Jesus' self-assertion: "He was not only pronouncing the name of God, which Jews normally did not dare to utter, but, even worse, he was claiming to be God."[110]

As several of the quotations cited above indicate, observations such as these led a host of exegetes not only to conclude that the *ego eimi* in this verse is a direct citation of the Old Testament divine name but also that it constitutes an ontological claim. Above all, Jesus is seen to be declaring that as deity he is characterized by timeless, static eternality. Barrett encapsulates this idea when he paraphrases Jesus' words: "Before Abraham came into being, I eternally was, as now I am, and ever continue to be."[111] Bernard adds his voice to this chorus: "It is clear that Jn. means to represent Jesus as thus claiming for Himself the timeless being of Deity, as distinct from the temporal existence of man."[112]

Exegetical considerations such as these are important, of course. Yet the conclusion that Jesus is claiming the divine name and therefore voicing an ontological assertion of timeless eternality as deity does not take us to the heart of the text. For this reason, our quest to determine the significance of Jesus' final utterance of the *ego eimi* in this chapter requires that we look at several clues that emerge in the context in which these words are spoken.

The beginning point for this search is the role of the figure of Abraham in the dispute between Jesus and his hearers.[113] I noted in chapter 4 that one exegetical tradition understood the "victor from the east" in Isaiah 41:2 as a reference to Abraham rather than to Cyrus. This interpretive tradition dates back at least to the intertestamental period, for the Aramaic translation of Isaiah (the Targum of Isaiah) interpolates Abraham into several verses that speak about Yahweh's impending provision of deliverance, even when these verses originally referred to Cyrus (e.g., Isa. 41:2; 43:12; 46:11; 48:15–16).[114] This interpolation indicates the elevated sense of the importance of Abraham in the story of salvation that had developed in Jewish thought by the first century. This high view of the patriarch's role might be what led Jesus' hearers to introduce Abraham

---

110. Kruse, *Gospel according to John*, 138.
111. Barrett, *Gospel according to St. John*, 292.
112. Bernard, *Critical and Exegetical Commentary on the Gospel according to St. John*, 2:322.
113. For a somewhat similar treatment of this theme, see Harner, *"I Am" of the Fourth Gospel*, 40–41.
114. J. F. Stenning, *The Targum of Isaiah* (Oxford: Clarendon, 1949), 134, 136, 158.

as a liberating figure into the dialogue. In response, Jesus claims to offer to his disciples an identity and a freedom that is greater than what the Jews so readily assert is theirs through physical descent from Abraham. Jesus' claim to superiority over Abraham reaches its climax with his declaration that he (and not Abraham) is the saving *ego eimi* not only of Second Isaiah but also of the tradition regarding the divine name associated with Moses' experience at the burning bush.

As I noted earlier, Jesus' hearers bring Abraham into the picture midway into the discourse. Hence, the discussion of Jesus' status vis-à-vis the patriarch is merely one aspect of a larger topic. For this reason, our journey toward understanding the climactic I AM saying requires that we read Jesus' words in the light of the overarching themes—his origin "from above," his relationship to the Father, and his mission on behalf of the Father—that John presents in this section of his Gospel. These various motifs are connected to, and even find their center in, the theme of eternal life that plays such a central role in the Fourth Gospel as a whole. In his sixth discourse, Jesus repeatedly casts his identity in terms of his possession of a unique quality of life. Read in this light, his response to the introduction of Abraham into the discussion involves a declaration that the crucial dimension that marks his superiority to the patriarch and therefore lies behind his superior ability to deliver his people is the kind of life that each of them possesses. Abraham's existence had a beginning point, indicating that his life is temporal and derived from another. Jesus' existence, in contrast, is like that of God. He is characterized by existence that does not "come into being" but simply "is." His life, therefore, is not temporal but eternal, and for this reason it is nothing short of the life of the Father.

This link to the divine life, in turn, provides the basis for Jesus' prerogative of conferring this very life, and hence eternal existence—the kind of life that never dies and the existence that never ends—to his followers. This suggests that, as Schnackenburg points out regarding the *ego eimi*,

> the importance of the statement is not its metaphysical significance for Jesus himself—it is not a Christological statement "for its own sake"—but its status as the basis of his promise of salvation to us. It is only as the Son who has always belonged to God and who "remains in the house" that Jesus can lead us to true freedom (v. 36) and give the life that overcomes death (v. 51).[115]

Jesus, therefore, is claiming to have what God alone has and to bestow what only God can grant. Thereby, he is staking a claim to a unique, divine identity, and is appropriating to himself the divine designation, I AM.

A similar perspective arises from a consideration of the present tense in John 8:58 viewed in contrast to the imperfect of the opening verse of the

---

115. Schnackenburg, *Gospel according to St. John*, 2:223.

prologue. Several exegetes have pointed out that in the sixth discourse, Jesus does not say "I *was* (there)" with reference to the span of time before Abraham existed. Instead, in keeping with his affirmation that Abraham rejoiced to see his day, Jesus offers a declaration in the present tense: "I *am*." Yet commentators have not always noted that these words are uttered by the *incarnate* Word, and not by some divine person isolated from, or viewed apart from the human, historical Jesus. The "I am" spoken here, therefore, is not a declaration regarding the eternal existence of the divine Word apart from his incarnation, apart from the story told by the Gospel writer. Rather, *ego eimi* comprises the manner in which Jesus voices his claim that his life, ministry, and impending death carry significance for all of time, including the entire sweep of history that is linked to Abraham's rejoicing, and therefore that he belongs to the eternity of God. It is in this manner, therefore, that Jesus is nothing less than the incarnate I AM.[116] Calvin states the point well when he declares regarding Jesus' I AM saying, "Some think that it simply applies to Christ's eternal divinity. . . . But I extend it much further, in that Christ's power and grace, inasmuch as He is the Redeemer of the world, were common to all ages."[117]

With this in view, we are in a position to return to a crucial aspect of the divine name that had been disclosed to Moses at the burning bush that I pointed out in chapter 4. Although it is presented as a noun, the I AM formula is in fact verbal in force. The God who discloses himself as the I AM is one whose being is his be-ing, above all, his be-ing present in the salvation of his people. Jesus' utterances of the *ego eimi*, therefore, (contra Lindars) are not references to a static name. Rather, Jesus is thereby linking himself to the active be-ing present throughout all the moments of time that was already present in the giving of the name at the burning bush. Jesus' continuing presence was evident not only at the exodus, to which he seems to allude in the language of freeing sin's slaves, but also already in the days of Abraham, the patriarch who foresaw the day of the incarnate one.

In this manner, then, the *ego eimi* emerges as the central thread that draws the entire sixth discourse together. John 8:58 forms a fitting climax to a chapter that runs from the significant "I am the light of the world" saying, through Jesus' appropriation of the Old Testament motif of Yahweh as the one who saves, to the claim that he participates in, and therefore mediates to others, the eternal life of the I AM who disclosed his presence to Moses at the burning bush. Moreover, the *ego eimi* of John 8:58 draws together the entire group of I AM sayings sprinkled throughout the Fourth Gospel. Just as by means of the announcement of his name Yahweh voiced to his covenant people his promise to be savingly present

116. For a somewhat similar perspective, see Ridderbos, *Gospel according to John*, 323.
117. Calvin, *Gospel according to St. John*, 1:235.

in their history, so also Jesus' appropriation of the *ego eimi* entails his appeal to them to listen to him as the one through whom the God of Abraham has come to them to fulfill his saving promises.[118] The fulfillment of these promises, in turn, involves his active presence in their story from this point forward as the one true bread from heaven that gives life to the world (6:35, 41, 48, 51; cf. 6:33), the light of the world that leads out of bondage to sin and into the promised land of true light (8:12), the door that opens the way to true life (10:7, 9), the good shepherd who cares for the life of his sheep (10:11, 14, 28), the resurrection that leads to eternal life (11:25), the true vine that mediates ongoing life (15:1, 2), and the way, truth, and life itself (14:6).[119]

Above all, however, the *ego eimi* of John 8:58 forms the central text, the heart of the series of I AM sayings of Jesus, that binds the Fourth Gospel itself into the narrative of the incarnate I AM. Taken as a whole, therefore, the I AM sayings—those found in John 8, as well as those scattered throughout the Fourth Gospel—constitute a new chapter in the ongoing saga of the I AM. These sayings embody Jesus' claim to fulfill a unique role in the divine, salvific narrative by embodying a unique mode of being that transcends human categories[120]—the mode of eternal life–divine life, which he mediates to all who believe in him. As Ethelbert Stauffer concludes, "From now on every step of the history will be a contribution to the revelation and glorification of the Son, to the fulfilment of the meaning of His *ego eimi*. . . . This is the final thrust of *ego eimi* without predicate. The *ego* of Christ is the Subject of the history of God, and this history will be nothing but a powerful self-proclamation of Christ."[121] In this sense, this theophanic formula becomes Jesus' purest, boldest, and profoundest declaration not only of what Jesus has accomplished on our behalf but also of who he in fact is.[122]

The I AM and the Revelation of the Divine Name

At the heart of the *ego eimi* sayings in John 8 is the question of Jesus' relationship to his Father. Actually, this issue comes to the fore repeatedly in the Fourth Gospel. And on several occasions, Jesus' declarations regarding this matter become the basis for his hearers accusing him of blasphemy (e.g., 10:31–33). Central to Jesus' assertions about his close connection to the Father is the claim that he is declaring what he has heard from the Father (e.g., 8:26) or what he has seen in the Father's presence (8:38). Statements such as these point in the direction of a crucial Christological theme of the Fourth Gospel. Jesus is the one who reveals the Father. In the Old

---

118. For a similar perspective, see Schnackenburg, *Gospel according to St. John*, 2:224.
119. A similar enumeration can be found in Schnackenburg, *Gospel according to St. John*, 2:88.
120. For a similar descriptor, see Schnackenburg, *Gospel according to St. John*, 2:80–81.
121. Stauffer, "ego," 353.
122. Stauffer, *Jesus and His Story*, 194.

Testament, Yahweh's self-disclosure to humans is generally accompanied by an announcement of the divine name. In the Fourth Gospel, Jesus continues this pattern. In fact, this feature marks what Gary Burge calls "the remarkable new step taken by the Fourth Gospel."[123] As the incarnate Word who reveals the Father, Jesus rightly discloses his identity by speaking the divine name.

What is left for us to explore in this chapter is the sense in which Jesus' mission includes the task of disclosing the divine name. In seeking an answer to this question, we will narrow our focus to the explicit statements that he makes to this effect in what has been known, at least since the writings of the sixteenth-century Lutheran theologian David Chytraeus (1530–1600)[124] and perhaps as early as Cyril of Alexandria,[125] as Jesus' "high-priestly prayer." In this prayer, which Hull acclaims as "the loftiest spiritual passage" in the Fourth Gospel, Jesus petitions the Father concerning the completion of his mission as well as on behalf of his followers.[126] He does so from the perspective of his ministry viewed as a whole, inclusive of his impending death,[127] and in anticipation of his return to the Father. As Brodie rightly concludes, "What is being portrayed, therefore, is a Jesus who is not exclusively either on earth or in heaven, but who in some sense is moving from one to the other, who is ascending and is coming closer to the Father.[128]

The Divine Name in the Prayer of Jesus

The lengthy prayer of Jesus brings together many of the central theological themes of the Fourth Gospel. Here we find such topics as the mutual glorification of the Son and the Father, the Son's prerogative to mediate eternal life, the Father as the source of the Son's mission and word as well as the origin of the Son himself, the connection between knowing and believing as the means whereby eternal life is received, and the Son's status as the one who knows the Father. In presenting these themes, the prayer becomes a summary of John's Christology, not only with respect to Jesus' work but also regarding his person as the Son who is united eternally with the Father.[129]

Jesus' high-priestly prayer is generally divided into three sections,[130] although some scholars separate off either verses 24–26[131] or simply verses

123. Burge, "'I Am' Sayings," 356.

124. See Bruce, *Gospel of John*, 328; Carson, *Gospel according to John*, 552.

125. For this historical note, see Lindars, *Gospel of John*, 516.

126. Hull, "John," 343.

127. For the basis of this view, see Hovey, *Commentary on the Gospel of John*, 337.

128. Brodie, *Gospel according to John*, 507.

129. For a somewhat similar perspective, see Barrett, *Gospel according to St. John*, 417.

130. Examples include Bernard, *Critical and Exegetical Commentary on the Gospel according to St. John*, 2:559; and Morris, *Gospel according to John*, 634. For a variant on the three-part division, see Moloney, *Gospel of John*, 459.

131. Beasley-Murray, *John*, 295–96; Carson, *Gospel according to John*, 553; Lindars, *Gospel of John*, 515; Schnackenburg, *Gospel according to St. John*, 3:167–69.

25–26[132] into a fourth. In the first section, Jesus focuses on the theme of the mutual glorification of the Father and the Son in view of his imminent death (vv. 1–5). He then turns his attention to his disciples, who will now face being in the world without his presence with them (vv. 6–19). The third section extends the scope of Jesus' prayer both to include all who will believe and to include his desire that they might all see his glory (vv. 20–24). As the prayer concludes, Jesus speaks about knowing the Father and the attendant goal of knowing the divine love, themes that have formed the heart of Jesus' mission (vv. 25–26).

Four times in the prayer, Jesus uses the term "name" (*onoma*) with reference to the name of his Father (John 17:6, 11, 12, 26). Furthermore, the prayer brings together the claims that Jesus declared elsewhere regarding the divine name. He had previously claimed to have come (5:43) and to have done works in the Father's name (10:25). In addition, earlier during Holy Week he had petitioned the Father to glorify his name (12:28), a supplication that referred to his looming death.

Jesus' four references to the divine name in the high-priestly prayer speak explicitly about two themes: revelation and protection. The latter is the topic of two verses lying in the center of the prayer, which set forth its occasion and ground. Jesus declares that he will soon be departing from the world, and when this happens, his disciples will be especially dependent on the Father's provision. With this in view, Jesus notes that while he was in the world he protected his disciples in the Father's name, a declaration that is reminiscent of his "I am the good shepherd" saying. Aware that his impending departure will mark the end of this ministry toward his disciples, Jesus petitions the Father to take over the task of providing providential care (vv. 11–12).

In a subordinate clause found in both his assertion and his petition, Jesus speaks of the protecting name of the Father as the name "that you have given me." Bernard notes that John 17:11–12 is the only place in the New Testament where the idea that the Father has given his name to Jesus is explicitly expressed, although the idea seems to be implicit in Philippians 2:9.[133] The possibility that the divine name might rest on someone or something is not completely foreign to the Old Testament. On the contrary, Yahweh instructs the people to listen to the angel sent to lead them to the promised land, because Yahweh's name is "in him" (Exod. 23:20). Similarly, through the Aaronic blessing, the priests could place the divine name on the Israelites (Num. 6:27). And the Israelites were to worship at the place (i.e., the temple) where Yahweh would choose to put his name (Deut. 12:5).

Yet John seems to be indicating something far greater than is declared in these various texts. In contrast to the Old Testament occasions of the

132. Barrett, *Gospel according to St. John*, 416–17; Kruse, *Gospel according to John*, 338–48.
133. Bernard, *Critical and Exegetical Commentary on the Gospel according to St. John*, 2:569.

placing of the divine name, the giving of the divine name to Jesus is unique. The perfect tense of the verb (*dedokas*) indicates the abiding effects of an action completed in the past. Hence, the point of the clause is to declare that Jesus possesses the divine name continuously. Moreover, as Paul indicates in his great christological hymn, the possession of the divine name, which has been given to Jesus by God, is what bestows on him the right to receive the universal homage that will one day be his (Phil. 2:9–11).

What does John intend by Jesus' comment that the Father has given him his name? En route to an answer we must look at the second theme presented in the high-priestly prayer, namely, that of the revelation of the divine name, which bookends it. Near the beginning, Jesus declares that he has revealed the Father's name to those whom the Father gave to him (John 17:6). He voices a similar assertion at the end of the prayer, this time adding that he will continue to do so, "so that the love with which you have loved me may be in them, and I in them" (v. 26). The idea of revealing the Father's name (v. 6) leads back to Jesus' role as the one who brings eternal life. In verse 3, eternal life is described as knowing the Father, who is the one true God, and Jesus whom the Father sent. The mention of "knowing" in this verse, in turn, anticipates the presence of the idea in verse 26, and links together linguistically Jesus' claim to reveal (v. 6) and to make known (v. 26) the Father's name.

Lost in some English translations (such as the NRSV) is the fact that a change in verbs occurs from the first statement to the second. John initially uses *ephanerosa*, the first-person aorist tense of *phaneroo* ("reveal"), whereas in the second *egnopisa*, the aorist of *gvorizo* ("know"), appears. Many exegetes find little significance in this change, treating the two as synonymous. Reynolds, however, is an exception. In his estimation, "'To make manifest' is not equal in potency with 'to make known, to cause them to know'; there is more direct work done in them and to them in order to effect *knowledge*."[134] Reynolds's case is strengthened by the addition of the phrase "and I will make it known" in the second assertion (v. 26). It is possible that Jesus is hereby distinguishing between the "making known" that he accomplished during his ministry and the deeper "making known" that is still to happen in connection with his passion. Yet, as Reynolds suggests, the text might also suggest an anticipation of the ongoing transformation into greater degrees of knowing the Father's name that will occur by means of Jesus' continual presence with his followers through the Spirit.

As with our quick look at verses 11–12, here again we are left with a question: In what sense does Jesus reveal and make known the divine name? This query and the one I raised previously converge in a single

134. H. R. Reynolds, *The Gospel of St. John*, 2 vols., in *The Pulpit Commentary*, ed. H. D. M. Spence and Joseph S. Exell (New York: Funk & Wagnalls, n.d.), 2:353.

exegetical question that relates to the high-priestly prayer as a whole: What is the meaning of "your name" as it is used throughout the prayer?

The Significance of the Divine Name

A person's name, of course, quite often stands for the whole person.[135] On this basis, many commentators connect the Father's name that Jesus mentions in John 17 with either the divine power[136] or the divine character.[137] The first option is most readily seen in connection with Jesus' petition for the Father's protecting care (vv. 11–12). The second possibility, in contrast, comes to the fore in Jesus' declarations regarding his role in making the divine name known to his disciples (vv. 6, 26).

Both of these senses fit well with the overall Christology of the Fourth Gospel. John presents Jesus as coming in the power of the Father and as manifesting the divine character. In Jesus' high-priestly prayer, the latter aspect is implicit in the close connection that Jesus repeatedly draws between his work in revealing the divine name and that of revealing the Father's glory. Viewing his ministry as a completed whole, Jesus declares that he glorified his Father on earth by finishing the work that the Father gave him to do (v. 4). This work, which includes making known the Father's name (v. 6), involves granting eternal life to his followers (v. 2), giving them the Father's word (v. 14), as well as passing on to his disciples the glory that the Father had given him (v. 22).[138] In this sense, Jesus' prayer contains some of the same elements that are present in one of Moses' theophanies. In response to Moses' request that he might see the divine glory, Yahweh revealed his goodness—that is, his character—and announced the divine name, Yahweh, as the one who shows compassion or mercy to those he chooses (Exod. 33:19; cf. 34:5–7).

At the heart of the revealed character of God is love.[139] In keeping with this theological understanding, the movement of Jesus' prayer leads to the climactic elevation of love, the love of the Father for Jesus the Son that Jesus desires likewise be in his followers, with which the prayer ends. Furthermore, this understanding provides the basis for John's relational perspective on the process of knowing God. Jesus declares that his knowing the Father (v. 25) is based on the relationship that he enjoys with the Father, a relationship that is characterized by love (v. 24). Because of this

---

135. See, for example, Morris, *Gospel according to John*, 88, 640.

136. See, for example, Bruce, *Gospel of John*, 332.

137. D. A. Carson, *The Farewell Discourse and Final Prayer of Jesus: An Exposition of John 14–17* (Grand Rapids: Baker, 1980), 184. See also Barrett, *Gospel according to St. John*, 421. It should be noted that Carson later expands his understanding to include the revelation of the divine name. Carson, *Gospel according to John*, 558.

138. For a sketch of the interpretive options regarding the meaning of the divine glory in this verse, see Hovey, *Commentary on the Gospel of John*, 347–48.

139. Lindars, *Gospel of John*, 524, 533.

relationship, Jesus is able to make his name known or reveal him to others—that is, he is able to lead them into a similar relationship in which
the Father's love is also in them (v. 26).

The idea that Jesus' possession and revelation of the Father's name
involves his disclosing the divine character does not exhaust the meaning
of these statements in the high-priestly prayer. On the contrary, John's language might be intended to lead the reader to recall the specific divine
name that Jesus both possesses and reveals.

This becomes evident when the four verses are read in the light of their
Old Testament and Jewish background. As the pronunciation of the actual
name of the God of the Hebrews came to be limited to the high priest in
the Holy of Holies, various euphemisms were developed to represent it.[140]
The most common, of course, was *adonai* ("Lord"). But "the Name" also
came to be used as a reverential substitute for the tetragrammaton. Furthermore, the Old Testament and the later Jewish writers anticipated a time
when the divine name would again be known. For example, in a prophetic
verse that I quoted in another context, Yahweh declared to the Jewish exiles,
"My people shall know my name; therefore in that day they shall know that
it is I who speak; here am I" (Isa. 52:6). Some ancient thinkers linked the
fulfillment of this prophetic promise to the coming messianic age.

According to the New Testament writers, in Jesus this age had dawned.
Jesus' words in John 17:6, 26 are a significant instance in which this theme
of fulfillment comes to the fore. Indeed, the language of Jesus' prayer
recalls what came to be seen as a crucial prophetic declaration that is found
in one of the central messianic psalms: "I will tell of your name to my
brothers and sisters" (Ps. 22:22). This verse, which in the Septuagint reads
diegesomai to onoma sou tous adelphois mou, was interpreted by the author
of the book of Hebrews as referring to Christ (Heb. 2:12). C. H. Dodd
summarizes the importance of Jesus' claim regarding his work in revealing the divine name in the light of this background: "We may recall the
rabbinic saying that while in this age the true name of God is unknown,
in the age to come it will be revealed. According to John xvii.6, 26, the
mission of Christ in the world was to make known the Name of God, and
this mission He fully discharged."[141]

This brings us to the crucial question: Is John suggesting that Jesus discharged this revelatory mission by enunciating the divine *ego eimi*?[142]
Critics aver that the likelihood that this is the case is diminished by the
main point of John 17:6.[143] Jesus declares that he disclosed the divine
name to those whom the Father gave him. In contrast to this statement

---

140. For this historical datum, see Barrett, *Gospel according to St. John*, 421.
141. Dodd, *Interpretation of the Fourth Gospel*, 96.
142. Ibid., 417 n. 2.
143. See, for example, Lindars, *Gospel of John*, 521.

regarding the restricted range of Jesus' revealing work, the *ego eimi* sayings were voiced publicly and to audiences that included his opponents. In response, some commentators suggest other possibilities for the specific name that Jesus might have disclosed.

One suggestion is that Jesus revealed the name "Father."[144] Although this suggestion has not evoked a wide following, it seems to point in the right direction. To see this requires that we interject a seemingly obvious observation. The name Jesus reveals and makes known is the same name as that which the Father has bestowed on him. This name, therefore, must be a name that he shares with the Father. The exegetical trail that we have been traversing in this chapter leads to the conclusion that, whatever else John might have in mind here, the revealed and bestowed name must be the divine I AM.[145] What Jesus has received from the Father is the Old Testament name of the covenanting God of Israel. Consequently, Jesus shares with the Father the great I AM self-designation. And just as the Father is rightly declared to be Yahweh, so also Jesus can rightly be identified, together with the Father, as the Yahweh of the Old Testament story. In this sense, then, patristic and medieval exegetes were not completely in error when they asserted that the one who appeared to Moses at the burning bush was Christ.

Although Jesus is the recipient of the divine I AM name of the Old Testament, which he shares with the Father, Jesus and the Father are not simply identical. The nonidentity of the two is evident in a crucial aspect of the manner in which Jesus reveals and makes known the Father's name. Throughout the Fourth Gospel, John is careful to present Jesus as manifesting the divine name of Father simply and always in that he himself is disclosed as the Son. It is important to note that the designation "Son" is actually a shortened form of "the Son of the Father." Moreover, "Father" is likewise a shorthand way of saying, "the Father of the Son." Hence, precisely in his work of being present in the world as the Son of the Father, Jesus discloses as well the one who is the Father of the Son. Reynolds states the point well: "By being and living on earth as Son of the Father, the Father was revealed. A full revelation of the Father involves and is involved in the manifestation of his own Sonship."[146]

According to Harner, a central aspect of the absolute *ego eimi* sayings of Jesus is the claim that they embody to the unity of the Son with the Father. To this end, he connects John 8:58 with Jesus' declaration, "I and the Father are one" (John 10:30), which Jesus then recasts in terms of the idea of mutual indwelling: "The Father is in me and I am in the Father" (10:38). Harner then concludes, "This theme of mutual indwelling

144. See, for example, Reynolds, *Gospel of St. John*, 2:344; Adolf von Schlatter, *Der Evangelist Johannes*, 3rd ed. (Stuttgart: Calwer, 1960), 319.
145. For a similar conclusion regarding the divine name in John 17, see Brown, *Gospel according to John*, 1:537, 2:755–56.
146. Reynolds, *Gospel of St. John*, 2:344.

expresses the dynamic aspect of the unity between the Father and the Son. It is a way of stating, in what we might call pre-Trinitarian language, that distinct 'persons' exist in mutual interrelatedness within the godhead."[147]

The eternal unity of the Son with the Father that Jesus voiced in John 8:58, which Harner rightly sees as pre-Trinitarian language, is readily evident in Jesus' high-priestly prayer. At the beginning of the prayer, Jesus speaks of the glory that was his before the world came to be (v. 5). As the prayer draws to a close, he repeats the idea, this time connecting his eternal experience of glory with the love that the Father has showered on him before the creation of the world (v. 24). He then declares that he has made the Father known to the disciples. His goal is that the love that the Father has for him might be in them as well and as a result that they might experience the ongoing presence in them of Jesus himself (v. 26). Furthermore, the prayer reflects the mutuality or reciprocity of the relationship between the Son and the Father. This note is sounded at the very beginning of the prayer. Jesus petitions the Father to glorify him as the Son, so that he as Son might in turn glorify the Father (v. 1). Read in this light, Bernard is correct when he declares that the giving of the divine name mentioned in Jesus' high-priestly prayer "is yet another way of expressing the essential unity of the Father and the Son."[148]

These considerations suggest that Jesus' high-priestly prayer provides a bridge between the I AM sayings of the Fourth Gospel and the trajectory that eventually leads to the development of a Trinitarian theology and soteriology. In addition to implicitly setting forth the unity of Jesus and the Father, the final petition of Jesus anticipates the coming of the Spirit and as such entails an allusion to the Spirit's future ministry.[149] In addition, the closing verses of Jesus' prayer reflect the idea that eternal life entails drawing believers into the very life of God, which is perfect love. Because the Father loves Jesus' followers in the manner that he loves the Son (v. 23), believers come to share in the eternal love of the Father for the Son.[150]

Beginning in chapter 7, we will pursue the Trinitarian theme. Then in the final chapter, we will draw out its implications for human life. Throughout part 3 of this volume we will need to take seriously Godet's insightful comment regarding John 17:24: "This saying of Jesus is that which leads us farthest into the divine depths. It shows Christian speculation on what path it must seek the solution of the relations of the Trinity; love is the key of this mystery."[151] Yet before we can explore this, we must add one more chapter to our saga of the I AM in the New Testament.

147. Harner, "I Am" of the Fourth Gospel, 41.

148. Bernard, Critical and Exegetical Commentary on the Gospel according to St. John, 2:569.

149. See, for example, Beasley-Murray, John, 304; Brown, Gospel according to John, 2:781.

150. See, for example, Kruse, Gospel according to John, 347. For a statement regarding the presence of this theme in John 17, see Bruce, Gospel of John, 335–36.

151. Frederic Louis Godet, Commentary on John's Gospel (Grand Rapids: Kregel Reprints, 1978), 903.

Chapter Six

From the Future to the Eternal

The Exalted I AM

In the Old Testament, the name of Israel's God, Yahweh, linked as it is to the language of I AM, denotes active be-ing or dynamic presence. Inherent in the name is the idea that the divine presence does not come and go; nor is it limited to certain particular events and hence bounded by a limited number of moments of time. Instead, Yahweh's presence is continuous, constant, and at hand at all times. The active presence of the God of Israel, in short, encompasses the entire narrative of Israel. In fact, the divine presence even includes the absence of Yahweh from Israel's history that occurs through the revoking of the I AM name. This is clearly evident through the revocation of the revocation that occurs, when the one who said "I am not your I am" returns to the exiled remnant as "I am (He)." According to the Old Testament, therefore, the divine eternality bound up with the name I AM entails being actively and savingly present throughout the history of Israel.

While focusing on the divine presence with Israel, the Old Testament does not limit Yahweh's eternality to Israel's story. In fact, the history of this particular people is cast within a larger narrative, ultimately, the history of Yahweh's relationship with all creation. As the creator of the world, Israel's God is singly God, and as a consequence the great I AM encompasses the dynamic story of all that is. Viewed from this perspective, Yahweh's eternality entails his being present to every moment in the ongoing history of the world.

The Old Testament perspective is carried to a new level in the Fourth Gospel, which presents the incarnate I AM. To this end, the Johannine I AM sayings disclose that Jesus is the one sent by the Father with a mission to bestow life. These sayings, therefore, naturally focus on the present work of the incarnate I AM. Yet the statement that forms the climax to the sixth Johannine discourse carries a note of timelessness, at least in the typical Hebrew sense of being present to all time and thereby transcending each of the moments of time. In so doing, this self-predication illumines the various I AM sayings of the Fourth Gospel, which, taken together, embody the claim that the God of the covenant is actively present in time in Jesus, who therefore is the incarnate I AM.

Despite this focus on the present, the Johannine I AM sayings do not end with the present. Instead, they also anticipate an eschatological future. This is especially evident in the texts that connect the I AM to the Son of Man.

The task of this chapter is to round out the saga of the I AM by looking at the central New Testament texts that speak about the exalted I AM. Our journey commences by looking in the direction toward which the Fourth Gospel points, namely, the eschatological future. This perspective, in turn, provides the orientation point that will allow us to gain a glimpse of the exalted I AM. As the curtain opens on the final scene of our saga, therefore, we find on center stage the *ego eimi* sayings in the Synoptics that hint at, or even anticipate, an eschatological future for the I AM. These statements prepare the way for the main characters of the chapter, the series of declarations in the final canonical book which portray the I AM from the perspective of the exaltation. In these texts, the exalted Jesus comes to voice, pronouncing what we might deem to be the loftiest I AM sayings of the Bible, for they are spoken from the perspective of the eschatological culmination of history and by the reigning Lord.

For this reason, we rightly anticipate from these sayings the final goal of the quest, which has guided us since the beginning of chapter 4. In them, we can expect to discover the sense in which the divine name entails a claim to eternal existence. Hence, we will look in these texts for the ultimate manner in which the great I AM designation provides a bridge between belief in the biblical God and the philosophical question of being.

The I AM of the Future

Unlike John, the Synoptic Gospels only rarely place the *ego eimi* on the lips of Jesus. Only twice does the expression occur with an explicit predicate. If we include Luke's second volume, Acts, we would add an additional three instances, all of which relate to Paul's Damascus road experience and incorporate the identical construction; *ego eimi Iesous* (Acts 9:5; 22:8; 26:15). The phrase without a predicate occurs six times in the Synoptics, and these six occurrences are spread across four incidents. In chapter 5, we viewed the first of these, Jesus' walking on the Sea of Galilee (Mark 6:50; Matt. 14:27), in conjunction with its parallel in John 6. In that discussion, we concluded that the Synoptic version of the incident carries strong theophanic overtones and that Jesus' pronouncement of the *ego eimi* is likely intended to carry overtones of similar events of divine self-disclosure found in the Old Testament.

We must now look at the remaining three incidents in the Synoptic Gospels. Our task is to seek to determine the extent to which they also present Jesus' utterances of the *ego eimi* as suggesting that he appropriated to himself the divine name.

One of these can be eliminated immediately. This instance occurs in an incident that marks Jesus' third postresurrection appearance in Luke's Gospel. The Jerusalem disciples are discussing with their colleagues who encountered Jesus on the Emmaus road when the risen Lord appears to the gathered company. Jesus' sudden appearance so surprises his disciples that his declaration "Peace be with you," engenders the opposite reaction. Luke reports that they were "startled," a verb used in the Septuagint to denote the response of the Israelites to the theophany on Mt. Sinai (Exod. 19:16).[1] Furthermore, they were "terrified," for they thought that they were seeing a ghost. Luke's goal in what follows is to assert the reality of Jesus' actual, physical presence[2]—that is, to confirm that the risen Lord in their midst is indeed the resurrected Jesus of Nazareth.[3] To this end, Jesus invites the gathered company to look at his hands and feet. In this manner, they could discern "that it is I myself" (Luke 24:39). As Luke Timothy Johnson succinctly explains, "The showing of hands and feet prove that this risen Lord is the same person whom they knew before."[4]

1. For this observation, see Luke Timothy Johnson, *The Gospel of Luke*, ed. Daniel J. Harrington, vol. 3 of *Sacra Pagina* (Collegeville, MN: Liturgical Press, 1991), 401.

2. Nolland sees as well "an incidental (but not unintended) affirmation of the inalienable materiality of the human body (resurrected or not)." John Nolland, *Luke*, vol. 35c *18:35–24:53*, of the Word Biblical Commentary (Dallas: Word, 1993), 1213.

3. See, for example, Malcolm O. Tolbert, "Luke," in *The Broadman Bible Commentary*, ed. Clifton J. Allen, 12 vols. (Nashville: Broadman, 1969–1972), 9:185; Johnson, *Gospel of Luke*, 401.

4. Johnson, *Gospel of Luke*, 401.

Insofar as Jesus' central purpose is to confirm his identity, it is highly unlikely that the *ego eimi* here is intended to carry any reference to the divine name. This conclusion is confirmed by the Greek construction.[5] The subordinate clause reads *hoti ego eimi autos*. Grammatically, the *autos* that follows the *ego eimi* comprises a predicate.[6] If this is the case, then this instance could readily be deemed an example of, or at least akin to, the *ego eimi*-plus-predicate construction.

The Imposters' Claim to the Divine Name

More significant is a group of three verses. Two of the verses (Mark 13:6 and Luke 21:8) incorporate the *ego eimi*-without-predicate construction in a Jesus saying that Matthew renders by means of an *ego eimi*-with-predicate (Matt. 24:5). The Jesus saying occurs in what is often denoted, at least when referring to its treatment in the first two Gospels, the "Olivet Discourse" (in contrast to Luke, who suggests a more public location in the temple). The difficulties in exegeting the discourse are well known. As Joseph Fitzmyer observes, the complexity of the materials makes it "one of the most difficult parts of the gospel tradition to interpret."[7]

The genesis of the discourse in all three Synoptic narratives lies in someone's offhand remark about the beauty of the temple, Jesus' prediction of its destruction, and the inquiry of his hearers (whom Matthew and Mark, over against Luke, narrow to the disciples) regarding the sign that will indicate that this event is imminent. The discourse itself opens with Jesus' cautionary response to this query. Initially, he warns his hearers not to be led astray by false claimants who would come in his name. In Mark's and Matthew's versions of the discourse, Jesus' goal is to prepare his followers for the distressing events that will precede the coming of the Son of Man. In the first section, he seeks to dissuade them from any false sense of the imminence of the Parousia that messianic claimants, military campaigns, and natural catastrophes might lead them to entertain. The warning against the first of these potentially deceptive developments is motivated by a danger present throughout salvation history, namely, that false leaders will be able to lead the people of God astray.

In his presentation of the Olivet Discourse, Mark offers the shortest version of Jesus' warning: "Beware that no one leads you astray. Many will

---

5. Actually, some commentators ignore the construction completely. See, for example, G. B. Caird, *Saint Luke*, Pelican New Testament Commentaries (Harmondsworth, UK: Penguin Books, 1963), 260; Norval Geldenhuys, *Commentary on the Gospel of Luke*, New International Commentary on the New Testament (Grand Rapids: Eerdmans, 1954), 640.

6. Philip B. Harner, *The "I Am" of the Fourth Gospel: A Study in Johannine Usage and Thought* (Philadelphia: Fortress, 1970), 31.

7. Joseph A. Fitzmyer, *The Gospel according to Luke*, 2 vols., Anchor Bible (New York: Doubleday, 1981, 1985), 1323. For a similar appraisal and an elaboration of some of the reasons for it, see Ray Summers, *Commentary on Luke* (Waco, TX: Word, 1973), 253–55.

come in my name and say, 'I am he!' and they will lead many astray" (Mark 13:5–6). This is the first of several "beware" or "take care" exhortations that punctuate Mark's version of the discourse and denote important transitional points in it (e.g., vv. 5, 9, 23, 33). Luke provides a slightly fuller account of the anticipated seductive words. He reports Jesus as saying that to the "I am he!" the false claimants will add, "The time is near." Luke likewise adds a second caution: "Do not go after them" (Luke 21:8). In both Mark and Luke, Jesus puts into the mouths of the anticipated impostors an "I am" claim that reflects the *ego eimi*-without-predicate construction. (The "he" added in many English translations is not explicitly present in the Greek.) Matthew, however, interprets the *ego eimi* for his readers by adding an explicit predicate, *ho christos*. Hence, the Matthew text reads, "I am the Messiah" (Matt. 24:5).

The central exegetical question that this construction raises is whether the *ego eimi* in Mark and Luke carries the absolute sense or is to be completed with an implied predicate. At first glance, the obvious solution is simply to read Mark and Luke in the light of Matthew. In this case, the construction anticipates the supplying of an implied predicate, and the predicate to be supplied is the designation "the Messiah."[8] According to this interpretation, all three Gospels present Jesus as declaring that prior to the end, messianic pretenders will arise. Indeed, many such claimants did emerge, climaxing in Simon Bar Kokhba, who led a revolt in AD 132–135 in which he was supported by Rabbi Akiva, who believed that if Bar Kokhba were successful he might be the long-awaited Messiah. Harmonizing the three accounts in this manner introduces into Mark and Luke the interpretive question implicit in Matthew: In what sense can the claimants be said to be coming in Jesus' name?

An alternative would be to draw the implied predicate in Mark and Luke from Jesus' statement, "Many will come in my name," interpreted as "Many will come representing themselves as being me" or "as though they were I."[9] In this case, Jesus is warning against those who will claim to be the returning Jesus. Luke might be seen as hinting in this direction when he adds that the impostors would also claim, "The time is at hand." Perhaps he has in view a situation similar to the one Paul indicates had emerged among the Thessalonians. Paul warns the church against those who were claiming, on the authority of Paul himself, that the day of the Lord had arrived (2 Thess. 2:1–2), and, presumably, that Christ himself had come.[10] Yet in

---

8. For this perspective regarding Mark 13:6, see B. Harvie Branscomb, *The Gospel of Mark*, Moffatt New Testament Commentary (New York: Harper & Brothers, n.d.), 234. For Luke, see A. R. C. Leaney, *The Gospel according to St. Luke*, 2nd ed., Black's New Testament Commentaries (London: A. & C. Black, 1966), 259; Nolland, *Luke*, 35c:991.

9. For an engagement with this possibility, see Harner, *"I Am" of the Fourth Gospel*, 32.

10. See, for example, W. Manson, "The *Ego Eimi* of the Messianic Presence in the New Testament," *Journal of Theological Studies* 48 (1947): 137–45.

this scenario we would anticipate that the false teachers would be making a declaration about Jesus (e.g., "He is here") rather than about themselves ("I am he"). As Morna Hooker notes in her dismissal of this interpretation, "Whoever these men are, they seem to be making claims for themselves, not claims about Jesus."[11]

It should be noted, however, that the text might not require that we choose between the two types of potential false teachers. On the contrary, in Matthew's account Jesus predicts the coming of a variety of false prophets, including both those who make messianic claims about themselves—"I am the Messiah" (Matt. 24:5)—and those who voice such claims on behalf of others: "There he is" (24:23–26).

As these considerations indicate, the intent of Jesus' statement is dependent on the meaning of the two phrases "in my name" and "I am (he)." The first was often used as a technical expression connected to the sending of an appointed emissary or personal representative. If this is the sense that Jesus has in mind, the phrase could be rendered here, "claiming to be sent by me."

At the same time, insofar as one's name can denote one's power and dignity, the expression can also mean "arrogating to themselves the title and authority which properly belong to me."[12] Moreover, it is possible that Mark and Luke used the *ego eimi* in the absolute sense. R. T. France dismisses the implications of such a reading on the basis of the lack of such an idea in first-century Judaism: "There is no plausible context in first century Judaism in which we can envisage anyone making a simple claim to divinity by adopting the divine name from Ex. 3:14, and in any case such a claim would be so blatantly false as to need no warning."[13] Yet, as I noted in chapter 5, some Old Testament and intertestamental Jewish writers anticipated a time when the divine name would again be known. For some, this would be a decisive characteristic of the age to come. Viewed from this perspective, the *ego eimi* becomes a kind of solemn pronouncement that the current age is ending and the messianic age is dawning.

Putting the two phrases together in this manner yields the conclusion that Jesus might be predicting the coming of those who would be taking upon themselves the prerogative of voicing the divine *ego eimi* and in so doing claiming messianic status,[14] as Matthew indicates by means of his

11. Morna D. Hooker, *The Gospel according to Saint Mark*, in Black's New Testament Commentaries (London: A. & C. Black, 1991), 309.

12. For this rendering, see Ethelbert Stauffer, "ego," in *Theological Dictionary of the New Testament*, ed. Gerhard Kittel and Gerhard Friedrich, trans. Geoffrey W. Bromiley, 10 vols. (Grand Rapids: Eerdmans, 1964–1976), 2:253.

13. R. T. France, *The Gospel of Mark: A Commentary on the Greek Text*, New International Greek Testament Commentary (Grand Rapids: Eerdmans, 2002), 510.

14. For a similar treatment of this possibility, see Harner, *"I Am" of the Fourth Gospel*, 32.

interpretation of Jesus' remark. William Lane is on the right track when he offers the following rendering of the meaning of the statement: "Jesus cautions his disciples that men will emerge in the crisis who will falsely claim to have the theophanic name and power of the Messiah and they will lead many astray."[15]

Viewed from this perspective, the phrase "will come in my name" does not necessarily refer to Jesus' own personal name, but rather to the *ego eimi* itself. In this case, the phrase might be understood along the lines of "usurping my name" or "claiming a prerogative to the name that is solely mine." Hence, Jesus' warning would embody a veiled claim to possess the right to the *ego eimi* self-designation, reminiscent of his declaration to his frightened disciples who saw him walking on the Sea of Galilee. By extension, the warning might also be meant to imply that his disciples should wait patiently for his own decisive, eschatological reiteration of the divine name.

The inclusion of the incident in the Synoptics suggests that by the time of the writing of Mark's Gospel, *ego eimi* had already become a technical formula carrying meanings associated with Jesus' own use of the phrase.[16] These occurrences indicate as well that the designation would likely have a crucial eschatological significance for the early church. This eschatological orientation is even more explicit in the other two incidents in the Synoptics in which Jesus voices the *ego eimi*.

The I AM on Trial

The most significant occurrence of the *ego eimi* in the Synoptics comes in Jesus' trial before the Sanhedrin. Although the hearing is reported in all three Synoptic Gospels, the *ego eimi*-without-predicate construction is found only in Mark and Luke.

The *Ego Eimi* and the High Priest's Confession

In contrast to Mark, who appears to suggest two hearings before the Sanhedrin (cf. 14:53 and 15:1), Luke's account presents only one.[17] Moreover, the hearing lacks the marks of a formal trial, but takes the form of a kind of pretrial investigation that has as its goal gaining whatever materials are necessary to launch a successful bid to have Jesus tried before the Roman prefect.

In Luke, the single question of the chief priest in Mark is divided into two. In this manner, the trial scene is reminiscent of the two declarations

---

15. William L. Lane, *The Gospel of Mark: The English Text with Introduction, Exposition, and Notes*, New International Commentary on the New Testament (Grand Rapids: Eerdmans, 1974), 457.

16. For a succinct overview of this aspect, see Stauffer, "ego," 353.

17. For an engagement with the issue of the two hearings, see Hooker, *Gospel according to Saint Mark*, 355–56. For the suggestion that Mark also presents only one hearing, see Nolland, *Luke*, 1107.

214 The Saga of the I AM

made by the angel in announcing to Mary who this child would be: the one to whom God would give "the throne of his father David" and the one who would be called "the Son of the Most High" and "Son of God" (Luke 1:32, 35). As Fitzmyer eloquently observes, "What was foreshadowed in the infancy narrative, where the chords were first struck . . . teaches with crescendo its climax in this scene, having been orchestrated in various ways in the Gospel up to this point."[18]

The council members first admonish Jesus, "If you are the Messiah, tell us." His response, "From now on the Son of Man will be seated at the right hand of the power of God" (Luke 22:69) is met with their follow-up query, "Are you, then, the Son of God?" or, following the Greek word order with its attendant emphasis, "You, therefore, you are the Son of God?" This occasions Jesus' cryptic response, *humeis legete hoti ego eimi*, which is usually rendered, "You say that I am" (v. 70).

In Luke's account, the context supplies a clear implied predicate—"the Son of God"—for the *ego eimi*. However, the phrase does not come as a direct personal claim voiced by Jesus. Some commentators view the statement as an idiomatic way of affirming the designation: "You yourselves are saying that I am what I really am."[19] But it is more generally viewed as a way whereby Jesus puts the burden on the questioners while not denying the charge.[20] In this sense, it might be cast in the form of a question: "Do you say that I am?"[21] Or, more likely it might be an affirmation that means simply, "You are the ones who use the designation, not I."[22] Used in this sense, it might also imply indirect, grudging assent to his interrogators' assertion, albeit with the suggestion that he thinks the questioners fail to understand exactly what they are asking[23] and, of course, do not believe what they are saying.[24] In any case, the council finds in Jesus' words sufficient evidence to warrant the desired conviction.

Insofar as this instance of the *ego eimi* is not uttered by Jesus in making an explicit claim regarding himself, it likely ought not to be read as a direct allusion to the divine name. At the same time, despite the exegetical correctness of this conclusion, we ought not to overlook a deeper meaning that might be at work in this text. Johnson uncovers this meaning when he writes, "The reader schooled in the LXX would be delighted to find the irony of the chief priest inadvertently terming Jesus *ego eimi*."[25]

18. Fitzmyer, *Gospel according to Luke*, 1463.
19. Summers, *Luke*, 293.
20. Johnson, *Gospel of Luke*, 360.
21. Nolland, *Luke*, 35c:1111.
22. For a similar suggestion, see Tolbert, "Luke," 175.
23. I. Howard Marshall, *Commentary on Luke: A Commentary on the Greek Text*, New International Greek Testament Commentary (Grand Rapids: Eerdmans, 1978), 851.
24. Fitzmyer, *Gospel according to Luke*, 1463.
25. Johnson, *Gospel of Luke*, 360.

The *Ego Eimi* in the Confession of Jesus

What is at best only implicit in Luke is explicit in Mark's account of Jesus' reply to his inquisitors, which is heavily influenced by the contrast that the evangelist seeks to draw between Peter's denials and Jesus' confession.[26] Mark presents the (first) hearing in a form that resembles an actual trial. The purpose of Jesus' inquisitors is to gain sufficient testimony to warrant a guilty verdict, before proceeding to Pilate for a trial in which the Jewish authorities act as accusers.[27]

In contrast to Luke's account, in which the council members pose two distinct questions to Jesus, Mark places in the mouth of the high priest only one query, "Are you the Messiah, the son of the Blessed One" (14:61). The two christological titles and the appositional manner in which they are put together is reminiscent of the manner in which some manuscripts render the announcement with which the Gospel opens: "The beginning of the good news of Jesus Christ, the Son of God" (Mark 1:1).

As the appositional character of the grammar suggests, the second title, which Jesus had already implicitly claimed for himself in the parable of the Vineyard (Mark 12:1–12), is closely connected to the first. The idea that the Messiah is "the Son of God" was apparently not foreign to first-century Judaism.[28] Consequently, the question at issue was whether Jesus viewed himself as the Messiah and if so, perhaps also what he might have meant by this claim.[29] If Jesus were to affirm this charge, his enemies would have a charge that could gain the ear of the Roman prelate. But they would also have from Jesus a clear declaration of blasphemy, insofar as no one would claim messianic dignity while standing helpless before his foes nor prior to God himself crowning him with this honor. A messianic claim by Jesus under present circumstances, therefore, would entail an infringement on the majesty of God and a diminishing of God's honor.[30]

Unlike the response reported by Luke ("You say that I am"; 22:70), which is even more equivocal in Matthew ("You have said so"; Matt. 26:64)

---

26. Nolland, *Luke*, 35c:1107. For a description of this contrast, see France, *Gospel of Mark*, 597–98.

27. For this characterization as well as its marked difference from Luke's presentation, see Nolland, *Luke*, 35c:1105.

28. France, *Gospel of Mark*, 609. Lane's characterization is even stronger, claiming that the Jews of Jesus' day viewed the idea of "son of God" solely in a messianic sense. Lane, *Gospel according to Luke*, 535 n. 133. Hooker, in contrast, claims that we lack clear evidence of any such association. Hooker, *Gospel according to Saint Mark*, 360. For this negative judgment, see also C. E. B. Cranfield, *The Gospel according to Saint Mark: An Introduction and Commentary* (Cambridge: Cambridge University Press, 1959), 443.

29. Marcus suggests that Jesus' identity was viewed as developing manner from a Son-of-David to a Son-of-God messiahship. Joel Marcus, "Mark 14:61: 'Are You the Messiah-Son-of-God?'" *Novum Testamentum* 31 (1989): 125–41. See also Marcus, *The Way of the Lord: Christological Exegesis of the OT in the Gospel of Mark* (Edinburgh: T. & T. Clark, 1999), 119–25. This view is rejected in Craig A. Evans, *Mark 8:27–16:20*, Word Biblical Commentary (Nashville: Thomas Nelson, 2001), 449.

30. For this insight, see Lane, *Gospel according to Mark*, 536, 538.

Jesus' response is unequivocal in Mark: "I am" (although according to some manuscripts Mark follows Matthew's account at this point).[31] Jesus then explicitly associates himself with the eschatological figure of the Son of Man, who, in turn, he closely connects to deity: "and you will see the Son of Man seated at the right hand of the Power, and coming with the clouds of heaven" (14:62). This statement marks a singular combining of language from two Old Testament texts: "The LORD says to my lord, 'Sit at my right hand until I make your enemies your footstool'" (Ps. 110:1), and "As I watched in the night visions, I saw one like a human being [a son of man] coming with the clouds of heaven. And he came to the Ancient One and was presented before him" (Dan. 7:13). In this short statement, Jesus begins with the figure from Daniel, then moves to the imagery from the psalm, and finally expands the imagery by the substance of the verse in Daniel. In this manner, the composite declaration offers a powerful assertion regarding an anticipated enthronement of the Son of Man.

Left unclear is whether this enthronement occurs at a single time or in two stages, such as at Jesus' resurrection and later in the Parousia.[32] If the latter is Mark's intention, then the saying carries implications not only in the context of Jesus' trial but also of the Marcan community itself. As Lamar Williamson declares, "Jesus' claims, incredible to the Sanhedrin, would be initially vindicated by the resurrection. Equally incredible to the contemporaries of Mark's first readers, these claims would be finally vindicated by the Parousia."[33]

In any case, the statement sets up a contrast between Jesus' present situation and his future vindication,[34] a vindication that, as the addition of "from now on" in Matthew's and Luke's accounts indicates, he declares will commence in the immediate future.[35] By means of this declaration, Jesus preempts the suggestion that his claim to messiahship is blasphemous, albeit in a manner that looks for a future confirmation from God.[36] The day will come, he asserts, when his accusers will see him enthroned

31. For a defense of the position that views this as the correct reading of Mark as well, see Vincent Taylor, *The Gospel according to St. Mark: The Greek Text with Introduction, Notes, and Indexes* (London: Macmillan, 1955), 568.

32. Reading the text in the light of Matthew and Luke, France sees only a single, heavenly enthronement motif at work here and denies that it involves a reference to an eschatological Parousia. France, *Gospel of Mark*, 611–13. Evans, in contrast, sees two horizons at work. Evans, *Mark 8:27–16:20*, 451–52. For a defense of the eschatological sense of the statement, see also Cranfield, *Gospel according to St. Mark*, 444–45.

33. Lamar Williamson, Jr., *Mark*, Interpretation: A Bible Commentary for Teaching and Preaching (Louisville: John Knox, 1983), 266.

34. For a similar characterization, see Hooker, *Gospel according to Saint Mark*, 562.

35. Gould interprets Jesus' remark as claiming that Jesus' rule over the affairs of the world from his heavenly throne would continue from that time on. Ezra Gould, *A Critical and Exegetical Commentary on the Gospel according to St. Mark*, International Critical Commentary (Edinburgh: T. & T. Clark, 1896), 279.

36. For a defense of the idea that Jesus did indeed claim to be the Messiah, see Taylor, *Gospel according to St. Mark*, 568–69.

by God and invested with the requisite dignity associated with God's Messiah. C. S. Mann encapsulates the meaning of the statement: "What Jesus claims in the text before us is that the glory and the exaltation belonging properly to the Anointed One will be his and will be seen to be his."[37] For the high priest, in contrast, the answer is not only a positive affirmation of the charge but an assertion of the possession of a unique authority, which brings into the open Jesus' exalted understanding of his identity.[38]

Upon hearing Jesus' declaration, the high priest tears his robes in a grand gesture of accusation. This response raises the question of what specific aspect of Jesus' statement comprised the blasphemy that his accuser is so certain that he heard. Matthew seems to suggest that the high priest interpreted Jesus' claim to be linked to the Son of Man as blasphemous. Luke, in turn, tends toward Jesus' ambiguous assent to the charge of claiming to be the Son of God. In Mark, in contrast, Jesus offers a composite confession, which includes the titles Messiah, Son of the Blessed One, and Son of Man, which is prefaced by his simple declaration, "I am." In this manner, Mark hints at the possibility that Jesus' voicing of the *ego eimi* was a contributing factor in the charge of blasphemy. Indeed, this would be the case if the Sanhedrin heard in these words an utterance of the divine name. And if they were following the stricter understanding of blasphemy as "pronouncing the name itself" that later became the norm, such a declaration would have been mandatory for gaining a condemnatory verdict. Williamson offers a forthright declaration of the point: "The accusation of blasphemy attests the theophanic function of 'I am' in the present text; a messianic claim would not in and of itself have been considered blasphemous."[39] In this interpretation, the *ego eimi* is deemed to be an example of the use of the phrase in the absolute sense.[40]

At the same time, it is not obvious that Mark is intending that the "I am" be viewed in this manner. On the contrary, this might be an instance in which an implied predicate is to be supplied from the context,[41] perhaps in the form of the twofold title, "the Messiah, the Son of the Blessed One." The *ego eimi*, therefore, might be merely Jesus' affirmative response to the question regarding his sense of personal identity and not a pronouncing of the theophanic formula.[42] And this declaration, indicated by

---

37. C. S. Mann, *Mark: A New Translation with Introduction and Commentary*, Anchor Bible (Garden City, NY: Doubleday, 1986), 626.

38. For a somewhat similar characterization, see France, *Gospel of Mark*, 601.

39. Williamson, *Mark*, 265–66.

40. For the likelihood that the *ego eimi* entails an invocation of the divine name, see R. A. Cole, *The Gospel according to St. Mark: An Introduction and Commentary*, Tyndale New Testament Commentaries (Grand Rapids: Eerdmans, 1961), 229; Hooker, *Gospel according to Saint Mark*, 362; Sherman E. Johnson, *A Commentary on the Gospel according to St. Mark*, Black's New Testament Commentaries (London: A. & C. Black, 1960), 245.

41. For this judgment, see Harner, *"I Am" of the Fourth Gospel*, 34.

42. For this judgment, see Lane, *Gospel according to Mark*, 536.

what is a natural Greek expression,[43] in turn opened the way for the Son of Man assertion that followed, which perhaps became the actual declaration that triggered the charge of blasphemy. This conclusion is supported by Darrell Bock's observation that in Jesus' day the Jews considered it unthinkable for anyone to claim for oneself the honor of sitting beside God and thereby equating oneself with God.[44] If Bock is correct, then this statement from Jesus would have been sufficient to confirm the suspicions of the Sanhedrin. Yet France might well offer the safest conclusion: "The blasphemy . . . is to be found not in any narrowly defined misuse of language, but in a total claim to which the whole of Jesus' public life and teaching has been building up, and which sets him irrevocably in conflict with the Jerusalem authorities."[45]

Despite these exegetical considerations, the question remains as to what connections Mark might intend that the reader make with his inclusion of the *ego eimi* at Jesus' trial. Mark has placed this phrase at three interesting points in the narrative. The first came in the context of the theophany that ensued when the disciples saw Jesus walking on the Sea of Galilee. This was followed later by Jesus' admonition to his disciples not to be drawn away by false claimants but (by implication) to await his future declaration of the "I am." And the triad reaches its climax at Jesus' trial in which he quickly moves to a prediction of a soon-to-be-fulfilled enthronement of the Son of Man. Reading these pericopes together draws us ever forward, until our gaze rests on a future time when the divine name will be fully known, because all will see the enthroned Jesus who as such is the *ego eimi*.

The I AM for All Time

The future time anticipated by the Synoptic *ego eimi* sayings is spelled out and declared to be "at hand" in the final book in the canon, the Apocalypse. For this reason, the saga of the I AM finds its culmination in the eschatologically oriented claims voiced by the postresurrection, postascension, heavenly Jesus found in that book.

There are six I AM sayings in the book of Revelation, albeit in one of these, the *eimi* is implied rather than actually present (22:13). In contrast to the use of the expression in the Gospels, in the Apocalypse the *ego eimi* never carries the absolute sense. Instead, in each occasion an explicit predicate in the nominative case is present. Revelation also differs from the Gospels in that as many as two of the I AM sayings in the final book of the Bible have

---

43. France, *Gospel of Mark*, 610 n. 34.
44. Darrell L. Bock, *Blasphemy and Exaltation in Judaism and the Final Examination of Jesus in Mark 14:53–65* (Grand Rapids: Baker, 2000), 183.
45. France, *Gospel of Mark*, 601; cf. 615.

God as the speaker (1:8; 21:6). Furthermore, although the other four (1:17; 2:23; 22:13, 16)—or possibly five—are uttered by Jesus, in each of these he now speaks as the exalted Lord rather than as the incarnate I AM.

The Exalted I AM

Of the six I AM sayings, two embody the claims of the exalted Jesus to possess or exercise lofty characteristics, even the prerogatives of deity. At the same time, unlike several of the declarations in the Gospels and especially in John, neither of these two sayings entails an actual utterance of the divine *ego eimi*. Hence, they do not involve a direct claim by Jesus to the divine name. Nevertheless, the characteristics that the exalted Lord ascribes to himself associate him closely with God. And they form an integral part of a series of assertions that, taken together, involve a claim to deity and hence to the status of being the bearer of the divine name.

The One Who Is the Shoot and Star

Perhaps the "I am"-plus-predicate statement that at first glance appears to be the least consequential is found in the epilogue of the Apocalypse. In fact, it forms the last *ego eimi* saying of Revelation. After the culmination of the book in the promise of the new creation, the exalted Lord authenticates the angel who has guided John through the various visions by declaring, "It is I, Jesus, who sent my angel to you with this testimony for the churches." Jesus then identifies himself further by voicing the *ego eimi* with a twofold predicate: "I am the root and the descendant of David, the bright morning star" (Rev. 22:16). Coming almost immediately after Jesus' highly significant I AM statement in which he designates himself as "the Alpha and the Omega" (22:13),[46] this assertion marks the second time that the exalted Jesus speaks about his identity in the epilogue to the Apocalypse. Moreover, the statement combines two designations that are linked to Jesus earlier in the book.

The first predicate in Jesus' self-identifying statement, *he hpiza kai to genos David*, echoes the angel's description of Jesus as "the root of David" (*he hpiza David*), which is voiced earlier in Revelation with regard to his status as the one who has conquered (Rev. 5:5). In this earlier reference, Jesus is declared to be the "Lion of the tribe of Judah" and the "root of David," two designations that according to George Eldon Ladd "sum up the totality of the Old Testament messianic hope."[47] In both occurrences of the latter phrase, the word *hpiza* refers to what comes from a root,

---

46. Although nearly all exegetes conclude that the speaker here is Jesus, there is some dissent from this near consensus. Ashcraft, for example, concludes that the content of the claim requires that God the Father be the speaker. Morris Ashcraft, "Revelation," in *Broadman Bible Commentary*, 12:359.

47. George Eldon Ladd, *A Commentary on the Revelation of John* (Grand Rapids: Eerdmans, 1972), 83.

namely, a shoot, rather than the root itself.[48] Moreover, both assertions entail allusions to Isaiah's prophecy, "A shoot shall come out from the stump of Jesse, and a branch shall grow out of his roots" (Isa. 11:1), in which the Messiah is viewed as descending from the line of David.

The elongated phrase in Revelation 22:16 poses a theological question that is connected to an underlying exegetical problem. Does the designation of Jesus as "root" indicate that as Messiah he is the source or origin of the Davidic line?[49] Are *hriza* and *genos* to be treated as two separate nouns, or are they in fact merely alternate ways of voicing a single designation? In response to the exegetical question, many commentators opt for the latter option.[50] David Aune, for example, considers this construction to be a hendiadys, in which *hriza* has a figurative meaning similar to *genos* and the *kai* functions epexegetically, so that the Greek phrase becomes, "the shoot, that is, the descendant."[51] If this is correct, then the designation is best translated, "the root and offspring from David." And the point of the declaration is to identify Jesus as the one who fulfills the Isaiah prophecy that a descendant of David will be the Messiah.[52]

The second predicate, "the morning star," is not applied directly to Jesus anywhere else in the New Testament.[53] It might be an allusion to the prophecy in Balaam's fourth oracle, "a star shall come out of Jacob" (Num. 24:17), and perhaps also to Isaiah's declaration, "Nations shall come to your light, and kings to the brightness of your dawn" (Isa. 60:3). Moreover, the star was a familiar messianic symbol in the intertestamental Jewish writings. In the conclusion of the fourth of the seven highly stylized epistles found in chapters 2 and 3 of the Apocalypse, the letter to Thyatira, Jesus promises to give the morning star to those of his followers who overcome (2:28).[54] The meaning of this promise is unclear. Some interpret it in the light of Revelation 22:16 to mean that those who over-

---

48. For this interpretation, see Robert H. Mounce, *The Book of Revelation*, rev. ed., New International Commentary on the New Testament (Grand Rapids: Eerdmans, 1998), 408 n. 29.

49. For the case for an affirmative answer, see George R. Beasley-Murray, *Revelation*, New Century Bible (Grand Rapids: Eerdmans, 1981), 342. See also G. B. Caird, *A Commentary on the Revelation of St. John the Divine* (New York: Harper & Row, 1966), 286; Dennis E. Johnson, *Triumph of the Lamb: A Commentary on Revelation* (Phillipsburg, NJ: P&R, 2001), 328.

50. See, for example, Leon Morris, *The Book of Revelation: An Introduction and Commentary*, 2nd ed., Tyndale New Testament Commentaries (Grand Rapids: Eerdmans, 1987), 94.

51. David Aune, *Revelation*, vol. 52c of the Word Biblical Commentary (Dallas: Word, 1997–1998), 1199.

52. For a summary of the various considerations that lead to this conclusion, see G. K. Beale, *The Book of Revelation: A Commentary on the Greek Text*, New International Greek Testament Commentary (Grand Rapids: Eerdmans, 1999), 1146–47.

53. For this judgment, see Aune, *Revelation*, 52c:1227.

54. For an extensive treatment of the nature and style of these epistles, see Aune, *Revelation*, 117–32. See also M. Eugene Boring, *Revelation*, Interpretation: A Bible Commentary for Teaching and Preaching (Louisville: John Knox, 1989), 86–91. For an extended engagement with this topic, see Colin J. Hemer, *The Letters to the Seven Churches of Asia in Their Local Setting* (Grand Rapids: Eerdmans, 2001).

come will receive Christ's presence,[55] Christ himself,[56] or perhaps Christ in the fullest sense.[57] But it could also refer to the exalted Lord's guidance and leadership during his followers' time of trial.[58] Or it might indicate that the Lord will share with his faithful followers his messianic status[59] by having them participate in his rule over the nations.[60] Hence, Austin Farrer comments, "in making us parties to his dominion Christ gives us the star of his empire."[61] In the epilogue, however, the designation seems to carry a somewhat different meaning. Its use as a description of the exalted Jesus entails the promise that "the long night of tribulation is all but over and that the new eschatological day is about to dawn," to cite Robert Mounce's helpful characterization.[62]

In this manner, Jesus offers an implicit claim to be the Lord of history, the one through whom the culmination of God's program for the ages comes to its preordained conclusion. This claim is especially powerful in that it comes as the climactic I AM declaration of the Apocalypse and thereby carries with it overtones of the various sayings that preceded it in the book. Yet it does not explicitly speak about the eternality of the one who voices the claim.

The One Who Searches Mind and Heart

A second instance of the *ego eimi*-plus-predicate construction leads to an even stronger conclusion. At the heart of the admonition of the letter to Thyatira is Jesus' threat to deal harshly with the "Jezebel" in their midst, as well as with those who follow her. Many commentators postulate that the reference is to a particular woman of stature within the congregation whose beguiling influence on the Christian community parallels that of the Israelite queen in the Old Testament who promoted idolatry in Israel. Whoever the woman may have been who evoked this nefarious descriptor from the lips of the exalted Jesus, the issue was likely her accommodating the faith to the trade guild–oriented culture of the city.[63] It likely centered on "Jezebel's promotion of the participation of Christians in the various

55. Morris, *Book of Revelation*, 74.

56. Caird, *Commentary on the Revelation*, 46, 286; Johnson, *Triumph of the Lamb*, 82.

57. Ashcraft, "Revelation," 270.

58. For this proposal, see Ray Summers, *Worthy Is the Lamb: An Interpretation of Revelation* (Nashville: Broadman, 1951), 119.

59. Aune, *Revelation*, 52a:212.

60. Craig R. Koester, *Revelation and the End of All Things* (Grand Rapids: Eerdmans, 2001), 62. Koester also suggests that the promise entails that the overcomers will receive Christ himself.

61. Austin Farrer, *The Revelation of St. John the Divine: Commentary on the English Text* (Oxford: Clarendon, 1964), 76.

62. Mounce, *Book of Revelation*, 409.

63. For a discussion of the problem of accommodation in the seven churches, see Boring, *Revelation*, 92–95.

acts of homage paid by the guild members to their patron deity[64] and might have included participation at guild meals dedicated to the deity."[65]

More important for our consideration is the additional purpose that the epistle's author declares that his act of judgment will serve: "And all the churches will know that I am the one who searches minds and hearts" (Rev. 2:23). This designation emerges as an outworking of that aspect of the seer's opening vision, in which the Son of Man's eyes are "like a flame of fire" (Rev. 1:14), which is repeated later in the description of the rider on the white horse (Rev. 19:12). In addition, it perhaps foreshadows the vision of the Lamb with seven eyes, which are said to be "the seven spirits of God sent out into all the earth" (Rev. 5:6).

As is confirmed by the concluding line of the assertion, "and I will give to each of you as your works deserve," the saying embodies an allusion to two statements in Jeremiah. In the first of these, Jeremiah declares regarding Yahweh, "But you, O LORD of hosts, who judge righteously, who try the heart and the mind, let me see your retribution upon them, for to you I have committed my cause" (Jer. 11:20). A similar declaration is later spoken by Yahweh himself: "I the LORD test the mind and search the heart, to give to all according to their ways, according to the fruit of their doings" (Jer. 17:10).

In the I AM declaration in the letter to Thyatira, Jesus ascribes to himself the prerogative of searching human minds and hearts.[66] Actually, the Greek word that designates the first object of the Lord's scrutiny literally means "kidneys." In this context, however, it is used metaphorically to refer to the center of a person's affections or emotions, and it is closely connected to the second term, which denotes the center of intelligence and possibly will.[67] Combining the two provides a poignant way of declaring that no deceit, no sophistry of any kind, can escape the notice of the exalted Jesus.[68] Repeatedly the biblical writers ascribe to God this lofty kind of knowledge (e.g., 1 Sam. 16:7; 2 Sam. 14:20; 1 Kgs. 8:39; 1 Chr. 28:9; 2 Chr. 6:30; Ps. 44:21; 139:1–6; Matt. 6:4, 6, 18; Acts 1:24; 15:8; Rom. 2:16; 1 Cor. 4:5; 14:25; Heb. 4:12–13). Although this text in the Apocalypse cannot be viewed as an instance of Jesus uttering the divine name or of developing directly the meaning of the divine eternality, it does present the exalted Lord as relegating to himself the same divine

---

64. See, for example, Beale, *Book of Revelation*, 260–61.

65. For a discussion of this issue, see R. H. Charles, *A Critical and Exegetical Commentary on the Revelation of St. John: With Introduction, Notes, and Indices also the Greek Text and English Translation*, 2 vols., International Critical Commentary (Edinburgh: T. & T. Clark, 1920), 1:69–70.

66. For the connection between this phrase and possible Old Testament parallels, including Jer. 11:20, see Charles, *Critical and Exegetical Commentary on the Revelation*, 1:72–73.

67. For this widely held interpretation, see Mounce, *Book of Revelation*, 88 n. 26.

68. For this interpretation, see J. Massyngberde Ford, *Revelation: Introduction, Translation, and Commentary*, Anchor Bible (Garden City, NY: Doubleday, 1975), 403.

prerogative that Yahweh voices in the Old Testament. As such, it becomes a basis for Jesus' claim to be the eschatological judge.

The Sovereign I AM

The *ego eimi* sayings in Revelation 22:16 and 2:23 do not involve any obvious or clear allusions to the divine name. Yet they embody an implicit claim on the part of the exalted Jesus to close association with God. What is implicit in these two I AM sayings is explicitly evident in another set of *ego eimi*-plus-predicate occurrences. These statements, which number four in all, incorporate three related phrases: "the first and the last," "the Alpha and the Omega," and "the beginning and the end." The three phrases, which do not all occur in each of the four verses, are examples of a figure of speech or a rhetorical device called a merism, in which polar opposites are stated with the purpose of highlighting everything that lies between them.[69] These phrases imply that the speaker is sovereign over history, and as a result emphasize especially his ability to bring history to an end in salvation and judgment.[70]

The First and Last

One of the four *ego eimi* texts includes only the designation "the first and the last." In this I AM saying, the sense of sovereignty is present. Yet the statement is closely connected to an attendant claim that sets out the basis for this exalted status.

The text comes in John's recounting of Jesus' act of commissioning him to write the epistles to the seven churches, a commission vision that is reminiscent of those found in several Old Testament prophetic books (e.g., Isa. 6:1–13; Ezek. 1:1–3:11). John reports that while he was "in the Spirit on the Lord's day," he heard a trumpetlike voice charging him with this task. Upon turning around, John saw "one like a son of man" but who in fact was the resplendent, exalted Jesus standing among seven lampstands. John immediately prostrated himself before the heavenly visitor in a manner in keeping with the way in which other biblical characters responded to similar visions (e.g., Ezek. 1:28; Dan. 8:17; 10:15; see also Matt. 17:6; Acts 26:14). At this point, the Son of Man touched his servant and spoke to him. His words took the form of an oracle of assurance,[71] which in this case was intended to alleviate the anxiety of the seer and to prepare the way for the exalted Jesus to relay the ensuing message to John. By being structured in this way, the entire scene follows the fourfold pattern evidenced in the book of Daniel (cf. Dan. 8:15–19;

---

69. For this definition, see Beale, *Book of Revelation*, 199.
70. Beale, *Book of Revelation*, 1055.
71. For this term, see Aune, *Revelation*, 52a:100.

10:2–11:2), in which the prophet sees a vision, prostrates himself out of fear, is strengthened by the heavenly messenger, and then receives additional revelation.[72] In this particular oracle of assurance, however, the speaker identifies himself in a manner that far exceeds the self-designation of any heavenly visitor in the Old Testament: "I am the first and the last, and the living one. I was dead, and see, I am alive forever and ever; and I have the keys of Death and of Hades" (Rev. 1:17–18).

In the Greek construction, the Lord's assertions are successively joined together by the copulative *kai*. The result is a rhythmically flowing array of descriptors for the exalted Jesus. Three of these ("the first," "the last," "the living one"), each of which is a substantival participle, provide the predicates for the *ego eimi* that introduces the statement. Each of the three participles is introduced by the definite article, indicating thereby that the author desires to emphasize that each is a distinctive characteristic of the exalted Jesus.[73] At the same time, the first two belong together as a typical merism. And the third predicate of the *ego eimi*, "the living one," in turn introduces the subsequent explanatory declarations regarding Jesus' resurrection into the kind of life that lasts forever and his possessing the keys to death and Hades.

Although parallels for the declaration "I am the first and the last" can be found in ancient Greek literature,[74] its more explicit background is Yahweh's similar self-predications in Second Isaiah (e.g., Isa. 41:4; 44:6; 48:12), which we surveyed in chapter 4.[75] The recollection of the Old Testament sayings in the Apocalypse indicates that the exalted Lord is being associated with the divine "I am (He)" of Second Isaiah. Jesus' self-predication, therefore, implicitly entails a claim to be the divine I AM. As the great I AM, he stands at both the inception and the consummation of history, and consequently he is the one who is sovereign over the procession of history. Like the recipients of Yahweh's self-designations given through the Old Testament prophet, John's readers can take comfort, for regardless of the vicissitudes of history that they might see around them, the purposes of the divine "I am (He)" have been and will be, and therefore are now being, served.

Jesus augments his claim by the declaration that he is "the living one." The immediate basis for this assertion arises from his resurrection, through which he entered into unending life: "I was dead, and see, I am alive forever and ever" (Rev. 1:18). Although the claim has a direct historical basis, even here the parallel divine self-predications in the Old

---

72. For this pattern, see Beale, *Book of Revelation*, 213.
73. Archibald T. Robertson, *Grammar of the Greek New Testament in Light of Historical Research* (Nashville: Broadman & Holman, 1947), 785.
74. For examples of references, see Aune, *Revelation*, 52a:102.
75. For a helpful delineation of the parallels, see Beale, *Book of Revelation*, 214.

Testament are not far from view. The claim to be "the living one" finds precedence in claims made by Yahweh or about Yahweh that he is "the living God" (e.g., Josh. 3:10; Ps. 42:2; 84:3; cf. Matt. 16:16; Acts 14:15; Rom. 9:26). Consequently, Jesus' claim to be the living one draws together into a sublime double entendre this traditional Hebrew designation for God with Jesus' status as the one who was victorious over death. In this manner, the assertion declares that his triumph has placed Jesus in a new state, namely, that of being eternally alive. As the one who can claim "I am alive forever" (literally, "unto the ages of the ages"), he is closely connected to "the one who lives forever" (Rev. 4:9, 10; 10:6; 15:7).

Yet the claim carries an additional significance, one that we discovered in chapter 5 to be an important theme in the I AM texts in the Fourth Gospel. Not only does the exalted Jesus participate in eternal life, but precisely because he does, he is also able to bestow life. In Revelation 1:17–18, the exalted Jesus explicitly announces this claim by asserting that he holds the keys to death and Hades (i.e., the abode of the dead). According to Jewish understanding, only God possesses these keys.[76] Consequently, Jesus' claim places him on the plane with God.

Although it is not an explicit *ego eimi* text, a second instance of Jesus' claim to be "the first and the last" ought to be mentioned in this context. The salutation to each of the seven churches describes the exalted Jesus by means of some appropriate characteristic that is taken from the initial vision of the Son of Man reported in the opening chapter of the book. The letter to the church in Smyrna is no exception. Drawing from Jesus' self-predication in Revelation 1:17–18, the epistle begins, "And to the angel of the church in Smyrna write: These are the words of the first and the last, who was dead and came to life" (Rev. 2:8). This epithet was perhaps especially appropriate for the church in this city, because Smyrna competed with Ephesus and Pergamum for the title "first of Asia."[77]

Here again, the idea of being first and last is juxtaposed with Jesus' resurrection. This event is denoted by *ezesen*, which is the aorist of *zao*. As an aorist, the verb views an occurrence as completed at a point in the past. Hence, it refers to the actual event of resurrection, in which Jesus came back to life.[78] This designation is intended to be a source of encouragement to the persecuted church in Smyrna, for it assures them that they can face possible martyrdom, knowing that the one who came back from the dead both has the prerogative to and actually will reward their faithfulness with eternal life.

76. For instances of this idea in Jewish literature, see Mounce, *Book of Revelation*, 61 n. 40.
77. Ford, *Revelation*, 394.
78. William F. Arndt and F. Wilbur Gingrich, *A Greek-English Lexicon of the New Testament and Other Early Christian Literature* (Chicago: Univerity of Chicago Press, 1957), 336.

The Alpha and the Omega/the Beginning and the End

On three occasions the sovereignty of the "I am" is declared by means of a claim to be "the Alpha and the Omega" (Rev. 1:8; 21:6; 22:13). In two instances (21:6; 22:13), the phrase is followed by "the beginning and the end," and in the second of these, the descriptor "the first and the last" is inserted between the other two.

The descriptor "the Alpha and the Omega" draws its significance from its incorporation of the first and last letters of the Greek alphabet. Implicit therein is the idea that the speaker stands at both the inauguration and the culmination of the process of history, and by implication encompasses it all. Some exegetes, however, look to the Hebrew equivalent—"aleph and taw"—for a further indication of the meaning of the phrase.[79] One (unlikely) interpretation suggests that these two letters stand respectively for the Urim and Thummim, which were used in the Old Testament by the high priest to determine the will of God.[80]

One Alpha-Omega declaration is especially noteworthy in that it comes within a short discourse in which God the Father is the speaker:

> And the one who was seated on the throne said, "See, I am making all things new." Also he said, "Write this, for these words are trustworthy and true." Then he said to me, "It is done! I am the Alpha and the Omega, the beginning and the end. To the thirsty I will give water as a gift from the spring of the water of life. Those who conquer will inherit these things, and I will be their God and they will be my children." (21:5–7)

The language of these verses, together with the vision of the river of life in the new Jerusalem (Rev. 22:1–2), echos several of the divine pronouncements in the Old Testament (e.g., Ezek. 47:1–2; Zech. 14:8). Perhaps the most significant of these for this particular declaration is Yahweh's declaration in Second Isaiah, "I am about to do a new thing; now it springs forth, do you not perceive it? I will make a way in the wilderness and rivers in the desert" (Isa. 43:19; cf. 44:3; 49:10). The statement is also reminiscent of Yahweh's invitation, "Ho, everyone who thirsts, come to the waters; and you that have no money, come, buy and eat! Come, buy wine and milk without money and without price" (Isa. 55:1).

Like the first of these texts in Isaiah, God's self-description in the penultimate chapter of the book of Revelation draws from the image of a spring of water, and the theme of both passages is the gift of new life. Moreover, the new life that God claims to give is linked to his status as Creator. God speaks the creative word that calls the new creation into being. God is able

---

79. For examples of the presence of this expression in Jewish literature, see Charles, *Critical and Exegetical Commentary on the Revelation*, 1:20.
80. For this possibility, see Ford, *Revelation*, 379.

to do this because he is "the beginning and the end." This phrase likely arises from Hellenistic religious and philosophical sources, in which it carries a cosmological rather than a temporal meaning.[81] And the former, that is, the status of being both the ground and goal of all that is,[82] is evident in this divine I AM saying. Wilfrid Harrington points out the implication: "He is at the origin of all and at the end of all; all things have tended towards God, and now all things are found in him."[83] The inclusion of the connection to the divine creative power links the claim in the Apocalypse to the "I am (He)" texts of Second Isaiah, which we surveyed in chapter 4. To cite one example, Yahweh declares, "Listen to me, O Jacob, and Israel, whom I called: I am He; I am the first, and I am the last. My hand laid the foundation of the earth, and my right hand spread out the heavens; when I summon them, they stand at attention" (Isa. 48:12–13). It should be pointed out, however, that God's work in bringing the new creation into existence indicated here takes the form of renovation and culmination, or re-creation, rather than of beginning anew. As Eugene Boring points out, "God does not make 'all new things,' but 'all things new.'"[84] The promise, therefore, is not that of a second *creatio ex nihilo*, but of the renewal and hence the completion of God's creative work that commenced in the beginning.[85]

A second Alpha-Omega *ego eimi* saying is clearly attributed to Jesus, who declares, "See, I am coming soon; my reward is with me, to repay according to everyone's work. I am the Alpha and the Omega, the first and the last, the beginning and the end" (Rev. 22:12–13). The I AM statement is prefaced by Jesus' assertion that his Parousia will entail judgment. The language of this part of the verse is closely connected to a text in Second Isaiah: "See, the Lord GOD comes with might, and his arm rules for him; his reward is with him, and his recompense before him" (Isa. 40:10). This connection indicates that the exalted Jesus is claiming that he will be exercising a prerogative that was prophesied regarding Yahweh. The exalted Jesus bases his right to be the eschatological judge on the fact that he has fulfilled his role in bearing definitive testimony as the word of God. As a result, he now bears the titles that go with the exalted status of being sovereign over history.

In this text the three designations occur in rapid succession. Plummer notes regarding this feature of the text, "All three titles are here combined, as if to finally gather up into one impressive assertion the titles hitherto used separately."[86] G. K. Beale, in turn, sees in this combination of the

81. Aune, *Revelation*, 52c:1126–27.
82. For this language, see Caird, *Commentary on the Revelation*, 266.
83. Wilfrid J. Harrington, *Revelation*, vol. 16 of *Sacra Pagina*, ed. Daniel J. Harrington (Collegeville, MN: Liturgical Press, 1993), 210.
84. Boring, *Revelation*, 220.
85. For a similar observation, see Harrington, *Revelation*, 208.
86. A. Plummer, *Revelation*, in *The Pulpit Commentary*, ed. H. D. M. Spence and Joseph S. Exell (New York: Funk & Wagnalls, n.d.), 547.

titles a clear intention to highlight the deity of the exalted Jesus. He then adds, "The titles figuratively connote the totality of polarity: Christ's presence at and sovereignty over the beginning of creation and over the end of creation are boldly stated in order to indicate that he is also present at and sovereign over all events in between. The emphasis of the bipolar names here at the end of the book is to underscore Christ's divine ability to conclude history at his coming."[87] This conclusion is strengthened when we observe that until this point in the book, the first and the third of these titles were voiced solely with reference to God. Consequently, this I AM saying seems to be emphasizing that the eschatological vindication of the exalted Jesus confirms that he has the authority to mediate the final divine judgment.

The Trinitarian I AM

Apart from the opening superscription with its attendant blessing to the obedient hearer (1:1–3), the book of Revelation takes the form of an extended epistle. As such, it begins with a typical salutation that identifies the author of the letter and includes the appropriate greeting that invokes divine "grace and peace" upon the recipients. Anticipated in this greeting, and then asserted just after the doxology, is what turns out to be the most significant I AM saying of the Apocalypse.

The greeting in the book of Revelation follows the standard protocol of the day. And it includes the typical Christian epistolary blessing, "grace to you and peace," that is found in nearly all of Paul's letters.[88] Yet John's designation of the God who grants these benefits is unique. Such grace and peace arises from a threefold source: "from him who is and who was and who is to come, and from the seven spirits who are before his throne, and from Jesus Christ, the faithful witness, the firstborn of the dead, and the ruler of the kings of the earth" (1:4–5). Because of the uniqueness of this language, each of the ingredients in this threefold source includes items of exegetical interest and carries weighty implications for the understanding of the I AM in the Apocalypse.

We will look at the three originators of blessing in the greeting in reverse order. In this manner, our discussion will climax with the three-tense designation that is repeated in the subsequent I AM statement (1:8).

---

87. Beale, *Book of Revelation*, 1138.

88. For a helpful listing of these, see Aune, *Revelation*, 52a:26–27. Boring concludes that the writer of the Apocalypse belongs within the broad stream of the later Pauline tradition. Boring, *Revelation*, 74. Schüssler Fiorenza, in turn, sees the entire prescript of the Apocalypse as written in the form of a Pauline epistle prescript. Elisabeth Schüssler Fiorenza, *The Book of Revelation: Justice and Judgment* (Minneapolis: Fortress, 1998), 71.

The Exalted Jesus Christ

The identity of the third member of the threefold source enumerated in John's greeting is the most obvious and least exegetically problematic. The exalted Jesus is here listed, albeit without the typical designation "Lord." Instead, John follows the name with a threefold title, perhaps drawn from one of the enthronement psalms (Ps. 89:27, 37),[89] by means of which he focuses on three moments in the story of Jesus.[90] The use of the psalm, in which David is presented as the king who will reign over his enemies and whose throne, through his offspring, will be established forever, indicates that John intends to elevate Jesus as the ideal Davidic king, who has been enthroned as the eschatological, eternal sovereign.

The first of the three descriptors, "faithful witness," which appears in expanded form in the address to the Laodicean church (Rev. 3:14), can carry two quite different meanings. The fuller idea associated with the designation, namely, that of bearing testimony faithfully to the point of death, suggests that the designation might refer to the entire life of the earthly Jesus, climaxing in his death, as being a witness to the truth of God. At the same time, the reference might focus on Jesus' witnessing function in the book of Revelation, whether that be his role as the revealer of the message that he has received from God (1:1) or as the exalted Lord who guarantees the truth of the entire revelation that John is transmitting (cf. 22:20).

The second descriptor, "the firstborn from the dead," is a christological designation that is found as well in Paul's epistle to the Colossians (Col. 1:18), a letter that he intended to be circulated among the seven churches of the Apocalypse, including Laodicea (Col. 4:15). The phrase speaks of Jesus as the first to experience resurrection. This does not only mean that he was the first temporally, but also that as the one who is victorious over death, he sets the precedent for those who will follow. As the resurrected Lord, therefore, he is the one who inaugurates a new creation. Caird, therefore, is correct when he notes, "Instead of being an honorific title, ['firstborn'] is the guarantee that others will pass with him through death to kingship."[91]

Furthermore, by virtue of his resurrection, Jesus is exalted to the position of firstborn son and is imbued with the sovereignty that this status entails.[92] The third aspect in his title, "ruler of the kings of the earth,"

---

89. For a delineation that follows this perspective, see Margaret Barker, *The Revelation of Jesus Christ: Which God Gave to Him to Show to His Servants What Must Soon Take Place* (Edinburgh: T. & T. Clark, 2000), 93–94; Aune, *Revelation*, 38–39.

90. For an example of this widely held division, see Robert W. Wall, *Revelation*, New International Biblical Commentary (Peabody, MA: Hendrickson, 1991), 58.

91. Caird, *Commentary on the Revelation*, 17.

92. For this insight, see Ladd, *Commentary on the Revelation of John*, 25.

encapsulates a consequent aspect of the exalted Jesus' prerogative as the firstborn son. As the enthroned Son of Man, he is destined to exercise sovereignty over all authorities, including his foes. By putting this designation here at the beginning of the book, John anticipates the manner in which this central aspect of the ongoing place of the exalted Lord will be played out more completely as the drama of the Apocalypse unfolds.

The Seven(fold) Spirit(s)

The meaning of the designation of the second member of the threefold source of blessing is more problematic. The Greek construction reads *apo ton hepta pneumaton ha enopion tou thponou autou*, which can be rendered quite naturally, "and from the seven spirits who [are] before his throne."

At first glance, this appears to be a reference to seven angels,[93] perhaps the seven "angels of the face" or throne angels, "who stand ready and enter before the glory of the Lord" (Tob. 12:15), mentioned and even named—Uriel, Raphael, Raguel, Michael, Saraqael, Gabriel, and Remiel (*1 Enoch* 20:1–8)—in the intertestamental literature. Martin Kiddle notes that the basis for this image of the heavenly court dates to the mythologies of Babylon and Persia, in which the sun, the moon, and the five known planets were worshiped as the seven spirits of the sky.[94] Viewed from this perspective, the seven angels might be the guardian angels of the seven churches, to each of whom the respective epistle is subsequently addressed. Moreover, the seer later refers specifically to seeing "the seven angels who stand before God" (Rev. 8:2).

Yet this seemingly obvious understanding is not without problems. For example, although the idea is well documented in the intertestamental period, its roots in the Old Testament itself are weak. In fact, the plural word "spirits" is never used in the Old Testament to speak about angels, nor is the plural phrase "spirits of God,"[95] although both occur as such in the Qumran documents.[96] A stronger objection is theological, arising from the location of the phrase between John's designation for God and his mention of Jesus Christ within the delineation of the threefold source of blessing. Nothing short of deity, it is argued, could be associated with God and Christ in such a close manner.[97] Supporters of the idea that angels are in view here point out that the legitimacy of the objection is

---

93. For a defense of this position, see Aune, *Revelation*, 52a:34–35; Charles, *Critical and Exegetical Commentary on the Revelation*, 1:11–13.

94. Martin Kiddle, *The Revelation of St. John*, Moffatt New Testament Commentary (New York: Harper & Brothers, n.d.), 8–9. Kiddle considers the subsequent occurrences of the term "the seven spirits" to be "a primitive formula for the Power whom we call the Holy Spirit" or at least "the complete, sevenfold power that belonged to the Messiah." Kiddle, *Revelation of St. John*, 86, 100.

95. For this observation, see Aune, *Revelation*, 52a:33.

96. For examples, see Aune, *Revelation*, 52a:34–35.

97. See, for example, Ladd, *Commentary on the Revelation of John*, 24–25.

diminished by the association of angels with God and Christ in statements such as the reference to the coming of the Son of Man "in his glory and the glory of the Father and of the holy angels" (Luke 9:26) and Paul's solemn admonition to Timothy, which he offers "in the presence of God and of Christ Jesus and of the elect angels" (1 Tim. 5:21).[98] In response, it should be pointed out that in neither of these texts are angels listed with God and Christ as the source of such gifts as grace and peace, which elsewhere in Scripture are presented as originating from deity alone.

An exegetical tradition that dates at least to Victorinus of Pettau in the late third century[99] sees "the seven spirits of God" as what Leon Morris calls "an unusual way of designating the Holy Spirit."[100] A. Plummer explains that John's choice of numbers is theologically significant: "The number seven once more symbolizes universality, plenitude, and perfection; that unity amidst variety which marks the work of the Spirit and the sphere of it, the Church."[101] Robert W. Wall offers a similar interpretation: "This phrase is a title for the Holy Spirit and suggests the wholeness of life which God continues to mediate through the Paraclete within the believing community."[102] Similarly, Caird concludes, "The seven spirits represent the Spirit of God in the fulness of his activity and power."[103]

The case for seeing theological significance in this designation is strengthened by the observation that the phrase "the seven spirits of God" occurs on four occasions in the Apocalypse. In Richard Bauckham's estimation, this is no accident:

> There are *four* references to the *seven* Spirits . . . because they represent the fullness of the divine power "sent out into all the earth." These four references to the seven Spirits correspond to the seven occurrences of the fourfold phrase for the nations of the earth. It is as the power of the church's prophetic witness to all the nations that they are sent out into all the earth. They also correspond to the 7 x 4 references to the Lamb, since the seven Spirits are very closely associated with the victorious Lamb.[104]

This terminology occurs next in the Apocalypse in the address to the Sardis church: "These are the words of him who has the seven spirits of God and the seven stars" (Rev. 3:1). The latter part of this designation of Christ refers back to the opening vision in which John sees the exalted

---

98. See, for example, Mounce, *Book of Revelation*, 47.

99. For this historical reference, see Mounce, *Book of Revelation*, 46.

100. Morris, *Book of Revelation*, 49. See also Johnson, *Triumph of the Lamb*, 84.

101. Plummer, *Revelation*, 3.

102. Wall, *Revelation*, 57.

103. Caird, *Commentary on the Revelation*, 15. For a defense of a similar view, see Johnson, *Triumph of the Lamb*, 15–16.

104. Richard Bauckham, *The Climax of Prophecy: Studies on the Book of Revelation* (Edinburgh: T. & T. Clark, 1993), 35, cf. 162–66.

Jesus as having seven stars in his right hand (1:16), which are then declared to be the "seven angels of the seven churches" (1:20). The *kai* in 3:1 could possibly be taken to be epexegetic rather than copulative. The verse then reads, "the seven spirits of God, even the seven stars," a reading which equates the seven spirits with the seven stars.[105] Although this rendering is exegetically possible, most scholars find it improbable.[106]

If the spirits and the stars are not the same, then this occurrence favors the idea that the phrase refers to something other than the angels of the churches. It should be added that the alternative idea, namely, that the designation refers to the Holy Spirit, leads some exegetes to see this text as a biblical basis for the idea of the double procession of the Spirit. Plummer, for example, observes, "The Son hath the Spirit, not as One who receives it from the Father, but as One who can impart it to men."[107]

The phrase "the seven spirits of God" is also found in two of John's visions of the throne room. In the former, the seer's gaze is drawn to seven "flaming torches" burning in front of the throne, which are then said to be the "seven spirits of God" (4:5). Roy Summers offers a typical explanation of the symbolism involved in this designation (albeit one that is not shared by all commentators[108]): "Lamps give light; '7' is the perfect number. Seven Spirits picture God in his perfect spiritual essence. Therefore, we must have symbolized here as a token of God's sovereignty the perfect operation of the Holy Spirit in his work of illumination and revelation to man of the things of God."[109] More common is the idea that the language here is meant to refer to the fullness of the Spirit's presence with God.[110]

The other vision is more complicated: "Then I saw between the throne and the four living creatures and among the elders a Lamb standing as if it had been slaughtered, having seven horns and seven eyes, which are the seven spirits of God sent out into all the earth" (5:6). Both this text and Revelation 4:5 appear to contain allusions to Zechariah's vision of the heavenly throne room, regarding which the angel offers this explanation: "These seven are the eyes of the LORD, which range through the whole earth" (Zech. 4:10). The close connection between the seven eyes/spirits of the Lord and the Lamb suggests a stronger reality than mere angelic creatures. In a manner somewhat akin to the seven horns representing the fullness of the Lamb's strength, power, or rulership,[111] the seven eyes seem to facilitate his cognition of events in the world. As Mounce suggests, the

---

105. For this interpretation, see Aune, *Revelation*, 52a:219.

106. See, for example, Mounce, *Book of Revelation*, 47.

107. Plummer, *Revelation*, 107.

108. Ladd, for example, agrees that the reference is to the Holy Spirit, albeit in "his work in the creation and preservation of the natural world." Ladd, *Commentary on the Revelation of John*, 76.

109. Summers, *Worthy Is the Lamb*, 132.

110. See, for example, Johnson, *Triumph of the Lamb*, 99.

111. This interpretation is widely held, even to the point of being nearly assumed. See, for example, Ladd, *Commentary on the Revelation of John*, 88.

seven eyes "speak of that completeness of vision which leads to perfect knowledge."[112] The vision, it would therefore seem, is of the Lamb as the one who is endowed with the fullness of the Spirit.[113]

The idea that "the seven spirits of God" is a reference to the divine Spirit is strengthened by a consideration of its probable Old Testament basis. More specifically, this designation arises from Isaiah's prophecy that the fullness of the Spirit would rest on the "shoot . . . from the stump of Jesse" (Isa. 11:1). The prophet declares, "The spirit of the LORD shall rest on him, the spirit of wisdom and understanding, the spirit of counsel and might, the spirit of knowledge and the fear of the LORD" (11:2). Whereas the Masoretic Text enumerates six aspects of the Spirit's endowment, in the Septuagint rendering of the verse the six are expanded to seven by the insertion of "and godliness" after "knowledge." The likelihood that John had Isaiah 11 in view when he composed the Apocalypse is heightened by the allusion to Isaiah 11:1 in Revelation 5:5, which occurs immediately prior to the third reference to the "seven spirits of God" in the book.

These considerations lead to the conclusion that this phrase is a reference to the Holy Spirit. This conclusion suggests that in this cryptic manner, John presents the Spirit as both one and sevenfold, a perspective that is in keeping with the complex and cumulative descriptions of unity and fullness of being that characterize the book of Revelation.[114] Moreover, this understanding suggests a rationale for the inclusion of the Spirit in this unusual manner in the epistolary greeting. The sevenfold descriptor of the Spirit indicates that the Spirit who blesses the readers is the one who empowers the church as a whole, here depicted as the seven churches, in its role of being the burning lamp of witness in the world.[115]

The Divine Designation

In contrast to the typical Pauline phrase, "from God the/our Father," John designates the first member of the threefold source of grace and peace by means of a nonpersonally oriented, three-tense descriptor: the one "who is and who was and who is to come" (*ho on kai ho en kai ho erchomenos*; Rev. 1:4). We might say that in this manner, the Fatherhood of God, which is readily evident in Paul's greetings, gives way to the divine longevity and universal sovereignty in the greeting of the Apocalypse.

In John's declaration, the three substantives all appear in the nominative case, even though they follow the preposition *apo*, which normally takes the ablative (or genitive) construction. The seer's purpose might be

---

112. Mounce, *Book of Revelation*, 133.
113. For this conclusion, see Barker, *Revelation of Jesus Christ*, 83.
114. See Barker, *Revelation of Jesus Christ*, 83.
115. For a similar interpretation, see Beale, *Book of Revelation*, 189; Caird, *Commentary on the Revelation*, 14–15.

to highlight the direct connection that he intends between this designation, or at least the first element in it (*to on*), and Exodus 3:14. Beale
explains the rhetorical principle that might be at work here: "It is possible that John employs such kinds of constructions here and elsewhere as
Hebraisms in order to create a 'biblical' effect and so to show the solidarity of his work with that of God's revelation in the Old Testament."[116] In
any case, the grammar of the verse suggests that the phrase "who is and
who was and who is to come" has become a fixed formula. In fact, it
appears that the three-tense formula is intended to denote the divine
name, and that John considers the name to be a single indeclinable noun.[117]

As I noted in chapter 5, the first of the three elements in the formula
(*to on*) emerged as a widely used designation for God. This arose in part
out of the Septuagint rendering of Exodus 3:14 as *ego eimi to on*. Jewish
influence might also have led to the appearance of the designation in the
Greek magical papyri.[118]

The three-tense formula is likewise not without its literary antece-
dents.[119] A similar formula was attested in Greek since Homer. Yet in
such writings, the phrase is not limited to deity but can also denote aspects
of the material world. For example, a passage in Empedocles declares
that from fire, air, and water "comes all that was and is and will be hereafter."[120] Similarly, the Targumim include references to both a three-tense
and a two-tense divine name,[121] many of which instances are expansions
from Exodus 3:14 or various texts in Second Isaiah. In each case, the
goal of the expansion is not merely that of describing Yahweh as present
at the beginning, middle, and end of history. Rather, these passages depict
Yahweh as the sovereign Lord of history and therefore as being able to
deliver his people, despite overwhelming odds, from wherever they might
be held in captivity—Egypt, Babylon, or "the nations."[122] In any case, the
phrase as a whole as found in Revelation is often deemed by exegetes to
be a paraphrase of the divine name disclosed to Moses at the burning
bush.[123]

Despite the apparent parallels, the exact relationship of the Apocalypse
to these literary traditions remains uncertain. This uncertainty is evidenced in the fact that in at least one important way John's three-tense

---

116. Beale, *Book of Revelation*, 189.
117. See, for example, Ford, *Revelation*, 376. On this construction, see Mounce, *Book of Revelation*, 46 n. 7.
118. For an extensive list of literary examples, see Aune, *Revelation*, 52a:30–31.
119. Horst Balz, "eimi," in *Exegetical Dictionary of the New Testament*, ed. Horst Balz and Gerhard Schneider, 3 vols. (Grand Rapids: Eerdmans, 1990–1993), 1:393.
120. M. R. Wright, *Empedocles: The Extant Fragments* (New Haven, CT: Yale University Press,
1981), 100–101, 177–79.
121. For examples in the literature, see Beale, *Book of Revelation*, 187.
122. Beale, *Book of Revelation*, 188.
123. For this interpretation, see Mounce, *Book of Revelation*, 45.

formula differs from that found in the Jewish writings.[124] Whereas the third element in the references to God in such texts tends to be "he who will be," in the Apocalypse it is "he who is to come." This future-oriented designation denotes the certainty of God's anticipated eschatological act that will bring about the consummation of history.

The future orientation of the designation is confirmed by two occurrences later in the Apocalypse in which the formula appears in a shorter, bipartite form. The twenty-four elders declare, "We give you thanks, Lord God Almighty, who are and who were" (Rev. 11:17). Later the angel of the waters asserts, "You are just, O Holy One, who are and were" (16:5). Both of these instances of the shorter form occur at points in the vision in which the end is being anticipated (11:17–18; 16:5–7). The omission of the third tense from the formula indicates that the last part of the triadic divine name is connected to the eschatological future, when God brings history to its culmination by overthrowing his enemies and establishing his eternal kingdom.[125] Viewed from this perspective, his coming is no longer seen as future, because he has already come and is reigning.[126] We might say that at these points, the God who is coming will have come.[127] In the light of this certainty, saints can now rest assured that if they persevere they will be rewarded by the God of history and that their persecutors will receive just retribution.

Earlier in the Apocalypse, the three-tense divine designation is repeated by the four living creatures, albeit with the first two elements transposed: "'Holy, holy, holy, the Lord God the Almighty, who was and is and is to come" (Rev. 4:8). In the subsequent verses, this title is associated with the idea that the one on the throne "lives forever and ever" (4:9–10) and is worthy of praise because he is the creator of all things (4:11).

More significant, however, is the repetition of the divine designation, albeit in an augmented manner, in a statement that is inserted between the christologically focused doxology (1:5b–7) and the vision of the Son of Man that forms the preamble to the letters to the seven churches (1:9–20): "'I am the Alpha and the Omega,' says the Lord God, who is and who was and who is to come, the Almighty" (1:8). Although John attributes these words to "the Lord God," the question remains as to whether the speaker here is Christ (as in 22:13), or the Father (as in 21:6).[128] If the latter is correct, which is much more probable, then this is the first of only two occasions in the Apocalypse in which God speaks directly.

124. For a discussion of this issue, see Aune, *Revelation*, 52a:32–33.
125. For this conclusion, see Beale, *Book of Revelation*, 613.
126. For a similar interpretation, see Mounce, *Book of Revelation*, 227.
127. For this insight, see Bauckham, *Climax of Prophecy*, 32. See also Kiddle, *Revelation of St. John*, 208.
128. Plummer believes that it is Christ. See Plummer, *Revelation*, 4–5.

This instance of the statement is noteworthy in that it combines the three-tense designation of God with the Alpha-Omega *ego eimi* saying that is repeated twice in the closing two chapters of the Apocalypse, as I noted previously. In fact, the first predicate of the *ego eimi* in Revelation 1:8 is the Alpha-Omega claim. Rather than coupling this phrase with "the beginning and the end" or even "the first and the last" as in the other two occurrences, here the designation is followed by not only the three-tense formula of verse 4 but also the explanatory predicate nominative, "the Almighty" (*pantokpator*). This constellation of designations indicates that the emphasis in all three lies in God's sovereignty over all history, which provides the theological basis for the certainty that the exalted Jesus will indeed bring about the consummation of the divine program for history as suggested by the application to him of Daniel 7:13 and Zechariah 12:10 that precedes this I AM statement (v. 7). Yet the inclusion of the three-tense allusion to the Old Testament divine name provides an additional aspect of this theological basis. This God is sovereign because, as the divine name itself indicates, he is everywhere present to time, and in that sense he transcends every moment of time and hence time itself. It is in this sense that we should understand the popular idea that the three-tense formula "gathers past and future into an eternal, immediate now," to cite Eugene Peterson's version of what has become a typical characterization.[129]

As this overview has indicated, the opening greeting of the Apocalypse is well-fashioned structurally to make the theological point that John is highlighting. This structure is enhanced by the introduction of each element of the threefold source of divine blessing by the preposition "from" (*apo*). Moreover, the first and third elements, which bracket a singly designated second element, each consist of a threefold designation.

Viewed in its entirety, the pronouncement of a threefold source of grace and peace within the greeting in Revelation resembles the New Testament Trinitarian blessings such as Paul's benediction, "The grace of the Lord Jesus Christ, the love of God, and the communion of the Holy Spirit be with all of you" (2 Cor. 13:13). Yet John departs from the standard formulation in that he mentions the Spirit between his references to God and to Christ. Perhaps his goal in this is to indicate a revelatory progression from the eternal God through the Spirit to Christ and thereby to indicate already in the greeting what unfolds as the case throughout the eschatological vision that comprises the book. In so doing, John declares that the threefold source of grace and peace is the God who is active and present in the world by his Spirit, but supremely so in Jesus Christ.[130] In this sense, the Spirit, as well as Christ, participates in the eternality of the one who is and who was and who is to come.

---

129. Eugene H. Peterson, *Reversed Thunder: The Revelation of John and the Praying Imagination* (San Francisco: HarperSanFrancisco, 1988), 21.
130. For this idea, see Harrington, *Revelation*, 47.

Epilogue: The Bestowal of the Divine Name

The seer prefaces his vision of the consummation of history with a powerful description of the divine name. Working initially from ideas that had emerged within the Jewish tradition that associated a second figure with God in the throne room of heaven,[131] John develops a description that brings together a threefold source of blessing in a manner that opens the way toward later formulations of the doctrine of the Trinity.[132] But of greater immediate relevance, John lays the groundwork for a Trinitarian understanding of the I AM divine self-designation, which runs through the biblical drama from the disclosure of the divine name to Moses to its complete, final, eschatological unfolding through the victorious, exalted Jesus. But we have not yet delineated fully the manner in which the theme of the final unfolding of the divine name comes to the fore in the Apocalypse. To this end, we must look at the references to the act of bestowing the name found in the book.

The Name and the Exalted Jesus

The most significant text that explicitly refers to the conferring of a name on the exalted Jesus occurs in John's vision of the conquering rider on the white horse set to do battle against the beast, the false prophet, and those who follow after them. The seer reports:

> Then I saw heaven opened, and there was a white horse! Its rider is called Faithful and True, and in righteousness he judges and makes war. His eyes are like a flame of fire, and on his head are many diadems; and he has a name inscribed that no one knows but himself. He is clothed in a robe dipped in blood, and his name is called The Word of God. . . . On his robe and on his thigh he has a name inscribed, "King of kings and Lord of lords." (Rev. 19:11–13, 16)

Although several suggestions have been proposed regarding the identity of the rider, most exegetes agree that the seer's vision is of the exalted Jesus, depicted as the conquering Christ. Several considerations point in this direction, including the inclusion here of descriptions that were predicated of the exalted Jesus elsewhere in the Apocalypse, especially in the opening vision of the Son of Man. Hence, in both visions the heavenly figure is characterized by eyes that are like a flame of fire (1:14; 19:12; cf. 2:18) and with a sharp sword coming from his mouth (1:16; 19:14; cf. 2:12).

---

131. For a helpful sketch of this development, see Charles H. Talbert, "The Christology of the Apocalypse," in *Who Do You Say That I Am? Essays on Christology*, ed. Mark Allan Powell and David R. Bauer (Louisville, KY: Westminster John Knox, 1999), 176–79.

132. Glasson goes so far as to see the greeting as a reference to the Trinity. T. F. Glasson, *The Revelation of John*, Cambridge Bible Commentary (Cambridge: Cambridge University Press, 1965), 17.

In the vision of the rider, three names or titles are explicitly assigned to the conquering Christ: "Faithful and True"[133] (v. 11), "The Word of God" (v. 13), and "King of kings and Lord of lords" (v. 16). The first two of these are designations by which the rider is "called," whereas the third is "inscribed" on his robe and his thigh.

This is the only instance in the Apocalypse in which Jesus is explicitly named "The Word of God." The other two titles, in contrast, do occur earlier in Revelation. The Lamb's status as "King of kings and Lord of lords," a title found in intertestamental Jewish writings where it is generally associated with Yahweh,[134] is elsewhere in the Apocalypse declared to be the reason that he will be victorious over those who will make war on him (17:14). Similarly, the title "Faithful and True" is reminiscent of the designation "the faithful and true witness" (3:14), by means of which Jesus identifies himself in the beginning of the letter to the Laodiceans, as I noted earlier. Moreover, this pair of adjectives is later predicated of the words spoken by God regarding the promise that he will "make all things new" (21:5) and then of the words of the angel insofar as they are commissioned by the exalted Jesus, "the Lord, the God of the spirits of the prophets" (22:6).[135]

As a christological title, "Faithful and True" might draw from the steadfastness exhibited by the earthly Jesus, when he bore witness to the truth to the point of death.[136] Yet a deeper meaning of the designation emerges when we view the presence of these twin attributes in the Apocalypse in the light of the Old Testament attribution of these terms to Yahweh. Hence, "faithful" is readily ascribed to Yahweh to denote his covenant faithfulness. This theme is evident in a central declaration in Deuteronomy:

> It was not because you were more numerous than any other people that the LORD set his heart on you and chose you—for you were the fewest of all peoples. It was because the LORD loved you and kept the oath that he swore to your ancestors, that the LORD has brought you out with a mighty hand, and redeemed you from the house of slavery, from the hand of Pharaoh king of Egypt. Know therefore that the LORD your God is God, the faithful God who maintains covenant loyalty with those who love him and keep his commandments, to a thousand generations, and who repays in their own person those who reject him. (Deut. 7:7–10)

In Ladd's estimation, the same meaning is associated with the second attribute, "true." He explains: "The Hebrew idea of truth was not basi-

---

133. In contrast to most translations, Moffatt renders the sentence, "His rider is faithful and true," thereby proposing that these words be understood as describing the rider's character rather than as a title. James Moffatt, *The New Testament: A New Translation* (London: Hodder & Stoughton, 1913), 467.

134. Aune, *Revelation*, 52c:953–55, 1063.

135. Charles, *Critical and Exegetical Commentary on the Revelation*, 2:217.

136. For a similar characterization, see Talbert, "Christology of the Apocalypse," 167.

cally correspondence to reality as in Greek thought, but reliability. The 'God of truth' (Jer. 10:10) is not the God who reveals eternal truth, but the God who can be trusted to keep his covenant." Ladd then applies this idea to the vision of the rider: "The return of Christ will be the reappearance of him who has already appeared among men to bring God's covenant promises to their final and full consummation."[137]

Placed between the first and second names attributed to the conquering Christ in this vision is a fourth, enigmatic designation. Like "Lord of lords," this title is inscribed on the rider. But unlike the other three, its actual content is not given. Rather, it is a name "that no one knows but [the rider] himself" (Rev. 19:12). Wall describes honestly the state of the exegesis of this cryptic text: "The precise meaning of the rider's unknown name is contested and insoluble."[138]

Perhaps the most widely held interpretation sees this name as a secret designation that remains forever withheld from all created beings. Various reasons have been proposed as to why the name must remain a mystery. One suggestion is that the name must be kept secret to preclude anyone from having power over the rider, in keeping with the ancient understanding that to know someone's name meant to be able to tap into the person's power.[139] Viewed from this perspective, withholding the name from his opponents gives to the rider a strategic advantage. Hence, Craig Koester explains, "as Christ comes to the great battle in Revelation, he keeps a name secret, so that he alone has access to the power and authority that it represents."[140] Dennis Johnson, in turn, concludes that the secrecy of the name means that "no opponent can get a handhold to overthrow him or slow his advance."[141]

Other exegetes theorize that name encapsulates the depth of the rider's identity or personhood. If this is the case, then it cannot be disclosed simply because no finite creature can fully understand who the rider is,[142] no human mind can fathom the depth of his essence,[143] or no set of adoring names ascribed to him can exhaust the mystery of who he is.[144] As Mounce explains, "There will always remain a mystery about Christ that finite minds will never fully grasp."[145] Drawing this idea together with the names that are voiced in this passage, Ladd concludes regarding the rider, "He is known to himself by his hidden name; he is known to the churches

---

137. Ladd, *Commentary on the Revelation of John*, 253.
138. Wall, *Revelation*, 230.
139. See, for example, Morris, *Book of Revelation*, 223.
140. Koester, *Revelation and the End*, 176.
141. Johnson, *Triumph of the Lamb*, 274.
142. For a similar interpretation, see Harrington, *Revelation*, 190.
143. Ladd, *Commentary on the Revelation of John*, 254.
144. Caird, *Commentary on the Revelation*, 242.
145. Mounce, *Book of Revelation*, 353.

as the Faithful and True, the Word of God; he is known to the world as King of kings and Lord of lords."[146]

The New Testament writers, however, repeatedly voice the hope that we will one day know such deep theological mysteries. We will see the exalted Jesus as he is (1 John 3:2), we will know fully even as we are fully known (1 Cor. 13:12), and we will see God's own face (Rev. 22:4). Consequently, we can also anticipate that the secret name will one day be revealed to the faithful followers of the exalted and conquering Christ. Beale, therefore, appears to be on the right track when he concludes, "The symbolic meaning of the 'unknown name' is the affirmation that Christ has not yet consummately fulfilled the promises of salvation and judgment, but will *thoroughly* reveal to all his character (i.e., his name) of grace and justice when he comes to carry out those promises in vindication of his followers."[147]

This understanding of the significance of the secrecy of the name fits well with the meaning of the three disclosed designations in the vision of the rider. In bringing history to its close in judgment and vindication, the exalted Jesus confirms that he is the ultimate fulfillment of the covenant faithfulness promised by Yahweh in the Old Testament, to which he has borne witness as the Word of God. And his eschatological victory is assured because of his exalted status as sovereign over all earthly sovereigns. Yet the rider inaugurates his eschatological mission bearing a secret name, because its full content can only become evident as history comes to its culmination in the completion of that mission.

Yet the question remains regarding the actual content of the name itself. What name brings "Faithful and True," "Word of God," and "Lord of lords" together, while going beyond any one of them? Perhaps a clue is given in the epilogue of the book. In his parting words, in which the exalted Jesus declares that he is coming soon in judgment, he names himself in what turns out to be the loftiest I AM saying that he speaks in the Apocalypse. In this statement, he claims for himself the very same designation that to this point in the book has been pronounced only by God himself (1:8; 21:6): "I am the Alpha and the Omega." The exalted Jesus then adds to this lofty self-predication the two related descriptors, "the first and the last, the beginning and the end" (22:13).[148] The secret name, therefore, that is inscribed on the rider can be nothing less than the divine name itself, the great I AM connected as it is to the ineffable name, the tetragrammaton.[149] Margaret Barker said it well when she concluded that

146. Ladd, *Commentary on the Revelation of John*, 256.

147. Beale, *Book of Revelation*, 956.

148. For a similar perspective, see Wall, *Revelation*, 230–31.

149. Farrer sees a link here to the divine name worn on the forehead of the high priest. Farrer, *Revelation of St. John*, 198.

the name known only to the rider is "the most secret name[,] . . . 'I am that I am,' which the LORD revealed to Moses at the burning bush."[150]

The Name and Jesus' Followers

Yet Jesus is not the only one who comes to bear the divine name in the eschatological vision of the Apocalypse. On the contrary, through him this great privilege is extended to believers as well. This is evident in the vision of redeemed followers standing secure with their Lord and in the promise that the exalted Jesus voices to his followers who are facing trials on earth.

John's vision of the Lamb and his faithful witnesses presents the reception of the name in a culminated manner: "Then I looked, and there was the Lamb, standing on Mount Zion! And with him were one hundred forty-four thousand who had his name and his Father's name written on their foreheads" (14:1). The exegetical difficulties in this text are well-known. In fact, Mounce goes so far as to assert regarding this passage, "Verses 1–5 are often referred to as in some respects the most enigmatic in the book."[151] The difficulties begin already with the identity of the 144,000.[152] One long-standing exegetical tradition sees this number as designating an elite group of believers who have attained a special spirituality by means of celibacy.[153] More likely, however, is the view that finds in this text reference to a spiritually "celibate" army of the Lamb, that is, to a company of believers who have not defiled themselves spiritually but have remained faithful to Christ, awaiting the heavenly marriage supper of the Lamb.[154] Viewed in this light, the throng of 144,000 standing with the Lamb becomes a symbol of the church in its purity.[155] But the question still remains as to the nature of the group that the symbol represents. Is it the totality of God's people throughout the ages viewed as the true Israel[156] or as the continuation of Israel,[157] in short, the total company of the redeemed?[158] Or is the reference to some smaller number, such as the faithful remnant of true believers,[159] those who undergo martyrdom, or the proportion of the church sealed by God for some special service?[160]

---

150. Barker, *Revelation of Jesus Christ*, 306.
151. Mounce, *Book of Revelation*, 263.
152. For an extended treatment of this issue in its connection to the vision of Rev. 7:4–8, see Charles, *Critical and Exegetical Commentary on the Revelation*, 1:191–203.
153. For a recent restatement of this view, see Glasson, *Revelation of John*, 85.
154. For a similar interpretation, see Mounce, *Book of Revelation*, 267–68.
155. Johnson, *Triumph of the Lamb*, 202–4.
156. Morris, *Book of Revelation*, 112.
157. Beale, *Book of Revelation*, 733, cf. 416–23. See also Boring, *Revelation*, 129–31.
158. Ladd, *Commentary on the Revelation of John*, 190, cf. 117–19.
159. Wall, *Revelation*, 116, 179.
160. Caird, *Commentary on the Revelation*, 96.

As important as this question is for the exegesis of the vision, more crucial for our purposes is the significance of the presence of the two names on the foreheads of this multitude. Commentators routinely find a connection between this feature and the earlier marking of the 144,000 with a seal on their foreheads (7:3),[161] which is commonly viewed as signifying both security and ownership.[162] This connection, in turn, is routinely deemed to open the way for contrasting both acts with the presence of the mark of the beast—that is, "the name of the beast or the number of its name," 666 (13:16–18)—on the hands or foreheads of the rest of the earth's inhabitants. Just as the followers of the beast bear his mark, so also the Lamb's soldiers have his name and that of his Father on their foreheads. With this in view, Beale goes so far as to assert that the two acts of naming and sealing are equivalent, explaining that "the 'seal' or 'name' empowers saints to persevere through adversity, which authenticates their profession of faith as genuine and shows that they truly belong to God."[163]

The two acts are indeed connected as Beale and others suggest. In fact, it might be that the seal consists of the two names.[164] Yet this connection ought not to obscure the difference that John seems to be drawing between the two scenes with their respective acts. The sealing and the bestowal of the divine name serve two somewhat different, albeit related, purposes. As the instructions to the four angels suggest (7:3), the purpose of the seal is to provide some type of protection to its bearers in the context of their presence on the earth.[165] This is brought into sharp relief when the passage in the Apocalypse is read in the context of what might form its Old Testament basis, for a similar marking occurs within Ezekiel's vision of the departure of the divine glory from the temple:

> The LORD called to the man clothed in linen, who had the writing case at his side; and said to him, "Go through the city, through Jerusalem, and put a mark on the foreheads of those who sigh and groan over all the abominations that are committed in it." To the others he said in my hearing, "Pass through the city after him, and kill; your eye shall not spare, and you shall show no pity. Cut down old men, young men and young women, little children and women, but touch no one who has the mark. And begin at my sanctuary." (Ezek. 9:3–6; cf. Exod. 12:23; Zeph. 3:12)

The presence of the divine name on the foreheads of the redeemed who stand secure with the Lamb on Mt. Zion, in contrast, might be an allu-

---

161. For an opposing viewpoint, see Glasson, *Revelation of John*, 85.
162. See, for example, Ashcraft, "Revelation," 289.
163. Beale, *Book of Revelation*, 734.
164. For this view, see Aune, *Revelation*, 796, 804–5.
165. For an appraisal of the proposals of what this protection entails, see Charles, *Critical and Exegetical Commentary on the Revelation*, 1:194–99.

sion to the provision in the Deuteronomic law that the phylactery containing the Shema should be "fixed . . . as an emblem upon your forehead" (Deut. 6:8).[166] Even more likely is its possible connection to the practice of writing God's name on the high priest's forehead, in accordance with the stipulation in the law that "Holy to the LORD" be inscribed on a gold plate placed on the front of Aaron's turban (Exod. 28:36–38). Later Jewish writings interpreted this as indicating that the divine name "Yahweh," the tetragrammaton itself, was written on Aaron's forehead.[167] This Old Testament context suggests that the presence of the divine names on the foreheads of the 144,000 is intended to indicate that they have truly been made "priests of God and of Christ" (Rev. 20:6; cf. 1:6; 5:10).

In any case, the presence of the 144,000 on Mt. Zion indicates that they represent those who have come through the time of trial and are now secure, because they are present with the Lamb. But rather than being the special prerogative of any one particular group of Christians, the reception of the divine name is promised to all who overcome. This is evident in the statement within the climactic description of the new Jerusalem, whose inhabitants "will see [God's] face, and his name will be on their foreheads" (22:4). Perhaps this reference includes the extending of the high priestly prerogative, signified by the wearing of the divine name on the forehead, to all who inhabit the new city of God.[168]

The vision of the new Jerusalem provides the context for the specific promises voiced by the exalted Jesus in two of the seven letters. To the Philadelphia church, he declares, "If you conquer, I will make you a pillar in the temple of my God; you will never go out of it. I will write on you the name of my God, and the name of the city of my God, the new Jerusalem that comes down from my God out of heaven, and my own new name" (3:12). Although exegetes routinely conclude that the three names mentioned in this promise share a common meaning and hence can be treated simply as synonymous,[169] their full significance only emerges as they are viewed as component parts within an interrelated whole.

Two of the three names are explicitly stated by the exalted Jesus. He promises that his faithful followers will bear the name of "my God" and of the new Jerusalem. Ford explains the cultural background that lies behind this metaphorical promise:

> Inscriptions on pillars were a common feature of ancient oriental architecture. Writing one's own name on a temple wall was thought to keep one in continual unity with the deity of the temple. It was

166. For this connection, see Ford, *Revelation*, 241.

167. For examples of the relevant literature, see Aune, *Revelation*, 52a:242–43; Beale, *Book of Revelation*, 1114.

168. For this connection, extended to Rev. 3:12, see Glasson, *Revelation of John*, 35.

169. Beale, *Book of Revelation*, 293.

> also customary for the provincial priest of the imperial cult to erect
> a statue in the confines of the temple dedicated to the emperor and
> to inscribe on it his own name, that of his father, the place of his
> birth, and his year of office.[170]

She then adds, "To bear the name of the city is a sign of citizenship of the
heavenly city of God, the new Jerusalem."[171] This background confirms
the idea that the eschatological salvation awaiting the overcomers is in
view here. The temple in which they will be placed like pillars is not the
earthly temple, of course, nor the Christian community as such, but the
eschatological temple of redeemed people in the new Jerusalem.[172]

Although placing the promise in its more immediate cultural context
is helpful, not to be overlooked is its Old Testament background. Hence,
for inscribed temple pillars John needed to look no further than Solomon's temple with its two named pillars, Jachin and Boaz (1 Kgs. 7:21).[173]
More importantly, Yahweh's declaration of a future time of salvation that
will include the foreigners and eunuchs speaks of the bestowal of a new
name in similar language to the promise in Revelation: "To the eunuchs
who keep my sabbaths, who choose the things that please me and hold
fast my covenant, I will give, in my house and within my walls, a monu-
ment and a name better than sons and daughters; I will give them an
everlasting name that shall not be cut off" (Isa. 56:4–5). Similarly, the
inscription of the name of the new Jerusalem is illuminated when it is read
in the light of the glorious vision with which Ezekiel's prophecy ends. The
prophetic book closes by announcing, "The name of the city from that
time on shall be, the LORD is There" (Ezek. 48:35).

This Old Testament background confirms that the first two names
promised to the overcomers incorporate within them the sacred divine
name itself. Believers will be stamped with the name of the God of the
exalted Jesus, which is the everlasting name of Isaiah's prophecy, and the
name of the new Jerusalem, which according to Ezekiel is "Yahweh is there."

But what about the cryptic third name mentioned in the promise—
"my new name"? This phrase takes us back to the secret name that only
the rider knows, to which this promise seems to allude. And it leads, in
turn, to the other promissory statement, the promise to the church in
Pergamum: "To everyone who conquers I will give some of the hidden
manna, and I will give a white stone, and on the white stone is written a
new name that no one knows except the one who receives it" (2:17). In a
manner that is even stronger than the phrase "my new name," spoken to

---

170. Ford, *Revelation*, 417. See also Aune, *Revelation*, 52a:242.

171. Ford, *Revelation*, 417.

172. For a similar interpretation, see Aune, *Revelation*, 52a:241.

173. Some commentators see this as the background for the statement in Rev. 3:12. See, for example, Farrer, *Revelation of St. John*, 81.

the church in Philadelphia, the promise to the Pergamum overcomers anticipates the vision of the rider on the white horse. In both texts we find a reference to "a name having been written, which no one knows except" the recipient.

Some exegetes conclude from this observation that the new name promised to overcomers is the rider's own secret name. By implication, the name written on the stone is not unique to each believer, but is shared by and known together by the entire community,[174] which suggests that the new name is a mark of membership in the community of the redeemed.[175] This understanding might find its basis in the ancient use of white stones as admission tickets to public festivals.[176] The stones held by overcomers convey to them access to the new Jerusalem. In the ancient world, white stones had other uses as well, above all, a judicial use. Ancient jurors sometimes denoted a verdict of acquittal or innocence by means of a white stone or pebble.[177] Drawing from this practice would imply that the name written on the white stone is unique to each person.[178] It is the name of the acquitted overcomer written in the Lamb's book of life, an act that exempts its bearer from condemnation at the final judgment.

Perhaps more significant than either of these secular uses, however, is the background in Old Testament texts that speak about the granting of a new name. One such text occurs within a messianic vision in Jeremiah: "The days are surely coming, says the LORD, when I will raise up for David a righteous Branch, and he shall reign as king and deal wisely, and shall execute justice and righteousness in the land. In his days Judah will be saved and Israel will live in safety. And this is the name by which he will be called: 'The LORD is our righteousness'" (Jer. 23:5–6). Jeremiah's prophecy declares that the Messiah will bear a new name, "Yahweh is our righteousness," that is clearly connected to the divine name, but more importantly to the saving presence of the God of Israel with his people. Read in the light of this verse, the statements promising that believers will share in the divine name found in the Apocalypse highlight the identity of the speaker himself, the exalted Jesus, as the fulfillment of Yahweh's promises regarding the future of the divine name disclosed in the Old Testament. The second Old Testament text connects a new name directly to believers. Yahweh promises that on the day of judgment and vindication, he will bestow a new name on his people: "For Zion's sake I will not keep silent, and for

174. Beale, *Book of Revelation*, 257.

175. Ibid., 255.

176. For a list of possible interpretations, see Hemer, *Letters to the Seven Churches*, 96–102; Mounce, *Book of Revelation*, 82–83. Charles also supplies a list and then opts for a connection between this text and popular superstition surrounding the use of engraved amulets. Charles, *Critical and Exegetical Commentary on the Revelation*, 1:66–67.

177. For this interpretation, see Ladd, *Commentary on the Revelation of John*, 49; Wall, *Revelation*, 76–77.

178. This view is preferred by Mounce, *Book of Revelation*, 82.

Jerusalem's sake I will not rest, until her vindication shines out like the dawn, and her salvation like a burning torch. The nations shall see your vindication, and all the kings your glory; and you shall be called by a new name that the mouth of the LORD will give" (Isa. 62:1–2; cf. 65:15).

The meaning of the new name in the Apocalypse emerges as we note the element that the various Old Testament prophecies regarding the name share in common. Specifically, they all connect the name bestowed on others to the divine name itself. Moreover, the names that are spoken in each case—such as "Yahweh is our righteousness" and "Yahweh is there"—are all promises of the saving presence of the God of Israel with his people. They anticipate a future instantiation of the divine be-ing with or being present that were readily associated in the Old Testament with the I AM.

Viewed from this perspective, therefore, the promise of the exalted Jesus to share his own name—the glorious I AM—entails the promise of a new, eternal "being present" of the sovereign God. The God of history and of all creation will be with those who bear the divine name at every moment of time and even into eternity. In this way, the promise of a never-ending presence of the covenanting God with the covenant people emerges in the Apocalypse as the central significance of the divine eternality disclosed in the *ego eimi.*

PART THREE
THE SAGA OF
THE TRIUNE NAME

Chapter Seven

From the I AM to the Trinity

The Meaning of the Divine Name

Part 1 entailed a three-chapter narrative of the saga of Being. This narration brought to light how the divine I AM name disclosed to Moses at the burning bush formed the linchpin for the attempt of Christian theologians to connect the God of the Bible to the Greek concept of Being. It indicated as well how the melding of Christian theology and Western metaphysics occurred on the basis of the concerns and the categories set forth by the philosophical enterprise. Christian thinkers tended to understand the God of the Bible in accordance with a conceptual framework derived from metaphysics. In short, they moved from philosophy (Being) to theology (God). The result of their efforts was the construction of what came to be called "onto-theology," a perspective in which God is understood on the basis of a prior knowledge of Being; God is made to fit within the concerns that motivated the discussions in classical ontology. The "saga of Being" ended, however, by noting how impulses over the last hundred years have spelled the demise of onto-theology.

Part 2 elevated to center stage the particular divine name to which the architects of ontology had appealed as the link between the biblical God and the Greek philosophical concept of Being. The "saga of the I AM" traced the journey of this name through the biblical narrative. In so doing, it revealed that the biblical witness is uniform: The God of the Bible is a God who has a name. The unfolding of this story led from the revelation of the I AM name to Moses, through the incarnation of the I AM in Jesus Christ, and ended with the exaltation of Jesus as the eternal I AM.

My goal in this third part is to determine how the divine name might once again become the basis for a conversation between theology and ontology. In inaugurating a renewed conversation, we must bear in mind the changed situation that the demise of onto-theology introduces. This demise, which characterizes the context in which any renewed conversation must occur, means that the flow of discourse can no longer move solely from philosophy to theology. Rather, if such a conversation is to have any bearing for theology this side of the demise of onto-theology, it must flow—at least initially—from theology to philosophy. The conversation, in other words, must entail a "theo-ontology."

If God Had a Name

One aspect of the connection between theology and ontology has not been altered by the demise of onto-theology. The beginning point for any renewed conversation remains the same as that which launched the initial construction of a grand synthesis of Christian theology and Greek philosophy: the name of God. Even here, however, the new context marks a radical change, in that the manner in which the discovery of the divine name is put to use cannot remain the same. For the patristic and medieval architects of the grand synthesis, what was most important about the name of the God of the Bible was its inherent connection to the Greek concept of Being. Drawing from the Septuagint rendering of Exodus 3:14, Christian philosophical theologians noted that the name disclosed to Moses, *ego eimi ho on*, carried within it the claim "to be the one who is." Once this discovery was made, the biblical narrative served no actual philosophical purpose; onto-theology had no need for the ongoing story of the relationship of God to a particular people, Israel.

A theo-ontology, in contrast, draws from the disclosure of the I AM name in a quite different manner. It views the narrative of the name of God as crucial to the ontological quest. Indeed, it develops its ontology on the basis of that narrative, because it deems the saga of the I AM as having far-reaching ontological significance.

The Divine Name in Theological History

The first step in inaugurating a renewed conversation between theology and ontology on the basis of the divine name is to explore the theological character and importance of that name. The beginning point for such an exploration, in turn, is to view the presence of the divine name in theological history.

The Subdued Interest in the Divine Name

Writing in 1946, Emil Brunner observed, "The small part the conception of the 'Name of God' plays in the dogmatic work of the Church is in striking contrast to the witness of Scripture, which shows—by the very fact of its frequent use—that it is one of the most important ideas in the Bible."[1] Brunner's point is well taken. The divine name has been surprisingly absent from the history of theology. Theologians have given only meager space to a consideration of the significance of the fact that the God of the Bible has a name.

In the patristic era and the Middle Ages, the divine name tended to be of interest largely insofar as it provided the means to connect the God of the Bible with the Greek concept of Being. Many modern critics lay the blame for this development at the feet of Augustine. Brunner's characterization is not atypical. He claims that Augustine concluded that Plato and the Exodus text were declaring the same basic idea. Brunner explains that under the influence of Neoplatonism, the church father identified the *summum esse* with the *summum bonum*.[2]

The idea of the divine name was clearly evident in work of the patristic author who assumed the name of Dionysius the Areopagite. Despite its promising title, *De Divinis nominibus*, however, the book in which we would expect to find an extensive treatment of the topic is in fact not a treatise on the divine name disclosed in Scripture. Instead, it engages the question of the extent to which our ideas regarding God—that is, the names by which we designate God—are true reflections of the divine reality. Dionysius concludes that all such names are inadequate to the task, for the divine nature is ultimately unknowable. Near the beginning of the treatise, the author states the point in the form of a question:

> But if It is greater than all Reason and all knowledge, and hath Its firm abode altogether beyond Mind and Being, and circumscribes, compacts, embraces and anticipates all things while Itself is altogether

1. Emil Brunner, *The Christian Doctrine of God*, vol. 1 of *Dogmatics*, trans. Olive Wyon (Philadelphia: Westminster, 1950), 128.
2. Ibid., 129.

> beyond the grasp of them all, and cannot be reached by any per-
> ception, imagination, conjecture, name, discourse, apprehension, or
> understanding, how then is our Discourse concerning the Divine
> Names to be accomplished, since we see that the Super-Essential
> Godhead is unutterable and nameless?

Dionysius then concludes, "Conscious of this, the Sacred Writers cele-
brate It by every Name while yet they call It Nameless."[3]

The situation of the perceived significance of the divine name did not
change markedly in the Middle Ages. Thomas Aquinas, to cite an especially illuminating example, speaks to the topic twice in part 1 of his *Summa
Theologica*. In question 2, article 3, he cites Exodus 3:14 as the basis for
claiming that God exists. Then in question 13, article 1, he responds to
the query of whether God can be named:

> I answer that, Since according to the Philosopher (Peri Herm. i),
> words are signs of ideas, and ideas the similitude of things, it is evi-
> dent that words relate to the meaning of things signified through the
> medium of the intellectual conception. It follows therefore that we
> can give a name to anything in as far as we can understand it. Now
> it was shown above (12, 11, 12) that in this life we cannot see the
> essence of God; but we know God from creatures as their principle,
> and also by way of excellence and remotion. In this way therefore He
> can be named by us from creatures, yet not so that the name which
> signifies Him expresses the divine essence in itself. Thus the name
> "man" expresses the essence of man in himself, since it signifies the
> definition of man by manifesting his essence; for the idea expressed
> by the name is the definition.[4]

As this response indicates, Aquinas was not interested in explicating the
divine name disclosed in Scripture. Rather, he was concerned about the
problem that Dionysius had raised: How can our words be predicated of
God? In this manner, Aquinas advanced the tendency that he had inherited to treat the "names" of God as equivalent to the divine attributes.

Aquinas's basic approach has remained influential into the present. For
example, the opening chapter of Thomas Oden's three-volume systematic
theology bears the title, "The Naming of God." Although Oden gives
at least passing mention to the various divine names found in Scripture,
he quickly moves to an enumeration of God's attributes. Thereby, the
chapter exemplifies Oden's belief that "the discussion of divine *attributes*
is best viewed as a fuller development and clarification of scriptural *names*
for God."[5]

3. Dionysius the Areopagite, *On the Divine Names* 1.5, in *On the Divine Names and the Mystical Theology*, trans. Clarence Edwin Rolt (London: SPCK, 1920), 59–61.

4. Thomas Aquinas, *Summa Theologica* 1.13.1, trans. Fathers of the English Dominican Province, 2nd and rev. ed., 5 vols. (Allen, TX: Christian Classics, 1981), 1:60.

5. Thomas C. Oden, *The Living God* (San Francisco: Harper & Row, 1987), 32.

Regarding the matter of how we can predicate attributes to God, Aquinas followed the method that had come to characterize much of medieval thought. This approach suggests that statements about God can be derived from what we know about creatures in three basic ways: the *via causalitatis* (or *affirmativa*), the *via negationis* (or *negativa*) and the *via eminentiae*. Twentieth-century Protestant theologians Emil Brunner and Otto Weber have pointed out that the theory of the three ways was actually derived from Dionysius.[6] Brunner asserts that its basis in Neoplatonism means that "the method of the '*via*' in the doctrine of God corresponds exactly to the 'method' in the practice of mysticism."[7] For this reason, Brunner rejects it categorically, claiming that it is "rational metaphysics . . . not Christian theology."[8] Similarly, Weber concludes that this approach is not theology but "a metaphysics of being and founds a mysticism of being which corresponds to such a metaphysics."[9]

In contrast to the medieval scholastics, theologians working in the wake of the Reformation routinely drew insight from the divine name disclosed in the Bible, which they tended to denote (erroneously) as "Jehovah." Yet although the Protestant scholastics elevated the divine name in their theological work, their interests generally ran in directions other than that of the significance of the biblical name of God.

One central task that concerned many theologians was that of uncovering Trinitarian overtones in the Old Testament. Their exegetical findings led some to conclude that the name "Jehovah" can rightly be predicated only of the first person of the Trinity. For example, writing in the closing years of the seventeenth century, the Dutch theologian Leonard van Rijssen observed that one such text, Exodus 3:2, contains a reference to three persons and attributes distinct operations to each: Jehovah exercises mercy or loving-kindness toward his people, the Angel of his presence carries out the work of redemption, and the Holy Spirit is the agent of anger and contention against the people of Israel.[10] In drawing this conclusion, Rijssen was following in the footsteps charted over a century earlier by Wolfgang Musculus, who in speaking about the difference between the essence and the substance of God, defined the former as "that which was common to all persons in the Holy Trinity," whereas the latter entails "that which . . . appertained to one person, that it could not be attributed unto the other two persons." He then determined that the Old Testament

---

6. Brunner, *Christian Doctrine of God*, 245; Otto Weber, *Foundations of Dogmatics*, trans. Darrell L. Guder, 2 vols. (Grand Rapids: Eerdmans, 1981, 1983), 1:412.

7. Brunner, *Christian Doctrine of God*, 245.

8. Ibid., 246.

9. Weber, *Foundations of Dogmatics*, 413.

10. Leonardus Rijssenius, *Summa theologiae didactico-elencticae* (Amsterdam, 1695), as cited in Richard A. Muller, *Post-Reformation Reformed Dogmatics: The Rise and Development of Reformed Orthodoxy, ca. 1520 to ca. 1725*, vol. 4, *The Triunity of God* (Grand Rapids: Baker, 2003), 225.

254 The Saga of the Triune Name

denoted the three substances by the words *Jahweh*, *dabar*, and *ruach*.[11] The equating of Jehovah with the first person of the Trinity came to a climax in eighteenth-century Britain, when Samuel Clarke argued that insofar as only the Father is to be identified as the Jehovah of the Old Testament, only the Father is fully and absolutely divine in himself and hence the bearer of all the attributes of deity.[12]

More widespread among post-Reformation Protestant theologians was the tendency to view the name Jehovah as referring to the one divine essence common to the three persons of the Trinity. Jerome Zanchi (1516–1590) paved the way in this direction, for he derived the unity of God from the name "Jehovah," whereas he claimed that the Trinity emerged from the descriptor "Elohim."[13]

Viewing "Jehovah" as the designation for the one God was especially crucial in the apologetic endeavors of orthodox theologians who sought to counter the arguments of the Socinians by proving the divinity of all three persons of the Trinity. The orthodox exegetes concluded that because Scripture connects the name "Jehovah" to the one God apart from any identification or determination of the three persons, the Bible could rightly also apply the name to Christ and to the Spirit. In support of this apologetic, these theologians pointed to texts (especially in the New Testament) in which a biblical writer clearly identifies Christ or the Spirit but that parallel passages (generally in the Old Testament) in which the person spoken of or about is Jehovah.[14]

The Protestant scholastic theologians also continued the tendency, inherited from their patristic and medieval predecessors, to link the tetragrammaton with the Greek concept of Being. Francis Turrettin provides a lucid example. He acknowledges that "God . . . does not need a discretive name; nor does a name properly belong to him, either appellative (which is of the distinct species of the same genus) or proper (distinctive of the individuals of the same species)." But, he adds, "because all our knowledge begins from a name, he assumes various names in Scripture to accommodate himself to us." Moreover, "the first and principal name is Jehovah, which is derived from his essence or existence."[15] Turrettin then explains that the Bible indicates that this name suggests three interconnected truths about God. First, it implies "the eternity and independence of God, inasmuch as he is a necessary being, and existing of himself, inde-

---

11. Wolfgang Musculus, *Loci communes sacrae theologiae* (Basel: Johann Herwagen, 1560), i, as cited in Muller, *Post-Reformation Reformed Dogmatics*, 4:205–6.

12. For this characterization of Clarke's position, see Muller, *Post-Reformation Reformed Dogmatics*, 4:130, 133.

13. Muller, *Post-Reformation Reformed Dogmatics*, 4:85.

14. For a helpful summary of this apologetic procedure, see Muller, *Post-Reformation Reformed Dogmatics*, 4:302–5, 357–59.

15. Francis Turretin, *Institutes of Elenctic Theology* 4.1, trans. George Musgrave Giger, ed. James T. Dennison, Jr., 3 vols. (Phillipsburg, NJ: Presbyterian & Reformed Publishing Co., 1992), 1:183–84.

pendent of any other, self-existent (*autoon*)—'I am that I am.'" Hence, he is called simply the being (*ho on*) as the ancient philosophers and Plato especially acknowledged. Second, it indicates "causality and efficience because what is the first and most perfect in each genus is the cause of the rest (for God is by himself so that he is the cause of being to all others)." And finally, it points to "immutability and constancy in promises because he really performs and does what he has promised by giving to his promises being (*to einai*), not only self-existent (*autoon*), but also essentially existent (*ousion*) and essence-making (*ousiopoios*)."[16]

Turrettin's conclusions found repeated echo among subsequent Protestant thinkers. One example is the lengthy treatise on systematic theology that the Puritan Baptist pastor John Gill (1697–1771) composed, as he himself notes, after he had completed "an Exposition of the whole Bible."[17] Gill treats the divine names in the first chapter of his doctrine of God. Reminiscent of Turrettin, he begins by noting that the divine incomprehensibility means that God cannot be named, whereas his status as the only God entails that he has no need of a name. In support of this contention, Gill cites Plato, who declared that God has no name and therefore called God *to on*. Gill links this designation to Exodus 3:14 and to the name Jehovah that he sees arising from this text.[18] The name "Jehovah," Gill adds, refers to God "as a necessary and self-existent being."[19] Noting that the divine name comes from the Hebrew root that signifies "to be," he then explains that it "is expressive of the essence of God; of his necessary and self-existence, for God naturally and necessarily exists." He then adds that unlike creatures, "God exists in and of himself, he is a self-existent and independent Being. . . . He is the Being of beings; all creatures have their beings from him and in him."[20]

In contrast to this long tradition of connecting the tetragrammaton to the Greek conception of Being, Christian theologians in the modern era tended to interpret the divine name in light of the progressive character of the economy of salvation. These thinkers aver that the tetragrammaton belonged to the preparatory stage of God's self-revelation. Consequently, they argue, it was rendered obsolete by God's fuller revelation to the church.[21]

The Renewed Interest in the Divine Name

The theological heritage as a whole has expressed little explicit theological interest in the significance of the fact that the God of the Bible is named. This lack of interest led to the discounting of the Hebrew name for God

16. Ibid. 4.5 (1:184–85).
17. John Gill, *A Body of Doctrinal Divinity*, rev. ed. (1839; Atlanta: Turner Lassetter, 1965), xxiii.
18. Ibid. 1.3.1 (25–26).
19. Ibid. 1.3.7 (28).
20. Ibid. 1.3.7 (29).
21. R. Kendall Soulen, "The Name of the Holy Trinity," *Theology Today* 59, no. 2 (July 2002): 246.

that came to characterize theology and biblical studies in the modern era. Yet the twentieth century also gave birth to important exceptions.

Among conservative Reformed theologians, an attempt at least to acknowledge that there is some theological significance in the divine name can be seen in Louis Berkhof's treatise on systematic theology published in the middle of the twentieth century. After treating the traditional topics—the existence of God, the knowability of God, the relation of the being and attributes of God—Berkhof moves to the names of God. He notes that when the Bible speaks of the name of God in the singular, "'the name' stands for the whole manifestation of God in His relation to His people, or simply for the person, so that it becomes synonymous with God." Berkhof then adds, "In the most general sense of the word, then, the name of God is His self-revelation. It is a designation of him, not as He exists in the depths of His divine Being, but as He reveals Himself especially in His relations to man."[22]

Perhaps the twentieth-century theologian who more than any other was concerned to rehabilitate the concept of the divine name for theology was Emil Brunner. In the initial installment of his three-volume *Dogmatics*, he launched his creative treatment of the doctrine of God (which he entitled, "The Eternal Foundation of the Divine Self-Communication") by looking first at "The Name of God."

Reminiscent of Dionysius, Brunner sets as his starting point the biblical idea that God is "a Mystery dwelling in the depths of 'in accessible Light.'"[23] But Brunner quickly moves away from the Neoplatonic perspective of the patristic writer, for he then adds that we can only understand the true depth of the divine mystery as we come to know God in his revelation. Consequently, Brunner asserts that the truly mysterious God is not the "Nameless One." Instead, "the Mysterious One is He who makes His Name known to us in His own revelation." Brunner then concludes, "Because the revelation of the Name is the self-manifestation of the God who is free, and exalted high above this world, it is this alone which confronts us with the real mystery of God. Hence, the revelation of the Name of God stands in the centre of the Biblical witness to revelation."[24]

Despite his attempt to make a new beginning, in the end even Brunner marches in step with the modern perspective regarding the temporary nature of the Old Testament divine name. He observes that initially in salvation history, the name of God was the proper name "Yahweh," which was necessary to distinguish the God of Israel from the gods of the other nations. But, he adds, later in Old Testament history, the idea of a plurality of gods disappeared and with it the need for a divine proper name.[25]

22. Louis Berkhof, *Systematic Theology*, rev. ed. (Grand Rapids: Eerdmans, 1953), 47.
23. Brunner, *Christian Doctrine of God*, 117.
24. Ibid., 119.
25. Ibid.

Brunner's goal, therefore, like that of most theologians throughout Christian history, is not that of exegeting the divine name.

At one point, Brunner does offer a quick comment on the disclosure of the name to Moses. He bemoans the translation of the name into the language of speculative thought and its transformation into a definition: "I Am He Who Is." According to Brunner, the sacred name should be seen as meaning, "I am the Mysterious One, and I will to remain so. . . . I am the Incomparable, therefore I cannot be defined nor named."[26] Yet even here, instead of exegeting the name, Brunner is concerned to draw theological significance out of the idea of the divine name.[27] Above all, he finds this significance in the idea that the name of God is "God in His Self-communication."[28] Drawing from the personalism that lies at the heart of Brunner's theological perspective, he asserts that the divine name leads to the realization that God is Person, our primary "Thou," rather than an "It." According to Brunner, this realization occurs as God discloses himself to us in a manner that allows us to call upon him in return and thereby reveals himself as the one who exists "for us."[29] For Brunner, this glorious event occurs ultimately in Jesus Christ.[30]

Brunner follows his discussion of the divine name by delineating the actual content of the nature of God that is disclosed in God's self-revelation. He asserts that from the biblical standpoint, God reveals himself as the Lord. On this basis, Brunner lauds the translators of the Septuagint for rendering the name "Yahweh" by the title "Lord."

In Brunner's estimation, the self-disclosure of God as Lord, and not some supposedly neutral definition of the Godhead, provides the genesis for dogmatic reflection.[31] He believes that this starting point reminds us that God is Subject addressing us, rather than a mere topic of human speculation. Brunner states the point unequivocally: "The God with whom we have to do in faith, is not a Being who has been discussed or 'conceived' (by man); He is not an *Ens*, a 'substance,' like the Godhead of metaphysical speculation; He is not an object of thought—even though in a sublimated and abstract form—but the Subject who as 'I' addresses us as 'thou.'"[32] In this manner, Brunner concludes that thinking about God must always start from what he calls the "original situation of faith," that is, from the perspective of God meeting us as the sovereign "I." In short, he is convinced that theology must begin with God's self-disclosure of

26. Ibid., 120.

27. According to Garrett, Brunner enumerates three decisive elements that are bound up with the divine name, to which Garrett adds a fourth. James Leo Garrett, Jr., *Systematic Theology: Biblical, Historical, and Evangelical*, 2 vols. (Grand Rapids: Eerdmans, 1990, 1995), 1:190.

28. Brunner, *Christian Doctrine of God*, 121.

29. Ibid., 121–24.

30. Ibid., 127.

31. Ibid., 138.

32. Ibid., 139.

"His personal Being as Subject," rather than from "any kind of neutral definition of being, such as that of the theology determined by Platonism, Aristotelianism, and Neo-Platonism."[33]

Writing in the wake of Brunner's work (as well as that of Karl Barth), Weber also seeks to determine what "can be derived dogmatically from the name Yahweh."[34] Like Brunner, he concludes that because God really has a name, God is not an idea but a person. Moreover, God remains a mystery in his name, which Weber sees as the chief significance of the older derivation of the divine aseity from Exodus 3:14.[35] But of greatest importance to Weber is the observation that the name "Yahweh" means that God is a covenanting God. Weber believes that the use of this name indicates that God acts concretely in the covenant agreements that God has made and hence that God is explicitly related to the history of the divine self-manifestation.

In Weber's estimation, this means that the older theological trajectory was incorrect in attempting to derive the nature of God from the divine names, whether in the biblicistic manner followed by the Protestant scholastics or in the speculative approach of the medieval theologians.[36] Rather than pursuing either of these two paths, Weber avers that theology must find its center in the one Name that God has given us for salvation. In his estimation, this name is not "Yahweh," which name belongs to the old covenant as is evidenced by the fact that it does not occur in the New Testament. Instead, the "new and eternal covenant" set forth in the New Testament "is accompanied by the New Name," Weber avers, and this name is "Jesus," the one in whom God has fulfilled what remained unfulfilled until the coming of the Son of God. For this reason, Weber concludes, "If the Church still wanted to say 'Yahweh' (or perhaps 'Jehovah'), then it would be denying what God has done."[37]

"Yahweh" and the "New" Divine Name

Theological proposals such as those articulated by Brunner and Weber, building as they do from the findings of modern biblical scholarship, underscore the seemingly surprising observation that emerges from a cursory reading of the New Testament. In contrast to the repeated use of the name "Yahweh" in the Old Testament, what for the Hebrews was the proper name for the God of Israel disappears completely from view in the New. Edgar Krentz states the point sharply:

33. Ibid., 141.
34. Weber, *Foundations of Dogmatics*, 1:418.
35. Ibid.
36. Ibid., 1:419.
37. Ibid.

> The Old Testament is rich in names and epithets for God. . . . That richness is not found in the New Testament. Even more striking is the complete absence of the Old Testament proper name of God from the New Testament. Thus the New Testament does not simply continue Old Testament practice in speaking of God. There is, for all of the lines of continuity, a break in the tradition.[38]

This observation and the conclusions Brunner and Weber draw from it raise the theological questions of why the name "Yahweh" is absent from the New Testament and whether the tetragrammaton is replaced by another name.

The Tetragrammaton in the New Testament

The background for the seemingly unanticipated disappearance of the name "Yahweh" in the New Testament is well known. I noted in chapter 5 that after the Babylonian exile, pious Jews—with the exception of the high priest in the Holy of Holies—gradually ceased to pronounce the name "Yahweh."[39] In the interests of this aspect of the developing reverential piety, the Jews devised various euphemisms to represent the divine name. A variety of designations, including "the Name," came to be used as substitutes for the tetragrammaton. Yet the most common circumlocution was the Hebrew word *adonai* ("Lord"), which was generally translated in the Septuagint by the Greek term *kyrios*. At the same time, certain Old Testament texts and the Jewish writings in the intertestamental period anticipated a time when the divine name would again be known outside the temple.

Despite the advent of the kind of reverential piety that viewed the divine name as inexplicable, the idea that the God of Israel had a name did not disappear. And even though by the time of Jesus the tetragrammaton no longer functioned as the personal name of the God of Israel, at least not in its expressed form, it is doubtful that the knowledge of the name itself was lost completely. On the contrary, the divine name— or the idea that God has a name—has played an ongoing, central role in Judaism. Jewish theologian Michael Wyschogrod offers a poignant reminder of this, when he indicates the insufficiency of simply viewing God as "Thou," as Martin Buber had proposed:

> When I address my friend as You, it is he who I am talking to, with his face and intonation, his gait and opinions. It is so ultimately

---

38. Edgar M. Krentz, "God in the New Testament," in *Our Naming of God: Problems and Prospects of God-Talk Today*, ed. Carl E. Braaten (Minneapolis: Fortress, 1989), 78.

39. For this historical datum, see C. K. Barrett, *The Gospel according to St. John: An Introduction with Commentary and Notes on the Greek Text* (London: SPCK, 1978), 421. For examples in the Jewish literature, see Krentz, "God in the New Testament," 78–80. For an extended study of the divine name in Judaism, see G. H. Parke-Taylor, *Yahweh: The Divine Name in the Bible* (Waterloo, ON: Wilfrid Laurier University Press, 1975), 96.

> specific that his name rather than the Thou is required. The name
> specifies his particularity. . . . The God of Israel is not just a Thou.
> *The God of Israel has a proper name.* There is no fact in Jewish theol-
> ogy more significant than this. And the tradition always understood
> the significance of this fact and so surrounded this name with end-
> less mystery, so that it became an ineffable name because it celebrated
> the most terrible of all recognitions, the personality of God.[40]

The reverential refusal to speak the name "Yahweh," therefore, ought not
to be viewed in and of itself as involving a diminishing of the importance
of the divine name to the Jewish religious perspective.

In the light of this, some contemporary scholars argue that the name
"Yahweh" was actually present, even in its unspoken absence, in the New
Testament.[41] They find this to be especially the case in the widely followed
manner of speaking that Joachim Jeremias terms the "divine passive."[42] One
place where the divine passive came to the fore was in the prayer language
of pious Jews, who used the passive construction as the means to avoid naming the one to whom their prayer was being addressed. Each time the divine
passive was used as the way of not voicing the tetragrammaton, the divine
name remained present as the word that was left unspoken, as the name that
rang clearly through the silence that surrounded the name of God.

Perhaps the most striking New Testament example of the divine passive occurs in the petitions of the Lord's Prayer. Each of these sup-
plications avoids referring directly to the one who is being petitioned.
Contrary to an exegetical tradition that dates at least to Augustine,[43] the
implicit subject of the petition is not humans but the God of Israel. In
fact, rather than suggesting any uncertainty or ambiguity in Jesus' mind
about whom he is calling upon to act, when understood in the context of
Jewish reverential piety, the passive voice indirectly but unmistakably
identifies Israel's God as the one to whom the petition is being directed.[44]
Seen in this light, the first petition calls upon the Father, who is initially
addressed in the prayer, to glorify his name—that is, to fulfill the eschatological promise that Yahweh voiced through Ezekiel: "I will sanctify my
great name, which has been profaned among the nations" (Ezek. 36:23).
The petition, therefore, parallels Jesus' prayer in the Fourth Gospel,
"Father, glorify your name" (John 12:28). Dale Allison explains the possi-

---

40. Michael Wyschogrod, *The Body of Faith: Judaism as Corporeal Election* (New York: Seabury, 1983), 91.

41. For an interesting study of the general phenomenon of anonymity in the Bible, see Adele Reinhartz, *Why Ask My Name? Anonymity and Identity in Biblical Narrative* (New York: Oxford University Press, 1998).

42. Joachim Jeremias, *New Testament Theology: The Proclamation of Jesus*, trans. John Bowden (New York: Charles Scribner's Sons, 1971), 9–14.

43. See, for example, Augustine, *Sermon on the Mount* 2.5.19, in *Nicene and Post-Nicene Fathers*, 1st series, ed. Phillip Schaff (1886; Peabody, MA: Hendrickson, 1994), 6:40.

44. Soulen, "Name of the Holy Trinity," 250.

ble purpose of the use of this construction in the Lord's Prayer: "The solemnity of this first request ensures that the intimacy conveyed by the address 'Father' will not degenerate into presumptuous familiarity."[45] R. Kendall Soulen, in turn, expresses the implication of this manner in which Jesus himself prayed: "So, the Tetragrammaton speaks. It speaks through periphrastic language to identify by name the One to whom Jesus prays."[46]

The presence of the divine passive on the lips of Jesus is not simply an expression of pious deference. It also voices Jesus' understanding of the significance of his mission in the eschatological activity of the God to whom he prays, about whom he speaks, and by whom he has been sent. The meaning that Jesus pours into the divine passive arises from his modification of the apocalyptic tradition, in which context this way of speaking first appeared. As Jeremias explains, "All those divine passives announce the presence of the time of salvation, albeit in a veiled way, for the consummation of the world has dawned only in a veiled form."[47]

When understood in the context of the manner in which the Jews of his day expressed pious reverence for God, Jesus' use of the divine passive in prayer is a vivid indication of the presence of the divine name even in the midst of its absence.[48] The tetragrammaton was also present in the New Testament through the use of the name "Lord." Indeed, as I have already noted, "Lord" (*kyrios*) is the typical Greek rendering of the Hebrew *adonai*, which emerged as the favorite circumlocution for "Yahweh." In the New Testament, *kyrios* is used repeatedly as a designation for God, as well as for Jesus Christ and for the Holy Spirit. Scholars are quick to see the name "Yahweh" lurking behind many of these New Testament references.[49] Viewed from this perspective, Brunner is on the right track when he asserts that "Lord"—understood, however, as the Greek translation of the most common Hebrew circumlocution for the unspoken Old Testament name—is the basic content of the divine name.

The trajectory charted in part 2 of this volume indicates that the presence of the divine name in the New Testament is not limited to the divine passive or to the Greek version of the reverential Hebrew designation *adonai*. More significantly, the name is voiced (even if at times only indirectly) in the I AM declarations that characterize Jesus' own self-designations, especially in the Fourth Gospel, and the I AM claims that reverberate throughout the vision of the seer of the Apocalypse. Viewed from this perspective, the Hebrew divine name continues to play a crucial

45. Dale C. Allison, *The Sermon on the Mount: Inspiring the Moral Imagination* (New York: Crossroad, 1999), 120.

46. Soulen, "Name of the Holy Trinity," 251.

47. Jeremias, *New Testament Theology*, 14.

48. For this insight, see Soulen, "Name of the Holy Trinity," 250–51.

49. For an overview of the scholarly opinion of the source and significance of the appellation *kyrios* as a designation for Jesus, see Parke-Taylor, *Yahweh*, 100–104.

role in the New Testament, for the narrative of this name provides the nec-essary background, the context, and the trajectory in connection to which the manner of addressing and designating the God of the followers of Jesus can be understood. Yet the question remains as to what emerges as the central Christian designation for the God who was disclosed in the Old Testament divine name.

The Tetragrammaton and the Name "Father"

As was delineated in the previous two chapters, except for the one signif-icant declaration voiced by God in the book of Revelation, all of the var-ious I AM claims are spoken by Jesus. Moreover, in every case, "I am" functions as a self-designation. Hence, Jesus never uses the expression to identify the God who had sent him.

At first glance this observation seems to add credence to Weber's claim that "Jesus" is the new name for the God of the covenant in the New Tes-tament. Moreover, this assertion appears to resonate with the conclusion that Adelheid Ruck-Schröder draws from her careful and exhaustive study of the name of God and the name of Jesus in the New Testament. She writes, "In this ascription of the concept 'Name' to both God and Jesus lies the specifically New Testament understanding of the divine name, in con-trast to the Old Testament and the Jewish understandings."[50] Yet Ruck-Schröder's exegetical conclusion also indicates that the situation of the New Testament is not quite as simple as Weber suggests. Even though Jesus is the recipient and the bearer of the divine name, the Old Testament name for God is not simply transformed into the name "Jesus" in the New.

The complexity of the divine name in the New Testament is evident in Jesus' own naming of God. Despite his careful avoidance of the Old Tes-tament divine name as a designation for God, which is evidenced even in his attention to the reverential practice of framing petitions by means of the divine passive, Jesus was not at all reluctant to speak directly to God or to name the God of Israel. More specifically, as was noted in chapter 5, Jesus readily called this God "Father."

Jesus' practice leads to the question as to the connection of "Father" to the divine name. More pointedly, does "Father" replace the tetragram-maton as the New Testament (and hence the Christian) name for God? A long line of Christian theologians has made just such an assertion. These thinkers are convinced that Jesus' act in naming God "Father" entails a reformulation of the divine name that was revealed to Moses and that played such a central role in the Old Testament.[51]

---

50. Adelheid Ruck-Schröder, *Der Name Gottes und der Name Jesu: Eine neutestamentliche Studie* (Neukirchen-Vluyn: Neukirchener Verlag, 1999), 260–61.

51. Although not stating the point directly, Packer suggests that "Father" is the Christian name of God. James I. Packer, *Knowing God* (Downers Grove, IL: InterVarsity Press, 1973), 183.

Proponents of this view routinely suggest that the supposed metamorphosis of God's name from "Yahweh" to "Father" arose out of Jesus' own designation of the God of Israel as *abba*. On the lips of Jesus, it is argued, "Father" became God's proper name. T. F. Torrance exemplifies this perspective when he declares that in the pages of the New Testament, "'Father' is . . . revealed to be more than an epithet—it is the personal name of God in which the form and content of his self-revelation as Father through Jesus Christ his Son are inseparable."[52]

As Torrance's remark indicates, often connected to the idea that the New Testament name for God is "Father" is the suggestion that naming God in this manner comprised the great theological innovation of Jesus. The prophet of Nazareth, it is argued, broke decisively with the Old Testament and Jewish conception of God by introducing the idea of God as Father, or at least by bringing what had been a marginal conception to center stage.[53] Claude Geffre states the point sharply: "The name 'Father' is the one best calculated to manifest the novelty of the God of Jesus, as compared not only with the God of the Greeks but with the God of the Jews."[54] Donald Guthrie, in turn, draws several of the prevailing ideas together when he declares confidently regarding *abba*: "It is a unique form, for it finds no parallels either in the OT or in Judaism as an address to God. Its use by Jesus shows how completely his view of God as Father is divorced from any formal approach. The Abba form conveys a sense of intimacy and familiarity which introduced an entirely new factor into man's approach to God."[55]

Beginning in the late nineteenth century, this conclusion was deemed to be an assured result of biblical scholarship.[56] But in recent years, it has become increasingly controversial. Scholars have (re)discovered the theme of God as Father in both the Old Testament and noncanonical Jewish writings.[57] Applying these developments to Jesus' perspective, Scot McKnight

---

52. Thomas F. Torrance, "The Christian Apprehension of God the Father," in *Speaking the Christian God: The Holy Trinity and the Challenge of Feminism*, ed. Alvin J. Kimel, Jr. (Grand Rapids: Eerdmans, 1992), 131.

53. Above all, this idea is generally associated with Jeremias. For his treatment of this theme, see Joachim Jeremias, *The Prayers of Jesus* (1967; repr., Philadelphia: Fortress, 1978), 11–65. For an engagement with the use and abuse of Jeremias's findings, see Marianne Meye Thompson, *The Promise of God the Father: Jesus and God in the New Testament* (Louisville, KY: Westminster John Knox, 2000), 21–34.

54. Claude Geffre, "'Father' as the Proper Name of God," in *God as Father?* ed. Johannes-Baptist Metz and Edward Schillebeeckx (New York: Seabury, 1981), 44.

55. Donald Guthrie, *New Testament Theology* (Downers Grove, IL: InterVarsity Press, 1981), 84.

56. For a late nineteenth-century example, see Wilhelm Bousset, *Jesu Predigt in ihrem Gegensatz zum Judentum: Ein religionsgeschichtlicher Vergleich* (Göttingen: Vandenhoeck & Ruprecht, 1892), 41–43.

57. See, for example, Jeremias, *New Testament Theology*, 65–67; Robert G. Hamerton-Kelly, *God the Father: Theology and Patriarchy in the Teaching of Jesus* (Philadelphia: Fortress, 1979), 21–38; Geza Vermes, *Jesus the Jew: A Historian's Reading of the Gospels*, 2nd ed. (London: SCM Press, 1983), 210–11; Scot McKnight, *A New Vision for Israel: The Teachings of Jesus in National Context* (Grand Rapids: Eerdmans, 1999), 54.

declares, "As we say with Jesus' teachings about God as inflexibly holy, so also here: there is nothing in Jesus' use of *'abba'* that was not also known in Judaism. Use of the term *'abba'* was certainly characteristic of Jesus. What he meant by *'abba'* is what it meant in Judaism."[58] Similarly, Brevard Childs asserts unequivocally, "Jesus brought no new concept of God." He then adds, "But he demonstrated in action the full extent of God's redemptive will for the world which was from the beginning."[59]

Although the idea that God is Father was already present in the tradition, references to God as Father in both the Old Testament and the intertestamental writings are somewhat meager, being overshadowed by a variety of other forms of designating and addressing the God of Israel.[60] Similar to the writings that he read, Jesus used a variety of designations to speak about God. Yet the designation "Father" became central. As McKnight puts it, "When he thought and taught about God, the term he preferred was 'Father,' and this in simple analogical terms."[61] What Jesus inaugurated, therefore, was the transformation of "Father" into the preferred designation. In his own praying and in his teaching, "Father" became the central manner of denoting and addressing God. And Jesus encouraged his disciples to follow his lead. Therefore, Jesus' use of the name "Father" as his central designation for God marked an innovation in degree, rather than in kind, from the practice of his predecessors and contemporaries; it involved a change in emphasis rather than in form and content.[62]

This observation raises the question as to the significance that Jesus (and consequently the New Testament community) attached to the name "Father" as used of God. Reading the designation in the light of its Hebrew and Jewish background suggests that the idea of God as Father was connected to the covenantal relationship between God and Israel and, by extension, between God and the new people of God.[63] The emergence of the name "Father" within a covenantal context conveys the idea that God became the Father of Israel by a historic act of election (an outlook that forms a glaring contrast to the idea of generation prominent in pagan myths).[64] Viewed from this perspective, the designation of God as Father carries a crucial element of exclusivity. H. F. D. Sparks pointed this out in

58. McKnight, *New Vision for Israel*, 55.

59. Brevard Childs, *Biblical Theology of the Old and New Testaments* (Minneapolis: Fortress, 1992), 358.

60. For a summary of some of these, see Jeremias, *New Testament Theology*, 63.

61. McKnight, *New Vision for Israel*, 57.

62. Ibid., 55.

63. Quell sees little connection between fatherhood and the covenant in the Old Testament. Schrenk, however, finds the connection to be strong in intertestamental Judaism. See Gottlob Schrenk and Gottfried Quell, "pater," in *Theological Dictionary of the New Testament*, ed. Gerhard Kittel and Gerhard Friedrich, trans. Geoffrey W. Bromiley, 10 vols. (Grand Rapids: Eerdmans, 1964–1976), 5:965, 978.

64. Carl E. Braaten, "The Problem of God-Language Today," in Braaten, *Our Naming of God*, 32.

1955, when, on the basis of his study of the divine fatherhood in the Gospels, he rejected the then-popular doctrine of the universal fatherhood of God: "The distinctively Christian Doctrine of the Divine Fatherhood, as evidenced by the gospels and supported by the rest of the New Testament, is that God is the Father of those, and only of those, who acknowledge the Messianic sonship of Jesus, who are incorporated into his new Messianic community, and who are thereby entitled to claim that they are sons of God through him."[65]

As Sparks's reference to the messianic community suggests, the name "Father" on the lips of Jesus carries a future-directed significance. Jesus' naming of the God of Israel "Father" was linked to his anticipation that the eschatological time had come near. The God of Israel would soon act to fulfill the covenant. Werner Kümmel hints at this eschatological orientation of the designation "Father," when he notes that by means of this term, Jesus "wanted to preach with specific urgency that God seeks to encounter man with fatherly love. And just as Jesus spoke of God's future appearance as king and judge, so also now he speaks of God's future actions as Father."[66] Kümmel then notes the presence of this perspective in the Lord's Prayer, which "by no means is oriented primarily to the needs of the present, but in the main to the Father's eschatological activity."[67] Jesus declared that the God of Israel was about to fulfill the covenant with Israel. God was about to restore Israel by means of the forming of an eschatological people, to whom God will be "father" and who will relate to God and to each other as God's children. Consequently, for Jesus' followers to refer to God as "Father" was considered to be a great privilege.

Despite the far-reaching importance associated with this designation, according to the New Testament "Father" is not, in fact, God's personal name, at least not when used singly.[68] Instead, this designation is more akin to the appellatives "Mom" and "Dad," which are not the actual public names of the persons so designated, but carry meaning only within the context of the familial relationships that they signify. Marianne Meye Thompson rightly points out, "The designation Father functions within the Christian family to speak of the one to whom the community owes its life and being and to remind them of their collective identity as the people called out by God."[69]

---

65. H. F. D. Sparks, "The Doctrine of the Divine Fatherhood in the Gospels," in *Studies in the Gospels: Essays in Memory of R. H. Lightfoot*, ed. D. E. Nineham (Oxford: Basil Blackwell, 1955), 261.

66. Werner Georg Kümmel, *The Theology of the New Testament according to Its Major Witnesses: Jesus-Paul-John*, trans. John E. Steely (Nashville: Abingdon, 1973), 40.

67. Ibid., 41.

68. That this is the case is evident from the variety of designations for God in the New Testament, together with the apparently minimal use of "Father" in the communities described in the book of Acts. On this latter topic, see Robert L. Mowery, "The Disappearance of the Father: The References to God the Father in Luke-Acts," *Encounter* 55, no. 4 (Autumn 1994): 353–58.

69. Thompson, *Promise of God the Father*, 178.

Many scholars have shown that the familial language of the Christian community finds its source in the ministry of Jesus. The survey of the *ego eimi* sayings in the Fourth Gospel in chapter 5 concluded by indicating in what sense Jesus discharged his revelatory mission in enunciating the divine *ego eimi* by disclosing the one whom he called "Father." In his work of being present in the world as the Son of the Father, Jesus disclosed the one who is the Father of the Son and with whom he enjoys unity as the incarnation of the one divine I AM name.

The Divine Name and the Triadic Baptismal Formula

As was delineated in chapter 6, the Johannine I AM christocentric sayings give way in the Apocalyse to a triadic conception of the divine name. In the eyes of some theologians, the triadic formula emerges as the New Testament name for God. Alvin Kimel speaks for many when he declares pointedly, "Father, Son, and Holy Spirit is our deity's *proper name.*"[70] This alternative is not devoid of New Testament precedence.

The New Testament writers explicitly connect the word "name," in the sense of the divine name, with two designations. The first of these, "Lord" (*kyrios*) is repeatedly used either as part of the longer designation "the name of the Lord Jesus Christ" (or some variant) or in contexts in which the one designated as Lord is assumed to be Christ (Jas. 5:7–10, 14; 3 John 7). The phrase "the name of the Lord" also occurs in quotations of Old Testament texts in which "Lord" is clearly a circumlocution for "Yahweh," as in Jesus' weeping over Jerusalem (Luke 13:39), the shouts of the people on Palm Sunday (Mark 11:9, 10; Matt. 21:9; Luke 19:38; John 12:13), Peter's sermon on Pentecost (Acts 2:21), and Paul's description of the way of salvation (Rom. 10:13). The phrase is also used as a description of Paul's preaching, as one who spoke "boldly in the name of the Lord" (Acts 9:28).

Although the phrase "the name of the Lord" is an important variant on the use of *kyrios* as a circumlocution for the tetragrammaton, more significant in providing a scriptural basis for the triadic formula as the new name for God is the second designation with which "the name" is linked. In the Great Commission pericope with which Matthew's Gospel concludes, Jesus instructs his disciples, "Go therefore and make disciples of all nations, baptizing them in the name of the Father and of the Son and of the Holy Spirit" (Matt. 28:19). This expansion of the simpler reports of baptism "in the name of Jesus" (Acts 2:38; 8:16; 10:48; 19:5; cf. Rom. 6:3; Gal. 3:27) is anticipated in the various triadic texts in the New Testament,[71] including the greeting found in the opening chapter of the book

---

70. Alvin F. Kimel, Jr., "The God Who Likes His Name," in Kimel, *Speaking the Christian God*, 191.

71. For a helpful listing of these texts and a summary of their significance, see Allen D. Churchill, "The New Testament and the Trinity," in *The Trinity: An Essential for Faith in Our Time*, ed. Andrew

of Revelation (explored in chapter 6) as well as the widely used Pauline benediction, "The grace of the Lord Jesus Christ, the love of God, and the communion of the Holy Spirit be with all of you" (e.g., 2 Cor. 13:13). Yet only in the command to baptize do we find the juxtaposing of a direct reference to the divine name with the three Trinitarian persons.

The very uniqueness of this expression has meant that it "has caused endless controversy among exegetes," as Leon Morris notes.[72] Commentators routinely point out that the Great Commission text is the only occurrence of a triadic baptismal formula in the literature of the first century.[73] This, coupled with the indications in the book of Acts that the New Testament community baptized "in the name of Jesus," leads most exegetes to question the authenticity of the Matthew formula as an actual saying of Jesus.[74] The uniqueness of the Matthean phrase, if its source is not Jesus himself, in turn raises the question of whether Matthew intends that the phrase be read as an actual liturgical form, which it later clearly became, or as a description of what he saw as being accomplished in baptism.[75]

One of the theories regarding the origin of the Great Commission pericope proposes that the canonical form is a Matthean reworking of an earlier midrash on the vision of Daniel 7:13–14. The controversial version of the theory proposed by Jane Schaberg adds that the triad "the Father and the Son and the Holy Spirit" is a development of the Danielic triad "Ancient of Days, one like a son of man, and angels."[76] Its apparent background in the vision of Daniel suggests that the triadic phrase is intended to be seen as an allusion to the eschatological exaltation of the Son to the heavenly throne of the Father, with the Holy Spirit representing the power that brings a person into the heavenly realm. In the act of baptism, in turn, the candidate is drawn into the transcendent realm. Drawing these themes together, Schaberg concludes, "In baptism in the name of the Father, and the Son and the Holy Spirit, the exaltation of Jesus becomes a communal

---

Stirling (Nappanee, IN: Evangel, 2002), 88–93. For an engagement with the question posed by the phenomenon of triadic texts and its relationship to Matt. 28:19, see Jane Schaberg, *The Father, the Son, and the Holy Spirit: The Triadic Phrase in Matthew 28:19*, SBL Dissertation Series (Chico, CA: Scholars Press, 1982), 5–16.

72. Leon Morris, *The Gospel according to Matthew* (Grand Rapids: Eerdmans, 1992), 747.

73. See, for example, Floyd V. Filson, *The Gospel according to St. Matthew*, 2nd ed., Black's New Testament Commentaries (London: A. & C. Black, 1971), 305. Filson notes that this is the case, unless *Didache* 7.1 dates from the first century.

74. Even some conservative commentators hold open the possibility that the phrase does not represent the actual words of Jesus. See, for example, Craig L. Blomberg, *Matthew*, New American Commentary (Nashville: Broadman, 1992), 432; D. A. Carson, "Matthew," in *The Expositor's Bible Commentary*, ed. Frank E. Gaebelein, 12 vols. (Grand Rapids: Zondervan, 1976–1993), 8:598.

75. For the latter proposal, see W. F. Albright and C. S. Mann, *Matthew: Introduction, Translation, and Notes*, Anchor Bible (Garden City, NY: Doubleday, 1971), 363.

76. See, for example, Donald A. Hagner, *Matthew 14–28*, Word Biblical Commentary (Dallas: Word, 1995), 888. For a summary of Schaberg's theory, see Schaberg, *Father, the Son, and the Holy Spirit*, 322.

experience, one that could be regarded as the keeping of the promise to Daniel's *maskilim* and their followers."[77] According to Schaberg's theory, Matthew incorporated into the midrash his own concern for discipleship, understood as obedience to Jesus' commands.[78]

Left unanswered by reconstructions such as Schaberg's is the question regarding the relationship between the divine name, expressed here in the form "in the name of," and the triadic name in the canonical version of the text. One feature of the text that sheds light on this question is the absence of the phrase "the name of" before each of the references to the individual Trinitarian persons. Indeed, "the name of" occurs only once, and it precedes the phrase "the Father and the Son and the Holy Spirit." This suggests that the triadic phrase ought to be taken together as designating a single name in connection to which candidates are to be baptized.[79] Understanding the baptismal formula as referring to a single, Trinitarian name might have been an important factor that led the church as a whole eventually to discard the practice of triune baptism that was followed by some congregations during the early centuries.[80]

The conclusion that the reference to the three persons is to be treated as a single unit or as one composite name is strengthened by the observation that of the prepositions *epi*, *en*, and *eis*, used in the New Testament baptismal references, the third is the term found in Matthew. Although exegetes offer slightly different proposals regarding the significance of the preposition, the common thread running through many of them is the idea that the word indicates that the baptized person is "going into" or "participating" in the triune life.[81] Hence, W. F. Albright and C. S. Mann declare, "The expression used in this verse describes an entrance into fellowship with the Father, the Son, and the Holy Spirit."[82] The Dutch bib-

---

77. Schaberg, *Father, the Son, and the Holy Spirit*, 327.

78. Ibid., 331–35.

79. This conclusion is not acknowledged by all commentators. See, for example, Claude Tresmontant, *The Gospel of Matthew: Original Reconstructed Translation and Notes*, trans. K. D. Whitehead (Front Royal, VA: Christendom Press, 1996), 596.

80. The *Didache* seems to make provision for trine baptism when it suggests that under certain circumstances the rite could be practiced by means of pouring water "on the head three times 'in the name of the Father, Son and Holy Spirit.'" *Didache* 7, in *Early Christian Fathers*, trans. and ed. Cyril C. Richardson (New York: Macmillan, 1970), 174. Similarly, early in the third century, Hippolytus reported the practice of having the candidate respond affirmatively to three questions coordinated with the three persons ("Do you believe in God the Father?" "Do you believe in God the Son?" "Do you believe in God the Holy Spirit?") with the candidate immersed in water after each response. Hippolytus, *The Apostolic Tradition* 21, trans. Geoffrey J. Cuming, in *Documents of Christian Worship: Descriptive and Interpretive Sources*, by James F. White (Louisville, KY: Westminster/John Knox, 1992), 154–55.

81. For a similar explication, see Thomas J. Scirghi, *An Examination of the Problems of Inclusive Language in the Trinitarian Formula of Baptism* (Lewiston, NY: Edwin Mellen, 2000), 163. For a surprising alternative suggestion, see Eduard Schweizer, *The Good News according to Matthew*, trans. David E. Green (Atlanta: John Knox, 1975), 532.

82. Albright and Mann, *Matthew*, 362.

lical scholar Herman Ridderbos adds that baptism "signifies an intimate relationship" with the triune God.[83] Donald Hagner, in turn, explains that "*eis*, lit. 'into,' the 'name' . . . reflects the Hebrew/Aramaic expression *lesem*, which has a cultic sense and means 'fundamentally determined by.'" Noting that this rite thereby stands in contrast to John's baptism, Hagner concludes that the act "beings a person into an existence that is fundamentally determined by, i.e., ruled by, Father, Son, and Holy Spirit."[84] Floyd Filson draws various strands of thought together in summarizing the theological significance of the text for the practice of baptism:

> Baptism "in the name of," means baptism which (1) clearly names Father, Son, and Holy Spirit; (2) confesses the full right of Father, Son, and Holy Spirit to worship and loyalty; (3) gratefully acknowledges the gracious blessings given by the Father through the Son by the working of the Holy Spirit; and (4) pledges obedience to Father, Son, and Holy Spirit.[85]

What is interesting in these interpretations of the text is the repeated focus on the dynamic of the triune life as the particular sphere into which the baptismal candidate is incorporated by this rite.

Also noteworthy is the use of the definite article before each of the three designations. Rather than "into the name of the Father, Son, and Holy Spirit," the baptismal text reads, "*the* Father, *the* Son, and *the* Holy Spirit." This grammatical device serves to particularize what are otherwise all common, generic nouns, nouns that can be predicated of many subjects. The definite article used before each of the three words restricts the referent of each designation. It reduces the subject to which the noun points from the many who might be designated by the name to one specific designee. Thereby, the baptismal formula stipulates that the reference here is to particular persons. There is but one who is rightly named "Father," one who carries the designation "Son," and one who can be referred to as "Holy Spirit." In this manner, the name into which candidates are to be baptized is specified in no uncertain terms.

Taken together, these various grammatical observations underscore the idea that the phrase "the Father and the Son and the Holy Spirit" functions in the baptismal formula as a single proper name.[86] The language of baptism indicates that through this act the candidate is placed into the sphere of, into fellowship with, or into the realm of participation in the one God who is understood to be "the Father and the Son and the Holy Spirit."

83. Herman N. Ridderbos, *Matthew*, Bible Student's Commentary (Grand Rapids: Zondervan, 1987), 555.

84. Hagner, *Matthew 14–28*, 888.

85. Filson, *Gospel according to St. Matthew*, 306.

86. Soulen, "Name of the Holy Trinity," 254–55.

Perhaps the decisive exegetical consideration in determining whether the triadic formula is the new, New Testament name of God is the question: Is "name" to be understood here as epexegetical? Hence, is the statement to be translated, "into the name, which is 'the Father and the Son and the Holy Spirit'"? In his treatment of the significance of Christian baptism, Karl Barth appears to assume just such an understanding:

> If the mention of Father, Son and Holy Ghost is to be regarded as an enumeration, it is the enumeration of the dimensions of the one name of God, i.e., of His one work and word, of His one act of salvation and revelation. . . . The words Father, Son and Holy Ghost, in their inseparability and distinction, together indicate the expansion of the one name, work and word of God.[87]

Carl Braaten is even more forthright in declaring that this is precisely the way that the verse is to be rendered. He asserts, "In Christian baptism, the name of God is invoked, and that name (singular) is 'Father, Son and Holy Spirit.'" Braaten then draws out the theological implication: "That is the Christian name of God, as JHWH is the proper name of God in the Old Testament."[88]

Although Barth's and Braaten's instincts are surely correct, the connection between "name" and the three Trinitarian names is likely a bit more complicated. Soulen avers that the phrase "the name of" does not simply refer epexegetically to "the Father and the Son and the Holy Spirit." In his estimation, it is an allusive and reverential reference to the unspoken tetragrammaton, which is the name "that belongs to the Father, and that the Father gives to the Son, and whose praise is evoked by the Holy Spirit."[89]

Even Soulen's insight, as helpful as it is, must to be taken a step further. It seems that the baptismal formula might best be rendered "into the name that belongs to 'the Father and the Son and the Holy Spirit.'" Reading the text in this manner suggests that the name that is the topic of the formula is the one particular name that the three persons of the Trinity share, the name that is theirs together. Reading the baptismal formula in the light of the narrative recounted in part 2 suggests that this name is the divine I AM name. It suggests as well that the great I AM name, together with the tetragrammaton to which it is connected, is a triune name. In short, the saga of the I AM is ultimately the narrative of "the Father and the Son and the Holy Spirit." The saga of the divine name, in other words, is the saga of the relationships among the three persons of the Trinity.

---

87. Karl Barth, *Church Dogmatics*, IV/4, *The Doctrine of Reconciliation*, ed. Geoffrey W. Bromiley and Thomas F. Torrance, trans. Geoffrey W. Bromiley (Edinburgh: T. & T. Clark, 1986), 96–97.

88. Braaten, "Problem of God-Language Today," 32.

89. Soulen, "Name of the Holy Trinity," 256.

What's in a Name?

As the previous two chapters indicate, the incarnation of the I AM in Jesus opens the way for a Trinitarian expansion of the meaning of the divine name. And the considerations that we pursued in the previous section augment the discovery that arose out of the biblical trajectory of the I AM. This leads us to two interrelated questions: What does it mean to assert that the God of the Bible has a name? And what is the significance of the suggestion that this name is triune? The place to begin the search for answers to these queries is with contemporary understandings of the nature of proper names.

The Significance of Naming

A proper name is "a noun that designates a specific individual or place,"[90] or a noun that denotes a being or an object that is considered to be unique. In his *Theory of Names* (1953), linguist Ernst Pulgram expands the typical dictionary definition and explicates the idea of proper names in greater detail. From his study of the phenomenon, he concludes:

> A proper name is a noun used *kat' exochen*, in a non-universal function, with or without current lexical value, of which the potential meaning coincides with and never exceeds its actual meaning, and which is attached as a label to one animate being or one inanimate object (or to more than one in the case of collective names) for the purpose of specific distinction from a number of like or in some respects similar beings or objects that are either in no manner distinguished from one another or, for our interest, not sufficiently distinguished.[91]

Pulgram opens his treatment of naming theory by explaining in an almost poetic manner the significance of being named: "The name of a man is like his shadow. It is not of his substance and not of his soul, but it lives with him and by him. Its presence is not vital, nor its absence fatal. If a man were to move in perennial darkness, he would have no shadow, and if he were content to dwell in solitude, he would need no name."[92]

Implicit in Pulgram's statement is the suggestion that proper names are closely connected to the act of referencing. Proper names facilitate the task of denoting particular persons, places, or things. John Macnamara states the point explicitly and succinctly: "Proper names are the paradigm examples of words that refer. They reach out, as it were, to objects and designate them for comment."[93] Similarly, Frank Nuessel declares, "One of the

90. *Webster's New World College Dictionary*, 4th ed. (Forest City, CA: IDG Books, 2000), 1150.
91. Ernst Pulgram, *Theory of Names* (Berkeley, CA: American Name Society, 1954), 49.
92. Ibid., 3.
93. John Macnamara, *Names for Things: A Study of Human Learning* (Cambridge, MA: MIT Press, 1982), 3.

primary functions of a name is reference. It is not possible to refer to an item or person without that item or person having a name." From this observation, he then draws a quasi-ontological conclusion: "In this sense, a name is a *sine qua non* for existence. Without a name, no linguistic means of reference is possible."[94]

The observation that proper names serve an important referential function has led a variety of thinkers to conclude that the relationship between names and their bearers is above all semantic. Writing in the mid-twentieth century, Rudolf Carnap encapsulated what by then had become the widely held scholarly understanding of the concept of naming: "The name-relation is customarily conceived as holding between an expression in a language and a concrete or abstract entity (object), of which that expression is a name. Thus this relation is, in our terminology, a semantical relation."[95] The standard understanding that Carnap articulated so concisely raises the question of the actual semantic status of proper names, as well as the ontological significance of naming.

The Focus of the Debate: Connotation versus Denotation

Although the debate over this question has piqued the interest of many philosophers during the last two hundred years, it is by no means new. On the contrary, it dates at least to the fourth century BC.

In his dialogue *Cratylus* (360 BC), for example, Plato explores this matter in the form of a conversation involving Socrates and two dialogue partners, Hermogenes and Cratylus, who stand at opposite poles on the issue. Lying behind the discussion in this particular dialogue is the suggestion, obliquely raised by Cratylus, that Hermogenes is misnamed. The name he bears means "son of Hermes." Rather than resembling the one for whom he is named—the god of good luck, wealth, and clever dealing—Hermogenes, in contrast to his wealthy brother Callias, is penniless and luckless.

Despite the glaring disparity between his actual financial state and the status that his name would intimate, Hermogenes defends the aptness of his name. In his estimation, names are mere conventions, and as such can be given and altered at will:

> I . . . cannot convince myself that there is any principle of correct-
> ness in names other than convention and agreement; any name
> which you give, in my opinion, is the right one, and if you change
> that and give another, the new name is as correct as the old—we fre-
> quently change the names of our slaves, and the newly-imposed

94. Frank H. Nuessel, *The Study of Names: A Guide to the Principles and Topics* (Westport, CT: Greenwood, 1992), 2.

95. Rudolf Carnap, *Meaning and Necessity: A Study in Semantics and Modal Logic*, enlarged ed. (Chicago: Phoenix Books, 1956), 97.

> name is as good as the old: for there is no name given to anything by
> nature; all is convention and habit of the users.[96]

In short, he demurs that regardless of its literal meaning and its linguistic derivation, "Hermogenes" is the right name for him, simply because he is called by this name and he answers to it.

Cratylus, in contrast, maintains (in the words of Hermogenes) that names "are natural and not conventional—not a portion of the human voice which men agree to use—but that there is a truth or correctness in them."[97] In his estimation, a word is either the perfect expression of a thing or a mere inarticulate sound, and hence a name is either a true name or not a name at all.

For his part, Socrates offers a mediating position between the two antagonists. He suggests that language is both arbitrary and natural. To explicate this, he first sides with Cratylus against Hermogenes in asserting that names are the expressions of, or the imitations in sound of, things and therefore that true names are those that carry a natural meaning. But Socrates then parts company with Cratylus. He adds that every copy, including vocal imitation, can be imperfectly executed and that this phenomenon introduces an element of chance or opens the way for convention in the process of naming.

Despite the fact that Socrates' arguments appear to carry the day in the dialogue, his proposed middle way did not bring an end to the philosophical debate. A mere ten years later, Plato's student Aristotle articulated a viewpoint that closely resembles the proposal set forth by Hermogenes. According to Aristotle, names do not arise by nature, but by convention. Hence, in defining the principle parts of speech in his *On Interpretation* (350 BC), he declares, "By a noun we mean a sound significant by convention, which has no reference to time, and of which no part is significant apart from the rest. . . . The limitation 'by convention' was introduced because nothing is by nature a noun or name—it is only so when it becomes a symbol."[98]

Twenty-two centuries later a debate somewhat similar to that which polarized Hermogenes and Cratymus once again erupted. One significant early voice in this reignited philosophical dispute and the person who is often cited as setting the context for the modern discussion was John Stuart Mill. In his *A System of Logic* (1843), Mill differentiated between the "denotation" and the "connotation" of a term. By the former he meant the object(s) to which a particular term applies. The latter, in contrast, is

---

96. Plato, *Cratylus* 384d, trans. Benjamin Jewett, in *Plato: The Collected Dialogues*, ed. Edith Hamilton and Huntington Cairns (Princeton, NJ: Princeton University Press, 1961), 383.

97. Plato, *Cratylus* 383b (p. 383).

98. Aristotle, *On Interpretation* 2.16a28, in *The Categories, On Interpretation, and the Prior Analytics*, Loeb Classical Library (Cambridge, MA: Harvard University Press, 1938), 116.

the meaning of the term, including the attributes that define it.[99] In Mill's estimation, proper names function in a purely denotative manner: "When we name a child by the name of Paul, or a dog by the name of Caesar, these names are simply marks used to enable those individuals to be made subjects of discourse. It may be said, indeed, that we must have had some reason for giving them those names rather than any others; and this is true; but the name once given is independent of the reason."[100] Mill then added, "A proper name is but an unmeaning mark which we connect in our minds with the idea of the object, in order that whenever the mark meets our eyes or occurs to our thoughts, we may think of that individual object."[101] For Mill, therefore, "proper names are not connotative: they denote the individuals who are called by them; but they do not indicate or imply any attributes as belonging to those individuals."[102] Or as W. F. H. Nicolaisen encapsulated the point, "Words *connote* and names *denote*."[103] Of course, a proper name might suggest certain properties to a speaker, but such properties are not part of the definition of the name.

Mill was an advocate of what has come to be called the "direct reference view" of names, or the "theory of direct reference." This theory postulates that proper names are directly linked to their bearers. Furthermore, such names have no meaning. They do not function as surrogates for descriptive expressions, but merely as tags or labels for the persons, places, or things that they designate. Many philosophers since Mill have not found this theory completely satisfying. Some critics advocate instead what can be termed the "descriptivist view," which theorizes that a proper name can designate a person (or another unique entity) only via intermediate descriptive properties. In this view, a proper name functions in a manner somewhat akin to a definition. Hence, the name "Aristotle" denotes by definition the person who satisfies certain relevant properties.[104]

Description versus Direct Reference

The pathway toward the development of modern descriptivist theories was paved by the work of Gottlob Frege (1848–1925), who is often hailed as the founder of modern logic and philosophy of logic,[105] a major source

99. For this characterization, see Maria Baghramian, introduction to *Modern Philosophy of Language*, ed. Maria Baghramian (London: J. M. Dent, 1998), xxxvii.

100. John Stuart Mill, *A System of Logic, Ratiocinative and Inductive: Being a Connected View of the Principles of Evidence and the Methods of Scientific Investigation*, 8th ed. (New York: Harper & Brothers, 1900), 1.2.5 (p. 36).

101. Ibid. 1.2.5 (p. 38).

102. Ibid. 1.2.5 (p. 36).

103. W. F. H. Nicolaisen, "Are There Connotative Names?" *Names* 26 (1978): 40.

104. For this description, see, for example, Howard Wettstein, "Causal Theory of Proper Names," in *Cambridge Dictionary of Philosophy*, ed. Robert Audi, 2nd ed. (Cambridge: Cambridge University Press, 1999), 125.

105. For this judgment, see Anthony J. P. Kenny, "Frege, Gottlob," in *The Oxford Companion to Philosophy*, ed. Ted Honderich (New York: Oxford University Press, 1995), 294, 296.

for twentieth-century analytical philosophy,[106] and one of the thinkers directly responsible for what is now known as the "linguistic turn"[107] in philosophy.[108] Frege rejected perspectives, such as Mill's, that assert that proper names have no meaning other than denoting a referent. Instead, in what has become an influential theory of meaning, he differentiated between a name's nominatum,[109] referent[110] or reference (the object that a name names), and its sense (the way in which the object is given by a name). Moreover, he asserted that two expressions can have the same referent, while not having the same sense.

Frege's theory, which he first outlined in his essay "Funktion und Begriff" (1891), was initially motivated by the debate among mathematicians of his day as to whether or not the equals sign ("="), such as in mathematical equations like "$(4 \times 2) = (11 - 3)$" expresses an identity. In response, Frege pointed out that "4×2" and "$11 - 3$" do indeed stand for one and the same thing, namely, "8," but that they do so in two different ways. In this manner, he differentiated between the actual number a mathematical expression such as "4×2" denotes and the way in which that number is expressed. He termed the former the "reference" (*Bedeutung*) and the latter the "sense" (*Sinn*) of the expression.

In his subsequent essay "Über Sinn und Bedeutung" (1892), Frege expanded his differentiation between reference and sense to the linguistic realm. In this essay, he asserts that an expression "denotes" its reference but "expresses" (or "connotes," to use Mill's language) its sense.[111] Furthermore, Frege claims that two linguistic expressions can have the same reference but different senses. That is, they can refer to the same object, but differ in the mode of presentation or the cognitive content associated with each of the references by means of which each points out the common reference.

To explain and substantiate his theory, Frege offers a variety of examples. The one most often cited is his observation that the expressions "the morning star" and "the evening star" share the same referent, namely, the planet Venus. Yet they do not have the same sense, for they refer to the planet in different ways, namely, in virtue of different properties that the planet has.[112] The distinction between reference and sense provided the way for

106. Thomas Ricketts, "Frege, Gottlob," in *Cambridge Dictionary of Philosophy*, 328.

107. For this nomenclature, see *The Linguistic Turn: Essays in Philosophical Method*, ed. Richard Rorty (Chicago: University of Chicago Press, 1992).

108. For this judgment, see Baghramian, introduction to *Modern Philosophy of Language*, xxx.

109. For this translation of Frege's term, see Carnap, *Meaning and Necessity*, 118.

110. For this rendering of Frege's term, see John R. Searle, "Proper Names," *Mind* 67 (1958): 166.

111. Frege uses this language in "Über Sinn und Bedeutung." See Gottlob Frege, "On Sense and Nominatum," trans. Herbert Feigl, in *The Philosophy of Language*, ed. A. P. Martinich, 3rd ed. (New York: Oxford University Press, 1996), 189. For an alternative translation of the essay, see Gottlob Frege, "On Sense and Reference," trans. Max Black, in *Modern Philosophy of Language*, ed. Maria Baghramian (Washington DC: Counterpoint, 1999), 6–25.

112. Frege, "On Sense and Nominatum," 189.

Frege to understand the distinction between two apparent identity claims: "The morning star is the morning star" and "The morning star is the evening star." The former sentence conveys no information but is merely a case of the law of self-identity, which is knowable a priori. The latter, in contrast, is not merely a statement of identity, for it also imparts some information that was discovered a posteriori by astronomical observation. According to Frege, the fact that the proper names "the morning star" and "the evening star" have the same reference makes both statements true by virtue of the planet's relation of identity to itself. But the fact that the two expressions do not have the same meaning accounts for the informative character of the second statement in contrast to the first.

Like Frege, Bertrand Russell also disagreed with Mill. Against his predecessor's belief that descriptions such as "The king who succeeded William the Conqueror" are many-worded names,[113] Russell averred that descriptions are not names.[114] Although he stood in the wake of Frege's rejection of Mill's proposal, Russell attempted to solve the problems that motivated Frege without appeal to the concept of "sense," which he deemed suspect. In his important essay "On Denoting" (1907), Russell suggests that proper names bear the same semantic structure as definite descriptions[115] and therefore are often simply disguised descriptions.[116] The theory of reference that Russell proposes in the essay implies that a proper name refers to its referent by means of descriptions associated with the referent. Moreover, it suggests that the meaning of a name is given by a definite description of the referent that it denotes, a description that is deemed to be unique to that referent.[117]

Several philosophers subsequently expanded Russell's seminal idea, even though they may have disagreed with aspects of the theory of reference that he had proposed. Thinkers such as John Searle, for example, took up the question of how we are able to refer to a particular referent by means of a name. In his response, Searle theorized that a proper name designates its referent indirectly, insofar as it is associated "in a loose sort of way" with a conjunction or cluster of descriptions that determines what particular referent (or specific individual) is designated by that name.[118]

---

113. See Mill, *Systems of Logic* 1.2.3 (p. 32).

114. For this judgment, see Bertrand Russell, "Mr. Strawson on Referring (1957)," in Martinich, *Philosophy of Language*, 245.

115. For this observation, see Robert M. Martin, *The Meaning of Language* (Cambridge, MA: MIT Press, 1987), 161.

116. Bertrand Russell, "On Denoting," *Mind* 14 (1905): 479–93. This essay is reprinted in Bertrand Russell, *Essays in Analysis*, ed. Douglas Lackey (London: George Allen & Unwin, 1973), 103–19.

117. For this interpretation of Russell's position, see Tim Valentine, Tim Brennen, and Serge Bredart, *The Cognitive Psychology of Proper Names: On the Importance of Being Ernest* (New York: Routledge, 1996), 12; Baghramian, introduction to *Modern Philosophy of Language*, xxxix.

118. John Searle, "Proper Names," *Mind* 67 (1955): 166–73. See also P. F. Strawson, *Individuals: An Essay in Descriptive Metaphysics* (Garden City, NY: Anchor Books, 1963), 194–99.

Articulating a somewhat similar proposal, Otto Jespersen summarized the idea by declaring that the meaning of a proper name is "the complex of qualities characteristic of the bearer of the name."[119]

Gennaro Chierchia and Sally McConnell-Ginet, in turn, provide a concrete example of this approach, which is sometimes known as the "cluster descriptivist theory."[120] In response to the question of what it might be to claim that the name "Pavarotti" denotes the particular individual Pavarotti, they declare:

> One kind of answer might be that Pavarotti can be uniquely identified by means of descriptions like *the greatest Italian tenor who ever lived* or *the tenor that performed in the Arena di Verona on July 7, 1986*. A proper name like *Pavarotti* might be thought to be associated with a cluster of such descriptions, Pavarotti being the individual that uniquely falls under them. Together such descriptions could be regarded as a criterion that uniquely picks out Pavarotti from what there is. As such they seem to form a plausible candidate for being the meaning of *Pavarotti*.[121]

To the objection that the cluster descriptivist theory runs aground when one of the descriptions in the cluster proves to be untrue, Chierchia and McConnell-Ginet reply that the theory retains its usefulness, at least in the case of common nouns:

> Yet notice that when our identificational criteria for applying such a noun do wrong, our mistakes do not change what it is we are talking about or referring to when we use the word. People used to think that whales were fish and not mammals, but it seems intuitively plausible that we, who are biologically more sophisticated than they and have different criteria, are nonetheless talking about the same creatures our ancestors were when we use the word *whale*. Suppose that *whale* used to "mean" a kind of fish. Then when these earlier speakers spoke about whales, they were not speaking about Moby Dick and his kin. But this seems wrong. They believed that the very same creatures we think are mammals were fish. It is not the meaning of *whale* that has changed but beliefs about the creatures included in its reference.[122]

Despite the attempts of promoters of this approach to amend the theory to meet the objections of its detractors,[123] by the late 1980s its difficulties had become so numerous—at least in the case of proper

119. Otto Jespersen, *The Philosophy of Grammar*, 2nd ed. (New York: W. W. Norton & Co., 1965), 67.

120. See, for example, Martin, *Meaning of Language*, 164.

121. Gennaro Chierchia and Sally McConnell-Ginet, *Meaning and Grammar: An Introduction to Semantics*, 2nd ed. (Cambridge, MA: MIT Press, 2000), 195.

122. Ibid., 106.

123. For a recent example, see Chierchia and McConnell-Ginet, *Meaning and Grammar*, 106.

names—that Robert Martin could conclude that most philosophers had become convinced "that the descriptivist theory, even patched up by the cluster notion, is mistaken."[124] As a result of this unhappiness with descriptivists approaches, the theory of direct reference received a second look.

One important voice in this redirection of philosophical orientation, Saul Kripke, denies the thesis proposed by both Frege and Russell (and reformulated by subsequent thinkers such as Searle) that proper names are semantically equivalent to definite descriptions. Kripke points out that the former do not have defining characteristics, whereas the latter do.[125] Or to use Kripke's language, proper names are "rigid designators" in that they refer to the same individual in all possible worlds.[126] Definite descriptions, in contrast, are not "rigid," for they can refer to different individuals depending on the circumstances.

Kripke's most widely known counterexample to the descriptivist theory looks at a hypothetical situation in which the only description that is commonly associated with the name "Gödel" is "the one who proved the incompleteness of arithmetic." What would happen, Kripke asks, if we would find out that in fact a Mr. Schmidt who had died mysteriously in Vienna had proved this theorem and that the discovery was subsequently attributed to Gödel? If the name "Gödel" is semantically equivalent to the definite description "the one who proved the incompleteness of arithmetic," as the descriptivist theory suggests, Kripke concludes, we are left in the odd situation in which anyone who uses the name "Gödel" is in fact referring to Mr. Schmidt.[127]

If proper names are not definite descriptions, as attacks such as Kripke's indicate, the question reemerges: What connects a present use of a name with a referent? Several philosophers have sought an answer to this crucial query. Keith Donnellan, for example, proposed what might be called a historical account of referring.[128] In his estimation, a proper name refers to a specific referent in the present because it is connected to that referent through a chain of previous uses of the name to designate the referent. In a similar manner, Kripke sought an explanation by means of an appeal to an ongoing chain of communication. Alluding to the practice of giving a baby a name at baptism, he presented what he deemed to be merely "a rough statement of a theory," one that is often (albeit perhaps erroneously[129]) termed the "causal theory of proper

124. Martin, *Meaning of Language*, 164.
125. For a helpful summarization of Kripke's argument, see Martin, *Meaning of Language*, 164–66.
126. Saul A. Kripke, *Naming and Necessity* (Cambridge, MA: Harvard University Press, 1980), 21 n. 21, 48–49.
127. Ibid., 83–84.
128. Keith Donnellan, "Proper Names and Identifying Descriptions," *Synthese* 21 (1970): 352–55.
129. For this judgment, see Wettstein, "Causal Theory of Proper Names," 124–25. It should be added that Robert Martin explicitly denotes this proposal as "the causal theory of proper names." Martin, *Meaning of Language*, 172–74.

names."[130] Kripke writes: "An initial 'baptism' takes place. Here the object may be named by ostension, or the reference of the name may be fixed by a description. When the name is 'passed from link to link,' the receiver of the name must, I think, intend when he learns it to use it with the same reference as the man from whom he heard it."[131]

Robert Martin added to Kripke's "rough statement of a theory" the observation that whatever the human "proper-naming procedures" may be, an actual connection must exist between the thing named and the circumstances establishing the proper name. This, he observes, sets proper names apart from definite descriptions, which can be established without such a connection. Once the proper name is established, however, the need for any sort of direct connection with the individual named evaporates. All that is then necessary, Martin concludes, is that there be "some history of the use of that name which, traced back far enough, leads back to the individual," which in his estimation forms a "causal chain."[132] In his response to Kripke, Gareth Evans formalized this theory in the following manner: "A speaker, using a name 'NN' on a particular occasion will denote some item *x* to which there is a causal chain of *reference-preserving links* leading back from his use on that occasion ultimately to the item *x* itself being involved in a name-acquiring transaction."[133]

The impasse between advocates of the descriptivist and the direct reference approaches has led several philosophers to consider ways of bringing the two perspectives together.[134] Several such proposals have had the added benefit of developing a more social understanding of proper names. Hilary Putnam pointed in this direction when in his epoch-making essay[135] "The Meaning of 'Meaning,'" he quipped, "There are two sorts of tools in the world: there are tools like a hammer or a screwdriver which can be used by one person; and there are tools like a steamship which require the cooperative activity of a number of persons to use. Words have been thought of too much on the model of the first sort of tool."[136]

Perhaps the most significant stride in this direction was taken by Gareth Evans. Evans agrees with Kipke that the referent of a name arises from an ongoing chain that links the original act of naming with the subsequent uses of the name. But he adds that the information and beliefs

130. For the attaching of this label to Kripke's theory, see Gareth Evans, "The Causal Theory of Names," in Martinich, *Philosophy of Language*, 271.

131. Kripke, *Naming and Necessity*, 96.

132. Martin, *Meaning of Language*, 173.

133. Evans, "Causal Theory of Names," 273.

134. The summary statement of Chierchia and McConnell-Ginet might be viewed as an example. Chierchia and McConnell-Ginet, *Meaning and Grammar*, 106–8.

135. For this accolade, see Hilary Putnam, "The Meaning of Meaning," in Baghramian, *Modern Philosophy of Language*, 223.

136. Hilary Putnam, *Mind, Language, and Reality: Philosophical Papers*, vol. 1 (Cambridge: Cambridge University Press, 1975), as excerpted in Baghramian, *Modern Philosophy of Language*, 238.

associated with the use of the name are important as well. In his essay "The Causal Theory of Names" (1973), Evans states his proposal as a formal theory. He postulates that a name (NN) can be deemed to be a name of a particular referent (*x*) if there is a community (*C*) in which it is commonly known that its members use "NN" to refer to *x* with the intention of referring to *x*, and in which the success of any particular use of the name to refer to *x* relies on the knowledge shared by the speaker and the hearer that this name is in fact used in the community to refer to *x*, rather than on knowledge that *x* satisfies some predicate embedded in the name.[137]

In the concluding chapter of his posthumously published book, *The Varieties of Reference* (1982), Evans develops this communal approach further.[138] Here he speaks about a shared or communal activity, the "proper-name-using practice," that entails the use of a name to refer to a particular person (or place or thing). Moreover, he theorizes that some participants in these practices function as "producers," whereas others act as "consumers." The former group consists of those who are involved in the initial naming, as well as those who have direct dealings with the named person and use the name when speaking of that person. The producers can be credited with knowledge of the convention that led to the use of the proper name. Producers also gather information about the person. As this information circulates among the community of users of the name, some of it comes to be information that almost everyone associates with the name. At the same time, some of the circulated information might in fact be false. Consumers, in contrast, are not directly acquainted with the person and therefore are not in a position to add new information about the person to the practice of using the name. Because they are not involved in the initial naming, consumers must be introduced into the proper-name-using practice. Yet their role in continuing the practice eventually becomes what sustains it.

Meaning and the (Triune) Divine Name

I noted earlier that in Otto Weber's estimation, theology must find its center in the one name that God has given us for salvation. Although in making this claim Weber brought to light the importance of developing a theology of the divine name, neither he nor Emil Brunner engaged fully in this task. Yet as Michael Wyschogrod astutely observed, "The God of Israel is not just a Thou. *The God of Israel has a proper name.*" With this in view, we must now bring together the diverse topics explored in this chapter into a response to the central question that we have been pursu-

137. Evans, "Causal Theory of Names," 279.
138. Gareth Evans, *The Varieties of Reference*, ed. John McDowell (Oxford: Clarendon, 1982), 373–404.

ing: What is the theological significance of the witness of Scripture that the God of the Bible is named?

The Act of Naming and the Narrative of the Divine Name

Implicit in recent attempts to synthesize the descriptivist and direct reference theories of naming is the seemingly obvious observation that proper names are not self-given, but received. In the act of naming, the named person is passive. A person becomes the recipient of a name by being named by another.

A long trajectory of theological thought could be cited in support of the contention that this understanding of the act of naming is inapplicable when the one being named is God. Thinkers from Dionysius in the late fifth century to Aquinas in the thirteenth aver that our names for God are inadequate to the task of naming the divine reality. Yet the weightiness of this theological warning ought not to obscure an important aspect of the biblical perspective regarding the divine name. Seen in this light, the acknowledgment that God lies beyond our ability to name is a reminder that God cannot be adequately designated by any humanly devised name. It does not, however, leave God wholly nameless. The import of the biblical witness is not that the God of the Bible is *un*named, but that God is *self*-named.

This perspective on the naming of God forms a central theme of the story of the self-disclosure of the divine name to Moses at the burning bush. Reading the account from the perspective of the larger narrative of the divine name yields the conclusion that Moses' request that he be given the name of the God who was sending him to the Israelites entails a tacit admission that he does not have the prerogative of naming the God who was addressing and commissioning him. By asking for the name of this God, Moses was in effect acknowledging that the only true God stands beyond his prerogative to name. Indeed, the true God is the God who cannot be named by humans. Moses' request takes the matter a step further, however. The fact that the true God is beyond being named by mortals does not leave this God unnamed. On the contrary, Moses' request that he be told the divine name assumes that the God who was confronting him in the burning bush is the self-naming God. In responding to Moses' petition by announcing the divine name, Yahweh confirms what Moses had implicitly announced through his request: God, and God alone, has the prerogative of determining the divine name. Consequently, the divine response to Moses' entreaty not only involves God disclosing the divine name to the human inquirer, but it also entails God naming God.

Even though it is voiced by Yahweh himself, at this point in the narrative the name that God speaks carries little in the way of explicit descriptive content. Instead, it functions largely as a designator. To use Mill's categories, it denotes but does not connote. As I noted in chapter 4, the name does connect the God who appears to Moses with the God whom the patriarchs had come to know as the one who enters into a promissory covenant. Nevertheless, the divine name disclosed to Moses remains open-ended and essentially mysterious. It begs to be filled with positive descriptors regarding the one that it designates, as is evident even in the ambiguous character of the designation itself, "I AM WHO I AM." It begs to fill out its denotive role with connotations.

In his work on the act of naming, Evans speaks of the bestowal of a name as inaugurating a process in which "producers" gather additional information about the named person and eventually share that information with "consumers." We might draw from Evans's theory the idea that a name moves from mere "denoter" to carrier of descriptive meaning— from its denotative to its connotative role—through a process of personal interaction with those who initially form the name-pronouncing community. That is to say, a personal proper name comes to take on descriptive meaning through a narrative of personal relationships.

Such insights shed light on the narrative of the self-naming God. The vagueness of the divine name given to Moses suggests that the divine self-naming that commences at the burning bush, like the giving of any proper name, does not come to completion in the exodus story. Rather, it anticipates an ongoing, fuller self-naming that unfolds through a history of relationships. Hence, the fuller identity of its bearer comes to light by means of an unfolding drama. Viewed from this perspective, the narrative of the burning bush inaugurates the narrative of the divine self-naming. In this narrative, Moses (and subsequently others) act as "producers." By means of their firsthand encounters in this ongoing story of their relationship with the God of Israel, they collect and pass on to others the relevant information about the God who is named "I AM WHO I AM." We must quickly add, however, that despite this human involvement as participants in the ongoing community of those who carry forward the use of the divine name, ultimately only God can fulfill the role of "producer." In the narrative of the divine name, God always remains the self-naming God. Only God can disclose the descriptive information regarding the meaning of the divine name.

Although the name disclosed to Moses in the exodus story is open-ended and mysterious, it hints at the central theme of the narrative of the divine self-naming. I noted in chapter 4 that at its heart the divine name disclosed to Moses points to Yahweh's be-ing present with Israel. Consequently, the story of the burning bush anticipates that the yet-to-be-disclosed content of the divine name will be closely tied to the ongoing presence of I AM WHO I AM in the journey with the people of the covenant. The divine self-naming, therefore, takes the form of a narrative, the saga of the divine name, which is the saga of the I AM. According to the New

Testament, especially the Fourth Gospel, the subsequent drama leads to the coming of Jesus, who is the incarnate I AM and, as the Son of the Father, the bearer of the divine name. The last book of the canonical Bible portrays the saga as climaxing in the eschatological sharing of the divine name with the redeemed, who are marked by that name and who come to be so marked through the work of the Spirit.

In this manner, the "be-ing present" suggested by the disclosure of the divine name shows itself to be the saga of "the name of the Father, and of the Son, and of the Holy Spirit" given in the baptismal formula of the Great Commission. Insofar as the Protestant scholastics who followed the trail charted by Jerome Zanchi articulated this insight, they were correct in asserting that the divine name is shared among the three Trinitarian persons. But they did not take the insight far enough. They did not develop the idea that the divine name is linked to God's own self-naming. Nor did they see that the divine self-naming is a triune act.

The Narrative of the Divine Self-Naming

Recent understandings of the way in which proper names become descriptive designators suggest that the divine name comes to be filled with content through an ongoing history of relationships. At first glance, this perspective leads us to look to the history of the covenanting God with the people of the covenant for the locus of the process by means of which the divine name gains description. This, however, is only part of the story. History is not only the narrative of the relationship between God and Israel (and by extension humankind). More importantly, it is the story of the relationship of God to God. That is, history is the narrative of the relationships among the Father and the Son and the Holy Spirit. This narrative, in turn, comprises the saga of God naming God.

At the heart of the narrative of the I AM through which God's self-naming occurs is the act of naming that occurs between God and Jesus, and in which the Spirit participates. During his ministry, Jesus moved to center stage the divine designation "Father" that was already in use, albeit in a limited manner, in intertestamental Judaism. In so doing, Jesus in effect named God. Alvin Kimel states the larger theological point succinctly: "The Father *receives from Jesus*, through the power of the Spirit, his hypostatic identity *as Father*."[139]

Jesus' act in designating God as Father did not occur at Jesus' own initiative, however. Rather, it was closely connected to his sense that God had named him "Son," a theme that is found repeatedly in the New Testament and that closely links Jesus to the messianic expectations articulated in the Old Testament. The opening chapter of the book of Hebrews,

139. Kimel, "God Who Likes His Name," 205.

to cite one especially explicit example, applies assertions from what had come to be seen as messianic psalms to indicate that as the one whom God named "Son," Jesus is exalted above the angels (Heb. 1:5–13). Likewise, the idea is evident in the various Johannine texts in which Jesus claims close affinity to God as his Father. But the incident in the Gospels in which the Trinitarian dynamic inherent in the act of naming is most readily evident is in Jesus' baptism. Mark narrates the story in stark simplicity: "In those days Jesus came from Nazareth of Galilee and was baptized by John in the Jordan. And just as he was coming up out of the water, he saw the heavens torn apart and the Spirit descending like a dove on him. And a voice came from heaven, 'You are my Son, the Beloved; with you I am well pleased'" (Mark 1:9–11).

A long-standing exegetical tradition sees the baptism of Jesus as a Trinitarian event. Already in the third century, Origen declared, "In Jordan the Trinity was manifested to man. The Father bore witness, the Son received witness, and the Holy Spirit gave an intimation."[140] More recently, Edmond Hiebert concluded, "In the baptismal scene, we have a clear manifestation of the Trinity. The Father spoke His approval from heaven; the incarnate Son stood ready to begin His mission; the Spirit descended to empower Him."[141] William Hendriksen, in turn, has offered this terse comment: "Gloriously the Trinity is here revealed."[142]

Central to the Trinitarian character of the story is the relationship between Jesus and his Father that it dramatizes. Since at least the early twentieth century, commentators have connected whatever messianic conception might be indicated in the text to Jesus' prior consciousness of his identity as the Son of the Father. In 1918, William Manson sounded this theme when he declared, "He came to His baptism already conscious of a unique relation to God, on which the Messianic idea was now superinduced."[143] Forty years later, C. E. B. Cranfield reiterated the idea:

> The voice does not proclaim Jesus' newly established status of sonship consequent upon his installation as Messiah; rather it confirms his already existing filial consciousness. In response to his self-dedication to the mission of the Servant, made in his submission to baptism, he is given a confirmation of his own consciousness of being the Son of God, that is at the same time a confirmation of his Servant-vocation.[144]

140. Origen, *Matthew* (*Possinus' Catena*), as cited in *Ante-Nicene Exegesis of the Gospels*, ed. H. D. Smith, 6 vols. (London: SPCK, 1925), 1:307.

141. D. Edmond Hiebert, *Mark: A Portrait of the Servant* (Chicago: Moody, 1974), 38.

142. William Hendriksen, *Exposition of the Gospel according to Mark*, New Testament Commentary (Grand Rapids: Baker, 1975), 42.

143. William Manson, *Christ's View of the Kingdom of God: A Study in Jewish Apocalyptic and in the Mind of Jesus Christ* (London: James Clarke, 1918), 126–27.

144. C. E. B. Cranfield, *The Gospel according to Saint Mark*, Cambridge Greek Testament Commentary (Cambridge: Cambridge University Press, 1959), 55. Cranfield is echoing a similar decla-

In recent years, the enthusiasm of earlier exegetes such as Manson and Cranfield has been blunted by commentators who have taken a more cautious stance toward the possibility of ascertaining Jesus' self-consciousness.[145] Whatever may be deduced from the Gospels about the advent and depth of Jesus' sense of being the Son of the Father, within the baptism pericope itself "the emphasis is on *God's* initiative and *God's* act," as Hugh Anderson points out.[146]

Anderson observes further that "the centre of gravity of the baptism story lies in God's assent to Jesus as Son."[147] This divine assent, which could be rendered woodenly from the Greek, "You yourself are the Son of me, the beloved," echos several Old Testament texts (Ps. 2:7; Isa. 42:1; Gen. 22:2), while quoting none directly.[148] The final word in the statement, *agapetos* ("beloved"), is generally used in the Septuagint to designate an only child.[149] Consequently, it speaks not only of the Father's love for the Son[150] but also of Jesus' unique status as the Son of the Father[151] which in several New Testament texts is presented as an eternal status. In keeping with this development, some commentators conclude that the subsequent statement, "In whom I am well pleased," refers to an eternal, rather than merely a singular or temporal, being-pleased. Hence, his conclusion that the verb is a timeless aorist[152] leads Hendriksen to declare in a picturesque manner, "In the quiet recess of eternity the Son was the object of the Father's inexhaustible delight."[153]

---

ration made four years earlier by Vincent Taylor: "The terms of the announcement do not include the more obvious Messianic expressions. . . . What is expressed is a new and vital relationship to God which transcends Messiahship as it was understood in Jewish thought. . . . The fundamental note of the saying is the filial status of Jesus; and the words are best understood as an assurance, or confirmation, of this relationship, rather than a disclosure or revelation." Taylor, *The Gospel according to St. Mark* (London: Macmillan, 1955), 162.

145. See especially Morna D. Hooker, *A Commentary on the Gospel according to St. Mark*, Black's New Testament Commentaries (London: A. & C. Black, 1991), 44–48.

146. Hugh Anderson, *The Gospel of Mark*, New Century Bible (London: Oliphants, 1976), 80. Harrington seems to point in this direction, while maintaining aspects of the older view, when he declares, "As Jesus is about to embark on his public ministry God solemnly affirms both his status and his call." Wilfrid Harrington, *Mark*, New Testament Message: A Biblical-Theological Commentary (Collegeville, MN: Liturgical Press, 1991), 8.

147. Anderson, *Gospel of Mark*, 78.

148. For a helpful summary of the connections to these verses, see R. T. France, *The Gospel of Mark: A Commentary on the Greek Text*, New International Greek Testament Commentary (Grand Rapids: Eerdmans, 2002), 80–82.

149. For this observation and its implication, see Hooker, *Mark*, 47–48.

150. For this understanding of the term, see Joel Marcus, *Mark 1–8: A New Translation with Introduction and Commentary*, Anchor Bible (New York: Doubleday, 2000), 162–63.

151. See Eduard Schweizer, *The Good News according to Mark*, trans. Donald H. Madvig (Atlanta: John Knox, 1970), 41.

152. For this understanding of the verb, see also D. Edmond Hiebert, *Mark: A Portrait of the Servant* (Chicago: Moody, 1974), 38; Vincent Taylor, *The Gospel according to St. Mark* (London: Macmillan, 1955), 161–62.

153. Hendriksen, *Exposition of the Gospel according to Mark*, 44. See also Douglas R. A. Hare, *Mark*, Westminster Bible Companion (Louisville, KY: Westminster John Knox, 1996), 18.

Not to be overlooked is the role of the Spirit in the baptismal drama. In Mark's version of the narrative, as Jesus comes up out of the water he sees "the heavens in the process of being ripped apart," to cite Lamar Williamson's vivid rendering of the phrase.[154] As this translation indicates, the evangelist depicts the opening of the heavens by means of a strong Greek term (from which arises the English term "schism"). This word is later used to refer to the tearing of the temple curtain in conjunction with Jesus' death (Mark 15:38). In both cases, the passive voice implies that God is the agent of the action. Moreover, the point of the act in both scenes is to indicate that something that had long been inaccessible is suddenly flung open. Anderson remarks regarding the use of the word in the baptism pericope, "This graphic piece of imagery signifies that God is about to communicate with or reveal himself to men, and in Mark it is the prelude to the final and decisive disclosure of God."[155] Consequently, the descent of the Spirit on Jesus comprises the fulfillment of the long-anticipated hope: "O that you would tear open the heavens and come down" (Isa. 64:1). As Anderson concludes, "Accordingly the Evangelist intends the descent of the Spirit upon Jesus to indicate that the days of Spirit-famine are ended, that the prophetic promises have now come true, and that the Spirit is potently active in this new and last epoch of the ministry of Jesus."[156]

Despite the dramatic manner in which the Spirit appears in the baptism pericope, commentators routinely elevate the Father's pronouncement to center stage. They highlight the importance of the voice from heaven in denoting the divine confirmation of Jesus' status and calling, and relegate the descent of the Spirit to a subsidiary role. Yet it appears that the evangelist has a somewhat different intent in view. James Dunn points in this direction: "In the accounts as we have them the words of proclamation are obviously intended to *explain* the descent of the Spirit: the Spirit anoints Jesus as Son."[157]

The Synoptics, especially Mark, connect Jesus' Sonship to the presence of the Spirit in his life and mission, which presence, according to the baptism pericope, comes about by means of the descent of the Spirit upon him. The overarching christological supposition of Synoptics, taken as a whole, is that Jesus is the Son in that God bestowed on him the Spirit, who empowered him to live in obedience to his Father and to fulfill his unique vocation as the Savior of humankind.[158] In this vocation, Jesus' role and

---

154. Lamar Williamson, Jr., *Mark*, Interpretation: A Bible Commentary for Teaching and Preaching (Louisville, KY: John Knox, 1983), 34.

155. Anderson, *Gospel of Mark*, 77.

156. Ibid.

157. James D. G. Dunn, *Jesus and the Spirit: A Study of the Religious and Charismatic Experience of Jesus and the First Christians as Reflected in the New Testament* (Philadelphia: Westminster, 1975), 65.

158. For a helpful articulation of this proposal, see David Coffey, "The Holy Spirit as the Mutual Love of the Father and the Son," *Theological Studies* 51 (1990): 202–3. See also David Coffey, *Deus Trinitas: The Doctrine of the Triune God* (New York: Oxford University Press, 1999), 37–41.

status is not limited to being God's servant after the manner depicted in Isaiah's prophecy of the Suffering Servant. More importantly, he is God's beloved Son, as the heavenly voice in the baptism drama declares.

Dunn rightly points out that the voice from heaven is to be understood as providing a divinely uttered commentary that brings to light the meaning of the descent of the Spirit. But the utterance is also to be viewed in connection with the sense that Jesus displayed throughout his earthly sojourn of being the recipient of the fatherly love of God. As a consequence, the declaration, "You are my Son, the Beloved," leads to the conclusion that the descent of the Spirit upon Jesus does not simply entail his reception of the divine power. More importantly, it involves his acceptance of the Father's eternal love. In this manner, the Spirit, who is presented in the Old Testament as the power of Yahweh, gains through the divine self-disclosure in Jesus the added dimension of being the divine love. Through Christ, therefore, the Spirit is revealed as the love of God for Jesus, a love that constitutes Jesus as his Father's beloved Son.[159]

The relationality that emerges from the triune divine self-disclosure in Jesus includes another aspect as well. Not only is the Spirit the one who guides and empowers Jesus. The Spirit is the love of the Father for the Son evoking from the Son the reciprocation of that love. Hence, the Spirit, who is the love of the Father for Jesus, becomes in Jesus the love of the Son for the Father. This reciprocated love forms the wellspring of Jesus' ministry on behalf of the Father.[160] In the words of the French Catholic theologian Antoine Birot, "The Spirit actively brings about in the Son the obedient response of love."[161] As Jesus thereby offers the Spirit, whom he has received from the Father, back to the Father, the Spirit becomes the love shared between God the Father and Jesus the Son.

The triune character of the drama that is evident in Jesus' baptism comes into clearer focus when it is read within the context of the dynamic of the patriarchal family from which the primary Trinitarian language of the New Testament is derived. Marianne Meye Thompson notes that in ancient Israelite society a father was assumed to fulfill several basic roles. Bound up with the status of father was the task of protecting and providing for one's children. Moreover, being father meant correcting or disciplining one's children when they disobeyed or went astray. But above all, the father functioned as the source or origin of a family or clan and, as a consequence, the one who bestowed the family inheritance upon his heirs.[162] Thompson's findings indicate that, rather than focusing

---

159. For a similar conclusion, see Coffey, "Holy Spirit as the Mutual Love," 205.

160. For a helpful explication of this theme in the New Testament, see Coffey, "Holy Spirit as the Mutual Love," 206–11.

161. Antoine Birot, "The Divine Drama, from the Father's Perspective: How the Father Lives Love in the Trinity," *Communio* 30, no. 3 (Fall 2003): 425.

162. Thompson, *Promise of God the Father*, 39.

primarily on either gender or procreation, in the ancient patriarchal society "father" is a relational term. The one who is father stands in a specific relationship to certain, specific other persons. Although this relationship includes functioning as originator, life giver or defender, the most significant function is that of possessing and then passing on the treasures of the family to those who are the heirs of this inheritance.

When viewed in this context, Jesus' use of the designation "Father" for the God of Israel carries far-reaching significance. By means of this term, Jesus was acknowledging that he is the recipient of the grand inheritance that his heavenly Father grants to him as heir. Moreover, the "treasure of the family" that the divine Father possesses and bestows on the Son is something that is inherently the Father's. It is something that belongs to the Father rightfully or essentially. This suggests that the "treasure" is nothing less than the Father's own character or essential nature, and hence the Father's own deity. Furthermore, in the Trinitarian drama, what the Son receives from the Father, he returns to the Father. In this manner, the "treasure" comes to be shared between the Father and the Son. The baptism pericope suggests that what the Father bestows on the Son is the Holy Spirit, who is likewise the love shared between the Father and the Son. This conception fits well with one particular conception of the Spirit that boasts a long pedigree in theological history: As the third person of the Trinity, the Spirit is the personal concretization of the very essence or the very deity of God, namely, love.

The Triunity of the Divine Self-Naming

When viewed within the context of the saga of the "I am," and hence the narrative of the divine self-naming, the inheritance that the Father lavishes on the Son is the treasured name that belongs to the Father. The Fourth Gospel suggests that the Father bestows the divine name upon the Son, who receives this name so that he might glorify the Father's name and return the glorified name to the Father. In this manner, the Son is glorified, and in being the recipient of this "name that is above all names" the Father is likewise glorified. Moreover, the glorification of the name is mediated through the Spirit, who glorifies the Son and with him the Father. In this manner, the giving/receiving and returning of the glorified divine name comprises the history of the relationships of the three Trinitarian persons.

This observation takes us back to the central insight that arises from recent attempts to synthesize the descriptivist and direct reference theories of naming. These attempts have underscored the observation that in the act of naming, the named person is passive. When viewed from the perspective of the relationship of God and the world, this understanding of the act of naming is inapplicable to the naming of God, for God always remains the self-naming God. But as we have seen, there is another aspect of the divine act of self-naming: God names God. In this act, God is both

active agent and passive recipient. It is at this point that the importance
of the triunity of the self-naming God becomes fully evident.

To see this requires that we recall an aspect of proper names that is
indicative of ancient societies, especially Israel. In such societies, a name
carried more than mere denotative significance. Rather, it was deemed to
be connected in the closest possible way with its bearer, even to the point
of becoming a kind of *alter ego*.[163] According to the ancient understanding, a name is essentially linked to and forms an indispensable part of the
personality of the one who bears it. It is a power that discloses the nature
of the bearer of the name, so that its pronouncement or invocation sets
in operation the bearer's own energy.[164] Consequently, rather than merely
facilitating the task of distinguishing the person from others, knowledge
of a person's name was deemed to mediate a direct relationship with the
person's nature or being.[165] A name was likewise viewed as an expression
of the individual character of its bearer to the extent that it not only stood
for the person but was even interchangeable with the person.[166] Barth
summarizes this ancient understanding and then explains the resultant
significance of revealing one's name to another:

> In the thought and speech of the Old and New Testament . . . a
> "name" is not given to its bearer accidentally or merely by way of eti-
> quette. . . . On the contrary, it is itself the bearer, his person, being
> and potency, his whole historical reality in its nature and essence, to
> the degree that there belongs inseparably hereto the power to reveal
> and disclose itself, to the degree that it is capable of communication
> and engaged in it. In his name a man, speaking or acting, makes him-
> self known to others as the man he is, the man who does what he
> does. In it he opens himself to dealings with others, he is engaged in
> such dealings, he goes among people and is with them. This means
> that in his name he becomes and is a person who can be addressed,
> but who can also be claimed.[167]

In Israel, this understanding of the significance of proper names led to
the conception of a close relationship between the divine name and the
very nature and reality of God. In fact, in the Pentateuch, the revelation
and continuous presence of God's name among the covenant people came
to be viewed as the central expression of God's self-communication to
Israel.[168] In this context, God's name became an interchangeable term for

---

163. See Walther Eichrodt, *Theology of the Old Testament*, trans. J. A. Baker, 2 vols. (Philadelphia:
Westminster, 1961, 1967), 1:207; Hans Bietenhard, "onoma," in *Theological Dictionary of the New
Testament*, 5:254.
164. Bietenhard, "onoma," 5:243.
165. Eichrodt, *Theology of the Old Testament*, 1:207; 2:40.
166. Ibid., 2:40.
167. Barth, *Church Dogmatics*, IV/4, 92.
168. Eichrodt, *Theology of the Old Testament*, 1:409.

God's person. Eventually the divine name even came to take on a certain independence from Yahweh; it was endowed with a hypostatic character of its own. This development reached its climax after the destruction of the temple. What was now denoted as the "Name" came to serve as the representative of the transcendent God and the means by which Yahweh assures his people of his presence with them and of the continuing efficacy of his power.[169] The Name as the divine power was deemed to have been exalted to the side of Yahweh in heaven and as such to be a proper recipient of cultic worship.[170]

The exalted status of the Name in the postexilic era forms the context for the New Testament idea of the Father bestowing the divine name on the Son. Through this act the very character, nature, and power—indeed, the very deity—that inheres in the Father rests on the Son as well. In the baptism pericope, this "resting" comes in the form of the Spirit descending from heaven upon Jesus. Jesus' life, ministry, and death, in turn, become a composite act of returning to the Father what the Son receives from the Father, namely, the Father's very nature as deity—that is, the Spirit, who thereby becomes the Spirit shared by the Father and the Son.

It is in this respect that the act of God naming God emerges as a triune or Trinitarian act. Present in this act of naming are Namer, Named, and Name. Moreover, all three are constituted by the act. The second of the three is constituted as the one who is Named by the Namer, of course. But the first is likewise constituted as the Namer of the Named, who receives back the bestowed Name. And insofar as the Name is bound up with the very essence of its bearer, the third emerges as the Name shared by the Namer and the Named. Exchanging substantive for dynamic language leads to the conclusion that the act involves Naming, Being Named, and Name Sharing.

What is presented in the New Testament as an event involving Jesus, his heavenly Father, and the divine Spirit suggests a transcendent, eternal dynamic of naming within the life of the triune God. Stating the dynamic in classical Trinitarian terms, the eternal Father of the Son bestows the divine name, which is his own, eternally on the Son of the Father, who eternally returns to the Father what he has received. And this Name shared by the Namer and the Named is concretized as the person of the Holy Spirit.

In this dynamic, "Name," "Love," even "Deity," are drawn together by the one designation "Spirit." The interconnectedness of language entailed in the divine act of self-naming, in turn, forms the bridge from the saga of the divine name, and hence from the God of the Bible, to the philosophical concerns explored in the traditional discipline of ontology. To this topic, we can now turn.

169. Ibid., 2:41.
170. Ibid., 2:43.

Chapter Eight

From the Trinity to Being

The Ontology of the Divine Name

In David Bentley Hart's estimation, a "theology that refuses to address questions of ontology can never be more than a mythology."[1] In this terse statement, Hart provides what at first glance appears to be an irrefutable apologetic for a theology that takes philosophy seriously. More specifically, he voices in a short, single statement a clarion call for an explicit, self-conscious, and unabashedly theological engagement with the question of Being.

Hart's comment does not stipulate the exact form that theology's interaction with ontological questions ought to take. Nevertheless, he seems to rule out immediately any suggestion that such an encounter might occur on the level of myth. Indeed, as I noted in part 1 of this volume, philosophy was born, at least in part, as an attempt to overcome mythology. The desire of the early philosophers was to discover the unifying truth

---

1. David Bentley Hart, *The Beauty of the Infinite: The Aesthetics of Christian Truth* (Grand Rapids: Eerdmans, 2003), 213.

of the cosmos and thereby dispel the belief that life is capricious that stood at the heart of the mythological stories of the gods that were widely propagated among ancient peoples. Viewed from this perspective we might even describe ontology as the intellectual critique of myth.

Yet hidden beneath this observation is a series of interrelated questions begging to be asked: In the process of overcoming mythology, did metaphysics enthrone yet another, albeit highly sophisticated, myth? Is there a sense in which ontology might be properly understood as the embodiment of the myth of Being? And if philosophy as a whole can in this respect be viewed as a new mythology—perhaps ultimately as the propagation of the myth of the prowess of the human mind—on what basis can we conclude without a doubt that the philosophical discipline has offered a story that is "better" than the stories of the gods, which it has sought to supplant?

The task of this chapter is to bring the story of one particular God—the God of the Bible who is the named God—into direct conversation with the central concern of ontology, its quest for Being. Contrary to how similar conversations have sometimes been conducted, my goal in this conversation cannot be that of supplanting the Christian story by the story of Being. Nor is my intent more simply that of bringing the Christian story in line with a supposedly overarching story of Being. All such attempts land us ultimately in the realm of onto-theology. Rather, the intent of these pages is to explore the possibility of devising what might be denoted a "Trinitarian ontology" and hence a "theo-ontology." What should emerge at the end of this chapter is a conception of Being that arises out of the be-ing present of the Christian. Or, placing our quest in the context of the story lines narrated in this volume, I will be pursuing a conception of Being that emerges from the narrative of the divine name, insofar as this narrative discloses the presence of the be-ing of God. Underlying the chapter, therefore, is the desire to respond to the question, What kind of ontology arises out of the realization that the God of the Bible is a named God and that the divine name is Trinitarian?

The Trinity and the Greek Philosophical Tradition

Rather than seeking a response to this query directly, we must pursue our goal by first journeying through yet another aspect of the saga of the triune name. We must explore how the understanding of God as triune developed in the context of the discussion between Christian theology and Greek philosophy, especially the tradition of Platonism. This requires that we retrace a segment of the territory that we traversed in part 1. This time, however, our gaze will not be focused on the saga of Being. My intent is not that of determining how the Christian God came to be linked

with the Greek concept of Being. Rather, we will traverse this t
with a view toward the manner in which the orthodox doctrin
Trinity arose in the context of the encounter with Greek ontological concerns. In short, our theme is now the saga of the triune name. And our
working assumption is that this seminal segment of the ongoing saga of
the triune name can offer us direction as we seek today to engage with the
legacy of the philosophical tradition that pursues as its central question
the nature of Being.

The Development of Orthodox Trinitarianism
in the Context of Philosophy

The writers of the New Testament nowhere delineate a formal doctrine of
the Trinity. Rather than arising out of explicit scriptural teaching, this
doctrine emerged from what Edmund J. Fortman characterizes as "three
centuries of gradual assimilation of the Biblical witness to God."[2] Nor was
the interest that eventually led to the formation of the doctrine of the Trinity initially philosophical. The primary goal of the early Christians was
not that of bringing the biblical witness to the triune God into conversation with the question of Being. Rather, the discussions that resulted in
the framing of the doctrine of the Trinity centered on issues that were, on
the whole, theological.

The process that eventually netted the church's teaching about God
as triune was generated by a theological puzzle that lay at the very basis
of the Christian community. The early theologians found themselves
grappling with a three-part question: How could the confession of the
lordship of Jesus and the experience of the indwelling Holy Spirit be
understood within the context of the nonnegotiable commitment to the
one God that the early believers retained from their connection to Israel?
Or, as William Rusch states it, "How is the church, in an intellectually
satisfying manner, to integrate the doctrine of one God, Father and Creator, inherited from the Old Testament and Judaism, with the revelation
that this God had disclosed himself uniquely in Jesus and had given the
Holy Spirit to the church?"[3]

Setting the Stage for Philosophical Trinitarianism

The process that led to the development of the doctrine of the Trinity,
therefore, had an explicitly theological orientation. Nevertheless, many of
the church leaders who participated in this process found themselves

---

2. Edmund J. Fortman, *The Triune God: A Historical Study of the Doctrine of the Trinity* (London: Hutchinson, 1972), 35.

3. William G. Rusch, introduction to *The Trinitarian Controversy*, ed. William G. Rusch, Sources of Early Christian Thought (Philadelphia: Fortress, 1980), 2.

engaging in the theological discussion with Greek philosophy, above all with the tradition of Platonism, clearly in view. In his *Confessions*, Augustine indicates the extent to which this philosophical trajectory was revered by many church leaders:

> To Simplicianus then I went,—the father of Ambrose (at that time a bishop) in receiving The grace, and whom he truly loved as a father. To him I narrated the windings of my error. But when I mentioned to him that I had read certain books of the Platonists, which Victorinus, sometime Professor of Rhetoric at Rome (who died a Christian, as I had been told), had translated into Latin, he congratulated me that I had not fallen upon the writings of other philosophers, which were full of fallacies and deceit, "after the rudiments of the world," whereas they, in many ways, led to the belief in God and His Word.[4]

It is not surprising, therefore, that the tradition of Platonism formed the context in which the theological delineation of the Christian conception of God came to be developed. In fact, we might say that the orthodox doctrine of the Trinity arose from a theological engagement regarding the mystery of the Christian experience of God that transpired within an intellectual climate that was dominated by Platonic thought. As Christian theologians sought to explain the mystery that they perceived at the heart of the faith, they drew from the intellectual tools that their context in the Greco-Roman world placed in their hands. These were largely Platonic in origin. For this reason, in its infancy Trinitarian theology was naturally cradled by Platonism. Throughout its history, orthodox Trinitarianism has never fully discarded the shape that its philosophical nanny provided during those formative centuries.

The move toward giving theological deliberations regarding matters of the triunity of God a philosophical cast was inaugurated as early as the second century. It emerged as a crucial concern that motivated the work of a group of Christian thinkers whose goal was to demonstrate the credibility of the faith of the church in the context of Greco-Roman culture. These thinkers, commonly referred to as the Apologists and whom Fortman elevates as "the Church's first theologians,"[5] presented Christianity as the true philosophy.[6] The Christian faith, they claimed, is that to which the Greek philosophers had pointed. Justin (c. 100–165), who is generally listed as the first of the Apologists, extolled philosophy itself as a means to the discovery of God. He declared, "Philosophy is, in fact, the greatest possession, and most honourable before God, to whom it alone

---

4. Augustine, *Confessions* 8.2.3, in *Nicene and Post-Nicene Fathers*, 1st series, ed. Philip Schaff (1887: Peabody, MA: Hendrickson, 1994), 1:117. (Hereafter this work is abbreviated *NPNF.*)

5. Fortman, *Triune God*, 44.

6. For a helpful summary, see Roger E. Olson, *The Story of Christian Theology: Twenty Centuries of Tradition and Reform* (Downers Grove, IL: InterVarsity Press, 1999), 54–67.

leads us and alone commends us; and these are truly holy men who have bestowed attention on philosophy."[7]

Christian thinkers such as Justin did not speak of God solely in biblical terms. Rather, their attempt to show the credibility of Christianity led them to portray the God of the Bible in philosophical categories. To this end, they described God as transcendent, unchangeable,[8] eternal, passionless,[9] and ineffable or nameless.[10] The central theological question that came to the fore in their deliberations, in turn, was that of the exact relationship between Jesus Christ and God. In fact, J. N. D. Kelly cites the Apologists as "the first to try to frame an intellectually satisfying explanation of the relation of Christ to God the Father."[11]

The Apologists' response took the form of what is often termed the "Logos christology." Drawing from the Stoic distinction between the *Logos endiathetos* ("the immanent Word") and the *Logos prophorikos* ("the expressed Word"),[12] the Apologists postulated that the Logos existed in eternity as God's mind or thought but that God spoke the Logos in creation and in revelation. In this manner, these theologians were able to maintain simultaneously the unity of the Logos with God and the distinction of the Logos, not only in name but also in number, from God.[13] Moreover, they used the language of generation to express the connection between God and the Logos as God's offspring.[14]

The Apologists evidenced less interest in determining the connection of the Holy Spirit to God.[15] This issue received more attention in the work of another thinker who sought to show the philosophical sublimity of the Christian faith, Clement of Alexandria (d. ca. 215). Clement even went so far as to suggest that Greek philosophy served as a "schoolmaster" bringing the Greeks to Christ.[16] In keeping with this perspective, he composed one of his works for the expressed purpose of dissipating the prejudice of his day against philosophy and theology.[17]

As a Christian, Clement believed, of course, in the God depicted in the Bible. But, like the Apologists, his interest in connecting Christianity with philosophy led him also to speak of God in philosophical terms as the

---

7. Justin, *Dialogue with Trypho* 2, in *Ante-Nicene Fathers*, ed. Alexander Roberts and James Donaldson (1885; Peabody, MA: Hendrickson, 1994), 1:195. (Hereafter this work is abbreviated *ANF*.)

8. Ibid., 1:167.

9. Ibid., 1:166.

10. Ibid., 1:165; Justin, *2 Apology* 6, in *ANF*, 1:192.

11. J. N. D. Kelly, *Early Christian Doctrines*, rev. ed. (New York: Harper & Row, 1978), 95.

12. See, for example, Theophilus of Antioch, *Apology to Autolycus* 2.10.22, in *ANF*, 2:98.

13. See, for example, Justin, *Dialogue with Trypho* 128.4, in *ANF*, 1:264.

14. See, for example, Justin, *Trypho* 62.105, 125, in *ANF*, 1:228; Justin, *1 Apology* 21, in *ANF*, 1:170.

15. For individual examples of this as well as a summary statement, see Fortman, *Triune God*, 47–51.

16. Clement of Alexandria, *The Stromata* 1.5, in *ANF*, 2:305.

17. For an example of this widely held judgment, see Arthur Cushman McGiffert, *A History of Christian Thought*, vol. 1, *Early and Eastern* (New York: Charles Scribner's Sons, 1932), 183, 197.

utterly transcendent, unnameable unity beyond unity.[18] As such, he averred, God cannot be described in terms of "genus, nor difference, nor species, nor individual, nor number."[19] Arthur Cushman McGiffert offers the following description of Clement's conception: "Following Philo and the later Platonists he emphasized the transcendence of God and carried it to extreme heights. God he identified with the philosophical absolute. He is unapproachable, inaccessible, unknowable, incommunicable, beyond space and time, and out of relation with all else that is."[20]

This God, Clement adds, can be known only through his Word. The Word, in turn, is essentially one with God, in that the Word is God's mind or rationality.[21] Moreover, the Word is the mediator between the transcendent God and the world which God contains.[22] Once again McGiffert provides a helpful characterization of Clement's perspective: "God in himself is so transcendent that neither creation nor revelation is possible to him nor can men attain to a knowledge of him." However, "in the Logos the abstract becomes concrete, the absolute enters into relations, and God creates the world and reveals himself to men."[23]

According to Clement, the Spirit is the power of the Word, who pervades creation and draws people to God. The Spirit is likewise the light issuing from the Word who enlightens or illuminates believers.[24] Clement's conceptions of God, the Word, and the Spirit fit together in a Trinitarian conception resembling the triad prevalent in what is often denoted as Middle Platonism.[25] One prominent Platonist of Clement's day, Albinus, depicted this triad as consisting of the unmoved First Mind (God), the Second Mind or World-Intellect through which God operates and which is set in motion by desire for the First Mind, and the World-Soul.[26] On the basis of this similarity, Kelly concludes regarding Clement's understanding of God, "Thus we have a Trinity which, though in all its lineaments Platonic, Clement unhesitatingly identifies with Christian theism."[27]

The attempt to delineate a conception of the Christian God by appropriating the tools of Platonic philosophy reached a new level in the early third-century Christian theologian Origen (185–232). McGiffert lauds Origen as the one who "became in course of time the greatest theologian

---

18. Clement of Alexandria, The Tutor 1.7, in ANF 2:223–24; Clement of Alexandria, Stromata 2.6.1, in ANF 2:353; 5.6, in ANF 2:452–54; 5.7, in ANF, 2:454; 5.8, in ANF, 2:457.

19. Clement of Alexandria, Stromata 5.2, in ANF, 2:463.

20. McGiffert, History of Christian Thought, 1:203.

21. Clement of Alexandria, Stromata 4.25, in ANF 2:438; 7.2, in ANF 2:524; Clement of Alexandria, Tutor 1.2, in ANF 209–10; 3.1, in ANF 2:271.

22. Clement of Alexandria, Stromata 5.1, in ANF 2:444; Clement of Alexandria, Exhortation to the Heathen 98.3, in ANF 2:195–97.

23. McGiffert, History of Christian Thought, 1:204.

24. Clement of Alexandria, Stromata 6.18, in ANF 2:519; 7.9, in ANF 2:538.

25. For a somewhat similar judgment, see Rusch, introduction to The Trinitarian Controversy, 12.

26. See Kelly, Early Christian Doctrines, 20.

27. Kelly, Early Christian Doctrines, 127.

and the most daring speculative genius of the eastern church" and who "published the first systematic work on Christian theology."[28]

Like Justin and Clement, Origen sought to engage the Christian theological vision with the philosophical currents of the day. As Peter Widdicombe explains, "Origen draws on biblical and Middle Platonist ideas about God to develop a distinctively theological statement about God's nature."[29] The result, according to Kelly, "was a brilliant reinterpretation of the traditional triadic rule of faith . . . in terms of the same middle Platonism."[30] Similarly, Fortman declares that Origen "tried to build a harmonious synthesis of strict monotheism and a Platonic hierarchical order in the Trinity." In Fortman's estimation, however, Origen failed in this project.[31] In any case, it would be fair to say that Origen was less interested in being a Platonist metaphysician than in advancing an understanding of the Christian faith that was based on biblical exegesis and served a soteriological goal.[32]

Like his predecessors, Origen viewed God as a solitary, incomprehensible, and "uncompounded intellectual nature."[33] His chief interest, however, was to set forth as God's most basic characteristic incorporeality,[34] and this perhaps in response to Christians who had been influenced by the Stoic teaching that fire and spirit are corporeal.[35] Origen's use of Scripture to shape his comments about God led him at times to speak about God as "he who is," "being itself," or *ho on*, and to contrast God with nonbeing (*oux on*). Yet he also declared that God "transcends mind and being,"[36] and he assigned the designation "being" to the Son, whom he also declared to be "being of beings."[37] Despite the seemingly obvious contradictory nature of these two descriptions, Origen might not have viewed them as standing in tension with each other, but simply affirmed both as biblical ideas. Moreover, his intent in voicing the latter is not so much to delineate a metaphysical postulate as to set forth the Son's unique function as the revealer of the Father.[38]

Whereas the Father is God in the absolute sense, Origen declared, the Son is God only derivatively. In a manner that seems to take its cue from Albinus's Platonism, Origen postulated that the deity of the Word is derived through the act of contemplation, through the Son's "remaining

28. McGiffert, *History of Christian Thought*, 1:208, 209.
29. *The Fatherhood of God from Origen to Athanasius*, rev. ed. (Oxford: Clarendon, 2000), 9.
30. Kelly, *Early Christian Doctrines*, 128.
31. Fortman, *Triune God*, 57.
32. Widdicombe, *Fatherhood of God*, 9.
33. Origen, *First Principles* 1.1.5, in *ANF* 4:243; 1.1.6, in *ANF* 4:243.
34. Widdicombe, *Fatherhood of God*, 13.
35. For this judgment, see Widdicombe, *Fatherhood of God*, 15.
36. Origen, *Against Celsus* 7.38, in *ANF* 4:626.
37. Origen, *Against Celsus* 6.64, in *ANF* 4:603.
38. Widdicombe, *Fatherhood of God*, 43.

always in uninterrupted contemplation of the depths of the Father," which entails participation in the Father.[39] Of greater importance to Origen, however, is the idea of the eternal generation of the Son. Origen theorized that the Son proceeds from the Father by means of an act of eternal generation, that resembles the emergence of will from mind, reason, or understanding.[40] The eternal character of the act of generation is crucial in Origen's overarching program. For him (as for many Greek philosophers) eternality was essential to his controlling theological concepts of divine incorporeality and immutability. Origen was convinced that what is postulated of the three divine *hypostases* must be viewed as eternal. Hence, the generation of the Son is eternal, just as the Father's fatherhood is eternal. Furthermore, the generation of the Son occurs through a continuous exercise of the divine will. In postulating this, Origen moved away from the Platonism of his day, which did not view the Mind as generated by the purposeful will of the One.[41] In Origen's estimation, the eternal generation of the Son marks the distinction between the Father's relation to the Son and his relation to the world, for this act indicates that the Father does not will the Son in the same way that he wills the existence of creatures.

Paralleling the Platonism of his day, Origen theorized that God brought into existence a realm of rational or spiritual beings (*logikoi* or *theoi*), who are likewise eternal. The mediator between the one God and the multiplicity of spiritual beings is God's Son or the Word.[42] The Son fulfills his mediator role by reflecting the Father to rational creatures and thereby establishing their relationship to God. In this sense, the Father produces the Son so that there might be a created universe.[43] Furthermore, the relation of creatures to the Son parallels that of the Son to the Father. As he is the image of the Father, so they, on a lesser level, are images of the Son and therefore can be called gods (*theoi*). The Holy Spirit, in turn, is the first among all that is originated by the Father through the Son.[44] The chief role of the Spirit is to promote holiness in Jesus' followers, that is, to effect sanctification.[45]

As these observations suggest, Origen's perspective leads to a Trinitarian theology that posits a series of hierarchical relationships that move from the Father to creation. In this hierarchy, the Father's action envelopes all creation, the Son's is directed toward rational creation, and the Spirit's work focuses on those who are being sanctified.[46] This downward move-

39. Origen, *Commentary on John* 2.2.18, in *ANF* 9:323.
40. Origen, *First Principles* 1.2.4, in *ANF* 4:247; 1.2.6 in *ANF* 4:247–48; 4.36, in *ANF* 4:380–81.
41. For this judgment, see Rusch, introduction to *The Trinitarian Controversy*, 13.
42. Origen, *Against Celsus* 2.64, in *ANF* 4:457.
43. For this understanding, see McGiffert, *History of Christian Thought*, 1:217.
44. Origen, *Commentary on John* 2.10.75, in *ANF* 9:328.
45. For this understanding, see McGiffert, *History of Christian Thought*, 1:221.
46. Origen, *First Principles* 1.3.1–8, in *ANF* 4:251–56.

ment of the triune God in revelation and accommodation to creatures leads, in turn, to a parallel upward movement of the soul in the process of coming to the knowledge of God. Following the basic Platonic framework of the ascent to a knowledge of truth,[47] Origen describes the soul's journey to perfect knowledge of God as passing through three stages. At the same time, he alters the Platonic framework by presenting the soul's final happiness as the contemplation of the three divine *hypostases* rather than of the forms.[48] Origen was convinced that the soul can only know the Father through participation in the knowledge of the Father enjoyed by the Son as mediated by the Spirit.[49] In keeping with this outlook, he anticipated a future restoration of all things in which "those who have come to God on account of His Word which is with Him" so that being "found by the knowledge of the Father, they may all be His Son, as now no one but the Son knows the Father."[50] This journey begins with participation in the Spirit, moves to participation in the Son, and climaxes in participation in the Father.[51]

The Cappadocian Philosophical-Theological Orthodoxy

Two crucial theological decisions forged in the crucible of the Arian controversy led to the actual formation of the doctrine of the Trinity. The first dispute brought to a head the debate regarding the exact nature of the relationship of Jesus to God that had been discussed at least since the second century. What triggered the settling of the issue in the form of church dogma was Arius's attempt to protect the absolute uniqueness and transcendence of God by temporalizing Origen's concept of the Father's generation (or begetting) of the Son. To this end, Arius postulated that the distinctions among the three persons are external to God, and hence that in the eternal divine nature God is one and not three.[52] At the First Ecumenical Council at Nicea in 325, the church unequivocally affirmed the full deity of Christ, a position summarized in the council's assertion that the Son is "begotten of the Father, of the substance of the Father, begotten not made, of one substance with the Father."[53] In this manner, the council set the christological foundation for the subsequent development of the doctrine of the Trinity.

47. For this judgment, see Widdicombe, *Fatherhood of God*, 44.
48. Robert M. Berchman, *From Philo to Origen: Middle Platonism in Transition* (Chico, CA: Scholars Press, 1984), 190–91.
49. See, for example, Origen, *Commentary on John* 2.10, in *ANF* 9:332–33.
50. Origen, *Commentary on John* 1.16.92, in *ANF* 9:305–6.
51. See, for example, Karen Jo Torjesen, "Hermeneutics and Soteriology in Origen's *Peri Archon*," *Studia Patristica* 21 (1989): 338.
52. Paul Tillich, *A History of Christian Thought: From Its Judaic and Hellenistic Origins to Existentialism*, ed. Carl Braaten (New York: Simon & Schuster, 1968), 61–79.
53. See "The Creed of Nicaea," in *Documents of the Christian Church*, 2nd ed., ed. Henry Bettenson (London: Oxford University Press, 1963), 24.

In his study of the road that led to Nicea, Bernard Lonergan concludes that what emerged as the Nicene theology marked an explicit movement away from Platonism and a return to the Christian categories of Creator and creature. At the same time, it entailed a definite movement away from the Platonic concept of agency and toward the use of the ontological category of substance. He writes that Nicene dogma "marks a transition from things as related to us to things as they are in themselves, from the relational concepts of God as supreme agent . . . to an ontological conception of the divine substance itself."[54] He then adds, "To the theological question, how God was to be conceived, an answer was given that set aside the sublime Platonic Ideas, reaffirmed the omnipotent Creator and went beyond the notion of God as agent to think of him in terms of the substance that causes all substances, the being that is for all beings the course of their being."[55]

Regardless of whether or not Lonergan has rightly characterized Nicea, the ascendancy of the language of consubstantiation did not end, but rather fueled the engagement of Trinitarian thought with the Platonic tradition. In fact, the Arian controversy heightened the connection, for the Arians drew part of their basis from an emergent reformulation of the reigning philosophical tradition, a reformulation known as Neoplatonism. As a consequence, the orthodox theologians found themselves looking to Neoplatonic thought for impulses by means of which to cast the doctrine of the Trinity.

This process unfolded in the context of a second theological debate, which emerged in the aftermath of Nicea and provided the corresponding pneumatological basis for the church's Trinitarianism. This dispute also had its roots in Arius's teaching. Just as Arius had asserted that the Son was the first creature of the Father, his followers theorized that the Holy Spirit was the first creature of the Son.[56] The dispute reached its climax in 381 when the Council of Constantinople sided against the pneumatological Arians and, in a statement popularly known as the Nicene Creed, announced that the Holy Spirit is to be "worshiped and glorified together with the Father and the Son."[57]

The way to Constantinople was paved by the attempt of the Cappadocian fathers—Basil, Gregory of Nyssa, and Gregory of Nazianzus—to postulate how the three persons constitute one God. John Zizioulas concludes that the Cappadocians mark a watershed in Christian Trinitarian theology and that they launched a revolution in Greek philosophical

---

54. Bernard J. F. Lonergan, *The Way to Nicea: The Dialectical Development of Trinitarian Theology*, trans. Conn O'Donovan (Philadelphia: Westminster, 1976), 136.

55. Ibid., 137.

56. Kelly, *Early Christian Doctrines*, 256.

57. See "The Constantinopolitan Creed," in *Creeds of the Churches: A Reader in Christian Doctrine from the Bible to the Present*, 3rd ed., ed. John H. Leith (Atlanta: John Knox, 1982), 33.

history, for they inaugurated an ontology of personhood that struck a balance between the one (i.e., nature) and the many (i.e., persons).[58] This balance is commonly denoted by the widely known formula *mia ousia, treis hypostateis*, which Joseph Lienhard points out "is, in fact, more a piece of modern academic shorthand than a quotation from the writings of the Cappadocians."[59] Indeed, according to Sarah Coakley, the term *prosopon* is more commonly found in Gregory of Nyssa's writings than is *hypostasis*.[60]

The Cappadocians developed their innovative proposal not only in response to Arianism but in the context of several debilitating heresies that were vying for the theological allegiance of Christians in the fourth century. One such heresy was Sabellianism. In response to the modalism of the Sabellians that portrayed the Trinitarian members as merely roles assumed by the one God, the Cappadocians asserted the full ontological integrity of the three persons of the Trinity. Zizioulas explains that to do so, they identified the Greek term *hypostasis* (which to this point had been a synonym of *ousia*) with *prosopon*, a concept with which *hypostasis* had enjoyed no previous connection in Greek philosophy. By connecting *hypostasis* with *prosopon*, Zizioulas concludes, the Cappadocians transformed "person" into the constitutive element of a being,[61] and the concept of Being itself became relational. As Zizioulas states it, "*To be* and *to be in relation* become identical."[62]

The Cappadocian innovation emerged likewise in the context of the orthodox response to a form of Arianism known as Eunomianism. In reflecting on the church's teaching about the generation of the Son and the procession of the Spirit, Eunomius raised the question as to the implications of the causative role of the Father. On the basis of his conclusion that being "ungenerate" or "unbegotten" must belong to the divine *ousia*, he surmised that the Son must be of a different *ousia* than the Father, in that sonship consists in being unbegotten. This meant, however, that the Son as well as the Spirit are ontologically subordinate to the Father. In arguing against this position, the orthodox thinkers distinguished between substance and person in God. They asserted that "unbegotten" refers to the personhood (*hypostasis*) of the Father and not to the divine substance (*ousia*). Furthermore, they declared that each of the three persons is defined

---

58. For a summary of his understanding of the Cappadocian contribution, see John Zizioulas, "The Doctrine of the Holy Trinity: The Significance of the Cappadocian Contribution," in *Trinitarian Theology Today*, ed. Christoph Schwöbel (Edinburgh: T. & T. Clark, 1995), 52–55.

59. Joseph T. Lienhard, "*Ousia* and *Hypostasis*: The Cappadocian Settlement and the Theology of 'One *Hypostasis*,'" in *The Trinity: An Interdisciplinary Symposium on the Trinity*, ed. Stephen T. Davis, Daniel Kendall and Gerald O'Collins (New York: Oxford University Press, 1999), 99.

60. Sarah Coakley, "'Persons' in the 'Social' Doctrine of the Trinity: A Critique of Current Analytic Discussion," in Davis et al., *Trinity*, 139.

61. John Zizioulas, "Doctrine of the Holy Trinity," 45–47; *Being as Communion: Studies in Personhood and the Church* (Crestwood, NY: St. Vladimir's Seminary Press, 1997), 27–39.

62. Zizioulas, *Being as Communion*, 88.

through a property (e.g., unbegottenness, begottenness, spiration) that is not shared with the other two. This understanding of the Trinity led the Cappadocians to the philosophical insight that a person is identified by means of his or her uniqueness rather than through a common "nature" or "substance."

The Cappadocian innovation emerged as well in response to tritheism. To avoid this error, the Cappadocians linked *ousia* with *physis*, which they understood as a general metaphysical category that can be applied to more than one person. This provided the Cappadocians with the philosophical basis for distinguishing between the one divine *ousia* and the three *hypostases*.[63]

To illustrate this distinction, they drew an analogy from the one human nature or substance that is shared by concrete human beings.[64] The Cappadocians were quick to point out the shortcomings of the analogy, however. The temporality of human existence in contrast to the eternality of God means that the interplay of the one and the many in humankind differs categorically from the interplay within the triune God. Humans share a human nature that preexists and is logically prior to them, whereas the divine nature does not precede the three Trinitarian persons. Rather than sharing a preexisting divine nature or being three instances of a "universal" (which would lead to tritheism), the three *hypostases* coincide with that nature. The three are to be differentiated from each other by means of causation. The Father is uncaused, the Son is caused by the Father, and the Spirit is caused by the Father through the Son. In this manner, the Cappadocians postulated that the one and the many coincide in God, for the three Trinitarian persons are united in such an unbreakable communion that none can be conceived apart from the others. This fundamental relationality among the Trinitarian persons undercut any suggestion that Father, Son, and Spirit are to be viewed as autonomous individuals.

We might summarize the Cappadocian proposal by saying that *hypostasis* designates personal uniqueness or "whoness," whereas *ousia* denotes shared essence or "whatness." The former term speaks of the Father, Son, and Spirit as three distinct, subsisting actors in the specificity of their particular existence. The latter, in contrast, focuses on the one nature or essence that is instantiated in each of them. But the Cappadocians were quick to add that the divine *ousia* does not exist except as concretely "enhypostasized" in each of the three *hypostases*.[65]

---

63. For examples of their use of these terms, see Gregory of Nazianzen, "Oration on Holy Baptism," *Oration* 40.41, in *Nicene and Post-Nicene Fathers*, 2nd series, ed. Philip Schaff and Henry Wace (1893; Peabody, MA: Hendrickson, 1994), 7:375; Gregory of Nazianzen, "Oration on the Holy Lights," *Oration* 39.12, in *NPNF*, 2nd series, 7:323.

64. See, for example, Basil, "To His Brother Gregory," Letter 38.2, in *NPNF*, 2nd series, 8:137. See also Gregory of Nazianzen, "On the Holy Spirit," *Oration* 30.19, in *NPNF*, 2nd series, 7:323.

65. For this insight, see Thomas Hopko, "Apophatic Theology and the Naming of God in Eastern Orthodox Tradition," in *Speaking the Christian God: The Holy Trinity and the Challenge of Radical Feminism*, ed. Alvin F. Kimel, Jr. (Grand Rapids: Eerdmans, 1992), 147.

This Cappadocian linguistic innovation cannot be understood apart from the Platonic overtones that lie behind it. Cyril Richardson points out the fundamental Platonic perspective that lies at the heart of their proposal: "Suffice it to say that the Cappadocians began their considerations of the threefold life of the Divine from the point of view of a plurality rooted in the unity of the divine essence. They looked at the matter Platonically: the one essence or *ousia* of the Godhead expressed itself in three *modes of being*, to which they applied the term *hypostaseis*."[66] Richardson then notes that the originator of this far-reaching use of *hypostasis* to distinguish items that share the same *ousia* was the Neoplatonic master, Plotinus.[67]

Trinitarian Theology and Neoplatonism

The Cappadocians provided leadership in devising the language for speaking about the triune God. To this end, they drew insights from the Neoplatonic thought of the day. Yet the arena in which Trinitarian theology and Neoplatonism initially came together most explicitly was not in the East but the West.

The Emergence of Neoplatonist Trinitarianism in Victorinus

In the Western church, Augustine emerged as the central theological architect. Yet he was not the first person to compose a systematic, philosophical exposition of the doctrine of the Trinity. This honor belongs to another theologian, Marius Victorinus (ca. 280–365),[68] whom Kelly lauds as "the most original and interesting figure . . . in the middle decades of the fourth century."[69] H. R. Swete characterizes Victorinus as "an African by birth, and a Roman by long residence in the capital."[70] Even Augustine pays tribute to Victorinus. In the *Confessions*, Augustine elevates him as one of three persons whose exemplary conversions were instrumental in his own journey to Christianity.[71] Augustine's description, which he reports to have received from Simplicianus, who claimed to have known Victorinus intimately at Rome, depicts him as a highly regarded teacher of rhetoric who became a Christian late in life and as a consequence lost his position.

After his conversion, Victorinus directed his literary efforts to the composition of theological and exegetical works. Above all, he sought to defend orthodox Trinitarianism against Neo-Arian ideas. This is evident in a series of treatises on the topic, the longest of which, *Against Arius*, comprises four

66. Cyril C. Richardson, "The Enigma of the Trinity," in *A Companion to the Study of St. Augustine*, ed. Roy W. Battenhouse (1955; repr., Grand Rapids: Baker, 1979), 237.

67. Ibid., 238.

68. Paul Henry, "The *Adversus Arium* of Marius Victorinus, the First Systematic Exposition of the Doctrine of the Trinity," *Journal of Theological Studies*, n.s. 1 (1950): 42–55.

69. Kelly, *Early Christian Doctrines*, 269–70.

70. H. R. Swete, *The Holy Spirit in the Ancient Church: A Study of Christian Teaching in the Age of the Fathers* (London: Macmillan, 1912), 305.

71. Augustine, *Confessions* 8.2.3–8.5.10, in *NPNF*, 1st series, 1:117–20.

books. In this work as well as in his three hymns to the Trinity, Victorinus seeks to respond to the Arian challenge by connecting the Christian conception of God as triune with the philosophical or ontological categories that were central to the controversy of his day. His overarching goal was that of defending the Nicene assertion that the Son (and subsequently the Holy Spirit) is of one substance, or consubstantial, with the Father.

Victorinus directed several of his writings against a thinker named Candidus, who some commentators now believe is a fictitious correspondent whose views Victorinus set up as a foil for his demolition of Neo-Arian thought.[72] Candidus defined God as "to be," and declared that inherent in the divine "to be" is the triad "to be," "to live," and "to understand." This idea, which was derived from Plato's *Sophist* 248e, was common currency among gnostic and Platonist philosophers during the early centuries of the Christian era.[73] Moreover, Candidus taught that God must be self-caused—that is, God must be the cause of his own "to be."[74] With this in view, Candidus proceeded to argue against the eternal generation of the Son on the basis of the postulate that insofar as generation involves movement and movement entails change, generation in God is impossible because there can be no change in God.[75] As a consequence, Candidus added, the Son must come from nothing, rather than from the being of the Father— that is, the Son must be the product of, or emerge as an effect of, the divine will. As "the first and original effect of God,"[76] the Son must likewise be the first substance, the one who is "made a substance and not from substance."[77]

In his response, Victorinus draws from Candidus's own basically Neoplatonic language to show the erroneous character of his denial of the Son's consubstantiality with the Father. He accepts his opponent's understanding of God as beyond existence, but then shows that the Son as the Existent cannot come from nothing. Rather, the Existent (*on*) arises from the God who is the Preexistent (*proon*), in whom the Existent is already present in potentiality.

This perspective facilitated Victorinus in asserting that far from being absent from God, motion is inherent in God, for God is not static. At the same time, not every movement involves change.[78] To indicate this, Vic-

---

72. See Mary T. Clark, introduction to *Theological Treatises on the Trinity*, by Marius Victorinus, trans. Mary T. Clark, Fathers of the Church: A New Translation (Washington, DC: Catholic University of America Press, 1978), 20.

73. For a summary of the gnostic idea of the divine Triple Power, see Curtis L. Hancock, "Negative Theology in Gnosticism and Neoplatonism," in *Neoplatonism and Gnosticism*, ed. Richard T. Wallis and Jay Bregman (Albany: State University of New York Press, 1992), 175.

74. *First Letter of Candidus* 3, in Victorinus, *Theological Treatises on the Trinity*, 49.

75. Ibid., 47–57; Victorinus, *Letter to Candidus* 30, in *Theological Treatises on the Trinity*, 81.

76. *First Letter of Candidus* 10, in Victorinus, *Theological Treatises on the Trinity*, 55.

77. *First Letter of Candidus* 11, in Victorinus, *Theological Treatises on the Trinity*, 56.

78. Victorinus, *Letter to Candidus* 30, in *Theological Treatises on the Trinity*, 81; Marius Victorinus, *Against Arius* 1.43, in *Theological Treatises on the Trinity*, 160–61.

torinus exchanges the dyad Preexistent-Existent for the dyad *esse-agere*.
The Father is pure *esse*; as such the Father is not "to be something" but "to
be" itself.[79] At the same time, the "to be" of God, the divine *esse*, entails
within itself "to act," or the divine *agere* (which in turn involves a second
dyad: living-knowing). "To act," then, is the reality within "to be."

Lying behind this aspect of Victorinus's proposal is the idea found
among some Neoplatonic thinkers, especially those influenced by the
second-century philosopher Numenius,[80] of the two states of intelligence:
intelligence in repose and intelligence in motion.[81] Viewed from this perspective, "to act" is "to be" in manifestation, whereas "to be" is "to act" in
repose. God, in turn, is active self-creation, and this action is not added
to the divine potency, but is already implicit in it. Hence, the divine
agere—the Son—is inherent in God's *esse*; that is, the Son is hidden
already in the Father. The begetting of the Existent, in turn, is merely the
actualization and manifestation of what is already present in the divine
Preexistent. Or, putting the idea in Christian theological terms, the coming forth of the Son is the manifestation in action of, and the expression
of, the hidden Father. As Mary T. Clark states Victorinus's point, "The
Father is the Son in potentiality; the Son is the Father in act."[82] Seen in
this light, the Son is clearly consubstantial with the Father.

Drawing from Candidus's Platonic triad now read through the lens of
the dyads "to be"-"to act" and "to live"-"to know," Victorinus portrays
God as an active, self-creating reality who encompasses three dynamic
characteristics or three powers. Victorinus describes the three in various
ways, including *existentia*, *vita*, and *cognitio*, as well as *substantia*, *forma*,
and *notio*. The differentiation between *substantia* and *forma* that lies at the
heart of this second triad places Victorinus in the patristic tradition that
underscores the primacy of the Father in the Godhead. Moreover, he
thereby views the Father as the divine "to be," as unconditioned, unde-
termined, and without form,. In the Son, this indeterminate, infinite substance comes to be determined. In the Son, therefore, what is beyond
form, without form, or nonrevealed form, takes form.[83]

The nomenclature that is most central to Victorinus's proposal and
in a sense encapsulates the others is Candidus's triad of *esse* (being), *vivere*
(living), and *intelligere* (knowing).[84] Whereas Candidus attributed the
entire triad to the one God, Victorinus sees in it the makings of the doctrine of the Trinity. Although asserting that all three items in the triad
belong to all three members of the Trinity, Victorinus connects each item

79. See, for example, Victorinus, *Against Arius* 4.20, in *Theological Treatises on the Trinity*, 280–81.
80. For this connection, see Clark, introduction to *Theological Treatises on the Trinity*, 13.
81. For this conclusion, see Clark, introduction to *Theological Treatises on the Trinity*, 13.
82. Clark, introduction to *Theological Treatises on the Trinity*, 21.
83. Victorinus, *Against Arius* 4.19–20, in *Theological Treatises on the Trinity*, 280–83.
84. Victorinus, *Against Arius* 3.3, in *Theological Treatises on the Trinity*, 226–35.

to a corresponding subsistence of the one God. Thus, Victorinus's understanding of the triunity of God begins with the power of *esse*, which he identifies with the Father. Implicated in this *esse* is life-in-action, *vivere*, the living actuality that eternally manifests and declares the pure potency. Victorinus links this actuality to the Son. Finally, what goes out from the divine *esse* as *vivere* returns as *intelligere*, contemplative knowing, which Victorinus connects to the biblical language of wisdom and spirit and consequently to the Holy Spirit.

As this summary suggests, Victorinus conceives of God's self-creative activity as occurring by means of two complementary, albeit logically successive, movements: unfolding and refolding, or self-revelation and reunion. The unfolding involves the generation of the Son, whereas the refolding entails the unifying dynamic of the Spirit. Paul Henry offers the following helpful description of this aspect of Victorinus's Trinitarian proposal: "The Spirit unites the Father and Son by reversing the linear process of emanation by, so to say, pushing back the Son's Life into the Father's essential Rest and thus procuring Beatitude for the Godhead."[85] Kelly, in turn, summarizes Victorinus's perspective in this manner:

> He seems to envisage the being of God as in a continuous process of unfolding and refolding (cf. *status, progressio, regressus*). If the Son, as the form and image of the Godhead, reveals the unknowable, in the Spirit the same Godhead knows Itself, and so returns back to Itself. The Spirit is thus the link, or *copula*, between the Father and the Son, completing the perfect circle of the divine being.[86]

In a manner that prefigures Augustine's work, Victorinus finds in the human soul with its consubstantial triad of *esse, vivere, intelligere* the best creaturely analogy of the Trinity.[87] On the basis of this insight, Duncan Reid elevates Victorinus as "the first Christian thinker to derive a Trinitarian model *directly* from an analogy from creation," that is, "without the need for any reference to the biblical history of salvation."[88] In an especially illuminating passage, Victorinus summarizes the connection between the human soul and the triunity of God, with its attendant proof for the consubstantiality of the members of the Trinity:

> Our soul is "according to the image" of God and of the Lord Jesus Christ. If indeed Christ is life and *Logos*, he is image of God, image in which God the Father is seen, that is, in life one sees "to be." For this is the image, as was said. And if Christ is life, but "to live" is the

85. Henry, "*Adversus Arium* of Marius Victorinus," 45.

86. Kelly, *Early Christian Doctrines*, 271.

87. See, for example, Victorinus, *Against Arius* 1.32, 1.61–64, in *Theological Treatises on the Trinity*, 141–43, 188–93.

88. Duncan Reid, *Energies of the Spirit: Trinitarian Models in Eastern Orthodox and Western Theology* (Atlanta: Scholars Press, 1997), 12.

Logos, and if life itself is "to be," and "to be" is the Father, if again, life itself is "to understand." And this is the Holy Spirit, all these are three, in each one are the three, and the three are one and absolutely *homoousia*.

If then the soul as soul is at once "to be" of soul, "to live" and "to understand." If it is therefore three, the soul is the image of the image of the "Triad on High."[89]

Victorinus's Trinitarian proposal raises the question of the extent to which he was dependent on the tradition of Platonism, especially the Neoplatonic thought of his day. He is generally cited as instrumental in mediating Neoplatonism to Western theology. And Joseph Tixeront declares that Victorinus's efforts mark him as the precursor "not only of St. Augustine, but of the boldest schoolmen."[90] Some commentators, however, take the matter a step further. They deem the dependence of Victorinus's proposal on the Neoplatonism of Plotinus (whose work Victorinus translated into Latin) and on the thought of Plotinus's successors to be so complete that in their estimation his doctrine of the Trinity is little more than a restatement of the Neoplatonic triadic conception.

Etienne Gilson, to cite one especially critical example, insinuates that Victorinus went on "thinking as a Neoplatonist after becoming a Christian."[91] Gilson's conclusion is based on his assumption that Victorinus equates the Christian Trinity with the triad of Plotinus. After depicting Victorinus's conception of God as "a non-being who gives birth to being," Gilson connects it to Plotinus: "In the doctrine of Plotinus, the One begets the supreme Intelligence who, being the sum total of all intelligibility, is at the same time the first and supreme being. All we shall now have to say is that God the Father begets, through an ineffable generation, both being (*existentia*) and Intelligence (*vous*)." Gilson then offers a terse appraisal: "With due respect to the memory of a convert who was certainly doing his best, one must say that, theologically speaking, this was a pretty mess."[92] Fortman presents a similar reading of Victorinus's Trinitarian theology:

> Influenced by Neoplatonism (likely mediated through Porphyry), Victorinus speaks of the relationship between the Father and the Son in language that is similar to Plotinus's perspective on the connection between The One and *nous*. According to Victorinus, the Father is the absolute, unconditioned, transcendent, invisible, unknowable One who is prior to being. The Son, in turn, is the "form" through which the Father defines himself, enters into relations with the finite

89. Victorinus, *Against Arius*, 1.63, in *Theological Treatises on the Trinity*, 191–92.
90. Joseph Tixeront, *History of Dogmas*, 3 vols. (St. Louis: B. Herder, 1910–1916), 2:271.
91. Etienne Gilson, *Being and Some Philosophers*, 2nd ed. (Toronto: Pontifical Institute of Mediaeval Studies, 1952), 31.
92. Ibid., 32.

and becomes knowable, and the image by which the Father knows
himself.[93]

Such interpretations read Victorinus's Trinitarian proposal as little
more than a theological restatement of what is generally deemed to be the
standard Plotinian triad, together with the commonly understood manner in which Plotinus related the One to Being. Recent studies, however,
have determined that Plotinus's theory of the One is not quite so simple
as it was once believed to be. In fact, this theory contains at least two, if
not three, perspectives on the relationship of the One to Being. Sometimes Plotinus speaks of the One as radically transcending Being, sometimes as being within Being, and sometimes as paradoxically Being and
Non-Being.[94]

Even more consequential are those studies that have concluded that
Victorinus's relationship to Neoplatonism was more complicated than
had previously been assumed to be the case. That Victorinus drew from
Neoplatonic philosophical categories is, of course, not disputed. Yet commentators are increasingly unconvinced that Victorinus derived his philosophical perspective directly from Plotinus.[95] Nor did Victorinus absorb
the Neoplatonism of his day into his theology unchanged.[96] As Clark
notes, "Victorinus found nothing ready at hand within his philosophical
milieu that did not require some good, hard, creative interpretation on
his part."[97] Similarly, Matthias Baltes concludes from his study of the difficulties that emerge from Victorinus's transference of Neoplatonic ideas
to the doctrine of the Trinity, "These difficulties indicate that Marius Victorinus did not simply take over the Neoplatonic teaching that he used,
but that he adapted these teachings in accordance with his own intention
and thereby altered them."[98] Indeed, Victorinus's characterization of the
first member of the Christian Trinity, the Father, differs dramatically from
Plotinus's conception of the One as transcending all categories.[99]

Like others before him who attempted to bring Christian faith into
conversation with the tradition of Platonism, Victorinus sought above all
to be an orthodox Christian theologian. His interests did not lie in prov-

---

93. Fortman, *Triune God*, 135.

94. For an explication of and engagement with this phenomenon, see Eugene F. Bales, "Plotinus'
Theory of The One," in *The Structure of Being: A Neoplatonic Approach*, ed. R. Baine Harris (Albany:
State University of New York Press, 1982), 40–50.

95. For a short summary of the history of this interpretive development, see Clark, introduction
to *Theological Treatises on the Trinity*, 7–8.

96. For a helpful summary of the points at which Victorinus's Trinitarianism is at odds with Neoplatonic thought, see Matthias Baltes, *Marius Victorinus: Zur Philosophie in seinen theologischen
Schriften* (Munich: K. G. Saur, 2002), 107–15.

97. Clark, introduction to *Theological Treatises on the Trinity*, 18.

98. Baltes, *Marius Victorinus*, 115.

99. For a helpful synopsis of Plotinus's conception of the One, see Hancock, "Negative Theology in Gnosticism and Neoplatonism," 168–74.

ing himself to be a metaphysician in the tradition of Platonism. Henry aptly sums up the situation:

> Although his whole outlook is Plotinian, Victorinus has taken great liberties with the Neoplatonic *Weltanschauung*. His systematic theology is not merely a transposition of dogma into metaphysical concepts or conceptions crudely borrowed from a heathen philosophy; at best, such a procedure would have supplied him with an Arian or Semi-Arian doctrine. To remain orthodox as a theologian he was forced to achieve some degree of originality as a thinker.[100]

This revised appraisal is closely connected to a reevaluation of the precise Platonic triad that formed a basis for Victorinus's Trinitarianism.[101] Recent studies have brought to light the development in the tradition of Platonism triads that differed remarkably from the hierarchically ordered, "vertical" triad of Plotinus, which posited three conceptualities, sometimes termed hypostates—the One (which was seen to be beyond Being and Mind), the Nous (the Second One or Being One), and the Soul (the Third One or All One)—and viewed each successive One as dependent on its higher predecessor for the perfection or unity that it lacks.[102] The most important of these alternative triads for Christian theology was the "horizontal" triad that sought to explicate the inner economy of power by means of which the Nous constitutes itself and thereby becomes an epiphenomenon of its source, the One.

In devising his Trinitarian response to the Arians of his day, Victorinus appears to have been drawing from this "noetic" triad, which had been articulated by Neoplatonists such as Porphyry and Iamblichus, recasting it in accordance with his commitment to Christian orthodoxy. Indeed, it seems to be this triad that he deems to be the pathway to overcoming the error of Arianism. In fact, the problem with the Arian proposal was its rigorous imposition of the vertical triad to the Christian conception of God.[103] What led Victorinus (and subsequently other Latin theologians) to adapt Neoplatonism in his deliberations regarding the triunity of God, therefore, was not so much the question of the relationship of Plotinus's One to Nous (that is, of the ultimate One to the Being One). His immediate concern was not

---

100. Henry, "*Adversus Arium* of Marius Victorinus," 48.

101. For a helpful delineation of this, see Peter Manchester, "The Noetic Triad in Plotinus, Marius Victorinus, and Augustine," in Wallis and Bregman, *Neoplatonism and Gnosticism*, 207–22.

102. Whether Plotinus considered the One to be a hypostasis is debatable. For an argument favoring connecting this term with the One, see John P. Anton, "Some Logical Aspects of the Concept of Hypostasis in Plotinus," in Harris, *Structure of Being*, 24–33. In his reply to Anton, Deck maintains that "hypostasis" can properly be predicated only of the Nous. He claims that the Soul, in contrast, is "the inferior hypostasis" and thus "less-than-a-hypostasis." The One, in turn, "is above hypostasis and is best described, when the word 'hypostasis' is used at all, as quasi-hypostasis." John N. Deck, "The One, or God, Is Not Properly Hypostasis: A Reply to Professor Anton," in Harris, *Structure of Being*, 39.

103. For the basis of this observation, see Manchester, "Noetic Triad," 214.

with the question of whether some absolute Godhead stands beyond the divine Trinitarian life of Father, Son, and Spirit. Rather, he was concerned about what Peter Manchester calls "mediation within the structure of self-constitution."[104] In short, Victorinus appears to have discovered in the horizontal triad of the self-constituting of the Neoplatonic *Nous* a way of articulating the Christian doctrine of God in a manner that could beat the Neo-Arians at their own Neoplatonic-inspired philosophical game.

The Ascendency of Trinitarian Theology

In 389, Augustine's friend Nebridius inquired as to how it is possible, given the fact that the three members of the Trinity engage in all of their activities as a unity, that the Son alone was incarnated. This question arose out of the development of Nicene theology, which by the 380s had come to conceive of the unity among the three Trinitarian members in terms of the idea that any action of any one of the three is an action of the three inseparably.[105] Initially, Augustine sketched out a preliminary response in the form of a short letter (*Epistle 11*) addressed to his friendly inquirer, which set the tone for his understanding of the doctrine of the Trinity. A decade later, he took up the challenge of presenting a full-blown treatment of the Trinity, which eventually took the form of his famous treatise *De Trinitate* (*On the Trinity*). Near the end of his life, Augustine returned one final time to this central topic of the faith, as he found himself confronted directly by the inroads of Arianism.[106]

Cyril Richardson articulates the consensus of historians, when he lauds *De Trinitate* as "one of the ablest presentations of the doctrine in Christian literature."[107] Kelly takes the matter a step further. He declares that this volume stands as the "mature and final expression" of the doctrine of the Trinity in the Western tradition.[108]

The main lines of Augustine's influential work are well-known. The fifteen books of *De Trinitate* are generally seen as constituting two major parts. The first seven books establish the doctrine of the Trinity on the basis of Scripture, together with the philosophical conceptuality of substance and relation involved in his proposal. Books 8–15 move from the assumption that humans are created in the divine image, understood as the image of the triune God, and as a consequence that the human person in some manner discloses the Trinity. His attempts to determine what

---

104. Manchester, "Noetic Triad," 214.

105. For this characterization, see Michel Rene Barnes, "Rereading Augustine's Theology of the Trinity," in Davis et al., *Trinity*, 156.

106. For a helpful treatment of this aspect of Augustine's work on the Trinity, see William A. Sumruld, *Augustine and the Arians: The Bishop of Hippo's Encounters with Ulfilan Arianism* (Selinsgrove, PA: Susquehanna University Press; London: Associated University Presses, 1994).

107. Richardson, "Enigma of the Trinity," 235.

108. Kelly, *Early Christian Doctrines*, 271.

aspect of the human person reveals the divine triunity leads Augustine to the human mind or, more specifically, to the mind actively engaging in the task of knowing. What follows in his literary masterpiece is an investigation of what the image of the triune God in the human mind reveals of God's inner life, together with a presentation of his understanding of the human vocation as imaging the Trinity.[109]

The second part of *De Trinitate* is mainly devoted to Augustine's highly controversial analogies of the Trinity. Because humans are created in the image of God, he declares, the human person displays "vestiges" of the Trinity and hence reflects God's triunity.[110] Augustine offers a series of these analogies, based on humans as the *imago Dei*. He proceeds by means of an ascent from the realm of the senses to the mind's contemplation of eternal realities, in which process the traces of the Trinity become steadily clearer.[111] These analogies emerge as the result of his desire to find ways to understand what is already believed, in accordance with his methodological dictum that theology is faith seeking understanding. To this end, he sought examples of how an absolute unity could nevertheless entail real distinctions in which the first begets the second and the third unites the other two.

Augustine finds the best traces of the Trinity in the human mind, which he believes provides him with a series of theological analogies. The first of these is the mind knowing and loving itself. Actually the basis for this triad lies in book 8, in which Augustine introduces love into the discussion in keeping with the biblical teaching that God is love. This biblical idea leads Augustine to consider the mind's love of itself. At first glance, this phenomenon appears to be a dyad: the mind and its love for itself. Its triadic character emerges, however, when we remember that the mind cannot love itself without knowing itself. With this insight in view, Augustine concludes, "And so there is a kind of image of the Trinity in the mind itself, and the knowledge of it, which is its offspring and its word concerning itself, and love as a third, and these three are one and one substance."[112]

Yet the analogy that Augustine found most useful, and consequently the one that became most influential in later Western theology, was the triad, developed in book 10, consisting of *memoria, intelligentia*, and *voluntas*, or the mind (memory or being), its self-understanding, and its self-love. From this triad, Augustine derived the highest vestige of the Trinity: the mind remembering, understanding, and loving God.[113] This move is

109. For this division, see Manchester, "Noetic Triad," 219; Mary T. Clark, "De Trinitate," in *The Cambridge Companion to Augustine*, ed. Eleonore Stump and Norman Kretzmann (Cambridge: Cambridge University Press, 2001), 92.

110. Richardson, "Enigma of the Trinity," 248–55.

111. See, for example, Augustine's statements regarding this way of proceeding in *On the Trinity* 15.3.4–5, in *NPNF*, 1st series, 3:200–202.

112. Augustine, *On the Trinity* 9.12.18, in *NPNF*, 1st series, 3:133.

113. Augustine, *On the Trinity* 14.12.15, in *NPNF*, 1st series, 3:191.

predicated on the assertion that only in loving God does the mind rightly love itself.[114]

The far-reaching significance and lasting influence of Augustine's articulation of the doctrine is, of course, beyond question. Less assured, however, is any consensus regarding the particular source of his innovative perspective on this central Christian doctrine and especially of the triadic conception that informed it. The standard view looks to Neoplatonism and to the Plotinian triad. Some historians even go so far as to claim that Augustine's conversion was actually to this philosophical tradition rather than to Christianity. Recently several scholars, most notably Michel Rene Barnes, have rejected the standard view and concluded instead that the basis for Augustine's Trinitarianism lay within the Nicene theology of the late fourth century.[115] Although both approaches to Augustine's work can claim a degree of historical merit, it seems that the question cannot be answered definitively. Barnes concludes, "Augustine, of course, has a *triadic* analysis of being—which is unlike Hilary of Poitiers and Gregory of Nyssa, but like Marius Victorinus. We cannot, however, say *where* that triadic analysis is coming from or what philosophical influence it represents."[116]

As Barnes's observation suggests, the closest parallel to Augustine's Trinitarianism lies in the work of Marius Victorinus. In his *Confessions* Augustine acknowledges his spiritual indebtedness to his predecessor. Moreover, his writings give indication that he viewed Victorinus not merely as the translator of Plotinus and Porphyry but also as a theologian in his own right. Despite his willingness to suggest an intellectual acquaintance with the work of his predecessor, Augustine never cites Victorinus as the source of his own Trinitarian proposal. Nor does he engage directly with Victorinus's analysis of the Neoplatonic noetic triad. Yet in several respects, Victorinus anticipated, and even paved the way for, Augustine's influential proposal.

Victorinus anticipated Augustine insofar as he inaugurated a movement away from a strictly "economic" exposition of the doctrine of the Trinity. While not abandoning a Trinitarianism that took seriously the actions of the one God in three persons in salvation, both Victorinus and Augustine were also concerned to speak about the relations within the divine dynamic.

Significant in this regard is Victorinus's focus on the one divine substance. In response to Candidus's basically Neoplatonic conception of the One, which led the Neo-Arian to conclude that the Father is not a substance but that the Son is the first substance, Victorinus forthrightly

114. For this observation, see Richardson, "Enigma of the Trinity," 253.
115. For a helpful delineation of this perspective, see Barnes, "Rereading Augustine on the Trinity," 145–76.
116. Barnes, "Rereading Augustine on the Trinity," 159.

attributed substance to the Father. And by presenting it as a substance that is shared with the Son as well as with the Spirit, Victorinus set forth the idea that there is only one divine substance. He then concluded that insofar as each of the three Trinitarian members is identical with the one substance, each possesses all of the divine attributes, including the attributes that belong properly to the other two Trinitarian members. Moreover, although Victorinus began his Trinitarian reflections with the divine *esse*, which he linked to the Father, he cast the doctrine of the Trinity as the self-creating of the one divine substance.

Like Victorinus, Augustine was interested in affirming the faith of Nicea in the context of the theological challenges to it. In keeping with this goal, he, again like Victorinus, set forth as his starting point the divine unity. Yet Augustine's beginning point lay in the traditional Nicene manner of conceiving of this unity, namely, as the inseparable activity of the three Trinitarian members. Augustine's goal was that of developing in a thoroughgoing manner the then-current theological belief that the external operations of the Trinitarian persons are the work of the one God, which belief Augustine deemed to be part of the received catholic faith.[117] In fact, the idea of the common activity of the three became the Trinitarian axis around which Augustine structured his theology, to which ought to be added the christological axis consisting of the Son as the revealer of God the Trinity.[118] This is evident, for example, in his contention that the Creator is the Trinity, in contrast to the tendency to identify the act of creation with the Father, which is reflected in the inclusion of the doctrine of creation in the article on the Father in the Apostles' Creed. The fact that the three persons share in the work of the one God indicates that they are in fact one substance (or essence or nature, to cite Augustine's preferable designations). Moreover, Augustine concluded that each of the three members of the Trinity possesses the divine essence entirely, yet in a particular manner that is proper to that Trinitarian member. It is in this sense that we might say that Augustine started with the unity of the divine substance and then moved to the triunity of the three persons. Moreover, this particular manner in which Augustine appropriated the Nicene theology of his day marks a significant manner in which he departed from Victorinus, who continued in the older tradition that looked to the Father as the source of deity and hence as the ultimate ground of the Trinitarian life.

Victorinus also anticipated Augustine's turn to the soul to discover vestiges of the Trinity. Some historians go so far as to claim that Augustine was directly influenced by Victorinus at this point. Henry, for example, concludes regarding this aspect of his thought that "Augustine is not the *commencement absolu* he is said to be, although his originality remains very

---

117. Augustine, *On the Trinity* 1.4.7 in *NPNF*, 1st series, 3:20.
118. For this insight, see Barnes, "Rereading Augustine on the Trinity," 168 n. 38.

great."[119] Peter Manchester, in contrast, avers that Augustine's triad of *memoria, intelligentia,* and *voluntas* is not an adaptation of the proposal of any particular Platonist thinker but emerged "from a direct intentional analysis of his own noetic experience."[120] Nevertheless, even Manchester finds this aspect of Victorinus's thought of far-reaching significance for Augustine's own work: "Where he does respond, and even dramatically build upon an opening in Victorinus, is in the thesis that human noetic life is an *image* of the divine noetic triad, and therefore offers *a via interior* for the argument to God as trinity."[121] Manchester then concludes, "It was not the content of his noetic analysis that Augustine took from Victorinus, but instead the sheer invitation to explore such an analysis as an image of the divine trinity."[122]

Regardless of who should be credited as its progenitor, the shift to the so-called psychological model of the Trinity that Augustine placed at the heart of his Trinitarian proposal was monumental. Earlier theologians drew from the biblical declaration that Christ is the primary image of God the idea that participation in the Logos is the central manner through which humans come to be in the divine image. Augustine's innovation was to postulate that the divine image entails the image of the Trinity.[123] In keeping with this insight, he suggested that the beatific vision in eternity will entail a gazing upon the entire Trinity,[124] in contrast to the earlier patristic postulate that this blessing will involve our participation in the vision of the Father enjoyed by the Son.

These considerations lead to the most significant manner in which Victorinus anticipated Augustine. Victorinus illustrated for his successors how Christian theology could appropriate Neoplatonism without becoming in the process nothing more than a baptized version of the reigning spiritual philosophy of the day. Henry puts it well when he concludes that Victorinus

> showed Augustine that Christianity could express itself "in terms of modern thought," and perhaps had to, if it was to remain orthodox, but only on one condition: that the philosophical categories adopted by theology were not to be servile reproductions of the prevailing "mode," but the outcome of deep, personal, and sometimes revolutionary re-thinking—the only way in which they could be rendered suitable for the expression of transcendent truth.[125]

119. Henry, "*Aversus Arium* of Marius Victorinus," 53–54.
120. Manchester, "Noetic Triad," 217.
121. Ibid.
122. Ibid., 218.
123. For an exposition of the innovative character of this theological development, see John Edward Sullivan, *The Image of God: The Doctrine of St. Augustine and Its Influence* (Dubuque, IA: Priory Press, 1963), ix.
124. See, for example, Augustine, *On the Trinity* 14.19.25, in *NPNF*, 1st series, 3:197.
125. Henry, "*Adversus Arium* of Marius Victorinus," 54–55.

Like Victorinus, in his response to Arianism, Augustine drew from the philosophical categories of his Platonist predecessors and contemporaries, even if his overarching perspective was that of an orthodox (i.e., Nicene) theologian as Barnes has pointed out. For example, he appealed to the concept of relation as set forth by Plotinus and Porphyry to overcome a cunning dilemma posed by the Arians, who claimed that any distinctions in the Godhead must either be classified under the category of accident (which was impossible in that nothing in God could be accidental) or of substance (which meant that the three Trinitarian members constituted three substances). Augustine averred that Father, Son, and Spirit are relations in the sense that each is who he is in relation to one or both of the others. This use of the category of relation opened the way for Augustine to conclude that the Spirit is the consubstantial bond, the mutual love, uniting Father and Son. On the basis of his reading of Scripture, Augustine postulated that the Spirit is equally the Spirit of both the Father and the Son. Insofar as the Spirit is related to both in the same manner, in relation to the Spirit the Father and the Son form one principle or a single source.[126]

Above all, however, the manner in which Augustine formed his triadic analysis of being, a concern that paralleled the interests of the Neoplatonic philosophers, is of far-reaching significance for the saga of the triune name. Contrary to the prevailing view, his triad of *memoria, intelligentia,* and *voluntas* should not be understood primarily as a psychological model of the Trinity. If anything, the triadic analysis of Being that Augustine developed in his attempts to advance the Nicene theology of his day is a noetic triad. And as such, it is closely akin to the adaptation to Christian Trinitarian theology of the horizontal Neoplatonic triad pioneered by Victorinus.[127] Understood in this manner, Augustine's triune God subsists on the level of the Plotinian second hypostasis, and the Trinity as he conceived it takes on the structure of the triad *on, nous, zoe.*

Under this theo-ontological impulse, in turn, the architects of the metaphysics of the Western tradition—whether or not they understood Augustine properly—came to view God as the *summum ens* (the highest being) and as a spiritual substance understood as mindlike being. Manchester provides an insightful summary of the far-reaching ontological implication of Augustine's innovation in Trinitarian thought:

> The effect of Augustine's original application of the noetic triad to the doctrine of the trinity was to claim the trinity for an emphatically kataphatic theology, a theology of "horizontal" self-constitution on the level of Nous. This theology not only broke with the old efforts to model the trinity in the vertical hypostatic series of Plotinus, but

---

126. See, for example, Augustine, *On the Trinity* 5.14.15, 15.17.29, in *NPNF,* 1st series 3:95, 216.
127. For this perspective, see Manchester, "Noetic Triad," 219.

dissolved the hypernoetic and hyperontic One entirely into the mystery of noetic or spiritual freedom. To the Plotinian intuition that even in the perfection of its unity the freedom was derived, not aboriginal, metaphysical trinitarianism would counterpose the "causa sui."[128]

Viewed from this perspective, Gilson is surely on the right track when he concludes that Augustine the Christian thinker broke with the Neoplatonism of his day, even if he was influenced by that Neoplatonism. Gilson writes, "What makes the greatness of St. Augustine in the history of Christian philosophy is that, deeply imbued with Neoplatonism as he was, he yet never made the mistake of devaluating being, not even in order to extol the One."[129]

The Eastern Orthodox Trinitarian Alternative

Augustine's use of the noetic triad as a means for understanding the triunity of God set the stage for the Trinitarian theologizing prominent among Western theologians.[130] It also sparked, however, a heated controversy between the Eastern and Western churches. In *De Trinitate*, Augustine went beyond the statement about the Holy Spirit that had been included in the creed devised at Constantinople. Although the ecumenical creed affirmed that the Spirit is to be worshiped and glorified together with the Father and the Son, it explicitly linked the procession of the Spirit only with the Father.[131] Augustine, in contrast, taught that the Holy Spirit proceeds from the Father and the Son.[132] Many historians cite Augustine's *filioque* Trinitarianism as the central theological issue that eventually led to the Great Schism. As important as the *filioque* controversy proved to be in the post-Augustinian era, it was actually an outworking of a deeper issue, namely, a difference in general approach to the doctrine of the Trinity. This difference, in turn, has continued to divide Eastern Orthodox and Western theologies even into the present.

Both traditions took up the task of making sense out of the biblical experience of the God who is revealed and yet hidden, active in the world yet complete within the divine being. In responding to this challenge, however, Greek and Latin theologians worked out two basic but divergent ways of speaking about the connection between God as hidden and God as revealed. Eastern Orthodox thinkers tended to solve the problem by differentiating God's eternal being from God's activity, leading to the doctrine of the energies. Thinkers in the West, in contrast, generally saw God's activity and being as identical, and as a consequence developed their theological proposals on

---

128. Manchester, "Noetic Triad," 220.
129. Gilson, *Being and Some Philosophers*, 31.
130. Fortman, *Triune God*, 141.
131. See Leith, *Creeds of the Churches*, 28–33.
132. The logic of Augustine's position is presented in Kelly, *Early Christian Doctrines*, 275.

the basis of the principle of identity.[133] In short, Western Trinitarianism emerged as the outworking of an a priori methodological principle, whereas Eastern Orthodoxy has been characterized by the acceptance of a doctrine.

Lying behind these two perspectives are two divergent ways in which Eastern and Western thinkers drew from a common set of Greek philosophical concepts, the most important of which were *ousia* (essence), *dynamis* (power or potential), and *energia* (energy or efficacy). The identity principle of Western Trinitarianism was linked to a distinction, attributable to Aristotle, between the two latter terms.[134] Although each of these could be connected with the first word, leading to a distinction between essence as potential and essence as actual activity, Western theologians tended to focus on the latter. As a result, they came to equate essence with activity and concluded that God is *actus purus*.

The doctrine of the energies, which developed by means of a line of thought running from the Cappadocians through John of Damascus to Gregory Palamas, who is often cited as the first thinker to formulate it in a systematic manner,[135] emerged in part from an alternate configuration of these three Greek philosophical terms. Eastern theologians tended to equate *dynamis* and *energia* and to differentiate both from *ousia*. In keeping with this linguistic perspective, these thinkers posited a thoroughgoing distinction between the inner reality, being, or essence (*ousia*) of the triune God, or God *ad intra*, on the one hand, and God's names (*onomata*), attributes (*idiomata*), or energy (*energia*), or God *ad extra*, on the other.

The Eastern view was influenced as well by Plato's distinction between the sensible realm and the intelligible realm (i.e., the realm of the forms) and his tendency to locate essence (*ousia*) in the former. Plato suggested that the form of a particular essence or being, which is the source of the being of that particular thing, is located in the realm of the forms and hence that it lies "beyond the essence" (*epekeina tes ousias*).[136] This Platonic perspective found its way into the Eastern teaching that God is supraessential *in se* and, by extension, that the divine *ousia*, in distinction to the *energia*, denotes this supraessential, ineffable divine reality. Thomas Hopko explains the meaning of this seemingly paradoxical designation: "The term, *hyperousios* in Greek, indicates that the *essence* of God understood formally is *supraessential* when understood ontologically. It means that God's being, abstractly or schematically considered, is to be beyond all categories of being, nonbeing, and becoming when God's essence is considered in terms of its metaphysical content and reality."[137]

133. For this stark differentiation, see Reid, *Energies of the Spirit*, 121.

134. See, for example, Aristotle, *Metaphysics* 1048b; 1065b–1066a, trans. Richard Hope (New York: Columbia University Press, 1952), 188–90, 237–40.

135. Reid, *Energies of the Spirit*, 4.

136. For this observation, see Reid, *Energies of the Spirit*, 8.

137. Hopko, "Apophatic Theology and the Naming of God," 150.

The idea of God's essence as supraessential provided a way of speaking about the incomprehensibility of God, who in early patristic thought is viewed primarily as the Father, while acknowledging that this God is known in his actions and energies in the world, by means of which God reveals himself through his Son and his Spirit. The idea that God is incomprehensible yet in some sense knowable played a prominent role in the thought of many patristic thinkers. Gregory of Nyssa, for example, declares, "Now the divine nature, as it is in itself, according to its essence, transcends every act of comprehensive knowledge, and it cannot be approached or attained by our speculation. Men have never discovered a faculty to comprehend the incomprehensible; nor have we ever been able to devise an intellectual technique for grasping the inconceivable."[138] Gregory then developed a type of mystical theology in which God is known not in the divine incomprehensible reality, not in God's hidden supraessence which by its very nature cannot be known, but in the multiplicity of the divine energies. Moreover, Gregory finds this very process at work in the experiences of a variety of biblical heroes, including Moses, David, and Abraham. Regarding the latter, Gregory theorizes that the patriarch passed through all the reasoning about the divine attributes that is possible for human nature to attain, but after he purified his mind of all such concepts, he came to know the incomprehensible Godhead who completely transcends any knowable symbol.[139]

The idea that God is ineffable in the divine essence but indwells creation in the divine energies, and with it the acceptance of a nonnegotiable differentiation between the divine essence and energies, has become a central hallmark of Eastern Orthodox theology. As Reid aptly summarizes the situation, "The distinction between the essence and the energies, or in other words, between the inner being of God the trinity and this God's economic activities, is thus since the time of John of Damascus a constant, if not always strongly emphasized, feature of Eastern Orthodox theology."[140] Consequently, Eastern Orthodox thinkers are careful to avoid any tendency to equate *ousia* with *energia*. Equating the two, they argue, makes God either so closely connected to creation that the divine ineffability is lost or so transcendent as to eliminate the possibility of a relationship between God and creation that allows the latter to experience a real participation in the divine life. This care is often evident even in discussions of the working of the energies themselves. Thus, theologians tend to speak of our participation in the divine life as the outworking of the energy of divine grace that is imparted by, but is not identical to, the Holy Spirit. As Gregory Palamas explains, this grace "is properly called 'Spirit'

---

138. Gregory of Nyssa, *On the Beatitudes*, Homily 6, in *From Glory to Glory: Texts from Gregory of Nyssa's Mystical Writing*, trans. Herbert Musurillo (New York: Charles Scribner's Sons, 1961), 98.
    139. Gregory of Nyssa, *Answer to Eunomius' Second Book*, in *NPNF*, 2nd series, 5:259.
    140. Reid, *Energies of the Spirit*, 21.

and 'divinity' . . . in-so-much as the deifying gift is never separate from the Spirit Who gives it. It is a light bestowed in mysterious illumination." Palamas then adds, "But the Holy Spirit transcends the deifying life which is in Him and proceeds from Him, for it is its own natural energy, which is akin to Him, even if not exactly so."[141]

The Eastern understanding of the doctrine of the Trinity is closely connected to the doctrine of the energies, with its attendant distinction between the divine essence and energies. The patristic Greek theologians theorized that the divine essence is "enhypostasized" in three distinct modes of existence, and these three are named Father, Son, and Holy Spirit.[142] Viewed from the perspective of the supraessential divine essence, the three are incomprehensible to human understanding. Yet through the divine energies, they are made known to humans for the sake of communion, contemplation, and imitation.[143] The distinction between the essence and the energies allowed the Eastern thinkers to conclude against their colleagues in the West that the inner being of God (the immanent Trinity) need not correspond exactly to the activities of God in the economy of salvation (the economic Trinity). More specifically, they averred that the sending of the Spirit by the Son in salvation does not necessitate that we affirm that the Spirit proceeds from the Son in the eternal dynamic of the triune life. In this way, their commitment to the doctrine of the energies precluded the Eastern theologians from joining their Western counterparts in seeing the necessity of adding the *filioque* to the creed.

The Trinity and Being

The motivating drive that launched the saga of Being was the quest for a better story than the story of capriciousness. But the saga of Being seems to have led to the demise of onto-theology and hence to the undoing of the story that ran from the ancient Greeks to the advent of the postmodern turn. This development raises the question as to whether there might be an alternative, theo-ontological story that can speak within the contemporary situation. Finding an answer to this question requires that we develop further the conception of Being that emerges from the "named" character of reality. But if the resultant story is to be truly theo-ontological, this development can only proceed from the perspective of, and in conversation with, what is deemed to be the primal phenomenon of God as named. In the quest for an alternative story, the chapter of the saga of the

141. Gregory Palamas, *The Triads* III.1.9, ed. John Meyendorff, trans. Nicholas Gendle (Mahwah, NJ: Paulist Press, 1983), 71.
142. Hopko, "Apophatic Theology and the Naming of God," 159.
143. See, for example, John of Damascus, *On the Orthodox Faith* 1.8, in *NPNF*, 2nd series, 9:6–11.

triune name that involves the delineation of Christian Trinitarian theology within the context of the engagement with Platonism becomes significant. To this theme we now turn our attention.

The Pathway to Trinitarian Being

Orthodox theologian John Meyendorff claims that historians of Christian thought and theologians of all confessional backgrounds are in agreement that the presentations of the Trinity offered by the Cappadocians and Augustine comprise "two distinct systems of thought."[144] Latin thinkers supposedly proceed from general nature to concrete person (and see the latter as a mode of the former) and in so doing accord priority to the divine unity, whereas Greek theologians move from person to nature (under the assumption that the latter is the content of the former) and thereby initially emphasize the plurality of divine persons. In recent years, some commentators have dared to question this standard historiography. David Bentley Hart, to cite one especially articulate detractor, demurs, "There is some minimal truth to this distinction . . . but it is more myth than reality, and has served little purpose in recent years but to feed Eastern polemic and Western insecurity, and to distort the tradition that both share."[145]

The preceding historical overview is in substantial agreement with Hart's conclusion. More consequential for the saga of the triune name, however, is a quite different parting of ways that developed within the Eastern and Western theological traditions. The Greek and Latin theologians shared the concern to speak meaningfully of the biblical experience of the God who is both hidden and revealed. Although this concern resulted in the emergence of the incomprehensibility of God as a basic theme in Christian thinking as a whole, it eventually led to two seemingly different ways of engaging in the theological task: the apophatic and the cataphatic. At first glance, the apophatic method appears to challenge any attempt to speak about a named God as providing the basis for a Christian theo-ontological engagement with the question of Being.

Theology and the Way of Negation

The apophatic approach, which is often denoted (somewhat inappropriately) "negative theology," arose in late antiquity and in the early Christian era.[146] At its core, apophatic theology is a philosophical as well as a

---

144. John Meyendorff, "The Holy Trinity in Palamite Theology," in *Trinitarian Theology East and West: St. Thomas Aquinas–St. Gregory Palamas*, by Michael A. Fahey and John Meyendorff (Brookline, MA: Holy Cross Orthodox Press, 1977), 25.

145. Hart, *Beauty of the Infinite*, 169–70. See also Michel Rene Barnes, "Augustine in Contemporary Trinitarian Theology," *Theological Studies* 56 (1995): 237–50.

146. For the inappropriateness of the label as designating the approach of Dionysius the Areopagite, see Jean-Luc Marion, "In the Name: How to Avoid Speaking of 'Negative Theology,'" trans.

theological stance. Moreover, it is generated by an intuition that runs counter to a central trajectory of classical Greek philosophy. The apophatic way rejects the dictum, dating to Parmenides, that declares that thought and Being are one. It replaces this assumption with the supposition that the divine reality cannot be known or defined because it is radically transcendent, and consequently that God is best approached by denials or by declaring what God is not.[147]

Ilse Bulhof and Laurens ten Kate note that negative theology reached its first high point "in the Neoplatonic philosophy and theology that held sway in the third century A.D. and for long afterward."[148] The theological motivation that lay at the heart of its reception in Christian theology—namely, the confession of the incomprehensibility of God—took on increasing importance in the fourth century during the conflict with Neo-Arianism. Viewed through the eyes of the Niceans, Neo-Arians such as Eunomius, by declaring that the human intellect could know the divine *ousia* through an understanding of the term "ungenerate,"[149] appeared to be claiming that humans could comprehend God in the manner that God comprehends himself. In response to this claim, orthodox theologians including Basil and Gregory of Nyssa averred that essences in general, but above all the essence of God, are ultimately unknowable.[150] In keeping with this perspective, Gregory, whose writings Bulhof and ten Kate describe as "an eloquent example of a Christian negative theology,"[151] suggested that the soul's pathway to God involves the realization that God is unutterably "Other." Only after both sense expressions and intellectual activity are stripped away, he advised, can the soul come close to God.

Although Gregory set the foundations for a "negative" approach to God, the step of actually distinguishing apophatic theology from its cataphatic alternative, and placing the latter in the overarching context of the former, is generally credited to Dionysius[152] (who actually advocated a three-element rather than a merely two-element theological method).[153] According to Dionysius, the cataphatic way entails the contemplation of God in God's relationship to creation and in this way views God as Good,

Jeffrey L. Kosky, in *God, the Gift, and Postmodernism*, ed. John D. Caputo and Michael J. Scanlon (Bloomington: Indiana University Press, 1999), 21.

147. For this perspective on negative theology, see Ilse N. Bulhof and Laurens ten Kate, "Echoes of an Embarrassment: Philosophical Perspectives on Negative Theology—An Introduction," in *Flight of the Gods: Philosophical Perspectives on Negative Theology*, ed. Ilse N. Bulhof and Laurens ten Kate (New York: Fordham University Press, 2000), 4–5.

148. Bulhof and ten Kate, "Echoes of an Embarrassment," 4.

149. Carabine, *The Unknown God: Negative Theology in the Platonic Tradition: Plato to Eriugena* (Louvain: Peeters; Grand Rapids: Eerdmans, 1995), 234–35.

150. See, for example, Gregory of Nyssa, *Against Eunomius* 3.6.250, in *NPNF*, 2nd series, 5:149.

151. Bulhof and ten Kate, "Echoes of an Embarrassment," 21.

152. See, for example, Roberta C. Bondi, "Apophatic Theology," in *The Westminster Dictionary of Christian Theology*, ed. Alan Richardson and John Bowden (Philadelphia: Westminster, 1983), 32.

153. On this aspect of his thought, see Jean-Luc Marion, "In the Name," 24–28.

Being, or Life. Yet names for God such as these, Dionysius added, are only provisional, for God lies beyond them all. Because God is incomprehensible, God is beyond being named. Because God is unnameable, God is also unknowable. And insofar as God is unknowable, God is indeterminate. For this reason, Dionysius concluded, the cataphatic approach can only serve as a prelude for the apophatic method, which approaches God by negating all such provisional names, that is, by asserting what God is not.

By speaking about God by declaring what God is not, the apophatic approach links God to nonbeing. It is for this reason that it is often designated "negative theology." Yet rather than being simply "negative," apophatic theology follows a particular type of negative method. Its goal is not merely negation, but a kind of double negation, in which negation serves to aid the mind in the task of transcending the normal limits of human understanding so that it might reach the knowledge of the God who stands beyond all descriptive affirmations or negations. Hence, Deirdre Carabine observes, "We may understand apophatic theology to begin with the assertion that God is unknowable to the human mind and that one must proceed by means of negations, ultimately, even to the negation of the negations in order to attain to some 'positive' knowledge of him."[154] This forms the methodological context for understanding the seemingly paradoxical or even self-contradictory expressions of apophatic theologians, such as the "negation of the negation" (*negatio negationis*), "unknowing knowing," and the "superessential essence." In reducing the cataphatic method to a moment within the apophatic way, negative theology becomes an all-encompassing stance toward knowledge itself. Mary-Jane Rubenstein indicates the breadth of this epistemological stance: "Negative theology removes 'knowledge' from its place of ontotheological privilege, so that presence is always inflected with absence, selfhood is only constituted through radical otherness, and knowing is only possible in and through unknowing."[155]

Under the influence of the Cappadocians and Dionysius, the apophatic approach became a hallmark of the Eastern Orthodox theological tradition. Yet the kind of negative theology that drank deeply from the Neoplatonic theological well was also influential in the West. Latin thinkers participated with their Greek counterparts in the debates as to whether the silence with which negative theology ends is an adequate portrayal of the divine self-disclosure in Jesus. Above all, proponents of mysticism in the West followed their cousins in Eastern Orthodoxy in responding affirmatively to the silence that emerges from the apophatic way.

Despite the manner in which mysticism welcomed negative theology, the prevailing mood in the West has been to greet this idea with suspicion

---

154. Carabine, *Unknown God*, 9.
155. Mary-Jane Rubenstein, "Unknow Thyself: Apophaticism, Deconstruction, and Theology after Ontotheology," *Modern Theology* 19, no. 3 (July 2003): 393.

or even hostility. Apart from a few notable exceptions, the apophatic method—where it did manage to take hold—came to be confined within a larger framework dominated by the cataphatic approach, with its assumption that God is fullness of Being. Carabine explains that the apophatic assertion that God is most truly known through not-knowing renders this pathway less categorical than its cataphatic alternative, and as a result "in its understanding of the divine nature, it is more open to misinterpretation."[156] In the modern era, an even sharper critique arose, which eschews the apophatic approach because it allegedly opens the door to atheism. The twentieth-century Parisian philosopher Claude Bruaire (1932–1986),[157] to cite one especially articulate critic, voices this unequivocal conclusion: "It is therefore necessary to assign negative theology its official place, to give it its exact status, apart from the pious sentiments which cover with a sensible outer layer, with religious scraps, the unalterable absolute, sign of the Nothing: negative theology is the negation of all theology. Its truth is atheism."[158]

Many theologians would echo the suspicions voiced by Bruaire. Nevertheless, the theological concern that motivates negative theology has been deeply ingrained in Western thought, even if it is accorded a secondary place in the tradition. Augustine forms a lucid example of this. Augustine's theology, like that of Gregory of Nyssa, was formed before negative theology had made its definitive entrance into Christian theology through the influence of Dionysius. Moreover, Augustine nowhere develops a definitive method of affirmation and negation. Yet his predominantly cataphatic theological orientation is not devoid of a deep awareness of the common Christian acknowledgment of the divine ineffability.[159] The sensitivity that this understanding produced in Augustine is clearly evident in a powerful passage in *De doctrina christiana* in which he grapples with the ineffability of God:

> Have I spoken of God, or uttered His praise, in any worthy way? Nay, I feel that I have done nothing more than desire to speak; and if I have said anything, it is not what I desired to say. How do I know this, except from the fact that God is unspeakable? But what I have said, if it had been unspeakable, could not have been spoken. And so God is not even to be called "unspeakable," because to say even this is to speak of Him. Thus there arises a curious contradiction of words, because if the unspeakable is what cannot be spoken of, it is not unspeakable if it can be called unspeakable. And this opposition

156. Carabine, *Unknown God*, 9.

157. For an exploration of Bruaire's ontology of gift, see Antonio Lopez, "Gift, Spirit, and Being: God's Love in the Metaphysics of C. Bruaire" (PhD diss., Boston College, 2002).

158. Claude Bruaire, *Le droit de Dieu* (Paris, 1974), 21. For this translation, see Marion, "In the Name," 49 n. 8.

159. For a helpful engagement with this dimension of Augustine's thought, see Carabine, *Unknown God*, 272–77.

of words is rather to be avoided by silence than to be explained away by speech. And yet God, although nothing worthy of His greatness can be said of Him, has condescended to accept the worship of men's mouths, and has desired us through the medium of our own words to rejoice in His praise.[160]

Although Carabine perhaps goes too far in interpreting this awareness as entailing an actual apophatic strand in his theology, she is on the right track when she concludes, "Augustine's use of negative theology, although by no means systematic, achieves a certain balance in theological method, one which is not found again in the Western tradition until Aquinas's re-evaluation of the role of negative theology in the thirteenth century."[161]

As Carabine's mention of Aquinas indicates, despite his preference for the cataphatic way, the great medieval scholastic nevertheless couched his theological conclusions about God in the context of the fundamental acknowledgment that God is ultimately ineffable. Reminiscent of the apophatic tradition that was indebted to Neoplatonism, Aquinas declared that to claim that one is able to put God into words would be to over-estimate the power of human reason and to underestimate the divine transcendence.[162] Consequently, he concluded that theological language could never embody in words the fullness of the divine essence. As we noted in chapter 7, he stated the point clearly in his *Summa Theologica*: "In this life we cannot see the essence of God; but we know God from creatures as their principle, and also by way of excellence and remotion. In this way therefore He can be named by us from creatures, yet not so that the name which signifies Him expresses the divine essence in itself."[163] Earlier in the same work, Aquinas offered a statement that reflects a central characteristic of negative theology: "Having recognized that a certain thing exists, we have still to investigate the way in which it exists; that we may come to understand what it is, that exists. Now we cannot know what God is, but only what He is *not*."[164]

Despite these (and other) parallels, at one crucial point Aquinas offers a quite different perspective on the *via negativa*. He declares that the reason that theology falls short of encapsulating the divine is because of God's surpassing greatness. Jozef Wissink states the point well: "Thomas does not speak negatively about God because he speaks about an emptiness, but because he speaks of an overabundant *fullness*."[165] It was his concep-

160. Augustine, *On Christian Doctrine* 1.6, in *NPNF*, 1st series, 2:524.
161. Carabine, *Unknown God*, 277.
162. For this judgment, see Bulhop and ten Kate, "Echoes of an Embarrassment," 26–27.
163. Thomas Aquinas, *Summa Theologica* 1.13.1, trans. Fathers of the English Dominican Province, 2nd and rev. ed, 5 vols. (Allen, TX: Christian Classics, 1948), 1:60.
164. Aquinas, *Summa Theologica*, introduction to question 3 (1:14).
165. Jozef Wissink, "Two Forms of Negative Theology Explained Using Thomas Aquinas," in Bulhof and ten Kate, *Flight of the Gods*, 116.

tion of the surpassing fullness of God that led Aquinas ultimately to the *via eminentiae*.

The concerns that give rise to the apophatic way have repeatedly bubbled to the surface of Western thought. In recent decades, however, that "bubbling" has swelled to a discernable stream. The current revival of interest in negative theology (understood in its broader philosophical sense) has also been fostered by the questioning of the metaphysics of presence and the rejection of onto-theology that came to the fore at the climax of the saga of Being. Some thinkers who stand in this stream look to the deconstruction of modern ontology as the occasion for a reconstruction of metaphysics. At the end of her grueling 560-page *Philosophy of Being*, Oliva Blanchette, for example, concludes that reason can only give rise to a negative theology: "The only kind of theology that is possible at the end of metaphysics is a negative theology, because that does not claim to say anything about *what* God is as God but only what God *is not*, from the standpoint of created and finite being."[166] Blanchette then explains:

> In the face of the totally transcendent Summit of being affirmed at the end of metaphysics, then, the situation of reason remains totally paradoxical, as Kierkegaard would say. It must affirm that something *is* and that it cannot know *what* this something is, even if God appears in history. It cannot go beyond its affirmation that God is, even though it can still *ask what* God is without knowing how to answer that question except in a negative way.[167]

Other thinkers reject categorically any suggestion of a reconstruction of metaphysics in the manner that Blanchette proposes. In their review of this phenomenon, Bulhof and ten Kate view the present discontent with Enlightenment thinking and with the "self-emancipating human subject" as comprising a fourth stage in the history of negative theology in Western culture. They add, however, that this stage differs in one dramatic manner from its predecessors: "Resistance to reason's 'hubris' either cannot or will not be translated into the confirmation of (and devoted respect for) a Supra-Essence."[168]

The difference that sets the apophatic approach of the fourth stage apart from the kind of method that characterized its earlier embodiments sheds light on the debate over the validity of negative theology that the work of Jacques Derrida has sparked.[169] Derrida charges that, despite the denials of its practitioners, the apophatic approach persistently makes

---

166. Oliva Blanchette, *Philosophy of Being: A Reconstructive Essay in Metaphysics* (Washington, DC: Catholic University of America Press, 2003), 551.

167. Ibid., 553.

168. Bulhof and ten Kate, "Echoes of an Embarrassment," 12.

169. For a set of essays regarding this theme, see Harold Coward and Toby Foshay, eds., *Derrida and Negative Theology* (Albany: State University of New York Press, 1992).

affirmations about God—in particular the affirmation of God's existence—and in so doing continues to think of God in terms of presence. Consequently, Derrida concludes, negative theology has not freed itself from the metaphysics of presence.[170]

Although Derrida's critique is not without merit, contemporary proponents of negative theology generally look to this method as a way of undercutting onto-theology. Actually, the apophatic approach has always stood as a crucial reminder that God is not connected to Being in the manner that creatures (beings) are. In keeping with this perspective, negative theology has historically functioned primarily as a means of underscoring the limits of any natural theology, that is, of any theological method that claims to be able to draw names for God from creatures on the basis of a supposed connection between God and creatures. Yet several recent instantiations of the apophatic way give evidence to a more radical application and outcome of this approach. What began as the desire to protect God's ineffability, when pursued relentlessly, leads to the ironic conclusion that all we are left with is silence. In this manner, the apophatic way gives rise to a radical, complete silence born out of the conclusion that we must stop speaking not only about God but about Being as well. Were all negative theology to end here, then Bruaire's suspicion would be confirmed, that the apophatic way leads eventually and inevitably to radical atheism.

The apophatic way need not be understood, however, as leading to complete silence. Rather it can be seen as opening the way for a special kind of silence, the respectful silence that the ancient prophet enjoins: "The LORD is in his holy temple; let all the earth keep silence before him!" (Hab. 2:20; cf. Zeph. 1:7; Zech. 2:13). This silence comes when, similar to the experience of the ancient prophet, our attempts to understand the mysterious ways of a holy God give way to the hushed silence of reverential awe in the presence of the divine majesty.[171] This silence arises from an acknowledgment of a profound awareness of distinction, separation, or Otherness. Hence, the ancient Hebrew sage admonishes, "God is in heaven, and you upon earth; therefore, let your words be few" (Eccl. 5:2).

Such silence before the transcendent, mysterious, holy Other paves the way for a special kind of speaking, namely, the speaking of revelation. This speaking can come as the paradoxical silent speaking of creation of which the psalmist wrote: "The heavens are telling the glory of God; and the firmament proclaims his handiwork. Day to day pours forth speech, and

---

170. For a similar summary of Derrida's critique, see Marion, "In the Name," 22–23. The essay then encapsulates Marion's response to Derrida.

171. For similar depictions of this text, see O. Palmer Robertson, *The Books of Nahum, Habakkuk, and Zephaniah*, New International Commentary on the Old Testament (Grand Rapids: Eerdmans, 1990), 211; Francis I. Andersen, *Habakkuk: A New Translation with Introduction and Commentary*, Anchor Bible (New York: Doubleday, 2001), 256; J. J. M. Roberts, *Nahum, Habukkuk, and Zephaniah: A Commentary* (Louisville, KY: Westminster John Knox, 1991), 128.

night to night declares knowledge. There is no speech, nor are there words; their voice is not heard; yet their voice goes out through all the earth, and their words to the end of the world" (Ps. 19:1–4). Yet above all, Christian theology looks to Jesus Christ for the speaking of revelation. Augustine stated the point well when he declared, "The unknown one is no longer unknown; for he is known by us, our Lord Jesus Christ."[172]

In this respect, negative theology could be viewed as paralleling metaphysics. Blanchette brings this similarity to light when she notes at the end of *Philosophy of Being*, "Without crossing over into the proper realm of religion, which superseded philosophy, metaphysics might be understood as ending in what might [be] called a religious expectation," that is, "a revelation in being over and above what is known about being as being from the totality of finite beings."[173] Like metaphysics, then, apophatic theology is anticipatory. It clears the deck of all pretentious claims to know God by means of simple and simple-minded analogy from creatures. In so doing, it prepares the way for the in-breaking of divine revelation and with it to a revelational theo-ontology.

The God Who Is Other and the Triune Name

Negative theology stands as a reminder that no one possesses a warrant for any pretentious claim to know God fully or completely. Not even revelation dispels the divine incomprehensibility, for even in the divine self-disclosure, God remains the hidden God. At the same time, insofar as the hidden God is revealed in the divine self-disclosure, the apophatic way anticipates the revelation of the self-disclosing God and the advent of theo-ontology. More specifically, it anticipates the revelation of the self-naming God who both determines and discloses the divine name. Yet we must ask, What does God disclose about God's own self, in speaking in this silent revelatory manner? And what is the connection, if any, between the God who is revealed as the triune one—that is, who is named through the dynamic of the relationality among the three Trinitarian persons—and the hidden God whose incomprehensibility, unknowability, and unnameability apophatic theology seeks to preserve?

We have noted that Dionysius's attempt to make sense of the divine unknowability led him to posit a solitary God who is undifferentiated and unrelated, who transcends all differentiations and relationships. This God, Dionysius added, is manifested in the world by means of an aspect of the divine nature that is, as it were, turned toward creatures. According to C. E. Rolt's interpretation of Dionysius's view, this means that the names of the three Trinitarian members do not denote God in God's

---

172. Augustine, *On the Psalms* 98.2, in *NPNF*, 1st series, 8:481.
173. Blanchette, *Philosophy of Being*, 556.

328   The Saga of the Triune Name

undifferentiated and absolute transcendence, but in the divine manifestation. The Trinitarian names represent distinctions in God's eternal manifestation and not in God's ineffable self. Rolt observes that according to
Dionysius, "The absolute Godhead is the Super-Essence; the eternally
Manifested Godhead is the Trinity."[174] Rolt then explains:

> Thus while in the Undifferentiated Godhead the "Persons" of the
> Trinity ultimately transcend Themselves and point (as it were) to a
> region where They are merged, yet in that side of Its Nature which
> looks towards the universe They shine eternally forth and are the
> effulgence of those "Supernal Rays" through Which all light is given
> us, and whence all energy streams into the act of creation. For by
> Their interaction They circulate that Super-Essence Which Each of
> Them perfectly possesses, and so It passes forth from Them into a
> universe of Being.[175]

Rubenstein, in turn, confirms this interpretation of Dionysius. She writes,
"Insofar as *none* of the divine names names what it names, the 'Trinity!'
to whom Dionysius addresses his *Mystical Theology* does not circumscribe
the divine."[176]

In his desire to promote the attainment of a union with an all-
transcendent Unity, a perspective that is actually deeply indebted to a
Greek-oriented mysticism of unity, Dionysius concludes that the God who
is beyond all names transcends even the Trinitarian names. The trajectory
of Scripture, however, by means of its focus on the divine Other before
whom the world is admonished to remain silent, provides an alternative.[177]

According to Robert Sokolowski, Otherness lies at the heart of far-
reaching innovation that the Christian faith introduced into the world of
Greek philosophy, an innovation that he denotes as "the Christian difference." Sokolowski points out that in the context of the ancient Greek belief
that the divine was one part, albeit the highest part, of a single cosmos,[178]
the Christian faith postulated that a fundamental distinction separated the
Creator from "everything." Specifically, the Christian understanding asserts
that God is distinguished from creatures in a manner that is different from
the way in which creatures differ from each other. Any creature is different
from any other creature simply by not being the other creature, and consequently the "being" of a creature consists in part in its being "other" than

---

174. C. E. Rolt, introduction to *The Divine Names and The Mystical Theology*, by Dionysius the
Areopagite, trans. C. E. Rolt (London: SPCK, 1940), 8.

175. Ibid., 10.

176. Rubenstein, "Unknow Thyself," 403.

177. For this distinction, see Bert Blans, "Cloud of Unknowing: An Orientation in Negative Theology from Dionysius the Areopagite, Eckhart, and John of the Cross to Modernity," in Bulhof and
ten Kate, *Flight of the Gods*, 75.

178. Robert Sokolowski, *The God of Faith and Reason: Foundations of Christian Theology* (Notre
Dame, IN: University of Notre Dame Press, 1982), 12–20.

the other being from which it is distinguished.[179] This is not the case, however, with God. God's "being" is not determined by God being "other" than any other or all others, for God would be the same God even if the world that is other than God did not exist. Consequently, the distinction between God and creatures is unique in that this distinction is only present because of one of the parties of the distinction: God. The distinction only exists because God (and God alone) permits it to arise.[180] Philipp Wolf offers a somewhat similar conception when he declares, "God . . . extends beyond human differentiations . . . being the difference making a difference."[181]

The way of approaching God by looking to the Other indicative of Sokolowski's proposal finds a parallel in several currents of contemporary thought. Above all, it runs in a somewhat similar direction as recent philosophies of alteriority or exteriority,[182] such as those proposed by Franz Rosenzweig (1886–1929) and more recently by Emmanuel Levinas (1906–1995). The latter belongs to what Victor Kal calls "the large and broadly subdivided family of French 'diffe[']rence thinkers.'"[183] Kal offers a helpful description of diffe[']rence thinking:

> Diffe[']rence thinking says, in brief, that the human subject does not merely dominate and dispose of the world, or rule over itself; this subject must tolerate something else outside itself over which it has no say and which it cannot grasp. This "other" shatters the illusion of complete autonomy in which the subject possibly lives, and puts the subject in the relationship it has always already served. Diffe[']rence refers to the *difference* between this other and this relationship, on the one hand, and, on the other hand, being as it is presented readymade by us to be observed and manipulated in our quasi-autonomy.[184]

In seeking to delineate what went wrong with Western thinking that allowed horrors such as the Holocaust and the Second World War to occur, Levinas elevates the concept of the "other." In his estimation, Western thinkers failed to pay sufficient attention to the Other and hence to the ethical dimension of responsibility. Bert Blans offers a helpful characterization of this central theme in Levinas: "Thought is in principle

---

179. Ibid., 32.

180. Ibid., 33.

181. Philipp Wolf, "The Ontotheology of the Literary Aesthetic: Historical and Systematic Aspects," *Literature and Theology* 12, no. 3 (September 1998): 302.

182. This term is present in the subtitle of what is perhaps Levinas's most widely read volume: Emmanuel Levinas, *Totality and Infinity: An Essay on Exteriority*, trans. Alphonso Lingis (Pittsburgh: Duquesne University Press, 1969).

183. This is not to overlook the important differences that separate Levinas from Derrida. For a discussion of the relationship between the two thinkers, see Graham Ward, *Barth, Derrida, and the Language of Theology* (Cambridge: Cambridge University Press, 1995), 177–99.

184. Victor Kal, "Being Unable to Speak, Seen as a Period: Difference and Distance in Jean-Luc Marion," in Bulhof and ten Kate, *Flight of the Gods*, 145.

totalitarian and violent when it does not start with the other and does not think of responsibility."[185]

To address this deficiency, Levinas develops a philosophy of ethics that attempts to go beyond what he perceives to be the ethically neutral tradition of ontology. Ontology is suspect, because in its quest to establish the supremacy of knowing, a task which requires that otherness be reduced to sameness, it eradicates otherness.[186] Furthermore, the pursuit of knowledge reduces everything to knowledge, but because knowledge is incapable of determining worth, value, or purpose, it remains indifferent to the true humanity of the human. Richard Cohen points out that Levinas brought to light the fact that the object of knowledge is "'difference' not excellence." As a consequence, Cohen adds, "In defending ethics *ethically*, insisting on an excellence rather than yet another truth or untruth, Levinas surpasses the entire enterprise of philosophy hitherto conceived."[187]

Levinas's goal, in short, was that of "exceeding ontology toward ethics," to cite Didier Franck's cryptic description.[188] To this end, he engaged in an analysis of the idea of "face-to-face" relation with the Other, a perspective that he derived in part from the work of Rosenzweig and Martin Buber. Levinas acknowledges that although the Other may be "unknowable," it nevertheless calls into question and challenges the complacency of the self through desire, language, and the concern for justice.[189]

The contemporary focus on the Other carries within it the seed of an alternative to the "mysticism of the One" that has been such a central aspect of the apophatic tradition. It does so insofar as it brings into view another, equally powerful dimension of the apophatic way, namely, the acknowledgment that God is totally "Other" that has stood alongside the emphasis on the One at the center of negative theology since at least Gregory of Nyssa. The chief theological concern that gave rise to negative theology is the preservation of the radical transcendence of the transcendent One. In its postmodern, Levinasian form, this long-standing motivation comes to the fore in the attempt to eliminate the tyranny involved in every use of language in which another is named. Despite the differences that separate thinkers such as Levinas from their patristic forebears, in both the traditional Dionysian and the more recent postmodern varieties a similar concern emerges: the interest in the integrity of the Other.

185. Blans, "Cloud of Unknowing," 77.

186. For a similar understanding of Levinas's point, see Oliver Davies, *A Theology of Compassion: Metaphysics of Difference and the Renewal of Tradition* (Grand Rapids: Eerdmans, 2001), 129–30.

187. Richard A. Cohen, *Ethics, Exegesis, and Philosophy: Interpretation after Levinas* (Cambridge: Cambridge University Press, 2001), 5, 6.

188. Didier Franck, "The Body of Difference," in *The Face of the Other and the Face of God: Essays on the Philosophy of Emmanuel Levinas*, ed. Jeffrey Bloechl (New York: Fordham University Press, 2000), 16.

189. For a helpful summary of Levinas's thought, see Steven G. Smith, *The Argument to the Other: Reason beyond Reason in the Thought of Karl Barth and Emmanuel Levinas* (Chico, CA: Scholars Press, 1983), 53–100.

There remains, however, a deeper dimension of the Otherness of the divine reality that talk about being face-to-face with the Other and even language about God as Other to creation does not exhaust. As Sokolowski's thesis confirms, God as Other cannot be determined simply by God being other than any or all others. On the contrary, a central postulate of Christian theology is the acknowledgment that God would be the same even if the world did not exist as the other-than-God that it is. For this reason, the Otherness that is God must be present within the divine transcendence; it must be present even within whatever hiddenness of God lies beyond human comprehension. And precisely this radical or thoroughgoing acknowledgment of the presence of Otherness within the Transcendent lies at the heart of the Christian doctrine of the Trinity.

This acknowledgment opens the way for an understanding of God as the one in whom Otherness is eternally present, an Otherness that is, in turn, freely given in God's gracious revelation. Hence, it opens the way to the acknowledgment that while God remains always incomprehensible, there is no God "above" the unity-in-multiplicity or the multiplicity-in-unity disclosed in the revelational saga of the divine name. Furthermore, the divine Otherness means that absolute unity—Oneness apart from Otherness—need no longer be posited as the highest principle of reality. Rather, unity and multiplicity—Oneness and Otherness—demand equal emphasis. Yet these are not to be affirmed as two independent or competing principles, but as interconnected and reciprocally related, as Oneness-in-Otherness and Otherness-in-Oneness. Gregory of Nazianzus states the point well: "No sooner do I conceive of the One than I am illumined by the splendour of the Three; no sooner do I distinguish them than I am carried back to the One."[190]

The Character of Trinitarian Being

This acknowledgment of the presence of radical Otherness within the dynamic of the triune life leads us back to the insight that arose out of the historical survey that occupied us in the first half of this chapter. The final task of this chapter is to indicate how the theological appropriation of the horizontal triad in the third and fourth centuries provides a way of viewing the triune God as the self-positing or self-naming God, who is self-naming eternally and in relationship to humankind.

The Self-Naming God and the Noetic Trinity

Reading the story in light of the engagement of Christian theology with the Platonic tradition leads to the observation that Dionysius's apophatic method finds its philosophical analogue in a Neoplatonic vertical triad,

190. Gregory of Nazianzus, "Oration on Holy Baptism," *Oration* 40.41, in *NPNF*, 2nd series, 7:375.

which in the opinion of many historians was likely mediated to the Christian mystic by Proclus. In Dionysius's appropriation of this triad, the incomprehensibility of God is deemed to lie at the level of the Plotinian One. Insofar as Dionysius understood the Trinity to be the face of the incomprehensible God turned toward creation—that is, to be God in the divine manifestation—Dionysius's Trinity lies on the plane of the Nous and to this extent on the level of knowability.

We saw earlier in this chapter that Victorinus and Augustine altered the manner in which the Platonic vision was to be appropriated in the task of delineating the Christian conception of God as triune. For the Plotinian vertical triad, they substituted the horizontal triad of the Nous, which had been proposed by other voices in the Platonic philosophical tradition. In so doing, they not only set the Christian conception of God as Trinity on the level of the Nous, but they also brought the incomprehensibility of God onto this level, thereby eliminating the need to posit a realm of the One beyond the dynamic of the triadic Nous. The effect of this seemingly slight yet radical shift is to link the divine incomprehensibility with the one God who is the Trinity, rather than the God who lies beyond the Trinity and whose face is hidden because it is turned away from creation.

In effect, the change inaugurated by the two Latin theologians divides God's unknowability from the incomprehensibility of God. For Victorinus, the divine unknowability is focused on the Father, the unformed Preexistent, the pure "to be." But, Victorinus adds, it is precisely this unknowable Father who becomes known and knowable in the Son through the Spirit. In this manner, the dynamic of the Trinity, located as it is in the realm of the Platonic Nous, becomes the dynamic of the coming-to-be-known of the triune God.

Victorinus's proposal leads inevitably to the question of the "location" of this coming-to-be-known. His interest in refuting the Neo-Arians of his day determined that he would view this as an eternal dynamic within the life of the triune God apart from the world. The saga of the I AM that I charted in part 2 of this volume would lead us to couple Victorinus's response to the narrative of the divine self-naming in the history of God with creation. Yet as the emergence of the concept of eternality in that saga cautions, we dare not do so in a manner that divides the eternal and the temporal as if they were two separate, unrelated stories. Rather, the saga of the I AM as the narrative of the self-naming God is a window into—or should we say, an icon revealing—an eternal self-naming within the immanent dynamic of the triune life.

Contemporary narrative theory begins with the declaration that humans are storytellers. Not only do humans tell stories, however, humans are in fact "storied." Biblical revelation takes this insight into the theological realm as well. The Bible presents God not only as a storyteller but also as "storied." In the divine self-disclosure, God comes to the fore as the story of the divine name, the saga of the I AM. The Bible narrates the story of the I AM in the world. This story shows itself to be the story of an ongoing dynamic involving God, God's Son, and God's Spirit. Although the story of the divine name focuses on three central actors, each of whom is divine, the saga forms one story, for it is ultimately the story of the one God. For this reason, we can rightly speak of the biblical narrative of the divine name as a Trinitarian story. Moreover, the story is the narrative of the one God—the Father and the Son and the Spirit—in covenant with humankind and all creation.

The story of the divine self-naming is not merely a temporal narrative, a story that occurs in time. Rather, it is simultaneously an eternal story. It is eternal in that the temporal story is eschatologically caught up into an eternal reality. In this sense, it may be said to occur within the context of an eternal dynamic, the dynamic of the relationality of the eternal God who is the Father and the Son and the Holy Spirit, to cite the language from the baptismal formula.

The foregoing observation takes us back to the ontological implications of the concept of "name." In chapter 7, we noted that proper names are ontologically significant, because names are connected with existence. To cite again Frank Nuessel's observation, "A name is a *sine qua non* for existence. Without a name, no linguistic means of reference is possible."[191] Insofar as proper names are connected with personal existence, they carry ontological weight. They have ontological ramifications. In short, "to be" is connected to "bearing a name." And, by extension, so is the ontological category of Being.

At first glance, Nuessel's assertion appears to suggest that Being's connection to name bearing is based on the denotive function of names. In a sense, this is the case. Yet the fuller understanding of proper names developed in chapter 7 suggests that the relationship is more complex. Rather than remaining static, the task of name bearing is a dynamic action. This ongoing dynamic process often finds its genesis in a single act of naming and hence begins with a simple act of denotation. Yet name bearing rarely remains at the purely denotive level. Rather, the relationship between the name bearer and the naming community adds connotations to the denotation bound up with the name. And this relationship has a history, which lends a narrative character to the act of name bearing. In this manner, the denotive function of a proper name comes to be intertwined with the name's connotative power. In this sense, we can say with Justin Kaplan, "Names penetrate the core of our being and are a form of poetry, storytelling, magic, and compressed history."[192]

191. Frank H. Nuessel, *The Study of Names: A Guide to the Principles and Topics* (Westport, CT: Greenwood, 1992), 2.
192. Justin Kaplan and Anne Bernays, *The Language of Names* (New York: Simon & Schuster, 1997), 13.

Our study of the concept of "name" yielded the realization that the phenomenon is communal. A proper name is connected to the community of those who stand in some relationship to the person so named, whether that relationship be primarily that of being "producers" or "consumers." Names, we must now add, are likewise eschatological. Insofar as a name moves from simple denotation to connotation, the act of naming becomes a process. Moreover, the naming process always incorporates new insights regarding, and experiences with, the person who bears it. In this sense, the act of naming awaits the completion of the narrative of the person denoted by the name. Only then does the name take on its full connotative power and with it gain the ability to name the person fully. And this narrative does not necessarily end when the person dies. Rather, the name can live on in the naming community, thereby adding new aspects to the narrative of the named person.

The communal, eschatological aspects of the dynamic of naming lie at the heart of the act of self-naming of the self-naming God and even arise from this dynamic. God's act of self-naming is both communal and eschatological, for it involves the dynamic of the relationality of the three Trinitarian persons. We noted in chapter 7 that as the Father bestows his own name on the Son, the Father is in turn named as Father by the Son, and in this process both are dependent on the Spirit who is the name they share. Insofar as the Father bestows his name—his very essence, namely, the Spirit—on the Son who is other than the Father, the Father also finds his name, his Spirit, in the Son (through a saga that is eternal yet temporal). In this sense, the communal and eschatological dimensions of the naming dynamic are already present in an archetypal manner within the history of the relationality within the divine Trinity, even as they come into view in the temporal history of the relationships of the three Trinitarian persons.

The connotative power that a name comes to carry suggests that knowing a name entails a certain kind of knowledge. This knowledge is not merely that of the possession of some supposed objective facts about the named person, but involves a type of personal connection to, or relationship with the person, whether the relationship take the form of being producers or consumers within the naming community. Insofar as names carry a knowledge-mediating function, naming is a noetic act. Insofar as God always remains the self-naming God, as we explored in chapter 7, the eternal dynamic of the divine naming becomes the noetic act of the eternal Trinity.

The eternal dynamic of the divine self-naming as self-knowledge entails the eternal analogue to a cryptic Jesus-statement that invades the Synoptic story like a "thunderbolt from the Johannine heaven," to cite Douglas Hare's picturesque description:[193] "All things have been handed

---

193. Douglas R. A. Hare, *Matthew*, Interpretation: A Bible Commentary for Teaching and Preaching (Louisville, KY: John Knox, 1993), 128.

over to me by my Father; and no one knows the Son except the Father, and no one knows the Father except the Son and anyone to whom the Son chooses to reveal him" (Matt. 11:27). The direction of the saying, of course, is to highlight Jesus' unique role as the mediator of knowledge of God to humans.[194] Jeffrey Ringer puts it well: "Like the signifier in language, Christ acts as a readable expression of the ineffable divine. Jesus renders expressible to humanity the concept of God, a concept or signified that is beyond human understanding." He then adds regarding Augustine's perspective, "It is the incarnate Christ, the Word of God, that offers humanity a means to comprehend the ineffable."[195] But this role of Christ as the incarnation of the I AM points toward the eternal noetic Trinity, toward an eternal dynamic of knowing and being known that is connected to the eternal self-naming within the triune God.

The use of the familial language in Jesus' saying indicates that the concern of the statement overflows the intellectual process of knowing to embrace the relational, intimate, bonded character of the personal knowing of one who is Other.[196] This personal knowing entails, as Levinas suggested, an ethically oriented noetic engagement. Indeed, the Otherness within the divine triune reality is not the objectivist, neutral otherness that Levinas decries. Rather, it is an ethical Otherness, that is, an Otherness that takes a stance of being "for" the Other to the point of finding one's own identity in the Other. The ethical engagement that lies at the heart of the dynamic of the triune God, therefore, is best characterized by the biblical term *agape*.

The Noetic Trinity and the Divine Love

Augustine's understanding of the Trinity incorporated an innovative alteration of the horizontal, noetic triad proposed by voices within the Platonic tradition. Yet he coupled this innovation with an equally far-reaching proposal: the idea that the Christian conception of God as triune ought to be understood in connection to the concept of love. In so doing, Augustine sought to go beyond the Greek elevation of goodness, toward which the philosophers viewed love as being directed, and to focus instead on the absolute value of love itself.[197]

Augustine introduces love as a Trinitarian concept in book 8 of *De Trinitate*. In his estimation, love provides a way of conceiving of the Trinity, in that the human mind knows love in itself and as a consequence

---

194. Donald A. Hagner, *Matthew 1–13*, Word Biblical Commentary (Dallas: Word, 1993), 320.

195. Jeffrey Ringer, "Faith and Language: Walter Hilton, St. Augustine, and Poststructural Semiotics," *Christianity and Literature* 53, no. 1 (Autumn 2003): 12, 13.

196. For hints in this direction, see Eduard Schweizer, *The Good News according to Matthew*, trans. David E. Green (Atlanta: John Knox, 1975), 270.

197. For this judgment, see Clark, "De Trinitate," 97.

knows God, for God is love. In his estimation, this leads to at least a preliminary sense of the character of God's triunity, in that love implies a Trinity consisting of "he that loves, and that which is loved, and love."[198] Despite its far-reaching implications and its strategic location in a transitional section of the treatise, the analogy plays a relatively minimal role in the work as a whole. Augustine invokes the metaphor from love as an initial step toward understanding the Trinity. It serves merely as a preparation for, or an initiation into, what he considers to be the more important analogies, which are based on the noetic process within the human mind. Hence, coming as it does at the climax of book 8 and as the prelude to books 9–15, this analogy is given, to cite Augustine's own description, so "that we may have, as it were, the hinge of some starting-point, whence to weave the rest of our discourse."[199]

Yet this agapaic "hinge" upon which the rest of De Trinitate turns is not insignificant. In his short but pivotal delineation of the metaphor, Augustine points out that for love truly to be a triad a relationality to the other is required. Self-love, he declares, involves only two: lover and love. Genuine love, however, the kind of love that characterizes God, is directed toward the other, thereby yielding the triad of Lover, Beloved, and Love. Viewed from this Augustinian perspective, the Father might be said to beget the Son to be the recipient of the Father's love. The Son, in turn, is the one because of whom love proceeds from the Father. The patriarchal background of the traditional Trinitarian language, which we reviewed in chapter 7, assists us in seeing the manner in which this can be understood. Such language is reminiscent of the idea of the Son being the inheritor of the treasure possessed by the Father, the gift shared by the Father and the Son, which designation Augustine uses earlier in De Trinitate to describe the Holy Spirit.[200]

Although many modern historians find here a point of disjuncture between Augustine and the Eastern tradition, the perspective that links the Trinity to the dynamic of love is in fact not completely foreign to the Greek theologians. Perhaps the strongest indication of a commonality of theological perspective is evident in a text from Gregory Palamas's Capita Physica: "The Spirit of the supreme Word is like a mysterious love of the Father towards the mysteriously begotten Word; and it was the same love which the well-beloved Word and Son of the Father has for the one who begot him. This love comes from the Father together with the Son and naturally rests on the Son."[201] This Augustine-like perspective is reiter-

198. Augustine, On the Trinity 8.10.14, in NPNF, 1st series, 3:124.
199. Ibid.
200. See Augustine, On the Trinity 5.11.12, in NPNF, 1st series, 3:93.
201. Gregory Palamas, Capita Physics 36, p. 150 col. 1144D–1145A, as cited in M. Edmund Hussey, "The Palamite Trinitarian Models," St. Vladimir's Theological Quarterly 16, no. 2 (1972): 83–89.

ated in a statement that in Jeremy Wilkins's estimation has "the effect of showing that the fissure between Greek and Latin theology is, at least at some points, not so wide as many assume."[202] In a section of his *Capita 150*, in which Palamas writes in a manner that Wilkins admits is "very unusual for Palamas"[203] but that according to Edmund Hussey entails a tight interweaving of "ontological" and "psychological" depictions of the Trinity,[204] the Eastern Orthodox theologian declares, "Our mind too, since it is created in the image of God, possesses the image of this highest love in the relation of the mind to the knowledge which exists perpetually from it and in it, in that this love is from it and in it and proceeds from it together with the innermost word."[205]

What is significant for our purposes is the manner in which Augustine's introduction of love into the triune equation facilitates him in taking the approach to God a step beyond the apophatic way. In reflecting on statements in Psalm 18:10, "He rode on a cherub, and flew; he came swiftly upon the wings of the wind," Augustine declares regarding God:

> And He was exalted above the fulness of knowledge, that no man should come to Him but by love. . . . And full soon He showed to His lovers that He is incomprehensible, lest they should suppose that He is comprehended by corporeal imaginations. . . . But that swiftness, whereby He showed Himself to be incomprehensible, is above the powers of souls, whereon as upon wings they raise themselves from earthly fears into the air of liberty.[206]

In keeping with this statement, Deirdre Carabine characterizes the Augustinian resolution of the problem of the knowledge of God as the *via amoris*.[207] Although the *via amoris* goes beyond the apophatic method, it does not bypass that method. Rather, it is predicated on the widely held patristic principle of the divine incomprehensibility. Even after penning a lengthy expose on the Trinity, Augustine found himself acknowledging his inability to fathom the depth of God: "But among these many things which I have now said, and of which there is nothing that I dare to profess myself to have said worthy of the ineffableness of that highest Trinity, but rather to confess that the wonderful knowledge of him is too great for me, and that I cannot attain it."[208]

202. Jeremy D. Wilkins, "'The Image of This Highest Love': The Trinitarian Analogy in Gregory Palamas's *Capita 150*," *St. Vladimir's Theological Quarterly* 47, nos. 3–4 (2003): 385.
203. Ibid., 383.
204. Hussey, "Palamite Trinitarian Models," 86.
205. Gregory Palamas, *Capita 150* c. 37, in *The One Hundred and Fifty Chapters*, by Gregory Palamas, ed. and trans. Robert E. Sinkewicz (Toronto: Pontifical Institute of Medieval Studies, 1988), 123.
206. Augustine, *On the Psalms* 18 (11), in *NPNF*, 1st series, 8:51.
207. Carabine, *Unknown God*, 272.
208. Augustine, *On the Trinity* 15.27.50, in *NPNF*, 1st series, 3:226–27.

Although Augustine readily admits that the human mind cannot fathom the divine essence, in his estimation God can be seen in and through the *imago Dei*, and this by means of love. For Augustine, the noetic journey toward knowledge of God follows a pathway that leads from the exterior to the interior (*ab exterioribus ad interiora*) or from the inferior to the superior (*ab inferioribus ad superiora*). Hence, it moves from creation to the soul and through the soul, in which the divine image is to be found, upward to the transcendent God.

Augustine's movement beyond the *via negationes* to the *via amoris* brings to light what is ultimately the central insight of the apophatic approach. Negative theology stands as a stark reminder that knowledge does not exhaust the theological task. Rather, the final goal of theology is love, just as the God who stands above every attempt to delineate the divine attributes comes to us not to be known in some objectivizing manner but in love and as love. In short, the noetic is servant to, and a moment within, the agapaic, and the *via amoris* completes the *via negationes*, for the mystery of love is the one dimension into which even negative theology affirms that a direct insight is possible.[209]

At one crucial point, however, the Augustinian *via amoris* is in need of a corrective. As significant as the turn to the soul might be deemed to be, the way *ab exterioribus ad interiora* is not the complete story; it is not even the main theological story. For this reason, Augustine's turn inward requires the corrective that the philosophers of Otherness, from the Cappadocians to Levinas, offer. God is not primarily found in the interiority of the soul, but in the exteriority of the other. The God who is Trinitarian love and who comes to us as this very love is most clearly evident in the love that is evoked in the face-to-face encounter with the Other in the other. It is in our relationality, therefore—that is, in relationship to the other—that we find the *imago Dei* and thus come to know the triune God who is love.

Moreover, our reading of the saga of the I AM as the self-naming act of the triune God leads to the conclusion that the *via amoris* must in fact draw from the dynamic of naming that involves the three Trinitarian members, into which we, in turn, are called to participate. The pathway to God, therefore, proceeds by means of our being caught up into the narrative of the relationality of the Trinitarian persons, which narrative is eternal yet temporal, for it transpires in the history of Jesus' relationship with his Father through the Holy Spirit. We participate in this dynamic as the Holy Spirit places us "in Christ" and thereby constitutes us together as co-heirs with Christ of the treasure—the love and the name—that the Father eternally lavishes on his Son. In this manner, the Spirit who is the personal concretization of the divine love leads us to love the Other in the other.

---

209. Bulhof and ten Kate, "Echoes of an Embarrassment," 6.

The *via amoris*, augmented in such a manner, forges the link from the Christian conception of God as triune to the ontological concept of Being. In fact, by undermining any attempt to allow theology to find its *telos* in anything short of love, the *via amoris* can save Being from being discarded with the bathwater of onto-theology. Rubenstein explains the basis upon which Being can be rescued:

> *As a divine name*, Being is no more or less inappropriate than any other divine name. It becomes problematic when it masquerades as The Divine Name, leading the ontotheologian to believe he comprehends God when he utters the word "Being." Being becomes a "problem," in other words, when it is the object of an objectifying epistemology, holding in place the knowing subject and the known "God." The error of ontotheology is not using the word "Being" to refer to the deity, but deifying being as knowledge, and by extension, deifying the knowing subject itself.[210]

By pressing knowledge into the service of love and placing the *noetic* within the *agapeic*, the *via amoris* prevents the deification of being-as-knowledge. The *via amoris* elevates the unfolding of love, and not the process of accumulating knowledge, as the thread that ties together what is other, for it speaks of the triad of knowing, being known, and knowledge within the context of a far greater triad: loving, being loved, and shared love. In this manner, the *via amoris* seeks the transformation of the knowing subject into a participant in the ongoing dynamic of love that embraces the quest to know while directing it to its proper *telos*.

The theo-ontological link that the *via amoris* forges centers on the dynamic of love. This conclusion leads us back to the saga of the I AM. The history of the divine name reveals the centrality of the act of be-ing present for the meaning of the divine name. Ultimately, God's be-ing present involves the presence—the present-ing—of Trinitarian love, which substantiates the other as person. Love substantiates the other as person in that the presence of love honors the other as other and thereby sets the other in a relationship that is personal.

The Christian conception of God as triune asserts that the primordial, eschatological act of present-ing and substantiating love is complete within the dynamic of the eternal divine life. Within the one God who is love, the three persons of the Trinity are substantiated by means of the establishment of the relationality of persons that characterizes the eternal divine reality. In contrast to causal relations, in which one partner is the object of the other's causal agency, personal relations require the agency of both partners, as well as the acknowledgment by both not only of the personal agency of the other but also of their own dependence on the other for establishing the relationship. More specifically, in the personal communion involved in the dynamic of love, one person can *offer* love to another but cannot *cause* the beloved to return it. At the same time, the beloved cannot return the love of another, unless the other has first *offered* love to the beloved.[211] The Augustinian doctrine of the Trinity, which speaks of God as encircling Lover, Beloved, and Love, provides the depth-grammar for this dynamic of mutual substantiation in the relationship of love.

The divine life, therefore, entails the ongoing act of what Hart calls "determinacy toward the other" understood as that perfect joy in the other by which God is God.[212] This dynamic, in turn, gives rise to beings and hence to Being. As present-ing love in the act of be-ing present, the triune God brings beings (and in this sense Being) to be. Insofar as Trinitarian love forms the basis for the be-ing of beings and the "to be" of Being, the eternal divine love emerges as "the ontological possibility of every ontic action, the one transcendent act, the primordial generosity that is convertible with being itself," as Hart concludes.[213] Just as the act of naming and the dynamic of love are Trinitarian, and hence communal and eschatological, so also the resultant theo-ontology views Being as fundamentally relational and narratival or storied, mysterious but not capricious.

Levinas proposed that religion be viewed as "the bond that is established between the same and the other without constituting a totality."[214] In his *Capita 150*, Palamas asserts that insofar as the Spirit is "common" to the Father and the Son "by mutual intimacy," he is their "pre-eternal joy."[215] In commenting on Palamas, Dumitru Staniloae writes, "Within the Trinity the Spirit is the one who brings the Father and the Son into unity (a unity of love, not of being), not the one who unravels this unity still more."[216] In these statements, these thinkers confirm what Augustine suggested, namely, that in some sense the Holy Spirit forges the connecting link binding the One to the Other. The Spirit is the love shared within the divine life and as such is the personal concretization of the very essence and character of the one God. As the divine love given by the Father to the Son and then returned from the Son to the Father, the Spirit is shared Gift. As Augustine noted, the Spirit is "the gift of God; for he is the gift of the Father and of the Son."[217]

211. For this characterization, see Vincent Brümmer, *What Are We Doing When We Pray? A Philosophical Inquiry* (London: SCM Press, 1984), 46.

212. Hart, *Beauty of the Infinite*, 166.

213. Ibid., 166–67.

214. Emmanuel Levinas, *Totality and Infinity: An Essay on Exteriority*, trans. Alphonso Lingis (Pittsburgh: Duquesne University Press, 1969), 40.

215. Gregory Palamas, *Capita 150* c. 36, in *One Hundred Fifty Chapters*, 123.

216. Dumitru Staniloae, *Theology and the Church* (Crestwood, NY: St. Vladimir's Seminary Press, 1980), 30.

217. Augustine, *On the Trinity* 5.11.12, in *NPNF*, 1st series, 3:93.

The concept of "gift" is ontologically significant in that it encapsulates the graciousness of the God who is eternally Other within the divine reality yet who nevertheless substantiates the "to be" of a host of others with whom this God wills to enter into relationship as Other. Viewed from this theo-ontological perspective, Being itself takes on the connotations of gift, and as a consequence becomes the Gift of Being.[218] As the Gift of God— the One who as the gift of the Father and of the Son is with the Father and the Son fully God as well as the shared name of God—the Spirit, in turn, is the Gift of the "to be" of beings and is ultimately the Gift of Being.

218. For a helpful philosophical engagement with Being as gift, see Arthur Witherall, *The Problem of Existence* (Hants, UK: Ashgate, 2002), 121–56.

Chapter Nine

From God's Triune Be-ing to Human Being

Our Inclusion into the Divine Name

The goal in this third triad of chapters is to indicate the manner in which the realization that the biblical God is named might form the basis for a renewed conversation between theology and ontology in the wake of the demise of onto-theology. My overarching task is to reengage the saga of Being that characterizes philosophical history with the saga of the I AM that stands at the heart of the biblical trajectory. But rather than finding the basis for forging such a connection in the concerns and concepts of ontology, my desire is to determine the contours of a theo-ontology, that is, of a conversation that finds its beginning point in the divine name. Because of the focus on the divine triunity that characterizes our approach to this enterprise, we are pursuing the task that occupies us in the three chapters that constitute the third part of this volume under the rubric of "The Saga of the Triune Name."

Our efforts began in chapter 7 with a discussion of the question of what it might mean to say that the God of the Bible is named. This task was inaugurated through a juxtaposing of the story of the absence of the divine name in theological history with a search for the presence of that name in the New Testament. In this manner we came to an awareness that the I AM is a shared name. It is shared initially and primarily among the three Trinitarian members. The chapter then moved to an exploration of the concept of being named, from which we determined that the divine self-naming is a communal, eschatological, narratival, connotative event, in which the three members of the Trinity are involved in a process of mutual naming.

In chapter 8, we turned our attention to a delineation of the ontology of the triune name. We began the task by narrating the story of the rise of the church's Trinitarian teaching as it emerged in conversation with the tradition of Platonism. The recounting of this story revealed the manner in which the Christian teaching provided an innovative way of understanding the triadic nature of the divine ground of all that is. It likewise provided the context for raising anew the question of apophatic theology. We noted that this philosophical-theological method clears the way for the mysterious speaking, denoted as revelation, of the God who is Other than the cosmos. As the triune God, this God is the one in whom Otherness is eternally present. The triune God, in turn, lets otherness be as "gift" to creation. Finally, the recounting of the story of the encounter of Trinitarian theology with Platonic philosophy provided the tools by means of which to see how it is that the God who is the triune one and who is love offers the "to be" of creatures as the gift of the Holy Spirit.

One additional piece of this puzzle yet remains. The goal of the biblical drama, with its focus on the divine name, is not merely the instantiation of that name. Rather, the movement of the self-naming God extends to God's creation. The intent of the triune God is to incorporate humankind, indeed all creation, into the dynamic of that eternal/historical self-naming. God intends to share the divine name with humans! For this reason, we must now turn our attention to a final aspect of the saga of the triune name. We now must seek to offer a theological telling of the story of the incorporation of human being in the dynamic of the triune name.

Human Being in God

What is perhaps the clearest assertion of a connection between human being and God found anywhere in the Bible occurs in Paul's speech before the intelligentsia of Athens. Commentators speak with one voice in extolling the importance of this address. F. F. Bruce, to cite one example, declares, "Probably no ten verses in Acts have formed the text for such an abundance of commentary as has gathered around Paul's Areopagus speech."[1] Ben Witherington adds that this text "has attracted more scholarly attention

1. F. F. Bruce, *The Book of Acts*, rev. ed., New International Commentary on the New Testament (Grand Rapids: Eerdmans, 1988), 333.

than any other passage in Acts."[2] Patrick Gray goes so far as to conclude, "Paul's address before the Areopagus in Acts 17 counts as one of the most celebrated passages in the NT."[3]

Despite the agreement among commentators regarding the importance of the Areopagitica, no consensus has been reached regarding Paul's (or Luke's) intent in framing the speech or concerning its actual intended audience. Gray underscores the diversity of interpretative approaches when he observes that the speech "has been read variously as an expression of natural theology rooted in Stoic thought, as a Christian sermon aimed at Gentiles yet steeped in biblical language and thought patterns, as a gauge of Luke's reliability as a historian, as a source for reconstructing Paul's *modus operandi*, and as evidence for or against its Pauline authorship vis-a-vis the epistles."[4]

Recent studies have sought to move the interpretive discussion forward by understanding the passage in the context of Luke's intentions as a historian and a theologian.[5] This concern provides the context for the manner in which the Areopagitica will be put to use in the following paragraphs. For the purposes of this chapter, the importance of the address arises from the window it offers into Paul's (or Luke's) understanding of the connection between the God of the biblical gospel and the philosophical concern for the question of human being. This New Testament perspective, in turn, provides an occasion for advancing the narrative of the inclusion of human being in the story of the divine name.

Our Being in God and the Philosophical Quest

The watershed incident that stands at the center of the book of Acts is the meeting of the Jerusalem council, which formulated the terms for the mission to the Gentiles (Acts 15:1–29). The subsequent narrative unfolds the ongoing geographical expansion of the gospel witness among Gentiles throughout the Roman Empire, especially as this process was facilitated by the "apostle to the Gentiles." In keeping with this theme, the book of Acts climaxes in Paul's presence in the capital city itself.

When viewed as a moment in this larger narrative, the scene painted in this section forms the apex of a drama that has been building from the very beginning of the book (cf. Acts 2:39; 3:25; 7:48; 10:34; 14:15–17;

---

2. Ben Witherington III, *The Acts of the Apostles: A Socio-Rhetorical Commentary* (Grand Rapids: Eerdmans, 1998), 511.

3. Patrick Gray, "Implied Audiences in the Areopagus Narrative," *Tyndale Bulletin* 55, no. 2 (2004): 205.

4. Ibid., 206–7.

5. For examples of this approach, see Paul Schubert, "The Place of the Areopagus Speech in the Composition of Acts," in *Transitions in Biblical Scholarship*, ed. J. Coert Rylaarsdam (Chicago: University of Chicago Press, 1968), 235–61; Witherington, *Acts of the Apostles*, 511–35; Gray, "Implied Audiences in the Areopagus Narrative," 205–18.

15:7; 15:14). Despite the focus on the Gentiles in this particular trajectory, however, Luke does not present Paul's endeavors as excluding the proclamation of the gospel to diaspora Jews. Nor does he allow his readers to presume that the Pauline mission had been highly successful. In the drama of the expansion of the good news, Jerusalem might have decided to accept the Gentiles, but this decision did not automatically mean that the Gentiles would accept Jerusalem's gospel.[6]

As the "first address Luke records of the 'official' Gentile mission," to cite Gray's apt description, Paul's speech before the Areopagus plays an important role in Luke's story. F. J. Foakes-Jackson encapsulates the incident as a whole by declaring, "We are prepared to hear a great speech, leading, however, to no great result."[7] By portraying Paul's Athenian sojourn in this light, Luke invites his readers to see the various characters who surround his hero in this scene as exemplifying the diverse ways in which the Gentile recipients of the message, quite similar to their Jewish counterparts, respond to the good news.

The Context: Paul and the Philosophers

In Luke's narrative, Paul's sojourn in Athens occurs almost by accident, as does his address to the intellectual elite of the city. Luke notes that his hero's aversion to the idolatry that he observed in Athens drove him initially to the synagogue. Not until he added the agora to his itinerary did he encounter the philosophers, whose awareness of and opposition to his teaching evoked the involvement of the Areopagus in the matter. Despite its apparent accidental nature, Paul's presence in this ancient center of Greek culture occasions what Foakes-Jackson considers "the earliest Christian 'apology' to the Greeks."[8] According to Steve Mason, one of Luke's central goals is to unite Christianity and Judaism, and one "essential element" in this Lucan strategy "is his portrayal of the church as a Jewish *philosophical school* alongside the Pharisees and Sadducees."[9] If Mason is correct, Paul's speech before the Areopagus must be seen as playing a central role in this larger strategy.

One crucial feature of the incident, therefore, is the manner in which Luke presents Paul as the missionary to an educated and philosophically sophisticated Gentile audience.[10] In the narrator's estimation, the Christian emissary proves himself to be quite capable of going head-to-head

6. For a similar description of the situation in Acts, see Gray, "Implied Audiences in the Areopagus Narrative," 207.

7. F. J. Foakes-Jackson, *The Acts of the Apostles*, Moffatt New Testament Commentary (London: Hodder & Stoughton, 1931), 163.

8. Ibid., 163.

9. Steve Mason, "Chief Priests, Sadducees, Pharisees, and Sanhedrin in Acts," in *The Book of Acts in Its Palestinian Setting*, ed. Richard Bauckham, vol. 4 of *The Book of Acts in Its First Century Setting* (Grand Rapids: Eerdmans, 1995), 153.

10. For this observation, see Witherington, *Acts of the Apostles*, 511.

with the intellectuals of his day. Indeed, in this particular scene of his drama, Luke casts Paul along the lines of a philosopher visiting the city of philosophers.[11] Some commentators even go so far as to find in the passage indications that for the purposes of this particular episode Luke patterns his central character after the great Athenian philosopher Socrates.[12] In fact, Luke seems to be presenting Paul in Athens as the new Socrates.

By casting Paul as a philosopher, Luke provides the backdrop in which to present the ambiguous manner in which Paul's "apologetic masterpiece," as Daniel Marguerat calls it, can be read.[13] The Areopagitica is open to both a Greek philosophical and a Jewish religious reading. This ambiguity remains unresolved only until the direction in which the address is intended to move the reader becomes clear at the end of the speech by the inclusion of a call to conversion on the basis of the Christian doctrines of eschatological judgment and resurrection.[14]

Paul's role as philosopher also occasions Luke's subtle attempt to highlight the ambiguous connection between the apostle's teaching and the main tenets of the prominent philosophical schools of the day, as represented by his learned hearers. Repeatedly throughout the episode, Luke portrays the intellectual leaders of Athens as rejecting Paul's message. The philosophers mock him as a *spermologos* ("babbler"), a strong term of derision referring to a person who is merely a philosophical dilettante. The word carries the idea of someone who has acquired only scraps of learning and therefore is able to convey nothing more than snippets of philosophical or religious knowledge. Such a person is compelled to babble, that is, "to talk long and persuasively to conceal the second-hand, second-rate quality of their doctrine," as E. M. Blaiklock characterizes the meaning of the Greek term.[15] In addition, the learned hearers of the teaching that Paul offered in the marketplace determined that he was dangerous. In their estimation, he appeared to be a herald of foreign gods, namely, Jesus and Anastasis ("the resurrection"). And he seemed to be the author of "new teaching" (v. 19). Precisely such charges had led to Socrates' demise four centuries earlier.[16]

11. Foakes-Jackson, *Acts of the Apostles*, 163.

12. Examples of commentators who find allusions to Socrates in the narrative include Luke Timothy Johnson, *The Acts of the Apostles*, ed. Daniel J. Harrington, Sacra Pagina (Collegeville, MN: Liturgical Press, 1992), 312–14; John B. Polhill, *Acts*, New American Commentary (Nashville: Broadman, 1992), 368.

13. Daniel Marguerat, *The First Christian Historian: Writing the Acts of the Apostles*, trans. Ken McKinney, Gregory J. Laughery, and Richard Bauckham (Cambridge: Cambridge University Press, 2002), 70.

14. For a similar understanding, see Marguerat, *First Christian Historian*, 70–71.

15. E. M. Blaiklock, *The Areopagus Address* (Bristol: University of Bristol Press, 1964), 6.

16. Plato, *Socrates' Defense (Apology)* 24b–c, trans. Hugh Tredennick, in *The Collected Dialogues of Plato Including the Letters*, ed. Edith Hamilton and Huntington Cairns (Princeton, NJ: Princeton University Press, 1961), 10. For a discussion of this connection, see Rudolf Pesch, *Die Apostelgeschichte*, 2 vols. (Zurich: Benziger, 1986), 1:135. See also C. K. Barrett, *A Critical and Exegetical Commentary on the Acts of the Apostles*, International Critical Commentary, 2 vols. (Edinburgh: T. & T. Clark, 1998), 2:830–31.

It should be pointed out that Luke's intent is to turn the tables on Paul's critics. To this end, he presents the Athenian intellectuals as the real dilettantes and as willfully ignorant.[17] By casting them in this light, the philosophers' response to Paul serves to diminish their stature in the eyes of the narrator's audience.

The fact that Paul's teaching in the agora triggered a negative reaction from the intellectual elite of the city did not dissuade Paul from sprinkling his address to the Areopagus with comments with which the philosophers of his day would have agreed. In fact, such appears to have been his deliberate strategy. This observation raises the question as to the makeup of the audience that Luke portrays as being on hand to hear the apostle's speech.

Of course, members of the Areopagus were present. This council, comprising the elite of the city,[18] served as the main governing body of Athens[19] and was empowered by the Romans with the authority to try cases of murder as well as to decide questions involving morality and religion.[20] Paul's speech was occasioned by the fact that his teachings had not gone unnoticed by this body. Yet the actual nature of his appearance before the Areopagus remains unclear. Some commentators note that the Greek verb *epilabomenoi*, which can carry the strong sense of "to take by force," suggests that Paul, reminiscent of Socrates,[21] was coercively taken before this tribunal, perhaps even having been arrested, so as to answer charges that were being leveled against him.[22] Other exegetes do not view the scene as a formal trial before the council itself, but as an informal meeting with the "education commission" of the Areopagus court, to cite Bertil Gärtner's playful allusion to a modern parallel.[23] N. B. Stonehouse surmises that "Paul was compelled to face the council to demonstrate that his appearance among the public lecturers of Athens was unobjectionable."[24] Bruce Winter, however, narrows the focus. He theorizes that the goal of this commission might have been to determine whether or not the two gods that Paul appeared to be representing, Jesus and Anastasis, should be added to the Greek pantheon.[25]

---

17. For this insight, see Gray, "Implied Audiences in the Areopagus Narrative," 210–11.

18. David W. J. Gill, "Acts and the Urban Elites," in *The Book of Acts in Its Graeco-Roman Setting*, ed. David W. J. Gill and Conrad Gempf, vol. 2 of *The Book of Acts in Its First-Century Setting*, ed. Bruce W. Winter (Grand Rapids: Eerdmans, 1994), 110.

19. David W. J. Gill, "Achaia," in *Book of Acts in Its Graeco-Roman Setting*, 441, 447.

20. C. S. C. Williams, *A Commentary on the Acts of the Apostles*, Black's New Testament Commentaries, 2nd ed., ed. Henry Chadwick (London: A. & C. Black, 1964), 202.

21. For this connection, see Ernst Haenchen, *The Acts of the Apostles: A Commentary*, trans. Bernard Noble and Gerald Shinn, rev. R. McL. Wilson (Philadelphia: Westminster, 1971), 517.

22. For a helpful discussion of this issue, see Witherington, *Acts of the Apostles*, 515–17.

23. Bertil Gärtner, *The Areopagus Speech and Natural Revelation*, trans. Carolyn Hannay King, Acta Seminarii Neotestamentici Upsaliensis 21 (Uppsala, Sweden: Almquist & Wiksells, 1955), 59.

24. N. B. Stonehouse, *Paul before the Areopagus and Other New Testament Studies* (London: Tyndale, 1957), 9.

25. Bruce W. Winter, "On Introducing Gods to Athens: An Alternative Reading of Acts 17.18–20," *Tyndale Bulletin* 47, no. 1 (1996): 80–83.

If this general view is correct, then rather than being a closed session of the council's education subcommittee, the event was probably open to other interested persons or perhaps the variety of stakeholders who shared in the task of overseeing the religious climate of Athens. Luke's intent, in any case, seems to be to characterize the event as a public informational session rather than an actual legal trial.[26] The public nature of the hearing is perhaps implied by Paul's opening salutation to the gathered group. By beginning his speech with the seemingly redundant declaration, *andres Athenaioi*, the apostle appears to be including not only the council members but also the philosophers and other curious listeners in attendance.[27]

The audience present at the public hearing was likely sufficiently diverse to allow for a variety of interpretations of, and responses to, Paul's ambiguous opening observation that the Athenians are *deisidaimenestepous* (v. 22). This characterization could be taken either as a complement ("extremely religious" [NRSV]) or as a mild rebuke ("too superstitious" [KJV]). If understood in the former manner, Paul's declaration fits with the view widely held in the ancient world that the citizens of this city were among the most religious people of the day.[28] Yet the ambivalence that the term carries renders it a masterful rhetorical choice. The negative connotations that it carries would have resonated with the sensitivities of the philosophically minded listeners among Paul's audience. For their part, the Stoics and Epicureans would have shared the implied antipathy for many of the religious practices of the Athenian populace. I. Howard Marshall offers a helpful summary of the manner in which Paul's critique of the piety of the Athenians paralleled concerns of the philosophers of his day: "The Epicureans attacked superstitious, irrational belief in the gods, expressed in idolatry, while the Stoics stressed the unity of mankind and its kinship with God, together with the consequent moral duty of man."[29]

By saluting his audience in this manner, Paul was able to gain standing with his audience while avoiding the temptation to offer a compliment with the hope of gaining the goodwill of the court, a tactic that the ancient writer Lucian declared must not be followed when addressing the Areopagus.[30] More importantly, by means of this ambiguous opening declaration, the apostle set the stage for his subsequent wedding of the philosophical criticism of popular religious practice to the long-standing Jewish rejection of pagan idolatry,[31] as well as his attempt to find common ground between his

---

26. For this conclusion, see Marshall, *Book of Acts*, 285.

27. For a similar judgment, see Witherington, *Acts of the Apostles*, 520.

28. For examples of the ancient literature in which this viewpoint is stated, see Bruce, *Book of Acts*, 335 n. 54.

29. I. Howard Marshall, *The Acts of the Apostles: An Introduction and Commentary*, Tyndale New Testament Commentaries (Grand Rapids: Eerdmans, 1980), 281–82.

30. Lucian, *Anacharsis*, 19, as cited in Bruce, *Book of Acts*, 335 n. 55.

31. For a similar characterization, see Gray, "Implied Audiences in the Areopagus Narrative," 213.

own biblically informed view of God's relationship to the cosmos and that of the Athenian philosophers in his audience. Furthermore, Luke might have intended that Paul's ambiguous manner of characterizing the people of his host city facilitate his readers in catching the irony of the situation. As Marshall explains, "For all their religiosity, the Athenians were in reality thoroughly superstitious and lacking in knowledge of the true God."[32]

It is in this context that Paul voices his appeal to traditional authorities that the Athenians themselves would acknowledge to substantiate his declaration regarding the existence of humans in God. His use of this strategy has led one modern commentator, Martin Dibelius, to bestow on the speaker of the Areopagitica the status of "precursor of the Apologists."[33] Yet Paul's ultimate goal was not simply that of engaging as a Christian with the "Greek mind," but to call his audience to repentance. For this reason, Bruce's appraisal is perhaps the more appropriate. He characterizes Paul's speech before the Areopagus as "an introductory lesson in Christianity for cultured pagans."[34]

The Central Content: The Proclamation of the Unknown God

Luke sets the scene for Paul's deliverance of his "introductory lesson" by noting that the apostle was "deeply distressed to see that the city was full of idols" (v. 16). The narrator captures Paul's mood by means of a word that was used in the Septuagint in contexts in which Yahweh's anger is provoked by Israel's sin, especially the sin of idolatry (Deut. 9:18; Ps. 106:29; Isa. 65:3; Hos. 8:5).[35]

Luke's comment raises the question of why Paul's spirit was so deeply provoked at the sight of the Athenian temples. The apostle was no stranger to the pagan cults of the ancient world. Yet what violated Paul's sensitivities might have been the blatant, overwhelming presence of religious shrines in the city that despite its decline in the first century BC[36] continued to be considered the cultural and intellectual center of the Roman Empire.[37] Richard Wycherley explains that upon entering the city, Paul would have found himself confronted by "a veritable forest of idols."[38] David Gill and Bruce Winter offer a more complete picture of the scene that might have drawn Paul's attention and grieved his spirit:

32. Marshall, *Acts of the Apostles*, 285.

33. Martin Dibelius, *Studies in the Acts of the Apostles*, ed. Heinrich Greeven, trans. Mary Ling (New York: Charles Scribner's Sons, 1956), 63.

34. Bruce, *Book of Acts*, 341.

35. For this insight, see Stonehouse, *Paul before the Areopagus*, 6.

36. For a synopsis of this decline, see Joseph A. Fitzmyer, *The Acts of the Apostles: A New Translation with Introduction and Commentary*, Anchor Bible (New York: Doubleday, 1998), 600–601.

37. Polhill, *Acts*, 365–66.

38. Richard E. Wycherley, "St. Paul at Athens," *Journal of Theological Studies*, new series, 19 (1968): 619.

Perhaps he was struck by the way that the temples of the main civic sanctuary on the Akropolis dominated the city. Perhaps as he was sailing from Macedonia to the Piraeus he was struck that as the ship sailed around Sounion, he could see the tip of the spear and the crest of the helmet of the colossal statue of the Athena Promachos which stood on the Akropolis to commemorate the Battle of Marathon. . . . For Paul a statue of a deity which could be seen from the sea was a daily reminder of the way that pagan religion, and especially Athena, dominated the life of the city.[39]

With this physical backdrop to Paul's Areopagitica in view, Foakes-Jackson encapsulates what he sees as the significance of the religious confrontation that Paul's address entailed:

Paul probably spoke to his audience facing the noblest monuments of Greek art and the most revered objects of Hellenic religion. It is in full view of the Parthenon, and of the statue of Athena with her gleaming spear, the light of which, when caught by the rising sun, was the first object the mariner saw on approaching Athens. The old religion in its glory and the new religion, represented by an insignificant-looking Jew, so to speak, confronted one another, and the great struggle between the Faith and the cults of the ancient world was in this way inaugurated.[40]

Commentators routinely divide the Areopagitica into four (or five) sections.[41] Witherington, for example, finds in the address four of the classical rhetorical elements: *exordium* (vv. 22–23), *propositio* (v. 23b), *probatio* (vv. 24–29), and *oratio* (vv. 30–31).[42] In a manner reminiscent of Dibelius's older study,[43] Marshall proposes a further division of the *probatio* based on what he sees as its main points: As lord of the world, God does not need human cultic ritual (vv. 24–25); as God's creation, humans need God (vv. 26–27); because God and humans are related, idolatry is foolish (vv. 28–29).[44]

Central to the bridge that Paul builds to his audience is his claim, articulated at the end of his *exordium*, to have seen in the city an altar dedicated to an unknown god. The apostle's claim has triggered a seemingly

39. David W. J. Gill and Bruce W. Winter, "Acts and Roman Religion," in Gill and Winter, *Book of Acts in Its Graeco-Roman Setting*, 85–86. E. M. Blaiklock claims that sailors could see the sun's glint on the point of Athena's spear some forty miles away. Blaiklock, *Areopagus Address*, 2–3.

40. Foakes-Jackson, *Acts of the Apostles*, 165.

41. For a five-part division that views the speech as following a chiastic structure (ABCBA), see Polhill, *Acts*, 370. Fitzmyer, in turn, finds in the speech a three-part body preceded by Paul's introductory words and followed by his conclusion. Fitzmyer, *Acts of the Apostles*, 602. For a division of the speech into two sections, see Hans Conzelmann, *Acts of the Apostles: A Commentary on the Acts of the Apostles*, trans. James Limburg, A. Thomas Kraabel, and Donald H. Juel, ed. Eldon Jay Epp with Christopher R. Matthews (Philadelphia: Fortress, 1987), 141.

42. Witherington, *Acts of the Apostles*, 518.

43. Dibelius, *Studies in the Acts of the Apostles*, 27.

44. Marshall, *Acts of the Apostles*, 282.

endless debate regarding the likelihood that such an altar existed in first-century Athens. Attempts at reaching any definitive answer to the question are frustrated by the fact that all relevant extrabiblical evidence postdates the first century. One such piece of evidence, the report of the mid-second-century travel chronicler Pausanias, indicates the presence in the city of altars to gods who are called unknown. His testimony, however, raises the question of whether he meant that each of these altars was dedicated to one god or to several gods.[45]

If Paul did indeed see at least one specific altar with the inscription "to an unknown god," its construction could have been connected to one of several possible purposes. Altars that had been partially destroyed through war or natural disasters so that the name of the original god was obscured were sometimes subsequently restored and rededicated, albeit with the inscription "to an unknown god" or "to an unnamed god."[46] Diaspora Jews, God-fearers, or even polytheistic Gentiles might have erected altars to the God of Israel, who was deemed to be unknown because this God could not be named or represented by an image.[47] Altars could also carry the inscription "to an unknown god" if they were so designated by persons who were unsure of the true name of a particular god and did not want to incur the god's wrath by misnaming the deity in question, or by persons who wanted to protect themselves against the jealousy and anger of unknown gods.[48] Occasionally an altar was placed on a grave that had been disturbed with the hope of placating whatever deities might otherwise take vengeance in response to the desecration.[49] This leads to the possibility that the item that Paul saw was not an actual altar but a hero shrine connected to one of the tombs surrounding the agora at which offerings were made.[50]

Regardless of the exact nature of the religious site that Paul witnessed, he uses this phenomenon as a point of contact with his audience. Then by raising matters that Socrates had earlier discussed[51] and by developing themes that the Epicureans and the Stoics had also enunciated, the apostle fulfills the "orator" aspect of his role as the new Socrates.[52]

The main point of the Areopagitica, which is recited in the *oratio*, is that the Athenians need to repent of their idolatry and receive instruction about

45. For a helpful treatment of this issue, see Pieter W. van der Horst, *Hellenism, Judaism, Christianity: Essays on Their Interaction* (Kampen: Kok Pharos, 1994), 165–202. For a succinct summary, see Witherington, *Acts of the Apostles*, 521–23.

46. For examples in the ancient world, see Bruce, *Book of Acts*, 336.

47. Horst, *Hellenism, Judaism, Christianity*, 187–90.

48. For this possibility, see Williams, *Commentary on the Acts of the Apostles*, 202; Horst, *Hellenism, Judaism, Christianity*, 190–93.

49. Marshall, *Acts of the Apostsles*, 286.

50. For this possibility, see Wycherley, "St. Paul at Athens," 620–21; Gill, "Achaia," 446.

51. See, for example, Socrates' discussion of piety. Plato, *Euthyphro* 11–15, in *The Dialogues of Plato*, 2 vols., trans. B. Jowett (New York: Random House, 1892), 1:392–98.

52. For this insight, see Witherington, *Acts of the Apostles*, 525–26.

the God who is unknown to them but whom they nevertheless worship. Forming the basis of Paul's argument, which comprises much of the *probatio*, is his contention, which draws together themes present in both Old Testament and Greek thought, that the God to whom the Athenians unknowingly pay homage is the Creator of the universe. As Creator, God does not dwell in humanly constructed shrines (v. 24; cf. 1 Kgs. 8:27). Nor is the Creator dependent on human religious activities (cf. Ps. 50:9–12), a theme that according to Dibelius was repeated in all the schools of Greek philosophy from the Eleatics to the Neopythagoreans and the Neoplatonists.[53] On the contrary, this God is the one upon whom humans are dependent. Indeed, God is the giver of "life and breath and all things" (v. 25).

Paul rounds out this part of the *probatio* by affirming the unity of humankind as the creation of God and then asserting that the divinely determined goal of human existence is that of inhabiting the earth and searching for God (vv. 26–27; cf. Deut. 4:28–29; 32:8; Isa. 55:6; Amos 5:6). The verb Luke uses to denote this human quest (*pselaphao*) paints a picture of a blind person or a person in the night attempting to discern objects in the darkness.[54]

Here again Paul could anticipate that his Stoic hearers would find themselves in basic agreement with him. Yet it is also precisely at this point in the Areopagitica that a hint is given that the two viewpoints in fact diverge. The philosophers would want to take Paul's point further, adding that because the divine principle was to be found in all creation, humans ought to strive to find the deity by cultivating reason, which comprised the presence of the divine within the human person. Luke's manner of casting the human search, therefore, occasions a contrast between the Stoic belief that nature could lead to knowledge of God and Paul's contention that human seeking does not result in such knowledge, which unhappy situation the apostle finds evidenced by the idolatry of the Athenians. Witherington states the point well: "The overall effect of this verse is to highlight the dilemma and irony of the human situation. Though God is omnipresent, and so not far from any person, ironically human beings are stumbling around in the dark trying to find God."[55]

For the author of the Areopagitica, therefore, the philosophical quest for God, though legitimate as an outworking of our God-designed nature as humans, cannot ultimately lead us to the God who is not far from any of us. Finding the unknown God of the Greeks—the God in whom we exist—Paul avers in the *oratio*, requires the kind of repentance that is in keeping with the self-disclosure of the no longer unknown God. Not

---

53. Dibelius, *Studies in the Acts of the Apostles*, 43. It should be pointed out that Dibelius concludes that the idea is thoroughly Greek and not rooted in the Old Testament.

54. See, for example, Richard C. Trench, *Synonyms of the New Testament* (1880; repr., Grand Rapids: Eerdmans, 1950), 58.

55. Witherington, *Acts of the Apostles*, 529.

explicitly stated yet strongly implied in this speech is the apostle's central conviction that the revelation through which the formerly unknown God has become knowable comes in the one by whom all humankind will be judged. Gärtner puts it well: "An altar to an unknown God conveys, to Paul, that the Athenians have acknowledged that God is unknown to them. . . . But now, with the coming of Christ, the unknown God is made known to all."[56]

Human Being in God

The introduction of the creation of humans for the sake of seeking God sets the stage for what for our purposes is the most important feature of the Areopagitica. This dimension arises out of the central concern of this section of the address. Paul has reminded his audience that the goal of human existence is to seek after God. The grammatical construction of the Greek text, especially the use of the optative mood, indicates that the ability of humans to attain this goal is not only not guaranteed but remains doubtful. Yet the task of seeking God is not an impossible quest, Paul adds, for God is already near at hand. The burning question that such an assertion raises is: How is this so? In what manner is God present? And what constitutes the confirmation of the divine presence? The apostle's answer is brief yet far-reaching. The divine nearness to human seekers is evident in the fact that God is the giver of "life and breath and all things."

God as the Giver of Human Being

At first glance, Paul's language invites the reader to see a Greek underpinning to the declaration. The triadic structure—"life, breath, all things"—was a common linguistic device in the religious literature of the day.[57] Moreover, the word for life (zoe) was routinely associated with the name of the Greek high god, Zeus. In keeping with this connection, Paul appeals directly to Greek ideas and literary sources to substantiate his point, sources that link Zeus with life itself. Specifically, he incorporates two sentences that possibly comprise two quotations from Greek literature: "In him we live and move and have our being" and "We too are his offspring" (v. 28).

The actual literary sources of the two quotations—assuming that Luke's new Socrates is indeed citing specific written works—is not entirely certain. The most likely candidate for the first citation, which some commentators have concluded is not in fact a direct quotation from an extant writing,[58] is an address to Zeus that occurs within a larger ancient Greek poem:

---

56. Gärtner, *Areopagus Speech and Natural Revelation*, 238–39.
57. Ibid., 201.
58. See, for example, Max Pohlenz, "Paulus und die Stoa," *Zeitschrift für die neutestamentliche Wissenschaft* 42 (1949): 101–4. See also Dibelius, *Studies in the Acts of the Apostles*, 187–88; Fitzmyer, *Acts of the Apostles*, 610.

> They fashioned a tomb for thee, O holy and high one—
> The Cretans, always liars, evil beasts, idle bellies!—
> But thou art not dead; thou livest and abidest for ever
> For in thee we live and move and have our being.[59]

The second line of this address, which appears in Titus 1:12, is attributed to a Cretan poet, Epimenides, by Clement of Alexandria.[60] The text appears in its entirety in a work of a ninth-century Syriac commentator and Nestorian church father, Ishodad of Merv, whose references were, in turn, likely based on the writings of Theodore of Mopsuestia.[61] Ishodad asserts that Paul's source for the inclusion of this line in his Areopagitica was Minos of Crete, who was supposedly the son of Zeus. Furthermore, Ishodad reports that the setting of the original poem was Minos's desire to attack the Cretan belief that Zeus had been lacerated by a wild boar and was buried on the island.[62]

The background to the second quotation is less obscure. The form in which it is found in the Areopagitica is likely drawn from the fifth line of the *Phainomena* composed by the third-century BC Stoic poet Aratus of Soli:[63]

> From Zeus begin the song, nor ever leave His name unsung, whose godhead fills all streets, All thronging marts of men, the boundless sea And all its ports: whose aid all mortals need; For we his offspring are; and kindly he Reveals to man good omens of success, Stirs him to labour by the hope of food, Tells when the land best suits the grazing ox, Or when the plough; when favouring seasons bid Plant the young tree, and sow the various seed.[64]

Aratus, in turn, might have taken the text that Paul quotes from the opening words of line 4 of Cleanthes' *Hymn to Zeus*,[65] which reads, "Thou, Zeus, art praised above all gods; many are thy names and thine is the power eternally. The origin of the world was from thee: and by law thou rulest over all things. Unto thee may all flesh speak, for we are thy offspring. Therefore will I raise a hymn unto thee: and will ever sing of thy might."[66] The apostle's declaration, "as even some of your own poets have

---

59. For this rendering of the poem, see Bruce, *Book of Acts*, 339.

60. Clement of Alexandria, *Stromateis* 1.19, in *Ante-Nicene Fathers*, ed. Alexander Roberts and James Donaldson (1885; repr., Peabody, MA: Hendrickson, 1994), 2:321–22. See also Witherington, *Acts of the Apostles*, 529; Marshall, *Book of Acts*, 288–89.

61. For this description, see Horst, *Hellenism, Judaism, Christianity*, 183. For the literary source see Dibelius, *Studies in the Acts of the Apostles*, 48.

62. Williams, *Acts of the Apostles*, 205.

63. For this description, see Colin J. Hemer, "The Speeches of Acts: II. The Areopagus Address," *Tyndale Bulletin* 40 (1989): 243.

64. For this citation, see Eusebius, *Preparation for the Gospel* 13.12 (p. 666b–c), trans. Edwin Hamilton Gifford, 2 vols. (Grand Rapids: Baker, 1981), 1:720.

65. For this judgment, see, among others, Bruce, *Book of Acts*, 339.

66. For this rendering of the hymn, see Blaiklock, *Areopagus Address*, 13.

said," suggests the possibility that he is aware of multiple sources of the quotation.[67]

The appeal to the saying(s) of Greek poets in substantiating the claims of this section of the address confirms in the minds of some commentators that Luke is thoroughly accommodating the message of his hero to the Greek philosophical tradition. In fact, so complete is the accommodation believed to be that the speech is viewed as completely Stoic in tone and content, and as such absolutely foreign to the thought of the New Testament.[68] This perspective was especially in vogue during the mid-twentieth century. For example, writing in 1939, Dibelius concluded regarding the Areopagitica, "It is a hellenistic speech about recognizing God, and about recognizing him philosophically."[69] Dibelius was convinced that the central theme of the speech is "knowledge of God, to which every human being can attain, since man's own position in the world and the affinity of his nature with God's inevitably head him there."[70]

Of course, it is quite possible that many in Paul's audience would have interpreted his speech in general and his use of the Greek poets in particular along Stoic lines. Rather than making the speaker a closet Stoic, however, the citation of Aratus places Paul in the company of the various Hellenistic Jews who sought to connect the Zeus of the Greek philosophers with the God of Israel. The patristic historian Eusebius cites as an example the Hebrew philosopher Aristobulus the Peripatetic, who claimed that his Greek counterparts actually drew their ideas from the philosophy of the Hebrews. In his address to King Ptolemy, Aristobulus reflected his practice of replacing the name of Zeus in the writings of Greek luminaries such as Aratus—which name in the genitive case becomes *Zios*—by *Theos*. The Jewish philosopher claimed as his rationale that *Theos* was what the original author actually intended.[71] Eusebius quotes Aristobulus as saying, "It is clearly shown, I think, that all things are pervaded by the power of God: and this I have properly represented by taking away the name of Zeus which runs through the poems; for it is to God that their thought is sent up, and for that reason I have so expressed it."[72]

Many commentators now conclude that the Areopagitica ought to be read in the light of this kind of Jewish literature. Rather than presenting little more than warmed-over Stoicism, therefore, Paul was following the custom of couching what are essentially Jewish religious concerns in a Hellenistic form, albeit with the addition of uniquely Christian

67. Marshall, *Acts of the Apostles*, 289.
68. For this judgment, see Dibelius, *Studies in the Acts of the Apostles*, 71.
69. Dibelius, *Studies in the Acts of the Apostles*, 81.
70. Ibid., 58.
71. Irina Levinskaya, *The Book of Acts in Its Diaspora Setting*, vol. 5 of *The Book of Acts in Its First-Century Setting*, ed. Bruce W. Winter (Grand Rapids: Eerdmans, 1996), 100 n. 101.
72. Eusebius, *Preparation for the Gospel* 13.12 (p. 666d), 1:720.

elements.[73] The manner in which Luke casts the scene seems to confirm this conclusion, for the narrator's intent appears to underscore the subtle yet highly significant difference that separated the new Socrates from the philosophers of his day. Paul's inclusion of Greek themes and Greek sayings into his speech, therefore, does more than appeal to sources that his audience would honor as a way of bolstering his case. It also facilitates him in the task of drawing these very themes and sources into the orbit of the Old Testament and Christian teaching regarding the relationship between God and creation, even though this perspective differs significantly from that of the Athenian philosophers.

Reading the Areopagitica in this manner suggests that the poetic sayings that the apostle quotes are not intended to be understood as statements of the Greek idea that divinity resides in human nature. Rather, the meaning that the author of the speech gives to the poets' lines emerges from their connection to his central contention that God is the giver of "life and breath and all things." Although this triad is not unique to Paul, for it is present in Greek religious thought of the day, the understanding that the apostle pours into it arises out of his commitment to the biblical doctrine of God as Creator.

This observation raises the question regarding the source of this triad, which plays such a central role in the address. For an answer to this query, some commentators look to a particular verse in Isaiah: "Thus says God, the LORD, who created the heavens and stretched them out, who spread out the earth and what comes from it, who gives breath to the people upon it and spirit to those who walk in it" (Isa. 42:5). Concerning the architect of the Areopagitica, Ernst Haenchen, for example, declares, "The speaker uses Isa. 42.5 freely. He first extracts from it a statement embracing the whole creation account of Gen. 1.1–23; then he constructs out of the Isaiah material a formula which expresses God's continuing lordship."[74] Haenchen then explains how the triad—life, breath, all things—emerged from the Old Testament text:

> So Luke alters Isa. 42.5: (a) he cannot say that God gives everyone *pneuma* without being misunderstood by Christians: God gives the spirit only to the believers! Therefore he exchanges *pneuma* for *zoan*, a word that is understandable to pagans as to Christians and prepares the way for verse 28; (b) for *to lao*, which in LXX means mostly the elect people, the inclusive word "all" is introduced; (c) finally "and everything" is emphatically added.[75]

---

73. Marshall, *Acts of the Apostles*, 282. See also Witherington, *Acts of the Apostles*, 524.

74. Haenchen, *Acts of the Apostles*, 522. For a defense of the conclusion that Isaiah lies behind these verses, see Edward Fudge, "Paul's Apostolic Self-Consciousness at Athens," *Journal of the Evangelical Theological Society* 14 (1971): 193–98.

75. Haenchen, *Acts of the Apostles*, 522 n. 7.

Whether or not Haenchen has determined the actual literary source of Paul's use of the triad, he is surely correct in highlighting the fundamentally biblical orientation that informs the Areopagitica at this point. Paul's central thesis here is that God is already near at hand, for this God is the Creator. This God is the giver of life, breath, and all things. It is, in turn, in this sense that Luke intends that the reader understand the subsequent citations from the Greek poets.

Read in this light, the first declaration, which is best translated "in him [or perhaps 'by him'] we live and move and are," affirms that God is the environment in which humans exist, not in the pantheistic sense taught by the Stoics, but as the personal God of Israel who gives us life, breath, and all things. The statement, therefore, is not primarily intended to affirm God's nearness in a spatial sense (although Paul does not deny this dimension), but to underscore God's relationship to humans as Creator.[76] The God who is near is the one who is the giver of human being.

Humankind as the Offspring of God

Like the first quotation, the line from Aratus is likewise to be read within the context of the biblical doctrine of God as Creator. Paul's intent is not to suggest that we are God's offspring in any directly ontological sense. Instead, he uses the well-known line from the poet to affirm that our connection to God is due to the fact that God gives us life, breath, and all things. In short, we are God's offspring, because God is our Creator.

The declaration that we are God's offspring by virtue of the act of creation takes us back to the problematic reference to the unity of humankind voiced earlier in the Areopagitica: "From one . . . he made all" (Acts 17:26). Similar to other statements in the speech, this assertion is ambiguous and, because of its ambiguity, open—at least initially—to either a Stoic or a Jewish reading.[77] The ambiguity in the meaning of this statement arises out of an exegetical ambiguity surrounding the gender of the noun in the Greek prepositional phrase *ex henos* ("from one"). The second word of the phrase could be seen as a neuter noun. In this case the statement in which it is found might readily be interpreted along the lines of the Stoic idea that humankind is the product of an original principle. It is more likely, however, that Luke intends that the noun be taken as masculine. This rendering would suggest that Paul might have the second creation narrative in view (Gen. 2:7), and if so, that he is affirming the unity of humankind through the connection of all humans to one particular person. But who is this person?

---

76. Ibid., 524–25.
77. For this observation, see Marguerat, *First Christian Historian*, 70.

The obvious conclusion is that the unnamed one is Adam, by means of whose creation as the progenitor of every human, all humankind is drawn together into a unity of origin. The doctrine of the unity of humankind in Adam is, of course, central to Paul's thought (e.g., Rom. 5:12–29; 1 Cor. 15:45–49).[78] Seeing *ex henos* as an allusion to the creation of Adam sheds light on the sense that the Areopagitica attaches to Aratus's statement that "we too are his offspring." Whatever its original Greek meaning might have been, in the mouth of the new Socrates it is to be understood in a manner in keeping with the way in which Luke brings to completion the genealogy of Jesus in his Gospel. In the first of his two-part historical narrative, the evangelist traces Jesus' lineage back to Adam, whom Luke designates "the son of God" in the sense that Adam was created by God (Luke 3:38).

The connection of the Areopagitica to the biblical theme of the unity of humankind through Adam leads not only to the second creation narrative, however, but also to the first. The center of this Genesis story is not the creation of all persons from a first human being. Rather, the narrative builds toward the creation of humankind in the divine image (Gen. 1:26). Viewed in this light, being God's offspring—as well as our unity as those who have been made *ex henos*—is connected to our status as the *imago Dei*.

That the narrator intends that the poet's line be understood in this manner is confirmed by the way in which the apostle draws his *probatio* to its pointed conclusion:[79] "Since we are God's offspring, we ought not to think that the deity is like gold, or silver, or stone, an image formed by the art and imagination of mortals" (v. 29). As this verse indicates, the belief that humankind is created in the divine image provides the crucial basis for Paul's critique of idolatry. In fact, the entire argument of the *probatio* moves toward this climactic conclusion. The relationship between God and humankind as God's image means that only humans—and no humanly constructed idols—can truly reflect the divine reality. Although this argument is unmistakably biblical in orientation, Paul might have rightly anticipated that it too could resonate with the Greek philosophers among his hearers. As Marguerat points out, "The affirmation that God does not resemble silver, gold or stone can fit with Jewish faith, in which all representations of the divine image are forbidden, but it can also be received by the Greek for whom the Living one can only be represented by a living person."[80]

With the apex of his *probatio* reached in the critique of idolatry, the new Socrates moves to the concluding *oratio* (vv. 30–31). The times of ignorance have now ended, he declares forthrightly. The unknown God is now known. As to the manner in which this has come about, the *ora-*

---

78. On this point, see Witherington, *Acts of the Apostles*, 526.
79. For a similar observation, see Johnson, *Acts of the Apostles*, 316.
80. Marguerat, *First Christian Historian*, 70–71.

tio only hints at an answer: God is made known in the apostolic proclamation with its call to repentance on the basis of the coming judgment
and the appointment of the eschatological judge. In an earlier episode in
the drama of the bringing of the gospel to the Gentiles, the narrator of
the book of Acts provided the basis for this glorious reality. The gracious
God who here is presented as the giver of life and breath and all things
has granted to the Gentiles "the repentance that leads to life" (Acts 11:18).

In calling his hearers to repentance, Paul breaks decisively with the
intellectual elite of Athens. By means of this radical disconnection, Luke
alerts the reader—finally—that the Areopagitica is in fact not ambiguous
at all, but quite forthright in its message. The openness of meaning that
to this point he has structured into the speech as a means for sparking the
inquisitiveness of the reader is now closed and settled.[81] The new Socrates
turns out to be the Christian evangelist. And the message he brings is one
of eschatological judgment, the certainty of which is confirmed by the resurrection of the one by whom the judgment will take place.

In this manner, the entire address reveals that it has all along been in
fact eschatologically oriented and christologically centered. Unbeknown
to the reader, throughout the address Paul has been reading the story of
the creation of humankind as a unity through the lens of the eschatological judgment of humankind by the risen and exalted Jesus. The unity of
humankind in eschatological judgment, and not simply the story of Adam
in the primordial past, therefore, forms the ultimate basis for the creation
of humans as those who are determined by their search for God. Like all
religious Gentiles everywhere, the Athenian hearers must repent. They
must forsake their inappropriate ways of seeking God and orient their
lives in accordance with the apostolic witness to the God whom they also
can now come to know in the one whom God raised from the dead.

Similar to the biblical narrative itself, Paul's speech begins with God the
creator of all and ends with God the judge of all.[82] Yet like the message that
emerges when the Bible as a whole is read canonically, the end—that with
which the address itself, as well as the biblical narrative that it encapsulates,
reaches its apex—provides the lens through which the beginning is to be
understood. The Areopagitica, therefore, is not to be seen as a discourse on
the first article of the creed, as some commentators are disposed to describe
it. Rather, like Paul's theology in general, it is a christologically centered,
eschatologically oriented presentation of the gospel.

For Paul, our being in God is likewise christologically centered and
eschatologically oriented. The goal of God's creation of humankind is that
we search for the God who is close at hand. Yet the divine closeness is not
based in some grand philosophical conceptuality but is related simply to

---

81. For a somewhat similar characterization, see Marguerat, *First Christian Historian*, 71.
82. For a similar observation, see Bruce, *Book of Acts*, 335.

God's gracious giving to us of life and breath and all things. Ultimately the gift that this triad entails is the Gift who is the Spirit. And the giving of this Gift is for the sake of our living in the one who is the way, the truth, and the life.

Read in this light, Paul's ambiguous declaration that God created all *ex henos* becomes a statement of a theme that is even more central to the apostle's thought than the unity of humankind in Adam and that forms the theme from which for Paul our unity in Adam takes its meaning: the unity of all in Christ, who is our true progenitor. This theme, in turn, occasions the ultimate distinction between the message that the new Socrates brings to his Gentile listeners and the teaching of the Athenian philosophers. William Neil pinpoints this difference and then sets it in the context of Paul's underlying Christology: "The Stoics believed that the divine Reason is immanent in man, i.e. 'God is in us'; what Paul is saying here is that 'we are in God,' which is in line with his general teaching that the Christian lives 'in Christ.'"[83]

God's Be-ing as the Basis for Our Being

My goal in this final chapter is to delineate the connection between the theo-ontology developed in the preceding chapter and human being. We began this process by creating a scriptural context for our deliberations by means of an appeal to the insightful lines lying at the heart of Paul's Areopagitica. The apostle declares that God the Creator is the giver of "life and breath and all things." In support of this assertion, he adds two statements that are reflective of, if not direct quotations from, the teachings of prominent Greek poets and philosophers. In so doing, he sets forth the idea that human being is related to the act of be-ing in God. According to the apostle, we live and move and are, insofar as we are in the one who gives us life and breath and all things. Our task now is to use this Pauline insight as the occasion for drawing our theo-ontology into a theo-anthropology. We must now set forth what it means to speak about our being in God.

Being "in Christ" as Our Being "in God"

As we noted earlier, William Neil has observed that Paul's declaration "We are in God" is in line with his general teaching that the Christian lives "in Christ." Neil's observation points in the direction that we must trod if we are to understand the manner in which human being arises out of our being "in God." Because for Paul, being "in God" is connected to being "in Christ," as Neil suggests, our search for what it means to be "in God"

---

83. William Neil, *The Acts of the Apostles*, New Century Bible (London: Marshall, Morgan & Scott, 1973), 191.

requires that we consider the biblical idea of being "in Christ." This concept, however, is related to another scriptural theme: the idea of the creation of humankind in the divine image, which takes us back to the topic of volume 1 of this series.[84]

The *imago Dei* as Our Vocation to Be in Christ

As noted in the previous section of this chapter, Paul appropriates the statement of the Greek poets "We too are his offspring" to serve his own purposes. Whatever the originator(s) of the saying might have had in mind, in quoting the poetic line, Paul intends that it be understood in connection with the biblical idea of our being created to be the divine image. This is evident in his use of this idea to provide the basis for his case against idolatry. But the idea of the *imago Dei* also forms the motif that underlies his assertion of the unity of humankind. We are all made *ex henos*, Paul declares. This unity involves a unity of vocation, a common calling to be the divine image. The *imago Dei* is not some obscure idea that the apostle himself devised. Rather, it forms a central motif in Scripture and provides one particular manner of telling the biblical story. Indeed, its implicit presence in the Areopagitica draws from and hence must be understood in connection with a particular narrative that runs through the Bible.

The opening scene of the drama of the *imago Dei* occurs in the first creation narrative: "Then God said, 'Let us make humankind in our image, according to our likeness' . . . So God created humankind in his image, in the image of God he created them; male and female he created them" (Gen. 1:26–27). This scene recounts the creative act of God "in the beginning" that destines humankind to be the representation of the divine reality on earth.

The background for the idea of the *imago Dei* lies in the idea that was present in many ancient Near Eastern cultures that images can function as representatives of the entity they designate. More specifically, images were thought to represent and even mediate the presence of one who is physically absent, especially the king whose throne is in a distant city but possibly also a deity whose abode is on the remote mountain of the gods.

Viewed in this context, the creation of humans as the *imago Dei* is intended to indicate that humankind somehow mediates within creation the immanence of the transcendent Creator. Consequently, verses 26 and 27 stand at the pinnacle of the first creation narrative with its focus on the God who creates a world that is external to God and who then places humankind within that creation as a creaturely representation of the

84. For a fuller development of the themes presented in this section, see Stanley J. Grenz, *The Social God and the Relational Self: A Trinitarian Theology of the Imago Dei* (Louisville, KY: Westminster John Knox, 2001).

transcendent deity. Furthermore, the story of the creation of humankind as the *imago Dei* serves to undermine the exclusive aspect of the royal ideology out of which the biblical concept emerged. In contrast to the reigning view of the ancient societies that elevated the king as the representative of whatever deity was deemed to be connected to the particular people over which he ruled, by extending the divine image to humankind as a whole, the first creation narrative—in a manner akin to Psalm 8—declares that the task of being the representation of, and of bearing witness to God on earth, is shared by all.

Although the first creation narrative presents the divinely given vocation to "image" the Creator as a universally human task, the text does not define precisely what this imaging entails. The quest to understand our common human calling to be God's image bearers leads to Jesus. The New Testament writers, especially Paul, present Jesus as the *imago Dei* and claim that his status as the divine image forms the center of the drama of the divinely purposed destiny of humankind.

Crucial in this regard is Paul's linking the idea of Jesus as the *imago Dei* to his role as the Second Adam, as is evident, for example, in 2 Corinthians 4:4–6. By means of this typological connection, the apostle connects the coming of Jesus to the Old Testament narrative of the creation of humankind in the divine image. A similar theme is sounded by the christological hymn in Col. 1:15–20, which emphasizes Christ's status as the *imago Dei* by asserting that he is the "firstborn" (*prototokos*)—the "firstborn of all creation" (v. 15) and, reiterating a theme found elsewhere in the New Testament, the "firstborn from the dead" (v. 18). By means of this repetition of the term "firstborn," the hymn links the "beginning" with the "new beginning," and it draws the entire creation/salvation-historical narrative into its central focus, namely, Jesus, who as the center of God's actions is the *imago Dei*. In this manner, the hymn declares that the Genesis story of humankind being created in the divine image can only be rightly understood when viewed in the light of the narrative of Jesus, who as the preeminent Christ is the *eikon* of God.

The opening four verses of the Epistle to the Hebrews offer an additional perspective. By declaring that Jesus is the reflection of God's glory and the imprint of God's being (Heb. 1:3), the author declares that Jesus manifests who God is. Yet Jesus does not do so by being a passive reflector of the divine reality, similar to a mirror that can only reflect the light issuing from another source. Rather, Jesus *is* this light. He is the pattern according to whom those who are stamped with the divine image are conformed. Moreover, the author of Hebrews links this to Jesus' status as the Son of the Father.

As the text in Hebrews indicates, the New Testament writers not only present Jesus as the divine image but also as the head of the new humanity destined to be formed according to that image, in fulfillment of God's

intent for humankind from the beginning. Consequently, the biblical narrative of the *imago Dei* does not end with the declaration that Jesus is the
image of God. Rather, the narrative comes to completion only as God's
intentions for humankind are realized in a community—the new humanity—through which the divine character that has been revealed in Jesus
truly shines forth. The biblical drama depicts the new humanity, therefore, as the final outworking of God's intentions for humankind "in the
beginning" to be the image of God according to the pattern disclosed by
Jesus, who is the true *imago Dei*.

In Romans 8:29, Paul articulates the point in christocentric language
reminiscent of Genesis 1:26–27. According to the apostle, God's intention is that those who are in Christ should participate in his destiny and
thereby replicate his glorious image. In fact, Paul declares that his readers
will be caught up in the Christ event and become copies of God's Son. In
this text, the clause "that he might be the firstborn" expresses the christological intent of God's foreordination, namely, the preeminence of Christ
among those who participate in the eschatological resurrection. The designation of these as Christ's *adelphoi* indicates the communal interest of
the text, which marks Romans 8:29 as the final exegesis of Genesis
1:26–27. The humankind created in the *imago Dei* that the first creation
narrative announces is none other than the new humanity conformed to
the *imago Christi*. In this manner, the narrative of the emergence of the
new humanity provides the climax to the entire salvation-historical story
and becomes the ultimate defining moment for the Genesis account of
the creation of humankind in the *imago Dei*.

In 1 Corinthians 15:49, Paul takes up the question as to the exact
nature of conformity to Christ. In this verse, he connects the *imago
Christi* with the resurrected new humanity by means of the Adam-Christ
typology and the correlate Second-Adam Christology found elsewhere in
the apostle's writings. Paul sets forth Jesus' resurrected body as the paradigm for all who will bear his image. To this end, he introduces an antithesis between the *psuchekon soma* and the *pneumatikov soma*, and then draws
a contrast between Adam and Christ as the representations of these two
corporate realities. In what might be described as a midrashic reflection
on Genesis 2:7, Paul suggests that the advent of the spiritual body was in
view at the creation, yet not as an aspect that was inherent within human
nature from the beginning but as the eschatological destiny of the new
humanity in Christ. Paul's Adam-Christ typology, therefore, indicates
that the creation of Adam did not mark the fulfillment of God's intention
for humankind as the *imago Dei*. Instead, this divinely given destiny
comes only with the advent of the new humanity, who participates in the
pneumakon soma by means of its connection to the Second Adam.

Viewing in the context of the biblical story of the *imago Dei* brings
to light the christological focus inherent in Paul's declaration in the

Areopagitica that humans are made by God *ex henos*. The *imago Dei* is the divinely intended vocation of all humankind and the shared goal of our existence. This vocation, in turn, defines our very being. God's intention is that we might experience eschatological transformation after the pattern of the resurrected Christ, who is the Second Adam. Or, viewing our destiny from another perspective, God desires that we find our being as we are caught up in the narrative of the Son. In this manner, the *imago Dei* emerges as the christologically focused and eschatologically oriented, universal human vocation.

The narrative of the *imago Dei* is not the ultimate story line of the Bible. On the contrary, it is a central plot within a larger drama involving a wider divine goal. The New Testament authors, such as Paul and John, speak of God's overarching intent as that of bringing creation to new creation. Moreover, they declare that the pattern for the divine purpose for all creation is Christ. These authors boldly assert that God created the world through Christ (Col. 1:15–16), who is the divine Word (John 1:3). Hence, Christ's role is cosmic in extent. He is the one in whom all things find their center (Col. 1:17). For this reason, he is the one in connection with whom all things participate in God's new creation.[85]

Being "in Christ" as Participation in God

Paul's citation of the line from the Greek poets, "We too are his offspring" can only be understood in the context of the biblical theme that our connection to God arises through the universal human calling to be the *imago Dei*. Nevertheless, the poetic statement also calls to mind the idea of participation in the divine life. We are God's offspring, because God intends that we draw our life from, or find our life within, the dynamic of God's own life.

The most explicit biblical statement of the idea that we are to participate in the divine life is found in a seemingly obscure declaration in the second epistle ascribed to Peter:

> His divine power has given us everything needed for life and godliness, through the knowledge of him who called us by his own glory and goodness. Thus he has given us, through these things, his precious and very great promises, so that through them you may escape from the corruption that is in the world because of lust, and may become participants of the divine nature. (2 Pet. 1:3–4)

These verses form an important part of the biblical basis for the idea of *theosis* (or deification) that has been especially central to the theological

---

85. See Helmut Thielicke, *Theological Ethics*, trans. John W. Doberstein, ed. William H. Lazareth (Philadelphia: Fortress, 1966), 1:383–451; and Dietrich Bonhoeffer, *Ethics*, trans. Neville Horton Smith (New York: Macmillan, 1965), 120–213.

understanding of the Eastern Orthodox Church. Thomas J. Scirghi encapsulates this perspective when he asserts, "It is the human destiny to share by grace in all which the Trinity possesses by nature."[86] As this statement suggests, Orthodox soteriology views the work of Christ as directed beyond merely rescuing fallen humankind from sin to the goal of effecting eschatological deification.

Lying behind the patristic emphasis on *theosis* is the idea that humans are theological beings. The patristic writers believed that this idea is evident in the biblical declaration that humans are created in the image of God. Linking this general anthropological theme to the biblical description of Christ as the *imago Dei* led the Greek fathers to conclude that Christ is the great archetype of humanity and that our essential nature lies in this archetype.[87] In this manner, the concept of *theosis* was closely bound up with human being "in Christ." Contemporary Orthodox theologian Panayiotis Nellas explains that deification actually entails Christification. This concept, he argues, is not to be limited to the kind of "external imitation" of Christ that involves merely "ethical improvement."[88] Rather, Christification is to be understood in the ontological sense indicated by the declaration of Maximus the Confessor: "God the divine Logos wishes to effect the mystery of His incarnation always and in all things."[89]

For the biblical basis for the connection between the idea of *theosis* and the theme of being "in Christ," Orthodox theologians look to New Testament texts such as Colossians 1:15, 28; 2:10; Ephesians 4:13; and 1 Corinthians 2:16. Important in this context, however, is also the biblical declaration that our participation in Christ entails sharing in his filial relationship with the one whom he called "Father." This is evident, for example, in Jesus' invitation to his disciples to address God as "Our Father in heaven" (Matt. 6:9) and in the instruction that the resurrected Christ gave to Mary Magdalene to tell his "brothers": "I am ascending to my Father and your Father" (John 20:17). The theme is reiterated in Paul's declaration that as God's children through Christ, we approach God as "Abba" or "Father" (Gal. 4:6; cf. Rom. 8:15)—that is, we have the privilege of speaking to God after the manner of Jesus himself. In fact, living and being "in Christ" emerges as Paul's favorite motif for describing the Christian life.

In both of these passages, Paul links the prerogative of addressing God as "Abba" explicitly to the presence of the indwelling Spirit, whom the apostle identifies as "the Spirit of [God's] Son." Furthermore, he declares

---

86. Thomas J. Scirghi, *An Examination of the Problems of Inclusive Language in the Trinitarian Formula of Baptism* (Lewiston, NY: Edwin Mellen, 2000), 7.

87. Panayiotis Nellas, *Deification in Christ: Orthodox Perspectives on the Nature of the Human Person*, trans. Normal Russell (Crestwood, NY: St. Vladimir's Seminary Press, 1987), 33–34.

88. Ibid., 39.

89. For this quotation from Maximus the Confessor, *To Thalassios: On Various Questions* 63, see Nellas, *Deification in Christ*, 39.

that the Spirit who leads those who are "in Christ" to address God as "Abba" likewise constitutes them as "heirs of God and joint heirs with Christ" (Rom. 8:17). Taken together, these Pauline observations imply that by incorporating the new humanity into Christ, the Spirit gathers them into the dynamic of the divine life as those who are placed by the Spirit "in the Son." Through the Spirit, those who are "in Christ" come to share the eternal relationship that the Son enjoys with the Father.

In his high priestly prayer, Jesus adds a further perspective, for he opens a window into the divine purpose in the act of creation: "Father, I desire that those also, whom you have given me, may be with me where I am, to see my glory, which you have given me because you loved me before the foundation of the world" (John 17:24). This assertion suggests that the dynamic within the triune life involves the glorification entailed in the reciprocal sharing of love. The Father eternally lavishes the unbounded divine love on the Son and thereby glorifies the Son. The Son, in turn, reciprocates the love received from the Father and in this manner glorifies the Father eternally, just as Jesus brought glory to his heavenly Father through the completion of his earthly mission (John 17:4). Because participants in this new community are by the Spirit's work co-heirs with Christ, as Paul declares, the Father bestows on them by virtue of their being "in Christ" what he eternally lavishes on the Son. Being "in Christ" by the Spirit means as well that those who are in the Son participate in the Son's act of eternal response to the Father. In this manner, the company of humans who by the Spirit are in the Son participates in the reciprocal dynamic that characterizes the eternal divine life.

By being drawn into the dynamic of the triune life, the new humanity participates in this eternal reciprocal glorification. Yet this destiny is not intended for us apart from creation. Rather, in the eschatological completion, the Spirit will gather the new humanity together with all creation into the Son, who is the Logos, the one in whom all things "hold together" in the sense of finding their interconnectedness (Col. 1:17). In this manner, the Spirit brings creation to completion in the new creation, and the coming to be of the eschatological new creation forms the ultimate instantiation of the glorification of the Father through the work of the Son and the Spirit. In that it is the divinely intended goal from the beginning, the coming to be of the eschatological new creation comprises the glorification of creation as well. Moreover, our role in participating in the great chorus of praise to the Father as those who are in the Son by the Spirit entails our glorification, because glorifying the Father as those who together with all creation are in the Son by the Spirit is the ultimate expression of the *imago Dei* and therefore marks the *telos* for which humankind was created "in the beginning."

God's intention for all humans, therefore, can be capsulized by asserting that we are created so that we might be the *imago Dei*. The fulfillment of this intent—our imaging of God—ultimately occurs by means of our participation in the divine life as those whom the Spirit places in Christ, who is the image of God. Just as God's goal is to bring all creation to new creation, so also the divine desire that we be the *imago Dei* is directed toward all humankind. The eschatological vision of the fulfillment of our destiny as those who are "in Christ" by the Spirit, in turn, provides the context for our being "in God" in the present. Even now all humans are given "life and breath and everything" with a view toward participation in the one human vocation that we all share. And this gift of living and moving and being "in God," this gift of being bestowed freely on us by the God whose very name entails the promise of be-ing present with us at every moment, is mediated to us by the gift of God who is the Spirit.

The Gift of the Spirit and Being Named "in God"

The declaration that our being "in God" is mediated by the gift of the Spirit leads us back to the conclusion, voiced at the end of chapter 8, that the Spirit is the gift of the "to be" of beings and as such the gift of Being. The idea that the concept of the Spirit as gift carries ontological implications has been noted by several thinkers in recent years.[90] Many of them look to the divine life itself for the basis for this understanding.[91]

The Spirit as the Gift of Life

The conception of the Spirit as the divine gift is not foreign to the Bible. On the contrary, several New Testament texts speak of the Spirit as the gift of God (Acts 2:38; 8:20; 10:45; 11:17; Heb. 6:4; cf. John 4:10). The same metaphor is suggested by the proto-Trinitarianism of the New Testament. The biblical writers hint at the possibility that the unbounded love lavished eternally by the Father upon the Son can be deemed to be the Holy Spirit, who is the personal concretization of the divine essence (love). In keeping with this understanding, Western theologians tend to see the Spirit as gift on the basis of the idea that the Spirit is the exchange of mutual love between the Father and the Son.[92] Those who are "in Christ," in turn, are the recipients in the Son of the eternal outpouring of the gift of the Spirit, who is the gift of love shared by the Father with the Son and reciprocated by the Son to the Father. This theological assertion

---

90. See, for example, Mary Timothy Prokes, *Mutuality: The Human Image of Trinitarian Love* (Mahwah, NJ: Paulist Press, 1993), 36. For a helpful engagement with John Milbank's important contribution to this discussion, see J. Todd Billings, "John Milbank's Theology of the Gift and Calvin's Theology of Grace: A Critical Comparison," *Modern Theology* 21, no. 1 (January 2005): 87–105.

91. See, for example, W. Norris Clarke, *Explorations in Metaphysics: Being, God, Person* (Notre Dame, IN: University of Notre Dame Press, 1994), 119–20.

92. Pope John Paul II, *On the Holy Spirit in the Life of the Church and the World* (Boston, 1986), 18, as cited in Prokes, *Mutuality*, 35.

finds its temporal precursor in the assurance that Jesus voiced to his disciples regarding the great love his Father has for them (John 16:26–27), coupled with his promise that the Father will graciously lavish the Spirit on all who ask (John 14:16; cf. Luke 11:13). Paul unites the present reception of the divine Gift with the eschatological promise when he declares that the giving of the Holy Spirit means that "God's love has been poured out into our hearts"(Rom. 5:5).

In recent years, several philosophers have explored the ontological theme that is related to this theological perspective, namely, the idea of being as the gift of Being. Arthur Witherall notes that many of the major answers to the fundamental ontological question "Why is there something instead of nothing?" share a similar structure, at the heart of which is the metaphorical postulate that "Being gives itself to beings." He argues that this postulate, in turn, views existence itself as a gift,[93] as "gratuitous bestowal."[94]

Our mundane experience indicates that human gift-giving occurs in many ways. Perhaps the manner that most readily comes to mind involves the basic procedure in which one person bestows upon a second person an object that is distinct from both. More significant as a metaphor for the ontological meaning of giving, however, is the act of parents giving life to their offspring through procreation or of a mother giving life to a child through the birthing process. But even the act of human life-giving falls short as a metaphor for its ontological counterpart, for as Witherall points out, "Ontological giving is a total involvement, and it is the absolute giving of oneself to another."[95] Witherall concludes that the ultimate picture of the ontological theme of "Being giving itself to beings" is the theological assertion that God gives life to creation.

The biblical writers link the life-giving act of God to the idea of Spirit. This connection is evident already in the Hebrew word *ruach* ("spirit") itself. Basic to the meaning of this term is the idea of "wind" (Gen. 8:1; Exod. 10:13) and hence "breath" (Ezek. 37:1–10).[96] The ancients were aware of the close connection between breath and life. They observed that breathing indicates the presence of life, whereas the cessation of breath means that life has come to an end. Consequently, *ruach* came to refer as well to the life principle in living creatures (Gen. 6:17; 7:15, 22). Because the Hebrews believed that all creaturely life found its source in God, *ruach* also denoted the divine power that bestows life. This theme is evident in the second creation narrative, which depicts God as breathing into Adam's nostrils "the breath of life," resulting in him becoming "a living being" (Gen. 2:7). The

93. Arthur Witherall, *The Problem of Existence* (Aldershot, UK: Ashgate, 2002), 123.
94. Ibid., 134.
95. Ibid., 128.
96. See, for example, Friedrich Baumgaertel, "*pneuma* . . . : Spirit in OT," in *Theological Dictionary of the New Testament*, ed. Gerhard Kittel and Gerhard Friedrich, trans. Geoffrey W. Bromiley (Grand Rapids: Eerdmans, 1968), 6:359–62.

Greek term *pneuma* reflects a similar range of interconnected meanings. Like its Hebrew counterpart it refers both to "wind" and "breath." It also denotes "life," for which breath is both the sign and the condition. And by extension it came to mean the divine life-creating power.

This constellation of meanings lies behind the biblical idea that God is Spirit (e.g., John 4:24). As "Spirit," God is the source of created life. Yet the affirmation also suggests that behind God's relationship to the world as the Giver of life is an eternal divine dynamic that marks God as the eternally living one. In the Fourth Gospel, Jesus offers an insight into this eternal dynamic: "For just as the Father has life in himself, so he has granted the Son also to have life in himself" (John 5:26). This declaration suggests that the focus of the divine vitality is the relationship between the Father and the Son. The divine vitality entails the eternal activity of the Father who as the fountain of life generates the Son to share in this life. The self-giving of the Father for the Son, in turn, is reciprocated in the Son's self-giving for the Father. This relationship between the Father and the Son is constituted by the Holy Spirit, who as the gift of life shared between the Father and the Son is the concretization of the essence of the triune God, namely, life.

The biblical writers came to focus on the life-giving function of God the Creator in the work of the Spirit of God, who bestows and sustains life. The role of the Spirit in the act of creation is suggested in the first creation narrative, which pictures the Spirit of God as sweeping, hovering, or brooding over the primordial "deep" (Gen. 1:2). Similarly, alluding to the connection between "breath" and "Spirit," the psalmist describes the breath of God's nostrils as carrying a creative effect (Ps. 18:15). And the presence of the Spirit is repeatedly said to be indispensable for human life (Gen. 6:3; Eccl. 12:7). The Spirit also emerges as the sustainer of life. When God removes the Spirit creatures die, but the sending of the Spirit results in the earth being renewed (Ps. 104:29–30; Isa. 32:15). Above all, the Spirit's abiding presence sustains human life (Gen. 6:3; Job 27:3; 34:14–15).

We might conclude, therefore, that the Creator's act of giving to us "life and breath and all things" occurs through the giving of the Spirit. Viewed from this perspective, we live and move and are in God insofar as we share in the Spirit of God, whose act of be-ing present constitutes our life and breath. In short, as the Giver of life, the Spirit is the Gift of Being, who bestows being on beings. This act of the Spirit is in keeping with the Spirit's prerogative in bearing the divine name, I AM, with its link to the idea of be-ing present not only with Israel, but with all creation.

The Spirit as the Gift of Name

The direction that we have pursued in these chapters suggests that the possibility that the theological idea of God giving life to creation might serve as the central metaphor for ontology and hence as the primary motif of a reformulated Trinitarian theo-ontology is closely tied to the process of naming. In chapter 7, we noted that the saga of the I AM is the drama of the self-naming of the self-naming God. Drawing from the saga of the I AM charted in part 2 of this volume, as well as the Marcan account of Jesus' baptism, we likewise observed that the drama of the divine self-naming is Trinitarian in character. In this drama, the Father bestows on the Son the treasured name (and hence the deity) that belongs to the Father. The Son receives this name so that he might glorify the Father's name and return the glorified name to the Father. In this process, the Son is likewise glorified. Furthermore, this mutual glorification is mediated by the Spirit, who glorifies the Son and, with him, the Father. On this basis, I concluded that the acts of giving/receiving and of returning the glorified divine name constitute the history of the relationships of the three Trinitarian persons, a history that is both temporal and eternal.

In the delineation of the significance of the divine name, we also viewed the drama of the self-naming of the self-naming God as the movement of the name of the one who is initially denoted as "I AM WHO I AM" (that is, the one whose identity is associated with be-ing present with Israel) from designation to connotation. According to the New Testament, this process reaches its apex in the coming of Jesus, who is the incarnate I AM and, as the Son of the Father, is the bearer of the divine name. The coming of Jesus, in turn, leads to the sending of the Spirit as the one who advances the process of glorifying the divine name. Although the apex of the drama came with the incarnation of the divine I AM name, the biblical texts present the story's climax as being yet future. The future, dramatic climax entails the eschatological sharing of the divine name with those who are marked by that name and who come to be so marked through the work of the Spirit. The eschatological act that stands at the end of the biblical story, therefore, entails the Spirit's act of drawing the new humanity to participate in the dynamic of the self-naming of the self-naming triune God.

Viewed from this perspective, human being arises from, and is integrally connected to, participation in the divine story, which is the story of the self-naming of the self-naming triune God. It is in this sense that Frank Nuessel was correct when he asserted, "A name is a *sine qua non* for existence."[97] The eschatological vision of our participation "in God" as the *imago Dei* that we outlined in the preceding section lends itself to being reformulated in accordance with the theme of our being named "in God."

Our study of naming in chapter 7 also brought to light the dynamic character of the name-giving act. Naming is an ongoing process that, although

---

97. Frank H. Nuessel, *The Study of Names: A Guide to the Principles and Topics* (Westport, CT: Greenwood, 1992), 2.

it generally begins with a single act of denotation, soon reveals itself to be a connotative narrative. This narrative is the history of the process whereby the name takes on the connotations that emerge through the interplay of the name bearer with the naming community. Moreover, a name is eschatological, insofar as the full content of what it connotes awaits the final completion of the process of adding connotations to the name.

The eschatological promise that stands at the end of the saga of the I AM, that of our divinely bestowed destiny to being brought to share in the divine name, lends a heightened perspective from which to view the eschatological character of naming. Jesus' promise offers the longest possible horizon for the process of a name taking on ever new connotations. The saga of the I AM leads to the conclusion that beyond any human naming-community stands the divine Namer, who by voicing the final connotation of our name that occurs as our name comes to be placed within the divine name, draws the narrative of our being named into the story of the self-naming God.

The divinely given promise that our name will be gathered into the story of the self-naming God does not find its fulfillment in us as solitary creatures. On the contrary, it includes our being named within a named community. And ultimately it occurs within the context of the divine plan to bring creation to new creation. The transformation of creation into new creation—that is, the bringing of all things to find their center in Christ—entails as well the placing of the story of creation into the story of God. Indeed, participation in the divine story is what in the end constitutes the story of creation, for it is from the perspective of its inclusion in the divine dynamic that creation—transformed as it will be into new creation—ultimately comes to be named.

This observation brings to light a central theme of pneumatology: The giving of the Spirit is always directed toward a *telos*. This is rightly said of the Spirit's role within the immanent Trinity, for within the eternity of the divine life, the Spirit as the gift shared between the Father and the Son is the *telos* of the Trinitarian dynamic. As a consequence, this also comprises the Spirit's place within the economic Trinity. The giving of the Spirit in and to creation is *telic* in orientation, for the Spirit is given with a view toward the divine purpose for creation and for creatures. The Spirit's presence, therefore, always carries the sense of being "unto" or "toward." And the "unto" toward which the Spirit is given is the eschatological participation of all things "in Christ" and thereby their ultimate being "in God."

The act of naming carries a similar sense of being "unto" or "toward." Just as was evident in the angelic annunciation to Joseph in Matthew's birth narrative, "You are to name him Jesus, for he will save his people from their sins" (Matt. 1:21), so also every name is given as a denotation with a view toward an unfolding process by means of which it will come to be filled with connotation. Viewed in this light, we might say that the act of naming is bound up with the reception of the gift of the Spirit. The Spirit, in turn, is the Gift of Being—the gift of "to be"—bestowed on all that is. We are given the gift of the Spirit, who is the gift of life and breath and all things, with the goal that we might come to be properly named. The divine intention is that we might come to be named in a manner that coincides with the goal of our naming, namely, our reception of the eschatological new name that the exalted I AM intends to share with us. In short, the gift of the Spirit is given so that we might receive the goal of our existence, which is being "in Christ" and hence "in God."

Jean-Luc Marion puts it well: "The Name no longer functions by inscribing God within the theoretical horizon of our predication, but by inscribing us, according to a radically new praxis, in the very horizon of God." Marion then makes the appropriate ecclesiological connection to the rite of baptism: "This is exactly what baptism accomplishes when, far from our attributing to God a name that is intelligible we receive our own."[98] Moreover, in this act of receiving our name, our personhood as an individual within the community is substantiated. As Paul Tournier observed, "What separates and distinguishes me from other people is the fact that I am called by my name; but what unites me with them is the very fact that they call me."[99]

The reception of any gift brings with it an attendant responsibility. Our being the recipients of the Spirit for the sake of coming to be properly named, in turn, carries the greatest responsibilities imaginable.

The reception of this gift calls us to sense a responsibility toward all others who, in a similar manner as we are, are also being gifted with being by the Gift of Be-ing Present who is the Spirit bestowed upon all creation. Our responsibility toward one another as gift recipients includes responding to each other with the respect, gratitude, and love that is due to the other, of course. But it includes as well the responsibility to respond to our ongoing encounters with each other with the kind of awe that arises when we sense that we stand in the presence of the depth of mystery that confronts us as the Other in every other.

The reception of the Gift of Being brings a responsibility to ourselves as well. The Spirit who wills that we be properly named calls us to participate in the process of determining who we will be; by means of the presence of the Spirit we are called to determine *who* we will be named. Furthermore the Spirit, who is the divine Be-ing continually present with us, invites us to engage in the ongoing task of discerning by whom we should properly allow ourselves to be named. In other words, the pres-

---

98. Jean-Luc Marion, "In the Name: How to Avoid Speaking of 'Negative Theology,'" trans. Jeffrey L. Kosky, in *God, the Gift, and Postmodernism*, ed. John D. Caputo and Michael J. Scanlon (Bloomington: Indiana University Press, 1999), 38.

99. Paul Tournier, *What's in a Name?* trans. Edwin Hudson (London: SCM Press, 1975), 4–5.

ence of the Spirit mediates to us the privilege and freedom to participate in the task of deciding which of the kaleidoscopic plethora of voices ought to be given the prerogative of naming us and which of the myriad of names ought to be appropriated in the ongoing task of defining our personal sense of being. In this process, the Spirit's goal is that we might come to see that our true being lies in the naming dynamic involved in our participation in the divine story and thereby that we are truly properly named only when we gain our sense of being from the name of the eternal I AM, that is, from the name that the Father desires to bestow upon us in the Son as the eschatological gift of the Spirit.

Yet the responsibilities toward others and toward ourselves that are entailed in the gift of the Spirit are merely aspects of the greater, joyous responsibility that we share in the presence of the one who gives us "life and breath and all things." Our ultimate responsibility is that of responding to the one in whom "we live and move and are" with gratitude for the gift freely bestowed upon us, the gift of the be-ing present of the Spirit who, together with the Father and the Son, is the I AM. For indeed, as Witherall put it, "the final significance of the gift lies in the way that we appreciate it."[100] In short, the reception of the Gift of Being who is the Spirit of the Father and of the Son is intended to lead us to enter into true doxology, as we are brought by the Spirit to declare with Paul, "Thanks be to God for his indescribable gift!" (2 Cor. 9:15).

100. Witherall, *Problem of Existence*, 156.

Index

absolutes, 62–63
Absolute Self, 85
Achtemeier, Elizabeth, 157
Acts, book of, watershed incident in, 344–45
actual occasions, 105–7
Adam, doctrine of unity of humankind in, 358
aesthetic process, contributing to self's overcoming of individuality fixation, 88
Against Arius (Victorinus), 303–4
Albinus, 296
Albright, W. F., 141, 268
Allison, Dale, 260–61
Alpha-Omega declarations, 226–28
Althaus, Horst, 95
Ambrose, 174
Anaxagoras, 23
Anaximander, 18–19
Andersen, Francis, 151
Anderson, Hugh, 285, 286
Andronicus of Rhodes, 3
Angst, 115–16
Anidjar, Gil, 129
Anselm, 45
Apologists, 294–95
apophatic theology, 11, 320–27, 330
Aquinas, Thomas, 45–50, 252–53
    addressing Platonic errors, 46–47
    apophatic approach, 324–25
    central ontological principle, 47
    elevating natural theology, 51–52
    God as highest object humans can know, 49
    on meaning of the divine name, 47
    Scotus's revision of, 53–56
    transforming Unmoved Mover into biblical Creator God, 48
Aratus of Soli, 354, 357
Areopagitica (Paul), 11, 343–60, 364
Arianism, 299–300, 315
Aristobulus the Peripatetic, 355
Aristotle, 27–33, 52
    Andronicus's collecting works of, 3
    concept of Unmoved Mover, 32–33
    describing four causes, 30–32
    determining dynamics of change, 30
    distinguishing potentiality and actuality, 31–32
    exploration of Being, 29–30
    father of logic, 28–29
    influence on Aquinas, 46, 47
    on names, 273
    Ockham bending natural philosophy of, 59
    overlap of ideas with Plato, 28, 30
    Scotus's revision of, 53–56
    understanding of substances and categories, 29
Arnold, William R., 141
Augustine, 38–44, 52, 294, 332
    addressing certainty, 39–41
    cataphatic orientation, 323–24
    central philosophical problem for, 39
    Christian God as highest good, 42–43

concluding that God is Being, 43–44
doctrine of the Trinity, 310–16
love as Trinitarian concept, 335–40
on meaning of the divine name, 47
ontology of, differing from Plotinus, 43
on presence of truth in the mind,
    41–42
response to Arianism, 315
response to problem of evil, 43
on role of sensation, 41
under Neoplatonic influence, 251
on Victorinus, 303
Aune, David, 220

Baal cult, 152–54
Baltes, Matthias, 308
baptismal formula, 266–70, 283
Barker, Margaret, 240–41
Bar Kokhba, Simon, 211
Barnes, Michel Rene, 312, 315
Barrett, C. K., 196
Barth, Karl, 270, 289
Basil, 300, 321
Bauckham, Richard, 231
Beale, G. K., 227–28, 240, 242
Beasley-Murray, George, 183
becoming
    interrelationship with being, 105
    world of, 26–27
being. *See also* be-ing, Being
    interrelationship with becoming, 105
    as philosophical term, 3–4
be-ing
    Parmenides' concept of, 21–22
    Yahweh's continuous act of, 143–45
Being. *See also* being, be-ing
    Aquinas's perspective on, 45
    becoming Christian, 33–50
    beginnings of, 16–17
    as Being, 29–30, 33
    birth of, 20–23
    changes within, 22
    Christianization of, 7–8
    Christian theologians linking to
        biblical God, 133
    confused with presence, 115
    connecting biblical God to, 249
    connection to name-bearing, 333
    demise of, 91
    as desire of Christian soul, 38–44
    Edwards reconnecting with biblical
        God, 78
    gestation of, 17–20

Gift of, 372–73
as *ipsum esse*, 47–48
last gasp of, 8
linguistic sources of, 15–16
linked with God, 339
as mystery, 118–20
Plotinus linking Intelligence to, 36
among pre-Socratic thinkers, 23
promotion to center of philosophical
    inquiry, 23–33
question of, in Heidegger's thought,
    112–16
and the realm of the forms, 24–27
recalling truth of, 119–20
secularization of, 89
as self-absorbed thinking, 27–33
soul's desire and, 34–44
synthesis of God with, 8
tetragrammaton linked to Greek
    concept of, 254–55
triadic analysis of, 315
Trinitarian, pathway to, 320
understanding biblical God in context
    of, 5–6
Being-in-general, 74
Being and Time (Heidegger), 113–14
Bergson, Henri, 101
Berkeley, George, 79
Berkhof, Louis, 256
Berlin, Isaiah, 69
Bernard, J. H., 176, 186, 196, 201
Bernard of Clairvaux, 49
Bible, narrating story of the I AM in this
    world, 333
Birot, Antoine, 287
Bittle, Celestine, "being" defined, 4
Blaiklock, E. M., 346
Blanchette, Oliva, 325, 327
Blans, Bert, 329–30
Bock, Darrell, 218
Boethius, 44
Bond, H. Lawrence, 67
Boring, Eugene, 227
Braaten, Carl, 270
Branscomb, B. Harvie, 179
Brodie, Thomas, 178, 200
Brown, Raymond, 178, 180, 184, 194
Browning, Douglas, 103
Bruaire, Claude, 323
Bruce, F. F., 180, 187–88, 343
Brunner, Emil, 251, 253, 256–58, 261,
    280
Buber, Martin, 259–60, 330

Bulhof, Ilse, 321, 325
Bultmann, Rudolf, 111, 175–76, 194
Burbridge, John, 98
Burge, Gary, 200
burning bush, 135–36, 174, 249, 282

Caird, G. B., 229, 231
Calvin, John, 169–70, 171, 173, 189,
    198
Candidus, 304
Capita 150 (Palamas), 340
Capita Physica (Palamas), 336
Cappadocian fathers, influence on
    Trinitarianism, 300–303
Caputo, John, 129–30
Carabine, Deirdre, 322, 323–24, 337
Carnap, Rudolf, 272
Carson, D. A., 178, 180
Cartesian rationalism, attack on, 101
cataphatic theology, 321–22
causation, efficient, 103
Celsus, 34
change
    of Being, 22
    illusionary nature of, 21
    perpetual nature of, 19
Chierchia, Gennaro, 277
Childs, Brevard, 135, 141, 147, 149–50,
    161, 264
Chopp, Rebecca, 6
Christianity, connecting with philosophy,
    293–99
Christian leaders, attitude toward Greek
    philosophical heritage, 33–34
Christian theology
    Aquinas's synthesis with Greek
        philosophy, 45–46
    connecting to Greek ontology, 8
    metaphysics and, 1
christophany, 135–36, 174
Chytraeus, David, 200
circularity, concept of, 26
The City of God (Augustine), 39
Clark, Mary T., 305, 308
Clarke, Samuel, 254
Clauberg, Johann, 5
Cleanthes, 354
Clement of Alexandria, 34, 295–96
Clements, Ronald, 137, 147
cluster descriptivist theory, 277–78
Coakley, Sarah, 301
Coggins, Richard, 139
Cohen, Richard, 330

Cole, R. Alan, 141
Confessions (Augustine), 43, 294, 303,
    312
Connell, George, 120
consciousness, Hegel's approach to,
    93–94
Copernican Revolution, 80
Copernicus, Nicolas, 80
Copleston, Frederick, 34, 50
    on Newton, 69–70
    on Ockham, 58
cosmology, naturalistic, 18
cosmos, as ever living fire, 19–20
Council of Constantinople, 300
Council of Nicea, 299–300
Cranfield, C. E. B., 284
Cratylus (Plato), 272–73
creatio continua, 76–77
creatio ex nihilo, 75
creation
    linking Jesus to narrative of, 362–63
    members of the Trinity participating in,
        313
    read through eschatological lens, 359
    rival understandings of, in Second
        Isaiah, 165
creativity, foundation of Whitehead's
    system, 109–10
Critique of Judgment (Kant), 86
Critique of Practical Reason (Kant), 82
Critique of Pure Reason (Kant), 80–82, 83,
    94
Cyril of Alexandria, 200

Das, Rasvihary, 102, 109
Dasein, 114, 116
Das Man, 116
Davidson, A. B., 136
Davies, G. I., 155
Davis, John J., 142
deconstruction, 120–21, 127–28
De Divinis nominibus (Dionysius the
    Areopagite), 251–52
De doctrina christiana (Augustine),
    323–24
deductive reasoning, 20–21
Delitzsch, Franz, 164, 165
Democritus, 23
de Raeymaeker, Louis, 3
Derrida, Jacques
    campaign against dualism separating
        philosophy and literature, 121
    contrasting speech and writing, 122

crusade against realist understanding of
   language, 121–22
deconstruction as tool of, 127–28
on *différance*, 124–26
earlier vs. later, 120–21
on metaphysics of presence, 122–23
treatment of religion, 129–30
work of, sparking debate on validity of
   negative theology, 325–26
de Santillana, Giorgio, 62–63, 65
Descartes, René, 67, 90–91, 124
descriptivist view, 274–75
Destruktion, 112–13
De Trinitate (*On the Trinity*) (Augustine),
   310–12, 316, 335–37
Dibelius, Martin, 349, 352, 355
différance, 124–26
differ[']rence thinking, 329
Dionysius the Areopagite, 38, 65,
   251–52, 253, 321–22, 327–28,
   331–32
divine identity, concern for, 135–38.
   See also divine name
divine incomprehensibility, 255
divine life, humans' participation in,
   364–67
divine name. See also divine self-naming,
   I AM entries
   addressed in the Middle Ages, 252
   Aquinas on meaning of, 47
   Augustine on meaning of, 47
   bestowal of, 237–46
   complexity of, in New Testament, 262
   connection of "Father" to, 262–66
   as expression of gratitude and petition
      for presence, 151
   importance of knowing, 137–38
   imposters' claim to, 210–13
   interest in, 10–11, 251, 255–56
   Jesus' followers and, 241–46
   linked to compassion, 149–50
   meaning and origin of, 145–47
   meaning of the giving of, 148–51
   narrative of, and act of naming,
      281–83
   need for secrecy of, 239
   ongoing role of, in Judaism, 259–60
   ontology's appeal to, 250
   place in theological history, 251–58
   reiteration of, 151
   renewed interest in, 255–58
   revelation of, 134–38
   revocation of, 9, 151, 155–59

self-disclosure of, 281
significance of, 203–6, 370
subdued interest in, 251–55
temporary nature of, 256
three-tense, 233–36
triadic baptismal formula and, 266–70
triunity of, 288–90
divine passive, 260–61
divine presence, theme of, introduced,
   149, 150
divine self-naming, 7–8, 281, 282–83,
   288–90, 331–35
divine substance, Trinitarian members
   identical with, 313
divine vitality, 369
Dodd, C. H., 180, 182, 204
Dogmatics (Brunner), 256
Donnellan, Keith, 278
double negation, 95
dualisms, Heidegger's attack on, 115
Dunn, James, 286–87
Durham, John, 135, 137

Eastern Orthodoxy, approach to
   Trinitarian theology, 316–19
Edwards, Jonathan, 72–78
   on *creatio continua*, 76–77
   Newtonian concept of space analogous
      to God's mystical presence, 77
   reconnecting link between Being and
      biblical God, 78
   Trinitarianism inherent in work of,
      77–78
   on ultimate goal of God's activity,
      74–75
ego eimi, usefulness of phrase to New
   Testament writers, 175
Eichrodt, Walther, 144, 147
El, 134
Elliger, Karl, 170
El Shaddai, change of name to Yahweh,
   148–49
Elwood, Douglas J., 74
Empedocles, 23
empiricism, 79–80
energies, doctrine of, 316–18
entitas individualis, 54–55
Epimenides, 353–54
Erigena, John Scotus, 44
eternality, 298
Eunomianism, 301
Eunomius, 301, 321
Eusebius, 355

Evans, Gareth, 279–80, 282
Evans, J. Claude, 127
evil
    Augustine's response to problem of, 43
    principle of, 36–37

Farrer, Austin, 221
"Father," as name for God, 262–66. *See also* Jesus, relationship with the Father
Feast of the Tabernacles, in Fourth Gospel, 184–85
Fichte, Johann Gottlieb, 83–86, 87, 92, 95
    on consciousness, 93
    linking self and will, 85–86
filioque Trinitarianism, 316
Filson, Floyd, 269
final causality, Ockham altering understanding of, 62
fire, image of, from Heraclitus, 20
First Cause
    decoupling Christian God from idea of, 58
    God as, 48
    knowing, 49–50
    undoing of, 65–71
first efficient cause
    God as, 71
    Ockham's two aspects of, 63
Fitzmyer, Joseph, 210
Foakes-Jackson, F. J., 345, 350
Foote, Patrick J., 57 n.18
form of the Good, 27, 35–36
forms, theory of, 24–27
Fortman, Edmund J., 293, 294, 297, 307–8
France, R. T., 212
Franck, Didier, 330
Franks, Robert S., 92
Freedman, David, 151
Frege, Gottlob, 274–76
Fremantle, Anne, 38
    on the Middle Ages, 44–45
    on Ockham, 58
    on Scotus, 56
Fretheim, Terrence, 135, 138, 140

Galileo, 68
Gärtner, Bertil, 347, 353
Gasché, Rodolphe, 127, 129
Geffre, Claude, 263

Geist, 97–100
Gift, of God and Being, 341
Gill, David, 349–50
Gill, John, 255
Gilson, Etienne, 4, 5, 39
    on Aristotle's perspective of Unmoved Mover, 32–33
    on Augustine, 316
    on marriage of theology and philosophy, 53
    on Victorinus, 307
Glenn, Paul, 3, 4
God
    active and passive in self-naming, 288–89
    as *actus purus*, 77, 317
    as Being, 43–44
    Being as Being, 50
    as Being-in-general, 74
    bringing into conversation with quest for Being, 292
    as Charity and object of charity, 42
    connecting Being to, 249
    connection with First Cause (Principle), 52
    connection with human being, 343–44
    decoupling of, from idea of First Cause, 58
    dipolar nature of, 107
    as divine despot, 109
    encompassing three dynamic characteristics (powers), 305
    finding place for, in post-Newtonian cosmology, 72
    First Cause of the world, 8
    foundational roles of, according to Whitehead, 107–8
    inability of human mind to fathom, 337–38
    inability for humans to name, 281
    incomprehensibility of, 318, 321–22
    ineffability of, 323–24
    life-giving act of, linked to Spirit, 368
    link with Being, 339
    name of, as designator rather than descriptor, 281–82
    name of, interchangeable with term for God's person, 289–90
    named character of, 7
    narrative of divine self-naming, 283–88
    omnipotence of, in Ockham's view, 58–60

of onto-theology, 119
of process philosophy, 107–10
self-disclosure of, 257–58, 287
as self-existent First Cause, 50
self-naming of, 7–8, 281, 282–83,
    288–90, 331–35
separating unknowability of, from
    incomprehensibility of, 332
sexual motifs in speaking about,
    153–54
statements about, three ways of
    deriving, 253
transcending Trinitarian names, 328
triunity of, connected with human
    soul, 306–7
Goder, Frederic Louis, 206
Gomer, children of, significance of names,
    156–58, 160
Grant, Edward, 45
gravitation, principle of, 70–71
Gray, Patrick, 344, 345
Great Commission text, origins of, 267
Greek metaphysics, central concern
    of, 18
Gregory of Nazianzus, 300, 331
Gregory of Nyssa, 300, 318, 321, 323
Grosseteste, Robert, 61 n.42
Guelich, Robert, 181
Guthrie, Donald, 263

haeccitas, 54–55
Haenchen, Ernst, 356–57
Hagner, Donald, 269
Hamlyn, D. W., 18, 58, 92, 103
Hanson, Paul, 172
Hare, Douglas, 334
Harner, Philip, 179, 183, 187, 191,
    205–6
Harrington, Wilfrid, 227
Hart, David Bentley, 291, 320, 340
Hawkins, D. J. B., 53
Hegel, Georg W. F., 92–101
    Hegelian dialectic, 95
    intimate connection between thought
        and life, 95–96
    linking formation of thought and
        reality with God of Christianity, 93
    philosophy divided into three major
        parts, 94
    reason emerging out of experience, 96
    self-consciousness as goal of world
        process, 93

three moments of divine reality in
    historical process, 98–99
Heidegger, Martin, 110–20, 122
    on artistic expression, 117–18
    central insight of, 115–16
    on Dasein, 114–16
    earlier vs. later, 110–12
    influence on Derrida, 127
    opening way to mystical idea of Being
        as mystery, 118–20
    plan for Being and Time, 113–14
    replacing representational thinking,
        116–17
Hendriksen, William, 284, 285
Henry, Paul, 306, 309, 313–14
Heraclitus, 19, 22, 104
Hiebert, Edmond, 284
Higgins, Kathleen M., 21, 23–24, 33, 69,
    81, 86, 93, 111
Hilary of Poitiers, 134
history, relationship of God to God, 283
History of Western Philosophy (Hamlyn),
    103
Honeycutt, Roy, 155
Hooker, Morna, 212
Hopko, Thomas, 317
Hosea
    altering features of Yahweh-Israel
        relationship, 152–56
    announcing hope for restoring Yahweh-
        Israel covenant, 159–61
    naming of Gomer's children, 156–59
    relationship with Gomer, 155–56
Hoskyns, E. C., 184
Houtman, Cornelis, 139, 141, 148–49
Hovey, Alvah, 194–95
Howells, Christina, 120, 121, 123–24
Hubbard, David Allan, 154, 159
Hull, William E., 178, 200
human beings
    christologically centered and
        eschatologically oriented, 359
    creation of, God's goal for, 359–60
    goal of existence, to seek after God,
        353
    as God's offspring, 357–58
    in hierarchy of being, 37
    misunderstanding own existence, 112
    naming of, drawn into naming of
        God, 371
human mind, traces of the Trinity in,
    311–12

Hume, David, 79–80, 91, 101
Husserl, Edmund, 114, 123–24
Hussey, Edmund, 337
Hyatt, J. Philip, 143
Hymn to Zeus (Cleanthes), 354
hypostasis, 309 n.102

I AM. *See also* I AM sayings, I AM sayings of
    Jesus
    Aquinas's presentation of, as scientific
        God, 52
    associations with Christ in the Old
        Testament, 175
    claim of, declaring sovereignty over
        history, 10
    as first and last, 168–73
    linking God to Being, 9, 134
    meaning of self-designation, 138–45
    phonetic connection with "Yahweh,"
        145
    revealing of the name, 135–38
    saga of, 282–83
Iamblichus, 309
I AM sayings
    in Revelation, 218–45
    three-tense, 228–36
    voicings of Hebrew divine name in
        New Testament, 261–62
I AM sayings of Jesus, 9–10, 175
    anticipating eschatological future, 208,
        218–45
    appearances in the Synoptic Gospels,
        209–18
    appropriating divine identity, 192–99
    in conversation with Samaritan
        woman, 177–79
    double meaning, 176–77
    as exalted Lord, 219–23
    future orientation of, 191
    in the garden, 182–84
    lifted up, 187–91
    revelation of the divine name, 199–206
    on the Sea of Galilee, 179–82
    as self-designation, 262
    as sovereign, 223–28
idem per idem construction, 139, 141
ignorance, knowledge of, 65
imago Christi, 363
imago Dei, 11
    as humans' vocation to be in Christ,
        361–64, 366–67
    as plot within larger drama, 364

indeterminacy, victory of, 130
inertia, law of, 71
infinity, 66–67
On Interpretation (Aristotle), 273
Inwood, Michael J., 118
Isagoge (Porphyry), 60
Ishodad of Merv, 354
Israel, relationship with Yahweh, 152–55

James, William, 101
Jehovah, denoted as divine name,
    253–54, 255
Jenson, Robert, 73, 75
Jeremias, Joachim, 260, 261
Jerome, 133–34
Jespersen, Otto, 277
Jesus. *See also* I AM sayings of Jesus
    addressing God as "Father," 262–64
    baptism of, as Trinitarian event,
        284–88
    confession of, I AM sayings during,
        215–18
    crucifixion of, 100
    exalted, 219–23, 229–30, 237–41
    high-priestly prayer of, 200–206
    "I am (he)" sayings of, 184–91
    identity of, developing from Son-of-
        David to Son-of-God messiahship,
        215 n.29
    inaugurating new exodus, 190
    incarnation of, 99
    naming God, 283
    as new name for God, 258, 262
    prior consciousness of identity as Son
        of the Father, 284–85
    relationship with the Father, 186–87,
        199–200, 203–4, 284, 286–88
    revealing the name "Father," 205
    use of divine passive, 260–61
Jezreel, significance of name, 156, 160
John, Gospel of
    double meaning I AM sayings in,
        176–77, 180, 183
    Jesus' prayer in, 260
    repeated use of *ego eimi* in, 175–76. *See
        also* I AM sayings of Jesus
John of Damascus, 317
Johnson, Dennis, 239
Johnson, Luke Timothy, 209, 214
Jones, W. T., 23, 38, 64, 80, 83
Justin, 294–95
Justinian, 38

Kahn, Charles
  on importance of Parmenides' work, 21
  study of *einai*, 16
Kal, Victor, 329
Kant, Immanuel, 80–83, 86, 87, 91, 119
  on pure reason, 94–95
  returning God to purview of critical
    philosophy, 82–83
  theory of knowing, 81–82
Kaufmann, Walter, 110–11, 116
Kearney, Richard, 121
Keener, Craig, 177, 178, 195
Kelly, J. N. D., 295, 296, 297, 303, 306,
  310
Kenites, 146
Kenny, Anthony, 20, 25, 34, 35, 69
Kepler, Johann, 68
Kiddle, Martin, 230
Kimel, Alvin, 266, 283
Knight, George A. F., 136, 161, 162
knowing, as fundamental human purpose,
  48–49
knowledge, pursuit of, 330
Koester, Craig, 239
Koole, Jan, 166, 170
Koren, Henry, 64
Kraus, Elizabeth, 104, 106
Krentz, Edgar, 258–59
Kripke, Saul, 278, 279
Kruse, Colin G., 196
Kümmel, Werner, 265
Küng, Hans, 97

Ladd, George Eldon, 219, 238–40
Lane, William, 213
language, as system of differential signs,
  124–26, 128–29
Lectures on the Philosophy of Religion
  (Hegel), 97–98
Lee, Sang Hyun, 77
Leibniz, G. W., 71 n.88
Leucippus, 23
Levinas, Emmanuel, 329–30, 335, 340
Lienhard, Joseph, 301
Limburg, James, 157
Lindars, Barnabas, 175, 177, 180, 194
Locke, John, 69, 78–79
logic, Aristotle as father of, 28–29
logocentrism, 120–24, 128
logos, overarching unity of, 20
Logos christology, 295
Lonergan, Bernard, 300

Lord's Prayer, divine passive in petitions
  of, 260–61
love, as Trinitarian concept, 335–40
Lucian, 348
Luther, Martin, 113

MacIntyre, Alasdair, 39 n.94
MacKenzie, John L., 171
Macnamara, John, 271
Macquarrie, John, 111
Magliola, Robert, 123
Maguerate, Daniel, 346
Malebranche, Nicholas, 74
Manchester, Peter, 310, 314, 315–16
Mann, C. S., 217, 268
Manson, William, 284
Margolis, Joseph, 124
Marguerat, 358
Marion, Jean-Luc, 372
Marrow, Stanley B., 185
Marshall, I. Howard, 348, 350
Martin, Robert, 279
Martyr, Justin, 33
Mason, Steve, 345
mathematics, aid in theological reflection,
  66–67
Maximus the Confessor, 365
Mays, James Luther, 155
McConnell-Ginet, Sally, 277
McGiffert, Arthur Cushman, 296–97
McKnight, Scot, 263–64
Mead, George Herbert, 84
Mellert, Robert B., 104
merism, 223
metaphysics
  Christian theology and, 1
  as "first philosophy," 29
  Ockham's approach to, 62
  origins of, 2–3
  of presence, 122–23, 129–30
  propriety of, as intellectual pursuit, 2
  questioning of, 2
  reestablishing, in scientific
    environment, 102–3
  renewal of, 91–92
  task of, 29, 62
  topics and concerns of, 3–4, 5
Metaphysics (Aristotle), 31, 48–49
Meyendorff, John, 320
Middle Ages, 44, 252
Middle Platonism, 35, 296
Milesian materialists, 18

Miletus, birthplace of philosophy, 17
Mill, John Stuart, 273–74
Miller, Perry, 73 n.97
Moloney, Francis, 178, 191
monism, 21
monist tradition, beginning of, 18
moral evil, 43
Morris, Leon, 195, 231, 267
Moses
  association with Kenites, 146
  God's annunciation of divine name to,
    133–38
motion, laws of, pointing to God's
    existence, 71
Mounce, Robert, 221, 232–33
Musculus, Wolfgang, 253
mysticism, welcoming negative theology,
    322–23

name, Spirit as the gift of, 369–73
name bearing, as dynamic action, 333
  descriptivist view, 274–76, 277–78
  significance of, 138, 333
naming
  act of, 281–83, 370–71
  attempts to synthesize descriptivist and
    direct reference theories, 279,
    288–89
  direct reference approach, 278–79
  eschatological nature of, 334
  passive nature of, 281
  producers vs. consumers in act of, 280,
    282
  significance of, 271–80
narrative theory, 332–33
natural philosophy, 68, 70
natural theology, 51–52, 57–64
Nebridius, 310
negation, 95
negative theology, 320–27, 330, 338
Neil, William, 360–61
Nellas, Panayiotis, 365
Neo-Arianism, 321
Neoplatonism, 34–44, 300
Neoplatonist Trinitarianism, 303–10
Neville, Robert, 102
New Testament
  complexity of divine name in, 262
  disappearance of name of Yahweh in,
    258–59
  tetragrammaton in, 259–62
Newton, Isaac, 68–72, 75
Nicene Creed, 300

Nicholas of Cusa, 65–67
Nicolaisen, W. F. H., 274
Nietzsche, Friedrich, 117–18, 127
Nobo, Jorge Luis, 105
nominalism, 60–62, 63
North, Christopher, 170
Noth, Martin, 141–42, 144
noumenon, 81
Nuessel, Frank, 271–72, 333, 370
Numenius, 305

objective formal distinction, 55
Ockham, William of
  proposing understanding of science
    unreliant on existence of universals,
    61
  revisiting Aristotle's fourfold causation,
    62
  two aspects of first efficient cause, 63
  understanding of God's omnipotence,
    58–60
Ockham's razor, 61
Oden, Thomas, 252
Old Testament
  fatherhood-covenant connection in,
    264 n.63
  messianic expectations in, 283–84
  Trinitarian overtones in, 253–54
the One, Plotinus's concept of, 35–38
Oneness, apart from Otherness, 331
ontology
  conversation with theology, 6
  destruction of history of, 112–13
  founding charter of, 20
  last gasp of, 8
  topics and concerns of, 4–5
  from Trinitarian perspective, 7
onto-theology, 119, 249
  de(con)struction of, 110
  demise of, 130, 250, 319
  destruction of, 122
Opus Oxoniense (Scotus), 56–57
organic mechanism, 104
Origen, 34, 284, 296–99
Oslon, Roger, 74
Otherness, 328–31, 335, 338
Owens, Joseph, 1, 47

Palamas, Gregory, 317, 318–19, 336–37,
    340
Parker, DeWitt H., 86
Parmenides, 20–23, 28, 321
Paul. See also Areopagitica

announcing eschatological judgment,
    359
role as philosopher, 345–46
Pausanias, 351
Pegis, Anton, 49
Peirce, Charles Sanders, 101
Phainomena (Aratus of Soli), 354
The Phenomenology of Spirit (Hegel),
    93–94
Philipse, Herman, 113, 120
philosophy
    Aquinas's synthesis with Christian
        theology, 45–46
    birth of, 18
    birthplace of, 17
    Copernican Revolution in, 80
    Derrida's critique of, 121
    father of, 17
    Hegel's three-part division, 94
    interwoven with theology, 73
    as means to discovering God, 294–95
    modern synthesis with theology,
        96–101
    monist tradition, 18
    of organism, 104
    starting point for, in Heidegger's terms,
        114
    target for deconstruction, 128
    traditional division of topics, 2–3
Philosophy of Being (Blanchette), 325, 327
Physics (Aristotle), 30–31
Pittenger, Norman, 108–9
Plato, 23–27, 33, 52, 304
    Aquinas addressing errors of, 46–47
    debt to pre-Socratic philosophers, 24
    dialogues of, in three groups, 24–25
    distinction between sensible and
        intelligible realms, 317
    form of the Good, 35–36
    God having no name, 255
    on names, 272–73
    overlap of ideas with Aristotle, 28, 30
Platonism
    influence on Aquinas, 46
    tradition of, effect on Trinitarianism,
        293–94
Plotinus, 35–38, 303, 307–8, 309
Plummer, A., 231
pneumatology, 371
Pope, Alexander, 69
Popkin, Richard H., 92, 93, 113
Porphyry, 35, 309
Powell, Samuel, 100

prehension, 106
presence, metaphysics of, 122–23,
    129–30
pre-Socratics, Plato's debt to, 24
principle of parsimony, 61
process philosophy, 101–2
    contours of, 102–7
    God of, 107–10
Process and Reality (Whitehead), 102, 105,
    109 n.112
Proclus, 38, 332
proper names
    connected to community, 334
    connotation vs. denotation, 273–74
    function of, 271–72
    meaning of, 276–77
    as rigid designators, 278
    set apart from definite descriptions,
        279
    taking on descriptive meaning through
        personal relationships, 282, 283
Pseudo-Dionysius. *See* Dionysius the
    Areopagite
Pulgram, Ernst, 271
Putnam, Hilary, 279
Pythagoras, 16–17

quidditas, 55

Raphael, 28
Rapp, Friedrich, 110
rationalist tradition, 91
reality
    built from four ultimate concepts,
        105–6
    first principle of, 18–19
reason, Middle Ages' emphasis on, 45
Reese, William, 102
Reid, Duncan, 306, 318
Renaissance, intensifying move from final
    to efficient causality, 68
representational thinking, 116–17
Revelation, climax of saga of I AM, 293
Reynolds, H. R., 202, 205
Richardson, Cyril, 303, 310
Ridderbos, Herman, 189, 194, 268–69
Ringer, Jeffrey, 335
Rolt, C. E., 327–28
Romanticism, 83–89
Rorty, Richard, 120
Roscelin, 60
Rosenzweig, Franz, 329, 330
Rowlinson, George, 142

Rubenstein, Mary-Jane, 322, 328, 339
Ruck-Schröder, Adelheid, 262
Rusch, William, 293
Russell, Bertrand, 276

Sabellianism, 301
Sanhedrin, trial before, I AM sayings
    during, 213–14
Santayana, George, on religious character
    of philosophy, 1–2
Saussure, Ferdinand de, 124–25, 128
Schaberg, Jane, 267–68
Schelling, F. W. J., 95, 110–11
Schmidt, Werner, 136, 147, 143–44
Schnackenburg, Rudolf, 180, 186, 193,
    195, 197
scholasticism, 45, 57
The School of Athens (Raphael), 28
Schopenhauer, Arthur, 83, 86–89
Schweizer, Eduard, 12
The Science of Knowledge (Fichte), 83–84
scientific materialism, 102–3
scientific mentality, rise of, 68
Scirghi, Thomas J., 365
Scotus, John Duns, 53–58
Search after Truth (Malebranche), 74
Searle, John, 276
Second Isaiah, 161–65, 181–82
self
    creating and determining own external
        world, 84–85
    relation to linguistic activity, 126
self-consciousness, examining, 87
sevenfold spirits, 230–33
Sherburne, Donald W., 105
Sidgwick, Henry, 46, 58 n.22
signs, expressive vs. indicative, 124
society of occasions, 107
Socrates, 24, 347, 351
Sokolowski, Robert, 328–29, 331
Solomon, Robert C., 21, 23–24, 33, 69,
    81, 86, 93, 111
Son
    establishing relationship between
        rational creatures and God, 298
    eternal generation of, 297–98
soul, Plotinus's view of, 36–38
Soulen, R. Kendall, 261, 270
Sparks, H. F. D., 264–65
Spirit
    bringing creation into completion, 366
    chief role of, per Origen, 298

as Gift of Being, 372–73
as gift of life, 367–69
as gift of name, 369–73
as theological gift, 12
Sprigge, T. L. S., 87
Staniloae, Dumitru, 340
Stauffer, Ethelbert, 179, 199
Stonehouse, N. B., 347
Stroll, Avrum, 92, 93, 113
Stuart, Douglas, 152, 160
Stumpf, Samuel Enoch, 17, 20, 113
    on Aristotle and Plato, 28
    on the Middle Ages, 44
    on Ockham, 61
subject-object dualism, 114–15
subject-superject, 106
substance, three basic types of, per
    Descartes, 91
Summa Theologica (Aquinas), 252,
    324
Summers, Roy, 232
Swete, H. R., 303
Synoptic Gospels
    connecting Jesus' sonship to Spirit's
        presence in life and mission, 286
    I AM sayings in, 209–18
A System of Logic (Mill), 273–74

Taylor, Charles, 39, 98
Taylor, Vincent, 285 n.144
telos, 31, 32, 52
ten Kate, Laurens, 321, 325
Tertullian, 34
tetragrammaton
    name of "Father" and, 262–66
    in New Testament, 259–62
Thales of Miletus, 17–19
Theodore of Mopsuesita, 354
theology
    conversation with ontology, 6
    interwoven with philosophy, 73
    modern synthesis with philosophy,
        96–101
theo-ontology, 250, 292
    development of, 11
    viewing narrative of God's name as
        crucial to ontological quest, 250
theophany, 181
Theory of Names (Pulgram), 271
theosis, 11–12, 364–65
Thilly, Frank, 24, 32
    on Nicholas of Cusa, 65

on Ockham, 64
on stages of scholasticism, 57
thinging, 118
thing-in-itself, 84, 87, 92
Thompson, Marianne Meye, 188, 265, 287–88
Tillich, Paul, 111
Tixeront, Joseph, 307
Torrance, T. F., 263
transcendental voluntaristic idealism, 86
triad, vertical, 331–32
triadic baptismal formula, divine name and, 266–70
Trinitarian being, character of, 331–41
Trinitarianism
    inherent in Edwards's approach to God's divine creativity, 77–78
    Neoplatonist, 303–10
    philosophical, 293–99
    Western vs. Eastern, 316–17, 320
Trinitarian model, derived directly from analogy from creation, 306
Trinitarian ontology, 292
Trinitarian theology
    ascendancy of, 310–16
    Eastern Orthodox alternative, 316–19
    rebirth of, 6–7
    as series of relationships moving from Father to creation, 298–99
Trinity
    Augustine's doctrine of, 310–16
    christological foundation for doctrine of, 299
    concept of relation applied to, 315
    doctrine of, connecting Christian God and *Geist*, 97–100
    doctrine of, Hegel's articulation of, 97–98
    historiography of, 320
    linked to dynamic of love, 335–40
    noetic, 331–41
    Otherness within Christian doctrine of, 331
    psychological model of, 314
triune name, apophatic theology's connection to, 327
Turrettin, Francis, 254–55

Unbeing, 21–22
universal solidarity, 105
universals, 60–62

Unmoved Mover, 32–33

Valla, Lorenzo, 44
Van der Veken, Jan, 109
van Rijssen, Leonard, 253
The Varieties of Reference (Evans), 280
via amoris, 338–39
Victorinus, Marius, 231, 303–10, 312–15, 332
The Vocation of Man (Fichte), 84
voluntarism, 56, 58–59
von Rad, Gerhard, 140, 142–43

Walker, Williston, 150
Wall, Robert W., 231, 239
Walsh, Martin, J., 32, 69, 83, 86, 94
Ward, James, 155
Warner, Rex, 24
Watts, John D. W., 163, 165
Weber, Otto, 253, 258, 280
Westermann, Claus, 170
Westphal, Merold, 119, 120
Whitehead, Alfred North, 101–10
    on metaphysics–Christian theology relationship, 1
    ontological principle, 106 n.88
    placing self in history of philosophy, 103–4
    system of, creativity at foundation of, 109–10
    understanding of the Deity, 107
Whybray, R. N., 164
Widdicombe, Peter, 297
Wilkins, Jeremy, 337
Willard, Dallas, 127
Williamson, Lamar, 216, 217, 286
Winter, Bruce, 347, 349–50
Wissink, Jozef, 324
Witherall, Arthur, 368
Witherington, Ben, 343–44, 350, 352
Wolff, Christian, 5
Wolff, Hans Walter, 153, 158
Wolff, Philipp, 329
Wolter, Allan B., 53
The World as Will and Idea (Schopenhauer), 86
Wycherley, Richard, 349
Wyschogrod, Michael, 259–60, 280

Yahweh
    active agent in Hosea's story, 156
    angel of, as christophany, 135–36

Yahweh (*continued*)
  comparing self to other gods,
    165–68
  disappearance of name, in the New
    Testament, 258–59
  etymological roots of name, 146–47
  knowledge of name before Israel
    established, 146
  name unspoken but present in New
    Testament, 260–61
  no longer I AM, 152
  referred to as "Baal," 152–54

relationship to history of entire world,
    208
  restoring name of, 160–61
  significance of name, 135–38
  tracing use of name, 134–35
  uniting name and reality, 150
Young, Edward, 166, 167, 171

Zanchi, Jerome, 254, 283
Zeller, Eduard, 19, 33
Zeno, 21
Zizioulas, John, 300–301